RELIGION IN THE MIDDLE EAST

THREE RELIGIONS IN CONCORD AND CONFLICT

GENERAL EDITOR
A. J. ARBERRY

SUBJECT EDITOR
C. F. BECKINGHAM

VOLUME 2
ISLAM

CAMBRIDGE UNIVERSITY PRESS
CAMBRIDGE
LONDON NEW YORK NEW ROCHELLE
MELBOURNE SYDNEY

Published by the Press Syndicate of the University of Cambridge
The Pitt Building, Trumpington Street, Cambridge CB2 1RP
32 East 57th Street, New York NY 10022, USA
296 Beaconsfield Parade, Middle Park, Melbourne 3206, Australia

Library of Congress catalogue card number: 76-11080

ISBN 0 521 20543 3 3 Volume 1
ISBN 0 521 20544 1 Volume 2
ISBN 0 521 07400 2 set of two volumes

First published 1969
Reprinted 1976, 1981

Printed in Great Britain at the
University Press, Cambridge

CONTENTS

PART 1: ISLAM

edited by C. F. BECKINGHAM

PART 2: THE THREE RELIGIONS IN CONCORD AND CONFLICT

edited by A. J. ARBERRY

PLATES

(*Plates are near the end of this book, following p.* 626)

PART I: ISLAM

MAPS

NOTE. In view of the changing nature of Israel's boundaries with neighbouring states, the 1948 armistice boundaries have been used and are drawn in fainter convention.

FOREWORD

Amongst the factors dividing and, to a certain extent, uniting the peoples of the Middle East, not the least interesting and noteworthy is the religions they variously profess and the sects within each religion by which they are further fragmented. The Middle East area (herein implying the lands of the Fertile Crescent, Arabia proper, and the territories to east and west, north and south affected by the Arab conquests and the spread of Islam) witnessed anciently, as is accepted for a commonplace, the rise of monotheism and its dissemination. Thereafter, and down to the present day, the three faiths predominantly concerned—Judaism, Christianty and Islam—have retained their separateness and have been in different degrees torn asunder by schisms; the "Two-and-Seventy jarring Sects" have long been distressingly notorious. Less well known, because less spectacular, has been the degree, admittedly modest, of co-operation between the three faiths and their multifarious sects, throughout history and even now.

What hopes can be entertained for a less turbulent future? The present symposium, conceived and planned before renewed crisis in the summer of 1967 rekindled always smouldering animosities, aims at giving a factual account of the three religions and their sects in this second half of the twentieth century. The table of contents is self-explanatory, and scarcely requires elucidation; experts from many parts of the world have written the individual chapters, and the whole work has been co-ordinated by a team of leading scholars. It should be said, however, that the writers in these two volumes were first invited to make their contributions in 1964 and had completed them by the end of 1966. At some points, recent developments in the Middle East might have led them to word some passages differently.

A very generous grant by the Spalding Trust underwrote a part of the expenses of this work. Cambridge University Press matched this grant by undertaking the costs of printing and publication. Grateful thanks is hereby rendered to both. G. M. Hinds of Cambridge University acted as the General Editor's assistant.

A few words are necessary to explain the system of transliteration employed. The editors have aimed at accuracy and consistency; it will be obvious, however, that complete uniformity, however desirable, remains unattainable, not least because of the great variety of source-languages involved. Contemporary proper names constitute a particular problem—Turkish proper names are a case in point, calling for more or less arbitrary decision; whilst the spelling of place-names is famously fraught with difficulty. A reasonable compromise has in practice been sought, as befits a work directed primarily at the general reader rather than the specialist.

A. J. ARBERRY

INTRODUCTION TO THE 1976 REPRINT

Religion in the Middle East was published in 1969 but all the contributions had been submitted by the end of 1966, only one or two notes being added and a few trivial alterations made subsequently. During more than nine years that have passed since then the history of the countries with which the book is concerned has been turbulent. There have been two fierce though short wars between Israel and the neighbouring Arab states, the Six Days' War of June 1967 and the Yom Kippur War of October 1973; their spectacular victory in the first raised the military prestige and confidence of the Israelis to a level from which they receded somewhat after the initial Arab successes in the second. The civil war in Yemen ended in 1967 with the withdrawal of the Egyptians and the new republic has been generally recognized. The British have relinquished their colonies and protectorates in the peninsula; the Federation of South Arabia was replaced by an independent republic in 1967 and the United Arab Emirates were established in the Gulf in 1971. In Oman a coup d'etat in July 1970 substituted the reforming Sultan Qabus ibn Taymur for his eccentric and reactionary father; the rebellion in Dhufar appears to have been suppressed, at least temporarily. King Faysal of Saudi Arabia was assassinated in March 1975 and was succeeded by his brother Khalid. In the sub-continent a new Islamic state was created with Indian help when, in 1971, Bangladesh became independent of Pakistan, where its secession was followed by the fall of the military government. Cyprus has been virtually and violently partitioned between the two communities after a conflict precipitated by the temporary ejection of President Makarios in 1974. In the autumn of the same year the ancient monarchy of Ethiopia was overthrown and a republican regime professing a Marxist ideology installed in its place. One of the most protracted and determined Kurdish revolts against the government of Iraq collapsed in 1975 when an accord was reached between the Shah and the Ba'thist government in Baghdad. More recently Spain has renouced its Saharan territories which have been divided between Morocco and Mauritania, though the authority of both states is being challenged by a guerrilla movement demanding independence. At the time of writing Lebanon is ravaged by a civil war of which the outcome is still in doubt but which will certainly entail important changes in the relations between the Christian and Muslim communities.

It is not the purpose of this chapter to describe or analyse these events, still less to revise the original work or repair its omissions. It is intended to do no more than consider how the political and military changes of these years have affected the status of religion in the Middle East. In fact, however dramatic some of the battles and revolutions may have been, the pre-eminent factors, problems, and tendencies have remained much the same. Politically, the grant of full independence to South Yemen and to the small states of the Gulf, like the Spanish abandonment of the Sahara, was only a continuation of the gradual dissolution of the European empires which has been in progress since the end of the Second World War so that now it is only in Central Asia that one of them can be said to survive in a much altered guise. Socially, the changes in Cyprus and now in Lebanon can be regarded as the last stages of the process begun in the last century by which the plural society of the Ottoman Empire has been transformed into what aspire to be national states. Both Judaism and Islam are confronted by serious and in some respects very similar difficulties in becoming the established religions of such states. The adherents of all three religions are threatened by secularism rather than by each other; Oecumenism has become a notable though not a universal feature of the relations between different Christian churches, to some extent between different Muslim denominations, between Christianity and Judaism, and between Christianity and Islam. It is likely that only an obtrusive political fact has prevented its development in the relations between Islam and Judaism.

Since the second quarter of the seventh century Islam has been the dominant religion of the Middle East, not in the sense that the majority of its inhabitants have been Muslims, which they were not until a few centuries later, but in the sense that the greater part of the area has usually been ruled by Muslims. It is for this reason that *Religion in the Middle East* accords to Islam rather more extensive treatment than it does to Judaism or to Christianity. Although it unfortunately proved impracticable to adhere to the original plan which would have allowed for chapters on Islam in South-East Asia and in China, the book nevertheless does include several chapters on Islam in countries which are not considered part of the Middle East, such as the U.S.S.R., the Balkan peninsula and the Indian sub-continent. It is important to remember, and the British are more liable than some other Europeans to forget, that although the Middle East is the home of Islam and contains its

Holy Places, the greater number of Muslims in the world do not live there. The two countries with the largest Muslim population are, in fact, Indonesia and Pakistan, in that order.

Throughout the greater part of their history Muslims had little experience of being a subject people; though they were sometimes a minority, as they were in the first centuries of the Caliphate and in their empires in India, they were a ruling minority. For two or three generations a few Muslims were subjects of the Crusading Principalities; for two or three generations again many Muslims in western Asia were subjects of the Mongols who, however, had no organized religion of their own but practised an eclectic paganism; in Spain some Muslims stayed behind in cities like Toledo when they fell to the Reconquista, but in the perspective of Islamic history, these were all untypical phenomena. The experience of uninterrupted retreat and of eventual subjugation by European powers which continued during the eighteenth and ninteenth centuries was something new and traumatic, something for which the thinkers and jurists of Islam had not prepared the community. By the end of the First World War there was hardly any Islamic country that was not, or did not appear about to become, a colony, protectorate or mandate, *de facto* if not *de jure*, of one of the European powers. This was intolerable to Muslim feeling. The attempts to resist the advance of European imperialism were of two kinds. There were those who saw in defeat the just punishment of sin and who advocated the total rejection of all that came from the West. This was the impulse behind a number of desperate, heroic and vain revivalist movements. Others, who were more successful, were ready to imitate Europe sufficiently to enable them to destroy its hegemony. This proved to necessitate much more than the first reformers had supposed, and it has presented Muslim statesmen with the recurrent dilemma of deciding how far they are justified in departing from the hallowed practices and precepts of Islam in order to achieve and preserve the independence of Muslims from alien domination. To a differing extent in different countries they have undertaken or sanctioned a drastic reconstruction of traditional Muslim society.

Anyone who has read *Religion in the Middle East* will realize that Islam like Judaism but unlike Christianity, is a religion with a few simple dogmas but with an elaborate code of behaviour. For most professing Muslims throughout history its distinctive feature has been the way of life that it prescribes, the rituals of prayer, fasting, and pilgrimage, its dietary laws, and the rules concerning marriage, divorce and inheritance. These have induced among Muslims a sense of fraternity far greater than has existed among Christians for a very long time and this sense of communal solidarity was an important factor in the Islamic empires. These were plural societies in which the divisions between the recognized religious communities, sometimes even between different segments of the communities, were in many respects more important for the daily lives of their subjects than the identity of the state to which they belonged or of the dynasty to which they gave their allegiance. Territorial changes, frequent and violent though they were, often affected the inhabitants less than a general election in a modern social democracy. In such societies the ruler, however arbitrary his power might be in some ways, was not in the same relationship to all his subjects. He was not in quite the same sense the ruler of those among them who did not belong to his own religious community. Whatever he might do to individual members of those communities, there were many matters affecting their personal lives in which he never interfered.

The plural society was not an Islamic invention; it had been a feature of the Hellenistic empires of antiquity. Islam had from the very first legislated for Jews and Christians living in Arabia under Muslim rule. In the Muslim states the same principles were followed and they are best known to us and were perhaps most elaborately enforced in the *millet* system of the Ottomans. Such a system is not, however, compatible with the demands which a modern industrial state makes upon its subjects, and the plural society has been gradually superseded by the national state. Ten years ago there were still two countries where something of the *millet* survived. The first was Cyprus where it had been preserved by British colonial rule, persisted precariously in the independent republic and has now perished in the convulsions that ensued after the coup d'etat of 1974. The history of the two principal communities in the island is instructive. These are not in origin ethnic or even linguistic, but religious. The "Turks" do indeed include the descendants of some Muslims from Anatolia who were introduced to repopulate the island after the Ottoman conquest in 1570–71. They also include Cypriots who were converted to Islam later and who continued to speak Greek at least until very recently. A Cypriot "Turk" is in fact a Cypriot who, whatever his mother tongue or racial origin, or even personal beliefs, comes from a Muslim family. What were once the adherents of two faiths have come to believe themselves to belong to two nationalities. The other important relic of Ottoman pluralism was the peculiar communal structure of the Lebanese polity and this seems now likely to disintegrate (March 1976).

These changes have not, however, resulted in the creation of secular societies as indifferent to religion as the European governments they sometimes aspire to imitate. The heritage of pluralism and the strong Muslim consciousness of belonging to a community have precluded this. In Turkey, for instance, which in theory became as secular as anywhere in the world, it is generally felt that anyone whose origins are not Muslim cannot be truly Turkish. To some extent Islam has come to reinforce and to identify itself with nationalism. Naturally there are aspects of traditional Islam which are not easily reconciled with the socialist and nationalist republican ideology so widely favoured today. This explains the frequent denunciation of "marabutism" by the Algerian authorities and the suppression of most of the dervish confraternities in Turkey.

Islam is still dominant in the Middle East. It never had much to fear from Christian missionaries and it has less than ever to fear now. But despite the strength of popular support which it still commands in many countries none of the important events of the past nine years has tended to strengthen it as a religion. The ruling classes may advocate Islam but they usually do so on the ground that it is conducive to social progress, or that it is morally valuable to the nation, not because it is the command of God given to mankind through His Prophet. Islam has zealous defenders in high places, but the arguments with which many of them defend it have nothing to do with religion. The late Denis Saurat, animadverting on the exhortations of Charles Maurras to the French to adhere to a faith which he personally rejected, once said "On ne peut pas exploiter Dieu". Many of the governments of the Middle East are trying to do precisely that.

C. F. BECKINGHAM

PART I

ISLAM

CHAPTER I

HISTORICAL REVIEW

> "Because of the characteristics of wildness in them (the Arabs), they are, of all peoples, too refractory for one to submit to another, on account of their toughness, pride, lofty ambition, and rivalry for supremacy. Rarely are their aspirations united (towards a single end). When, however, religious law (*dīn*) exists, through prophetship or sainthood, the restraining of them (the Arabs) comes from within themselves, and the character of haughtiness and rivalry passes from them."
>
> IBN KHALDŪN, *Muqaddima*

Islam, as a religion and a culture, we recognize as fundamentally *one*, despite its many varying aspects, whether it be encountered in Morocco or China, South Africa or Poland, or in Arabia where it was born. It is not always in the ascendant, and often inconsistent in its practice, but insists always on certain basic principles and doctrines. Yet Islam remains adaptable on the one hand to the needs of highly cultured peoples like the Indians, Chinese, medieval Spaniards, and the Hellenized Middle East which so greatly shaped its development outside the confines of Arabia, while on the other it is capable of proselytizing in pagan Africa without the shock and dislocation often caused by occidental Christianity. Although of course the subsequent development of Islam is of a kind that Muḥammad and his immediate successors could not possibly have envisaged, the primitive Islam of Mecca and Medina has the simplicity of universal appeal. The personality of Muḥammad the Prophet, powerful yet attractive, revealed with its shortcomings and faults as well as its virtues by Arab writers themselves more patently than that of the founder of any other world religion, has won the hearts of both soldier and mystic for fourteen centuries.

Till recent years it was difficult to form a clear conception of the milieu and society into which Muḥammad was born, but with the far greater knowledge of Arabia and new expertise in interpreting the ever-growing number of pre-Islamic inscriptions a much more intimate understanding of Muḥammad's career is possible. This implies that the early history of Islam must be entirely re-written, and this introductory sketch, embodying recent researches, still remains provisional. Hitherto Western writers, preoccupied with Jewish and Christian writings, have frequently neglected the specifically and dominating Arabian nature of the Qur'ān which resorts to Jewish and Christian matter for illustration rather than ideas.

MUḤAMMAD FOUNDER OF ISLAM—AN ARABIAN RELIGION

Along the east and west flanks of the Arabian peninsula run two great trade-arteries from Europe to the Far East, the Persian Gulf and Red Sea routes; parallel with the latter there runs a north–south caravan route skirting the eastern edge of the Ḥijāz–Yemen mountain range. Prior to Islam Persia and Byzantium contended for their mastery, but Byzantium could succeed only in controlling indirectly the Red Sea routes in loose alliance with the Abyssinians, Christians, who from early times had settled colonies, the Ḥabashāt, in the Tihāma, that have left a lasting mark on its population. Shortly before Islam however (A.D. 622) the Persians even managed to bring the Yemen within their sphere of influence. Northern Arabia was hemmed in by the Roman *limes* and buffer Ghassanid state, while the Persians long supported the buffer state of Ḥīra on the Mesopotamian borders of Arabia. Although Persia and Byzantium probably only maintained spheres of political influence in Arabia the material culture of the Hellenistic world had penetrated to and influenced civilized south-west Arabia. Within Arabia in many larger centres, especially those of the trade routes, were Jewish communities remounting to pre-Christian times. Christianity had also widely penetrated Arabia in the form of cults or communities in the north and south-west, Najrān, Ḥaḍramawt, etc. There were Jewish proselytes among Ḥimyar and other tribes. The majority of Arabians were however pagans.

Where the social organization of the Arabians is concerned, from ancient to contemporary times the population has consisted basically of a welter of tribal groups, normally at war, dominating and holding in subjection the cultivators, artisans, merchants, fishermen, and foreign settlers. The tribesman is free (*ḥurr*) and possesses nobility (*sharaf*), armed and strong (*qawī*) as opposed to the subject groups unable to defend themselves and reckoned weak (*ḍaʿīf*). The tribes accord protection to the subject classes, the *mawālī* or clients. Slaves are a simple possession but well treated. Everywhere in Arabia there were sacred enclaves such as the *ḥaram* of Mecca where feuding tribes could meet on neutral holy ground, go to market, perform acts of religion, confer, and seek decisions on their endless disputes. The sacred enclaves were dominated by "holy" families recognized by the tribes as endowed, through their knowledge of the supernatural, with nobility (*sharaf*) and virtue (*faḍl*) superior to their own, so they dealt in tribal affairs and became repositories of the law of the country known as *ṭāghūt*. Each group of tribes had its god and was linked to a particular sanctuary by treaties obliging the tribe to recognize the inviolability of the sacred enclave or *ḥaram* and protect it by force of arms; the sacred enclave could in turn extend its protection to others. The South Arabian temples (*maḥram*) appear to have been organized according to this pattern. Names such as Taym al-Lāt (Taym of the Goddess al-Lāt) and 'Aws Manāt, are no doubt to be understood as referring to the tribal deities of these tribes.

Mecca was one of these sacred enclaves demarcated by stone pillars (*anṣāb*), containing a Ka'ba, a cube-like building perhaps originally a black tent,[1] executed as it were, in stone; there was another at Najrān. In one corner of the Ka'ba is set the sacred black stone; litholatry in a wide variety of forms is still practised in Arabia. By the seventh century it seems to have become a kind of Pantheon, but it could well be that it was originally simply the sanctuary of a god called Allāh (the name derived from the Syriac 'Allāhā?)[2] to whose cult had been added an accretion of cults of other lesser gods.

Quraysh, the "holy" family of Mecca, was at the earliest known time the sacred house of the Kināna confederation, living scattered within it, descended from an ancestor Fihr b. Mālik. In later times, let it be remarked, a view was widely held that the *imām* or head of the Muslim community could be any one of the descendants of Fihr, that is, any member of the original "holy" family. Genealogists however distinguish the line in which is the "house" (*bayt*), meaning the nobility (*sharaf*), from the other houses of Quraysh.[3] Quṣayy was the first of Quraysh to gain control of the Meccan *ḥaram* and its lucrative offices, guardianship of the temple keys, the collection of the tax to supply food for the pilgrims, watering them, the care of the council chamber, and the banners. The family of his eldest son 'Abd al-Dār, that is, Servant

[1] Cf. the suggestions in my "Ma'n Gypsies", *Anthropos* (Posieux-Fribourg, 1961), vol. LVI, p. 737.

[2] I am indebted to the Rev. David Brown for this suggestion.

[3] Ibn Ḥazm, *Jamharat ansāb al-'Arab*, ed. É. Lévi-Provençal (Cairo, 1948), pp. 11, 12.

of the Temple, inherited these rights, but they were later contested by the family of another son 'Abd Manāf, and the latter gained the right to collect the tax and water the pilgrims, though the guardianship of the Ka'ba and council-chamber remained with the 'Abd al-Dār branch. This clearly shows that it was the senior house despite what genealogists may assert to the contrary. The 'Abd Manāf branch divided into two important houses, that of Hāshim who took charge of feeding the pilgrims, and that of 'Abd al-Shams, ancestor of the Umayyad house. Important as these two families were on the eve of Islam they were not the only powerful Quraysh in Mecca.

The extent to which the "holy" Quraysh group had extended its ascendancy over the tribes may be surmised from the statement that all merchants coming from the Yemen and Ḥijāz used to take safe-conducts (for which they would doubtless pay escort fees) from Quraysh while they were in Muḍar territory because Muḍar (tribes of the north Arabian group) would not molest merchants of Muḍar, nor would an ally of a Muḍarī, such as Kalb, Ṭayyi' and Asad,[1] disturb them. By the latter years of the sixth century Mecca had become a flourishing caravan city sending caravans to south Arabia to meet the Indian trade fleet in the winter monsoon, and despatching merchandise up to Syria during the summer. The house of Umayya soon profited from these happy circumstances whereas the influence of Hāshim may have suffered a decline.

Into this society about the year 570 was born Muḥammad b. 'Abdallāh . . . b. Hāshim, of the noble house of 'Abd Manāf. Orphaned at an early age and brought up by his uncle Abū Ṭālib, he appears at first to have been of little consequence in Mecca, a lesser scion of the noble house of Hāshim. His very marriage to Khadīja, a rich widow, older than himself, though also of noble family, may indicate that his family was not prepared to meet the costlier dowry required for a young virgin. Muḥammad is said to have followed the religion of his ancestors till aged about forty, when, as tradition has it, he had a sudden burst of conviction that he was called upon to proclaim the word of God. God's command to Muḥammad, it is agreed, comes as chapter XCVI of the Qur'ān which opens with the verse, "Recite thou, in the name of thy Lord who created". Henceforth the Qur'ān continued to be revealed to him piece-meal, and to judge by the descrip-

[1] Ibn Ḥabīb, *al-Muḥabbar* (Ḥaydarābād, 1942), p. 264. Cf. M. J. Kister, "Mecca and Tamīm", *Journal of the Economic and Social History of the Orient* (Leiden, 1965), vol. VIII, pt. ii, pp. 113–63.

tions, in a state of ecstasy, a physical manifestation of which is a violent shaking of the entire body; it is tempting to compare this with similar ecstatic states one occasionally encounters in Arabian religion today.

Those parts of the Qur'ān revealed at Mecca contain a limited set of themes—the unity of God which is the great fundamental tenet of Islam, the numerous signs of his bounty, the impossibility that he should have sons and daughters as other faiths assert. Monotheism and the concept of a supreme God were not new ideas in Arabia, for, Judaism and Christianity apart, the Qur'ān itself alludes to the *ḥanīfs*,[1] those who followed the pure religion of Abraham who was neither a Jew nor a Christian but a *ḥanīf muslim*, not a polytheist (*mushrik*). In fact the only serious point of doctrine at issue with the Meccan hierarchy at this period seems to have been that they made other gods share with Allāh in divinity while reckoning him supreme. It might be that Muḥammad arrived at monotheism through his wish to institute, or it may even be *to revive* the exclusive worship of Allāh at Mecca. One major point of difference with the lords of Quraysh was Muḥammad's claim to be the recipient of revelation which they ridiculed. Had they conceded this it need not have been difficult to alter their religious belief and practice, but his iconoclastic revelations cannot but have impressed them as both irreligious and as undermining their position. His natural reaction to their rejection of his claims seems to be linked to the injunction to treat the poor and the orphan well, for it seems that Muḥammad felt that the rights to which his birth rendered him an aspirant were not suitably recognized by the influential office-holders of the Meccan hierarchy.

Consequently much of the early chapters of the Qur'ān consists of self-justification and of drawing parallels between the prophets of former times and his own position; it is here, in reiteration of his theme, that he resorts to episodes culled from Jewish and Christian literature and legend, as well of course as Arabian history, but he points each story with a moral of his own.

The moral teachings of the Meccan period—kindness and respect to parents, payment of dues to kindred, charity to the poor and traveller, courtesy, generosity, keeping to covenants, not being over-bearing, considering meanness (*bukhl*) as a sin, are typical tribal virtues. "Full measure", "just balance", and thrift, on the other hand, smack more of

[1] Cf. Y. Moubarac, "Abraham dans le Coran", *Etudes musulmanes* (Paris, 1958), vol. v, p. 74, for suggestions as to the sense of *ḥanīf*.

the code of commerce. Only such few injunctions as that against the exposure of female infants and adultery may be to some extent original to Muḥammad.

In his Meccan period there develops the idea of a Book in Arabic to act as a scripture for the Arabians, just as Jews and Christians had their sacred books. The Qur'ān is indeed a curious compilation. Western techniques of literary criticism have not long been applied to it, but a prominent critic has formulated the hypothesis that it is a welter of written documents, probably penned by Muḥammad himself, revised, added to, altered, during the Prophet's lifetime; but Muḥammad, he maintains, did not live to complete the Book in the final form he had envisaged.[1]

In Mecca Muḥammad made little headway. While he attracted a few adherents from the nobility most were drawn from the classes under tribal protection, some even slaves. His opponents could not touch Muḥammad himself without creating a *casus belli* with his family Hāshim, but the resentment of the tribal lords of Quraysh at what they considered unwarranted interference and sedition among their dependants was vented on the converts among the latter. Since Hāshim refused to restrain Muḥammad, Quraysh resorted to a common Arabian device, and banned them from trading, and, perhaps with intent to diminish their status, from intermarriage with Quraysh tribes. This, like other measures, failed, but seeing he could make no impression on Mecca, Muḥammad had begun to look elsewhere. After some failures he found acceptance and protection with the Arab tribes of Medina.[2]

Following a disastrous war, the tribes of Medina, Aws and Khazraj, found in Muḥammad a third and neutral party who would maintain peace between them. No obscure person could fill such a position, and it was natural to resort to a member of a holy house. The fact that Muḥammad was alienated from the Quraysh lords may have made him the more eligible to the Medinan tribes to whom he was also distantly related on the maternal side. So twelve headmen, the *naqībs*, each representing a separate sub-tribe of Aws and Khazraj took him under their protection, undertaking to associate no other gods with Allāh, and conform to certain other requirements. By degrees his Meccan adherents left for Medina, and when Quraysh decided to make common

[1] Cf. Richard Bell, *The Qur'ān* (Edinburgh, 1937–9), preface; *Introduction to the Qur'ān* (Edinburgh, 1953).

[2] The fullest account of this part of the Prophet's life, replete with interesting detail, is probably that of al-Iṣfahānī, *Dalā'il al-nubuwwa* (Ḥaydarābād, 1950), pp. 236 ff.

cause against Muḥammad to kill him and force Hāshim to accept blood-money in compensation, he too went secretly to Medina. This is the *hijra*, usually rendered as "migration" or "flight", but it may be more correct to understand it in the sense it still has in the Yemen,[1] whereby a member of a holy family settles with a tribe under its protection, the tribe gaining, in its turn, the benefit of the sanctity (*baraka*) of his presence.

Soon after his arrival the Prophet concluded two agreements between the *mu'minūn* and *muslimūn* of the "Emigrants" (*muhājirūn*) and "Supporters" (*anṣār*), treating the Quraysh Emigrants a tribe like the Aws and Khazraj Supporters. These treaties have become lumped together with several later documents, the whole known in Europe under the erroneous title of the "Constitution of Medina".[2] The two agreements are fundamental as establishing the basis of the nascent Islamic community. Entirely political, they set out to establish a system of security. The opening clause declares these groups a separate *umma*, that is, a confederation, probably, one should understand, theocratic in nature. Each confederate tribe is to settle its disputes within its own ranks, doubtless by reference to its *naqīb* or headman. The *mu'minūn*, "Believers", but perhaps it also means tribal guarantors of security,[3] who are distinguished from the *muslimūn* who would include non-tribal persons, are to act as a body against any aggressor from among themselves, even if it be one's own son. They are to act as a unit against external foes, and form a single group in dealing with questions of blood-money, vengeance, peace, etc. The Jews who follow the *mu'minūn* are accorded protection and just treatment; this indicates an inferiority in status *vis-à-vis* the Arab tribes, though their exact social standing before and after Islam is not yet quite clear. The second agreement, amplifying the first, contains the provision that any *mu'min* aiding or sheltering an aggressor shall have God's curse upon him till the Day of Resurrection, that is, he would be spiritually (and physically) outlawed.

The latter document concludes with a clause commanding that, wherever differences arise between the parties to it, they shall be referred to God and Muḥammad. The Prophet then is the *maradd*

[1] See p. 292.

[2] I have dealt with the analysis of this set of documents in a preliminary study, "The Constitution of Medina", *Islamic Quarterly* (London, 1964), vol. VIII, pts. i–ii, pp. 3–16.

[3] Cf. Abū Ḥātim Aḥmad b. Ḥamdān al-Rāzī, *Kitāb al-Zīnah*, ed. Ḥusayn al-Hamdānī (Cairo, 1956–8), vol. II, p. 70.

which in present-day south Arabia means an authority on customary law to whom recourse is sought for a verdict.[1] Muḥammad, a member of the Meccan holy house can hardly but have been well versed in customary law in which indeed his grandfather ʿAbd al-Muṭṭalib was a renowned judge. So it is to be expected he would follow existing law except in such cases where he resolved to establish precedents, *which were very few*, and those probably justified by a Qur'ānic revelation. There are indications that the two agreements are based on patterns already long in existence, as a comparison with certain pre-Islamic inscriptions, were it made, might conceivably demonstrate. Indeed the whole attitude of Arabia, the Prophet and Islam itself is to hark back to precedents, to reject innovations. The very word we render as "heresy" (*bidʿa*), has the sense of a novelty. Ideologically, at Mecca, he wished to restore the simple uncorrupt worship of Abraham.

Muḥammad's career in Medina has two aspects, his struggle to consolidate his internal power, and his campaign to expand the external influence of his theocratic state, first by winning for himself the influence wielded by Quraysh of Mecca, and secondly by gathering Arabia as a whole within the security system devised in the two Medinan agreements. To realize the latter purpose he had first to achieve the former, but the two objectives are inseparable. He was immediately faced by the necessity of obtaining revenues to discharge his function as Lord of the theocracy, and he had to enforce his authority as ultimate arbiter, representing Allāh, in matters of dispute. The incorporation of the Jewish communities within the state, and their extreme reluctance to pay into the treasury of Allāh constituted another problem.

The opponents of Muḥammad are known as the *munāfiqūn*, the original sense of which was, I propose, "those who share in contributing *nafaqa*", that is, "maintenance money". *Nafaqa* was, it seems, a term used for contributions paid to Muḥammad for his public and private use; in Arabian society the two are barely distinguishable. Ṭabarī's commentary[2] on Qur'ān XIV. 294, says of the *munāfiqūn*, "Only their declaring themselves to be quit of Allāh prevented the acceptance of their *nafaqa*", whether voluntary, or taken by force. The leader of the

[1] Cf. my "Two tribal law cases", *J. Royal Asiatic Society* (London, 1951), p. 159; H. F. Jacob, *Perfumes of Araby* (London, 1915), p. 57.

[2] *Tafsīr al-Tabarī*, ed. Maḥmūd and Aḥmad Shākir (Cairo, 1374 H.), vol. XIV, p. 294. The Jews also paid *nafaqa* and gave loans to Allāh, i.e. Muḥammad, on which they charged interest. Cf. A. Guillaume, *The Life of Muhammad* (Oxford, 1955), p. 263.

munāfiqūn was 'Abdallāh b. Ubayy, the lord (*sayyid*) of Khazraj before Islam who had been on the point of becoming temporal lord of both Aws and Khazraj when he was displaced by the successful intrigue of the tribal chiefs, the *naqībs*, to invite Muḥammad to Medina. Though, I believe, signatory to the two federation treaties it is not surprising to find him heading those opposed to the new regime, some of whom only became Muslims after the battle of al-Khandaq. The equivocal role of the *munāfiqūn* has given their very name the sense of "Hypocrites". That the influential Medinans who opposed Muḥammad were tenacious of their function as judges can be perceived from Qur'ān IV. 62, where after the *mu'minūn* are exhorted to obey Allāh, his Apostle, and their leaders (presumably the *naqībs*), and to refer (*radda*) their disputes to Allāh and his Apostle, certain of them are taxed with taking their cases for arbitration to the *ṭāghūt* from which they had been ordered to declare themselves quit (*kafara*). The *ṭāghūt*, as can be perceived from Ṭabarī,[1] is customary law as exercised by the temple priests (*kuhhān*, sing. *kāhin*), and *ṭāghūt* has survived to this day to mean tribal chiefs who exercise law, and tribal customary law itself.[2]

The internal struggle in Medina could not be resolved as between the principals without disrupting the federation, and they resorted to other means. The *munāfiqūn* encouraged their Jewish clients to try to confute Muḥammad's claims to prophetship, and Muḥammad, perhaps opportunely more than by design, cut the ground from under their feet by eliminating the Jewish tribes one by one, gaining an accession of strength in each case by confiscating their wealth. The Jews moreover had commercial ties with Mecca so that Muḥammad's policy of breaking with Quraysh there cannot have been to their advantage. He was the arbiter in their inter-tribal disputes also. The struggle of course ranged over a wide field of activities, allegiances being changing and confused, but the Prophet, with the inherited skill in political manipulation of a "holy house", was invariably able to turn the ever-present rivalry of Aws and Khazraj to his own advantage.[3]

The Medinan tribes were reluctant to commit aggression against Quraysh, but became involved by taking part in the attempt to capture the Quraysh caravan returning from Syria. The Meccans, though they outmanoeuvred them and saved the caravan, suffered a reverse at the

[1] *Tafsīr al-Ṭabarī*, vol. VIII, pp. 461 ff.

[2] In the editors' note to al-Ānisī, *Tarjī' al aṭyār* (Cairo, 1369), p. 252, a *ṭāghūt* is a tribal chief who judges the tribes by customary law (*'urf*).

[3] A. Guillaume, *The Life of Muhammad*, p. 482.

hands of Muḥammad's expedition. For Quraysh this event, known as the battle of Badr, was a serious thrust at the security of their caravan-trade, protected by their sanctity rather than force of arms.

After Badr comes the first expulsion of the Jewish allies of the Medina tribes. An affray in the market of the Banū Qaynuqāʿ, who as artisans, silversmiths, can scarcely have had tribal status, appears to have originated from a petty misdemeanour of one of them. The Prophet was prevented from drastic action against the Qaynuqāʿ by the intervention of ʿAbdallāh b. Ubayy who as lord of Khazraj, their protectors, stood up to the Prophet on their behalf, but his action was opposed by a *naqīb* of his own tribe, the Banū ʿAwf, and the upshot was that the Qaynuqāʿ were expelled, leaving their property behind them. Thus the Prophet obtained control of the market of Medina.

This incident may have influenced ʿAbdallāh b. Ubayy to desert the Prophet, with about a third of the Medinan force, when he next encountered Quraysh who had mounted an expedition to avenge Badr and joined battle with the Prophet at Uḥud near Medina. The Prophet's side got the worst of the battle and he himself escaped up the mountain slightly wounded. Notwithstanding his defeat at Uḥud the Prophet felt strong enough to strike a shrewd blow at his internal foes when he accused the Banu 'l-Naḍīr of attempting to assassinate him[1] and blockaded them in their fortified houses set amid palm-groves. The Banu 'l-Naḍīr were, of the three Jewish tribes, those most near to tribal status for, until the Prophet established parity between them and Qurayẓa, they received from Qurayẓa twice as much blood-wit for a man of theirs slain by the latter, as they would pay Qurayẓa in like circumstance. Though the Banu 'l-Naḍīr were allies of Aws, ʿAbdallāh b. Ubayy of Khazraj and his faction of the Banū ʿAwf had promised them assistance, notwithstanding that Aws had already apparently consented to their expulsion. These *munāfiqūn* however were unable to honour their promises and so the Banu 'l-Naḍīr were forced to abandon their property and move north to Khaybar, with the honours of war, fully armed and with drums beating. Muḥammad distributed their property among his Meccan supporters, the *muhājirūn*, thereby relieving the *anṣār* and himself of any further necessity to support them.[2]

[1] This episode has been well discussed by M. J. Kister, "Notes on the papyrus text about Muḥammad's campaign against the Banū al-Naḍīr", *Archiv orientální* (Prague, 1964), vol. XXXII, pp. 233–6, referring to Nabia Abbott, *Studies in Arabic literary papyri* (Chicago, 1957).

[2] Muḥammad had established a sort of brotherhood between certain *anṣār* and *muhājirūn* whereby the former divided their possessions with the latter. Cf. Sir J. B. Glubb, *Story of the*

Banu 'l-Naḍīr did not however remain quiescent but persuaded the far from unwilling Meccan Quraysh with their allies, the Ghaṭafān tribe, to invest Medina. In defence of their homes the Medinans dug a ditch (al-Khandaq, from which this episode takes its name) to prevent mounted raids into the scattered houses and plantations. Wearying of the intense cold, hunger, and inaction, the Bedouin besiegers, Arabian fashion, drifted away, but for the Prophet it was a near-run thing. So desperate had the situation been that he had all but agreed to buy off Ghaṭafān with a third of the Medina date-crop. In an agreement concluded prior to the attack all parties in Medina including the Jewish Qurayẓa tribe had agreed to support one another against anyone attacking Yathrib as it was called and not to conclude a separate peace. Unfortunately for Qurayẓa their chief was persuaded, against his better judgment, to introduce the besiegers by treachery into the quarter, so exposing the women and children to danger by opening the defence on the south side. The Prophet now dealt with them by blockade, until in desperation, they agreed to surrender to the judgment of Sa'd b. Mu'ādh, paramount chief of Aws. As clients (*mawālī*) of Aws they hoped for lenient treatment. It is characteristic of the lack of executive authority of the chiefs, even of Muḥammad himself, that Sa'd forced Aws to swear in advance to accept his ruling be what it may. His verdict, that the adult males be executed, is still customary law in such cases today in South Arabia. Though recognized as just, or at any rate appropriate, Sa'd's decision was unpopular with Aws.

When Yathrib had shown its sacred personality, for holy cities like Mecca are felt to have a personality, by saving itself, in the face of an overwhelming foe, the Prophet declared it to be his *ḥaram* or sacred enclave, probably on this occasion naming it *madīnat al-nabī*, the City of the Prophet, although some traditions place this event after his raid to Khaybar.[1] Like the *ḥaram* of Mecca the sacred enclave was demarcated by stone pillars.

The Prophet's power continued to increase until, in the year 628, he felt strong enough to make the pilgrimage to Mecca, which he had every right to do, since during the pilgrimage month all hostilities were in abeyance. He avoided Quraysh attempts to intercept him, arriving

Arab Legion (London, 1948), p. 153, where tribes divide up their own property with a tribe that has lost its possessions when raided. "Arab honour prescribes that the warrior must give his poor neighbours precedence before his nearest relations." This viewpoint is expressed also in an early Tradition of Islam.

[1] al-Samhūdī, *Wafā' al-wafā'* (Cairo, 1326 H.), vol. 1, p. 76.

before Mecca wearing pilgrim dress, leading sacrificial animals, and announcing his peaceful intent. Quraysh remaining obdurate, he concluded a stand-still truce with them out of respect for the sanctuary, and it was agreed he should make the pilgrimage the following year. A series of expeditions or demonstrations in various directions enhanced his position, and in 630 he found cause to enter Mecca *vi et armis* unopposed, but he paid the greatest reverence to the sanctuary, confirming its inviolability and Shayba of 'Abd al-Dār[1] as keepers of the keys of the Ka'ba. Though recorded to have removed idols from the Ka'ba and declared the blood of certain murderers and blasphemers as lawful, he otherwise behaved with remarkable clemency. His policy turned to conciliating Quraysh who began to play a new role as his supporters in the expanding theocracy now consisting of two sacred enclaves—*al-ḥaramān*.

By methods mainly diplomatic, backed by occasional use of force Muḥammad proceeded to extend the security of his theocracy to the entire Arabian peninsula. He defeated the Hawāzin tribe, the sacred house of which was probably Thaqīf.[2] In 630/1 Thaqīf, that had originally rejected Muḥammad, accepted Islam, and, after protracted negotiation, allowed their idol al-Lāt to be destroyed, but the Prophet had to accept a treaty agreeing to the inviolability of the sacred grove and animals of Wajj.[3] The same year is also designated the "Year of the Embassies" for in it arrived deputations of tribes from all over Arabia to come to terms with the Prophet. He met opposition however from such personages as Musaylima in al-Yamāma of central Arabia, Ṭulayḥa of Asad, and al-Aswad al-'Ansī of Ṣan'ā' of the Yemen, dubbed false prophets by the Arabic sources, but from the sparse information surviving, one surmises they were rival theocratic lords on the same traditional pattern as Muḥammad's confederation (*umma*). Musaylima, it is known, established a *ḥaram* among the Banū Ḥanīfa. Tradition says Muḥammad dispatched missions even to foreign rulers like the Byzantine and Sasanian emperors.

When he had attained the height of his power after the "Year of the Embassies", Muḥammad insisted that the Bedouin perform the prayer, pay the *zakāt* tax, and destroy idols; later he prohibited the heathen from performing the pilgrimage, a measure in which there was

[1] Ibn Ḥazm, *Jamharat ansāb al-'Arab*, p. 118.

[2] According to Ibn Ḥazm, p. 254, it had the "honour" (*sharaf*) and held the banners.

[3] A. Guillaume, *op. cit.* p. 617; Muḥammad Ḥamīdallāh, *Majmū 'at al-wathā'iq al-siyāsīya*, 2nd ed. (Cairo, 1956), p. 206.

something of social and economic outlawing of those unwilling to conform to his requirements. These nevertheless were extremely simple, and most Arabians would not find Islam difficult to accept as it required so few changes, especially since, as research has shown, so much formerly thought to be specifically Islamic was already in being. Whereas Quraysh may have encouraged the establishment of a pantheon in Mecca in furtherance of their influence over the tribes, Muḥammad achieved a unity by turning the names of many of the pre-Islamic gods into attributes of Allāh. This can be ascertained by comparing the 99 names of Allāh with the god-names of the pre-Islamic inscriptions.[1] For the rest, to pay taxes to a Muslim tax-collector, and accept the Ḥijāz scale of penalties for misdemeanours and crimes involved little dislocation.

Muḥammad was still in process of extending his power when he fell ill and died at Medina in the year 632 while preparing an expedition for the north to avenge his reverse before the Byzantines at Mu'ta.

Western writers frequently tend to display sympathy with Muḥammad during his Meccan period, but censure his conduct in Medina, contrasting the lofty style of the early Qur'ān with its legal–political content in the latter period. If however the Arabian setting is fully understood it will not seem inconsistent that on assuming the theocratic function hereditary in his family, leading a life perpetually in public, surrounded by those with business to contract, Muḥammad was concerned with affairs rather than contemplation. His ethics are those of Arabian life. His attachment to Mecca and to the house of Hāshim did not waver. Muḥammad was no social reformer or egalitarian—that he cared for his non-tribal followers is not in itself evidence of a desire to create a new form of society—as the regulations for *kafā'a*, that a girl should marry an equal, and his acceptance of slavery in some degree demonstrate. He succeeded in his aim of purifying the ancient Arabian religion of Abraham, he incorporated the pilgrimage into Islam, made Ramaḍān the month of fasting, and established the *jihād*, or Holy War, to extend the power of the theocracy. He applied, if only for a fleeting period, the theocratic state principle to much of Arabia, however loose the link often was.

In sum, the emergence of Islam starts from differences between members of a hierarchy in an Arabian town, a sacred enclave, centre

[1] Cf. Y. Moubarac, "Les noms, titres, et attributs de Dieu dans le Coran et leurs correspondants en épigraphie sud-sémitique", *Le Muséon* (Louvain, 1955), vol. LXVIII, pp. 93–135, 325–68.

of a theocracy, and a flourishing caravan city—Muḥammad's struggle to win power from established authority. A strange chance it is that this particular conflict should give rise to a world religion, but the complex structure of Islam, as we now know it, developed long after Muḥammad's death.

ISLAM AND ARAB EXPANSION AFTER THE DEATH OF MUḤAMMAD

The tendency to disintegrate following upon the Prophet's decease was immediately manifest in Medina itself when the *anṣār*, or Supporter tribes all but elected a prominent *naqīb* and *sayyid*,[1] or chief, to an office unspecified by the sources, only to be frustrated by Muḥammad's two most prominent Quraysh Companions, Abū Bakr and 'Umar. Abū Bakr was elected by acclamation, and in due course his designation of 'Umar as successor to him was accepted. From the outset, however, the Prophet's cousin 'Alī, of holy Hāshimite stock, and his son-in-law, distinguished in the wars, would have been, by all Arabian precedent—offices being hereditary and elective—appropriate to elect in his place, yet, whatever 'Alī's qualities or defects, it is plain that he lacked Muḥammad's ability to grasp political opportunity. By force of the *fait accompli* he was unwillingly obliged to acquiesce in Abū Bakr's election and later in his being succeeded by 'Umar.

On accession Abū Bakr was confronted with the dissolution of the hold of the theocracy over the Arabian tribes, the so-called "apostasy" (*ridda*),[2] but it consisted mainly in their attempts to rid themselves of the duty of paying taxation, the *zakāt*, to the Prophet's representatives, and their rejection of any centralized authority, however light. Even before the Prophet's death three local theocratic leaders, backed by their tribes, as has been stated, had come out in opposition to him. These and other movements were reduced in a series of brilliant campaigns.

Politically, external events favoured Islam which could otherwise have flourished and died within the confines of Arabia like so many other religious movements. Shortly before Muḥammad's *hijra* the

[1] Cf. Ibn 'Abd al-Barr, *K. al-Istī'āb* (Ḥaydarābād, 1318–19 H.), vol. II, p. 562 where he is described as *sayyid fī 'l-anṣār*, *muqaddam*, *wajīh*, and as *muṭ'im*, i.e. providing entertainment for the guest.

[2] Cf. W. Hoenerbach, "Waṯīma's Kitāb ar-Ridda aus Ibn Ḥağar's Iṣāba", *Akad. d. Wiss. und der Literatur* (Wiesbaden, 1951), vol. IV.

Persians had been momentarilly successful in the continuous struggle with Byzantium, and occupied Egypt and Asia Minor. Though the Byzantines soon recovered these provinces both empires seem to have suffered from military exhaustion. The monophysite Christians of Egypt were harshly treated by the Orthodox Byzantine rulers, and the Christian Aramean population of Iraq was alien to the Persian Zoroastrian aristocracy. Making skilled use of the desert and their mobility the Arab forces, dispatched from Medina, were able to defeat the professional armies of the Persians in Iraq and Iran, and those of the Byzantines in Syria and Egypt. Within the first century of the *hijra* the Arabs controlled an empire extending from Spain and Morocco in the west, to Sind and Turkestan in the east. One need attribute no great religious zeal to the tribes which moved out of Arabia to campaign and settle. They have always displayed considerable cynicism about religion, but they were motivated no doubt by their natural rapacity, controlled by the Quraysh theocracy, to acquire a great empire. Within this empire they constituted a numerically small military aristocracy, leaving the administrative system largely as they found it, and drawing pensions from the Muslim Treasury. Though tribal rivalries were subordinated to the control of the theocratic state according to the principles of the two Medinan agreements, they were held in leash rather than eradicated, and Quraysh caliphs are to be reckoned successful when able to turn tribal energies to their own advantage. One may discern from the time of Muḥammad himself a certain hostility between the tribes and the religious element in Islam, professional or otherwise, an element which was to expand so much later on.

THE CALIPHATE OF ʿUTHMĀN: DISSENSION IN ISLAM

During the overlordship of Abū Bakr and ʿUmar the theocratic centre was able to exert its loose control over the Arabian tribes preoccupied with conquest and plunder beyond the peninsula, but as the tide of expansion slackened the third Caliph ʿUthmān, chosen by the electoral élite of Medina in opposition to ʿAlī, began to have trouble with them. The tribes resented Quraysh dominance—as ever when their interests clash with those of a "holy" family—and ʿUthmān's diversion of property, revenues, and booty in Iraq and Egypt to Quraysh, especially his relatives, aroused their bitter antagonism. The appointment of his

Umayyad relatives to high office in the provinces, able as they often were, like Muʿāwiya, whetted the envy of the other Quraysh families. Certain of these officials had been active opponents of Muḥammad's faction in Mecca, and so the religious element disapproved of them. The religious were further antagonized by ʿUthmān's "definitive" edition of the Qur'ān which not only offended certain of their religious sensibilities, but probably affected the interests of the Qur'ān reciters (*qurrā'*) who later flocked to ʿAlī.

ʿUthmān was driven to temporize with tribal discontent in southern Iraq, but, from Egypt, a party of malcontents marched on Medina to protest against his conduct of affairs. In the tangle of Quraysh and tribal intrigue following their arrival ʿUthmān was assaulted and killed; the two principal murderers appear to have been South Arabians, though others including Muḥammad, son of the caliph Abū Bakr, were involved. To aggravate so serious a crime ʿUthmān had been attacked with weapons, as Muʿāwiya said, in the sacred enclave of the Apostle of Allāh.[1]

ʿUthmān was a Hāshimī on his mother's side, though descended from the house of Umayya, and, like ʿAlī, a son-in-law of the Prophet. ʿAlī, who was elected with the support of the *anṣār* and Nakhaʿī chief al-Ashtar, a South Arab from Kūfa, himself linked with the murder of ʿUthmān, had to face opposition from the Umayyads and other Quraysh rivals. It is suggested that he had no choice but to accept election (and however superficially different the forms in which the caliphs were appointed may seem to have been, all, even ʿUmar in a sense, may be said to have been elected). The course of events however from the murder of Uthmān to that of ʿAlī is bedevilled by the partiality of the sources and remains obscure.

The Umayyads were clearly entitled to have those implicated in ʿUthmān's murder brought to justice, so Muʿāwiya, governor of Syria, as representative of the family and his most powerful relative, demanded of ʿAlī that they be handed over before he acknowledged him as caliph. He does not seem to have contested the election in principle, but asked that ʿUmar's precedent be followed in setting up a council (*shūrā*), and he uses, in demanding the murderers be handed over to be killed, phrases which are identical with those in the first Medinan agreement of Muḥammad.[2] ʿAlī was quite unable to

[1] Naṣr b. Muzāḥim al-Minqarī, *Waq ʿat Ṣiffīn*, 2nd edn. (Cairo, 1382), p. 87.
[2] al-Minqarī, *Waq ʿat Ṣiffīn*, pp. 127, 326, *passim*.

comply since the conspirators were his supporters, and he had no force to set against them, yet a substantial body of opinion undoubtedly felt that in this the law was being transgressed.

ʿAlī left Medina for his supporters in Kūfa and moved up the Euphrates to attack Syria, encountering Muʿāwiya at Ṣiffīn. ʿAlī and Muʿāwiya were both much at the whim of the tribes whose support of the two Quraysh opponents was often lukewarm, for they knew they were manipulating the tribal factions. Khathʿam of Syria indeed proposed to the Khathʿam chief on ʿAlī's side that they should let ʿAlī and Muʿāwiya fight it out and join the victor.[1] Eventually a demand by the tribes of the Syrian faction that reference be made to the arbitration of the Qur'ān appealed to the Iraq faction, which forced ʿAlī, much against his will, to consent to this procedure. In accepting arbitration ʿAlī really automatically deposed himself for if, according to the Medina agreements, in disputes final reference must be made to Muḥammad, representing Allāh, and *ergo* after his death to his caliphs, no arbitration could be possible. A group of ʿAlī's supporters, enthusiastic for arbitration at first, speedily perceived this illogicality, and now desired ʿAlī to reject it, their slogan "Only God can arbitrate" meaning that the outcome of battle should decide the dispute.[2] These are known as the Khārijīs (seceders) but it may mean "those who emerge from impropriety".

ʿAlī under the circumstances could not revoke, and both parties bound themselves to accept the decision of two arbiters who were to refer to "the custom (*sunna*) of Allāh which unites".[3] On what was to be judged by them the sources almost conspire to silence, but the indications are that it was whether ʿAlī's actions had contravened the fundamental law of the Islamic community—in cruder terms—did ʿUthmān's conduct, if unconstitutional, justify ʿAlī in sheltering and making common cause with those implicated in ʿUthmān's murder? The very result of the arbitration is dubious, but the subsequent setting up of a council (*shūrā*) seems to indicate that Muʿāwiya's view that ʿAlī's relations with the murderers disqualified him as caliph, prevailed.[4] ʿAlī availed himself of an escape clause in the arbitration treaty to reject it, but his career was closed a few years later in 661 with his

[1] al-Minqarī, p. 257.

[2] This sense of the phrase is clearly brought out in the accounts of the battle of al-Khandaq, as in Muḥammad Ḥamīdallāh, *Majmūʿat al-wathā'iq al-siyāsiya*, p. 29.

[3] al-Minqarī, p. 505.

[4] E. L. Petersen, *ʿAlī and Muʿāwiya in early Arabic Tradition* (Copenhagen, 1964), p. 193.

assassination by a Khārijī. His son al-Ḥasan literally sold out to Mu'āwiya who had already been acclaimed caliph at Damascus in 658. Thus the caliphate passed to the Umayyad branch of the holy house of 'Abd Manāf which claimed virtue (*faḍl*) equal to that of Hāshim.[1] Umayyad genius, well exemplified in Mu'āwiya, lay in a knack of manipulating tribal politics to their own advantage, and the ultimate fall of this house may be ascribed largely to a weakening of this technique, especially in coping with dissensions between North and South Arabs over the eastern empire.

The rash venture of al-Ḥusayn, 'Alī's other son by Fāṭima, the Prophet's daughter, terminating in his martyrdom at Karbalā' at the hands of Umayyad troops, established an enduring legend of hopeless courage, but the Shī'a or Legitimist Party of 'Alī continued to plot against the Umayyads. It may be at this stage that the characteristic Shī'ī principle of *taqiyya*, or religious dissimulation in face of overriding political conditions was first formulated. It was however the collateral branch of the house of Hāshim, descended from Muḥammad's uncle, al-'Abbās, which chiefly disseminated Hāshimite propaganda from its base south of the Dead Sea. It was too the 'Abbāsid house which introduced a new military element, the non-Arab troops of Khurasan in east Persia, and wrested the empire from the Umayyad grasp.

Succession to office in Arabia, broadly speaking, is hereditary and elective—hereditary within a family, elective as to the branch and individual. So it could be that 'Alī, by incompetence and his virtual deposition after Ṣiffīn, al-Ḥasan by his renunciation, al-Ḥusayn by his failure, were felt to have failed to substantiate their claim to office, whereas the politically competent 'Abbāsid branch, which seized the caliphate, had not. In turn the 'Abbāsids soon commenced persecuting the 'Alids whose pretensions to the Imamate were dangerous to their regime.

Always politically suspect to the central government the Shī'a formed sects around various of 'Alī's numerous descendants. 'Alī's entourage contained a number of non-tribal persons (*mawālī*) scorned by the tribes, and it is curious to see that as the focus of discontent Shī'ism attracted for example the heavily burdened peasants of south Iraq, still Shī'ite to this day. The central doctrine of Shī'ism holds that the *imām* chosen by God as part of the Divine Being is the leader

[1] al-Minqarī, p. 471. "We are the Banū 'Abd Manāf, there being no superior virtue (*faḍl*) of one over the other, except a virtue by which a noble person is not demeaned."

towards salvation, but the Shīʿa disagree on the line of succession, some distinguishing seven, others twelve *imāms*, after which no more are manifest. They believe the guided *imām* (*al-mahdī*) will return on the Last Day—so hence Shīʿī leaders are often not ʿAlids but claim to be missionaries (*dāʿī*) of the Hidden Imām.

So it was that there sprang from the train of political events touched off by ʿUthmān's murder and culminating in the ʿAbbāsid caliphate which was to endure for five centuries, the great divisions of Islam, at first purely political, but later to develop into sects often bitterly antagonistic to each other. The original solidarity of the Islamic community had been irrevocably breached.

PRIMITIVE ISLAM BECOMES A DEVELOPED RELIGIOUS SYSTEM

To discuss, now, the mainstream of the development of Islam (from which Shīʿism may be regarded as a major divergent), it is necessary to retrace our steps a little. Emerging from Arabia, Islam entered a world predominantly Christian and Hellenist though it later came in contact with numerous other influences—Manichaeism, Zoroastrianism, even Buddhism, influencing the proliferation of heretical and ephemeral sects often holding beliefs remote from and opposed to those of the founder of Islam. Both in Umayyad times, and later even at the ʿAbbāsid court, one finds Christian and Muslim theologians debating their religious beliefs, for Christianity had by this period built up an imposing structure of dialectical theology through an amalgamation of Christian tenets and Greek philosophy. Surrounded by these influences, Islam now entered a formative period during which the primitive, apparently illogical and often contradictory revelations of the Qurʾān were, by a process of re-interpretation, change of emphasis, and other means, welded into a coherent, consistent, and workable religious system.

The great centres of Islamic culture were firstly at Damascus, the Umayyad capital, but chiefly in ʿAbbāsid Iraq with the great cities of Baṣra, Kūfa, and Baghdad, but of course the Holy Cities, Mecca and Medina also had an important part to play. The Islamic faith was created specifically for Arabian conditions, but the Arab tribes who brought their religion and culture to the settled countries of the Fertile Crescent were themselves largely sedentary, living in houses and cultivated districts. They were distinguished from the population of the conquered countries which entered Islam as clients (*mawālī*) on the same pattern as the protected *mawālī* of pre-Islamic Arabia, by their higher social standing, not major cultural differences—they were not destructive like the pastoral Hilālī tribes who migrated to North Africa in the eleventh century. Racial assimilation, the diffusion of Islam, the evolution and extension of its laws and characteristic culture took place for the most part in the ʿAbbāsid period.

Under the ʿAbbāsids, Orthodox Sunnī Islam, following the custom (*sunna*) of the Prophet, gradually took shape, and Shīʿism, which might have become the orthodox attitude, failed to do so. From the Khārijīs eventually stemmed the Ibāḍī sects, in practice inimical to the ʿAlids, holding however that any pious believer is eligible to become the *imām*, or head of the Muslim community. The Murji'īs who were, at the very least, tolerant of the Umayyads, have disappeared, and the Qadarīs, or exponents of the doctrine of Free Will, merged early with the Muʿtazilites.

The Muʿtazilites, those early Believers, who stood aside from ʿAlī yet had no sympathy with the Umayyads, were to play an important role. Their attitude was summed up well in the statement "ʿUthmān was killed and we do not know whether his blood was lawful or not for he had committed misdemeanours (*aḥdāth*), then you (i.e. ʿAlī) besought him to repent, and he repented, then you were involved in his murder when he was murdered, and we do not know if you are right or wrong".[1] Early Muʿtazilism as it developed must be regarded as the theology of the ʿAbbāsids—it was indeed their official school for at least a century. Politically they found it in their interest, being themselves Hāshimites, to diminish the position attributed to ʿAlī, while not breaking their link with the Shīʿa. Muʿtazilites, adopting the logical method of Aristotle and making it the foundation of their dogmatics, can be described as the "rationalists" of Islam. During the eighth–tenth centuries, often under direct patronage of the ʿAbbāsid caliphs, Syriac translators were rendering Greek writings, including Aristotle and Plato, into Arabic. The Muʿtazilites came into conflict with the Traditionists who supported their dogmas by Traditions remounting to the Prophet and attempted to adhere to the Qur'ān and the Sunna, that is, the practice of the Prophet, as their pious ancestors had done. So, in dogmatics and jurisprudence the Traditionists advocated a return to the Qur'ān and Sunna, a cry to become

[1] al-Minqarī, p. 551.

familiar with reaction or reform throughout subsequent centuries, and by way of evidence they compiled a vast collection of Traditions of ancient practice.

An outstanding issue between the official Mu'tazilite school and the Traditionists of the early ninth century was whether the Qur'ān was created, as the Mu'tazilites held, or not. The celebrated Ibn Ḥanbal, founder of one of the four Orthodox schools or rites (*madhhab*) of Islam, taught that it was uncreated. "The Qur'ān is the speech of Allāh, written in the copies, preserved in the memories, recited by the tongues, revealed to the Prophet. Our pronouncing, writing and reciting the Qur'ān is created, whereas the Qur'ān itself is uncreated." Ibn Ḥanbal suffered for his doctrine, but it was left to a later theologian, al-Ash'arī, to formulate the Orthodox tenets on an intellectual basis. Turning his back on Mu'tazilism in which he had been trained, he used its dialectics to combat it. Orthodoxy nevertheless grew less hostile towards dialectic as time went on.

Out of the Sunna, the customary practice of the Prophet, grew the system of Islamic law known as *sharī'a*, though obviously much of it must simply be ancient Arabian tribal, market, and peasant law continuing with minor modification. In early Islam the Sunna, or custom, allegedly of Medina, held a very high place, practically equal to the Qur'ān in authority. This corpus of legal precedent was however handled a little differently by the several Orthodox rites of Islam. It is the author of the earliest surviving law-book of Islam, the scholar Mālik b. Anas (fl. eighth century), who has given his name to another of the four schools, the Mālikī rite, which today flourishes in North Africa, the Sudan, and Nigeria. Mālik's aim was to survey law and religious ritual according to the *ijmā'*, or general consensus of Islamic opinion at Medina.

By the end of the eighth century the Islamic system was being worked out from the Qur'ānic and Traditional elements, but *sharī'a* law is not only fundamentally the same in the four Orthodox schools, but even in the Shī'a law schools which sprang up at Kūfa and Baṣra, and differences lie mainly in points of not very important detail. In the process of formulation of *sharī'a*, a most notable name is that of al-Shāfi'ī (d. 820) who insisted that only a Tradition with a chain of narrators remounting to the Prophet could be regarded as fully valid. The effect of this requirement with regard to documentation was to render the *sharī'a* somewhat inelastic by sanctifying it with the Prophet's authority. Nevertheless the school which bears al-Shāfiʿī's name had, before the Ottoman expansion in the sixteenth century, won the central lands of Islam. It still predominates in Egypt, Syria, south Arabia, Malaysia and Indonesia, and prevailed in the Ḥijāz until the conquest of the Ḥanbalī Wahhābīs.

The remaining Orthodox school is that known as Ḥanafī after Abū Ḥanīfa, a Kūfan scholar (d. 767), the adherents of which are mostly to be found in India and Turkey. It is regarded as the most liberal of the schools and was the official rite of the ʿAbbāsids, and, later, of the Ottoman Turkish empire.

The period of the formation of the orthodox schools is regarded as the age when individual opinion (*ijtihād*) was formed in matters of law and theology, based of course on certain criteria. In later times the only right that experts in legal matters had was to give a legal view (*fatwā*) on questions put to them, but the Shīʿa, on the contrary, can still exercise the power of personal opinion up to the present time.

Probably from very early days, the mystics, quietists, little concerned with the formalist side of theology and law, seem to have existed within the ranks of the Muslim community. Their attitude to the law, which they averred had no weapon against religious hypocrisy, incurred them the enmity of the professional theologians and legists of the major Islamic sects. These Ṣūfīs, or *mutaṣawwifūn* as they are called, gradually coalesced into an authoritarian system of Ṣūfī orders in which initiates pass through various stages of development guided by experienced *shaykhs*. Ṣūfism in this form has long come to terms with, and been incorporated in orthodoxy, and the Ṣūfī orders (*ṭarīqa*) have spread over the Islamic world. With the Ṣūfīs are generally associated saint cults. In saint cults which are very widely spread in Muslim countries and a focus of popular religion there frequently survive practices, clearly of a pagan nature, for which the orthodox criticize them. Not all Ṣufī orders of course are associated with saint-cults, and many Ṣūfīs have been persons of high intellectual and moral stature.

The disaster of the abrupt end of the ʿAbbāsid caliphate in the thirteenth century did not for long impede the progress of Islam, though, when the Mongols under Hülegü Khān murdered the last ʿAbbāsid caliph in 1258 and sacked Baghdad, its cultural capital, they dealt it, it is true, a blow of a most serious nature. But by now the powerful Islamic civilization had taken a well established shape, deriving from an amalgam of multifarious elements. On the intellectual side the great disciplines of theology, law, science, and even technology were established. Arabic, the language of the Qur'ān, had become the vehicle of these disciplines from Spain to India, and had, beside, a vast literature. In the arts and material culture a very high level had been attained. Islamic civilization in many of its aspects exerted considerable influence upon medieval Europe. Islam, despite its internal divisions, was able to repel the Crusader and convert the Mongol savages who damaged it so severely. The Arabians of course had long lost political control of the caliphate to other races though their language had spread over many lands, not always displacing the native tongues. Notable men in all ranks and professions during the 'Abbāsid period were drawn from a multiplicity of races. While acknowledging a vague spiritual authority to the 'Abbāsid caliphs, the Islamic world had disintegrated into provinces and petty states politically independent of the centre. Often these were controlled by Hāshimī descendants of 'Alī such as the Sharīfs of the Ḥijāz and the still existing dynasties of Morocco and Yemen.

THE TERRITORIAL EXPANSION OF ISLAM[1]

At this point the physical expansion of Islam by the thirteenth century may appropriately be considered and the spread of the faith after that time.

In Africa Islam slowly penetrated Christian Nubia and the Sudan via Egypt and the Red Sea coast (though Christianity survived until about the sixteenth century), and hence to the neighbouring regions of Africa, but the great expanse of West African Islam has also been influenced by contact with Arab and Berber North Africa conquered in the first century of Islam. Spain (in which Muslim states survived for a period longer than the era dating from the Reconquista to the twentieth century) was an important cultural centre of Islam till the Moors departed. Sicily, Malta, the Balearics, parts of southern France and of Italy came, for shorter or longer periods, under Muslim rule. From Persia Islam had spread into Turkestan and other parts of Central Asia by the tenth century, and following the Mongol conquest of the thirteenth century large numbers of Muslims were taken across from

[1] Cf. Sir J. B. Glubb, *The Great Arab Conquests* (London, 1963); *The Course of Empire* (London, 1965), for detailed information.

Persia by the Central Asian route to settle in China. From very early 'Abbāsid times Muslim communities existed at Canton, the eastern terminus of the sea-route to China. In Eastern Europe the Tatars who invaded Poland and Hungary in the thirteenth century became Muslims and have left small groups there to this day. On the earliest Arab invasions of Sind information is meagre, but over the centuries that have elapsed since that time the Indian sub-continent has come to contain the largest number of Muslims. The coastal territories of the Indian Ocean and Far East have been exposed to peaceful Muslim penetration by trading communities from the eighth century onwards, though again the history is obscure. East Africa is predominantly Shāfi'ī because of the efforts of Sayyid missionaries from Ḥaḍramawt who also played an important part in the conversion of Malaysia, Indonesia—now containing nearly 80 million Muslims, and the Philippines. It appears that it was an Indian type of Islam with a strong mystic flavour that first reached Indonesia, but this was displaced by Arab Shāfi'ism, the bulk of the conversion having taken place about the fifteenth and sixteenth centuries. With the fall of Byzantine Constantinople to the Ottoman Turks in 1453 the last obstacle to Islamic expansion in the Balkans was removed, the Turks advancing up to the very gates of Vienna. Though the Ottoman tide has now ebbed it has left pockets of Muslims in those countries, such as the Muslims of Yugoslavia and Albania.

ISLAM IN MODERN TIMES—THE NINETEENTH AND TWENTIETH CENTURIES

Indeed the central lands of Islam had themselves, by the mid-sixteenth century, fallen to the Ottoman Turks whose capital city was Constantinople and whose sway extended from Algiers and Tunisia eastwards to the Persian Gulf. Into the protracted economic decline and stagnation of the last century and a half of the Ottoman empire there came the shock, in 1799, of the Napoleonic invasion of Egypt which, brief as it was, may be taken as heralding the modern age. It may also be regarded as initiating the process of colonization of the Islamic countries. The signing of the Versailles Treaty in 1919 left but few remaining independent Muslim states. In the nineteenth century the conservative Islam of the time not only suffered from the dislocation caused by the technical superiority of the West and from Western conceptions at variance with it, but was directly attacked by Christian missionaries under European protection.

Within Islam itself however, during the course of the nineteenth century, movements of importance still took place, some of which might be distinguished as backward-looking, seeing in a reversion to a Golden Age—in this case the lifetime of the Prophet and his Companions—the ideal solution to all problems, and those other movements which attempt to come to terms with our present time, though both would claim to go back to an idealized past.

There is, first of all, the Arabian Wahhābī movement (founded actually in the mid-eighteenth century) aiming at a return to Arabian Islam in its pristine purity devoid of innovation. Its monotheism attacks cults connected with saints' tombs—considered by the Wahhābīs as polytheism—and it advocates strict practices like compulsory attendance at prayer, etc. By contrast the Sanūsiyya, also backward-looking, does not attack saint (marabout) cults, though it aimed at restoring the original society of the Prophet in the north African steppe. It is an order of Ṣūfī mystics of the North African Mālikīs, the Sanūsī, its founder, himself being an Algerian descendant of the Prophet. A movement whose ostensible motive was the elimination of pagan practices among the West African Hausa was the *jihād* of the Fulani reformer 'Uthmān dan Fodio who, like the Wahhābīs was opposed to saint cults. The messianic belief in the *mahdī*, a member of the Prophet's family who will manifest himself at the end of time, was particularly widespread among Muslims of North Africa, and Muḥammad Aḥmad the Dongolawi (Dunqulāwī) of the Sudan, who claimed to be this person, consciously modelled himself on the pattern of the Prophet Muḥammad, though in fact he stands in the direct line of tradition from the scholars and saints of his own country. Nowadays his original movement has become transformed into a more or less orthodox order (*ṭarīqa*).

In our present age however it seems no more possible for a Muslim to solve any given contemporary problem merely by recourse to searching through the Qur'ān and *ḥadīth* than it is for a Christian automatically to find a solution by reference to the Gospels, though of course one can extract any answer one wishes from a religious book provided one ignores the interpretation carefully worked out by objective scholarship and supplies a subjective, perhaps emotional, sense instead. Nevertheless during the nineteenth century movements developed in Egypt and India to reinterpret the Qur'ān and Tradition so as to bring practice in Islam into general conformity with certain aspects of Western thinking of that time.

The initial inspiration of the Egyptian movement stemmed from that stormy champion of Islam the Sayyid Jamāl al-Dīn al-Afghānī, champion of the ideal of Pan-Islam, the union of all Muslim states into a great Muslim empire. This ideal was adopted by the opportunist and reactionary Turkish Sultan 'Abdülḥamid who, in fear of the overthrow of the Ottoman dynasty, laid emphasis on the Ottoman claim to the office of caliph in succession to the early caliphs of Islam whose names are revered over most of the Islamic world. It was al-Afghānī's pupil Muḥammad 'Abduh, an Egyptian of the peasant class, a Ṣūfī and a *shaykh* of the ancient Islamic University of Cairo, the Azhar, who gave the main impetus to the modernist movement which sought to find an accommodation between Islam and the age. He was convinced that only by a thorough reform of the whole Islamic system, amounting in fact to an evolution of a new Islam, could it prove its inherent adaptability to conditions of the day, though to him this meant but a return to its original form. He saw no conflict between religion and science, for he held that both are based on reason, and he even tried to introduce modern science into the Azhar, the stronghold of Islamic conservatism.

In nineteenth-century India (under British rule), the conservative *mullās* resolved on the disastrous policy of boycotting Western institutions, especially secular education, until the efforts of such men as Sir Sayyid Aḥmad Khān showed Indian Muslims the mistake of avoiding contact with the Christian West. With Sayyid Amīr 'Alī and the poet Iqbāl, he was largely responsible for the introduction of Western science into the Muslim educational system, and, by degrees, a modernizing movement, parallel to that of Egypt, grew up in Muslim India. A new emphasis was laid on the personality of the Prophet to portray him as the Perfect Man, influenced strongly by missionary presentation of Jesus. It should be remarked here that in Syria the educational and polemical activities of Christian missionaries provoked an Islamic reaction leading to readjustment of thinking, though of course as in all Islamic countries conversion from Islam to Christianity is as rare as the reverse process. So then, nineteenth-century Muslims could not ignore attacks on their faith—in which they endeavoured to show true humanity, reason and morality. Because of the greatly differing stages of evolution in these various countries modernist movements took place contemporaneously with revivalist movements of a most reactionary type.

The Indian continent is also the home of the Aḥmadiyya, regarded widely as heretical, and often arousing the violent opposition of other Muslim groups. Their founder, Ghulām Aḥmad, is considered a prophet by some, by others only a reformer. They display a marked acknowledgement of Western ideas which they attempt to fit into an Islamic framework, and they give the Qur'ān an interpretation of their own. The movement is characterized by strong missionary activity.

After 1920 when most Muslim countries were ruled by colonialist powers which could not be dislodged, Muslims everywhere realized more acutely than ever that their backwardness, especially in technical spheres, was due to a lack of education of the type and diffusion obtaining in the West. So everywhere the demand for modern education spread, triumphing over the prejudices of all but the most extreme reactionaries. The abolition of the caliphate by the Turkey of Mustafa Kemal, a severe blow at pan-Islamism, was disturbing to all Islamic countries, to none more so than India, and a stimulus to the existing trend towards nationalism of a secular kind.

Mustafa Kemal introduced anti-Islamic measures of a sort that no colonialist power would have dared to suggest, the abolition of the *sharī'a* courts, the introduction of monogamy, the secularization of education, and the like, in many of which he has been followed of latter years by Jamāl 'Abd al-Nāṣir of Egypt. So, after the Kemalist revolution, Egypt replaced Turkey as the spiritual capital of Islam, and the Azhar University grew enormously in prestige, though Jamāl 'Abd al-Nāṣir's recent radical changes and secularization of the Azhar, coupled with the too great use of it for political ends by the Egyptian Republic, might conceivably diminish this influence and may not ultimately be to its advantage. Over the last forty years the Azhar has however sent many purely religious and educational missions to Islamic and other countries to maintain and disseminate the knowledge of the faith, and conservative though its teaching may be, it has undeniably played an important role in the diffusion of religious education during that time.

The conservative type of Azharī outlook in Egypt, with its counterpart in other Muslim countries, has found political expression in the Muslim Brethren (*al-ikhwān al-muslimūn*). The movement was founded at Ismā'īliyya in 1928 by Ḥasan al-Bannā', himself descended from a scholarly family; it courts the professional religious of the Azhar group and is opposed to the secularism of the Egyptian of Western outlook. The Ikhwān held a great appeal for the masses, and constituted a powerful and well-organized reformist movement of a somewhat conservative type. They were dissolved by Jamāl 'Abd al-Nāṣir in 1954 after an attempt on his life, but remain widespread and active with a centre in Switzerland; recent disturbances in Egypt would seem to show that they have still a following there, by no means negligible.

During the last decade Islam has suffered devastating attack, not from the foreign Christian missionary effort (*tabshīr*) which is receding as Islamic missionary activity (*tablīgh*) is growing, so that it is an important influence no longer, but from within the ranks of Muslims themselves. In so many Muslim countries secular military governments, controlled by juntas of army officers who have seized political power, tend to regard traditional Islamic institutions as reactionary, an obstacle to progress, and a potential source of opposition to themselves. The essentially theocratic nature of Islamic society is rejected and ideals of nationalism, already somewhat outmoded in Europe, replace it. Education is no longer moulded on traditional Islamic ideals, but on secular Western lines, and though religion is taught it has perhaps often little impact compared with the injection of national socialism given at the same time. On the other hand, for one reason or another, Islamic countries have mostly rejected Communism. Islam of course is still immensely strong, and within its ranks it contains many men of high intellectual calibre conscious of the problems that face their religion and society. Moreover it is still very much alive, and nowadays there are Muslim communities in every country, to say nothing of a great variety of sects, including a recent movement, the Black Muslims of the United States, perhaps not to be accounted very Islamic in the traditionally understood sense.

CHAPTER 2

ISLAM IN EGYPT

Egypt is a country upon which fourteen centuries of Islam have left a deep impression. Of the 26 million inhabitants recorded by the 1960 census, it is estimated that Muslims represented 24 millions. The Egyptian Muslims are nearly all Sunnis; most of them belong to the Shāfiʿī and Mālikī rites. Most of the rest of the population belong to the Christian minority of orthodox Copts. These proportions of Muslims and Christians should however be treated with some caution since, at the present time, there are no recent, reliable and undisputed statistics on this point.

The traveller will at once be struck by the Muslim character of Egyptian social life. Nothing survives from the times of the Pharaohs, Greeks and Romans except ruins, splendid it is true, but dead. Christian churches are to be found in certain quarters or certain districts in Egypt. On the other hand, mosques and minarets can be seen everywhere. In Cairo, for example, these places of prayer, which for centuries were also centres of social life and study, serve to remind us that Islam was introduced on the banks of the Nile at a very early period. Thus, there is the mosque of ʿAmr at Fusṭāṭ, rebuilt on the very spot where the conqueror of Egypt, ʿAmr b. al-ʿĀṣ, had erected the first important mosque in Africa, in 643; or the mosque of Ibn Ṭūlūn, built in 876; or that of al-Azhar (970–2). Several still very flourishing sanctuaries, such as Sayyida Zaynab, Sayyida Ruqayya, Sayyidnā Ḥusayn, etc., are centres of devotion to the family of the Prophet, this devotion having in the past been encouraged by the Fāṭimid caliphs. Others contain the remains of Muslim scholars, such as the Imām al-Shāfiʿī, the jurist with whom one of the four orthodox rites is connected, in the southern cemetery of Cairo: these places also are frequented by the common people. Perhaps this is because Islam has always encouraged respect for religious knowledge and veneration for the learned, the *ʿulamāʾ*: "Among His servants, only the Learned fear God", says a well-known verse of the Qurʾān which many authors are fond of quoting.[1] In Egypt, incidentally, Cairo has a virtual monopoly of Muslim historical monu-

[1] Qurʾān xxxv. 25–8.

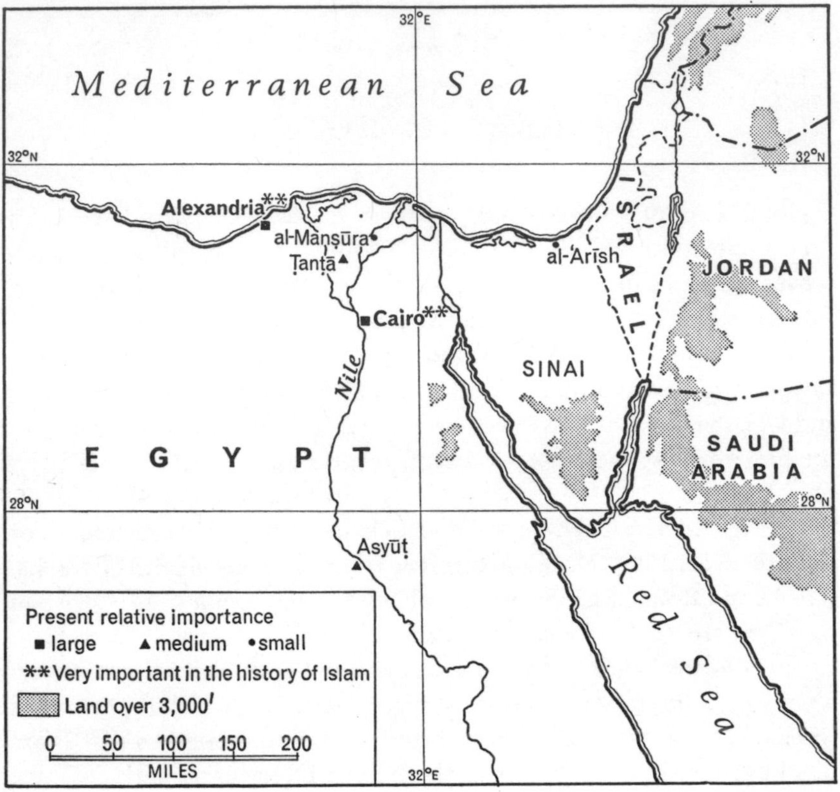

Egypt.

ments, and masterpieces of ancient Muslim architecture outside the capital are extremely rare. On the other hand, sanctuaries visited by the faithful are to be found throughout Egypt. Some of these are small tombs in villages, but others, like that of Sayyid al-Badawī at Ṭanṭā, are particularly famous, and their festival attracts tens or hundreds of thousands of Muslims annually.

It is not only in religious buildings that the influence of Islam is evident; it is clearly visible in everyday life. There is no need here to take note of all the ordinances imposed by religion, since their observance in Egypt does not differ in essence from that of neighbouring Arab countries; we shall return to the subject at the end of this chapter. For the moment, it is only necessary to say that religious practice can everywhere be readily attested, whether it is a question of prayer or the fast of Ramaḍān. As for the pilgrimage to Mecca, it was estimated that, until recently, in normal times from 25,000 to 40,000 Egyptian believers took part in it each year; only during the years of political tension or war, when transport has been affected, has this figure been considerably reduced.

Even in certain picturesque minor details, apparently peculiar to Egypt, the people's attachment to their religious traditions is revealed. In country districts or in crowded quarters of towns, to emphasize the importance of the pilgrimage, people often decorate the outsides of houses inhabited by pilgrims to Mecca with naïve pictures; thus, when the newly returned pilgrim comes back to his home, he finds the train, the ship, the mosque, even the aeroplane painted round his doorway. This fresco will last for many months, a reminder to all passers-by of the holy places of the Ḥijāz; dust from the desert or a new coat of whitewash will in time efface it.[1] Similarly, with Ramaḍān, side by side with the customs common to all Muslim countries some will be noted that appear to be peculiar to Egypt. Such is the practice of giving children small lamps, a kind of miniature lantern, as toys, recalling the time when children accompanied their elders on nightly visits, through the dark streets of the medieval city.[2]

The ascendancy of Islam also appears in another sphere. In recounting the struggles of the past and in setting before the young the example of their forebears, and that of Saladin in particular, it is, once more, the Muslim history of Egypt that the teachers and school textbooks are evoking.

Nor should we forget the actual presence of Muslim students who have come from Africa or Asia to enroll in Cairo at al-Azhar or in one of the faculties of the state universities; their presence is a symbol of the mission which many Egyptian Muslims feel themselves called upon to fulfil in relation to the rest of the world. Lastly, the political influence achieved by means of press, radio and the publication of Arabic books exported to all the Arab countries as well as to Black Africa has made Cairo one of the most important capitals of the Muslim world.

Thus, whatever some may have thought or said, Islam still continues to make its imprint on the public and private lives of the majority of Egyptians. The important fundamental values which constitute the moral beauty of a human life (trust in God the Creator, respect for one's

[1] J. Jomier, *Le Mahmal et la caravane égyptienne des pèlerins de la Mecque* (Cairo, 1953), plate VI.
[2] Jomier and Corbon, "Le Ramadan au Caire en 1956", *M.I.D.E.O.* vol. III (1956), pp. 1–74.

parents, family solidarity, the idea of mutual assistance, forgetfulness of self when put to the test, endurance, patriotism, etc....) are all visualized by the Egyptian Muslim through the eyes of Islam.

In spite of everything, this traditional aspect of the faith in Egypt is not the only one. The industrial revolution which brought about a radical overthrow of the material conditions of life throughout the whole world had its repercussions in the religious sphere. The real problem facing Islam in Egypt is that of its place, considered as a religion, in the modern world; on the banks of the Nile; in a society now in the process of transformation. What will Islam become? And as the present situation cannot be understood without some consideration of the past, it will be helpful to look back to the period when Egypt's awakening began. We shall then see how reformist circles preached a religious revival as part of a general revival. Later, we shall note that this reform movement has become out of date, now that several of its objectives have been attained. Finally, we shall try to envisage the future.

The modern awakening of the Muslim countries began tragically and brutally, in a way that wounded the sensibilities of many and that will take long to forget. The first shock came when the most discerning suddenly became aware of the scientific and industrial advance being made by the countries of western Europe. This advance was enabling those who profited by it to adopt an aggressive policy and to lay hold upon the wealth of vast regions overseas. Thus, in Egypt, Bonaparte's expedition (1798–1801), and later the occupation of the country in 1882, opened the eyes of many; but it was very late, and in any case too late to save them from having to endure a foreign presence on their native soil. Incidentally, the same phenomenon was occurring everywhere, throughout the whole world. But, in an Islamic country, it was an even more painful experience since, until the eighteenth century, Islam had never ceased to expand, except in Spain and the islands of the western Mediterranean where it had been driven back. In the Islamic countries, victory had always been regarded as a sign of divine protection: "We had pledged ourselves to give victory to the believers", says a verse of the Qur'ān speaking in the name of God.[1]

What was taking place? The state of bewilderment can be seen in the recollections of an Egyptian *shaykh* who, in one of his books, referred

[1] Qur'ān xxx. 47.

to the religious crisis which he had suffered in about 1882, at the age of twenty, and which incidentally he later overcame. All the foundations of his convictions were crumbling, and when a railway line had been laid not far from his village, he pondered "These railways on which trains are now running are not the work of Muslims. What do the Europeans who have done this work have to say?"[1] The leading Muslims in Egypt were realizing the utter lack of adaptation in their traditional educational system; after allowing themselves to be outdistanced, they had to make good the ground they had lost. It was then that the genuinely Muslim attempt to bring about a revival was made; it followed several courses (we are not referring here to the attempt to bring about the general modernization of Egypt, undertaken by Muḥammad 'Alī, though the reader must keep this attempt constantly in mind):

(1) in the matter of apologetics, to restore the Muslims' confidence in Islam and in the excellence of their civilization, and also to justify in the eyes of the traditionalists, who were opposed to all innovations, an evolution of society which was becoming increasingly necessary;

(2) in the field of educational institutions, starting with the attempt to reform the ancient mosque-university of al-Azhar; then, when the task proved too difficult, creating a whole series of establishments for advanced education in whose syllabus religious subjects took their place alongside scientific and technical subjects;

(3) finally by resorting to political and military activities, in varying degrees. While some leaders followed a purely national line, rallying round them Copts and Muslims, others immediately adopted a Muslim politico-religious programme which the Palestine war, first underground and then overt (1947–8), and the struggle against the occupation seemed to justify in the eyes of its supporters.

It is important to understand the exact character of the mosque-university of al-Azhar referred to above, so that it should not be confused with the state universities of the Western type founded during the last fifty years. At the beginning of the nineteenth century, al-Azhar was the only place in the whole of Egypt where an advanced education was given. Since that time, despite the existence of other universities, it has remained the principal establishment for the training of professional men of religion, the *'ulamā'*. This mosque has now been in existence for a thousand years. It was built between 970 and 972, and

[1] Quoted by Jomier, "Le Cheikh Ṭanṭāwī Jawharī", *M.I.D.E.O.* vol. v (1958), p. 125.

thus dates from the conquest of Egypt by the Fāṭimids and the building of their new capital al-Qāhira which was at once undertaken, this name soon embracing all the neighbouring townships and being perpetuated in the modern name Cairo. Al-Azhar was the congregational mosque of this new city. In the immense medieval city of Cairo, teachers taught under its porticos, as they also did in many other schools and mosques. When the Turkish occupation of Egypt (sixteenth to eighteenth centuries) hastened the decline of population and intellectual decadence, all these centres except al-Azhar fell into decline. Thus the resurgence of intellectual life that came later took place under the aegis of al-Azhar and in a centralized manner. It was therefore only after the eighteenth century that al-Azhar became a university, incidentally including elementary and intermediate classes, in short a system that was at once primary, secondary and advanced, if these terms are permissible. In the nineteenth century it was to al-Azhar that the rulers of Egypt went to seek out the most gifted students, who could be sent to Europe to specialize and after that made to work to modernize the country. At that time no other intellectual élite except that of Azharists was in existence. But, for its part, al-Azhar was for long to remain impervious to all modern ideas, and it was only very slowly that it later became open to them. It was outside al-Azhar, and sometimes indeed in opposition to the actions of its most conservative teachers, that everything evolved. While many reformers were attempting to breathe new life into the curriculum and into Muslim thought, al-Azhar continued its traditional role of training professional men of religion, and thereby its conservative influence was brought to bear on the people. It also affected certain circles in other Muslim countries through the medium of former pupils from those countries who had come to study there. Thus it was always the policy of the rulers of Egypt to foster this establishment, particularly during the time of the khedives and the monarchy. Despite everything, the reforms at al-Azhar were effected slowly. The last and most radical of them dates from 1961. With its application, the situation may be changed in the near future.

As for the reformers themselves, their role has been variously interpreted. They did not constitute a true school of thought, nor did they produce any genuinely original work; but, being situated in the midst of an intelligentsia itself affected by the course of evolution and by so many upheavals, they advocated a few simple ideas and sounded the key-notes to guide the reforms, thus restoring confidence to many of their co-religionists. They were in some measure the conscience of their period, formulating more precisely and disseminating those ideas that were beginning to appear. Were they carried forward by the new wave? Or, on the contrary, did they create this wave? It is difficult to say. The fact still remains that the ideas which they defended were eventually accepted by almost everyone, whilst they themselves were gradually consigned to oblivion. If, since 1940, several authors had not devoted themselves to the task of making them known and if school textbooks, such as the new collections of biographies, had not mentioned them, it is probable that silence would have obliterated their memory. One fact is clear, in any case; it is very rarely that anyone reads their books today, except perhaps the treatise on Divine Unity of Muḥammad ʿAbduh which was used as a textbook for classes at al-Azhar some years ago.

In this brilliant company of reformers, the name most deserving of recognition is that of an Afghan, Jamāl al-Dīn al-Afghānī (1839–97), whose origins are still shrouded in obscurity and who lived in exile for the last thirty years of his life. Impetuous, argumentative and cultured, he had read many of the great works of medieval philosophy but at the same time he was capable of attempting assassination. He plunged into a relentless struggle, giving himself three objectives—to put an end to the occupation of the Muslim countries by the colonial Powers, to fight on the territory of Islam against those Muslim sovereigns who were opposed to reforms, and lastly to challenge the materialistic European ideas which were then penetrating the East. He was no stranger to the history of modern Egyptian Islam since he lived for eight years on the banks of the Nile (1871–9). His activities made a profound impression upon a whole group of young men, several of whom were later to play an important part in the revival of modern Egypt. He encouraged them to found newspapers and reviews and to write, with the object of influencing public opinion, uniting them all in a masonic lodge which he had founded. Exiled in 1879, he stayed for a time in India and then, in Paris in 1883, he again met one of his disciples, the Egyptian Imam Muḥammad ʿAbduh, with whom he was to direct a review *al-ʿUrwa al-Wuthqā* (The Indissoluble Bond). The eighteen numbers that they jointly published in 1884 exerted a certain influence almost everywhere in Islam; in them was expounded the whole modern body of argument of the reform circles, such as was to be repeated without any significant change until our own time.

After the failure of this review when publication had to cease (the very strict censorship prevented its entry into India and Egypt), Jamāl al-Dīn once again set out on his travels, a tireless pilgrim in the struggle for the freedom of Islam. After visiting Persia, Russia and England he ended his life in Istanbul where he had been brought in 1892 by Sultan 'Abdülḥamid; he died there in gilded captivity in 1897.

Of his disciples, the one who followed the most religious line was Shaykh Muḥammad 'Abduh (1849–1905). Born of an Egyptian country family and sent by his father to attend the ordinary classes at al-Azhar, Muḥammad 'Abduh found in Jamāl al-Dīn al-Afghānī the support and guidance that he had hitherto lacked. He attached himself to the older man while the latter was living in Egypt. Then, on being appointed chief editor of the *Egyptian Gazette*, he became involved in 'Urābī's revolt (1882); arrested like so many others during the repression of the rising, he was sentenced to three years' exile. In Paris, where he had been summoned by Jamāl al-Dīn, he helped to edit the review *al-'Urwa al-Wuthqā*. On the cessation of this review, he separated from his master and thereafter pursued a more peaceful career which was more in keeping with his temperament and, in any case, the only one open to him in the circumstances. After staying for three years in Beirut, he returned to Egypt in 1889. From then onwards, he endeavoured to stir the conscience of his co-religionists and to promote a more spiritual conception of Islam, based on fidelity to the spirit of the Qur'ān to which above all it was important to return. Henceforward he gave particular attention to reforms which he considered capable of immediate realization, such as the reform of the Shar'ī courts of justice (courts applying the Qur'ānic law) and that of al-Azhar. In the latter instance he succeeded in getting a first series of measures adopted. He became Grand Muftī of Egypt in 1899 and died in 1905. He wrote several works of religious doctrine, such as his treatise on Divine Unity, and a commentary on the Qur'ān as far as Sūra IV. His dignified and simple literary style helped to bring about the abandonment of the elaborate style fashionable in his youth. In politics, he believed that the prime enemy of all reforms was the khedive who nevertheless seemed at times to support the reform movement. With the object of more effectively counterbalancing the khedive, he therefore came to be on closer terms with the British during the last years of his life. Certain nationalist circles which had adopted other views reproached him for this attitude.

A Lebanese Muslim, Sayyid Rashīd Riḍā (1865–1935), a refugee in Egypt where he found the liberty that the Ottoman Empire denied him, disseminated the ideas of Muḥammad 'Abduh as well as his own in the monthly review *al-Manār* (the Lighthouse) which appeared in Cairo from 1898 to 1935 and which was read in all the Arab countries by a Muslim religious élite. "This review became the organ of the reform movement which it to some extent took over, and exercised a considerable influence until the death of its founder."[1] Each number contained, among other articles, a continuous modern commentary on the Qur'ān which is certainly the most interesting of those that appeared in Egypt in the nineteenth and the first half of the twentieth centuries.

One could give a whole list of names of others who worked with the same purpose, for the most part Egyptians but also some Syro-Lebanese Muslim refugees in Egypt. Among these was 'Abdallāh Nadīm (1848–96), a disciple of Jamāl al-Dīn al-Afghānī, who, both by his writings and his stormy life, many years of which were spent in hiding after the occupation of Egypt in 1882, gave encouragement to a whole generation of readers. Others were Qāsim Amīn (1865–1908), the champion of feminine rights, and Farīd Wajdī (1875–1954), an apologist, some of whose semi-scientific concordist views seem very out of date today. Among those whose activities were more overt were Shaykh Muṣṭafā 'Abd al-Rāziq (who died in 1947) or, more conservative than the reformers and an excellent preacher, Shaykh Maḥmūd Shaltūt (1893–1963), both of whom were rectors of al-Azhar when they died.

Efforts to modernize al-Azhar have in fact been made since the beginning of this century, with varying results. Successive laws were promulgated to introduce a whole series of reforms in 1908, 1911, 1930 and 1936. The last law, in 1961, completely remodelled the curriculum of primary and secondary courses at al-Azhar, bringing them into line with the corresponding courses in the governmental schools. This is certainly the most important aspect of the measure; for the receptiveness of adults depends to a very large extent upon the primary education that they received as children. In addition, new faculties (commerce, administration, engineering, medicine, etc.) have recently been introduced at al-Azhar. It is still too early to be able to evaluate the significance of such changes.

The Muslim revival led also to the forming of various associations.

[1] 'Abd al-Jalīl, *Brève histoire de la littérature arabe* (Paris, 1943), p. 232.

Some of these, being basically political in character, do not concern us here. There are others, however, which must be mentioned, such as the Association of Muslim Youth which was started in Cairo in 1927. But the association which proved most controversial was the "Muslim Brethren". Founded in 1928 by Shaykh al-Bannā', it represents a more advanced experiment in the field of reform. Sermons, catechisms, meetings in cafés and mosques, the publication of pamphlets and reviews, the setting up of clinics and various small model industrial establishments lasting for some months or years—all these appeared outwardly to be the practical work of the association which, in about 1946, included nearly a million members and sympathizers. For many, this movement certainly provided an opportunity to devote themselves to God and to rediscover, in fraternity and prayer, the taste for spiritual realities which the modern world has so often caused to be forgotten. The Brethren also launched some paramilitary organizations which fought in Palestine (1947–8). It was the attitude of a minority of extremists which destroyed them. As the result of several criminal outrages in Cairo committed by these groups, the movement was banned for the first time in December 1948, while the political police procured the assassination of Shaykh al-Bannā' (1949). The movement resumed its activities in the years that followed, but an attempted assassination, this time aimed at President Jamāl 'Abd al-Nāṣir in Alexandria in 1954, proved fatal to it. Several of the Brethren were condemned to death and executed; many others were interned, and in Egypt the movement was banned. This was still the situation in May 1965.

One of the best series of modern Egyptian novels[1] took as its setting the life and evolution of three generations of a family in Cairo between 1917 and 1944. The author personifies the tendencies of the younger generation by embodying them in three young men. The first is the politician who marches with the old political parties, the second is the Muslim Brother, the third is the Marxist. In 1945 it certainly seemed that the Brethren was the movement with the greatest vitality capable of attracting young people concerned about their faith. At that time there were murmurs, even among the Azharists, that al-Azhar had failed in its mission and that the Brethren would raise the flag of Islam once more.

[1] Group of three novels often designated by the name of *al-Thulāthiyya* [The Trilogy], published in Cairo in 1956–7 by Najīb Maḥfūẓ; cf. *M.I.D.E.O.* vol. IV (1957), pp. 78–83.

In a country as densely populated as Egypt, it is quite understandable that other trends should have manifested themselves besides those of reformers properly so-called, whether moderate reformers or the Muslim Brethren. Many educated Egyptians, reflecting on their faith or traditions, published works on religious subjects. The great mass of leaflets, reviews, etc., unquestionably derived from active associations such as the Muslim Brethren or from traditional institutions like al-Azhar, or even from small devotional groups, confraternities, etc. Nevertheless, a certain number of independent individuals wrote works some of which were widely read. It should be noted that the majority of these people helped to establish the universities or else attended lectures at them. One of the most important features of modern society in Egypt is indeed the existence of these state universities. The first to be founded was the University of Cairo (in 1925 at Giza). Others followed, such as those at Alexandria, ʿAyn Shams (in fact the second state university of Cairo), Asyūt, al-Manṣūra, Ṭanṭā, etc. Now, in these universities, the staff of teachers included some sincere believers, and a good number of these wrote books on Islam or Muslim civilization, in the first instance for their students but ultimately for a wider public also. The foundation of these universities so clearly marked a new stage in the life of Egypt (whether Muslim or Copt) that Najīb Maḥfūẓ, the novelist referred to above, spoke of entry to the university as the starting-point of the evolution of a whole generation.

In the religious sphere, it must be confessed, these writers, even when members of the universities, remained highly traditional. There are few works of any originality to record. Among these, we should in particular note the work of Maître ʿAlī ʿAbd al-Rāziq on the caliphate and the separation of the spiritual and temporal powers which he advocated for Islam (1925), or that of Muḥammad Aḥmad Khalaf Allāh who, in 1947, to some extent introduced the idea of literary genres in the Qur'ān. The antagonism that both encountered showed that public opinion did not accept their views. However, Muḥammad Khalaf Allāh's work is now officially on sale and is in its third edition. We should also note various works on the life of Muḥammad and the beginnings of Islam (especially the first caliphs) by the best living writers. These reflect the image of their past which cultivated circles now entertain; in these works, fervour and devotion often influence the choice of the traditions that are dealt with. A place apart must be given to the very fine and highly spiritual essay of Dr Kāmil Ḥusayn, in which he envisages the problems of conscience of those who decided to condemn Jesus on Good Friday.[1]

Since 1945, and particularly since 1952, events in Egypt have succeeded each other so much more rapidly that many things are in process of being changed. The reform movement seems to be entirely out of date, now that many of its objectives have been attained—the opening of the modern world to Muslims who at the same time retain their faith in the Qur'ānic message, the independence of the Muslim colonized countries, the replacement of sovereigns who resisted reforms, the establishment of institutions whose function is the dissemination of the Muslim message throughout the world. It is particularly evident in the realm of feminism. Running parallel with the world-wide movement for the emancipation of women (the spread of education of girls, work for women outside their homes, their participation in political and military campaigns), the reform movement had preached the stability of the home and the limitation of polygamy and had called for a restriction of divorce. It relied on a text of the Qur'ān which requires that the husband should be just to his wives and that, if he cannot be so with several, he should remain monogamous. And it emphasized the point that, in the present day, no justice is possible without monogamy, save in exceptional cases. The reform movement had also secured acceptance of science, technology and industrialization in order to be strong and to restore its former glory to Islam. On the question of banks and loans on interest, the reformers temporized, and modern life has succeeded in legitimizing what the doctors hesitated to admit. Only the Muslim Brethren really faced the problem and, to finance their commercial and handicraft enterprises, they issued shares yielding dividends but absolutely refused to countenance those yielding fixed interest.

The other opinions held by the reformers have been made especially clear in their propaganda. To the West, they wished to demonstrate that Islam was in no way inferior in respect of civilization, and that Qur'ānic principles were even superior to what could be found elsewhere. The main themes they developed were those of Islam as the religion of reason, fraternity, strength, democracy, peace, unity, socialism, etc. It is unnecessary to dwell upon this aspect of things. It will be enough if those who live in daily contact with Muslims remain

[1] This work has been translated into English by K. Cragg under the title *City of Wrong* (London, 1959).

aware of it, so that they should not be caught unprepared. This apologetic is of such a systematic and often suggestive, and at times even factitious, character that many Muslims for their part reject it. On this apologetical aspect of modern Muslim thought Sir Hamilton Gibb has made certain observations which apply to Egypt. He noted, in about 1945, to what an extent this attitude was leading to a loss of objectivity and, in existing circumstances, what a serious obstacle it constituted to the evolution of thought in Islamic territory.[1] The example of the propaganda practised in so many European countries can only strengthen this tendency. Only the intellectual courage of the best teachers can ensure that the rising generation feels concern for truth for its own sake, and for the whole truth.

In practice, it is perhaps in legislation that the clearest indication of the evolution of the Muslim world, in Egypt as elsewhere, should be looked for. This evolution had begun more than a century ago. With the era of the recovery of independence it assumes a deeper significance. One cannot find fault with the laws for having been imposed from without; it is the Egyptian authorities who wish them to be what they are. Political power has always played a large part in Islam, and there was a time when the 'Abbāsid caliphs intervened with their full authority in theological debates, such as that on whether the Qur'ān was created or uncreated. At the present time, the part played by this power in the evolution of the Muslim world is considerable. It does not seem to be suffering any diminution; on the contrary, with the centralization of the socialist states, one may expect to see the political authority continuing to legislate on religious matters. Modern laws in Egypt long ago proclaimed the equality of all (for military service, taxation, etc.). Certain traditional positions of the medieval doctors, such as the law according to which a non-Muslim could not inherit from a Muslim, were partly modified: it is now laid down by law that the Christian widow of a Muslim official should receive the same pension as if she were Muslim. As for the right of free choice of religion, the law recognizes this officially for every Egyptian who has attained his majority, even when Muslim. Some of these laws, the last in particular, still meet strong social resistance, so habitual has religious discrimination become after so many centuries of medieval life; but these laws exist and have already been put into operation.

The revolution of 1952 was to give this legislation a new impetus

[1] H. A. R. Gibb, *Modern Trends in Islam* (Chicago, 1947), particularly the last chapter.

from which Islam benefited. The revolution in Egypt was directed against a certain order of things, characterized by foreign domination (both economic and military), and against those who were accused of favouring that domination. If there were Muslims among the Egyptians who were removed, they were not the principal targets; it was against the foreign communities that the movement was at first directed. Islam was not on the side of these communities; throughout the whole occupation period, al-Azhar had remained the bastion of the teaching of the Arabic language, in the face of attacks by those who wished to see it reduced to secondary rank. In national crises, in 1919 and again in 1956, it was in the mosque of al-Azhar that people and leaders came together spontaneously. Thus the disappearance of the former ruling class did not give rise to any anti-religious measures, in contrast to what had so often occurred in European revolutions.

The new government was opposed only to certain aspects of traditional Islam and wished to modernize everything in the Muslim religious system that lagged too far behind. It abolished property in mortmain (private *waqf*) from which certain individuals were beneficiaries, swept away religious courts and set up an administrative system dependent on the State. At first glance, it may seem to amount to a secularization of the state; in fact, it was a question rather of transferring to centralized governmental bodies work which previously had been performed by professional men of religion, in separate groups. In the old Constitution, Islam was declared to be the "state religion", and this is still the case in the new one. The government also encouraged feminist trends which ran counter to the practices of medieval society but which were in no way opposed to the Qur'ānic law. Thus the right to vote granted to women, their presence in the National Assembly and in many positions, even that of minister, are signs of the times; they will be seen as the logical conclusion of the admission of young women to the university thirty years ago.

But, in addition, part of the resources of the now socialist and centralized state were placed at the disposal of Islam, while the state assumed full responsibility for the intensification of the anti-colonialist struggle as had earlier been strenuously demanded by the Muslim Brethren. Thus the government and in particular the Ministry of Religious Worship set up a whole series of bodies concerned with publication and popular religious education by pamphlets, reviews, gramophone records, etc. A permanent "Islamic Congress" was founded in 1953 in Cairo, to help to reinforce and disseminate Islam. Radio and television have increased their Muslim programmes. Since 1964 a special radio station, the Voice of the Qur'ān, transmits, from 6 a.m. until 11 p.m. with a pause at about midday, a complete chanted recitation of the Qur'ān, the whole of the text thus being given in two days. Grants are awarded to African and Asian Muslim students to study at al-Azhar, in addition to those given for study at the state universities; a vast university city has been created for the benefit of these foreign Azharites in Cairo.

More deeply significant than all these external manifestations, it can be observed that, for some twenty years—that is to say, since the time of the founding of the Arab League (1945)—Egypt has been increasingly committed to the path of Arab nationalism. How is this nationalism to be evaluated in relation to Islam? Arab Christians often insist upon the distinction to be drawn between Arabism and Islam: they are not Muslims but Arabs, they remind us.

Muslims, on the other hand, have envisaged Arab nationalism from several points of view. At the beginning of the century Egyptian reformers did not speak of Arab nationalism; the universality of Islam under the caliph appeared to be a sufficient ideal. However, when Turkey, the seat of the caliphate, adopted a Turkish nationalist policy after 1908, a great many Arab Muslims renounced that country and adhered to the Arab nationalist movement. They justified their decision on the following grounds. Islam needs the Arabic language and Arab culture; as the Turks are now rejecting this language and this culture it becomes necessary to create an independent Arab fatherland where these values indispensable to Islam can flourish.[1] Atatürk's nationalistic policy and the suppression of the caliphate in 1924 made this course even more imperative. For Egyptians under the influence of the reform movement it is essentially in these politico-religious perspectives that Arab nationalism is seen.

Beside this impetus to reform there are other tendencies among Egyptian Muslims. Even though everything that is written, said or preached on the religious plane is in practice marked by the ideas and apologetics of the reformers, we should not forget the silent attitude of those who are saying nothing just now, but are preparing the future, especially in the field of legislation. For a large number of Egyptian Muslims Islam is first and foremost a community. Whatever the extent

[1] Rashīd Riḍā in *al-Manār* (Cairo), vol. xx, pp. 33–47.

of their religious practice as individuals, they all want to see Egypt's political and economic development within the framework of the great Arab fatherland (*al-waṭan al-ʿarabī*). To strengthen their country, which is Muslim, is to them the best way to serve Islam. They do not care about justifying each of their actions by juridical arguments; they are wary of the casuistry that might impede action, and they feel estranged from men of religion, whom they consider old-fashioned. In the past this Arab nationalism frequently spoke about parliamentary democracy. Today, though a fairly large number of Muslim intellectuals and even of intelligent workers cultivate the ideals of liberty, parliamentary democracy and laicism, their voice is seldom heard. Since 1952, Egypt has formally abandoned parliamentary government based on the multi-party system, and since 1961, the year of the wholesale nationalization of Egyptian undertakings, there has been far less talk of *qawmiyya ʿarabiyya* (Arab nationalism) and far more of *ishtirākiyya* (socialism).

As for the clash with Communism, Egyptian Islam is acquainted with that too. No doubt, politically and economically speaking, it is above all to Western capitalism that, since 1952, Egypt has been opposed, and it is striking to note in the press today the wholly different tone employed when speaking of the Western world and of the Communist world. It is to the second that their sympathies are extended. Despite all this, Muslim believers have realized the danger that threatened their faith from Marxist atheism. The Muslim Brotherhood were the first to react, in pamphlets, in about 1945. After the revolution of 1952 and in particular after 1955–6, as a result of aid received from the Communist bloc, a damper was put on the publication of studies of Marxist atheism. But certain writers such as ʿAbbās Maḥmūd al-ʿAqqād were not afraid to speak. And in 1959, when a pro-Nāṣir movement in Iraq was crushed with the help of Communists, the circumstances made it possible for some Muslim religious reviews to publish articles on the danger from Marxist atheism. One of these even quoted an earlier occasion when President Jamāl ʿAbd al-Nāṣir had referred to this so-called "religion" of Marxism, for which the Muslims would not abandon their own.[1] In general, the most characteristic points of view were those of the authors who believed that the socialism of Islam was its best protection against Communism.

Must we conclude, as is sometimes done, by saying that Egyptian

[1] *Majallat al-Azhar*, vol. xxx (May 1959), p. 944. See also p. 986 for the social rôle of property in Islam.

Islam is at present apologetic and political? Without doubt, it is above all in these two directions that the reformers have reacted. And yet, despite the impressions left both by so many demonstrations and also by international congresses, such as that of the *'ulamā'* held in Cairo in March 1964, this conclusion would be incomplete and would overlook the essential feature. In religion, as in other things, there is both what one says and the way one lives. Apologetics and politics have tried to restore its former glory to the Muslim community. But there still remains the essentially religious attitude of man, face to face with God.

Looking beyond the various events that we have noted, we are at the present time witnessing a profound transformation of the world, in Egypt as elsewhere. On the one hand, this evolution is resulting in some of those concerned being cut off from religion, or at least from religious practice. Whereas, in the country, almost everyone gathers at the mosque for the Friday prayer, in the large towns only a fraction of the population attends. On the other hand, this minority of confirmed believers seems to be more conscious of its duties. It consists of souls who are searching for God, whether students or members of the ruling classes. Here can be seen a sign of the religious vitality of this minority which is opposed by another irreligious or atheistic minority, and, between the two is the great mass of the people, whose religious observance varies in degree but who nevertheless are still believers.

The fact remains that the faith of the Muslim is simple. In regard to the Unicity of God the Creator, it involves certain essential truths which do not need a great literature for their exposition. This faith is nurtured in the family, in traditions, in the practice of prayer, good works or devotion inspired by their surroundings and by divine grace. Perhaps too it can select instinctively the essential passages in the books that are read and overlook the rest. And thus, whatever the developments of apologetics and the implications of politics may be in Egypt, there still remains among the higher minds the one essential, this faith in God, the only God, the Creator and the Good, together with devotion to the Prophet and all the positive acts that this faith inspires.

CHAPTER 3

ISLAM IN THE COUNTRIES OF THE FERTILE CRESCENT[1]

> The heart of the Middle East is the Fertile Crescent...Since most of the religious, linguistic and national minorities are to be found in this area, the Fertile Crescent has the most heterogeneous population in the Middle East.[2]
>
> JOANNE E. HOLLER

The area with which this chapter deals includes the countries now known as Iraq, Syria, Lebanon, Jordan and Israel, the last two comprising the "Palestine" of most of the last three millennia. In any effort to estimate or reappraise the value of religion in the region in this century account must be taken of the paramount faith of the inhabitants for nearly fourteen centuries as well as of the events of the past seventy years. In times of stress people tend to look back to "the rock from which (they) were hewn, and to the quarry from which (they) were digged". There is a quarry-like solidarity in the Islamic world, though some loosened stones are sometimes in evidence. The Fertile Crescent, for all the extension of Islam since the seventh century and in ever expanding circles throughout Asia and Africa, remains closest to the rock from which Arabism and Islam were hewn. Some of the components of the area have hardly known for the past 5,000 years the direction of the next invasion, political or religious; but most of them would never have credited the possibility of the most recent, with the recapitulation of the first Israelite invasion of Canaan, connected with the names of Moses and Joshua—much less have expected it to have the deliberate support of Western imperialisms, even of the United Nations. It is this fact which has bedevilled human relationships and cut at the roots of revealed religion in the very home of monotheism, with the horrors of polytheism eliminated.

[1] The text of this chapter was completed in 1965, so that no cognisance of the events of June 1967 has been possible. In view of these, there are details which might require revision; but the main conclusions and contentions remain, in some cases heightened by the tensions caused by recent occurrences.

[2] *Population Growth and Social Change in the Middle East*, vol. 1 (The George Washington University, D.C., 1964).

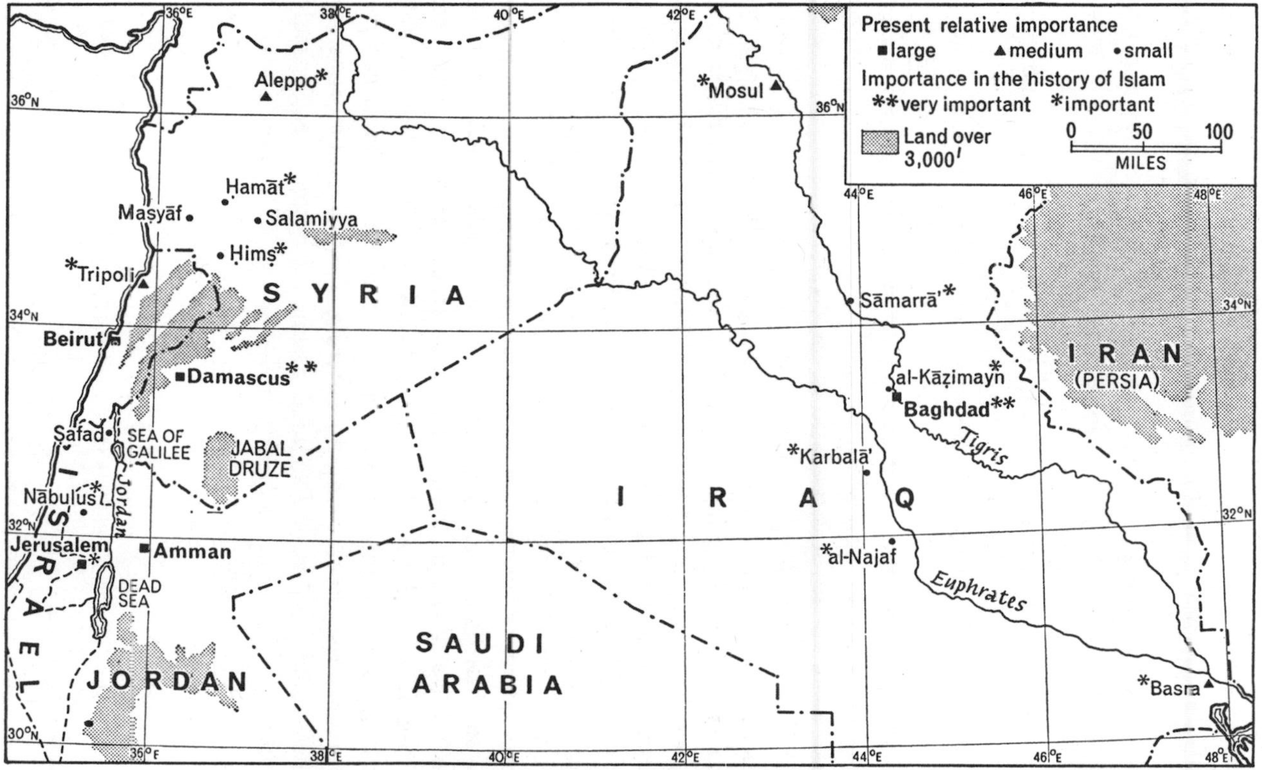

The Fertile Crescent.

It is probably true that the Islamic world of the Mediterranean region has felt the onslaught more than the Christian. While some Muslims of the modern generation have sought solace in secularism, others filled with a mixture of dismay, depression and disillusionment have returned in thought to Medinan days of Muḥammad's ministry rather than the Meccan. "When Muḥammad became head of a state, it was not a temporary expedient but the essence of Islam"[1] (Kenneth Cragg). Back in 1922 a missionary with decades of service behind him[2] remarked "You will find that this country (Palestine) has not yet recovered from the Crusades". But the Crusades constituted a minor episode compared with the disastrously mistaken policies of the twentieth century. The overwhelming tragedy of 1948 has meant more than frustration or resentment, alike for those who anticipated some such issue and for those who never dreamed that it could ever be. Till this fact is realized, nothing is gained by asking the victims to overlook the past. They don't.[3] Iraq has lost a Jewish community, integrated into the life of the country since the days of the Babylonian exile. Syria, Lebanon and Jordan have had fantastic frontiers imposed on them, along with other disabilities. The results of a wayward policy are not rubbed out by financial grants or higher education. Even if the validity of the calamity could remain unquestioned, its effect upon ordinary religious outlook is a more serious phenomenon. The end is not yet.

Anyone driving in the 1960s from Jerusalem down to Antioch, or in the reverse direction, would negotiate three national boundaries. The road through Haifa along the coast is off. There remains the roundabout route across the Jordan, then north to Damascus for Aleppo or some other point for entering Turkey. Nonetheless the traveller would echo more than once, despite the boundaries, the sadly true verdict of Heraclius, as he quitted Antioch, "Farewell Syria my fair province". Lebanon, though by-passed, adds to the beauty of it all. In Heraclius' day, and before him back to St Paul there were no

[1] *Islamic Surveys* 3. *Counsels in Contemporary Islam* (Edinburgh, 1965), p. 118. (Quoting al-Ghazālī in *Min hunā na'lam*.)

[2] The Reverend F. Carpenter who worked in Jaffa and Nazareth. Cf. Kenneth Cragg, *The Call of the Minaret* (New York, 1956), p. 265.

[3] Cf. Nevill Barbour in an address given to the Royal Central Asian Society, 15 December 1964 (*J.R.C.A.S.* vol. LII (April 1965), p. 110), "No such justification can...be made for our action in accomplishing (the establishment of Israel) at the expense of a people entrusted to our care; nor is it possible to turn a whole nation out of their country, and then ask them, as we seem to do, to let bygones be bygones".

such obstacles as frontiers, even when times were not incontestably peaceful. Today the changes in the structure of the political situation have been allowed, if not assisted, to become distressful, as in parts of Africa, and impracticable to the point of being ludicrous. "Who will show us any good?"

For Apostle and Emperor it was Syria—all of it—from the Orontes to the Jordan, from Aleppo to the Brook of Egypt. When Saladin ruled the area there was a sort of U.A.R. stretching from Cairo to Damascus. It nearly happened again in the earlier decades of the nineteenth century. To Antioch *in Syria* St Paul returned to make his missionary reports; St Luke is always careful to differentiate other "Antiochs". This was Syrian like the Lake southwards, of which Whittier wrote as the "Syrian Sea". *That* Syria no longer exists; though for four centuries she had been a cohesive entity within the Turkish Empire. But in 1919 Lebanon, Palestine and Transjordan were carved out to suit the imperial preferences of France and Britain, with Iraq too under Mandate of the latter. There was no self-inflicted tragedy as in the case of Pakistan. Just before the Second World War the Sanjak of Alexandretta, including *Antioch in Syria*, was ceded to Turkey. Six years later Palestine was deliberately lacerated in the interests of Western diplomacy. This alliance with (political) Zionism would seem to have been one of the most dangerous blunders of the century (so far), morally wrong in itself, and with religious ramifications wider than the Arab world. There is no rational appeal to any unifying forces of monotheism in the Fertile Crescent today. Like the erstwhile road through Haifa, that is "off"—for how long few would venture to prognosticate, or presume to offer any solution. The "Jerusalem that now is", and "is in bondage with her children", is both example and proof.[1]

Before the U.N. decision on partition as the method of resolving the Palestine problem, the principality (later kingdom) of Transjordan had been brought into being. In due course it absorbed, as the Hāshimite kingdom of Jordan, that section of central Palestine which had not succumbed to the pressures of Zionist invasion. Not for nothing does its statistical guide state that the kingdom is "separated from Occupied Palestine by the Armistice Line" (1962).[2] This left one

[1] Gal. iv. 25. The context interestingly is Arabian.

[2] Amman, 1962, p. iv. In *The Times* (19 May 1965) a Jordan government official is reported as saying that "the Palestine case is based on Creed and Principle—not on benefit and interests"

hundred and eleven villages in one country with their lands in another. The tragedy has cut across not only the physical geography of western Asia, but constitutes a constant threat to national securities, and (for the time being) renders nugatory the (missionary) progress of half a century towards the removal of religious misunderstandings and antagonisms. The Fertile Crescent has known too much of differing religious formulae during its history: it has perhaps experienced too much of the interplay of religious affiliations with political tenets within and without: though this must seem to many the second time in the Christian era that the European continent has interfered of set purpose in the life and prospects of the eastern Mediterranean. To understand the situation in this chiefly Islamic milieu it is essential to grasp realistically this basic fact and recognize the injustice done to national sovereignties—a sense of justice is as indigenous to the area as the ubiquity of the olive—coupled with western responsibility for the refugee calamity, involving the lives and usefulness of a million and more innocent men, women and children. This has transpired in a society which has always found difficulty in discerning the line of demarcation between the political and religious arenas. One early lesson the Prophet learned from the Jewish and Christian communities in Arabia was that monotheism made for unity in tribal life. Polytheism spelled discord and disruption. It does still. But this discovery was one of the phenomena his genius passed on to Islam, though other prophets before him had been confronted by a seemingly innate Semitic inability to co-operate. It was a fecklessness that he and his immediate successors eradicated; and the first countries to come within the orbit of this doctrine were those of the Fertile Crescent. "Peace is not the absence of tension but the presence of justice."

Domestically, however, it is not polytheism, as such, nor any brand of distracting Christian heresy (other than a school of prophecy) with which Islam has been confronted. The issue is not joined here, but in the combination of secular life, as elsewhere, and the revolt against orthodoxy. So besides these things that are without, Islam must tackle the inertia, indifference and unrealism that are engendered from within. It is here that the monotheists of the Fertile Crescent, Muslims, Jews and Christians, do sometimes find themselves in the same *wādī*. Except on occasions when feelings run high, are the mosques more frequented by young Muslims on Fridays than the churches by young Christians on Sundays? In how many of the Jewish collective colonies in mandated Palestine was there a synagogue? Since the followers of Islam and Christianity are considering similar problems from their teens onwards, it might be worth examining the proposal of one Muslim participant at the Muslim–Christian Convocation at Bḥamdūn (Lebanon 1954) that for communal needs which can be met by community action, there should be a centre (especially in areas of population growth and new housing estates) with a church and a mosque respectively abutting on the wings. Each sacred building should have one wall flush with the centre piece.[1] In *doing* things together the rising generation of Muslims and Christians might well discover the inspiration that lies behind—or should lie behind—any motivation to social service. Another participant from Damascus went a stage further in exclaiming that were it in his power he would found a mosque in which both Muslims and Christians would pray together.[2] In this context the denizens of the Fertile Crescent have the advantage of a common language. In their struggle for the modern expression of the Islamic soul, with all the inheritance of group loyalties, these countries have suddenly found themselves freed from foreign power-politics; free once more and at short notice to discover the right way through the unsettling movements and the intellectual disarray resulting from scientific and technological advance. Time was when their forebears were contented to know that God had expressed himself in the tongue of the Arabs and the brain of the Franks. This has gone for good and all. With "alien control ejected" the Muslims of the Fertile Crescent have shared with their Asiatic brethren generally in the "overall endeavour to reassert their community in the contemporary world" (Cantwell Smith).[3] Western research, scholarship and most of all friendship are welcomed; not political overlordship. Have not promising students throughout the area flocked westwards to imbibe part of what Europe and the U.S.A. have had to offer—to make them better doctors or more efficient engineers? If the events of recent years have turned their thoughts towards impending problems of defensive armament, Islam as Christianity is conscious of living *sub specie aeternitatis*. But just where does the authority of the Qur'ān express

[1] It is worth noting in this connexion that church and mosque at Lydda have a common wall between the Christian third and the Muslim two-thirds. The dedication is to St Georges Khiḍr.

[2] *Proceedings of the First Muslim-Christian Convocation, Bhamdun, Lebanon, 22–27 April 1954*, p. 78.

[3] *Islam in Modern History* (Princeton, 1957), p. 74.

itself in this whirlpool, or the influence of *ḥadīth* (tradition)? This is one of the burning questions.

Perhaps it is true to say that there are three main attitudes amongst Near Eastern Muslims in these days. There is a *Fundamentalism*, which reveals its loyalty in resistance to change and adherence to the Written Word. The Islam of the centuries is not dormant. Members of the Muslim Brethren will pull paperback copies of the Qur'ān out of their pockets—in English! Others seek to interpret Islam in a *liberal* spirit, with a modernist approach, knowing too that westward in Egypt and North Africa and eastward in Pakistan there are thinkers concerned for the reconstruction of Islam. There may not be enough re-examination of the Qur'ān critically and historically, such as that to which the documents of Christianity and Judaism have been subjected. And there are *simpler* believers too whose sense of the superiority of Islam is not lessened through the inroads of new learning. "The Arab Muslim", says Cantwell Smith, "is...proud of his faith: no other religion in the world has been so successful...in eliciting a confessional pride in its adherents."[1] "Islamic Unity", writes a former Iraqi Ambassador in London, "is more comprehensive and extensive than Arab Unity." In other words, since Muslims all through the world are one, how much more those of the Fertile Crescent. "Many Christian Arabs", he adds, "who are deeply conscious of their Arab nationalism look upon Islam with much understanding."[2]

As in other communities the world over, there are Muslims who have thrown over the religious side of the Islamic credo whether as *īmān* (belief), or *i'tiqād* (intellectual concept), and so tend to express their loyalty to the Faith through what is not quite correctly termed "nationalism". For the countries of the Fertile Crescent in their current fragmentation this hardly connotes the unification desired, which does not materialize through statehood. Michael Ionides has suggested "peoplehood" as approximating to the facts. There is a feeling of *Arabness*, not to be gainsaid—"a thing of the Spirit and not of territories".[3] "In the Arab's case [so Cantwell Smith] this pride in Islam is not separate from his national enthusiasm, but infuses it and gives it added point." Despite the deserts and the division the Fertile Crescent presents an Islamic unity of *Arabness*, not invariably manifest in other parts. Profound differences do not obscure this underlying *Arabness*.

[1] *Op. cit.* p. 230. [2] *Al-Bazzaz on Arab Nationalism* (London, 1965), pp. 70, 71.
[3] *Divide and Lose: The Arab Revolt of 1955-58* (London, 1960), p. 94.

The Euphrates flows through Syria to reach Iraq. Arabic has become a way of life as much as Latin or Hebrew. If the question remains whether Islam can meet once again the consequent striving after unity of culture and deeper religious living, and so give the answer to what the outside world regards as a lack of unity, this does not *per se* imply any absence of the desire for unity, but disappointment that the formula has not yet been discovered. After all serious differences exist in Western Christendom. With its language holy and irreplaceable this Islamic quest can scarcely be eliminated, much less ignored. It is here that the phenomenon of Islam impinges on that of Arabism. The question of which came first seems to be exercising the minds of Muslim thinkers in contemplation of the past and confrontation of the future.[1]

The Qur'ānic dictum that Abraham (Ibrāhīm) "was not a Jew, neither a Christian; but he was a *muslim* and one of pure faith, certainly he was never of the idolaters",[2] might well have more prominence and approval, historically at least, in the lands of the Fertile Crescent than anywhere else in the Islamic world, Mecca alone excluded. How many places westward and southward of Ur of the Chaldees have not been blessed with fragrant memories of the Patriarch—Aleppo, Shechem (Nābulus), Jerusalem, the Plain of Jordan, Hebron, where the Friend of God remains in veneration of the devotees of monotheism almost in unison. There is something eternal here. "Your Father Abraham rejoiced to see my day."[3] No one else could claim to be the patron saint of the Fertile Crescent, which in Abraham's day seems to have been very close to the border of Egypt. It is no wonder that he is singled out in the Prayer-rite of the Muslims.

> Make us, O Lord, the comrades of Muḥammad and
> Abraham Thy Friend and 'Isā (Jesus) Thy Spirit.

"Surely the people standing closest to Abraham are those who followed him and his Prophet (Muḥammad) and those who believe." Abraham used to hear "the throbbing and boiling of his heart during his prayers" (Constance Padwick).[4] More than that Abraham is pre-eminent in the total Islamic world as the builder of the Ka'ba. The pilgrims cannot forget the connexion of Ismā'īl and his father—'Arafāt, Ṣafā and Marwa,

[1] *On Arabism 'Urubah and Religion*, by Ismā'īl Fārūqī, is largely concerned with this problem (Amsterdam, 1962).

[2] Qur'ān III. 67. Abraham was not a *Muslim* before Muḥammad, but a *muslim* in the sense of one surrendering to the Divine Will.

[3] John viii. 56.

[4] *Muslim Devotions* (S.P.C.K., London, 1961), pp. 169 ff.

Zamzam—Abraham is there, no matter the intervening centuries of *jāhiliyya* (the Days of Pre-Islamic Ignorance).[1] What better incentive than all this for reinstating the Patriarch in the countries of the first great nomadic trek in Semitic history. Five thousand years later with his reputation enhanced the Arab armies poured out of their peninsula into the Fertile Crescent: and "these Arab conquests of the first century of Islam have remained Arabic in culture and predominantly Muslim in faith"[2] (C. F. Beckingham). Can the example of Abrahamic *ijtihād* (initiative) reassert itself? Is it here in the realm of initiative that Arabism joins forces with Islam, its latest exponent? Islam has been long enough in the world to be reckoned by those who hold it a matter of experience, not just experiment.

One institution with several hundred students with a fair percentage of Muslims records that while the serious keeping of Ramaḍān affects over 50 per cent, "one very very rarely sees a Muslim student reading a Qur'ān". Must the general impression be that the sway of Islam over the hearts and minds of the rising generation is waning; in other words that Muslim youth is no more attentive to the religion of its fathers than Western Christian youth? Is the trend towards secularism inevitable and conscious? Is it possible to obliterate the ingrained inheritance, without something virile and vital taking its place? One observer in Syria remarks that there seems some concession to Ramaḍān; and very few would break the fast in the presence of friends. No one deliberately wants to defy tradition or jeopardize reputation. "Whatever happens", writes Fayez Sayegh, "must depend on developments less connected with the ideas of Arab nationalism and Arab unity than with *Islam and its place in the hearts and minds of Muslims.*"[3] The struggle for the redemption of Islamic society, for the recovering of the Abrahamic initiative, the *ijtihād* which took him west and south, must lie with the *Ishmaels* of today rather than their fathers, and chiefly in the context of education, theoretical and practical. If it be true that as in our West many young people recognize no urge for the reconciliation of science and religion, boys and girls alike, Christians might well cultivate sympathetic recognition of the fact that in all the turmoil of the nineteenth century the Industrial Revolution by-passed the eastern Mediterranean. Words of the President of the U.A.R. are as true for the

[1] Aḥmad Kamāl, *The Sacred Journey* (first published in Great Britain, 1964), pp. 5, 50, 57 ff.
[2] *Atlas of the Arab World and the Middle East* (London, 1960), p. 48.
[3] *Arab Unity: Hope and Fulfillment* (New York, 1958), p. 94.

Fertile Crescent as for Egypt: "Our minds were trying to catch up the advancing caravan of humanity from which we fell back five centuries and more."[1] Here is a handicap with the seriousness of which neither Western Christianity nor Western culture had to contend when the twentieth century dawned. Darwinism was under weigh; while fundamentalism does not seem to work in quite the same way in the two religions. In this connexion recent trenchant words of Kenneth Cragg demand consideration:

For Muslims education tends to segregate two fields of discipline into two types. The mosque-school...style of training all too little serves the critical and knowledgeable fashion of mind, while the "secular" state-school, state university stream of students are all too often intelligently ignorant about their precise doctrinal heritage. With them Islam tends to be an allegiance of will and assumption, rather than an alert conviction. Only slowly is the educational duality brought into one.[2]

These words are quoted from a western Islamicist deeply concerned for the involvement of the Christian presence in Islam. They serve to emphasize words of a Lebanese Christian ten years ago, when the late Edward Atiyah wrote:

There is the problem of the gulf which is inevitably being created between the recipients of the modern secular education, with its basis in Western civilization, and those Muslim Arabs who are still receiving the traditional education...at mosque schools...This problem involves the deeper one of the Muslim Arabs in the modern world.[3]

In this educational dilemma the lands of the Fertile Crescent are probably better placed than other countries—from their position at the crossroads alike of history and geography. The standard of higher and general education was reached earlier. Even if touch with the West was commercial to start with, for Edward Pococke, the first Professor of Arabic at Oxford, served for six years as Chaplain of the Levant Company at Aleppo, Syria–Lebanon have been able to hold a key position in the development of relationships more important than the commercial. For fifty years and more in the widest sense Syrians have been employed as teachers, 1,000 miles from home. There were more graduates from the American University in Beirut at the inauguration

[1] Gamal Abd El-Nasser, *The Philosophy of the Revolution* (Cairo, 1951), pp. 42, 43.

[2] *Islamic Surveys*, 3, p. 61. Cf. Beckingham *op. cit.* p. 57. "...Arabs who will defend their religion fervently while ignoring its precepts and remaining ignorant of most of its tenets..."

[3] *The Arabs* (Pelican Books, 1955), pp. 230, 231.

of the United Nations in San Francisco than from any other university. A century ago a fresh translation of the Bible was undertaken in Beirut, when American missionaries solicited the help of Arab scholars, Muslim and Christian. The revision is now in progress in Cairo. This century has been described as one of "sudden and drastic changes".[1] At the other end of the scale it was in this area some thirty years ago that the initial effort was made to tackle the problem of illiteracy through the method connected with the name of Laubach. In this endeavour to "feed the minds of millions" Islam and Christianity have co-operated. The camps of refugeedom have not been neglected. This does not mean *eo ipso* the decline of the influences of oral tradition. But the growth in reading must lead to the emancipation of urban populations faster than that of the *fallāḥīn* and Bedouin. The injunction—"He that readeth (the *qārī'*) let him understand"[2] (what he is reading to others) remains as valid as ever. There may not be any nomads to cater for in Lebanon; but Syria (proper) is faced with the need for wider agricultural education, following on the gradual extinction of feudalism. Jordan is faced with a refugee peasant population which had educational advantages for fifty years, denied to her own. The Fertile Crescent has always reverenced the calling of the Teacher.

Lebanon as the lineal descendant of Phœnicia has maintained its mercantile reputation—with four ports compared with Syria's one; but the latter can boast of a greater proliferation of political parties, and with the great string of historical cities from Aleppo to Damascus, the last with memories of Saul of Tarsus and Yaḥyā b. Zakariyyā[3] and many a noted Muslim worthy of a later date. There has been more Arabism in both countries than further south; for the hierarchy of the Orthodox Church as of lesser communities has been Arab, while in the Jerusalem patriarchate control has remained over long in Greek hands. Jordan however may be better placed for research into Islamic influences. Amman has been enriched by the advent of Muslim intelligentsia from Palestinian directions, with a university already beyond the embryonic stage. Nābulus is one of the thoughtful Muslim centres between Cairo and Baghdad. The mushroom growth of Amman since 1948 has meant the need for new mosques; the city has passed the

[1] Beckingham, *op. cit.* p. 55.

[2] Mark xiii. 14. Cf. Rev. i. 3.

[3] The Church was not transformed into a mosque till the eighth century; but Yaḥyā was regarded in Islam as a prophet (Sūra 3).

200,000 mark since 1960. The peasant population still finds its spiritual sustenance met by an Islam its forebears knew and valued. The bulk of the refugees belong in this group of the more traditionally-minded. The same is roughly true for the Bedouin tent-dwellers, whose numbers are dwindling both through encouragement to settle and recruitment in the Arab army. What effect on this section of the community as on the influence of traditional Islam will these changes have? It is the urban group whom the outreach of secularism has touched; their sons and daughters may have gone further, in not treating the problem of science and religion as "an either-or".[1] "Prove all things; hold fast that which is good." Popular religion holds much of the allegiance of the villagers and the nomads. The inroad here, if such it be, is Pre-Islamic. Customs of long standing are hard to surrender as when Stephen roused the ire and enmity of the Sanhedrin. The peasant, rich or poor, is as wedded to his land as was Naboth the Jezreelite. This was centuries before the advent of Christianity and then Islam, but should help in the understanding of the refugee attachment to the Land of their own lands, and the consequent longing for return.[2] Grateful for work, as in the Jordan Valley, refugees are reluctant to leave concrete shelters for anything better, lest this might prejudice their ultimate restoration. *This attachment is religious*: not necessarily Islamic, though there are descendants of families settled in the reign of ʿUmar the Great, who are possessed of something of the same nature of emotional stress. These are factors which Islam should not write off as liabilities.

There is another cult which has held sway in much of the area of the Fertile Crescent for centuries, and which neither Judaism nor Islam nor Christianity has succeeded in sublimating—the cults of saints. Some of the *baalim* of the Old Testament would seem to have become the *awliyāʾ* of much later times. The number of places with *nabī* (prophet) in their names may be some proof. The cult is not as widespread in the open deserts of Syria as further south. The same system of devotion appears in oriental Christian life; the identification of Mār Elias with Mār Jirius is sufficient evidence. The fact remains that in village life the saint looms larger in the realm of worship and intercession than the more distant and transcendent Deity of Islamic faith. *Nabī* "whoever-he-may-be" is more accessible and knowable. Folklore stretches back

[1] In a personal letter where such are described as "completely self-sufficient materialists".

[2] This has been emphasized in refugee poetry. See translation of excerpts by A. L. Tibawi (*J.R.C.A.S.*, 1963).

into the days long before the birth of Christianity, let alone Islam. In more recent centuries characters eastern or western have become part and parcel of the saga. This is a problem with which none of the monotheistic religions has dealt satisfactorily—partly because they have had it so long.

There are two links in the Fertile Crescent, apart from the largely Iraqi attachment to the House of 'Alī, with the family in Arabia from which the Prophet sprang. Besides the King of Hāshimite Jordan (the last King in Iraq belonged in the same clan) the Great Mosque in Ghazza (Gaza) is dedicated to the memory of Hāshim, great-grandfather of Muḥammad. Hāshim was not a Muslim even in the Abrahamic sense; yet he has remained the *walī* of the area, which, despite its vicissitudes, is more solidly Muslim than almost anywhere else in the Fertile Crescent. In talking with anyone in Gaza whose name was not known it was customary to address him as "*Yā Hāshim*"—like the complimentary "Muḥammad" in other places. The ancient city is swollen to twice its size since mandate days, while the "Gaza Strip" is home to a quarter of a million dispossessed but patient Palestinians (Philistines). Most of these would express their faith in the agelong, "I am a Muslim, praise be to Allāh". Without this religious conviction and this characteristic patience, with potentialities human and divine, history these past two decades would have been far more serious than has been the case. If Jordan's ratio of Muslims to people of other faiths is fifteen to one, Gaza and the Strip have a population of which the merest fragment is non-Muslim. But it is this narrow fringe along the Mediterranean seaboard that has the prior right to the retention of the name of "Palestine"—Gaza being still the leading city of the Philistine confederation as in the centuries B.C. Islam has an unparalleled opportunity down this restricted *tihāma* (coast-land) of less than 100 square miles. People do not forget. God is with the patient.

Perhaps few countries have had to grow at the rate forced on Jordan in two decades, her reclamation of refugeedom balanced or offset by the reclamation of the desert, through the diversion of the Yarmūk. Jordan too has its importance for biblical scholarship and historical associations to counteract uncertainty for the future and (sometimes) isolation. Islam has become once more the guardian of Bethlehem and Jerusalem, with Nābulus the centre of the tiniest monotheistic community, the Samaritan, its biblical connexions antedating the Christian era, its credal formula closest to the Islamic. Through the Samaritans

Jordan stresses the place of Moses in the development of belief in the Unity of God.[1] It meets too with an angelology as detailed as that of Islam. The guardianship of Holy Places renders the little country important to the world of politics because important to the world of religion.

Jordanian minorities may be interesting, but they are negligible in comparison with the inter-community contacts with which Lebanon has to contend. Here are groups whose religious life seems at times too self-contained. Beirut has its small community of Jews. What contacts there are are superficial when they are not commercial.[2] Beirut too has more outside influences at work than other Near Eastern capitals. The margin between the Christian and the non-Christian inhabitants is narrowly drawn. But the country has received two influxes of refugees —the Armenians first, then the Palestinians. This has served to increase the autonomy of the various religious groupings, faced as they all are with the expanding of secularization. Here, remarks one observer, is "a weakening of the saint-cult", only practised by a remnant; while ordinary people are deprived of their former spiritual basis. Islamic Orders seem to have disappeared. "Religious values are weakened because they are not relevant to new goals of society" (Holler).[3] This may be part-reason for the decline in polygamy except in some rural districts of Syria at its widest, but in Lebanon it is practically extinct though for the Muslim marriage remains a religious obligation. For the younger and sophisticated groups all through the area monogamous marriages have long been the recognized rule. This is one of the subjects touching the position of women in Islam over which there ought to be much less generalization.[4]

In this connexion of religious values it is interesting to know that "the Mufti of Syria lectures weekly for an hour on television. This is a popular programme amongst Muslims and Christians...His position is quite ironic as he seeks to apply Islamic principles to current social concerns". Religion is a subject in official government examinations (Christianity being required for Christians). In Syria too *awqāf* are in some places wealthy enough to support mosques, orphanages and old people's homes. Religious people conserve past values; for the simple-minded (as elsewhere) there is the danger of syncretism—including

[1] John Macdonald, *The Theology of the Samaritans* (Philadelphia, 1964), *passim*.

[2] al-Fārūqī writes of the "Phoenicianism" of Lebanon (*op. cit.* pp. 140 f.).

[3] *Op. cit.* p. 11.

[4] Cf. discussion in Kenneth Cragg, *The Call of the Minaret*, pp. 165 ff.

Christmas celebrations! But Unity is regarded as of the whole Islamic world; but since there is a shared culture with the Jewish and Christian minorities, "Zionism" is regarded as "almost exclusively a political problem".

It is sometimes stated that the refugee problem would be lessened, if the refugee birth rate were reduced in volume. This merely begs the question. Nonetheless each of the sister countries in the Fertile Crescent has faced the problem in varying degrees and with partial solutions in specific circumstances. There is no possibility of any concerted plan. Jordan has received over half a million Palestinians, hence one out of every three inhabitants is a refugee, all of whom have been granted nationality. This does not mean absorption, since other problems connected with employment are created, while the Cis-Jordanians have for long had educational facilities that were not the privilege of Trans-Jordanians whose nomad life was more widespread. Lebanon has been unable to give nationality without disturbing the balance amongst her own communities. Syria like Lebanon has received about a fifth of the number who flocked to Jordan, but has given citizenship in many cases and proved more independent in making provision for the refugees. But one way or another Palestinians have been made aware of being reckoned *ahl al-bayt* (people of the household). For each country there is a moral issue involved. This includes responsibility for the care of displaced persons, which Muslims naturally assume. Ramaḍān helps the believer to sympathize with the less fortunate, and act accordingly. Furthermore there is the historic fact that by what has transpired a dagger has been thrust into the heart of Islam, so that the people of the Fertile Crescent, including the Iraqis with far fewer refugees, have had to re-examine their attitude to the outside world—Zionism in particular. As time has gone on with no implementation of the resolutions of the United Nations and consequent acceptance of the presence of refugees in each country almost as a matter of course, the refugees as such tend to have been forgotten; and thought becomes centred on the future of the host countries, forced into the sharing of a tragedy which was none of their making.

In terms of Christian thinking a million Muslims in the heartlands of the Islamic world have been pressured into the crucible of suffering. What is the answer of Arabism and Islam? For a thousand years and more Jerusalem has found room within its walls for the Dome of the Rock and the Church of the Resurrection. In the same square mile they have represented differing ways of life which have yet to converge. This actuality of modern Islamic history with the *Via Dolorosa* and the million Palestinians innocent and mostly Muslim walking in it cannot but affect the outlook of Muslim intelligentsia. But this is no struggle of Islam with Christianity—rather a joint endeavour to discover which way *Arabness* points. Both are assessing their values again; as in some Western countries ideas of God have undergone a change. In the clash of cultures Islam should be ready to accept as valid the experiences of Christianity. In days when both are deeply affected by Communism in its diverse forms, Islam must be asked to concentrate on its own constructive assets. We shall not do anything to counteract the hardening process resulting from the memories of the Crusades and the more recent laceration of the Holy Land (for which the Christian West must accept its share of responsibility) unless we are prepared to enter the *Via Dolorosa* of set purpose. Otherwise "if they do these things in the green tree, what shall be done in the dry?" The *Via Dolorosa* converges with the *Via Strata*, the Way of Arabism, not just Islam.

Islam as a world faith in the midst of conflict and confusion, with something to learn in the clash of cultures and something to teach in the clash of colours, should return not so much to medieval dogma as to those ethical principles which are the valued characteristics of any religion. Reminded of the divine *raḥma* (loving-kindness) in the daily reiteration of the *bismillāh*, the human counterpart of liberalizing tendencies should be envisaged too. Muslim believers should bear in mind the Islamic veneration of whom or what deserves respect or appreciation—by-products, as Temple Gairdner called them.[1] There is the traditional attitude to parents and the older generation as a whole, against which secularization seems to militate; there is the already emphasized resignation (*islām*) under (undeserved) affliction; there is the struggle it would be well to share with other faiths against the various aspects of usury and gambling, or the fight against the prevalence of alcohol—older legislation needing modernizing, not abrogation (*naskh*); there is an abhorrence of idolatry not always appreciated by those of other religions; and, as an inheritance from the once all-powerful mosque schools, the religious education of the rising generation in terms that can be understood; there is the genius for self-propagation—but what sort of Islam do Muslims of the Fertile Crescent

[1] Summed up in a paper prepared by Dr Eddy of the American University, Cairo, for presentation to the International Missionary Council in 1928, and later published privately.

desire to see passed on to animists throughout Africa? It has been estimated that of every ten African animists who come over to Monotheism, seven opt to become Muslims.

Internally the peoples of the area have an opportunity presented for the exercise of Islam ethically in the growing need to study the interests of the minorities—not so much the Christians for they too belong in a world religion, but the lesser groupings—Yazīdīs, Druzes, Mandaeans, Bahā'īs and their own sects, strong and virile in Iraq, but less so in Syria and Lebanon. The clash in Muslim beliefs may be inevitable—there is nothing against this in Islam any more than in Christianity—but a decline in ethics need never be.

In this connexion there is the Islamic remnant in the Israel of today—some 200,000 in all—in minority status, second-class citizens in their own country, many with their lands confiscated. In the history of the Fertile Crescent this has been something new for Muslims. The refugees are after all subjects of or subject to governments which are Islamic to a greater or less degree. But what should be the advice of Muslim leadership to this dispossessed and bewildered minority? In this situation to which Palestinian Muslims are unused, the problem becomes one of adaptation despite resentment. Here is a moral issue of an unexpected kind. In 1953 a Damascus professor published a booklet in which there is a section devoted to "Moralities" (*al-ādāb*).[1] Three aims are stressed; first, the strengthening of individual personality for rising to the assumption of duties and the bearing of life's hardships, even the enjoyment of the taste of sacrifice and effort in the pursuit of truth and good: secondly, the increase of the spirit of unification and co-operation amongst fellow-nationals, and the proscription of a spirit of selfishness and isolation in individuals: thirdly, the forbearance of the individual so far as his own rights are concerned, and his exertion for the rights of the community. These sentiments could as well have come from a convinced Christian as from this convinced Muslim. He would add the consequent rulings for the conduct of life—an Islamic conception which governed human existence in the effort to follow the Prophet in the smallest details. These Damascene counsels are supported by quotation from different collections of *ḥadīth* or by Qur'ānic precepts. As with other religions the practical issues of Islam must be the main concern of the community, ushered into an arena of

[1] Mustafa al-Siba'i, *Religion and State in Islam* (*This is Islam*, booklet 2) (Beirut, 1953), pp. 39 ff.

convulsing changes. These are changes which (in the words of Sir Hamilton Gibb) "have been accompanied by new political and social philosophies, which are not yet integrated with the deep rooted social ideologies in the Islamic world or with its economic life and potentialities...This has produced a complex of physical and emotional reactions which generate and perpetuate a broad era of instability, particularly marked in political life".[1]

It may then prove easily reasonable for Islam in the Fertile Crescent to study afresh and implement its theological basis—the things which belong in the realm of *dīn* rather than *dawla*. Or from another angle political fragmentation demands the effort to reach greater religious unification. "He who is not concerned for the matter (*amr*) of the Muslims is not of them." In past centuries, Islam was able to borrow and make its own cultures previously foreign, taking over (as Professor Grunebaum has reminded Muslims and others) medicine and mathematics from the Indians, logic and philosophy from the Greeks, to which might be added law from the Romans and prophets (chiefly) from the Hebrews, and this century's scientific and technological ideas from the West. Is it too much to think that the impact of modern cultures from the religious direction, rather than accelerate any process of de-Islamization, should lead to the realization of there being more things in common on the plane of *dīn* than has always been realized? The crux in Christian–Muslim relationships lies in the respective attitudes to Jesus Christ. At the Bhamdūn Convocation (1954) more than one reference was made to the fact that Islam, alone of the great non-Christian religions, found a place for the historic Jesus. Yet the total picture of Jesus as He was is different in Islam from what it is in Christianity, with all the latter's domestic divergences. The ethical teaching of Jesus is not the proper possession of Islam. It has been claimed that the Sermon on the Mount is all in the Qur'ān. Be that as it may, Islam from the Christian angle, needs more examination of the Gospel portrait of Jesus on lines already laid down by Muslim scholarship in Cairo and elsewhere.[2] The Fertile Crescent is better placed for an undertaking of this nature than other areas. Likewise there is need for an Islamic assessment of St Paul, an unknown quantity in the Qur'ān. The Islamic discovery of St Paul as *ṣūfī* before the Ṣūfīs might

[1] G. Grunebaum (ed.), *Studies in the Civilisation of Islam* (Boston, 1962), p. 337.

[2] Kāmil Ḥusayn, *Qarya ẓālima* (translated by Kenneth Cragg under the title *City of Wrong* (London, 1959).

well lead to a rediscovery of Jesus Christ. Looking elsewhere does not imply any policy of defeatism but the signification of a future and a hope.

Within the foreseeable future Islamic scholarship may well have to undertake a revision of the traditional attitude to the place of the Old Testament in Divine revelation. This is germane to the whole problem of the position of the Qur'ān. The doctrine of the supersession or abrogation of revelations previous to the Qur'ānic must be examined in the light of the last half-century of events in the Fertile Crescent. As in Christianity, factors which present themselves as unethical, and therefore not reconcilable with the Christian revelation of God, will have to be so considered from the standpoint of Qur'ānic ethics. There seems to have taken place a beginning in such books as Ismā'īl Fārūqī's *Arabism and Religion*. "The genuine voice of the early prophets of God", he writes, "stands out audibly in the Old Testament."[1] The modern Muslim has the right to be aware of what these prophets said and to appraise their validity and relevance in the light of the knowledge and events of the twentieth century. The names of several are mentioned in the Qur'ān; but readers should be alert to what they said in relation to their times as in the place they occupy in the divine economy.

So to the place of the Qur'ān. It is more than historically interesting that the question of the nature of the Qur'ān—the created or uncreated Word of God—seems to have derived from the aftermath of the Christological controversies succeeding the rise and fall of Arius. It is more important that the Qur'ān speaks of Jesus as the "Word of God". In the latter case the Qur'ānic *kalima* is the echo of the Johannine *Logos*. For Islam the declaration that this is the case comes with the greatest authority that Islam has known, *kalām Allāh*—the "Speech of God", which is a divine attribute from eternity. In Pre-Islamic times this discussion over the Person of Christ operated mostly in the lands of the Fertile Crescent; Justin Martyr taught in Rome but he belonged in Samaritan Shechem (Nābulus); Tatian hailed from Iraq; Theophilus was Bishop of Antioch (Syria); Apollinarius was the son of a schoolmaster of Berytus (Beirut); they and others were deeply involved in "the relation of the Logos to the Divine Being".[2] They could, if from differing backgrounds, have made their own the words of Athenagoras

[1] *Op. cit.* p. 17.

[2] J. F. Bethune-Baker, *An Introduction to the Early History of Christian Doctrine* (1903), pp. 124–9, 240.

that "it is the chief concern of the Christians to know God and the Logos who comes from Him". *Mutatis mutandis* the Muslims in the Fertile Crescent would echo the phraseology *vis-à-vis* Allāh and the Qur'ān, which is His speech. It looks as if Islamic scholarship must make research into the origins of the Qur'ān as a historical document, so of its relationship to the Divine Being. The problem of the *kalām* may not be far removed from the problem of the *kalima*. Some 900 hundred years ago a Muslim scholar, al-Nasafī, wrote in his Creed:

The Qur'ān, the Speech of Allāh, is uncreated and it is written in our volumes, preserved in our hearts, recited by our tongues, heard by our ears, (yet) is not a thing residing in them.[1]

As long again before that "in a recall to Fundamentals", it was written in a pamphlet by an unknown author not so far away from the Fertile Crescent:

It was there from the beginning: we have heard it; we have seen it with our own eyes; we looked upon it and felt it with our hands; and it is of this we tell. Our theme is the word of life.[2]

Should any change transpire in Islamic scholarship in this century as to the nature of the Qur'ān, the Fertile Crescent might well be the scene of another "Council of Nicaea".

[1] E. E. Elder, *Commentary on the Creed of Islam* (New York, 1950), p. 58. Cf. Cragg, *Islamic Surveys* 3, pp. 168–73.

[2] I John i. 1 (New English Bible).

CHAPTER 4

ISLAM IN TURKEY

"We hear now and then that the Turks are repudiating Islam. A greater lie was never told." Thus wrote Muḥammad Iqbāl, the spiritual father of Pakistan, in 1937,[1] the very year when the Türkiye Cümhuriyet Halk Partisi (CHP) had officially included the principle of laicism in their programme, and Islam seemed to disappear from the country. Yet Iqbāl was right, and still today the large majority of Turkey's inhabitants "feel honoured by being Muslims" (thus Kasim Gülek, general secretary of the CHP, in the newspaper *Ulus* on 15 February 1951). How can this situation be explained?

Already since the reforms of 1839 the importance of the religious law in the Ottoman Empire had been cut down to a certain extent, and, strangely enough, it was precisely the *'ulamā'*, the religious leaders who had helped in advocating some modernization.[2] Western influences became visible in new currents of literature which started blending liberal and social ideas with romantic dreams of the ideal Turkish culture, and Żiya Gökalp (d. 1924) proclaimed the threefold goal of Westernization, Turkization and Islamization. The framing of a constitution (after the abortive attempt of 1876) in 1908 was a further step away from the *sharī'a*-bound life though in the 31 March incident (13 April 1909) some people demanded the setting up of an administration that would conform to the sacred law of Islam.

The revolution under Mustafa Kemal, welcomed by most of the Muslim countries as a step against Western Imperialism, changed the situation completely. It seems that the turning point in the relations of the revolutionary army and the caliphal shadow-government was the *fatwā* of Sheykh ül-Islâm Dürrizade who in 1920 denounced Mustafa Kemal and his army as "a gang of common rebels whom it was the imperative duty of any loyal Muslim to kill".[3] The new leader, however, was by no means opposed to the religion of his people yet wanted

[1] *Speeches and Statements*, ed. Shamloo (Lahore, 1948), p. 217.

[2] U. Heyd, "The Ottoman Ulama and Westernization in the time of Selim III and Mahmud II", *Scripta Hierosolymitana*, vol. IX (Jerusalem, 1961).

[3] D. Rustow, "Politics and Islam in Turkey" in Richard N. Frye, *Islam and the West* (The Hague, 1957), p. 75.

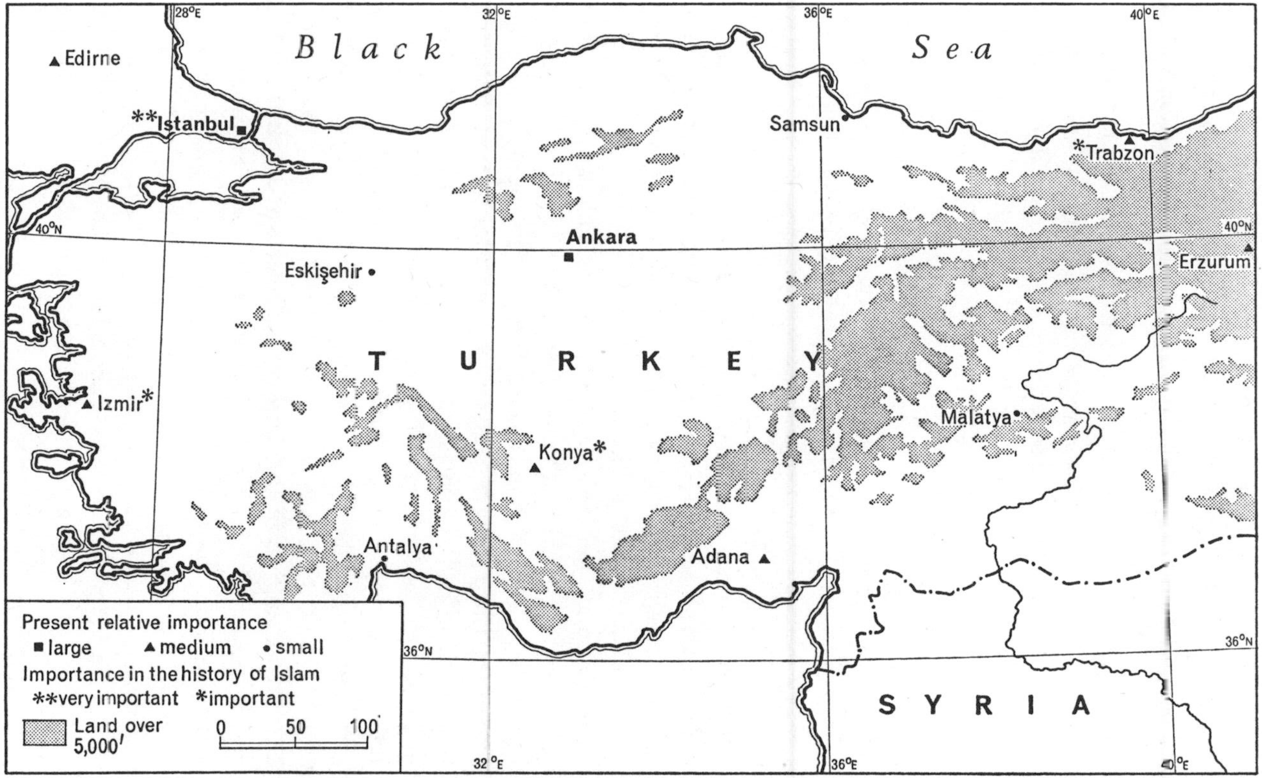
Black Sea
Edirne
**Istanbul
Samsun
*Trabzon
Ankara
Erzurum
Eskişehir
TURKEY
Izmir*
Malatya
Konya*
Antalya
Adana
SYRIA
28°E
32°E
36°E
40°E
40°N
36°N
Present relative importance
large
medium
small
Importance in the history of Islam
**very important *important
Land over 5,000′
0 50 100

Turkey.

to shake off the centuries-old fetters of traditions that hampered freedom and progress. It is significant that he addressed (7 February 1923) the people of Balikesir from the minbar of the Pasha Mosque, reminding them that in early Islam national affairs and social problems had also been the subject of Friday sermons and discussions in the mosque. (That was also a hint at the necessity of preaching in the Turkish mother-tongue.) He assured his audience that "our religion which gave the human race the spirit of progress is the last and most perfect religion",[1] and no less than seventy-three religious leaders were members of the first Great National Assembly (BMM). One year later, Mustafa Kemal attacked superstitions in the field of jurisprudence as a nightmare that prevented the nation from awakening; this was two days before the announcement of the abolition of the caliphate (3 March 1924). Aḥmed Emin Yalman describes the reaction of Atatürk's confidants at the first disclosure of this idea: "This man Mustafa Kemal had proved up to now that he had superior vision, but had he not suddenly gone mad?..."[2] But the daring leader told them: "The abolition of the caliphate is a part of a general scheme to end every vestige of theocracy in our public affairs..."

For this reason another serious blow to the Islamic way of life was given that very day by the promulgation of the Law for Unification of Education (below, p. 76). One month later (8 April 1924) the religious courts were abolished (Law No. 469); the new constitution, declaring Turkey a republic, its religion Islam, was accepted on 26 April 1924. The Civil Code on the Swiss model was introduced on 4 October 1926; only in some questions of the administration of Pious Foundations the *sharīʿa* remained valid.[3] But "to the villagers the Civil Code is irrelevant".[4]

Meḥmed ʿAkif, author of the Turkish national anthem, had left the country, disappointed by this uprooting of Islamic traditions, but Westernization went ahead: European dress was introduced (2 September 1925), the wearing of the fez (not of the women's veil!) prohibited, a measure which caused a much more violent reaction than the abolition of the 1,300 centuries old caliphate...[5] The side-by-side use of pure lunar *hijra*-years and (since 1789) financial solar years was

[1] Cf. Jäschke, in *Die Welt des Islams*, n.s. vol. II, pt. 4 (1953), pp. 272 f.

[2] Ahmed Emin Yalman, *Turkey in my Time* (Oklahoma, 1956), pp. 137–40.

[3] Cf. for the following paragraphs: G. Jäschke, "Der Islam in der neuen Türkei", *W.I.* n.s. vol. I (1951).

[4] Cf. Stirling, *Turkish Village* (London, 1965).

[5] Cf. Geoffrey Lewis, *Turkey* (New York, 1955), p. 92.

ended with the introduction of the Christian era on 1 January 1926; Friday as the weekly holiday (introduced officially in 1924) was replaced by Sunday on 27 May 1935 (Law No. 2739). The most important step towards a break with the Islamic past was the introduction of the Latin alphabet, even now regarded by many villagers as "infidel letters" (1 November 1928; Art. 526 of the Penal Code prohibits the printing of Turkish books in Arabic letters). Instruction in Arabic and Persian was banned from the schools (29 August 1929). In 1928 the mention of Islam as the state religion was dropped from the constitution; religious forms of oaths were no longer valid.

Laicism meant, according to prime minister Receb's "Statement" (16 January 1931) that religion should remain a matter of personal discretion, only concerned with the individual conscience, not with state affairs or public life. This betrays a fundamental misconception of the ideal of Islam which sees in religion and state only two aspects of the same reality.[1]

However, the need for a modification of this anti-Islamic attitude was felt at least after World War II. The cultural changes which were almost universal among the upper classes had scarcely reached the villagers. It began to be felt that too little tolerance had been shown to the Muslims in the practice of their faith, and attempts were made to prove that the Turkish revolution was anti-clerical but not anti-religious. The ten years of the Democrat party's rule (1950–60) mark a steady progress toward a revaluation of Islam, and in 1958 the official Democrat paper *Zafer* expressed the opinion that "the pure form of Islam as formulated by our Prophet has been the guide and the auxiliary of science, progress, virtue and good morals".

How has Turkey, since 1924, tried to solve her religious problems? First, there was the question of religious organization. In 1849 a Ministry of Law and Pious Foundation (*sherī'a ve evqaf vekaleti*) had been founded which acted under the direct supervision of the Grand Vizier but was sometimes administered by the Sheykh ül-Islâm in personal union. With the abolition of the caliphate it was converted into two separate offices (Law No. 429), one of them being the *Diyanet Işleri Reisliği* (sometimes *Bakanlığı*), DIR, now the official and legal authority on Islam. Its president is appointed by the President of the Republic

[1] But cf. the different attitudes of reformers in E. I. J. Rosenthal, "Some reflections on the separation of religion and politics in modern Islam", *Islamic Studies*, vol. III, pt. 3 (Karachi, 1964), and the same author's *Islam in the Modern National State* (Cambridge, 1965).

on the recommendation of the Prime Minister on whose budget the office depends. Besides there is the Directorate General of Pious Foundations (*Evkaf 'Umum*—later *Vakîflar Genel—Müdürlüğü*, EUM).

The DIR was at first in charge of the administration of mosques and dervish lodges, the nomination of *imāms*, preachers and other religious functionaries; but these duties were entrusted by Law No. 1827, 8 June 1931, to the EUM. The DIR which had representatives in forty-nine of Turkey's sixty-five provinces was "ultimately restricted chiefly to licensing preachers, to supervising the contents of their sermons, and to rendering an occasional advisory opinion on canon-law wherever it was applicable".[1]

After Börekçizade Meḥmed Rif'at (d. 6 January 1942) and the well-known orientalist Şerefeddin Yaltkaya (d. 23 April 1947) Aḥmed Ḥamdi Akseki became President of the DIR, a man whose deep piety has been praised by one of his co-prisoners from the 1920s: "According to him religion was a rule for life and social behaviour. He worshipped God out of love..."[2] In his time the political changes made greater activity by the DIR possible. On 23 March 1950, Law No. 5634 again entrusted the administrative control of the clergy to this office. It now appoints and pays *muftīs* who have to control and license *imāms* in each of Turkey's 487 administrative districts. Villages, however, must pay their *imāms* out of local funds. An important new activity was the broadcasting of Qur'ān recitations and of sermons. Many of them have been published; those of Kemal Edib Kürkçüoğlu excel by their oratorical beauty. The DIR also censors the illicit printing of "religious" books which propagate doctrines contrary to the Qur'ān, or aim at widening the gap between the Sunnite and the Alevite communities.

The numerous publications which the DIR issues include a journal, introductions to the ritual prescriptions of Islam, studies in Islamic law, pamphlets against Christian missionary activities, biographies of Muslim leaders, and confrontations of Muslim and Western thinkers. A special character marks the publications of General Sa'deddin Evrin, sometime vice-president of the DIR who tries to show the conformity of Qur'ānic revelation and modern science—fruits of a painstaking labour but partly of a very peculiar logic.[3]

[1] Rustow, *loc. cit.* p. 83.

[2] Şevket Süreyya Aydemir, *Suyu arayan adam* (Ankara, 1959), pp. 406 f.

[3] *Müsbet Ma'neviyyat Etüdleri*, 2nd ed. (Ankara, 1956). Cf. also his *Kur'an-i Kerim Açîklamasî, Fatiha ve Baqara Sureleri* (Ankara, 1962).

A. H. Akseki's (d. 9 January 1951) successor was Eyyüb Ṣabri Hayîrlîoğlu who was pensioned because of "reactionary thinking" after the revolution of 27 May 1960. He was succeeded by 'Ömer Nasuḥi Bilmen, Mufti of Istanbul since 1943; he, in his turn (1962) by Ḥasan Ḥüsnü Erdem; since 15 October 1964 Tevfik Gerçeker has been President of the DIR. In the centre fifty-three officials are now working, and the budget of the Presidency reached, in 1964, £T 83,220,000. As to the EUM where, in early 1965, 196 officials were employed, its budget amounted to £T 51,184,400.

Many complaints have been raised against the appointment and payment of *muftīs* and religious functionaries by the state-controlled DIR, which seemed to contradict the principles of both laicism and religious freedom. Prime Minister Menderes rejected these accusations in the BMM (22 February 1951). But the *Millet Partisi* as spokesmen of the orthodox wing included in their programme the demand that the DIR be taken out of the Prime Minister's budget and the revenues of the Pious Foundations handed over to this Presidency. However the long expected law concerning the reorganization of the DIR still awaits enactment.[1]

These discussions lead us to the complicated problem of religious reform with all its implications. Already in 1929, the Faculty of Theology in Istanbul had issued a reform programme in which it declared:

> ...it is almost impossible with the modern views of society, to expect such a reform...from the working of mystic and irrational elements. Religious life like moral and economic life must be reformed on scientific lines...First of all the form of worship...sanitary conditions...The language of worship must be Turkish...The character of worship—singers and imams equipped with a fair knowledge of music, instruments of music...The intellectual side of worship...the important thing is a philosophical view showing the human and permanent nature of the Islamic religion...The New Turkey will be the guide to freedom and progress of all the Muslim countries which are still enslaved and backward in civilization...[2]

Such a programme excited the protest of the orthodox, and the committee had to be called back. However, on one point the discussions continued, that is the language of worship.

[1] Rustow, *loc. cit.* p. 103. Cf. Ali Fuat Başğil, *Din ve laiklik* (Istanbul, 1962), and Jäschke in *W.I.* n.s. vol. IV, p. 282 and *idem*, vol. VIII, pt. 4 (1963), pp. 252 ff.

[2] According to L. Levonian, *The Turkish Press 1925–1931* (Athens, 1932), pp. 123 ff., quoted in full by Jäschke, "Der Islam in der neuen Türkei", pp. 66 f., and H. A. Reed, "The Faculty of Divinity at Ankara", *The Muslim World*, vol. XLVI, p. 300.

Żiya Gökalp—who had heavily attacked Turkey's dependence on the *sharīʿa* in his poem "Meşîhat"—had dreamt in his poem "Vatan" (1918) of a country where the Qur'ān would be recited in Turkish and the *adhān* sung in Turkish. And on 30 January 1932 one could hear for the first time the call *Allah büyükdür* from the Fatih mosque in Istanbul. In November 1932 the DIR adopted the wording *Tanrî uludur* which was—in vain—criticized since Tanrî, the old Turkish High God, does not correspond to *Allah*—if anything, then the word *Çalap*, common in medieval mystical texts, should have been used. Every muezzin who did not sing the new *adhān* was liable to imprisonment (Art. 526, Penal Code), and after 2 June 1941 even the recitation of the Arabic wording on any occasion could be punished. It was a most ingenious idea of Menderes to reintroduce the Arabic call to prayer on 16 June 1950 so that it could be sung on 17 June, corresponding to the first day of Ramaḍān! Since the "words of the *adhān* have been revealed to the Prophet by Divine inspiration", their translation is by no means acceptable to the orthodox.[1]

Likewise the question whether ritual prayer can be offered in Turkish has always been answered in the negative by the pious, and if a modernist like Osman Keskinoğlu thinks it permitted according to Abū Ḥanīfa he is told that those who do not offer their prayers today in Arabic surely will not offer them in their mother tongue either.[2] Of course, a translation of the *sūras* used in prayers for illustrating their meaning is necessary, as Akseki has shown in his booklet *Namaz surelerinin türkçe tercüme ve tefsiri* (Ankara, 1949).

The *khuṭba*, the Friday sermon, is now delivered in Turkish after recitation of the Qur'ānic verses in Arabic.

These questions are connected with the central problem: whether the Qur'ān can be translated? J. K. Birge wrote in 1951: "I do not remember having talked with a single Turk who likes the Qur'ān read in Turkish."[3]

That is true. The Qur'ān is, as Kürkçüoğlu has stated, the word of God, and as such not Arabic (*arabça*) but Lord's language (*Rab'ça*—an old word-play of the mystics). On the other hand there may just be the feeling that a certain "magical" quality is lost in translation, for the verses of the Holy Book are still used as protecting charms, written in

[1] *Din' de Reform Meselesi* (Ankara, 1957), p. 47; cf. Jäschke, *loc. cit.*, and *W.I.* n.s. vol. VI, pts. 3–4 (1961), about a new attempt at Turkizing the *adhān*.

[2] *Monthly Islam* (Ankara, 55/46).

[3] D. S. Franck (ed.), *Islam in the Modern World* (New York, 1951), p. 44.

shops, in cars, recited at the beginning of a journey together with the blessings on the Prophet, and carried as a talisman. And again, even a sophisticated Turk will enjoy a *ḥāfiẓ*' recitation of the Arabic text which is often of unsurpassable musical beauty. The different kinds of reciters, mentioned in detail by Jäschke,[1] are working under the supervision of the EUM; but there are many other Turks—their number is estimated at about 200,000—who know the Holy Book by heart.

Still, a large number of Turkish translations of the Qur'ān have been published since 1923, not for liturgical use, but for elucidating the meaning. None of them, however, aims at being the "generally accepted" version. The BMM allotted the DIR in 1932 the small sum of £T4,000 for the preparation of an official translation as well as translations of the Prophetic traditions, but only in 1961 did the Presidency begin to issue a Turkish translation which is not for sale (copies of the Qur'ān must never be sold, their price is called *hediye*, gift!). It was prepared by two assistants in the Faculty of Theology under the supervision of the DIR and an editorial committee, and is modestly called "perhaps the most correct" among over a hundred existing attempts to make the contents of the Holy Book known.[2] Among these "integral translations" the most important is that of 'Ömer Riza Doğrul (1934, 1947), the son-in-law of Mehmed 'Akif whose *Kur'andan ayetler* were published in 1944. The version by Elmalîlî Meḥmed Ḥamdi (1935–8) was often used. There are also translations by Besim Atalay and Şerefeddin Yaltkaya. The translation by Ḥasan Başrî Çantay, in three volumes, is considered the best and was reprinted four times between 1953 and 1964. Abdülbaki Gölpînarlî shocked the public by publishing a translation of the Qur'ān serially in a newspaper; later, the newspaper *Tan* also published a translation by Haci Murad Sertoğlu. The luxuriously printed translation by Besim Atalay (1962) contains so many strange Turkish words that the author had to add a dictionary.[3] In order to show the continuity of Turkish translations of the Qur'ān, interesting inquiries into the oldest Turkish versions have been made by 'Abdülkadir Inan and Zeki Velidi Toğan during recent years.[4]

Those who advocate the use of a Turkish translation of the Qur'ān

[1] Jäschke, *loc. cit.* pp. 82 ff.

[2] Cf. Jäschke, *W.I.* n.s. vol. VIII, pts. 1–2 (1963), pp. 59 f.; cf. *W.I.* n.s. vol. IV, p. 282, his remarks about the idea of introducing the Arabic Qur'ān in Latin letters.

[3] On the translation of Ismayil Hakkî Baltacîoğlu, 1957, see Kürkçüoğlu, *op. cit.* p. 54.

[4] A very useful booklet on this subject is Muḥammad Ḥamīdallah and Macit Yaşaroğlu, *Kuran-i Kerim Tarihi ile Türkçe Tefsirler bibliografyasî* (Istanbul, 1965).

often quote Luther's name in order to support their views so that false reformers can be styled simply *sakhte Lüther'ler*. It is, as W. C. Smith remarks in his article "Modern Turkey, Islamic Reformation?" (which has been translated in the *Quarterly of the Faculty of Theology*, vol. II, pt. 1, 1953) "startling to hear the name of Luther on many Turkish lips that could scarcely discourse on the work of al-Ash'arī or al-Ghazzālī or Iqbāl."[1] Indeed a strong predilection for the German reformer, to whom Meḥmed Emin had once dedicated a poem, is felt in Turkey, and a critical approach towards him by a German Protestant like me completely embarrassed my Muslim students in Ankara.

The main problem on which all these questions converge is that of religious education.[2] The Law of Unification of Education (*tevhid-i tedrisat*), published the very day of the abolition of the caliphate, orders that all *madrasas* and those primary schools which were administered by the Evkaf Ministry or existed as private *evkaf* were, like any secular school, to come under the supervision of the Ministry of Education. Attendance at secular elementary schools became compulsory in 1930. Since 1927 the attendance of pupils for religious instruction has been dependent on the wish of the parents; then religious classes were abolished in the middle schools in September 1931, but continued to be recommended in primary schools up to 1935. The following thirteen years passed without any official religious classes; only some books like that of Şerefeddin Yaltkaya, *Benim Dinim* (1943) were meant for home instruction in religion.

The government realized, however, that the complete suppression of religious instruction might cause a lack of ethical and moral qualities. The first parliamentary debate on this subject was opened on 24 December 1946, and in July 1947 some ideas for a programme were put down by Muḥiddin Baha Pars and Ḥamdullah Subhi Tanrïöver (Minister of Education in 1925) who resigned from the CHP shortly after his proposal: "Let us train at least one tenth the number of men that secular states (in Europe and America) are training to serve the Turkish nation in her religious institutions."

For the new Democrat party, Fuad Köprülü, once Dean of the Istanbul Faculty of Theology, and Adnan Menderes proposed private religious classes for children who had finished primary school. The

[1] Cf. the chapter "Turkey: Islamic Reformation?" in his book *Islam in Modern History* (Princeton, 1957).

[2] Cf. for the following: Howard A. Reed, "Turkey's new Imam-Hatip schools" *W.I.* n.s. vol. IV (1955), pp. 2–3; cf. also Jäschke, *W.I.* n.s. vol. IX, pp. 260 ff.

Millet Partisi accepted religious education into their programme, and even some members of the CHP spoke in favour of official religious instruction. Thus, on 15 February 1949, religious instruction by approved volunteer teachers became facultative in the fourth and fifth grades of primary schools, following a syllabus prepared by the DIR and the Ministry of Education jointly. One year later these classes were incorporated into the regular curriculum; in the textbooks (*Din dersleri*) special stress is laid upon the ethical values of Islam. "The reintroduction of religious education classes in the primary schools had been a very potent factor in stimulating increased attendance throughout the country in the villages."[1]

Five days before his death, 4 January 1951, Akseki, the president of the DIR, demanded religious instruction in the middle schools too, and five years later, such classes were introduced by Law No. 9406. Now (1965) even a scholarship for studying the methods of religious education in Germany has been granted to a young teacher, a former graduate from the Faculty of Theology.

Besides, we still find the indigenous religious training in Turkey. In the old *dār al-qurrā'* or *dār al-ḥuffāẓ* the Qur'ān was memorized without any attempt to study Arabic grammar; even one of my highly educated *ḥāfiẓ* friends gently refused my proposal to teach him Arabic. The *ḥāfiẓ* courses continued, authorized by law, after the revolution. From 1932 onwards, the number of teachers and pupils grew steadily until in 1949 it reached 130 teachers, and 6,403 male and 2,303 female students. In order to avoid misuse, the DIR made the provision that only those who had finished primary school be admitted to these courses. Many of the future *ḥāfiẓ* were recruited from poor families so that a special organization for their welfare was founded (*Kur'an kurslarinin yardim derneği*).

Statistics show that the majority of *imāms* and preachers are still very backward (the "Oflu Imam", named after some very reactionary inhabitants of the Black Sea coast is proverbial and the tension between the *imāms* and the modern schoolteachers still forms a grave problem in the villages), and thus the production of "enlightened" religious people (*aydin din adamlari*) has become an important problem. More than thirty training schools for *imāms* and preachers were left open in 1924, but in 1932 only two of them were still working, and these too had to be closed for lack of teachers. Thus in the villages the influence of

[1] *Ibid.* p. 154.

illiterate *imāms* continued in spite of Atatürk's reforms. However, "the survival of Islam as a vital force in Turkey could be assured only to the degree that the problem of religious leadership training is solved".[1] The Minister of Education had announced in 1947 a plan for training *imāms* in private seminaries with a total of at least eight years of previous education. On 15 January 1949 courses for graduates of middle schools were opened in a number of cities. Yusuf Ẓiya Yörükan, whose clear exposition of Islamic faith, *Müslümanlîk* (1957), has been styled as the semi-official creed of Turkey, and Ḥasan Ḥüsnü Erdem led the first courses which lasted ten months but were later extended to two years. The first regular schools for *imāms* and preachers were founded in 1951 "as a co-operative effort by the ministry of Education in response to and in collaboration with private organizing efforts in interested groups... They were begun on the three year middle school curriculum which was slightly reduced and to which was added a fairly heavy vocational training program, the whole course taking four years".

In 1956 there were sixteen "imām-hatip" schools in different district towns. That of Konya had, in 1962, more than a thousand pupils, but even "infidel Izmir" boasts of a great number of students; in 1964 the number of "īmām-hatip" students in Turkey was estimated at around 12,000, who wholeheartedly take upon themselves the rather complicated curriculum. Many private groups raise funds for buying the ground or erecting buildings.

The problem is the insufficient number of teachers for the ten vocational and seventeen general courses; for the latter, teachers are borrowed from secular schools; now, even some ladies are teaching vocational classes. The administration is with the directorate of special schools. None of the principals has a special religious training, nor are the students obliged to offer their prayers; that is left to their conscience. In 1954 a *lise kîsmî* was added to the "imām-hatip" schools so that the pupils had to undergo instruction in all classes of a normal Turkish *lycée* plus the vocational classes. Astonishingly enough they are not permitted to enter the Faculty of Theology where they would constitute a most useful element. The schools are now being converted into Islamic institutes, and a commission has once more discussed the principles of the instruction of future religious officials.

By Law No. 7344 (10 June 1959) a Higher Islamic Institute was

[1] H. E. Allen, *The Turkish Transformation* (Chicago, 1935), p. 184.

founded at Istanbul. The curriculum of 1962 shows that the stress lies here upon the vocational classes; in 1965, 28 teachers and 311 pupils were working there. A similar institute was set up in Konya, and there are tendencies to convert them into real Islamic faculties (*Islam ilimleri külliyesi*).

Yet there exists a rather large group of not specially trained persons who may qualify themselves by an examination (whose details are found in Law No. 5634, 23 March 1950, and its implementation schedules of 21 April 1952)[1] for the offices of *imām*, preacher, mosque-caretaker (*qayyūm*), *mathnavī-khwān*, *Bukhārī-khwān*—I remember, for instance, an engineer-preacher, an administration officer-*imām*, etc. The government has further organized continuation courses for *imāms*; meetings of the Federation of Societies of Religious Employees (*Hayrat Hademesi dernekleri*) and of the former pupils of "imām-hatip" schools have been arranged since 1963.[2]

In the training of these religious employees, again, the lack of qualified teachers is the greatest obstacle. An attempt was made to solve this problem, at least in part, by opening a Faculty of Theology.[3] Such a faculty had been attached to the first Turkish university between 1900 and 1919, and was reopened after 1924 for training advanced religious specialists. That faculty has issued an interesting quarterly since 1926, and was responsible for the above-mentioned Reform Programme. In 1933, it was converted into an Institute of Islamic Research, attached to the Faculty of Letters; this, in its turn, was closed between 1942 and 1955; then it was made again a pure research centre, headed by Zeki Velidi Toğan.

First formal suggestions concerning a new Faculty of Theology (*Ilâhiyat Fakültesi*) were made in January 1948, and found a wide echo, though the draft programme issued by the DIR was rather utopian. Deputies and the Minister of Education mostly agreed that such a faculty had "to work against reactionary trends". Eventually, Law No. 5424 (passed 4 June 1949) authorized the creation of this unique faculty which was opened in Ankara on 31 October 1949. Only two members of the staff, Y. Z. Yörükan and O. H. Budda, had already served in the former Istanbul faculty.

[1] Jäschke, *W.I.* n.s. vol. II, pt. 2, p. 131.

[2] Jäschke, *W.I.* vol. VIII, pt. 3, pp. 196 f., cf. *idem*, vol. IX, p. 304, about Hifzî Oğuz Beğata, *Aydîn Din Adamlarî* (Ankara, 1962).

[3] For the following cf. Howard A. Reed, "The Faculty of Divinity at Ankara", *The Muslim World*, vol. XLVI, pt. 4 (October 1956); vol. XLVII, pt. 1 (January 1957).

The programme was well designed, containing not only purely Islamic subjects but also History of Religion,[1] Psychology and Sociology of Religion, etc. But it was quite impossible to find qualified teachers for all these subjects. The deaths of four eminent professors during the first years added to the difficulties the new faculty had to face.

Professors from Morocco, Yugoslavia and other Islamic countries were invited and some stayed as permanent members of the staff. Five years' teaching experience made me acquainted with the problems of this faculty: not enough reliable textbooks, and the students suffering from a very poor knowledge of western languages in spite of foreign language classes; as to Arabic the students had to learn it during their four years' studies, not in a preparatory course. Nevertheless, they were very eager to gain knowledge about foreign religions, and lively discussions were held in my classes on problems of Christian dogmatics.

Next to no importance was given to "practical theology". Only once a class for Qur'ān recitation was held by a high official from the Home Ministry, a well-known *ḥāfiẓ*. A research institute with its own magazine (*Islam Ilimleri Enstitüsü*) was added in 1959. Homiletics were not taught. The faculty issues a quarterly which was welcomed in Europe as "scientific, critical, and original".[2] Both textbooks and research work are being published. I am quite sure that some of the former assistants, trained in Europe and Canada, who have now joined the staff, will eventually provide this faculty with the dreamt-of combination of Western scientific methods and personal piety.

Oddly enough, prayer was not offered regularly, and fasting not observed by all members of the staff, but, I think, by the overwhelming majority of the students.

We once made the students explain the reason for their entering the faculty. One girl wrote a poem in which she said "...with the wish to lay open in the right way before the new generation this religion that teaches humanity even to the wildest people, have I entered this faculty...".

The number of students during the first years was always between seventy and ninety, among them on the average fifteen girls; in 1959 the figures had increased to 141 boys, thirteen girls; in 1964 to 348 boys, thirty girls; so that a new building was required. About sixty students

[1] Cf. *idem*, vol. II, p. 25; Ḥikmet Tanyu, "Türkiye'de Dinler Tarihi Tarihçesi", *Ilâh. Fakültesi Dergisi*, vol. VIII (1960), pp. 109–24.

[2] Cf. Taeschner, *W.I.* n.s. vol. II, pt. 2 (1953).

are receiving scholarships from different organizations, like DIR, EUM, sometimes also from the army where the young men will serve as religious and moral leaders attached to military units. Only a limited number of those who have completed the course have joined the "imām-hatip" schools; others have become *muftīs*; some girls are religious teachers in middle schools. I may add that there was no discrimination against women either in the staff or among the students.[1] Since 1966, some of the graduates have been appointed "religious attachés" at Turkish embassies abroad, e.g. in Germany and Austria, to look after the religious problems of the Turkish workers in these countries.

In the classes on the history of religions the problem of missionary activities was sometimes touched upon; certain colleagues were even afraid lest a lecture on Osiris delivered by a Dutch theologian might conceal missionary tendencies!

But this "mission-complex" was palpable in the more secularized rather than in orthodox circles, whereas the attitude towards Israel[2] (which had granted three scholarships to the Faculty of Theology), and towards the Jews was more negative among orthodox circles, which did not even refrain from including the *Dönme*, the group of Sabbatay Zwi's followers in Salonica who had turned Muslim, in their antipathy, even hatred.

Relations with Greek Orthodox members of the community were always affected by political considerations.[3] In the very small Armenian groups in central Anatolia I found quite friendly personal relations between the staunch Muslims of that area and their Christian neighbours.

Concerning the group of Alevis who form a considerable minority in southern and eastern Anatolia it seems to be the policy of the DIR and the government to minimize the difference between the Sunnite majority and these heterodox groups; "tauḥīd means to declare God as One and to make the people one", not to exaggerate the differences between the children of one mother-soil.[4]

How does a Turkish Muslim live? From my personal experiences in middle-class families I should answer as follows: Every act, even the

[1] Cf. about this problem Jäschke, "Die Frauenfrage in der Türkei", *Saeculum*, vol. x, pt. 4 (Freiburg, 1959).

[2] Cf. *The Muslim World*, Karachi, 20 February 1965 on Arab–Turkish Relations.

[3] Cf. C. F. Beckingham in D. Grant, *The Islamic Near East* (Toronto, 1960), p. 209.

[4] Cf. H. A. Reed, "Religious Life of Modern Turkish Muslims" in R. N. Frye, *op. cit.* p. 120; and Kemal Edib Kürkçüoğlu, *Imanda Birlik, Vatanda Dirlik* (Ankara, 1953); and Ḥasan Başrî Çantay, *loc. cit.* p. 280.

conjugal act is begun with the *basmala*, and the child, immediately after its birth, is welcomed by the recitation of the *takbīr*, the *adhān* and the *fātiḥa*. Then it is given a name, a *göbek adî*, and the name by which it will be called. Though many of the old Muslim names are replaced by "Turkish" names, the *göbek adî* is still mostly Muslim. If a child is born thanks to a vow made at some sacred place it is either called after the saint (thus near Rihaniya we find hundreds of "Ökkeş", named after 'Akkāş), or it is metaphorically "sold" to the lodge or tomb of the respective saint. Then a boy is called *Satîlmîş* (sold), a girl *Satî*. Sometimes a pious or saintly friend of the family is asked to find an auspicious name.

Circumcision (*sünnet*) is practised between the seventh and eleventh year, and is still considered a big family feast. Sometimes a number of boys are put together into a big room and are diverted by shadow plays or films or amused by light music and the visit of many friends.

When the time of marriage arrives, in smaller towns it is still arranged by the parents and celebrated according to tradition.[1] The introduction of the Swiss Civil Code in 1926 made civil marriage in the presence of a mayor or a person of similar status obligatory. The minimum age of marriage has been altered according to the requirements of a southern country (first to the age of 18 for boys, 17 for girls; in 1938 it was reduced to 17 and 15, but girls under 14 are still married). Essentially, civil marriage corresponds with Islamic law according to which wedlock is only a contract, not a sacrament. However, for the common man marriage without a short sermon and the *nikâḥ duasî*, the prayer of an *imām* (which is essentially of no importance) is considered invalid, because "only the *imām's* prayer can prevent the enemies from succeeding in rendering the groom impotent by magical knots". Civil marriage does not mean anything for the villagers who continue to marry before the *imām*, though according to Penal Code Art. 765 (1 March 1936) every *imām* who performs the *nikâḥ duasî* without a preceding civil wedding is liable to imprisonment, and in 1946 Law No. 3038 included even the couple who asked for religious wedding ceremonies without a civil wedding. Since people in the villages did not care for these restrictions (which were directed mainly against polygamy) the government had to promulgate several laws (26 October 1933; 30 April 1945; 1 February 1950; 30 January 1956) by which the offspring of these

[1] Cf. Jäschke, "Zur Form der Eheschließung in der Türkei," *W.I.* n.s. vol. II, pp. 133–214, and "Die Imam-Ehe in der Türkei", *ibid.* vol. IV, pts. 2–3; Reed, *loc. cit.* p. 125.

marriages was recognized as having the status of legitimate children (which they had always enjoyed in the eyes of the villagers).

If possible the married couple hang a copy of the Qur'ān over the conjugal bed in order to secure heavenly blessings on the marriage. Life, then, is interwoven with religious duties; and Turkish conversation, even about the most elementary topics, is always a fabric of religious expressions, and from the regularly used *inshallah* and *mashallah* to thanking or to informing you of sad news, the name of Allāh is always on the lips of the pious. And just as the newborn baby is greeted with the religious formula, so a dying Turk will like to have around him his friends and relations who continue for hours and hours the recitation of Qur'ānic verses and of the confession of faith. The corpse is prepared for burial according to Islamic law, and the burial prayer recited. Even when Atatürk died, his sister urged his closest friends to have the burial prayer recited which was accordingly done on 19 November 1938 at a small gathering in Istanbul.[1] It is touching to witness the deep trust in God with which the death of the nearest relations is accepted; and the strong feeling that even in this cruel incident the wisdom of the Almighty is visible, and, though perhaps not understandable, is always prevalent. This religious attitude, to accept everything as sent by God who knows best what is good for his servants, makes the Turks such excellent soldiers, neither affected by brain-washing nor by any danger; and here lies, according to my experiences, the deepest source of strength of the Turkish Muslims, condensed in the often-quoted verse of Ibrahim Ḥaqqî Erzerumlu:

> *Görelim Haqq ne eyler—n'eylerse güzel eyler*
> Let us see, what God does—whatever He does, He does well.

"All rules and commandments of the *sharī'a* concerning beliefs, prayers, and morals, are in force and observed by the people", writes Ḥasan Baṣrî Çantay.[2]

The first obligation is ritual prayer (*namaz*), which can be, and is indeed, performed at home or elsewhere. As to the mosques their upkeep was entrusted to the EUM in 1924, and a remarkable number of them had to be closed according to the detailed restrictions announced on 25 December 1932; a mosque was to be at least 500 metres from the next mosque, otherwise it would be used for non-

[1] Cf. *W.I.* n.s. vol. IV (1963), p. 256.
[2] In K. Morgan, *Islam, The Straight Path* (New York, 1958), p. 280.

religious purposes (Law No. 2845, 15 November 1935, the year when Aya Sofya was made a museum). Thus, some mosques had even been converted into military barracks.[1] After World War II, however, a growing interest in the repair and reconstruction of places of worship made itself felt, and between 1950 and September 1954 the state assumed responsibility for maintaining 2,997 additional mosques.[2] In 1953 the EUM spent approximately £T22½ millions for the repair of mosques, and repair by private means is not at all an exception. Even in the residential quarters of Ankara that had been completely devoid of religious buildings, new mosques came into existence in the 1950s, all of them constructed after classical Ottoman models, without an attempt at creating a new style. In spite of their growing number one could meet every Friday noon in the old quarters of the capital, around the Mosque of Ḥaci Bayram in the religious centre of Ankara, large crowds performing their prayers on the pavement, using even newspapers as prayer-mats, for "the knowledge that the Democratic Government is not hostile to organized religion, as its predecessor was felt to be, has further increased attendances at mosques".[3] Even younger ladies were among the worshippers, though the attendance of women at public prayer is quite rare. It has even happened that ladies in Western dress have been hindered from entering a mosque like *hirka-i sherif* in Istanbul. But nobody marvels at people, men and women, who perform their prayer on the steamer, in a corner of the school court-yard, or even in a minibus.

Modernists have often objected to the outward forms of *namaz* from considerations of modern hygiene (for the face to touch a prayer-mat upon which thousands have trodden before, etc.). A narrow clinging to the details of outward ceremonies in prayer among the Turkish orthodox was witnessed even by Pakistani Muslims (for example in the details of *wuḍū'*, which is, according to westernized people, scarcely practicable in a modern industrialized society).

As to *zakāt*, there is no organization which could collect it, and sometimes it is given to private social welfare funds. Fasting in Ramaḍān is obeyed at least in the countryside by a fairly large part of the population. The offices are not closed during that month, yet a certain number of the officials keep the fast; in the smaller places in central Anatolia it is difficult to get a warm meal in daytime, though private hospitality

[1] Jäschke, "Der Islam in der neuen Türkei" (*W.I.* n.s. vol. 1; Leiden, 1951), pp. 88 f.
[2] Reed, *loc. cit.* p. 115.
[3] G. Lewis, *loc. cit.* p. 133.

offers the guest even then the most delicious food. We often admired the zeal of my maidservant who, after having been unable for health reasons to fast in 1958, fasted in the following year the three months preceding Ramaḍān, and then that month too—she thought it *çok sevab*, very meritorious—and continued her hard work with unfailing joy. Even some of those who do not intend to fast during the whole month will try it at least during the first or last three days of Ramaḍān, or before *Kadîr gecesi*, the Night of Power (the 27th of Ramaḍān), a night which is celebrated everywhere with great enthusiasm.[1] The breaking of the fast with a sip of water and some olives and similar small things is in tune with the customs everywhere, to put the *iftār*-food early on the table, is thought meritorious: then "the food is praising Allāh". The *tarāwīḥ* prayers are partly performed at home, partly in the mosque; one may perform a full recitation (*hatm*) of the Qur'ān during the holy month. Many newspapers now issue special Ramaḍān editions. The longed-for *'īd al-fiṭr, sheker bayramî*, is as well as the *'īd al-aḍḥā, kurban bayramî*, recognized as an official national holiday.

As to the *ḥajj*, the first pilgrims from Turkey visited the Ḥijāz, after years of prohibition, in 1947, and the number had increased in 1954 to more than 10,000, including a group of newspaper reporters from the widely read paper *Hürriyet*. *Ḥājīs* crowded the airports of Istanbul and Ankara carrying their small bundles and the big water jar, enthusiastically seen off by their relations, hailed on their return. However, no official Turkish leader has partaken in the pilgrimage. Emel Esin's admirable book *Mecca the Radiant, Medina the Glorious* seems to me symptomatic of the feelings of a large group of Turks who preserve Islamic ideals in harmony with modern Western education.

In Turkey the demand for sacrificial rams for the *kurban bayramî* increased in the 1950s; the meat was mostly given to the poor, the hide to some national welfare organizations. It may be mentioned, by the way, that on solemn occasions too, like the foundation of a house, a ram is sometimes sacrificed, not forgetting the thousands of animals, even camels, that were slaughtered when the Prime Minister Adnan Menderes returned safely to Turkey after the plane-crash of 17 February 1959.

Besides the two big holidays, people are very fond of celebrating the Birthday of the Prophet (the 12th of Rabī' al-Awwal) which had been declared an official holiday in 1910, but is now only privately celebrated.

[1] Cf. Taeschner, *W.I.* n.s. vol. IV, pp. 2–3, 202 f.

Pious people spend the day fasting, and at night the lights on the minarets are lit (*kandîl*), as they are during Ramaḍān, on *ragaib gecesi*, the night of Muḥammad's conception, in Rajab, and *berat gecesi*, the night of the revelation of his mission to the Prophet, mid-Sha'bān. Especially on the Birthday of the Prophet the deep veneration of the Turkish Muslim for Muḥammad is visible, a feeling which is shared by intellectuals and peasants; the former see in him the leader towards a rational and logical religion, and the people still hope for his intercession on Doomsday. Of course there are even enthusiasts who try to make him a Turk! A Turkish professor of medicine who repeated the theory of Muḥammad's being an epileptic[1] was vehemently attacked by the Press, and the book of the would-be reformer Osman Nuri Çerman, *Dinde Reform* (1958), caused a violent discussion in Parliament about the necessity of protecting the honour of prophets against abuse. An emendation of Art. 175, Penal Code, according to which the blasphemy and slandering of prophets would have been punishable was, however, not passed, because the question was raised whether such a law would include the protection of non-Muslim sacred persons and objects: "should we also punish abuse of the Virgin Mary or of the Holy Cow of the Hindus?"

Among the Alevi population '*āshūrā*' is celebrated, after days of fasting. On this day (the 10th of Muḥarram) a certain sweet, made of different pulse grains, raisins, sugar, etc., is offered the guest even in some Sunnite families in remembrance of the last meal of Imam Ḥusayn at Karbalā'.

One of the most touching religious ceremonies in Turkey is the recitation of a *mevlud*, the Turkish poem composed by Süleyman Çelebi of Bursa (d. 1423) in honour of the Prophet's birth.[2] Though during the centuries many similar epics have been written this simple and sweet poem is still enjoyed by everybody. The *mevlud* can be read at home or in public; it is recited by special readers, interspersed with prayers and recitations from the Qur'ān. It is usually recited forty days after the death of a relative, and on the anniversaries of the death, but the gathering can also be held to fulfil a vow. The sexes sit separately, the women covering their heads; a special beautiful scarf (*mevlud örtüsü*) is often used. Afterwards one offers sherbet and distributes sweets. The heavenly reward of the recitation is ascribed to the de-

[1] Enver Behcet Kamay, *Adli Tîbb* (Ankara, 1955).
[2] Translated by F. Lyman MacCallum (London, 1943).

ceased whose memory is being celebrated. The reciters are given some money together with the sweets. There is no clause which restricts the recitation to Muslims; yet it was amazing that a Turkish mystical leader, Ömer Fevzi Mardin, read a *mevlud* for Evita Perón (9 December 1951) in the new mosque of Şişli, Istanbul. On 14 November 1954 a *mevlud* was recited for the first time in memory of Atatürk, arranged by his sister in the Süleymaniye mosque in Istanbul with the assistance of the most celebrated singers; the celebration was broadcast and millions of Turks could listen to it. A *mevlud* in honour of Jalāl al-dīn Rūmī in the Alaeddin mosque in Konya (18 December 1955) was attended by nearly 8,000 persons, the ladies sitting in the outer courtyard.

In the development of Turkish Islam mystical currents have played a more important role than the official orthodox creed, and the amalgamation of mystical brotherhoods and their sometimes rather heterodox ideas under the rule of orthodoxy was only achieved from the time of Selim I onwards. The influence of Ṣūfism on Turkish cultural life cannot be estimated highly enough, and it is quite natural that even today Turkish religious feeling is more imbued with mystical feelings than is the case in other parts of the Islamic world.

Yet, it cannot be denied that mysticism, however noble and edifying its ideals were, has often degenerated in the hands of pseudo-religious leaders who made religion a mere snare for the simple villagers and knew well how to use "mystical" means for securing their private gain. A European can scarcely imagine how great the influence of such "shaykhs" has been, and it was only after I had witnessed some of them during the Menderes period that I understood the reasons for Atatürk's drastic measures against the religious orders. He formulated his ideas in this respect in August 1925:

> To expect help from the dead is disgraceful for a civilized society...The Turkish Republic can never be the country of *shaykhs*, dervishes and disciples of a religious order (*ṭarīqa*); the straightest and finest order (or: way, *ṭarīqa*) is that of civilization.

Is it sheer accident that the inscription on the first faculty building of Ankara University reads: "The truest leader [*murshid*, the common expression for the mystical leader!] in life is science"? Atatürk further declared: "I cannot accept the existence, in the civilized Turkish community, of people so primitive as to seek their material and spiritual well-being through the guidance of any old shaykh..." These ideas were given legal form on 30 November 1925 in Law No. 677. The dervish lodges (*tekke*) were closed and their administration was entrusted to the DIR. The heads of the lodges were allowed to stay in the *tekke* until they died, if the foundation-deed contained this stipulation; thus, in the Mevlâna Museum in Konya old Meḥmed Dede was living in his modest cell till 1957.[1] The establishment of new rooms for the cult, or the use of rooms for religious ceremonies, or the use of the traditional dresses and headgear was liable to at least three months' imprisonment or a £T50 fine.

But, as the thirteenth-century mystic Yunus Emre says in a very frequently quoted line:

Dervişlik dedikleri hîrqa ile tac degil,
Gönlün' derviş eyleyen hîrqaya muhtac degil...
What they call dervish-life is not by the patched frock and headgear,
He who makes his heart a dervish does not need a patched frock...

The substantial spiritual values of Turkish mystical tradition were preserved after the outward abolition of the order, and perhaps developed in a purer form than before, as R. Hartmann had predicted already in 1927 after his visit to Konya.[2]

Unfortunately some reactionary elements have tried again and again to make religion, especially the fraternities, their shield: "With the advent of democracy and liberty in Turkey, certain fanatic elements undertook a revival of excessive religious zeal, to invoke again the Islamic laws of the *sharīʿa* and to foment hatred against the secular state."[3]

The Naqshbandī group which had led a rebellion in Menemen in 1925, later became active in eastern Anatolia. Seventeen of their leaders were arrested in Mardin (1954) where they had gathered secretly. Much more important were the Tijānīs, active since 1949 in Turkey where they had come from North Africa. They "took forceful action in destroying public monuments of living creatures, notably a number of statues of Atatürk",[4] because acccording to Sūra IV. 92 the making of an image is forbidden. Their leader, the well-to-do Ankara businessman Kemal Pilavoğlu, was sentenced in July 1952 to ten years heavy imprisonment, and in 1958 banished to an island.

[1] Cf. *Anît*, vol. v, pt. 25 (Konya, 1960): Ankaralî Mehmed Dede Sayisî.

[2] Cf. R. Hartmann, *Im neuen Anatolien*, p. 110; Samiha Ayverdi, *Istanbul Geceleri* (Istanbul, 1952), p. 183. (A very fine analysis of this problem.)

[3] Yalman, *loc. cit.* p. 240.

[4] Howard A. Reed, "Revival of Islam in Secular Turkey", *Middle East Journal*, vol. VIII, pt. 3 (1954), p. 183.

Another group was led by a strange poet and gambler, Necib Fazîl Kîsakürek, whose daily paper *Büyük Doğu* (Great) East, had a strong reactionary bias, and whose followers became notorious by their criminal attempt against the well-known progressive editor and writer Aḥmed Emin Yalman in Malatya in the autumn of 1952.[1]

During the 1950s, another group of fanatic Muslims was active even in university circles; the Nurcus, followers of Said Nursi, a Kurd, an old agitator for Kurdish separatism, says Yalman. The DIR stated officially that his ideas did not contradict the Qur'ān but his 150 books and pamphlets, the *risale-i Nur*—published in cyclostyled form, contain a strange mixture of mystic ideas, influenced by Ibn 'Arabī, of cabbalistic wordplays (*jafr*) and similar devices. Several times sentenced to prison he was set free since "misuse of religion for personal and political purposes" (Penal Code Art. 163) was not proved. He died in Urfa, 87 years old, on 23 March 1960. About this trend Fuad Köprülü wrote (*Vatan*, 9 May 1958):

> Both the Government and the opposition must work together against reactionary manifestations which will cause disputes and hatred among citizens and will drag the nation back into darkness and a morass of ignorance and fanaticism.

Yalman (*loc. cit.* p. 250) thinks, no doubt erroneously, that all these organizations which carried on an increasingly vituperative campaign against secularism were directed from a common secret Communist centre.

There were, however, in all classes of the community others who kept alive the torch of real mystical piety. Would one expect an Air Force General to compose mystical quatrains, a high bank official to spend two hours every night in meditation, a simple joiner to utter words of deepest wisdom? This interior life could not be changed by outward measures. It became visible again after the reopening of the most important shrines on 1 March 1950 (addition to Law 677).

Among those shrines was also that of Mawlānā (Mevlâna) Jalāl al-Dīn Rūmī, the great mystical poet and inspirer of the order of the Whirling Dervishes who died in 1273 in Konya where his tomb has always been a centre of popular veneration. The Mevlevi order had played an important role in the cultural development of Turkey in music, poetry, calligraphy, etc., and its leader used to gird the Ottoman sultan with

[1] *Idem*, p. 295; cf. Rustow, *loc. cit.* pp. 98 ff. He attests that Yalman is a *dönme* (whence the aversion of orthodox circles); and Yalman, *loc. cit.* ch. 21.

the sword. In 1925, it still had twelve centres in Turkey, four of them in Istanbul. After a small local celebration of the anniversary of Rūmī's death in 1953 the authorities for the first time permitted a commemoration on 17 December 1954. Speeches were made (I was the first European to address the gatherings), and the mystical dance (*sema'*) was shown on the stage. The dervishes, coming from all parts of the country, displayed an amazing ability in performing the long-forbidden *sema'* which has been described in detail by H. Ritter.[1] Many members of Parliament, including the Minister of Education and his wife, attended the festival which in the following years became an institution, and has today more of a tourist attraction than of a religious experience. Now, Mevlâna-days are celebrated in different towns; the main musical part and speeches are broadcast on 17 December.

The growing interest in the works of Rūmī, who wrote in Persian but is proudly claimed by the Turks as a Turk, can be judged by the number of books written about him, and of translations from his works.[2]

Another mystical poet who is venerated in even wider circles is Yunus Emre, the greatest medieval poet of Anatolia (d. about 1321) who used for the first time the Turkish idiom for expressing mystical thought with unsurpassable beauty. His poetry is still understood without difficulty, and even in the Village Institutes which Atatürk had set up for the modern education of the villagers, Yunus has been celebrated as the representative of truly "Turkish" religious feeling; some of his sweet songs belong to the stock of school books. Now, his anniversary is celebrated in May in a small town, bearing his name, near Polatlî. And one of the finest expressions of modern Turkish music is the oratorio written on the basis of his poems by Adnan Saygun.[3]

Yunus Emre created that type of Turkish mystical poetry which was used by the poets of the Bektaşi order and that, in spite of its strange mixture of Shī'a elements, was very influential because of its connexion with the Janissaries. The songs and the jokes of the broad-minded unorthodox Bektaşis are still commonly known and loved; the order itself seems to exist under the surface; thirty Bektaşi leaders were

[1] "Die Mevlânafeiern in Konya vom 11–17 Dezember 1960", *Oriens*, vol. xv (Leiden, 1962), p. 249.

[2] Cf. H. Ritter, "Neue Literatur über Maulānā Celāluddīn Rūmī und seinen Orden"; *Oriens*, vols. XIII/XIV (1960/61), pp. 432 ff.; cf. esp. the important studies of Abdülbaki Gölpînarlî.

[3] A. Schimmel, "Yunus Emre", *Numen*, vol. VIII, pt. 1 (Leiden, 1961).

arrested in October 1952. One can assume that the Bektaşi novel *Nur Baba* by Ya'kub Kadri (1922) which unveiled some of the rather licentious practices of a number of "religious leaders" in Bektaşi circles, was not without influence on Atatürk's measures against the orders.[1]

In spite of the official verdict, saint-worship and popular superstitions continue in the whole of Anatolia, and even in the towns. Ḥikmet Tanyu has made an exhaustive study of the places near Ankara where vows are being made, including the different kinds of vows.[2] The field work was not easy since a number of shrines and tombs had been destroyed in 1939–40 by police or other persons (who, as people told, were all afflicted by illness and other calamities). Even society ladies took part in the superstitious customs though (or because) their knowledge of the dogmatic side of Islam was very poor. In Ankara one is accustomed to bring brushes to the mosque of Haci Bayram; one may light candles or—a modernization!—give electric bulbs to the shrine. Some places are visited only by women (thus Karyağdï Sultan in Ankara), others only on certain days. Very often the slaughter of an animal, preferably a cock, is vowed and the meat is distributed to the poor. Sometimes letters are put under the cover of the coffin and rags are bound to the windows or doors (in the shape of cradles if a child is asked for). Interesting is the *Zakarya sofrasï* which was introduced after 1923 and consists of a silent meal (mostly in the month of Sha'bān), which contains forty-one kinds of food. After the recitation of Sūra XIX, whosoever has a wish lights a candle and vows to arrange a similar meal next Sha'bān.

We may mention here the verses and prayers which are recited when the new moon is seen for the first time (important relic from the Islamic lunar calendar), or the importance given to dreams: according to traditional Islam dreams are part of prophecy; thus the belief in their truth is deeply rooted even in modern society.

In the countryside the number of superstitions is innumerable; people live with their demons and angels, fearing the Evil Eye, and both the bitter accusations of the enlightened schoolteacher Maḥmud Makal and P. Stirling's *Turkish Village* show the backwardness of most of the villagers; the lords of the country (*memleketin sahibleri*) are not,

[1] German translation *Flamme und Falter*, by A. Schimmel (Gummersbach, 1947).

[2] Cf. A. Schimmel, "Das Gelübde im türkischen Volksglauben", *W.I.* n.s. vol. VI (1959), pp. 1–2.

as Atatürk wanted it, the villagers but, as Makal puts it ironically, the spirits who rule daily life.

Sometimes "saints" from the villages came down to Ankara. I remember an Alevi from Malatya district who was said not to have eaten for twenty-one years because of an order from Ḥażrat 'Alī. Living only on a cup of tea a day he had walked three times to Karbalā'. A very strange uncouth radiance emerged from him for he was a living skeleton, the skin sticking to his bones...The irritating man told us that he was going to Germany to preach Islam there.

But more important and influential are the mystical currents among the intelligentsia. There is a strong feeling that mysticism, strengthening of the "inner life" rather than stress on details of law is needed in the country. We may mention here in the first place the group around Ken'an Rifa'i (d. 1950) who has been praised in a very instructive book by his four foremost disciples, all of them ladies of very high culture and well-known as writers, among them a Christian.[1] The influence of this mystical leader whose aim was the resuscitation of the spiritual values of Islam in his disciples is seemingly very deep. Samiha Ayverdi, after his death spiritual leader of the group, has tried in her beautiful books to show the marvellous achievements of the Turkish Islamic life, idealized in some way but no doubt important at a time when literature in Turkey mainly concentrates on rather unspiritual aspects of modern life.

Another leader of mystical tinge was 'Ömer Fevzi Mardin (d. 1953) whose warm liberal personality is praised by all those who have met him. He kept in touch with orientalists like L. Massignon, and tried to bridge the gap between the Muslims and the *ahl al-kitāb* by a rather personal exegesis with the desire to revive not only Islam but all monotheistic religions. In more than twenty-five books and pamphlets, among them a collection of Prophetic traditions, he tried to lead Turkish youth to an ethically based faith, full of love of God and mankind.[2]

There is also Ḥasan Luṭfi Şuşuṭ whose instruction aims at leading mankind through strict asceticism, constant fasting and night medita-

[1] Samiha Ayverdi, Nezihe Araz, Safiye Erol and Sofi Huri, *Kenan Rifai ve yirminci asrın Işığında Müslümanlık*(Istanbul, 1951); cf. Reed, "Religious Life", p. 139; "Revival of Islam", pp. 274–6; A. Schimmel, "Samiha Ayverdi—eine Istanbuler Schriftstellerin", *Festschrift Otto Spies* (Wiesbaden, 1967).

[2] I mention here the booklet *Ehli kitap ailesi* (Istanbul, 1952), which has been translated into Greek by Paul Hidiroghlu (Athens, 1962).

tions, to a level which is beyond the traditional conceptions of *unio mystica*. He holds that *taṣawwuf* is the realization of Not-Being, an idea which he derives from what he calls Turkish or Northern Ṣūfism; he has detected the earliest representatives of this type who have abstained from "second-range ideas like monism, love, union, beatific vision", etc., in the early Naqshbandīs of Turkestan.[1] Publications of "spiritual" character are mostly financed by private enterprise.

In the countryside we still find folk poets who sing their religious songs as has been done since the days of yore. Most interesting is the case of Ismail Emre, called by his admirers Yeni Yunus Emre, the new Yunus: an illiterate locksmith from Adana who, as we witnessed, recites at times in a state of trance mystical poems in the simple folk-style with the usual rhyme-pattern without knowing what he is singing. This modest man now and then gives spiritual advice, maintaining the essential unity of prophetic experience in all religions.[2]

A similar case of automatic writing is that of Turgut Akkaş, a high bank employee who has brought out a quarterly *İç Varlık* (since 1954) with articles combining mystical and spiritualist tendencies, and poems which were "dictated" to him in the last part of the night.

Here the frontiers of spiritualism are wide open; such is the case of Enis Behic Koryürek (1892–1949), an official in the Foreign Office, known as a poet who was seized by a spirit called Süleyman from mediéval Trabzon under whose influence he wrote a series of fine mystical poems which have been commented upon by 'Ömer Fevzi Mardin.[3] Thus it is not astonishing that a "Metaphysical and Spiritual Society" was founded in Istanbul in 1952; phenomena like cardiognosy, telepathy, etc., well-known to every student of mysticism, have to some extent been given this "scientific" form. The question of how far certain aspects of Ṣūfism are preserved in the Freemasons' lodges (founded in 1927 and 1933, dissolved in 1935, and reopened from 1948 onwards), or whether a relation exists between Bektaşis and freemasons, cannot be answered adequately.[4] Modern Turkish literature rarely reflects religious feeling. Sometimes the simplicity and daring language of the old Bektaşi poetry is imitated where the poet quite frankly tells God the miserable condition of this world. Ḥasan 'Ali Yücel, the CHP minister of Education, who was accused of leftist

[1] *Faqir sözleri; Islam taṣavvufunda khajegan Khanedani* (Istanbul, 1958).
[2] *Yeni Yunus Emre ve doğuşlari* (Istanbul, 1952).
[3] *Varidat-i Süleyman şerhi* (Istanbul, 1951).
[4] Cf. Dr Kurdoğlu, *Bektaşilik ve Batinilik* (Türkiye Mason Dernegi, 1955).

ideas, dedicated beautiful poems to Mevlâna Rūmī. Now and then poems of ethical content, or encomia on Rūmī, Yunus Emre, etc., are composed.

The continuing discussion of religious problems makes the Turkish intelligentsia sensitive to the work of other Muslim reformist authors. There are translations of books published first in the Azhar Mosque of Jamāl al-Dīn al-Afghānī and the Indian Aḥmad Sirhindī (d. 1624, venerated especially in Naqshbandī circles), and a particular interest is now perceptible in the work of Muḥammad Iqbāl. The fact that Iqbāl uttered bitter criticism of Turkish modernism in some of his poetical works was far outweighed by his appraisal of the Turkish solution of the form of government in his *Six Lectures* where he also examined the different strands of modernist thought in Turkey.[1] Meḥmed 'Akif, the poet of glorious Turco-Islamic hymns, had become acquainted with Iqbāl's poetry during his stay in Egypt, and admired both his style and his ideals. But the real interest in the poet-philosopher started after the foundation of Pakistan when the traditional friendship between the Indo-Pakistani Muslims and Turkey manifested itself again. Many translations were made from his works, by 'Ali Nihat Tarlan, Sofi Huri and the present writer. The way Iqbāl developed his ideas of reformation, his deep interest in the dynamic character of Islam and in human activity made him quite suitable for the reformist-minded Turks who aimed at a revaluation of human activity. He became even more attractive for the Turkish Muslims by his admiration for Mevlâna Rūmī.

It is difficult to judge the situation in Turkey today. We still see the different trends side by side. In Jäschke's words we have the 150 per cent Kemalists who want the *basmala* of a Turk to be "In the name of God who has created Atatürk..." and think that Atatürk's mausoleum should be the Ka'ba of the nation; then the 100 per cent Kemalists who dream of religious teachers who act according to the ideals of Atatürk in leading people towards a brilliant future, free from medieval fetters, not concerned with the *sharī'a* but with living faith; and last the orthodox with their different grades of possible modernization.[2]

The return to a more Islamic way of life during the Menderes period which sometimes led to strange manifestations of popular piety,

[1] Cf. A. Schimmel, *Gabriel's Wing. A Study into the religious ideas of Sir Muhammad Iqbal* (Leiden, 1963), esp. p. 245.

[2] Cf. Jäschke, "Vom Kampf der Islamisten und der Kemalisten in der Türkei", *W.I.* n.s. vol. VIII, pt. 4 (1963).

created also a new image of Atatürk; one tried, as Jäschke says so appropriately, to save Atatürk for Islam, showing him only as an enemy of superstition and the like.[1] Thus the prayer in the *Kadîr gecesi* which was celebrated in the Süleymaniye mosque in 1955 implores God's blessing for the soul of Atatürk "who had made it his highest goal to bring up a *faithful*, living, revolutionary generation".

After Menderes who had even been styled a kind of *walī Allāh*, friend of God, the revolution of 27 May 1960 turned back again to a stronger Atatürkist line. Yet one feels that the consolidation of religious feeling is the best preventive against Communist infiltrations, and the participation of Turkey in international Muslim congresses, her firm friendship with Pakistan and close relations with Iran show that the common glorious Islamic past is by no means forgotten. The new government, taking over in February 1965, is expected to support religion (in a country with 98 per cent Muslim population!) and to enlarge the circle of enlightened religious teachers who are supposed to oppose the disastrous influence of reactionary fanatics, as S. H. Ürgüblü stressed in his speech on 26 February 1965.

A Turk may be as far as possible from the outward acceptance of Islamic dogma or of approval of the *sharī'a*, yet he will surely not change Islam for another religion, and the hopes of certain groups who suppose Turkey after Atatürk's revolution to be a ready field for Christian mission will always be frustrated. A Turkish friend whom I asked in the spring of 1965 whether the currents in the country tended more towards Turkism or towards Islam gave an answer which seems to me symptomatic of the feeling of large parts of the population:

> The Arabs struggled 150 years for Islam and died for it. The Iranians never did. But the Turks no sooner accepted the Islamic religion than they started fighting for their faith, and still, the Turkish nation dies lovingly (*seve seve*) for their faith. For the Turk has riveted his religion and his national feeling into each other, has blended them completely, has made them into a single thing.[2]

[1] Jäschke, "Die Bedeutung der Religion für Mustafa Kemal (Atatürk)", *Kairos* (1963).

[2] The reader will readily understand how greatly the present writer is indebted to Prof. Dr Gotthard Jäschke's articles and to his unfailing help in answering questions.

CHAPTER 5

ITHNĀ 'ASHARĪ SHĪ'ISM AND IRANIAN ISLAM

HISTORICAL BACKGROUND

Persia is one of the most overwhelmingly Muslim countries in the world and has been one of the major centres of Islamic civilization since the inception of Islam.[1] The life of the vast majority of Persians today is dominated and moulded by Islam while at the same time the religious life of the people reflects the long history of the Persians. Having accepted Islam wholeheartedly, the Persians nevertheless succeeded in preserving their linguistic and cultural identity and in fact were able to bring to life in the universal perspective of Islam the most positive elements of their pre-Islamic past. To understand the present-day religious life of the Persians, particularly Ithnā 'Asharī or Twelve-Imam Shī'ism which is dominant in Persia today, it is necessary to cast a brief glance at the religious history of the people who have lived on the Iranian plateau during the past three thousand years.

Persia has been both a centre from which major religious influences have radiated and a cross-roads in which the religious traditions of the Mediterranean world and Asia have met, resulting often in new currents of religious life. Having originally belonged to the same ethnic and linguistic stock as the Aryan conquerors of India, the early Iranians who settled on the plateau possessed a religion akin to that of the Vedas. From this early background there arose the reform of Zoroaster and the establishment of the specifically Iranian religion of Zoroastrianism. Although the dates of Zoroaster are still much debated, there is no doubt that in the fifth century B.C. his teachings became the official religion of the Persian empire. The sacred book of Zoroastrianism, the Avesta, is the most precious religious document of the early history of Persia as well as a basic source for the study of the Iranian languages. Zoroastrianism, with its firm belief in the angelic

[1] Although no exact recent statistics are available, the last consensus shows that of the over 24 million population of Persia about 98 per cent are Muslim, the rest being comprised of Zoroastrian, Christian and Jewish religious communities as well as of the Bābī and Bahā'ī movements. Of the Islamic population about nine-tenths are Shī'ite and one-tenth Sunnī.

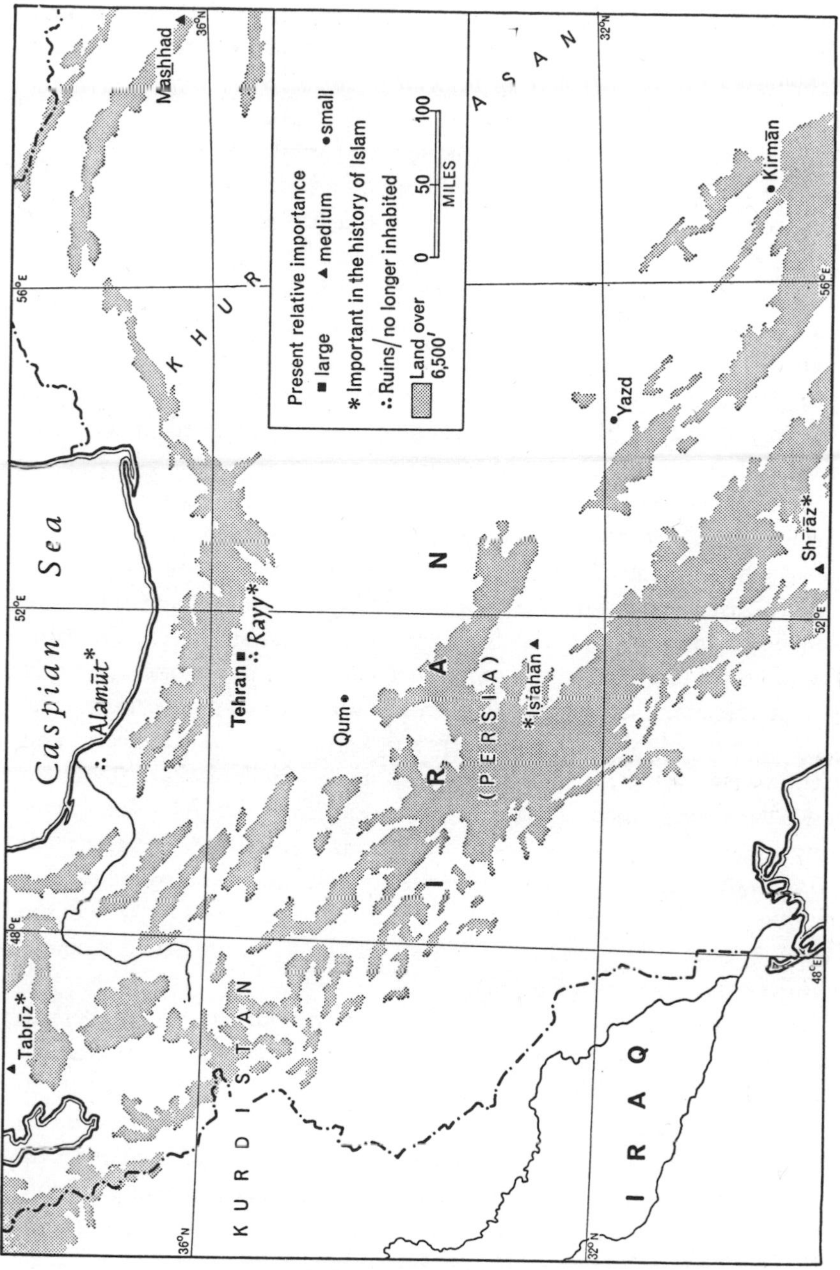
Caspian Sea
Alamūt*
Tabrīz*
Tehran
Rayy*
Qum
Mashhad
KHURASAN
KURDISTAN
IRAN
(PERSIA)
*Iṣfahān
Yazd
Kirmān
Shīrāz*
IRAQ
36°N
32°N
48°E
52°E
56°E
Present relative importance
large
medium
small
* Important in the history of Islam
Ruins/no longer inhabited
Land over 6,500′
0
50
100
MILES

Iran.

world, the moral quality of human existence, the reality of the after life and Last Judgment, the purity of the elements and the sacred character of human life, left an imprint both on the later religious life of western Asia and on the general outlook of the Persians.

The positive qualities which this religion implanted in the souls of the Persians survived and became transmuted into the Islamic mould after Zoroastrianism itself had decayed and lost the spiritual struggle against the new forces of Islam. For example, the care that devout Persians take in keeping their clothing, food and habitat clean in a ritual sense, sometimes even over-emphasizing this element of religion, is an old Zoroastrian teaching reinforced by the emphasis of Islam upon cleanliness. Whatever survived of Zoroastrianism in the Persian soul was, however, thoroughly Islamized and interpreted in the light of the unitary point of view of Islam.

From the matrix of Zoroastrianism, which is the stable and orthodox background of Iranian religions, there grew several religious movements which had world-wide repercussions and also shook the foundations of Zoroastrianism itself. With the fall of the Achaemenian Empire Hellenistic influences spread throughout the domain of the Persians. This cultural movement was combined with a religious one known as Mithraism which itself contained important Hellenistic elements. The mystery cult of Mithra, which spread as far west as Germany and Scandinavia, was a synthesis of Zoroastrian, Hellenistic, Babylonian and Anatolian elements. If for the world at large this religious movement meant the spread of Iranian religious elements, for Persia itself it implied perhaps more than anything else the establishment of a religious sanction for the syncretic cultural life through which the Persians were now passing as a result of the conquests of Alexander and the establishment of Seleucid rule.

During the Parthian period Zoroastrianism and the proper Persian cultural tradition began to reassert themselves until with the advent of the Sāsānids the religion of Zoroaster became once again the official state religion and remained in this position until the fall of the Sāsānid empire. Nevertheless, its authority did not go unchallenged even on the religious plane. In the third century A.D. a second world-sweeping Iranian mystery religion, Manichaeism, came into being. Its founder, Mani, first found favour with the Sāsānid ruler but was finally put to death through the opposition of the Zoroastrian priesthood. His cult nevertheless spread from China to France and in Persia itself gained many adherents. At once a socially revolutionary and religiously mystical movement, it marked a major protest against established religious institutions. Although some of its cosmogonic and cosmological teachings found a place in certain forms of Islamic philosophy, for Persians of the later period Manichaeism has appeared as a rebellion against religious authority. It has never enjoyed the same status as Zoroastrianism from which it came into being and against which it revolted.

The Sāsānid period was also witness to other religious movements such as Mazdaḳism, a "religious communism" known today mostly through what its enemies both Zoroastrian and Christian wrote against it. This movement, which was soon crushed, was again a protest against the Zoroastrian social order and foretold the collapse of this order which occurred with the coming of Islam. Also at this time there developed within Zoroastrianism the philosophico-religious school known as Zurvanism which indicates a blend of Iranian religious thought with certain Greek philosophical ideas. Finally, it must be remembered that out of rivalry with the Byzantines, the Sāsānids encouraged dissident Christian sects especially the Nestorians. These sects were given a free hand to establish schools and missions throughout the Sāsānid empire with the result that notable Christian communities came into existence in Persia and became an important minority religious community in the Islamic period. The Jews also had had several centres in Persia from Achaemenian times and continued to thrive under both Zoroastrian and Muslim rule. The tolerance toward minority religions shown by Cyrus the Great has been with few exceptions the rule in the religious history of Persia.

The major spiritual transformation in Persia came with the advent of Islam. Although the military defeat of the Sāsānids before the Arab armies was a sudden and rapid process, the spiritual struggle between Islam and Zoroastrianism was a gradual one, a process that did not really terminate until the tenth century. This fact itself indicates that the Persians accepted Islam not through force but because of an inner spiritual need. When they regained their political independence from the caliphate there were still very sizeable Zoroastrian communities in Persia. But rather than showing any inclination to return to this tradition, the newly independent Persian rulers became themselves the champions of the spread of Islam while insisting on the independence of the literary and cultural life of Persia. Most of the Muslim lands of Asia have in fact been Islamicized through the Persian form of Islam.

And to this day when a Persian thinks of the domain of "Persian culture" he sees before him nearly the whole of the eastern lands of Islam from the western borders of the Iranian plateau to western China with Iraq as an intermediary realm where the Persian, Arabic and later Turkish elements met.

During early Islamic history Persia was dominated by the Sunnī form of Islam. In fact it is from Khurasan that the theological defence of Sunnism was made during the tenth and eleventh centuries when many other lands of Islam were dominated by Shīʿism. Yet, certain centres in Persia such as Qum were from the beginning Shīʿite and the Persians in general had a particular reverence for the household of the Prophet of Islam. The figure of Salmān al-Fārisī, the Persian who in search of the ideal prophet journeyed all the way to Arabia to meet the Prophet and became so close to him as to be called "one of the members of the household" (*ahl-i bayt*) of the Prophet, has the deepest significance for the religious consciousness of Islamic Persia. During the early centuries therefore, Persia was at once a major centre of Sunnī Islam, producing such scholars and theologians as al-Bukhārī, al-Ghazālī and Fakhr al-Dīn al-Rāzī, and a land within which important centres of Shīʿism existed, where many of the greatest early Shīʿite theologians such as Ibn Bābūya and Kulaynī saw the light of day.

Before the Mongol invasion, which meant such a devastating material and social calamity for Persia, the forces of Ismāʿīlism were also strong in this land. Although the centre of their power was in the Yemen and later Egypt, from the ninth century onward there were outstanding philosophers and theologians of this school in Persia, men like Abū Ḥātim al-Rāzī and Nāṣir-i Khusraw who have left us so many doctrinal works on Ismāʿīlism. Moreover, with the "resurrection of Alamūt" Ismāʿīlism gained major political power in Persia and continued to exert political pressure until the destruction of Alamūt by Hülegü.

Between the Mongol invasion and the establishment of the Ṣafavids Persia moved gradually toward Shīʿism through both social, political and purely religious factors marked by the activity of certain Ṣūfī orders and several outstanding Shīʿite theologians. Yet, at the time of the establishment of the Ṣafavids and the recognition of Shīʿism as the official state religion, most of Persia was still Sunnī. The change, however, was made relatively rapidly and soon the country became predominantly Shīʿite while noticeable Sunnī elements have survived to this day in such areas as Khurasan and Kurdistan.

Persia was also from the beginning of Islamic history one of the lands in which Ṣūfism, the esoteric and mystical dimension of Islam, spread rapidly and expressed itself in most striking literary and artistic forms. Some of the greatest early Ṣūfīs, like al-Bisṭāmī and al-Ḥallāj were Persian and later the direct influence of Ṣūfism transformed Persian poetry into one of the most universal forms of literature. Both through the direct presence of Ṣūfī orders and the effect of Ṣūfism upon Persian literature, music, architecture and other forms of art as well as certain social organizations, the spirit of Ṣūfism has left an indelible mark upon many facets of the life of the Persians. It must be remembered, however, that being esoteric in character, Ṣūfism has always preserved its inner teachings for those who have been qualified to follow the Ṣūfī path. It is only the external manifestations of Ṣūfism that have a general cultural and social bearing and are so noticeable a strand in the fabric of Persian life and culture.

RELIGION AND THE GENERAL WORLD VIEW

The world view of the Persian is determined more than anything else by religion, and more specifically by the teachings of Islam. Like other Muslims, the Persian is born, lives and dies with the verses of the Holy Qur'ān echoing in his ears. He sees the world about him in the light of the conception of the divine and his creation as delineated in the Qur'ān. There is, in fact, in spite of the secularist tendencies of the past fifty years, still no conception of a way of life of which religion is only an element or of a world view of which the religious factor is only one dimension. The total world view is religious and even the apparent negation of religion in certain domains has itself a religious significance.

The universe in which the Persian lives, like that of all Muslims, is one that is created and sustained by Allāh, the Omnipotent and Omniscient Creator, Who is at once the origin and end of all things, the first and the last. His will reigns supreme over both the world of nature and the lives of men and their societies. He has knowledge of all things and his majesty melts into nothingness all that is beside him. Yet he has given man free will to pursue his own life and to choose the "right path" (*al-ṣirāṭ al-mustaqīm*) on his own accord without compulsion. The secret of man's life lies between these two logically contradictory assertions of the absolute omnipotence of Allāh and man's free will and responsibility before him as the supreme judge.

Every Muslim is aware throughout his life of the ultimate significance of his actions beyond this world of change and corruption. The Persian Muslim, like his other brethren in faith, may sometimes live a life that is mundane and even directly against a divine injunction because of his own weakness, but he never doubts for one moment the presence of the divine command and his responsibility to follow it. There are some who do not heed the voice of the divine but there is practically no one who doubts the presence of "His voice". That is why after a life of debauchery a man suddenly becomes devout and even in the midst of the most profane life is aware of the presence of the transcendent dimension of life.

Inasmuch as the will of God is manifested in Islam in the form of a concrete and all-embracing law, the *sharīʿa*, the Persian is always aware of the religious character of all facets of life. The *sharīʿa* covers all aspects of human life, and to the vast majority of the Persians all laws which they encounter and all acts which they perform during their daily lives possess a sacred character even if non-sharīʿite laws have been promulgated in certain domains. Most Persians feel that they are performing a religious duty when they work to make a living even if the particular work they perform is not itself of a traditional religious nature. By contrast the small Western-educated classes that have been affected by the Western distinction between the religious and the secular often do not attach a religious significance to their daily work. For them the *sharīʿa* is identified with specific acts of worship. But they are a small minority. For most Persians, both the uneducated and educated, the all-embracing nature of the divine will that governs all facets of man's life through a sacred law is very much of a reality and a permanent factor in their general world view.

The divine will is also seen in the world of nature of which the phenomena, in conformity with the teachings of the Qur'ān, are considered as the "signs of God". There is no ultimate distinction between the divine law governing men and the laws governing nature, between religious and natural law as understood in the West. Nature is a complementary aspect of the religious reality that is revealed directly through revelation. It can therefore incite the deepest intellectual and contemplative response in the Persian who turns to it both as a source of enjoyment and the background for the spiritual life. The very austerity of nature, the high mountains, the vast deserts, the green valleys hidden high in mountain ranges evoke an awareness of the transcendent. The visible itself is but a veil for the invisible and the laws of the world of nature but a part of the universal law which of necessity governs all things.

The Persian is also keenly aware of the transient nature of things, a point so often emphasized in Islam. He lives with the reality of death and a realization of the instability of all that surrounds him. For him the angelic world, the hierarchy of spiritual beings that stands above the world of material forms, is a constant reality, one that is emphasized in both the ancient religions of Iran and Islam. If this world is impermanent and transient there stands beyond it the permanent and luminous world of angelic substances.

This awareness of the transient nature of this world is combined with a great joy in life and its beauties which reflect the beauty of the higher orders of existence. Few people are given as much to the enjoyment of life's pleasures and beauties as the Persians, but this attitude is always compensated by the realization that a moment once gone never returns and all that is physical and sensual has an ephemeral character about it. These two attitudes are reflected even in distinctly religious activity in which frequent sessions of chanting of the Qur'ān at which people weep and are carried beyond worldly cares are held in the most beautiful gardens where the best refreshments are served and the voice of the reciter itself possesses the best musical quality. Carried to its most spiritual level this attitude is reflected in all Persian Ṣūfī poetry wherein one is constantly reminded that the infinite reflects an aspect of its beauty at each moment but because of its infinity its theophanies (*tajalliyāt*) never repeat themselves.

There is also an element of tragedy which characterizes the Persian and which is seen fully in the ethos of Shīʿism. This is not like the humanistic tragedy of the later Greeks, a rebellion of man against the gods, but is a spiritual quality. The tragic and sad element, which does not at all negate the aspect of joy in life, is always of a religious character and a basis for contemplation. It is most directly reflected in classical Persian music where the apparently sad quality is in reality a nostalgia for the divine. It is a tragedy based on the realization of the human condition as containing an apparent contradiction. Man is in desperate need to realize the divine and become aware of his own spiritual nature. Yet, this realization is made well nigh impossible by the distance that separates him from the divine and his need to await divine assistance to accomplish this end.

Closely connected with this point of view is the concept of the intermediary and the expectation of a future saviour, both so important to Shīʿism. Man is in need of an intermediary between himself and God. Even after the descent of a revelation, the role of the intermediary must continue. Therefore, after the Prophet of Islam there must be Imams who act as intermediaries between men of later generations and God. There must also be a future saviour, the *mahdī*, who will redeem the world from its state of corruption. He too is an Imam, in fact the twelfth Imam of Shīʿism, but an Imam who comes in the future, to expect whom (*intiẓār*) is itself a religious virtue. The idea of appealing to saints and Imams and of the patient awaiting of one who will in the future redeem injustice and corruption and therefore end the hardships of present-day life are constant elements of the Persian religious outlook.

RELIGIOUS INSTITUTIONS AND ORGANIZATIONS

The most important religious centre in the life of the Persians is the mosque whose size varies from the colossal Friday mosques of major cities to single rooms in small towns and villages. Its architecture also varies from ornate tiled mosques to mud structures whose walls are covered by whitewash. In all its forms the mosque is the centre of both religious and social activity in the community. Its door being always open, it remains a calm centre amidst the turmoil of daily life, a place where people wander in to say their prayers as well as to consider a transaction or simply to relax with friends in the contemplative and peaceful atmosphere which the mosque creates. In the cities in fact the bigger mosques are nearly always situated in the bazaars and are an inseparable part of daily life.

The mosque is also used for congregational prayers, particularly those of Friday, as well as for special occasions of religious mourning or feasting or funerals. The Friday prayers, however, are less emphasized in Persia than in other Muslim lands where Sunnī Islam predominates. This is because in the absence of the *mahdī*, the Friday prayers do not carry any political significance and their importance is not greatly emphasized by the *ʿulamā'*. Rather, the religious climate is such that the canonical prayers performed individually and often at home are considered as important as prayers at mosques so that many who do not go regularly to mosques nevertheless do perform their prayers and other religious rites.

The role of the mosque in the life of country and city dwellers as well as traditional and modern Persians is not the same. In the countryside the *imām* of the mosque often acts as teacher for elementary education, especially early religious education, and he is the arbitrator in most disputes. After daily prayers people usually gather about him to pose questions about problems which would otherwise have to be taken to court. In the smaller cities these traits subsist to a certain degree but in larger cities both functions, elementary education and judging cases, are performed outside the mosque, although in the second case the arbitrator is himself usually a religious authority. The larger mosques in big cities also perform an educational service on a higher level in that they are usually affiliated with a religious school or *madrasa* in which more advanced religious education is carried out.

As for the modern educated classes, particularly those who have been educated directly in the West, as a rule they do not go to mosques except on special occasions. They do make pilgrimages, participate in the mourning of Muḥarram or funeral rites, all of which are usually connected with mosques, but they rarely attend their local mosques for daily prayers. Although there are notable exceptions, one can say that in this aspect of religious life they are sharply distinguished from the rest of Persian society.

The *madrasa* system which has its roots in the early centuries of Islamic history is the means whereby the intellectual aspect of the religious tradition is kept alive. In these schools which are endowed and usually connected with a major mosque, students who have undergone an early religious education continue their studies. They are fully supported by the *madrasa*, receiving accommodation on the premises as well as board and other expenses. There is no pressure on them to finish their studies in a certain period nor are any specific degrees conferred upon them. Some stay for their whole life and if competent become teachers in their turn. The students mostly choose the field of the transmitted (*naqlī*) sciences, studying law, the principles of jurisprudence, Qur'ānic exegesis, *ḥadīth*, etc. Some, however, choose the intellectual (*ʿaqlī*) sciences and pursue logic, Islamic philosophy, theology, etc.

The largest *madrasa* system today, which is in Qum, has over six thousand students and there are other major centres in Mashhad, Tehran, Iṣfahān and several other cities. Moreover, besides the official lessons taught in the *madrasa*, classes are often held in the homes of individual professors and masters, these often being in more advanced phases of study. These classes are particularly important in the field of traditional Islamic philosophy or theosophy (*ḥikma*) as well as gnosis (*ʿirfān*). In these private circles many who do not belong to the *madrasas* also participate, including often some who have had a modern rather than a purely traditional education. One could even say that most of the teaching of the Islamic intellectual sciences in Persia is performed outside formal institutions and in private circles.

Shrines which consist of tombs of the Shīʿite Imams, their descendants and Ṣūfī saints play a major role in the life of all classes of Persians. They consist usually of a mausoleum and mosque, often with a *madrasa* and library attached and supported by endowments and donations. Of those within Persia itself the most important is that of the eighth Imam, ʿAlī al-Riḍā, in Mas͟hhad which is visited by hundreds of thousands of people every season. It has a vast complex of mosques and courtyards around the central mausoleum as well as dispensaries, hospitals, a major library, museum, *madrasa*, etc. A thousand people are fed at each meal free of charge and there is no time of the year when the shrine is not completely filled with throngs of the faithful. Next to Mas͟hhad, the holy city of Qum is important inasmuch as it is the site of the tomb of Imam Riḍā's sister, Ḥaḍrat-i Maʿṣūma. It too is frequented by many pilgrims throughout the year. The tombs of Ḥaḍrat-i ʿAbd al-ʿAẓīm near Tehran in Rayy, Shāh Chirāgh in Shīrāz, Shāh Niʿmat-allāh Walī, the famous Ṣūfī, near Kirmān, are all shrine institutions of first-rate importance. Other shrines are located on tops of mountains in difficult locations, in awesome sites of nature connected with the traditional science of sacred geography. There is no city or town without a site of pilgrimage and a saint to whom the people turn in their moments of trial as well as moments of thankfulness.

All of these shrines play a fundamental role in daily religious life inasmuch as people turn to these saints as intermediaries to God and ask through them what they wish to ask of God. There is hardly anyone in Persia, even the most modern, for whom the power of the grace or *baraka* of these shrines has been broken.

The Ṣūfī centres, called *khāniqāh* in Persian, are also major centres of religious life although Ṣūfism itself transcends the exoteric dimension of religion and contains within itself the esoteric teachings of Islam. The *khāniqāh* is usually either the home of a living Ṣūfī master or the tomb of a dead one which has become the centre of the order. In either case it is a complex of buildings in which the *fuqarā'* or dervishes meet for their sessions of spiritual practice and where there are rooms for travelling dervishes as well as cells for those who make spiritual retreats. On special religious holidays such as the birthdays of the Prophet and 'Alī as well as during days of mourning the *khāniqāhs* open their doors to all who come to benefit from the ceremonies held there. Even at other times the *khāniqāh* acts as a pole of spiritual attraction for the community itself, even if those outside its organization are not completely aware of all that is taught to disciples within the fold of each Ṣūfī brotherhood.

The major Ṣūfī orders in Persia today are the Ni'matallāhī with many branches throughout the country; the Gunābādī centred in Khurasan; the Dhahabī with its major centre in Shīrāz; the Qādirī powerful mostly in Kurdistan and the Persian Gulf region, and the Naqshbandī also having its centre in Kurdistan. These orders, many of which have close contacts with branches in other Muslim lands continue to influence the general structure of society and cultural life, in particular literature, music and miniature painting. The very presence of a living gnostic path of spirituality also has its effect on intellectual pursuits especially traditional Islamic philosophy, which for this very reason is not just a rational form of knowledge but a theosophy or *hikma*, ultimately a means of spiritual realization.

The institution of religious endowment (*waqf*) which is an important Islamic institution is the means whereby the above-mentioned religious organizations as well as many others are supported. Usually cultivated lands but also pastures, wells, trees, etc., are given as an endowment for a particular religious institution. A person is chosen to act as keeper and executor of the endowment and under his direction the income is to be spent in accordance with the will of the founder. Today a certain amount of organization has been given to this matter through the establishment of a department of *waqf* by the government. But the institution is far from being government controlled and in most cases it is still the person in charge of the endowment or his family who hold power in their hands.

SOCIAL ORGANIZATIONS CONNECTED WITH RELIGIOUS LIFE

In traditional Persian society, as in other traditional societies, every social institution possessed religious and spiritual significance. In modern times although some of these institutions no longer have a direct religious colouring, others have a religious connexion even if they are not, strictly speaking, religious organizations. Of these the guilds (*aṣnāf*) are of great importance. Existing in all the bigger cities, the guilds draw members of a particular occupation such as bakers, bricklayers or carpet-weavers into an organization which still preserves in many fields its original connexion with Ṣūfī orders and the chivalrous brotherhoods or *futuwwāt*. Most of the guilds have a particular reverence for ʻAlī, the traditional patron saint of all Islamic guilds, and possess a strong feeling of fraternity. Even labour organizations which most resemble unions in the Western sense possess some of the characteristics of the guilds and it is difficult in most cases to draw a line between the guild and the union.

Some social significance in certain quarters still pertains to the remnants of orders of chivalry centred around gymnasia called *zūr khāna*. Again closely connected with the name of ʻAlī, these orders served traditionally to enhance the spirit of chivalry (*jawān-mardī*) and to build up moral and spiritual character along with bodily exercises that are performed to the beating of a drum and the chanting of religious and epic verses. Traditional Persian cities, like other Muslim cities, have had local strong men who have kept the peace and protected the "morals" (*nāmūs*) of their quarters of the city. Such types have usually been connected in Persia with the *zūr khāna* and still perform this function in many cities although in the modernized parts of Tehran they stand in rather stark contrast to some of the westernized youth who are completely devoid of the traditional virtues of chivalry inculcated by these orders.

Finally, mention must be made of certain modern organizations usually connected with bureaucratic professions and some affiliated to Ṣūfī orders. There are also lodges of Freemasons which in the Persian climate have in certain cases gained a Muslim colouring, while some are even connected to *khāniqāhs*. In a few cases there has come into being a Persian version of an organization resembling these lodges but of a more directly religious character and attracting many from the modern educated classes. In all these cases a religious element is present, though it varies from one organization and even from one individual to another.

RELIGION IN SOCIAL, ECONOMIC AND POLITICAL LIFE

Because of the all-embracing nature of the sacred law or *sharīʻa* there is in reality no aspect of social life which is completely divorced from religious principles, even if modernism and older historical forces have removed certain aspects of social life from the direct jurisdiction of the *sharīʻa*. Those domains of social life in which the *sharīʻa* is still directly applied in Persia are personal law such as marriage, divorce, etc., as well as much of civil law. In this domain, even what was taken from European codes was done under the jurisdiction of the *ʻulamāʼ* and integrated into the matrix of the *sharīʻa* through the practice of "independent juridical opinion" or *ijtihād*. Moreover, those who practice law and administer it are nearly all either products of the *madrasas* or the law schools and theological faculties where they have been exposed to Islamic jurisprudence (*fiqh*).

It is rather in the domain of economic life that non-sharīʻite practices are to be seen. In the field of taxation other systems have been used from Umayyad times in addition to the Islamic religious tax which in Shīʻism consists of *zakāt* and *khums*. Many wealthy men, especially merchants in bazaars, do, however, continue to pay the religious taxes in addition to those demanded by the government. The religious tax is in fact a major source of support for centres of Shīʻite learning in such cities as Qum.

The religious attitude manifests itself in economic life not so much in specific norms as in attitudes. The Islamic view of the permitted (*ḥalāl*) and forbidden (*ḥarām*), the condemnation of usury, of amassing wealth in gold and silver, of usurping the right of orphans and many other injunctions even if not practised by all, penetrate subtly into economic life. Also the more philosophical attitude of uncertainty about what tomorrow will bring, of distrust of purely human causation, of the feeling of the impermanence of things, all play their role in fields of economic life where specific religious norms may seem to be absent.

As for political life, since Shīʻism does not accept the religious legitimacy of the institution of the caliphate and believes monarchy to be the best form of government in the absence of the *mahdī*, the Persian monarchy has a positive religious aspect. Ever since the establishment of Shīʻism as the official state religion by the Ṣafavids, the monarch has been considered as the legitimate ruler who should rule with the consent of the "religious scholars" or *ʻulamāʼ* and whose duty it is to uphold the *sharī'a* and promulgate Islam. The connexion of the monarchy with the religious structure of Shī'ism in Persia is a persistent element and gives a religious tone to political life even if parliamentary government is not itself an Islamic institution.

RELIGION IN INTELLECTUAL AND CULTURAL LIFE

The encounter of religious and modern, secular norms is best seen in the educational system in Persia. There are in fact two systems of education, one the *madrasas* which produce religious scholars, lawyers, *imāms* of mosques, etc., and the other the modern educational system leading to university degrees in different fields. Here religion is taught as a subject among others in the elementary and secondary school curricula, but one does not find the pervasive religious character of all education that has always existed in traditional Islamic society. In the universities also, besides faculties of theology, subjects connected with religious philosophy, law, etc., are taught in faculties of letters and law but here again other subjects are left outside the religious sphere. There is a direct encounter between religious and "secular" disciplines of learning which did not exist in the traditional Islamic world view where every science, be it natural, mathematical or philosophical, has possessed a traditional and sacred aspect and has never been divorced from the total religious and intellectual life of Islam.

As far as philosophy is concerned it is important to note that traditional Islamic philosophy is still very much alive in Persia. Non-religious European schools of philosophy are also taught in universities but have had little effect upon the general intellectual life of the country. In fact the very presence of a living Islamic intellectual tradition has prevented facile and shallow modern interpretations of Islam which are found in some other Muslim countries. Moreover, even modern philosophical discussions once presented in Persian have had to take cognizance of the presence of the Islamic philosophical tradition.

In literature, architecture, the plastic arts, music, theatre, and other forms of artistic and cultural life traditional forms which have a completely religious and spiritual basis subsist, while modern forms have been introduced with varying degrees of success among certain classes. In such cases as the theatre where the traditional form consisted solely of passion plays, Western forms of theatre depicting problems of Western man have had little appeal to the vast majority of the population and few attempts have been made to use Persian and Islamic themes and motives. In the other arts the traditional forms have sometimes been used in new contemporary settings. But by and large the traditional religious forms of artistic and cultural expression subsist and in certain cases dominate while the modernized minority in Persian society surrounds itself with certain aspects of Western artistic expressions and forms.

RELIGIOUS PRACTICES IN DAILY LIFE

The most important religious practices of Persians like those of all Muslims are the rites of prayers, fasting, pilgrimage and sacrifice with the local colour that the secondary aspects of these rites have acquired against the background of Persian culture. Their essential element is that of the universal norms of Islam itself. The daily prayers, which most Shīʿites usually perform three times a day by combining those of noon and afternoon as well as of evening and night, punctuate the rhythm of daily life. It would not be an exaggeration to say that the conception of time and the flow of life itself is determined by these canonical prayers which are considered as the pillar of Islam. In addition the very devout perform supererogatory prayers (*nawāfil*) and there are special prayers connected with hope, fear, expectation, etc.

Fasting as a religious rite is connected particularly with the holy month of Ramaḍān, although again many devout people fast on different occasions throughout the year, especially the beginning, middle and end of the lunar Islamic month. During Ramaḍān the rhythm of life changes and there is a perceptible transformation of the most external aspects of daily life. Many of the modernized Persians, however, do not fast, but on the whole the fast is observed throughout the country. During the holy month days become calm and sombre and the evenings gay. Many more social calls are made to relatives during the evening and at this time after the breaking of the fast religious and social life become completely intertwined.

The climax of the holy month comes during the nights of the 19th to the 21st, the period during which the first Imam ʿAlī was struck on the head while praying in the mosque at Kūfa and died of the wounds two days later. During these nights all amusements and parties are halted and mourning is observed in both homes and mosques. The period culminates in the night of the 21st called the "night of vigilance" (*aḥyā'*) during which mosques are thronged until the morning hours. People perform a hundred prostrations (*rak'a*) of prayer and chant litanies and supplications until the rising of the sun.

Pilgrimage, as already pointed out, plays a major role in Persian religious life. The obligatory pilgrimage is of course that made to Mecca (*ḥajj*) by virtue of which man crowns the religious performances of his life. Since making this pilgrimage requires financial means and the ability to provide for one's family in advance, those who make the *ḥajj* (the *ḥājī* in its Persian pronunciation) are identified with a certain wealth and economic well-being. The *ḥājī* is respected by all devout people, but, in the bazaar particularly, to be a *ḥājī* also confers social and economic advantages. And since all *ḥājīs* in the bazaar are not always beyond reproach in their dealings, some criticism of them can be sensed among the modernized classes. For many years in fact making the *ḥajj* had become rarer in the modern educated segment of Persian society. But this has changed completely in the last decade and now the annual *ḥajj* caravan includes people from every walk of life.

The other places of pilgrimage, especially at Najaf, Karbalā', Sāmarrā', al-Kāẓimayn in Iraq and Mashhad and Qum in Persia are also of the greatest significance in daily religious life. These centres as well as the smaller sites connected with different saints bring the *baraka* of the centre of Islam and of the Prophet to the outer territories. These centres are all echoes of the supreme centre where heaven and earth meet. There is hardly a Persian who does not make at least a few pilgrimages to a tomb of some saint with the continuous hope of being able to visit the more "central" ones whenever possible. Although some pilgrimages involve special hardship, the centres being in mountains or places with a bad climate, most pilgrimages combine religious asceticism with the enjoyment of God's bounties and beauties of art and nature. For a large segment of the population such a pilgrimage is the most enjoyable experience of the year, although it is also a time of the most intense purification, a period of prayer and forgiveness that leaves its mark upon the person long after the pilgrimage has come to an end.

The *ḥajj* terminates with the feast of sacrifice (*'īd-i aḍḥā*) or (*qurbān*) commemorating the sacrifice of Abraham. During this day not only in Mecca but throughout the Muslim world sheep are sacrificed. Herds are marked with special colours and brought into the city before the occasion and on the morning of the *'īd* the sacrifice is made, the meat being given to the poor and to neighbours. But besides this, sacrifice is made throughout the year. First, all meat that is used for daily food is slaughtered ritually and sacrificed, and secondly on almost any joyous occasion, such as the arrival of a traveller from a long journey, the birth of a child (particularly a son), the arrival of an honoured guest, sacrifices are made, usually of sheep but sometimes of other lawful animals including, occasionally, camels.

A religious practice that is particular to the Shīʿite world, especially Persia, is the *rawḍa* which was developed in its present form during the Ṣafavid period. The *rawḍa*, which means literally garden, consists of sessions during which sermons are delivered combined with the chanting of verses of the Qur'ān and religious poems with special emphasis on the tragedy of Karbalā'. These sessions are held most of all during the two-month period of Muḥarram and Ṣafar revolving around the death of al-Ḥusayn and its aftermath. Much religious and moral preaching to the public takes place on these occasions. The *raaḍa* is held in mosques as well as in private homes. On the crucial dates of the 9th and 10th of Muḥarram on which the tragedy of Karbalā' itself occurred there are even government sponsored *rawḍas* throughout the country. The sessions are marked by sobbing and wailing particularly on the part of women as all discourse is brought back periodically to the theme of the death of the members of the household of the Prophet.

Religious practice also enters into daily life at the critical moments of birth, marriage and death as in other religions. At the moment of birth there is the simple recitation of the "testimony of Islam" or the *shahāda* in the ear of the new-born child. In the case of boys the rite of circumcision is perhaps even more directly connected with religious practices than birth itself. As for marriage, although it is a contract and not a sacramental act, nevertheless since it is made valid by virtue of the *sharīʿa*, it is definitely a religious act. The verses binding the contract are usually read by one of the *ʿulamā'* although any male Muslim can perform this and other functions of a priestly nature.

It is naturally at the moment of death that religious rites become most vividly remembered and seriously practised. The acts of washing the body and burial are all performed in accordance with Islamic law. Afterwards a funeral service is held which men attend in a mosque, and another where women gather in the home of the deceased or of one of his relatives. Since to attend those services is a social duty and most men have many friends and relatives, attendance at funeral services in mosques is a regular event throughout one's life. The sermon delivered after the chanting of the Qur'ān is the best means available to religious authorities to reach the higher strata of society especially those who hold political power in their hands. That is why a funeral service held for a member of the government or a person of high reputation holds a special significance in the religio-political life of Persia. In fact several political assassinations and attempts toward this end have been made on such occasions during the modern history of Persia.

There is also a practice called preparing a *sufra* popular among women at which a table is laid full of all kinds of food to which friends and neighbours are invited. During the "feast" a person specializing in performing the *rawḍa*, called *rawḍa khwān*, chants the Qur'ān and religious poems and preaches on religious themes. The rest of the food is then given to the poor and some taken to each participant's home and given to friends and relatives as an object possessing *baraka* (*tabarruk*). The *sufra*, being especially for women, is usually connected with important events in the lives of women in the household of the Prophet such as Fāṭima and Zaynab. The whole process of preparing the table which is done with the greatest care and best taste is considered as a religious labour, one in which once again denial of the world is combined with the enjoyment of God's bounty.

The *sufra* as well as pilgrimage and many other religious acts are often performed as a result of a vow and solemn promise to God (*nadhr*) in return for which the person asks something of God. The practice of *nadhr* is very popular in all segments of Persian society. Women make a vow to pay so much money to the poor or set a *sufra* if they bear a child or if their daughter finds a suitable match. Students often vow to fast or perform a certain pilgrimage if they pass their examinations. Merchants in the bazaar make the *nadhr* to sacrifice so many sheep if their business transactions succeed. There is continuous "religious barter" in which Persians, like other traditional people, ask of God something in exchange for which they perform acts pleasing to Him. One can hardly understand the psychology of the Persian and the tensions of hope and fear within him without understanding his attitude toward *nadhr* and the "barter" he makes continuously with the Creator. Only the saintly man acts thus without asking anything in return. But this highest spiritual attitude does not in any way invalidate the general religious attitude involved.

POPULAR MANIFESTATIONS OF RELIGION

Besides religious practices that have been sanctioned and protected by the *ʿulamāʾ* and represent the conscious, intellectual aspects of Islamic tradition there are many popular practices which are often combined with the most intense religious fervour and enthusiasm. During the month of Muḥarram long processions are organized by men who, wearing black, celebrate the passion of Karbalāʾ by chanting religious poems and often beating themselves until they fall into a state of frenzy. Occasionally these practices are carried to extremes, some beating themselves with chains and even swords until they faint from loss of blood. Most processions, however, march through the streets of cities to the solemn rhythm of drum beats and the harmony of human voices choking with grief. In larger cities the sight of thousands of men and boys marching behind religious emblems and symbols of the family of the Prophet is a most moving religious experience.

There is also the passion play (*taʿziya*) which, although developed into an aristocratic art in Ṣafavid and Qājār times, is essentially a popular religious manifestation. It is not usually encouraged by the *ʿulamāʾ* although they do not oppose it since it is the medium of profound religious expression. Varying from simple versions in the villages to elaborate ones in big cities, the *taʿziya* depicts the events that led to the martyrdom of Ḥusayn at Karbalāʾ. The climax is usually performed at high noon on the day of *ʿāshūrāʾ*, the 10th of Muḥarram, when the third Shīʿite Imam, al-Ḥusayn, died and was beheaded. In a city like Qum where several thousand people participate in the performance of the drama and thousands more flock from the countryside to join the population of the city in observing the *taʿziya*, one sees one of the most overwhelming manifestations of religious life in Persia.

Finally, among popular religious phenomena one cannot overlook the practice of omens, magic and other occult arts. Islam opposes the practice of magic but that has not prevented people, especially women, from practising it often in combination with specifically Muslim practices. Furthermore, there is a complete traditional science of the "magical" use of Qurʾānic phrases, that is, the recitation of formulae for appropriate occasions. Although this science is itself far from being popular in the usual sense, it has a widely extended field of application in daily life. There are also prayers (*duʿāʾ*) connected with the names of Imams and Ṣūfī saints which people carry about with them or recite on different occasions. Besides their purely religious aspect, practices of this kind have also acquired a kind of magical quality. The "prayer writer" (*du'ā' niwīs*), like the practitioner of geomancy (*rammāl*), is a permanent fixture in the life of Persian women in the city and countryside combining strictly religious elements with all forms of fortune telling and both occult and pseudo-occult sciences.

RELIGIOUS EVENTS IN THE CALENDAR

The rhythm of life in Persia is determined by a number of holidays, many Islamic, some derived from ancient Persia and a few celebrating modern national events. Both the Islamic and ancient Persian dates have a wholly religious aspect. Even the ancient Zoroastrian *naw-rūz* or "New Year" which marks the Persian new year to this day has acquired a completely Islamic colour. At the moment of the vernal equinox people place the Qur'ān on their tables along with the seven objects beginning with the letter "s" (the *haft sīn* or seven s's) that have survived from Zoroastrian days. Prayers are also said and benedictions invoked upon the Prophet and his family.

As for the Islamic religious dates, the festivities of *aḍḥā* at the end of the *ḥajj*, *'īd-i fiṭr* at the end of Ramaḍān, the date of the birth of the Prophet, the birthday of 'Alī and *'īd-i ghadīr*, when according to Shī'ite belief 'Alī was chosen by the Prophet as his successor, are widely celebrated as joyous occasions. Also of great importance is the date of birth of the *mahdī* when all cities are illuminated with countless lights.

The calendar is also dotted with tragic events, the most important being the 10th of Muḥarram, the death of al-Ḥusayn, the 21st of Ramaḍān, the death of 'Alī, the 28th of Ṣafar, the death of the Prophet and the second Imam al-Ḥasan, as well as the dates of the deaths of other Imams and Fāṭima. All these dates mark an intensification of religious life and a transformation of many aspects of daily life. The tragic element in the Persian soul meets its spiritual need at the highest levels during these occasions which have the effect of cleansing the individual and society from the dross of negligence of their religious vocation.

ISLAMIC SECTS IN PERSIA

There exist in Persia today a number of sects which are identified by their emphasis upon a certain aspect of Shī'ite teachings at the expense of other elements and their ensuing separation from the main community. Of these the Ismāʿīlīs are perhaps the oldest, being the remnant of the much larger Ismāʿīlī community of early medieval times. In religious beliefs they are close to the Twelve Imam Shīʿites except of course in the question of the Hidden Imam or *mahdī*. Theologically of particular interest are the Shaykhīs, centred mostly in Kirmān, and founded by Shaykh Aḥmad Aḥsā'ī two centuries ago. They emphasize the role of *ta'wīl* or spiritual hermeneutics and have a special reverence for the Imams. The ʿAlī-Allāhī and Ahl-i Ḥaqq have followers in Kurdistan, Mazandaran and some of the southern provinces. Some even go to the extreme of believing in re-incarnation.

The significance of these sects from the point of view of the general religious life of Persia is that most of them belittle the practice of the *sharīʿa* and some do not even perform the daily prayers in the usual manner. In most cases they represent Ṣūfī orders that have become politicized or have taken on an external social character resulting in the destruction of the equilibrium which characterizes the orthodox Muslim community, Sunnite and Shīʿite alike. They are nevertheless Islamic sects in that they are still within the total matrix of the Islamic tradition. Such is not, however, the case with Bābism and Bahā'ism, particularly the latter, which broke completely away from the structure of Islam and cannot in any way be considered as an Islamic movement or sect.

CONCLUDING REMARKS—RELIGION IN PERSIA TODAY

The Persian psyche possesses an elasticity that makes the study of religion in Persia based on external forms difficult. From outward signs one sees the superimposition of a modern, Westernized class more or less torn away from religious practices, upon the traditional Persian society nearly all aspects of whose life are dominated by the religious spirit. Even pre-Islamic norms have become in this case Muslimized. But even among the modernized who outwardly seem completely secularized there exist many traditional religious tendencies which in a people of less elastic mentality would not be conceivable. One often sees women who dress in the latest European fashions and try to act like Western women but who at the same time display a completely traditional religious attitude at moments of sorrow or on different religious occasions. Likewise, many men who present a rationalistic front indifferent to religion become totally transformed in holy places of pilgrimage or at moments of participation in religious ceremonies.

It can therefore be said that contemporary Persian life is dominated in its universal principles as well as daily acts by the spirit and form of the Islamic revelation which also integrated into its world view elements of older religions which were in conformity with its own principles. Moreover, whereas certain domains of life have drawn away from the orbit of traditional religious life as a result of the advent of modernism, even in these domains religious elements and attitudes persist. The religious truths by which Persians have lived and died for centuries continue to dominate the horizon of their lives today even if occasional clouds momentarily obscure the horizons from some eyes. But the clouds are never permanent and there is hardly any one who during his lifetime does not gain some kind of vision of the horizon which has co-ordinated and oriented the lives of Persians throughout the ages and continues as the most abiding reality.

CHAPTER 6

ISLAM IN AFGHANISTAN, INDIA AND PAKISTAN

This area came into contact with Islam very early, at first by sea. For centuries there existed a brisk maritime trade between Arabia and India. Consequently, Muslim Arabs arrived on India's coast in the wake of their pagan ancestors. Thana, a small port near Bombay, is said to have been seized in the year 636 by order of the governor of al-Baḥrayn. By land west Afghanistan, with Herat as its principal city, was the first province to become acquainted with the strength of Muslim arms (642). In 664–5 Indian territory was reached by an army under the command of al-Muhallab, a general of the Caliph Muʿāwiya. In 711–12 followed the conquest of Sind by Muḥammad b. Qāsim. Kabul, the present Afghan capital, seems to have come under Muslim rule only in the year 871. The Ghaznavids, a powerful dynasty of Turkish origin, resided in Ghazna (east Afghanistan) from 977 till 1187. Its most famous representative Maḥmūd (d. 1030) extended his dominion in the east into the Panjab. Making incursions into India from Afghanistan became a tradition of many Muslim kings, and was resumed in the days of the decline of Mughal power. Thus successful raids were made by Nādir Shāh, who sacked the Indian capital in 1739, and carried with him from Delhi the famous Peacock Throne and the Kōh-i nūr diamond, and by Aḥmad Shāh Durrānī[1] who in 1761 defeated the Hindu Mahrattas[2] at Panipat (about fifty miles north of Delhi). The regular influx of Afghan soldiers may account for the great number of Muslims on the subcontinent of Afghan extraction. In the *Muslim World* of April 1928 S. M. Zwemer reports: "It is estimated that six millions today are of Afghan or Pathan blood, three hundred thousand of Persian, and a similar number of

[1] A king who was not a foreigner. Afghan historians today, therefore, like to point out that in the year 1747, the date of the assassination of Aḥmad Shāh's predecessor Nādir Shāh, Afghanistan became for the first time a national monarchy. In modern times the country obtained full independence in 1919.

[2] This energetic, militant and pious people, mainly consisting of peasants, inhabits the region east of Bombay and Poona. In the eyes of Muslims they are barbarians. The Urdu verb *marahṭī karnā* (*lit.* "to behave in the manner of Mahrattas") is an equivalent of "to plunder, ravage".

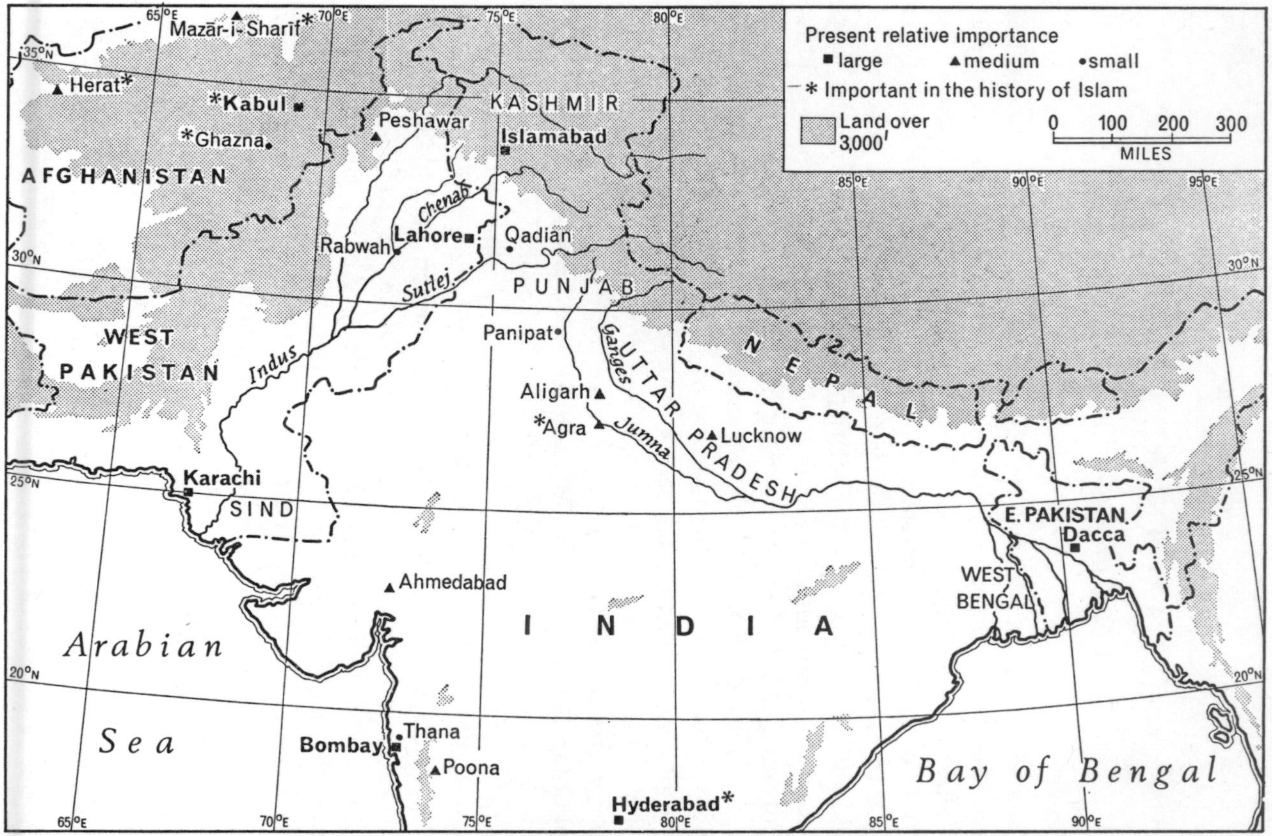

Afghanistan, India and Pakistan.

Turkish or Arab ancestry. The remainder may be roughly described as of Hindu-Arab origin." However, Islam did not succeed in obtaining a permanent hold on Indian soil till 1206, the year in which Quṭb al-Dīn Aybak, by birth a slave of Turkish descent, was invested as Sultan of Lahore. With the beginning of the so-called Slave Dynasty India became a Muslim State.

Though Islam reached Afghanistan and India almost simultaneously, the eventual results of proselytization proved completely different. Afghanistan became wholly islamized. In India Islam acquired for centuries a strong and predominant political position, but without achieving religious conquest. At the census of 1941, less than one fourth of the total population of pre-partition India proved to be Muslim. In the course of thirteen centuries Islam has been continuously confronted with the staunch bulwark of Hinduism, which always extends hospitality to foreign religions, absorbing them smoothly into its own syncretistic system, but from which believers are enticed with difficulty, bound as they are to its close cultural and social pattern.

Yet the significance of Islam in the Indo-Pakistan subcontinent should not be underestimated. It comprises nearly a third of the total number of Muslims in the world. It is worthwhile to examine how this monotheistic creed through alternate assimilation and repulsion of Hindu as well as Buddhist thought and practice has won its more than hundred millions of adherents on a subcontinent with an area like that of Europe without the USSR.

Before the establishment of stable Muslim rule, the northern parts of India had been overrun time and again by Turkish warriors and other adventurers in consequence of the emigration of races from Mongolia and Central Asia. They were driven to these lands by population pressure rather than religious zeal. Accordingly in India conversions to Islam have been effected more by intermarriage and preaching than by compulsion and the sword. Indicative of this is the fact that in the United Provinces of pre-partition India, including as they did the historic seats of Muslim government, only 14 per cent of the inhabitants professed Islam.

Since foreign Muslim soldiers and merchants did not object to Hindu wives, intermarriage functioned as an easy medium of islamization. On the other hand, it equally became a major factor in the transference of Hindu customs and beliefs into Muslim social classes.

The most favourable cause of the spread of Islam, however, has been the peaceful penetration of the country by Muslim saints and mystics. They could intermingle freely with the lower sections of the Indian population. Often the latter found in Muslim brotherhood a happy refuge from the rigid caste taboos. But it also happened that Hindus of higher castes were attracted to the new faith, though their number was much smaller. Another important factor in favour of conversion was the deplorable state of Buddhism. Proselytizing, it should be remembered, has been a continuous process. Thus even at the beginning of this very century conversions in mass to Islam took place in East Bengal, which now contains one third of the total Muslim population of the subcontinent.

In other words, it is Ṣūfism that has given Islam in India its original growth, its extension and its depth. It possessed all the fine properties and spiritual assets for a proper adaptation to the Indian atmosphere, so much inclined to meditation and asceticism. The maxim of Ṣūfī missionaries was *ṣulḥ-i kull* (peace with all). In particular the Chishtī order understood how to assimilate Indian conditions. It adopted many Hindu fashions, like the customs of bowing before a spiritual teacher and of shaving the head of new entrants to the mystic circle. The exercises *maḥmūda* and *naṣīra*, in which the eyes are made to converge on the tip of the nose and towards the middle of the forehead, which this order recommended for mystical concentration, are very similar to yogic *samādhi* practices. The division of the day by a Chishtī saint with fixed periods for meditation, meals and the reception of visitors, closely resembles that practised by Buddhist monks. Like his Buddhist colleagues the Chishtī subsisted mostly on *futūḥ*, the gratuitous supply of sustenance, permitting his disciples to circulate *zanbīl*, a bowl made of a dried and hollow gourd, and to collect food. Music, beloved by the Indian people in general as much as rejected by Muslim orthodoxy, was almost a tenet of faith with the Chishtīs. Sultan 'Alā' al-Dīn Khaljī (d. 1316), under the spell of this order, was a great patron of music. In the imperial storehouse a golden idol from the temple of Koyilolahu, was kept, captured at the time of an invasion of southern India. The priests of the sanctuary when informed that the sacred object had not been destroyed, approached the Delhi Sultan, and in his presence displayed their skill in music and dancing. Thereupon the king, enraptured by their performance, kindly restored the idol.

Another peculiarity of the Chishtīs was their avoidance of political authorities. When the said Sultan expressed his longing to visit the famous mystic Niẓām al-Dīn Awliyā (d. 1325), he received from the Chishtī saint the unequivocal message: "There are two doors in my house. If the Sultan comes in by one door, I shall quit by the other."

Indifference to politicians and aloofness from political dealings, however, were not features common to all Muslim orders. On the contrary, Ṣūfīs of other *ṭarīqas* could sometimes exercise considerable influence on affairs of state. Thus members of the Suhrawardī order consorted with kings. In this way they sought opportunities to help poor people in getting their grievances redressed by the Sultan, etc. Conversely, the royal court required the support of the Ṣūfīs, so popular with the masses, in their fight against the Mughals who in the thirteenth century repeatedly raided the Indian frontier provinces. Again in the first half of the seventeenth century Ṣūfīs became active in the political field. Then Shaykh Aḥmad Sirhindī (1564–1624), an initiate of the Naqshbandī order, tried to influence indirectly the Mughal emperor Jahāngīr by writing long epistles to nobles of the court. These *maktūbāt*, discussing in an exalted style all kinds of problems of Islamic faith and practice, aim in effect at the elimination of syncretistic heresies like those of Akbar.

In mystical speculative thought there exists in India the never-ending controversy between the advocates of a *waḥdat al-wujūd* and of a *waḥdat al-shuhūd*. From the beginning Ibn al-ʿArabī's ontological monism touched a responsive chord among the Indian Ṣūfīs presumably because of its similarity to Vedanta philosophy. It was briefly expressed in the term *waḥdat al-wujūd* ("unity of being") which indicates that the totality of the world is nothing but the divine mind (= all the attributes together) reflected in the mirror of God's being. God's essence (*dhāt*) is identical with his attributes; and they unfold themselves in manifestations or modes which are the world and its objects. Accordingly, things in themselves are not contingent but "necessary" and existence is not something that comes to them; they simply have it. Over against this monistic view, the aforesaid Aḥmad Sirhindī attempts to vindicate the contingency of the world, existing externally to God's mind as well as to his being. As his major argument he adduces revelatory mystical experiences. Under the spiritual guidance of his teacher, the famous Naqshbandī saint Shaykh Khwāja Bāqī billāh, he reached—it was in the year 1598—the stage that everything else except God went out of his consciousness. He did not "see" anything save God. But this was not the final stage. After two days this state was replaced by another wherein God and the world emerged as clearly distinguishable from one another. So Sirhindī recognized the "adumbrative" character of his earlier experience, and he realized that beforehand not an ontological but merely "an experimental unity" (*waḥdat al-shuhūd*) had been attained. He had been so immersed in emotion that it was *as if* he were one with God. But it was no more than a subjective feeling.

This difference in mystical perception between the *wujūdīs* and the *shuhūdīs* also has important consequences in the field of ethics. Metaphysical monism tends to weaken also the dichotomy of good and evil. "I mean by good", Ibn al-ʿArabī declares, "that which is conducive to someone's purpose and is in harmony with his nature and temperament, and by evil that which contravenes his purpose and is contrary to his nature and temperament." (*Fuṣūṣ al-ḥikam.*) In the context of *waḥdat al-shuhūd* and a separation between God and the world, a much clearer distinction can be made between the holy and the unholy, the truly good and really bad. With Sirhindī the essence of the world is non-being and evil, in need of correction and reform. Because of this, the mystics, after their spiritual journey into higher spheres, ought to return to the earth. If they think it beneath their dignity to be occupied with worldly affairs, then competent *ʿulamāʾ* who follow the lead of the Prophet are to be considered superior to them.

Concomitant with Islamic mysticism is worship at holy shrines. In spite of violent protests from puritanical or enlightened circles, up to the present the tombs have remained centres of ardent devotion. The main ones in Pakistan are supervised by the government, and money given by believers is collected by a civil servant and spent for the repair of mosques and similar purposes. Usually on Thursday evenings, small earthenware lamps are lit and placed on the tombs. Flowers are offered as is done by Buddhist pilgrims at their respective places of blessed memory. Often there is a flag on a long pole affixed to the shrine. The worshipper communes in his heart with the saint, telling him his troubles and desires. Rags and threads are attached to the shrine in testimony of prayers having been answered. Here again Muslims and Hindus meet. Thus on the occasion of the festival which celebrates the anniversary of a saint's death, called *ʿurs* (*lit.* "marriage", i.e. the union of the deceased holy man with the supreme spirit), Hindus too may gather round the grave. Reciprocally, Hindu saints find Muslim recognition. In Kashmir Hindu shrines became the graves of Muslim saints who never existed. Shāh 'Abd al-'Azīz of Delhi, a noted theologian and *muftī* (1746–1824), being asked his opinion of Krishna, cautiously replied: "One might do better to be silent about these matters. But from the Bhagavadgītā, a holy book of the Hindus, it appears that Krishna does belong to the *awliyā* (Saints)."[1]

Not only was Krishna styled a saint, but the Hindus themselves were sometimes distinguished as *ahl-i kitāb* ("possessors of the Scripture"), the well-known qualification in Muslim law, usually reserved for Jews and Christians. In a plea for it, the Naqshbandī mystic Mīrzā Jānjānān Maẓhar (1701–81) argues:

> All the schools (of Hindus) unanimously believe in the unity of the most high God. And the secret of their worshipping is this: there are certain angels who exercise power, by order of God, in our transitory world... Of these they make representations and on them they concentrate their thoughts. This practice recalls the sufis of Islam meditating the form of their spiritual guides[2] and getting grace of them. The only difference is that outwardly the Ṣūfīs do not set up an effigy of their *shaykh*.

Of a similar apologetic tenor is the "discovery", made by other Indian Muslims, of the doctrine of metempsychosis in the Qur'ān. To this end they cite the passages where it is told that God changed breakers of the Sabbath into apes.[3]

A policy of religious tolerance was pursued by the Mughal emperors. In a confidential testament which Bābur, the first of the Mughal rulers in India, left to his son Humāyūn, the father advised *inter alia*: "In particular refrain from the slaughter of cows. You should never destroy the places of worship... Treat the different peculiarities of your subjects as the different seasons of the year." The famous eclectic emperor Akbar (1542–1605) promulgated a self-made *dīn-i ilāhī* (divine Faith), a syncretistic hotchpotch of symbols and ordinances picked up from the religions of which he knew. Dārā Shukōh, the eldest son of Shāh Jahān (1615–59), himself made a Persian rendering of fifty-two Upanishads which, in his opinion, represent "the earliest of the heavenly books" and are hinted at in Sūra LVI. 77 as the "concealed scripture". Even the emperor Awrangzīb (1618–1707) who is reputed to have been an orthodox fanatic, did not deem it improper to participate in Hindu festivals like *Dasahrā* (held in honour of Durgā), and

[1] Muḥammad Ikrām, *Rud-i kawthar* (Lahore, 1958), p. 569.

[2] This refers to the ritual known as *taṣawwur-i shaykh*, an essential part of the training of Naqshbandī novices. Presumably the practice is of Hindu origin.

[3] II. 61, VII. 166 and V. 65.

appointed more Hindus to high offices of the state than any of his predecessors.

Another indication of Muslim Indian religious flexibility might be the preference given to the Ḥanafī school of religious law. Its eponym, Abū Ḥanīfa, was not very fond of utilizing *aḥādīth* (traditions). "Probably this attitude", K. A. Nizami surmises, "was born of a conviction that the *ahadis* related to particular conditions of time and space and could not be indiscriminately applied to the new conditions."[1]

Besides all this conscious and unconscious assimilation to the Indian environment, however, there are equally numerous instances of Muslim aversion for its antipode, as Hinduism essentially is, with its impudent parade of *shirk*, idolatry. Usually the first impulse of the early Muslim invaders was an urgently felt need to desecrate the hideous idols, destroy Hindu temples, or at least convert them into mosques, as happened, for example, in Amroha and Sambhal in Uttar Pradesh. Thus Maḥmūd of Ghazna was a zealous iconoclast, but he was no barbarian. He enriched his own capital with a great mosque, aqueducts and libraries, built from the spoils of India. But in the course of time Muslim rulers thought it more prudent to follow a policy of compromise, especially with respect to the redoubtable Hindu warrior caste of the Rajputs. Thus we see Akbar furthering intermarriage with the Rajputs. On the other hand, it is the same Akbar who prohibited compelling an unwilling widow to burn herself as a *satī* ("virtuous wife") on the funeral pyre of her husband.

Next the imposition of *jizya*, the poll-tax levied on non-Muslims was a humiliating measure, introduced by several sultans, emperors and kings in various parts of India; and again frequently abolished by their successors. Over and above that, many Muslim rulers collected a pilgrimage tax at Hindu religious fairs. Yet this institution in fact represented a compromise, viz. between the strict injunction of Muslim law not to tolerate public celebration of pagan practices and the desire of a vast Hindu population to perform their religious rites. Then sumptuary laws were sometimes enforced. Sultan 'Alā' al-Dīn Khaljī forbade Hindus to wear rich dresses, ride horses and drive in carriages and palanquins, so that they should look humble.

Occasionally, forced conversions to Islam took place. Thus a Muslim historian records that after Aḥmad Shāh Durrānī's victory over the Mahrattas at Panipat "about ninety thousand persons, male and female,

[1] K. A. Nizami, *Some Aspects of Religion and Politics in India* (Aligarh, 1961), p. 36.

were taken prisoners, and obtained eternal happiness by embracing the Muslim faith".

Another, perhaps more "civilized", aspect of Muslim disapproval of the Hindu way of life is the movement to purify Islam of Hindu accretions. As a rule, this starts at a time of *political* decline. This is typical of Islam. Muslims read God's favour and anger from historical events. Islam at the height of power means divine approval of His community, whereas defeat and ruin point to heavenly wrath. In the latter case it is incumbent to make a critical analysis of the religious situation.

After the death of Awrangzīb (1707) Muslim power collapsed at a rapid pace. On 5 May 1731, while he was meditating in the sacred precincts of the Kaʿba, it was revealed to Shāh Walī Allāh of Delhi (1703–62) the most original and comprehensive Muslim thinker of the eighteenth century, that he was charged with a divine mission to give himself to the uplifting of his country. He admonished his co-religionists "to abstain from non-Arab customs and the usages of the Hindus". Among the abuses adopted he reckons the custom of not allowing a woman to remarry after the death of her husband, fixing much too high amounts for a *mahr* (dowry), and lavish expenditure at weddings, on account of which families were ruined. Though the Indian reformer, unlike the Wahhābīs, does not condemn the worship of saints as such, he passes the following criticism on it:

> Some people assert: "We do not mean to attribute to holy men partnership with God...but because of their abiding in the vicinity of the heavenly court we pay such exceeding honour to them, so that they may bring us near unto God..." Virtually, however, these people worship saints to get rid of misfortune and they consider them capable of complying with their wishes!

In Bengal the masses of peasant Muslims are of Hindu and Buddhist extraction. Therefore many Hindu institutions and beliefs like the caste-system and astrology remained current in Muslim society. Muslim bards sang hymns breathing the spirit of Hindu *bhakti* and faith. Consequently, the situation called for reform movements. At the beginning of the nineteenth century the Taʿayyuniyya was established by Karāmat ʿAlī and the Farā'iḍiyya by Ḥājjī Sharīʿat Allāh. The former attacked *inter alia* music and dancing, the ceremony of *ʿurs* and the offering of *fātiḥas* (the custom of reading the opening chapter of the Qur'ān over the deceased for forty days after his death), while the latter prohibited among other things the pomp and ceremonial that had been introduced into the very simple, austere rites of Muslim marriage and burial, the offering of fruit and flowers at tombs, etc.

The most important Indian Muslim reform movement with a wider range than Bengal alone, however, is that of the Ahl-i ḥadīth. For their faith and religious practice the adherents of this sect wish to rely only on the Qur'ān and the authentic traditions. Their main object is to get rid of the authority of the four *fiqh* schools. In this way they try to restore the original simplicity and purity of Islam. Emphasis is laid on the reassertion of *tawḥīd* (unity of God). Occult powers and knowledge of the "hidden world" (*al-ghayb*), they state, are not within the grasp of human beings. Belief in saints is thus implicitly refuted. Though the group as a distinct sect appeared only at the end of the nineteenth century, its roots reach back to much earlier times. In his efforts to re-examine Islamic principles and to find out on what authority the legal schools could base their regulations, Shāh Walī Allāh had already rejuvenated the study of *ḥadīth*, tradition. Although he did not go so far as to reject the *fiqh* schools, nevertheless he taught that anybody was free to choose a particular decision different from that taken by the school to which he belonged himself, if he was convinced that the case was better confirmed by *ḥadīth*, that is, the practice followed by the Prophet and his companions. By their adversaries the Ahl-i Ḥadīth are often called Wahhābīs, an appelation which is not quite correct, since the latter follow the school of Ibn Ḥanbal.

In the "East" modern times really began when people realized that it was no longer possible to ignore Western civilization. This process of acculturation took and takes time; for religious people especially, conservative by instinct as they are all over the world, it is extremely hard to apprehend the need for adaptation to changed social structures and new ways of expression. In the West itself Christianity has been and still is involved in difficulties of reorientation, but it has the advantage over eastern religions that the major changes in *Weltanschauung* and patterns of culture proceeded from and developed in its own environment. More time is left for reflexion and a reply to the challenge.

In view of this very unfortunate situation for the religions of the East, it is the more intriguing and fascinating that in India Islam produced a genius who already in the middle of the eighteenth century intuitively foresaw the problems Islam was to be faced with in the future on account of the encounter with the West. Though there is no trace of any contact with Europeans, Shāh Walī Allāh, far ahead of his times, indicated to later generations a helpful way of reinterpreting Islam so that it might appeal again to people who could no longer draw inspiration from traditional belief. In Pakistan today his significance has been rediscovered, and he and Iqbāl are the most frequently quoted authorities on matters of faith and life.

In times of transition old values are viewed with a suspicious eye. The most vital contribution of the Delhi divine to the present Muslim generation is therefore his concern to demonstrate rationally as well as in religious terms *why* there is sense in accepting a certain article of faith or observing a particular religious duty. Thus in his *magnum opus*, called *Ḥujjat Allāh al-bāligha*, he discusses the "deeper meanings of religion" (*asrār al-dīn*). Against rising criticism, doubt and indifference religion has, so to say, to render an account of the trustworthiness of its doctrines and the expediency of its ordinances. Another striking feature of contemporary thought is the increasing regard for the human side in the interrelation of God and mankind. Shāh Walī Allāh's interest in the psycho-sociological aspects of religion is also remarkably "up to date".

> Prophets [so he explains], were each confronted with different situations and had to adjust their measures of reform accordingly...And as inhabitants of countries in which malicious elephants are met with picture jinns and Satans in corresponding fearful forms—and not in the forms of animals which are found in other countries—so revelatory documents make use of traditions and customs current in the country to which they pertain...Likewise for a prophet it is the best and easiest way to frame religious, civil and social laws according to the usage of his own people; not so rigidly as to prove a hardship for those who come later, but so that on the whole they might abide by them. The first believers will be drawn to the acceptance of that *sharī'a* (law of God) out of inner conviction and because it corresponds with their customs, while later generations will be drawn by the attraction of the exemplary lives of the religious leaders and sovereigns of the state.

But another century was to pass in India before the first *deliberate* attempts were made by a Muslim leader to interpret Islamic principles in the light of Western thought. Aḥmad Khān (1817–98) who had started his work of improving the backward conditions of his community by the introduction of educational institutes, recognized the subsequent need for what he defined as a modern *'ilm al-kalām* (apologetics), "by which we should either refute the doctrines of modern science, or undermine its foundations, or show that they are in conformity with the articles of Islamic faith". The immediate danger was that the young Muslims who received English ideas and had to absorb the enlightened ideas of the West, would lose their faith in Islam and its teachings. The first important apologetic writing Aḥmad Khān published: *A Series of Essays on the Life of Muḥammad* (1870) was virtually a refutation of Sir William Muir's *Life of Mahomet* which had made a deep impression on the English-educated Muslims because, as Aḥmad Khān's biographer Hālī remarks, "Sir William Muir had not adopted the worn-out methods by which the missionaries criticized Islam and which were never successful, but he argued with historical facts". In his attempts at reconciling Islam with contemporary European thought (read: English deism) our apologete arrived at rather radical conclusions. Thus he doubts the possibility of an actual response to prayer (*du'ā'*): everything is conditioned by the immutable divine decrees. But the benefit of prayer is that it may overcome man's restlessness and uneasiness in time of affliction. Aḥmad Khān's ideas met with vehement opposition. Thus, for example, Mīrzā Ghulām Aḥmad, founder of the Aḥmadiyya movement, attacks this last doctrine by comparing the efficacy of prayer with the efficacy of drugs: "If doubt arises when some prayers seem to have no result, then I say that this also happens with medicines: do medicines keep the gate to death closed? But in spite of this, who can assert that they are without effect?"

In Pakistan today, however, Aḥmad Khān (or "Sir Sayyid" as he is called on the subcontinent) enjoys high esteem, not so much for his religious ideas or educational achievements as for his political views; a separate Muslim nation would have been the eventual realization of what he already had in mind. It is true that the Muslim leader was continuously apprehensive of the domination of a Muslim minority by a Hindu majority. But it is to be doubted whether he would have hailed the establishment of Pakistan as the ideal solution of Hindu–Muslim communal clashes.

The next important contribution to Indian Islam we owe to the celebrated poet-philosopher Sir Muḥammad Iqbāl (1876–1938). From the past he kept the valuable heritage of mysticism. For the actual moment he felt the urgent need to lash men into furious activity. Accordingly he hankers after a kind of dynamic mysticism:

> Give me the bold, adventurous eye,
> And in love's transport let me die.[1]

[1] *Persian Psalms* (Lahore, 1948), no. 47, tr. A. J. Arberry.

Thought, with its potentiality of dynamic self-expression, is to him the link between the finite and the infinite: "It is in fact the presence of the total Infinite in the movement of knowledge that makes finite thinking possible."[1] In the cosmic process of a continuous stream of creativity two complementary ends are to be achieved: the integration of human personality and the reconstruction of Muslim society. For the former, prayer is the proper instrument. By prayer "the searching ego affirms itself in the very moment of self-negation, and thus discovers its own worth and justification as a dynamic factor in the life of the universe".[2] In this perspective it is that Iqbāl entrusts man with the task of acting as a second creator:

> God made the world, man made it more fair,
> And is man God's competitor to be.[3]

The appeal of Iqbāl to the Muslim community to take the world as "something to be made and remade by continuous action"[4] is really impressive. Unfortunately, in pointing out the implementation of it in society and politics he fails, and evades the critical issues with a vague romanticism. "He is great", as W. C. Smith acutely defines, "because he achieved in theory a realist religion. But he never achieved it in practice...on the specific questions of women, Islamic customs of eating and drinking, and so on, he hesitates to innovate."[5]

Nowadays Sayyid Abu 'l-A'lā Mawdūdī (born in 1903) is considered by the average Muslim in Pakistan the most prominent theologian of the country. At any rate he is the most formidable opponent of the government which he criticizes for its too liberal political principles. From the very beginning the Sayyid was not much in favour of the concept of Pakistan. Already in February 1941 he wrote that the advocates of a separate Muslim nation "are completely in error in the supposition that if in those provinces where Muslims are in a majority there were set up an independent state on democratic lines this would contribute in the end to the establishment of a government based on God's absolute sovereignty". This attitude was typical of many conservative and traditional Indian Muslims. As rigidly orthodox Jews kept aloof from the Zionist movement, a considerable number of orthodox Muslims in India were very suspicious of the Jinnāḥ ideals,

[1] *The Reconstruction of Religious Thought in Islam* (Lahore, 1954), p. 6.
[2] *Ibid.* p. 92. [3] *Lāle-i Ṭūr*, vol. II, tr. A. Schimmel.
[4] *The Reconstruction of Religious Thought in Islam*, p. 198.
[5] *Modern Islam in India* (London, 1946), pp. 133 ff.

fearing that the future Pakistani state would not be much different from Kemalist Turkey. Consequently, the puritanical divines of the Deoband seminary, the largest religious institution of the country, remained in India. And only later on, after much hesitation, did Mawdūḍī join Pakistan.

In spite of all denunciation, if not vilification, of Mawdūdī and his party, the *Jamā'at-i Islāmī*, from the controlled Pakistani press and high officials, sympathizers are numerous all over the country, among students as well as petty shopkeepers. There is in Pakistan a general feeling of uncertainty and discontent. Mawdūdī is a commanding personality—he has an impressive beard—a good orator, and he wields a powerful pen. Moreover he knows how to be looked upon as a man of all-round education. In his journal *Tarjumān al-Qur'ān* of August 1939 he deals with the philosophy of Hegel and Marx, comparing their system of thesis, antithesis and synthesis with a curved line, in contradistinction to the straight line which would be the proper symbol for the way pointed out by the Qur'ān. In short he is fairly up-to-date in style. This is the great advantage he has over the *'ulamā'* who also oppose him, though they can only accuse him (and that is significant!) of a few minor deviations from the classical creed. Typical of his attitude of mind and way of reasoning is the following exposition in an article, published in the *Voice of Islam*, October 1962. He begins with a seemingly liberal view, stating that there is a "vast range of human affairs about which the *sharī'a* is totally silent...This silence is by itself indicative of such matters at their own discretion and judgment". But then it turns out that this personal discretion of *ijtihād* merely comes to the "maximum effort to ascertain a law and the intention of Islamic injunction in a given problem or issue. Its real object is to understand...supreme law and to keep the legal system in conformity with its fundamental directions, abreast of the conditions obtaining in the world from day to day." That means—to mention one practical conclusion drawn—that Mawdūdī allows his daughter to matriculate at the Panjab University, but at the same time she is held to observe strict *pardah*.

A more appropriate understanding of the spirit of the times is displayed by Ghulām Aḥmad Parwez, born in the same year and living in the same city (Lahore) as Mawdūdī. The chief concern of this gifted and amiable teacher is to interpret the Qur'ān in the light of modern thought and to derive from the Holy Book adequate answers to topical questions like evolution, family planning, and so on. His audience consists for the greater part of students, lawyers, engineers and government officials. A valuable aspect of his movement is that young people with Communist sympathies are often attracted to it. Though Parwez himself disapproves of Communism because of its atheism and its "basing equality of men on equality of the belly", he enunciates plain socialistic principles:

The *millat* [community founded on divine rules] has to provide Paradise which not only embraces the hereafter but this world's life just as well. It is realised, if for example, somebody who earns five rupees but needs ten for his daily requirements, receives five more, whereas somebody who earns ten rupees but needs only five, gives the remainder which the Qur'ān calls *al-'afw*, to the public weal.[1]

Ṭulū'-i Islām, the institute of Parwez, obtained a certain notoriety in Pakistan for denying any authority to *ḥadīth* in faith and practice. An interesting discussion has been carried on upon this issue by Mawdūdī and Parwez.

It speaks well for divine wisdom [Mawdūdī argues] that revelation has come down to us in two forms: as Qur'ān with the principles and as *ḥadīth* with the elaborations of the principles. Had it so turned out that the "concealed revelation" (*waḥy khafī*) with all its details of *ṣalāt*, etc. had been inserted in the Qur'ān it would have been as big as the Encyclopaedia Britannica.

To this Parwez replies:

This difficulty of a too bulky book could have been removed, if two volumes of one work had appeared: Part I with the principles, and Part II with the details of the principles. But the trouble is a different one! All kinds of contradictions would prove to exist between what is stated in the Qur'an and what is in *ḥadīth*. The "manifest revelation" (*waḥy jalī*) declares that a man is free in essence and can choose between belief and unbelief. The "concealed revelation" says: No. A Muslim who apostatizes deserves capital punishment; and so on.

As for the Qur'ān, however, Parwez takes up the traditional fundamentalist stand. So the problematic issue of the Qur'ān's relation to science is quickly settled by the truism: "If research agrees with the exposition of the Qur'ān it will be a cause of due pride and great joy for the research workers...But if the result of their research does not agree with the Qur'ān they should continue their work."[2]

[1] *Salīm ke nām*, vol. I (Lahore, 1959), pp. 156 ff.

[2] *Ma'rif al-Qur'ān*, vol. II, pp. 5 f.

It might be relevant now to point out succinctly some striking and characteristic features of the spirit and way in which Islamic tenets and injunctions have been reinterpreted from the days of Aḥmad Khān till the present.

In his periodical *Tahdhīb al-akhlāq* ("Social Reform") of the year 1879, Aḥmad Khān sets the religious thought of former days against the ideas to be conceived at the present time.

> Before now, man was given for the sake of religion; today, religion is given for the sake of man. Formerly, people started from the assumption that man ought to purify his soul; at present the soul is regarded as pure of itself; therefore it is man's duty now to activate its specific abilities (This is what is called in the language of the prophets "repentance" and "atonement").[1] In former times, the principle of world-renouncing was highly respected; nowdays it is considered imperative to make the most of the benefits the world offers man.

The postulate that lies at the root of such views is the conception of the *analogia entis*: "In our essence Divinity is mirrored."[2]

And the divinely appointed task of man is to build his personality in complete analogy to the Divine personality: "Be aware that I am God; you should be God's counterpart, an incarnation in little of the divine attributes."[3]

In conformity with the supposed resemblance between human and divine properties is the equally stressed and repeated claim that Islam is the religion of nature... "Some people talk of the conflict of science with religion, science representing the study of nature and religion dealing with supernatural realities. Islam resolves that conflict by identifying itself with nature."[4] It is through Islam that man succeeded in "divesting the forces of nature of that divine character with which earlier cultures had clothed them".[5] Hence reason plays such a dominant part in this religion. And the "balance" sent down from heaven (see Qur'ān LVII. 25) is, according to the elucidation of Sayyid 'Abd al-Laṭīf, nothing else but "the rational basis on which the Kitāb, the Revelation, is to rest and help mankind 'to observe equipoise' or live a balanced life".[6]

[1] An observation Aḥmad Khān made before in the *Tahdhīb al-akhlāq* of 9 May 1872.
[2] Muḥ. Iqbāl, *Asrār-i khūdī*, vol. XVII, 1615 (Lahore, 1944), rev. tr. R. A. Nicholson.
[3] Muḥ. 'Ināyat Allāh Khān al-Mashriqī, *Tadhkira* (Amritsar, 1924), vol. I, p. 84.
[4] Khalīfa 'Abd al-Ḥakim, *Islamic Ideology*, 3rd ed. (Lahore, 1961), p. 30.
[5] Muḥ. Iqbāl, *Reconstruction*, p. 127.
[6] *The Mind al-Quran builds* (Hyderabad, Deccan, 1952), p. 36.

By virtue of its being the religion of nature, Islam is also the true universal religion for and from all times. It was to throw this particular aspect into relief that Abu 'l-Kalām Āzād (1888–1958), the well-known Minister for Education in independent India, wrote his widely praised *Tarjumān al-Qur'ān* (1930).[1] In this work he explains that the Qur'ānic term *al-hudā* is the essential concept for the universal religion, and it denotes "the universal guidance of the divine revelation which is granted from the first day to the world for all men".[2] In a survey of the history of religions the author speaks with appreciation of W. Schmidt's theory of a universal "Urmonotheismus". According to Āzād this view agrees exactly with the testimony of the Qur'ān: "People were one community once; then they disagreed."[3] But, it might be objected: "If Islam be so universal, how is it that such a fierce resistance and opposition to the message of the Qur'ān was offered by Jews and Christians?" To this objection our commentator replies:

> The true cause of resistance by adherents of other religions was not because the Qur'ān declared that their religion was false, but because it did not do this. Followers of every religion want to claim the truth for themselves and to regard everything else as false, whereas the Qur'ān wished to uphold the truth of every religion, without exception; and therefore nobody could be pleased with the Qur'ān. The Jews were delighted with the Qur'ān's confirming of the truth of Moses. But the Qur'ān did not stop at that. It also confirmed the truth of Jesus, and with that conflict arose...[4]

"Outward distinctions", so Āzād expounds in another passage, "are indeed met with in the various religions. That is so, because religion itself aims at happiness and prosperity of human society. And the conditions and patterns of human societies neither are nor can be uniform in every epoch and in every country."[5]

Thus there was a difference in respect of the conditions under which the precepts of Christ and the Qur'ān had to be explained and the form in which they had to be clothed (in essence, however, they come to the same thing). For Christ it was sufficient to lay stress on ethics and purity in heart, since the Mosaic Law was available. But the Qur'ān had to explain at the same time ethics and regulations. Therefore it chose a mode of expression in which precepts and regulations were explained in clear, practical and precise wording, instead of in metaphors and similes (as Jesus did).[6]

[1] Some years ago this Qur'ān commentary was reprinted in Pakistan, although its author had proved to be a fierce antagonist of the establishment of a separate Muslim state.
[2] Vol. 1, p. 180.
[3] Qur'ān x. 20 (vol. 1, pp. 128–31).
[4] Vol. 1, p. 311.
[5] Vol. 1, pp. 186 ff.
[6] Vol. 1, pp. 109 ff.

For the sake of his policy of reconciliation between the Muslims and the British[1] and in illustration of striking similarities recognizable in the Muslim and Christian sources of faith, Aḥmad Khān once betook himself to the composition of a commentary on the Bible, an undertaking unique in the Muslim world. In this *Tabyīn al-kalām* (1862) the exegete quotes in columns side by side with the Bible text sayings derived from the Qur'ān and *ḥadīth* which are of similar content. Along with it, by means of the Bible text, he pointed out mistaken conceptions of Christian theologians. So in his comment on chapter 4 of St Matthew, he remarks: "If Christ were God, what then could be the purport of the trials by the Devil?" (iii. 84).

For every Muslim on the Indo-Pakistan subcontinent, however bold his theories may be, the Qur'ān is absolutely perfect and comprehensive. It is the latest and last edition of the heavenly books; consequently, it has revised, if not superseded the Bible. This can be easily deduced from its reproducing in a much superior way stories both of them have in common. So, for instance, Mawdūdī refers to the Qur'ānic version of Nathan's parable to David (II Samuel xii. 1–23). In it, the rich man requests: "Make me her keeper"[2] (Qur'ān XXXVIII. 22); in other words in contrast with the way the matter is narrated in the Bible, there is no question of a *violent* snatching away of the poor man's single ewe. The point is, that in fact David did not commit adultery.[3] He only asked Uriah to repudiate his wife, a friendly office not unusual among the Israelites. Similarly, it was under the influence of the same Jewish usage that in Medina some "helpers" (*anṣār*) repudiated their wives on behalf of the men who emigrated with Muḥammad from Mecca (*muhājirūn*).[4]

The perfection of the Qur'ān, however, has been called into question because of Western historical criticism and Western standards of morality. In consequence, a good deal of effort is spent in showing that the Qur'ān does not contain notions originating from an antiquated *Weltanschauung*. Aḥmad Khān, though at times he may be equally guilty of this kind of apologetics, has made some sensible observations on this point which are in line with ideas expressed by Shāh Walī

[1] Unlike Abu 'l-Kalām Āzād, who in his fight for an independent *united* India, strove for a rapprochement between Muslims and Hindus. That may have been the concomitant political background of his universalistic views.

[2] The verb used is *kafala* IV: with 2 acc.—"to make a person a keeper, guarantor for".

[3] And could not have done so, since in the eyes of the Muslims David is a prophet; and an Islamic prophet is protected from great sins.

[4] *Tarjumān al-Qur'ān* (September 1938).

Allāh (see p. 129). In a comment on the seven heavens mentioned in the Qur'ān he declares that the Qur'ān was revealed in congruence with the sphere of thought of the ancient Arabs.[1]

It should be noted that Aḥmad Khān does not propound the theory that eternal truths from God received a phrasing in contemporary idiom from the prophetic genius. No; according to him, heaven itself adopted for the wording of the Qur'ān the language spoken by a seventh-century Arab. Against the view of Shāh Walī Allāh who asserts that only the conceptual content (*ma'ānin*) and not the literal text of the Qur'ān has come down from heaven, Aḥmad Khān argues: "A subject of thought (*madmūn*) devoid of words represents a logical absurdity."[2]

Equally numerous and unconvincing as the attempts at proving the modernity of Qur'ānic cosmology and physics are the explanations intended to show that the Qur'ānic ethics really prescribe monogamy, disapprove of slavery, etc. Less sophisticated and more discriminating, however, is the solution proposed by Ismā'īl Rāgī al-Fārūqī. This scholar wants to distinguish "axiologically superior Qur'ānic values" from lower ones. In this manner it is possible to consider, for example, as irrelevant the injunction of cutting off the hand of the proven thief (cf. Qur'ān v. 42), "as long as a just distribution of wealth does not obtain in our society (so that out of poverty somebody might be induced to steal)...In doing so, we would be obeying the higher command (of *falāḥ*, social justice, given in Qur'ān II. 137) affirming its higher order of rank as compared with the lower."[3]

If the authority of the Qur'ān as the Word of God is no point of discussion for the Indian and Pakistani Muslim, it is otherwise with *ḥadīth* as the authoritative word of the Prophet and his companions. The incorporation of a *ḥadīth* in one of the six canonical collections or the correctness of the chain of traditionalists is no longer sufficient guarantee for everybody of the authenticity of a tradition. Even Mawdūdī admits that a somewhat critical attitude towards the tradition is still desirable: "One should keep in mind that even the excellent work of the *muḥāddithūn* (compilers of tradition) has been the work of man, and thus not faultless."[4] But, as this divine states confidently: "through a good deal of study and exercise a gift in man might be developed by which he becomes familiar with the disposition of the

[1] *Tandhīb al-akhlāq* (Lahore, 1874).
[2] *Taḥrīr uṣūl al-tafsīr* (Lahore, 1892), p. 33.
[3] *Islamic Studies* (Karachi, March 1962), p. 48.
[4] *Tarjumān al-Qur'ān* (May 1937).

Apostle of God and the true spirit of Islam. If then he views a tradition, he perceives immediately whether the Prophet said so, or not." But when certainty has been acquired about its containing the very words of Muḥammad, the question is still how to apply the prophetic rule to present-day conditions. Faḍl al-Raḥmān, the director of the Central Institute of Islamic Research in Pakistan, is of the opinion that the problem of legal *ḥadīth* must be handled on the "principle of situational interpretation, by resurrecting the real moral value from the situational background". And incumbent at the moment, so he concludes, is "to recast the *ḥadīth* into living *Sunnah* terms by historical interpretation so that we may be able to derive norms from it for ourselves through an adequate ethical theory and its legal re-embodiment".[1]

One of the basic pillars on which the authority of Muḥammad rests is the Qur'ānic claim that he is the "seal of the prophets" (Qur'ān XXXIII. 40), which singles him out as the culmination of all previous divine messengers. Muḥammad closes the series of prophets. Hence, so Iqbāl and Parwez infer, Islam proclaims the finality of the institution of prophethood. To Parwez this means that after Muḥammad, "personality" as the decisive and most important factor has been concluded, and the "ideology" written down in the Qur'ān has been left to us. And how relevant this is for the present appears from the fact that in the world of today there is not a fight between personalities, but between ideologies.[2] For Iqbāl this implies that Islam has given inductive intellect the place of prophetic divination in gaining access to the secret springs of life and reality.[3]

In respect of the rules for religious practice, Indian and Pakistani Muslims like to stress the utility of the prescribed duties. With an allusion to Darwinian evolution, Āzād argues that the Qur'ān denotes the permanence of the most useful, not the survival of the fittest, since in its view the fit is above all the useful.[4] Mawdūdī characterizes prayer, almsgiving, fasting, pilgrimage, etc., as "training courses", while *jihād* is said to be meant for the "reconstruction of the social order of the whole world".[5] In the opinion of Parwez the very purport of pilgrimage, through which representatives from all over the Muslim world are brought together, is to serve as a "broadcasting station" for the divulgation of the revolutionary principles of Islam.[6]

[1] *Islamic Studies* (Karachi, June 1962), pp. 32 and 34.
[2] *Salīm ke nām*, vol. I, p. 235.
[3] Muḥ. Iqbal, *Reconstruction*, p. 126.
[4] *Tarjumān al-Qur'ān*, vol. II, pp. 278 f.
[5] *Tarjumān al-Qur'ān* (July 1935).
[6] *Ma'ārif*, vol. IV, p. 763.

In a society, however, on which the impact of Western life becomes increasingly stronger, it is still not enough that Islamic institutions should be founded on rational grounds of social utility. The situation calls for concrete legal reforms. This is understood by the government of Pakistan. It began in 1955 by forming a commission on marriage and family laws. The ordinance, suggested by this commission, imposes restrictions on the exercise of man's privilege to take more than one wife at a time. It tries to ensure that divorced women can under law claim proper guarantees of maintenance, and it upholds the woman's right to assert her will in the marriage contract. There is also provision for the registration of marriages. Finally, the law grants the children of a predeceased father the right (not given by the Ḥanafī school) to inheritance in their grandfather's property. The commission bases these proposals on the principle that "what is not categorically and unconditionally prohibited by a clear and unambiguous injunction (of the Qur'ān or *sunna*) is permissible, if the welfare of the individual or of the society in general demands it". This smooth shift from "obeying what is explicitly and implicitly ordained by the Qur'ān and *sunna*" (the orthodox standpoint) to "permissible is what has not been forbidden expressly" is typical of Muslim liberalism. It is obvious that in this way a much wider scope is secured for the introduction of changes and improvements. Though in the opinion of the commission itself it did not introduce "new rights for women which the Qur'ān and *sunna* had not already granted them", and it had "proposed only to implement those rights and make them more secure by a better procedure", this modernist approach to the family law of Islam, as it is qualified by its opponents, met severe criticism. If the principles of this commission were acted upon, it would be easy enough "to 'liberate' us from most restrictions of the *sharī'a*", Mawlānā Amīn Aḥsan Iṣlāḥī remarks sarcastically. "Religion", so the same critic argues, "they seem to contend, means belief in just a few simple, eternal and unchanging basic principles of life", but "anybody with any knowledge of the Qur'ān knows that the Qur'ān is not merely a collection of certain principles. It has also...envisaged a pattern of human society."[1] In short, this single instance of the agitation about the proposed marriage and family laws may demonstrate that Pakistan

[1] Cf. Khursheed Ahmad (ed.), *Studies in the Family Law of Islam* (Karachi, 1961), pp. 101, 131 and 133. This book gives the text of the Marriage Commission Report and a critical appraisal of it by Mawdūdī and some of his partisans.

has become an interesting and important laboratory for practical experiments in the adaptability of Islam to changing socio-economic patterns. In government circles liberal-minded people set the tone. But the government is cautious and takes time; the feelings roused must be ventilated.

The condition of the Muslims in India at present is totally different. Circumstances are far from being appropriate for reforming Islamic law. To begin with, the body which in a secular state might be most qualified to do it is the Indian Parliament. But in that case Hindus would join in discussions on matters which are of a specifically Muslim nature. Irrespective of the unpleasant implication that a legal procedure to amend Islamic law would entail, the fact of the matter is that the Muslims are not exactly in the mood for it. Their attention is too much monopolized by the issue resulting from the unhappy complications ensuing from the Partition in 1947. Their situation is extremely delicate. On the one hand, they feel deserted by their co-religionists who chose Pakistan; as a result the minority percentage of the Indian Muslims was reduced by more than 50 per cent ("We did not want the establishment of Pakistan, since it could never become a solution for *all* the Muslims", is the bitter comment given). On the other hand, "the irony of the situation" seems to be "that the state they created with their blood will be of no use in their difficulties". For, at the root of their troubles lies the bare truth that "their destiny is tied up with their fellow-countrymen who have their own ambitions and aspirations".[1] And the worst of it is that the average Hindu fairly easily falls a prey to the temptation of abusing the strong position he has.

The main grievances of the Indian Muslims are these:

(*a*) That they are regarded by their compatriots more or less as immigrant foreigners: "There is afoot a campaign to present the history of our land in a manner as if the Muslim era in India was an era of foreign, imperialistic domination."[2] The Muslims, on their part, are at great pains to discover all kinds of conformities in Islam and Hinduism. Thus it is claimed that in Sūra CXIV. 1 ff. there are echoes of *Bhagavadgītā* IX. 32;[3] that in the Upanishads the system of *isnād* (adding a chain of the transmitters) has been applied just as in the Muslim traditions.[4] More than that, there are remarkable instances of historical

[1] Ziya-ul-Hasan Faruqi, *The Deoband School and the Demand for Pakistan* (Bombay, 1963), p. 125.
[2] Abul Hasan Ali Nadwi, *Muslims in India* (Lucknow, 1960), p. 3.
[3] Hashim Amir Ali, *The Student's Qurān* (Bombay, 1961), p. 105.
[4] Muḥammad Zubayr Ṣiddīqī, *Hadīth Literature* (Calcutta, 1961), p. 133.

interaction. On the development of the Hindu cult of *bhakti* Islam had a major influence. "Like the Reformation in Europe, the Reformation in Hinduism in the Middle Ages owed a great debt to Islam."[1]

(*b*) Obstacles which are experienced in the field of missionary activities (Islam, like Christianity, is essentially a proselytizing religion).

(*c*) Steadily increasing efforts to eliminate the Urdu language. To deprive the Muslims of the language, in which nearly their entire religious literature has been written, is "not very different from depriving them of their social and cultural identity and their spiritual inheritance".[2]

(*d*) An unjust and partial system of education. "The books recommended for general study...are such that they deal solely with the ancient heritage and the heroes of a particular community, and ignore everything that is Muslim."[3]

(*e*) In appointments to government offices Muslims are placed at a disadvantage: "the proportion of Muslims in public services is falling day by day."[4]

Still, apart from these grievances, the most vital point for the Muslim Indian today is how to maintain Islamic identity in an environment which for the slightest cause of dissatisfaction accuses him of "communalism". Nevertheless it remains his sincere wish to prove himself a loyal citizen of a democratic secular India. In particular, a valuable contribution to public weal is given by the Jāmiʿa Milliyya Islāmiyya at Delhi. This national Muslim University was founded in 1920 to counterbalance the influence of the Aligarh University which was considered a servile acolyte of the British. (One of its most prominent principals was Zākir Ḥusayn, the present President of India.) It pays special regard to the training of teachers intended for educational projects in the much neglected rural areas.

Finally, a few general observations should be made. First, from the survey offered the reader should not conclude that the "theology" of the average Muslim in these countries consists of tenets enunciated by personalities like Iqbāl, Āzād or Parwez. This is like assuming that the average member of the Protestant Church would be thinking in terms of Tillich, Karl Barth or John Robinson. As ever the masses remain traditional in their religious outlook. Yet, even there differing shades

[1] Yusuf Husain, *Glimpses of Medieval Indian Culture* (Bombay, 1962), p. 31.
[2] Abul Hasan Ali Nadwi, *Muslims in India*, p. 133.
[3] *Ibid.* p. 129. [4] *Ibid.* p. 138.

can be distinguished. So in India a movement exists, the so-called Barelawī School, which not only encourages saint-worship but accepts also without any qualm the prevailing superstitions and corruptions. Beside it, there are the puritan activities of the Tablīghī Taḥrīk ("Movement of Promulgating", *sc.* the path of life as set in the Qur'ān and *ḥadīth*), introduced by Mawlānā Muḥammad Ilyās of Delhi (d. 1943) and continued by his son Mawlānā Yūsuf. In its *tarbiya* ("soul training") centres at Raywind (near Lahore) and Delhi small missionary teams are formed, and spread over India and Pakistan (some of them are sent abroad and visit countries like Nigeria, Indonesia, Japan, Turkey, England, Germany and U.S.A.). By pure life and stimulating example the members of such a "promulgating team" (*tablīghī jamā'at*) want to rouse common Muslim people to a more faithful and stricter obedience of the moral and ritual injunctions of Islam.

Secondly, a visitor to the Indo-Pakistan subcontinent is deeply impressed by the piety found among all strata of the Muslim society. No doubt, secularism has its impact, especially on the new generation of students. But the great majority of Muslims observe, more or less regularly, the *ṣalāt* and keep the Ramaḍān fast. In Pakistan the press pays much attention to discussions on matters of faith. People are proud of having divines in their families, and they very much like talking on religious subjects.

So variegated and lively a picture as Islam in India offers to the student, so dull and monotonous is the scene which Muslim life and thinking present in Afghanistan. The only variation is given by the wars of succession, inevitable as they are in Muslim countries because the *sharī'a* has not fixed definite rules for the delegation of political power in case of an empty throne. But no theologian of any repute, no clash of opinions of any interest does a surveyor of its history come across. For ages the country, isolated by high mountains and deep rivers, remained immune from cultural influences. No rival religion stimulated a reinterpretation of doctrines or institutions. Its population, consisting for the greater part of pious and simple-minded tribesmen, is dominated by the single authority of orthodox *mullās*, country parsons, who afford them mental stability by their age-old tenets of faith. If disease comes or crops fail they are willing to supply the proper charms. To be qualified to fabricate amulets, a *mullā* subjects himself to the *chillā* rituals. During a period of forty days he must shut himself in some cell or pass the time in a mosque. He eats little food and spends the greater part of the night and day in prayer and meditation. As the days pass, the result of the spiritual training is manifested in the appearance of figures who try to frighten him. If he succeeds in resisting these fearsome forms, they will at the end of the stipulated time kneel down before him with folded hands and receive his commands.

Charms are utilized for all purposes. Thus a tourist can find them attached in a motor-bus near a notice-board stating that travellers at the periods of *ṣalāt* are permitted to ask the driver to stop for the performance of their prescribed prayers.

Then, faith is kept alive by numerous shrines. By far the most important spiritual centre in Afghanistan is the shrine at Mazār-i Sharīf, believed by the Afghan Sunnīs to be the site of the tomb of ʿAlī, the son-in-law of Muḥammad.

The power of the *mullās* was until recently almost unlimited. If anyone dared to disregard them, he was excommunicated, which means that he may not enter a mosque, and can neither be married nor buried with Muslim rites. Many a banished "heretic" crossed the Indian border for refuge. Missionaries of other religions, including the Aḥmadiyya, are not allowed in Afghanistan. The building of churches is forbidden by the government though it does not object to the presence of a Roman Catholic chapel within the walls of the Italian embassy. Two priests, attached to the staff of the same embassy, enable foreigners to observe their religious duties. Hindus and Shīʿīs are tolerated, but Hindu women should wear a red-coloured *burqaʿ* (a long strip of cotton, veiling the whole of the face and reaching nearly to the feet) as a distinctive dress.

Rigid puritanism is demonstrated by the fact that the chief Afghan mosques, unlike those in India and Pakistan, are plain structures, devoid of any ornamentation, because the Prophet is said to have forbidden decoration in building. Fridays are regarded as general holidays in the government offices (in the Indo-Pakistan subcontinent the Sundays of former British rule continue to serve). The *ḥajj* is very much in favour. *Zakāt* is in most cases controlled and disbursed by the governments of each Afghan province. In older times *muḥtasibs* (superintendents of the police) roamed about armed with whips to take direct action against the violation of Ramaḍān, the Muslim Lent.

Besides the common people, the Afghan monarchs have been frequently forced to succumb to the tyranny of the *mullās*. In this century already three kings have lost their throne or life in their too hasty endeavours to introduce social and educational reforms. But nowadays the situation seems to be undergoing a remarkable change under the strong government of Muḥammad Ẓāhir Shāh. This king defies the *mullās*. Progressive upper circles set the tone. In the streets of present-day Kabul more ladies are seen cycling than in the whole of Pakistan and India. In the last five years a considerable number of women have put off the veil. Democracy is given a fair chance. For the first time the formation of political parties has been allowed. Elections for the members of the "House of the People" are secret, general and direct. Members of the "House of the Elders" (House of Lords) are to be elected by representatives of the provinces. The king keeps the right of nominating the prime minister and he is entitled to dissolve the parliament. All this sounds rather strange and it is hard to imagine that some day reactionary forces will not raise their heads again. But time will show.

CHAPTER 7

ISLAM IN THE USSR

The estimated total of Muslims in the USSR is about 25 million. This estimate is based on historical and cultural data rather than on statistics, for the Soviet census does not provide any information about adherence to the various religions known to be practised in the USSR. It can be assumed that if the question "what is your religion?" were put to all the peoples of which this estimated total is made up, the reply of the vast majority would be "Islam", although as elsewhere this would not necessarily mean that they were all practising believers.

Regionally the Muslims of the USSR fall into three groups: about three fifths of them are in Soviet Central Asia and Kazakhstan, one fifth in the Volga and Ural regions, and one fifth in the Caucasus. Apart from about three million Azerbayjanis belonging to Shīʿī sects, some small communities of Ismāʿīlī Shīʿīs in the Pamir region, some followers of various Ṣūfī *ṭarīqas* and a few adherents to the Shāfiʿī rite mainly in Dagestan, all the Muslims of the USSR follow the Ḥanafī rite. Racially, the Muslims can be divided into three main groups: Turkic—21 million located mainly in Central Asia and Kazakhstan, but also in the other regions; Iranian—2 million located mainly in Tajikistan and Uzbekistan, with small communities in the North Caucasus and Transcaucasia; Ibero-Caucasian—1¾ million located in the Caucasus. There are also in Central Asia some small communities belonging to other races such as Arabs and Dungans (Chinese Muslims).[1] In addition there are small numbers of Georgian Muslims (Ajars, Ingiloys), Armenian Muslims (Khemsins), Finnic Muslims (Udmurts, Maris and Mordvin Muslims), and some Tzigane (gypsy) and Chuvash Muslims.

Elements of Islamic culture can be observed in all the main Muslim communities, but the great reduction in the number of mosques, the total abolition of the Muslim *maktabs*, the absence of religious instruction in the state schools, and the abolition of the Muslim canon and customary legal systems have undoubtedly reduced the cultural cohesion which to some extent existed among the geographically separated

[1] For a list of the peoples making up these groups, see the table at the end of this chapter.

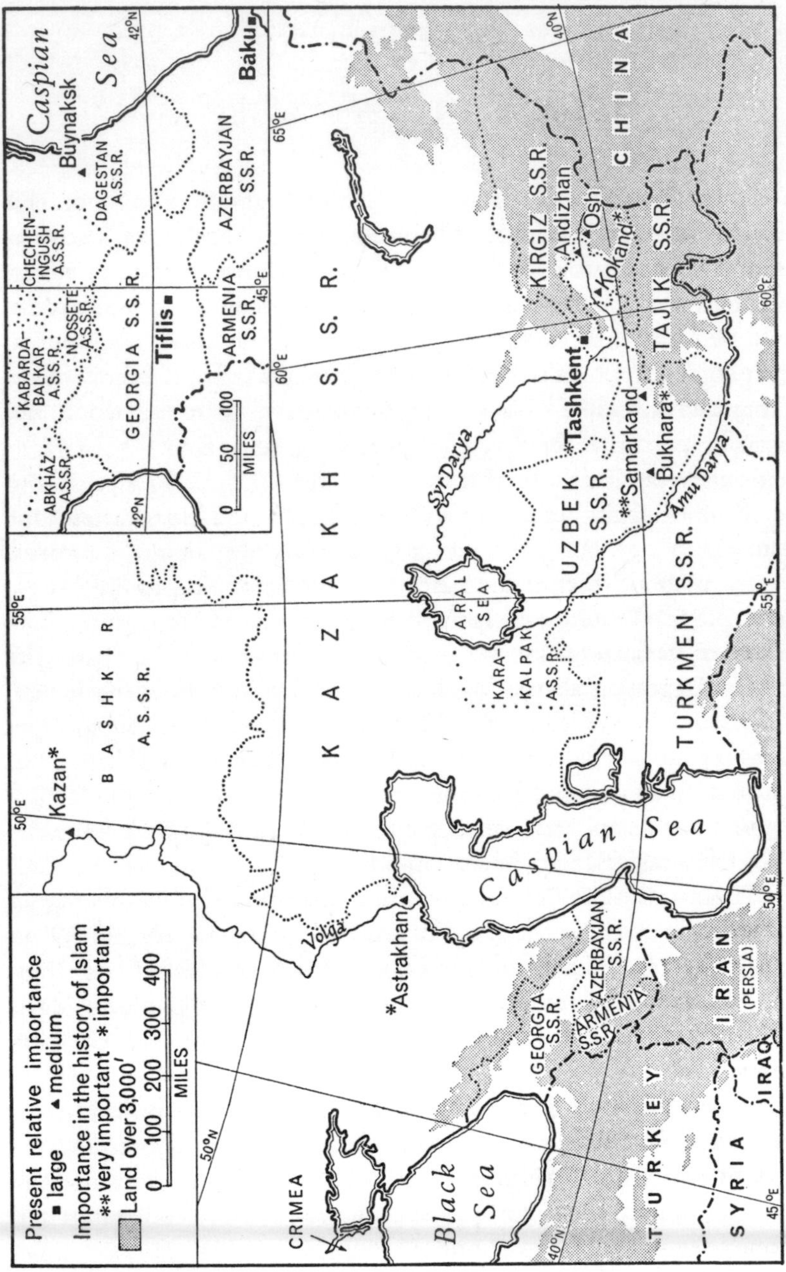

Soviet Central Asia and the Caucasus.

groups in Tsarist times. Before the Revolution, although the number of educated Muslims was very small—in Central Asia probably less than 2 per cent—literacy almost always included some knowledge of Arabic or Persian. Nowadays, however, the vast majority of even highly educated Muslims are quite ignorant of these languages and even of the Arabic script in which their own languages were formerly written. On the other hand, greatly increased literacy has brought with it a much more widespread knowledge of the Russian language. This, together with improved communications and the linking of communities in various all-Union enterprises may have resulted in the various Muslim communities knowing more about each other than they did previously. At the same time, Soviet linguistic reforms have in some instances had the effect of separating rather than uniting such closely allied communities as the Kazakhs and the Kirgiz.

Islam was established in the southern Muslim borderlands of the Soviet Union during the seventh and eighth centuries. The Arab invasion reached Transcaucasia in 642 just before the Umayyad caliphate. That of Māvarannahr or Transoxania was mounted from Khurasan, but direct Arab rule over what was then thought of as Turkestan came to an end with the rise of the ʿAbbāsid caliphate in 750. Later, Transoxania, and in particular the cities of Samarkand and Bukhara became part of the territory of the Sāmānid dynasty of Persia. Islam did not spread northward into the Kazakh Steppes until very much later, probably during the fifteenth century. It reached the Volga region and the North Caucasus during and after the Mongol invasions in the thirteenth and fourteenth centuries, the Mongol armies having included large numbers of Turks recruited in Central Asia, of whom many were Muslims. The first Muslims to fall under Russian rule were those of the Tatar khanates of Kazan and Astrakhan which were overrun in the middle of the sixteenth century and were thereafter considered as an integral part of Russia rather than of the Russian empire. The remaining Tatar khanate of the Crimea was annexed by Russia in 1783, when a large part of the Muslim population emigrated to Turkey. The Caucasus was a bone of contention between Turkey, Persia and Russia during the eighteenth century but by the 1870s the whole region had come under Russian rule. The first Russian encroachment into what is now Kazakhstan was along the Ural river at the end of the sixteenth century, but the annexation of the Steppe Region did not begin until the middle of the eighteenth century and was not completed until the middle of the nineteenth century. With the capture of Tashkent in 1865 the extension of Russian rule to the Chinese, Afghan and Persian frontiers became a foregone conclusion. It was completed in 1884, except for the khanates of Bukhara and Khiva which retained a semi-independent status until 1921. In 1924 they were incorporated in the Soviet Union as part of the new republics created in that year.

Until the coming of the Russians Islam was the overriding cultural influence to which the peoples of the North Caucasus, the Crimea, Azerbayjan, the Kazakh steppe and Turkestan had been subjected. During the Tsarist regime considerable efforts were made to eradicate this influence, but without success except in so far as Bukhara and Samarkand, and to a lesser extent Kazan, began to lose their status as great centres of Islamic learning and culture. The policy of the Tsarist regime towards Islam was inconsistent. During the early stages of the Russian advance into Kazakhstan, the Russian government regarded Islam as a stabilizing influence and actually ordered the building of mosques in the Kazakh Steppes. Later, however, Russian governors and in particular General Kaufman, Governor General of Turkestan (1867–82), looked on Islam as a baneful and dangerous influence which could best be countered by a policy of indifference. It was thought that Islam when confronted with a superior civilization would gradually wither away. Two circumstances, however, caused the Russian authorities to change their tactics. The first was a fanatical outbreak in Andizhan in 1898; and the second the emergence at the beginning of the twentieth century of a Muslim reformist movement known as Jadidism (from *uṣūl-i-jadīd*, or "new method"). The Andizhan revolt was a small affair which was suppressed in two days; but it greatly alarmed the Russians who assumed that powerful underground forces were at work. Jadidism, which aimed primarily at the modernization of Islamic educational methods, was regarded by the Russians as a potential challenge to their own culture and to counter it they formed what Barthold has described as "an alliance between Russian conservatism and old-style Islam".[1] The government began to take an interest in the *madrasas* and even considered the introduction of compulsory primary education. In spite of this, however, Jadidism grew apace not only in the Volga region and the Crimea, but in the Steppe Region, Turkestan and even in the khanate of Bukhara.

[1] *Istoriya Kul'turnoy Zhizni Turkestana* (Leningrad, 1927), pp. 143–4.

In the Caucasus the Russians encountered much more serious and violent opposition to their rule mainly in the shape of a revolt led by Shamil who constituted himself as *imām* and his followers as *murīds* in the prosecution of a holy war against the infidel conquerors. He harassed the Russians for nearly thirty years until his final surrender in 1859. The widespread revolt of the Central Asian Muslims against Russian authority which broke out in 1916 was destined to predispose the people to some extent in favour of the new regime which was to appear a year later. The underlying cause of the revolt was undoubtedly maladministration, the worst feature of this being the preference shown to Russian settlers over the Muslim population in the matter of land and of irrigation water; a decree calling up able-bodied men for labour service in World War I merely fanned smouldering discontent into a flame. On balance, however, the record of the Tsarist administration of the Muslim population of Russia was by no means wholly discreditable. In spite of what appeared to be grave shortcomings in administration and attention to the people's welfare, Russian rule imparted to the Muslim lands a degree of peace and security which had been unknown for centuries; the standard of living of the peasantry does not, on the whole, seem to have been much lower than that of the peasantry in some parts of European Russia; and in the matter of civic freedom, the Central Asian Muslims were in some respects better off, notably in that of conscription, to which they were not subjected until 1916, and then only for service in back areas.

The attitude of the Soviet regime towards religion in general was entirely different from that of the Tsarist government. Since Islam involved belief in the supernatural it came under the general fire directed against all such beliefs; but since it also had claims to universality it was considered potentially more dangerous than, for example, the Orthodox Church. As a way of life Communism regarded Islam as more dangerous and objectionable than any branch of Christianity. The Reformation and the Renaissance had enabled Christianity to come to terms, as it were, with modern life; but no similar reforms had ever set Islam free from the bonds of medievalism and the Soviet leaders therefore saw it as backward, as militating against material progress and as having been promoted and perpetuated, first by feudal oriental despots and later by Western imperialists for their own unethical ends.

The ruthless suppression of the 1916 revolt had undoubtedly aroused

Muslim religious feeling against the Russians and accordingly one of the first acts of the Soviet leaders was to issue in December 1917 a conciliatory appeal which assured the Muslims that "henceforward your beliefs and customs, your national and cultural institutions, are declared free and inviolable". The full force of the anti-religious campaign was not opened against Islam until after the end of the Civil War and it was mainly directed against the less fundamental aspects of Islam: the veiling of women, pilgrimages to holy places and tombs, festivals which interrupted work, and such practices as circumcision. Lenin himself was well aware of the inexpediency of crude attacks against cherished beliefs and in 1921 tried to put a curb on the more violent activities of the League of the Godless. In general, however, the momentum of the anti-religious campaign has been maintained, although foreign reports of persecution and suppression have been considerably exaggerated. The practice of Islam in accordance with Qur'ānic precepts was never formally forbidden and in its campaign against what it regarded as harmful customs the Soviet government never went to such lengths as the nationalist governments of some non-Soviet Muslim countries. On occasions anti-Islamic propaganda was deliberately played down; for example, when Germany attacked the USSR in 1941 the support of Islam, as of other religions, was actually enlisted. Although anti-Islamic propaganda is nowadays more calculating and "scientific", the Soviet government has never attempted to conceal its hostility to Islam and its concern at its obstinate survival.

In spite of their uncompromising hostility to Islam as a way of life, the Soviet leaders at first looked upon the Muslims of Russia as a political force which should be humoured, organized and enlisted as an ally, perhaps only temporarily, against the imperialist West. Whether they ever considered the possibility of some kind of permanent federation of Russian Muslim peoples which would merely be associated with the Soviet Union is doubtful; but they certainly intended that the spreading of the Revolution to the Muslims, and particularly to those of Central Asia, should be postponed until later.

During the Tsarist regime, no Muslim political organizations had been officially tolerated. Indeed, the desire to create such organizations could hardly be said to have arisen until 1905 at the time of the first Russian Revolution. In that year the first All-Russian-Muslim congress met secretly in Nizhniy Novgorod and thirty-six Muslim members were allotted to the first Duma or parliament. But in the third Duma elected in November 1907, the number was reduced to ten and these did not include any deputies from the Steppe Region or Turkestan. Political activity among the Muslims had certainly increased before the outbreak of the 1917 Revolution, but apart from a few extremist intellectuals, Muslim aspirations did not include political independence or self-determination but were restricted to such matters as the cessation of Russian colonization of their lands, freedom of religious teaching, freedom to publish books and newspapers, and the right to elect deputies.

In January 1918 Stalin, as chairman of the Commissariat of Nationalities, created a body called the Commissariat of Muslim Affairs under the direction of three Tatar intellectuals—Mulla Nūr Vakhitov, Mīr Sa'īd Sulṭān Galiyev and Sharīf Manatov. This Commissariat proceeded to establish bureaux and committees throughout the Muslim areas and in June 1918, Vakhitov formed the "Russian party of Muslim Communists". This, however, was dissolved after a few months, and the functions of its central commitee taken over by the Central Bureau of Muslim Organizations of the Russian Communist party. In March 1919 the words "Muslim organizations" were replaced by "organizations of the peoples of the East", and shortly afterwards the Muslim Commissariat itself disappeared. Muslim reactions to the Communist revolution had quickly shown the Soviet leaders that any recognition of the Muslim peoples of Russia as a corporate political, or even as a cultural entity would spell disaster for the new regime and might involve the loss to it of the vital oil and cotton resources situated in the Muslim lands.

Muslim reactions to the Revolution were neither uniform nor co-ordinated. Although there was a fundamental ideological incompatibility between atheistic Communism and theocratic Islam, this was not the overriding cause of the antagonism which developed between the Soviet government and the Muslim peoples of Russia in the early years of the Revolution. There was in Russia no central Muslim hierarchy which could represent the views of the Muslims as a whole or around which they could rally, and the organizations mentioned above were too short-lived to exercise any influence of this sort. The underlying cause of the antagonism was most probably xenophobia which was manifested in three ways all of which were in varying degrees dangerous or irksome for the new regime. The most formidable type of opposition was that offered by those Muslim intellectuals, mainly Tatars, who while they eagerly accepted Communism as a principle, thought that the German and Russian interpretation of Marxism was unsuited to the Muslim world. The principal exponent of this school of thought was Sulṭān Galiyev who, although a convinced Communist, held ideas which were bound up with Islamic tradition. He aimed at the creation of a Muslim state on the middle Volga which would eventually be joined first by all the Turkic Muslims of Russia and later by the other Russian Muslims. This state or federation would organize the propagation of Communism in the non-Soviet east and eventually form what he called "a colonial international". Owing to his important position in the Commissariat of Nationalities and his editorship of the magazine *Zhizn' Natsional'nostey* (The Life of the Nationalities) in which he propagated his ideas, Sultan Galiyev gained a considerable following in Central Asia and the Caucasus. This drew attention to the potential danger of his movement and in 1923 he was denounced, arrested and dismissed from the party. He ultimately disappeared and is thought to have been executed. Whatever the extent of Sulṭān Galiyev's movement, it was the last expression of what might be called an All-Union Muslim point of view. In Soviet eyes its danger was twofold: it could have resulted in all the Muslims of Russia "ganging up" against the new regime; and it might have extended into Asia as a purely Asiatic form of Communism which would eventually evade Moscow's control.

The second form of opposition was that known as "bourgeois nationalism". This was the name given by Communists to the activities of those groups which sought to use the Revolution not for the purpose of prosecuting the class-war, but in order to create nation-states on the Western model. In Central Asia, owing to the tribal organization of society, the intermingling of the various nationalities and the very low percentage of literacy, the aims of these groups were ill-defined and at the outset encountered the opposition not so much of the architects of the Revolution as of the hostile and chauvinist Russian colonists who in 1917 amounted to over 2 million in the Steppe Region and Turkestan alone. By 1924 the various attempts at creating individual nation states whether on a regional and Islamic basis like the shortlived Kokand government which came to an end in 1918, national governments like that of the Alash Orda in Kazakhstan, or Peoples' Republics like those based on the former khanates of Bukhara and Khiva had all foundered and the basis of the present five Socialist Soviet Republics was laid down by the central government.

In Transcaucasia an independent Azerbayjani republic was established in 1918, but it was overthrown by the Red Army in 1920. Azerbayjan was included in the Transcaucasian Federal Republic in 1922 and finally created a Union Republic in 1936. There were short-lived nationalist movements in Tatarstan and Bashkiria, but in 1920 both were included in the USSR as Autonomous Republics.

The third form of opposition was that evoked by Soviet agrarian, legal, educational, linguistic and social reforms, some of which were salutary and long overdue, but all of which struck at the heart of Muslim tradition and the Muslim way of life. The determined and often ruthless application of these reforms and the atheistic propaganda which accompanied them created great resentment and in the first five or six years of the new regime brought about frequent outbreaks of violence culminating in the widespread and long-sustained Basmachi revolt. This last is sometimes represented as a positive Turkestani nationalist movement aiming at independence from Soviet Russian rule; but it is possible that it was more the despairing reaction of the people to inefficient and oppressive authority and interference with their cherished customs. Many of the Basmachi leaders were not intellectuals or nationalists, but conservative reactionaries, some of them little more than brigands, who were as much opposed to the Muslim Jadidist reformers as they were to the Russians. Active resistance to the new regime had ceased by 1930 and even the Great Purge of 1935–8 with its thousands of executions and arrests did not give rise to any serious disturbance.

Doctor Baymirza Hayit, an Uzbek who grew up in Soviet Uzbekistan, has recorded that in spite of the Soviet assault on the Muslim traditions and way of life, "it was not until 1937 that the social life of Turkestan was determined by Communism. Up to then, the Turkestan Communist leaders had tried to let the people live in their own way, and at the same time to fulfil Soviet State plans. Therefore the people were able to live either secretly, or frequently quite openly, according to their own customs."[1] Doctor Hayit describes how all this changed after the purge of the party and state machinery which took place in 1937, and which coincided with the abolition of national military formations and the introduction of universal conscription in the Soviet armed forces. Since 1956 when Stalin was formally repudiated, responsibility for the

[1] Baymirza Hayit, *Turkestan im zwanzigsten Jahrhundert* [Turkestan in the Twentieth century] (Darmstadt, 1956).

violence and injustice which accompanied the purge has been squarely placed on his shoulders, and some of those executed on charges of nationalism have been posthumously rehabilitated. This process, which was still continuing in 1965, may have been part of a policy of propitiating the Muslim population in general, but it has never been accompanied by any change in the generally hostile Soviet attitude towards Islam as a way of life. Stalin was also made responsible for the uprooting and deportation from their homes of nearly a million Muslims from the Crimea and the North Caucasus for alleged collaboration with the Germans during the last war. In 1956 it was announced that the North Caucasian deportees would be repatriated and this has to some extent been carried out; but no mention has ever been made of the Crimean Tatars, some two hundred thousand of whom are still in Uzbekistan and Kazakhstan.

Since World War II, the material condition of the Muslims in the USSR has greatly improved and such small purges of highly placed Muslim officials as have taken place have been mostly concerned with charges of local patriotism, nepotism, inefficiency in relation to production and the like. Even those apparently found guilty or at any rate accused of large-scale corruption do not appear to have been arrested but only relieved of their posts. Muslim party officials are frequently taken to task for such reactionary practices as attending religious funerals, but there is no record of their being victimized. It is significant that of recent years the only case of a highly placed Muslim party official being actually punished for political offences was that of Bagirov, the first secretary of the Communist party of Azerbayjan, who was executed in 1956. So far from being a supporter of Muslim doctrine and practice, he was well known for his atheistic and anti-Islamic writings.

Accurate information on the subject of religious organization, the numbers of mosques and officiating clergy, religious education and publications, and the prevalence of religious practice is extremely difficult to obtain.[1] This is, of course, due to the generally hostile official attitude towards all religions and the consequent exclusion of information on religion from literature and the press. The present administrative organization consists of four spiritual directorates

[1] Probably the best available account is that given by Hélène Carrère d'Encausse in *L'Afrique et l'Asie*, no. 4 (52) of 1960 under the title of "Organisation officielle de l'Islam en URSS".

known as *nezārāt*, or in Russian as *dukhovnoye upravleniye*. These were founded in 1941, are recognized by law and are now under the control of the Council for the Affairs of Religious Cults attached to the Council of Ministers of the USSR. This Council deals with all matters affecting religious sects other than the Orthodox Church. It is represented in each Union or Autonomous Republic by a similar Council attached to the Republican Council of Ministers. The jurisdiction and location of the spiritual directorates are as follows: (1) The Directorate for Sunnī Muslims of European Russia and Siberia with headquarters at Ufa (Bashkir ASSR). Up to December 1948 the president of this directorate was regarded as the supreme spiritual leader of all the Muslims of the USSR. Its administrative language is Kazan Tatar. (2) Directorate for the Sunnī Muslims of Central Asia and Kazakhstan with headquarters in Tashkent. The administrative language is Uzbek. (3) Directorate for the Sunnī Muslims of the North Caucasus and Dagestan with headquarters at Buynaksk (Dagestan ASSR). Owing to the large number of languages in this region, no single language could have precedence, and in all probability Russian, or perhaps Arabic, is used. (4) Directorate for the Sunnī and Shīʿī Muslims of Transcaucasia with headquarters at Baku. The authority of this directorate extends to the whole Shīʿī community of the USSR to which the president belongs. The vice-president acts as *muftī* of the Sunnī communities of Transcaucasia. Smaller sects such as the Ismāʿīlīs, the Bahāʾīs and the Yazīdīs have no officially recognized spiritual directorate.

Each spiritual directorate is administered by an executive committee of from seven to nine members, who are elected by a regional congress composed of both clergy and laymen. The precise role of the directorates is difficult to determine as is also the process by which they came into being. From June 1942 there have been a series of Muslim congresses held at irregular intervals in Ufa, Tashkent and Baku. It was apparently at the second of these held in Tashkent in December 1948 that the directorates were instituted and at the same time the decision announced to reopen the Mīr-i-ʿarab *madrasa* in Bukhara. This was originally founded in 1535 by Khān ʿUbaydallāh on behalf of Shaykh ʿAbdallāh al-Yamanī. At the time of the Revolution it had been closed and was not officially reopened until 1952 as the "higher ecclesiastical institute" of the Spiritual Directorate of the Muslims of Central Asia and Kazakhstan. This was the only Muslim seminary for the training of Muslim clergy in the whole of the USSR until 1958, when another *madrasa*, that of Barak Khān, was opened in Tashkent; but it is not clear to what extent this functions independently of the Mīr-i-'arab. The latter can only accommodate about 100 pupils, whom it trains only for the offices of *qārī'*, *mu'adhdhin* and *khāṭib*. Arabic is taught, the medium of instruction being Uzbek written in the Arabic character.

No clue to the number of officiating clergy and functioning mosques can be found in any Soviet reference book, and information provided by various Muslim dignitaries is highly contradictory. At the outbreak of the Revolution, there were in Russia (exclusive of the semi-independent states of Bukhara and Khiva) a total of 45,339 Muslim clergy.[1] No figures are available even for the officially registered clergy at the present time, but the number is unlikely to exceed 9,000 for the whole of the USSR. It is probable, however, that there is in addition a large number of unofficial *mullās* who function at such ceremonies as circumcisions, marriages and funerals. The material condition of the officially recognized clergy appears to be satisfactory, their salaries being provided by contributions from the various congregations but actually disbursed by the Spiritual Directorates.

The number of functioning mosques is equally difficult to determine. In 1913 there were reported to be 26,279 mosques in the Russian empire excluding the khanates of Bukhara and Khiva; but this figure may have included small shrines without regular congregations. In 1900 it was estimated that in the province of Turkestan alone, there were 1,503 congregational mosques and 11,230 parish mosques, that is, approximately one mosque for every 470 believers. After the purges of 1936–8 there were very few mosques left even in the large cities of Central Asia. Since then, and particularly since the last war, the situation may have improved. In 1942 Soviet *War News* reported that there were 1,312 mosques open in the whole of the USSR. In 1956 Edouard Sablier, editor of *Le Monde*, reported two entirely different figures: according to the president of the Council for the Affairs of Religious Cults in Moscow there were 8,000 mosques and meeting rooms; while the presidents of the four Directorates reported a total of 1,800. Even in the large cities regularly visited by tourists reports of the numbers of functioning mosques vary widely. In Tashkent a city with at least half

[1] M. S. Rybakov, "Statistics of the Muslims in Russia on 1st January 1912", an article in *Mir Islama*, no. XI (1913), pp. 269–71. A. P. Savitskiy in *Trudy SAGU* (1956), pp. 53–71, gives a total of 12,499 mosques in the province of Turkestan alone in 1900.

a million Muslim inhabitants, the existence of only four functioning mosques has been fully confirmed; but there are reports of totals varying from sixty to ten. In Samarkand, which had more than 100 mosques before the Revolution, there appeared to be only three open in 1960, including that at the mausoleum of Shāh-i-Zindah. Bukhara, which had 360 mosques in 1917, had not more than six in 1960.[1] Information about mosques in the smaller towns of Central Asia and in the Caucasus is even more difficult to come by. Few towns seem to have more than one mosque: Kokand, whose population of 105,000 is predominantly Muslim, has only one mosque in place of the 247 open in 1917. As regards rural districts, there appear to be more mosques in the small towns and villages of the Caucasus than in those of Central Asia. The building of new mosques is occasionally reported: for example in 1957 Moscow radio reported the building of a new mosque at Osh in Kirgizya.

Although under article 128 of the Soviet Constitution of 1936 religious instruction in state schools is forbidden, the existence of schools exclusively devoted to religious instruction is legally permissible. In fact, however, between 1917 and 1941 all Muslim religious schools were closed and it is only since 1942 that the *madrasas* mentioned earlier have been opened. Inquiries by visitors have elicited the information that a certain amount of private religious instruction is carried out by *mullās*.

In Russia before the Revolution there were said to be twenty-three Muslim printing presses, eighteen religious periodicals and 196 libraries specializing in Muslim literature. At present, there appears to be no Muslim printing press and publishing is confined to the Qur'ān (whose publication was first permitted in 1948), a few religious calendars and one or two books. Apart from the Qur'ān, the only book whose publication has been announced is one called *Musul'manskoye Bogosluzheniye* (Muslim Form of Service). This was included in *Knizhnaya Letopis'* (Book Chronicle) no. 39 of 1957 and was said to contain 69 pages of text in Tatar printed in Arabic charaters. Mention has been made of two periodicals in Arabic characters, one in Tatar published at Ufa and another in Uzbek published in Tashkent; but no copy of either of these journals has ever been seen by any Western scholars.

[1] A pamphlet published in French at Tashkent in 1964 gave the total number of large mosques in Central Asia and Kazakhstan as only 250, while the *Propagandist and Agitator's Handbook* (Moscow, 1966) gives the total number of mosques in the USSR as about 400.

Although there are now no Muslim libraries in the Soviet Union, a Pakistani visitor reported that the library of the Spiritual Directorate in Tashkent contained 8,000 volumes of which 250 were in Arabic.

The restrictions and controls outlined above coupled with the invalidation of the *sharī'a* have unquestionably resulted in a lessening of the influence exercised by Islam on the daily life of the people. There are, however, certain other circumstances which must be taken into account. As in all other Muslim countries the observance of the five "pillars of the faith" has tended to diminish with the spread of education on modern lines irrespective of whether it contains an element of religious instruction. Among the Muslims of the Soviet Union general, technical and higher education has reached a far higher standard than in any other Muslim country in the world. Quite apart, therefore, from the special attitude and measures adopted by the Soviet government towards Islam, its observance could be expected to fall in proportion to the rise of education. As regards the spiritual and cultural hold of Islam on the hearts and minds of men, however, it may be doubted whether this is any less in the Muslim lands of the Soviet Union than it is in some of the modernized countries of the Middle East, and particularly in those where nationalist governments have deliberately curbed the influence previously wielded by the clergy. Although in the Soviet Union it is possible to find many educated Muslims who are ready to scoff at religious practice in a way which would not be tolerated in other Muslim societies where observance is no less lax, the number of such people who would actually deny that they were Muslims at all is likely to be extremely small. The fact remains that Islam is the most penetrating spiritual and cultural influence to which the indigenous peoples of the Asian part of the Soviet Union have so far been subjected and in spite of the headway made by westernization and Communism this influence remains strong.

It is difficult to speak with any degree of precision of the outward manifestations of Islam in the Muslim lands of the USSR. Except on Fridays in the few remaining mosques men are seldom if ever seen at prayer; veiled women are seen only occasionally; the *adhān* is certainly not heard regularly and has probably suffered the same fate as church-bells. But these and other similar lapses refer only to the larger towns which foreigners are allowed to visit; and things may well be different in rural districts. Even in the large towns, moreover, the traveller feels himself to be in a Muslim country, a feeling induced by such typical characteristics as the modest and dignified demeanour of the women, the almost universal wearing of some sort of Muslim headdress such as the *tyubeteyka* or *kalpak* by the men and the tendency to visit shrines on holidays.

Apart from the formal religious obligations, beliefs and line of conduct enjoined by Islam the Soviet authorities include in their condemnation of religion a number of beliefs, practices and traditions which are not related to Islam, or indeed to any religion, except in so far as they are rooted in a belief in the supernatural. Such practices include the visitation of tombs and shrines, most of which are thought to have curative properties, the practice of medicine and magical rites by *mullās* and the adoption of patron saints by such relatively new trades as chauffeurs and tractor drivers. More serious than these in the eyes of the authorities is the persistence of unorthodox sects (sing. *ṭarīqa*) and fraternities (sing. *ẓāwiya*) such as the Yasaviyya and Sulṭāniyya. Most of the practices of these sects have little to recommend them, but they are much more difficult to control than formal religious observance and their persistence is in great part due to the fact that they have become a kind of substitute for more fundamental religion. In the same way, stubborn adherence to such practices as *kalym* (bride-price) and child marriage, which have no connexion whatever with supernatural belief, is a kind of protest against cultural and social regimentation by foreigners.

In those regions which became Muslim as a result of the Arab conquest or of incorporation in the Persian empire social organization remained almost entirely Muslim until the coming of the Russians. Such matters as the ownership of land and other property, taxation, inheritance, justice, family life and particularly the status of women were regulated by *sharī'a* and *'āda*. Society also remained Muslim in the Volga region which had come under Russian domination in the sixteenth century. The nomads of the Kazakh Steppe probably remained untouched by Islam until the end of the fifteenth century, but by the coming of the Russians their social organization was largely Muslim, although the *sharī'a* had little application. During the Tsarist regime there was only minor interference with social structure and in 1917 the unit of Muslim society was still the communal family life consisting of the parents, the married sons (who remained in the family until the death of the father), unmarried daughters and grandchildren. The Soviet regime, on the other hand, considered that the very nature of Islamic society militated against the building of socialism, and therefore took active steps for its destruction such as the stabilization of the nomads, socialization of land and water rights, and finally, collectivization. Polygamy and the marriage of girls under eighteen were forbidden by law. Endogamy and the veiling of women were not actually made illegal, but were made the subject of vigorous propaganda campaigns. There is no doubt whatever that over forty years of regimentation, secular education, segregation from the outside world and service in the predominantly Russian armed forces have had a considerable effect on Islamic society. The old clan and joint family loyalties have almost, although not entirely, disappeared; the prescriptive right to own land, one of the most formidable obstacles encountered by the Revolution, is no longer recognized; and the Western way of life is everywhere gaining ground. But these are phenomena which are occurring all over the Muslim East, usually without any coercion or even encouragement on the part of governments. In the Muslim lands of the Soviet Union there has not only been coercion and encouragement to adopt a more modern and Western way of life, but the whole structure of society has been changed by the phenomenon of the artificially formed nation. The Muslims are now grouped not by tribes and clans as formerly, but by "nationalities". A nationality officially regarded as possessing a common language, territory, culture and economy qualifies as "a nation", and is constituted a Union Republic or an Autonomous Republic. Union Republics are those which border on foreign states with which they are in theory, but not in practice, allowed to have relations. There are six Muslim Union Republics and eight Autonomous Republics of which the titular, although not necessarily the majority nationalities are Muslim. Of the Autonomous Republics, however, only five bear the names of peoples who are regarded as nations, the Kabardians, also a nation, being combined with the Balkars (not a nation) in the Kabarda–Balkar ASSR. Some of the "nations" are only partly Muslim like the Ossetes and the Abkhaz.[1] Apart from the nationalities regarded as "nations", there is another category known as *narodnost'* which possesses some, but not all, of the criteria necessary for a nation. For example, the Chechens and Ingush possess only a territory and a literary language, while a whole range of other nationalities, mainly in the Caucasus, possess a literary language but no national territory.

[1] For the names of the various SSR and ASSR see the table on p. 170.

Officially all the Union and Autonomous Republics are said to be "fully sovereign", but this does not mean that they have any control over their affairs, the overriding authority being the Soviet government working through the agency of the Communist party. By any standards other than Soviet the creation of "nations" and *narodnost'* seems purely arbitrary, since some of the nations do not fulfil the four criteria and their very existence is dependent upon Moscow. Thus, during the Second World War, the Crimean Tatar, Kabarda–Balkar, and Chechen–Ingush Autonomous Republics were abolished and the peoples whose names they bore no longer had any status even as "nationalities", their very names ceasing to appear in any Soviet reference book. Since 1956, however, when all these people, with the exception of the Crimean Tatars, were rehabilitated and their ASSRs reconstituted, there has been no arbitrary creation or liquidation of ethnic formations.

The result of this re-grouping of peoples by nationalities, *narodnost'* and nations is not easy to determine. Although formed artificially, some of the Republics and particularly those in which the titular nationality has remained in the majority, have acquired a certain reality. This is partly due to forty years of indoctrination and propaganda, and partly to the fact that with the break-up of the old grouping of tribe and clan, the peoples have accepted the only form of grouping now permitted to them, namely, the nation. The whole matter is complicated by the Soviet principle that although nations may exist, nationalism must not, and that while the Republics may possess all the outward trappings of nationhood—national flags, national languages and national literatures—there is no such thing as national patriotism or national citizenship. In 1960, signs began to appear that the Soviet government had become dissatisfied with the artificial structure which it had so carefully created. The party programme adopted at the 22nd Party Congress of 1961 outlined a plan by which the same national distinctions which had previously been strongly emphasized were to be gradually eliminated until a single Soviet people with a single Soviet culture came into being. Since then, however, a note of indecision has been discernible in Soviet writing on the subject and at the time of writing (March 1965) it is impossible to say what the long-term plan of the Soviet government in respect of the Muslim nationalities is. As regards the attitude of the Muslim peoples themselves, it must be said that in the absence of any means of changing it, they accept the present situation with resignation.

Something which can be called national consciousness unquestionably exists in the sense that the people resent alien rule and alien colonization and attempts to regiment their ancient cultures. Somewhat ironically this consciousness has been partly awakened by Soviet education and propaganda which seem, however, to have failed to awaken an overriding or even corresponding Soviet patriotism. It is still difficult to say whether this national consciousness is a corporate feeling common to all Muslims, whether it operates independently among nationalities or groups of nationalities, or whether it centres on the artificially formed but by now partially crystallized republics.

Marxist–Leninist ideology takes the view that the highest form of culture is socialist culture which, having developed in different national forms and being profoundly international in character, ensures rapid adherence to a progressive culture, allows nations to preserve the best features of national cultures to the fullest extent, and contributes to their mutual enrichment. The standard Soviet description of the ideal culture for the Muslim as for the other republics of the Soviet Union is that it should be "national in form and socialist in essence". Up to the Revolution it would probably have been correct to say that the culture of the Muslim peoples of Russia was tribal or communal in form and Islamic in essence. Today, largely as a result of education and the development of national languages the *form* of culture is much more national than tribal. Whether it is more socialist or Soviet than Islamic in *essence* is doubtful. Some of the so-called socialist features of culture which have been introduced are merely modern accretions which have found their way into many non-Soviet Muslim countries and are accepted as a matter of course. If, according to one definition, "our culture is what we are, our civilization is what we use",[1] it could be said that the culture of the Muslims of the USSR is still Islamic, but that their civilization is rapidly becoming Soviet. Many convinced Muslim Communists, however, would probably prefer to think, if not to say, that their culture was national both in form and essence.

The steps taken by the Soviet regime to eradicate Islamic and establish socialist or Soviet culture include the development of education, linguistic reform, the organization of the creative arts, and atheistic propaganda. Taken as a whole the effect of these steps on the life of the Muslim peoples of the USSR has been very marked and a few words must be said about them. The development of technical and

[1] MacIver, *The Modern State* (London, 1926), p. 325.

general education among the Muslim peoples of the USSR is one of the most remarkable achievements of the Soviet regime. At the outbreak of the Revolution the average percentage of literacy among all the Muslim peoples, including the relatively advanced Tatars and Crimean Tatars, was probably not more than four or five. Today over 90 per cent literacy is claimed for the Muslim Republics, and although this may be an exaggeration and leaves out of account the fact that the population includes over 7,000,000 non-Muslims from the western part of the Union, there is no doubt that the standard of education is far higher than in the great majority of the Muslim countries of the Middle East and South Asia. The type of education is open to criticism on the ground that it is illiberal and is a complete breakaway from Muslim tradition. Much compulsion was necessary in the early years of the Revolution, but by and large the educational facilities now offered are eagerly sought after and have distracted attention from, if they have not actually compensated for, some of the less palatable restrictions imposed by the regime. In particular, the uniformity of the primary, secondary and higher educational systems throughout the Union has brought much more equality of opportunity than exists in other colonial empires.

From the beginning the Soviet regime attached the greatest importance to the question of language and the efforts which it has deployed in this matter have been prodigious. Three basic aims have been declared throughout: first, the "completion" and "enrichment" of existing languages, the widening of their scope and the transformation of tribal and community languages into developed national languages with a rich terminology and vocabulary; secondly, the removal of the large Arabic and Persian loan vocabulary inherited from the Muslim conquests; and thirdly, the establishment of Russian as "a second native language". Some progress has been made towards the achievement of all these aims, but most, perhaps, in the first. The first step taken was the abolition of the Arabic script in which all the languages of the Muslim peoples were written in so far as they were written at all. In 1929 a so-called Unified Latin Alphabet was introduced for all languages but this was replaced some ten years later by modified forms of the Cyrillic alphabet. School textbooks, grammars and dictionaries have been written for every language, a large part of Russian literature and most of the Communist classics have been translated into the vernaculars, and there is a growing if artificial literature in each of them. The effort to eliminate the Arabic and Persian element in Muslim languages has made less progress than was expected, even less, in fact, than has been made in Turkey. All new words taken into the languages are nowadays borrowed from Russian rather than Arabic and Persian as formerly; but a high percentage of words derived from the latter two languages remain and continue to give the languages an Islamic flavour. The third aim, that of making Russian "a second native language" has been pursued with great vigour, and the ultimate aim of Communist planners is undoubtedly that Russian should eventually become the *first* language in a multi-national State. Owing to the universal teaching of Russian in the primary and secondary schools and its indispensability for professional advancement, it has penetrated much more deeply into all walks of life in the Muslim lands of the USSR than English did in India during the British period. Although it is still theoretically possible for degree courses to be taken in local languages, Russian is in practice the medium of instruction in higher and technical education. The 1959 census shows a slight increase in the number of Muslims who declare Russian to be their "mother tongue", but the vernacular languages are displaying a remarkable staying power. They naturally vary very much in their adequacy as means of education and expression in a scientific age, and some of the smaller and less-developed languages are probably doomed to extinction. But they will not necessarily be supplanted by Russian, especially where they exist side by side with some relatively advanced language such as Azeri. It is noticeable, incidentally, that in Azerbayjan Russian is seldom the preferred language in scientific discussions. Generally speaking, it is improbable that the present position will change as long as the vernacular languages remain the medium of primary instruction in the schools.

The impact of the Soviet regime on the creative arts traditionally practised by the Muslims of Russia has been very great. Here the Soviet aim has been to remould these arts on socialist—and to a large extent—Russian lines. While showing deference to the achievements of the past in such fields as literature, architecture, ceramics and carpet-weaving, Soviet reformers have made it clear that the old motifs and styles are inapplicable to the present age and must be replaced. They have also been at pains to stimulate the practice of certain arts such as the drama, painting and sculpture which, owing mainly to Muslim inhibitions, were hitherto unknown. In literature the aim has been to create "national literatures" and "national presses" written mainly in the newly systematized national languages, although the idea of national literatures written in Russian has recently received some encouragement. Some idea of the enormous increase in writing and publishing can be gained from the following statistics for Kazakhstan: in 1913 13 books were published in Kazakh with a total print order of 4,000; in 1965, 569 books were published with a total print order of 8,137,000. In the same year there were in circulation 101 newspapers and seventeen periodicals. The technical literary quality of modern Soviet Muslim literature in the 1960s is probably as good as that of most other Muslim countries; but its artistic scope and the extent to which it reflects the progress of ideas either in the Soviet Muslim lands or in the world in general are limited by the Marxist–Leninist principle that the purpose of literature is the propagation of the great ideals of Communism and by the fact that writers are required to produce works of a characteristic national flavour about nations which are supposed to be rapidly losing their distinguishing national characteristics. When, however, they look for such characteristics in the past, they are apt to be accused of reactionary tendencies. It is, however, too early to pass judgment: the control of literature in respect of both of its contents and its forms by hierarchies of one kind or another, is not a new phenomenon. It has occurred before in the Islamic world and has not prevented the eventual emergence of vigorous and representative writing.

Great efforts have been made to encourage and develop the drama, music and fine arts; but only in the first two have these efforts met with a spontaneous public response. But while plays, operas, and concerts draw large Muslim audiences the marked preference for historical and literary themes and for traditional musical idiom is noted with disapproval by the authorities. The decline in traditional craftsmanship has been greater than elsewhere in the Muslim world, but there is now some hope that if the "cult of personality" continues to be condemned, carpet-weaving and wood-carving may be rescued from the curse of political portraiture. The entirely new arts of painting and sculpture are widely encouraged, but under present restrictions seem unlikely to form representative vehicles for native genius.

There are nowadays few Muslim countries where culture and the creative arts have not been affected to some extent by westernization. Only in the Soviet Union, however, is the conviction openly and constantly expressed that realization of the material benefits of modern civilization necessitates a complete transformation of traditional cultures and the dropping of all practices which conflict with the Western or Soviet notion of progress. The Soviet regime has from the beginning insisted that productivity and material welfare in the Muslim lands of the USSR are in direct proportion to the "sovietization" of culture and the decline of Islam.

The strict official control maintained inside the USSR over the practice of Islam and the relentless propaganda campaign waged against Islamic culture and the Islamic way of life naturally preclude any effective contact between Soviet Muslims and those of the outside world. A certain number of Muslims have been allowed to visit other Muslim countries for such purposes as pilgrimage and study in al-Azhar University and to hold posts in Soviet diplomatic missions. Like all Soviet citizens serving or travelling abroad such persons are very carefully selected and represent the Soviet attitude towards Islam in the USSR as one of complete toleration. At the same time, considerable efforts are made to convey the same impression of toleration and even of respect for Islam to delegations from non-Soviet Muslim countries to the USSR. Although the deleterious effect of the practice of Islam on the culture and economy of non-Soviet Muslim countries is a common theme in literature published in the Soviet Union, no such suggestion can be found in propaganda directed towards those countries. While the Soviet government is unquestionably right in thinking that any form of anti-Islamic or atheistic propaganda would not be tolerated in the outside Muslim world, it probably tends to overestimate the temporal power of Islam as a unifying political force among the countries professing it. This is certainly the impression gained from the articles on Islam in the Soviet *Philosophical Encyclopaedia* (1962) and the *Historical Encyclopaedia* (1964) written by the late Ye. Belyayev, a leading Soviet authority on Islam. The first of these articles states that "the national bourgeoisie, which holds sway in Muslim countries after having gained political independence, uses Islam as a spiritual instrument of power". After explaining that "in the period of the decline of the colonial system they [the pan-Islamists] aligned themselves with a pro-imperialist conception of Islam as 'a third force'—enrolled to fight simultaneously against Communism and Imperialism", the article goes on to say that now "the bourgeois ideologies of Islam, under the influence of the struggling masses, take part in the anti-imperialist movement and endow with the sanctity of religion such events as the establishment of Republican order in Egypt, the nationalization of the Suez Canal, and the formation of the UAR".

At one time the Soviet Union seems to have visualized its Muslim Republics acting as a kind of cultural bridgehead for the spread of Communism throughout the Muslim world. This plan, however, involved certain risks and seems to have been abandoned in favour of leaving Communism to develop in the non-Soviet Muslim countries by means of local Communist parties. On the surface, the results achieved by these parties are not great: in the middle 1950s the total party membership in the Arab countries and Turkey did not exceed 50,000 and the number has probably decreased since then. But Communist ideology has certainly made progress in the sense that its existence is now accepted and is considered—not necessarily correctly—as the motive force behind the Soviet Union and China. It is often regarded as certainly no worse and sometimes even as better than what is still thought of as Western imperialism. Muslim Communists both inside and outside the Soviet Union occasionally argue that there is a certain compatibility between Islam and Communism and that the two ideologies can therefore co-exist; but this view has been firmly rejected by orthodox Islam and Communism alike.[1] Alexandre Bennigsen, a leading French authority on the subject, has stated that co-existence is difficult to realize since it would be "possible only if the two doctrines were placed on an equal footing, which is the case neither in Soviet Russia, where Islam is relegated to the fringe of society, nor in the Middle Eastern countries, were life is still dominated by Islam". Any kind of *rapprochement* between the two ideologies inside the Soviet Union would be regarded by the authorities as tantamount to "national Communism" and as likely to lead in the same direction as the movement of Sultan Galiyev mentioned earlier.

Apart from the 47,000,000 Muslims of India, the Muslim peoples of the USSR constitute the largest Muslim community living in a state the majority of whose population is non-Muslim. It is not, however, correct to describe the Muslims of the USSR as "minorities",[2] since they are for the most part living in their own territory which was forcibly annexed by Russia during the eighteenth and nineteenth

[1] An article by ʿAlī Yalā, general secretary of the Moroccan Communist Party, in *Afrika i Aziya Segodnya*, no. 8, 1966, suggests a recent change of policy. See *Central Asian Review*, vol. xv, no. 1, p. 1.

[2] According to the Soviet definition the term minorities can be applied only to those people who live outside their national republics or who do not have such republics.

centuries. Compared with Muslim communities elsewhere their position displays many unusual and some unique features. Although the practice of Islam as a religion is not prohibited, as an ideology and as a way of life it is subjected to constant official criticism and even denigration. Religious instruction is completely excluded from the educational curriculum at all levels; the clergy are not regarded as having any social or intellectual status and are, apart from a handful of selected pilgrims to the Holy Places, effectively segregated from all contact with the outside Muslim world. By closing mosques, by restricting the number of clergy and by a number of other measures the Soviet regime has endeavoured to reduce the part played by Islam in the everyday life of the people. On the other hand, the standards of material existence, of general and technical education and of public health are generally speaking far higher among the Muslims of the USSR than in any other Muslim community in the world. Briefly, then, it can be said that while spiritually the Muslims of the USSR are under heavy restrictions, materially they are far better off than their co-religionists elsewhere. The orthodox Communist view is that eventually materialist considerations will prevail and that Islamic doctrine, practice and culture will be relegated to the limbo of outworn beliefs and superstitions. Up to the present, however, Communist expectations in this respect have not been fulfilled: the rapid and systematic westernization which has been part and parcel of the Soviet regime has probably had a greater effect on Muslim society in the USSR than elsewhere in the *dār al-Islām*, but the Islamic ways of life and of thought are still holding their own just as they did against the physical ravages of the Mongol invasions, of which scarcely a trace remains today.

Although there is no doubt about the hostile attitude of Communism and of the Soviet regime towards Islam, it is impossible to speak with precision of the corresponding attitude of the Muslim peoples of the USSR. Since the final suppression of the Basmachi revolt in the late 1920s, there has been no evidence of any organized resistance to the present regime on the part of the Muslims. It is now known and admitted by the Soviet authorities that the Great Purge of 1936–8 was not evoked by any nationalist movement either in the Muslim republics or elsewhere in the Union; but it was unquestionably the cause of the large-scale defections of Muslim soldiers to the Germans during the war. Only a very small proportion of these soldiers were able to avoid repatriation and the ultimate fate of the remainder is unknown. Since the war, material conditions have greatly improved; there are far more facilities for education and recreation, and life has generally become much easier for the Muslims as for the other peoples of the USSR. But quite apart from the memories of past trials and tribulations which must remain, there is undoubtedly an endemic resentment against alien rule and against the cultural regimentation which has resulted from it. Whether this resentment could find expression in nationalist movements of the kind which have shaken other colonial empires remains an open question. Those movements arose in circumstances which have not so far been present in the Soviet Union, circumstances which included the existence of easily identifiable national leaders with some freedom of speech and movement; the growth of liberal opinion in the metropolitan country; and moral and material aid from abroad. It must also be remembered that the 25,000,000 Muslims of the USSR are spread over a vast area and that among them are settled at least 10,000,000 non-Muslims, mostly Russians. But except for the last, all the existing conditions are susceptible of change, and in the meanwhile two positive circumstances persist: the staying power and resilience of Islamic culture and the relatively good material conditions of the Muslim peoples of the USSR.[1]

[1] The following items of information have been made known too late for inclusion in the text.

In 1966 it was officially stated in *Spravochnik Propagandista i Agitatora* [Propagandist and Agitator's Handbook] that there were in the USSR 400 mosques and "about 1,000 unregistered groups practising [Muslim] religious observances in their own homes".

In September 1967 a decree of the All-Union Supreme Soviet was published which "rehabilitated" the Crimean Tatars, who were described as "citizens of Tatar nationality who had formerly lived in the Crimea". Nothing was said about their return to their homeland or about the reconstitution of the Crimean ASSR. The majority of those deported in 1945 are now said to be living in the Uzbek SSR.

Muslims of the USSR

Nationality	Number (1959 census)	Political status	Main location
		I. TURKIC PEOPLES	
Uzbeks	6,004,000	Nation	Uzbek SSR
Tatars	4,969,000	Nation	Tatar ASSR
Kazakhs	3,581,000	Nation	Kazakh SSR
Azerbayjanis	2,929,000	Nation	Azerbayjan SSR
Turkmens	1,004,000	Nation	Turkmen SSR
Bashkirs	983,000	Nation	Bashkir ASSR
Kirgiz	974,000	Nation	Kirgiz SSR
Kara-Kalpaks	173,000	Nation	Kara-Kalpak ASSR
Kumyks	135,000	Narodnost'	Dagestan ASSR
Uygurs	95,000	Narodnost'	Kazakh and Kirgiz SSRs
Karachays	81,000	Narodnost'	Karachay-Cherkess Autonomous Oblast
Balkars	42,000	Narodnost'	Kabarda–Balkar ASSR
Nogays	41,000	Narodnost'	Karachay–Cherkess A.O
		II. IRANIAN PEOPLES	
Tajiks	1,397,000	Nation	Tajik SSR
Ossetes (partly Muslim)	410,000	Nation	North-Ossete ASSR
Kurds	59,000	Foreign minority or Narodnost'	Armenian SSR
Iranians	21,000	Foreign minority	Soviet Central Asia
Tats	11,000	Narodnost'	Azerbayjan SSR
Baluchis	7,800	Foreign minority	Turkmen SSR
		III. IBERO-CAUCASIAN PEOPLES	
Chechens	418,000	Narodnost' developing into nation	Chechen–Ingush ASSR
Kabardians	204,000	Nation	Kabarda–Balkar ASSR
Ingush	106,000	Narodnost'	Chechen–Ingush ASSR
Adyges	80,000	Narodnost's developing into nation	Karachay–Cherkess A.O.
Cherkess	30,000		
Abkhaz (partly Muslim)	74,000	Nation	Abkhaz ASSR
Abaza	20,000	Narodnost'	Karachay–Cherkess A.O.
Avars	268,000	Narodnost'	Dagestan ASSR
Lezgins	223,000	Narodnost'	
Dargins	158,000	Narodnost'	
Laks	64,000	Narodnost'	
Tabasarans	35,000	Narodnost'	
Aguls	8,000	Narodnost'	
Rutuls	7,000	Narodnost's in process of disappearing	
Tsakhurs	6,000		
		IV. MISCELLANEOUS	
Dungans	21,000	Narodnost'	Kazakh and Kirgiz SSRs
Arab	8,000	Foreign minority	Soviet Central Asia
Albanians (partly Muslim)	5,000	Foreign minority	—

CHAPTER 8

ISLAM IN NORTH-WEST AFRICA (*MAGHRIB*)

Maghrib is an Arabic word which denotes the place where the sun sets. The *Jazīrat al-Maghrib*, that is to say literally "the Island of the setting sun", consists of that part of Africa which includes Morocco, Algeria, Tunisia, Cyrenaica and Tripolitania. This geographical entity, often called Barbary by European historians on account of its inhabitants, and bounded by the Mediterranean on the north and by the Atlantic on the west, is in fact isolated from the African continent to the south by the great stretches of desert sand which the Arabs, with their sense of poetry, have said to be of tawny colour, *ṣaḥrā'*, from which the geographers have derived the word Sahara.

In the pages that follow, the term Barbary will be restricted to the long narrow quadrilateral containing the three countries which used to form what, until recently, was known as French North Africa or simply as North Africa.

Because the African inhabitants of these regions, being for the most part rustics and nomads, in general proved hostile to their system of civilization, the Romans termed them barbarians, whence comes the word "Berbers" retained by the Arabs. Closely attached to their Atlas mountains, scattered throughout the high plains and plateaux of their "island", these highly independent peoples, devoted to their traditions and liberties, tough and warlike, have never succeeded in establishing for any length of time a political unity comparable with that of European countries.

They saw in succession on their territory, from ancient times until the first half of the seventh century, first Phoenicians, then Romans, Vandals and Byzantines. The first, being simply merchants, were content to set up trading stations on their coasts. The second, on the other hand, occupied militarily that part of the country that seemed to them the most useful and the easiest to govern. There they maintained troops, built military posts, laid down roads, introduced their urban civilization and established a strong administrative organization. Christianity had followed romanization. Thus, in the middle of

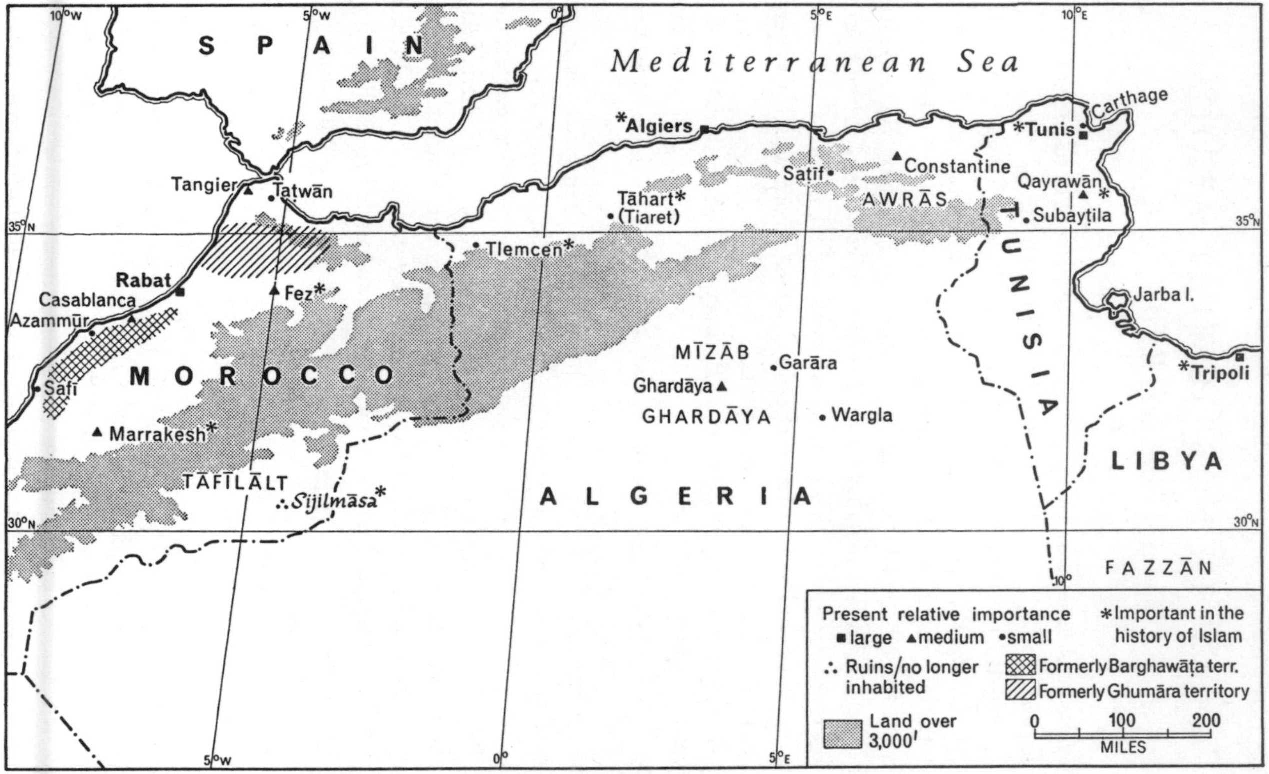

North-West Africa.

the third century, there were some twenty bishoprics in Numidia alone; and, from its base at Carthage, facing Rome, the teaching of Christ spread out over Africa.

The weakening of Rome and the Vandal invasions, during the first quarter of the fifth century, resulted in the birth of a strong Berber resistance which relied on sedentary elements in Numidia and on nomadic camel-drivers from Tripolitania. In fact, the events which were to follow showed that fifteen hundred years of history had flowed over the Berbers without altering their character. Neither Phoenicians nor Romans, Vandals nor Byzantines had succeeded in conquering them or in making any lasting impression on them. Innovations brought into their "island" they either rejected or allowed to perish in oblivion. In the towns to which Rome had brought her administrative tradition, her concept of civilization and her language, they adhered only for a while to this way of life which soon fell into decline. Elsewhere, in rural and nomadic circles, the *imazighen*, the freemen, the nobles, as they styled themselves, remained completely faithful to their own nature, unconquered and as it were suspended outside history.

It is a fact worth noting that there seems to have been a total incompatibility between the European genius of Rome and that of the Berbers. The religion of Christ, though gentle and tender in its tenets, was deeply riven in Barbary by the appalling convulsions of Donatism, the episode of the Circumcelliones, and the excesses of the Vandals' Arianism; in these storms it was torn apart, like a worn-out garment. The Berbers, who with their lack of imagination never invent anything, though they assimilate readily, showed in these circumstances that they could forget just as easily. Perhaps a sure biological instinct impelled them to do so. Islam, victorious where Rome and Christianity had failed, seems to represent the universe best suited to their character, and in any case it is thanks to Islam alone that they have been brought into history as a nation. Moreover, the Arabs who introduced this religion among them and whom they fought tenaciously, resembled them from many points of view. They were rough nomads, barbarians like themselves by Roman standards. Their unqualified monotheism, stated simply in the profession of faith, the *shahāda*—"There is no other god than Allāh, and Muḥammad is His prophet"—was admirably suited to their mentality. The Arabs did not interfere with their customs. The idea of making the inhabitants become sedentary, as the Romans had done, could not have occurred to them. Muslim universality and the Arabs' nomadic instinct could never have conceived the marking out of a *limes* in the Roman fashion; that is to say, a frontier between the territories won over for civilization by religion and those given over to barbarism for administrative reasons or on account of non-profitability.

The triumph of Islam in Barbary is the result of an ideological conquest for, in the last resort, the Berbers remained victorious on the battlefield. We do not find an Arab kingdom being set up in that country, with a strong administrative framework and maintained by a powerful, disciplined, well-organized army to rule over a conquered nation. Except for the relatively short period of the history of the Arab invasion during which the natives had to endure the yoke of foreign governors, the eastern caliphs did not succeed in subjecting Barbary to their authority. And yet, where Rome had only been able to transfer her legions and to be confined to the towns together with Christianity, Islam was to conquer the masses of countryfolk and peasants and to spread its teaching and its faith, slowly but with certainty, in successive infiltrations.

The whole process of conquest lasted about seventy years. The time taken would have been less if the eastern caliphate had not also had to face serious internal difficulties. But in fact these seventy years, which were to overthrow the political equilibrium of the Mediterranean, seem little when one thinks of the negative outcome of the preceding fifteen hundred years of history. From the Phoenicians, from Rome, from Byzantium, all that remained in Barbary was ruins, archaeological memories. The century of Vandal domination had left no trace. One true conqueror alone appears on the threshold of this new age, Allāh-Yahveh, the holy God, the God of battle of the Old Testament. At the head of modest contingents of pillaging Bedouins, he conquered the old Baal of Carthage and overthrew the cross of Christ, victoriously brought fire and sword to a country which, never before having had the chance to develop its own individuality, appeared, in order to achieve this, to be awaiting the mystical and bloodstained union of the Berber people with Islam.

After taking three-quarters of a century to force an entry into the Maghrib, Islam was then to gain a hold over both hearts and minds, but after what vicissitudes! The most resolute and best organized resistance came from the latinized Berbers and the Byzantines. The obscure masses of animist pagans without historical consciousness were the easiest to win over to the teachings of the new faith. But this docile receptiveness was fraught with danger, and the Arabs realized how deceptive it was when they found with what eagerness the neo-Muslims apostatized. Although accepted as a creed, the Arabs' religion aroused the distrust and anger of the natives when it meant their subjection to arrogant and avaricious governors, heavy taxes unfairly levied and all the exactions of a contemptuous and brutal Arab soldiery. The first move was immediately to apostatize. Instances are recorded of tribes which apostatized as many as eight times. But this reaction which in a sense was negative and unfruitful and raised dangerous possibilities was very soon to dwindle away and disappear. Around towns such as Qayrawān, Tunis, Tlemcen and Fez (which was founded at the beginning of the ninth century) Islam established itself with missionaries, theologians and jurists gathered together beside their mosque. Ifrīqiya, that is to say the province corresponding to the modern Tunisia and the region of Constantine, the earliest to be occupied, was the first to be islamized. In the eighth century it made a final break with its Punic, Roman and Greek past. At the same time, at the other end of Barbary, Islam was infiltrating the Jewish and pagan tribes, from the bases of Fez and Tlemcen, thanks to the dynasty of the Idrīsids founded by Idrīs I, a descendant of the family of the Prophet. One can imagine what difficulties the propagandists of the faith had to face simply as a result of their ignorance of the Berber dialects and of the difficulty that the natives had in taking to Arabic. Indeed, for them religion could only consist of ritual and practice. For any considerable participation by the Berber element in juridical and theological studies in the towns and suburbs, we have to wait until the ninth century; moreover, this observation applies particularly to Ifrīqiya, where ancient cultural traditions existed.

But if the progress of orthodox, or Sunnī, Islam encountered great difficulties, this fact was also due to the impassioned religious temperament of the Berbers and their love of independence. Every time they thought they had discovered in some schismatic form of the religion a way of escaping from the overlordship of the East, they plunged into it with the zeal, warlike ardour and mortal fury that had been shown by their schismatic Christian ancestors.

It is, however, to the schisms in particular that we must direct our attention, since the movements to which they gave rise made a positive contribution towards the islamization of the Maghrib, preparing the ground for the complete triumph of orthodoxy.

The earliest of them, that of the sect of Khārijites, had plunged the east in bloodshed without, however, succeeding in bringing about the creation of a theocratic state, as in Africa. The followers of this sect took their origin from the quarrel that led to armed conflict between 'Alī, son-in-law of the Prophet Muḥammad, and Mu'āwiya, the powerful governor of Syria. Their doctrine was made up of a juxtaposition of conservative and revolutionary ideas. On the one hand, they maintained that the caliph could only bear the title of *imām* which, in its narrowest sense, signifies director of prayer, and that it was necessary for him to preserve the strict tradition of the Prophet, and his first two successors at the head of the community, Abū Bakr and 'Umar; on the other hand, unlike the aristocratic doctrine of Sunnī Islam, they believed that this same caliph could be chosen from any social class whatever. It is possible for a negro slave, they said, to seek to win the title and to secure it, provided he be worthy of the office.

The Khārijite ethic is of the utmost strictness. Faith is not sufficient without works and without great moral purity. Any sullying of the conscience, such as evil thoughts or lying words, leads to excommunication or even death. As revolutionaries, democrats, intransigent puritans, the Khārijites found in Barbary a setting eminently favourable for their enterprise. The populace, cruelly oppressed and humiliated by despotic governors, were ready to rise at the slightest signal.

In 740 the rising broke out in Morocco, in the region of Tangier, under the leadership of a humble water-carrier named Maysara. From this bloody episode were born the Khārijite kingdoms in the region of Tlemcen, from Tāfīlālt to Sijilmāsa, and in particular around the town of Tāhart, near the modern Tiaret, founded by an eastern prince of Persian origin, Ibn Rustam. This last kingdom survived from 761 until 909. Throughout this period, Tāhart was a centre of religious studies which contributed powerfully to the spread of Islam in the central Maghrib.

The second eastern schism to meet with great success in the Maghrib was the one instigated by sectarians fanatically devoted to direct descendants of the Prophet through Fāṭima, his daughter, and 'Alī, his son-in-law.

Of the Shī'ī doctrine, one aspect alone was of a kind to appeal to the Africans, namely the profound veneration that it professed for the

Prophet's descendants. But the imprecations and curses heaped upon his pious successors Abū Bakr, 'Umar and 'Uthmān, the modifications made in the orthodox form of worship, the scandalous conduct of certain Fāṭimid caliphs and their dire need of money were a serious obstacle to the spiritual conquest of the natives. Towards the middle of the eleventh century, the Berber feudatories of Qayrawān broke away from their masters who had settled in Cairo. It was the end of the Shī'ī schism in Barbary. It had indeed never succeeded in taking root in the centre and west, or in really winning over the jurists and scholars of Ifrīqiya whose influence over the whole country was at that period preponderant.

This repudiation had extraordinary consequences for the people of the whole of Barbary, from the social, economic and religious aspects. In order to punish his Berber vassal for his action, the Fāṭimid caliph sent forward against the Maghrib the dreaded Arab tribes of the Banū Hilāl and the Banū Sulaym who were then infesting Upper Egypt. Henceforward, by means of a slow but continuous advance, these nomadic Arabs were to settle down in Barbary itself. From Ifrīqiya to the western Maghrib, for several centuries, they spread out over the countryside and the desert regions, impoverishing the great urban centres, holding the inhabitants to ransom and transforming rich, cultivated and well-wooded areas into steppes. However, they did not drive back the inhabitants as they went; in the end, they became fused with them in such a way that, in all the parts of the Maghrib accessible to them, a new Arabo-Berber population came into being. For the same reason, the Arabic language which, before this new invasion, had been spoken only in the towns and surrounding suburbs was to penetrate deeply into the country. What the Arabs of the conquest had been unable to achieve, these barbarian nomads were to bring about. The arabization of the Maghrib was to leave the way wide open for islamization.

In short, through the Arabic language Allāh, the god of nomadic shepherds, the same God whom the patriarch Abraham, fleeing from the abhorred great cities, had worshipped, was certain of ultimate triumph in the Maghrib on account of these tribes, even though their devotion to the Muslim faith was tepid and their religious convictions nil. Once again, history proved to be the accomplice of Islam.

At the very moment when the Hilālian and Sulaymite hordes were spreading out over Ifrīqiya, in southern Morocco some Berbers, also nomads, who had come from the Sahara and who closely resembled the modern Tuareg, embarked upon the methodical conquest of Morocco. In this instance it was not a matter of anarchic masses seeking for a home, but rather of a strictly orthodox reform movement. These warriors of the faith had been trained in the strict discipline of religion and the holy war in one of the fortified monasteries called *ribāṭ* in Arabic. The persons gathered together at one of these centres were given the name *murābiṭ* from which the name "Almoravid" is derived, denoting those Berbers who were veiled and rode on camels.

The Almoravid dynasty, founded and advanced by the talented Yūsuf b. Tāshufīn (1106), established its domination over the Maghrib as far as the meridian of Algiers and added the territories of Muslim Spain to its African possessions.

Established Maghribī Islam is indebted for certain of its general characteristics to these Saharans—uncompromising orthodoxy, devoted adherence to the narrow conservative juridical school of Mālik b. Anas, and marked hostility to the spirit of philosophy and free enquiry. Almoravid Islam, denuded of spiritual life and with a notorious anti-mystical trend, was in fact the Islam of the caste of jurists, the *fuqahā'*, who were more concerned with the administration of legal procedure than with spiritual elevation. It lasted only about a hundred years, from the second half of the eleventh century until the second half of the twelfth, but its reign is very important, for it inaugurated Berber participation in the development of North African Islam.

Far more complex and richer from the doctrinal point of view, the Almohad reform movement was launched during the first quarter of the twelfth century by the Berber theologian Ibn Tūmart (d. 1130), a native of southern Morocco. Small in stature and deformed, but with an indomitable will, leading an ascetic life, preaching and writing in Berber, translating the Qur'ān into that language, this leader of the new reform represented himself as the *mahdī*, infallible, impeccable and entrusted with the hidden verities handed down by the Prophet to his son-in-law 'Alī. The Shī'ī side of the doctrine did not fail to influence the mountain-dwellers of the Atlas.

But the fundamental point of this teaching was the assertion of divine unicity. The term "Almohad" which is applied to these new sectarians derives from the Arabic expression *al-muwaḥḥid* which means "the proclaimer of divine unicity".

As the Almohad theologians conceived it, the divinity was wholly abstract. Its attributes—sight, hearing, speech—could not be regarded as distinct from its essence, any more than they could lead to an anthropomorphic representation. Nothing resembles God, they maintained; he occupies no place in space; and man attains knowledge of him by means of reason.

Intellectualism and rationalism were the weak points of the system. They were ill-suited to the religious mentality of the Berbers, who love and search for a concrete divine presence. This they were to find through the help of men who loved God, the saints both living and dead, the recipients of the divine influx, of the mysterious *baraka* which protects human beings from the actions of malevolent powers.

In addition, the *mahdī* called into question the works of jurisprudence (*fiqh*) of the juridical schools founded by the great exegetes, who could be regarded as the fathers of the Muslim church, four of the most celebrated of these being acknowledged and respected by the whole community. In the eighth and ninth centuries these pious and scholarly men had defined, with certain differences of method, the legislative bases upon which Muslim society was to be constructed, starting from the Qur'ān, the Tradition of the Prophet and of the Companions. The writings of one of them, Mālik b. Anas (d. 795) author of a famous work, the *Muwaṭṭa'* (the level path), were received as authoritative in the Maghrib and in Andalusia. Mālikism, the juridical system of Mālik, had been accepted first in Ifrīqiya, then in the rest of the country, thanks to the works of Qayrawān scholars. Ibn Tūmart advocated a return to the direct study of the sources of law. He rejected Mālik's authority and violently condemned the Mālikī *fuqahā'*. He reproved them, and indeed with reason, for their pedestrian spirit, their dry casuistry and the pecuniary profits that they made from their exalted position. He accused them of ruining all spirituality in Islam, of tolerating anthropomorphic beliefs and evil habits, and of inspiring the persecutions directed by the authorities against the followers of the great eastern mystic al-Ghazālī (d. 1111), the originator of a doctrine that sought to integrate Ṣūfism (*taṣawwuf*), that is to say the spiritual exercises and methods of prayer of mystics, into Islam.

On overcoming the Almoravid dynasty in about 1147, the Almohads founded a vast Berber and Muslim empire, a unique and glorious moment in the history of the Maghrib. The Almohad rule extended as far as Tripolitania and included Muslim Spain. But, when in about 1270 the splendid edifice began to crumble, the doctrinal system of the *mahdī* had ceased to exist for some thirty years. The eighteenth caliph of the dynasty, al-Ma'mūn, had specifically condemned Ibn Tūmart's claims to rank as impeccable *mahdī*, and proclaimed everything that he and his successors had done to be heretical.

In the political sphere, Barbary was returning to anarchy. From the religious point of view, it was officially returning to orthodoxy.

The history of the Muslim Maghrib is as much the history of a religion as of a people. From the time of the penetration of Islam into this part of Africa until the thirteenth century, the wars which took place there were exclusively wars of religion. The constitutions of kingdoms and empires were based upon the religious idea. They defended themselves, they attacked, they built, they destroyed in the name of religion. We do not find any single state or group of states being established outside the sphere of religious disputes. By reason of its fundamental character, which makes no distinction between the sacred and the secular, Islam tolerated only the theocratic state. This perished together with the dynasty which had founded it; as for the dynasty, it relied on the ethnic group which had brought it to power. As soon as the clansmen degenerated and lost their warlike spirit, the dynasty's power declined and its reign came to an end. In this way historical events served to illustrate the sentiment deeply rooted in the Muslim soul, that there is no eternity save that of God, and that there is no conqueror other than He.

The Almoravid and Almohad dynasties, in roughly two centuries, assured the final victory of orthodoxy. Heresies were extirpated. The Shī'ī schism miscarried. All that remained of Khārijism was two small communities, in Mīzāb in southern Algeria and in the Tunisian island of Jarba. This situation was not altered when, from the fifteenth century, the Turks settled in Algiers and Tunis, but they did introduce the juridical school of Abū Ḥanīfa into the central and eastern Maghrib.

On account of its adherence to orthodox Islam, the Maghrib therefore welcomed the official text of the Qur'ān established by order of the third caliph after the Prophet, 'Uthmān (d. 656), and later put into its definitive form during the tenth century through the efforts of seven specially chosen doctors.

Of the four principal juridical schools, that of Mālik b. Anas gained recognition, as has been said, owing to the work of a revered scholar of Qayrawān, named Ṣaḥnūn (d. 854). To elaborate his system, Mālik naturally relied on the Qur'ān, and afterwards on the Tradition of the Prophet and the Companions. In addition, he invoked the customary law of the town of Medina and the commonly held opinion, or consensus (*ijmā'*) of the doctors of that town. The part allotted to personal opinion (*ra'y*) was reduced to a minimum; the same was true of the principle of analogy (*qiyās*) since he envisaged only occasional resort to these procedures, in contrast to the practice in the school of Abū Ḥanīfa, where it was precisely the speculative methods of elaboration of the law that had to preponderate. It will also be noted that, in comparison with the school of another jurist, al-Shāfi'ī (d. 820) who, for his part, extended the consensus of doctors to include the whole of a given period, the *madhhab* of Mālik is characterized by a quite clearly marked conservative tendency very much to the taste of the Maghribīs. The way in which, for centuries, the Māliki manuals such as the *Risāla* of Ibn Abī Zayd al-Qayrawānī (d. 896) or the *Mukhtaṣar* of Sīdī Khalīl (d. 1374) were constantly repeated in the mosques and *madrasas* reveals a cast of mind which is still the despair of modern teachers.

As regards the idea of God, the orthodox and very prudent thesis which recommends acceptance of the dogma without asking too many questions and without trying to establish dangerous comparisons (*bilā kayfa wa lā tashbīh*) has also been accepted. God sees and hears. Has he eyes and ears like human beings? Are his attributes distinct from his essence? Generally speaking, the reply is—"No allegorical interpretations. Keep to the text of the Qur'ān". After that, if a certain anthropomorphic tendency appears in the minds of simple, ingenuous believers of no great culture, that is no reason to put whole tribes to the sword, as the Almohads did.

Similarly with the other problems put before the Muslim community by rationalist theologians in the eighth and ninth centuries, whether it was a question of choosing between the thesis of the creation of the Qur'ān, or of its eternal character; of man's free will or of the divine compulsion which influences him in the performance of his actions, the definitive solutions proposed by orthodoxy in the tenth century were welcomed in cultured circles, and integrated into the Muslim creed in Africa, without difficulty. The idea that the Qur'ān is eternal, like Allāh, and that the latter is the all-powerful master of men's actions seems to the Berber mentality to be better founded and more worthy of the divine majesty than any other doctrine which held the contrary view. One merely has to see with what care old men of the faith will pick up, in the streets, scraps of paper bearing Arabic characters and put them in a safe place to realize the reverence felt for the language used by Allāh to reveal to men their sacred book. Very similarly, the acquiescence in God's will expressed by the popular *maktūb*, the "it is written", which so shocks the modernists and activists of nationalism, remains one of the foundations of the fatalistic philosophy of the people and perhaps their greatest consolation.

But, to be frank, an Islam of this kind, even though tinged with anthropomorphism, and a God so aloof and difficult of approach who removes every intermediary between himself and his creatures, could not fully satisfy the religious needs of the Berbers. From the eleventh and twelfth centuries, in the most remote parts of the countryside as well as in the towns, certain individuals appeared among the people whose behaviour was different from that of scholars and jurists. These new men preached in the open air; they fasted, and lived like hermits. They took a vow of poverty, their clothes were patched. They wandered along the roads, apparently aimlessly, leaning on pilgrims' staffs. Sometimes they settled in isolated hermitages. For the most part they were not learned men or intellectuals. In any case, they were poor and humble, and ultimately their witness was worth more than mere knowledge. Such were the *awliyā'*, the neighbours of God, His friends. They made the presence of the divinity become more perceptible and closer to the poor. They were the direct product of those associations of celebrated Ṣūfīs, made illustrious by the great names of Muslim mysticism, and whose teaching spread from the east to Andalusia and the Maghrib.

The Ṣūfī teaching proved fruitful. From it came the worship of saints, both living and dead, and the astonishing proliferation of *ikhwān* (brothers) and *fuqarā'* (poor men) grouped into confraternities. These religious associations came into being through the creation of houses of instruction and residence, the famous *zāwiya* which, for this church of mystics, are the counterpart of what the *madrasas* of orthodox Islam are for the *fuqahā'* and the *'ulamā'*.

In the *zāwiya* the methods of prayer proper to the order were practised, and the respect due to men of God observed. But we must not deceive ourselves. The adoration of the saints entrusted with the *baraka* was not disinterested. What was expected of the saint was that he should protect the clan, and their homeland from the schemes of any possible enemies or, for example, from the exactions of the governor representing the central power. He was asked to intercede with Allāh to obtain good harvests, rain in times of drought and protection for herds and orchards. The saint was in fact a replica of the magician or healer of pagan antiquity. His mausoleum often stood close to a spring, among trees held to be sacred or on the top of a hill. Thus, though duly islamized, the old nature cults dedicated to the woods, streams and caves, the magic rites for securing the help of beneficent powers and the techniques for warding off evil forces still survived.

This explains how it is that the *baraka* takes a leading place in the Arabo-Berbers' daily life. But to realize its full importance, it is necessary to bear in mind that, for these simple people who have remained close to ancient ancestral traditions, the sublunary world is a mysterious ground in which all kinds of good or evil forces are at work.

Pre-eminent among these is the influence of the *jinns*, whose existence is attested by the Qur'ān. These creatures haunt the undergrowth, rivers, cemeteries and rocks. They can assume the forms of animals and humans. Some of them are even Muslim. The evil eye is a constant threat, from which people protect themselves by wearing amulets. The most efficacious of these talismans is a small hand, made of silver, which jewellers offer for sale and which still enjoys great success. The five fingers of the talisman obstruct the injurious rays emitted by an envious or covetous eye, or the eye of an old woman, or an eye rendered suspect by its colour. This ancient belief is widely spread over a large part of the world, and in Africa it assumes all the more importance in that the Qur'ān has also incorporated it in the Muslim faith.

In such a life, in which people are daily compelled to ward off misfortune and, in the last resort, to direct it against others, oaths, blessings, and curses form part of the ordinary round. Conversations, disputes, quarrels, and promises are always full of them. Men swear by God the Immense, by a saint, by the Qur'ān. They pour a stream of curses on their enemies, wishing them the worst calamities; but they call for God's blessing on their parents and friends. Very fortunately, the *baraka* protects those in whom it dwells, and others who live in contact with these privileged persons.

The first to have enjoyed the divine benediction was the Prophet. This he transmitted to his descendants, the *shorfa* (classical Ar. *shurafā'*, pl. of *sharīf*). In Morocco, the dynasty of the Sa'dīs and the present dynasty of the 'Alawīs which succeeded it are reputed to be Sharīfian, which means that since the beginning of the sixteenth century the *baraka* has to some extent been officialized in the person of the sultan and the actual ruling prince. Algeria and Tunisia, having been occupied by the Turks, did not have the opportunity to follow the same path.

The *baraka* can be acquired by a pious life, the recital of the Qur'ān, the observance of the five daily prayers and the fast of Ramaḍān, and by the pilgrimage to Mecca. It was in this way that the saints acquired it when they did not inherit it from the Prophet. Possession of it is attributed to certain animals, such as the horse, the ram and the camel, to some extent; to the bee, the cicada, the swallow, the eel; to some vegetables, such as the cereals; to some fruits, for example the date. The uneven numbers one, three and seven and certain proper names also benefit from it.

The cult of the saints, transformed into human fetishes known as marabouts (from the dialectal Arabic *mraboṭ*), and Sharīfism, that is to say the veneration shown for the *shorfa*, were of great assistance to the Moroccans when, in the fifteenth and sixteenth centuries, they had to face the Portuguese attacks on the coasts of Morocco. It will be recalled that Algeria and Tunisia were at that time occupied by the Turks. These two provinces then became dependencies of an eastern sultanate which, however, was powerful and possessed a good army and navy. Morocco, for its part, faced the enemy alone, and the central authority was incapable of organizing an effective resistance. It was the marabouts and the religious confraternities who took the lead. The popular holy war which followed gave Maghribī Islam a very pronounced tinge of fanaticism and xenophobia which remained one of its characteristic features until the coming of the French to North Africa.

At a very early time orthodox Islam had fought against ancient beliefs or practices which were looked upon either as pre-Islamic survivals or as detestable innovations (*bida*ʿ). The spread of public education and the powerful reform movement inaugurated in the last century by the Afghan Jamāl al-Dīn and his Egyptian disciple Shaykh Muḥammad ʿAbduh greatly helped to purify the faith among the bourgeois elements. The political role of the confraternities was now reduced to a minimum, but the worship of saints was maintained intact at popular levels. Prolonged contact with the West has not weakened the faith; indeed, on the contrary, it has strengthened it when it has not made it more fanatical. A section of the Maghribī intelligentsia does in fact incline towards agnosticism or atheism, but the great majority remains no less faithful to the Muslim community. Having lost its content, Islam is turning into a will to rule. If the practice of the five daily prayers seems fairly lax, the celebration of the canonical festivals, the Great Festival (*al-'īd al-kabīr*), marked by the sacrifice of a ram, on the tenth day of Dhu 'l-Ḥijja, the Lesser Festival (*al-'īd al-ṣaghīr*) which ends the month of fasting of Ramaḍān, the birth of the Prophet (*mūlūd*, classical Ar. *mawlid*) and *'ashūrā'*, which falls on the 10th of Muḥarram, are all occasions of great popular rejoicing. The pilgrimage to Mecca would draw crowds if it were less onerous. The return of pilgrims from the east gives rise to the most effusive family festivities. The fast of Ramaḍān enjoys a respect which no one would deliberately dare to imperil. In regard to this social rite, local pressure is so strong that everyone knows what he is risking when he braves popular sentiment by starting to eat in public, or to light a cigarette in the street during the daylight hours when fasting is imposed. Wearing the veil is mostly practised by townswomen and is tending to be given up by the younger generations who have attended schools. In modernist circles it is admitted that polygamy is an outmoded institution. The eating of pig's flesh is for the most part regarded with stubborn disgust. The same can hardly be said of alcoholic beverages. But the ancient Semitic pact of alliance with God, circumcision, still remains a firmly established custom.

The proclamation of independence in the three countries of the Maghrib opens a new period in the history of the ancient Barbary. The two republics of Tunis and Algiers and the venerable Moroccan monarchy, realizing that the formulae of the caliphate and imamate are out of date, are trying to preserve the structure of the State built up by France, while at the same time doing their utmost to fashion institutions that meet the national aspirations of peoples responsible for their destiny.

In this creative effort, it may be said that there has been constant recourse to Islam. The Tunisian Constitution affirms that the state religion is Islam and that its head must necessarily be Muslim. The same is true of Morocco. Different articles in the Fundamental Law of 2 June 1961, promulgated by the king, proclaim that Morocco is an Arabic, Muslim kingdom and that education provided in the country must be Arabic and Islamic. The republican Socialist Algeria is no exception. She declares herself to be Muslim and an integral part of the Arab world. Such is the power of this religion in this part of Africa, such is the prestige of the language and culture to which it is bound, that the Berber Maghrib wishes to be Arab.

The taste for reverie, the attraction of all forms of violence and the passion for justice and independence are all so strongly felt by the Maghribīs that the most widely varied and unexpected doctrines have the possibility of achieving success there, even if only ephemeral, provided only that Islam has furnished them with a reassuring aspect or imbued them with its own substance.

In the Maghrib, the history of Islam still continues.

CHAPTER 9

ISLAM IN THE SUDAN[1]

During the last 150 years Sudanese Islam has been exposed to four different influences from four different ruling institutions.

The Turco-Egyptian regime which dominated the territory from 1820 to 1881 gave Sudanese Muslims not only their first experience of unification under a single political authority but their first introduction to the Islamic establishment of the Ottoman empire, Sunnite, doctrinally orthodox, unfanatical. Throughout these years the judges, largely recruited from Egyptian, and latterly Sudanese, graduates of al-Azhar University, Cairo, administered the official Ḥanafī code in a country whose Muslim inhabitants were Mālikīs. The Ṣūfist ingredient in Sudanese Islam, represented by the local *faqīhs* and the *ṭarīqas*, the religious brotherhoods, were discountenanced by the official *'ulamā'* who, as elsewhere in the Ottoman realm, were generally public servants and consistent upholders of the government.

A new influence was that of Muḥammad Aḥmad b. 'Abdallāh al-Mahdī whose theocracy replaced the Turco-Egyptian rule in a violent upsurge. Wahhābite in his puritanism, the Mahdī was hostile on the one hand to the moral laxity of the Turks and on the other to the Ṣūfist tendencies of the popular religion. He imposed the doctrine of his own Mahdīship and a scripturally-inspired social and legal system. He freed the judges from adherence to any of the four codes and the people from the obligation to make the pilgrimage to the Holy Places of Arabia.

The Anglo-Egyptian Condominium, in power from 1899 to 1955, brought a third influence to bear on Sudanese Islam. This regime restored the primacy of the Azharite *'ulamā'* and the use by the judges of the Ḥanafī code. The British, the dominant partners in the Condominium, confined the Islamic law to the realm of Muslim private

[1] This chapter was written in 1965 and consequently lacks comment on such later developments as the emergence of the Muslim Brothers as a popular force in the struggle for political power; the tensions within the Mahdist community; the possibility of a modification of the present secular state by the adoption of a constitution inspired by Islamic principles; the assumption in 1966 of full University status by the *Ma'had al-'Ilmī* as the Islamic University of Omdurman, and the recent efforts by the government and the Christian churches to reach a settlement of outstanding issues in the Southern Sudan.

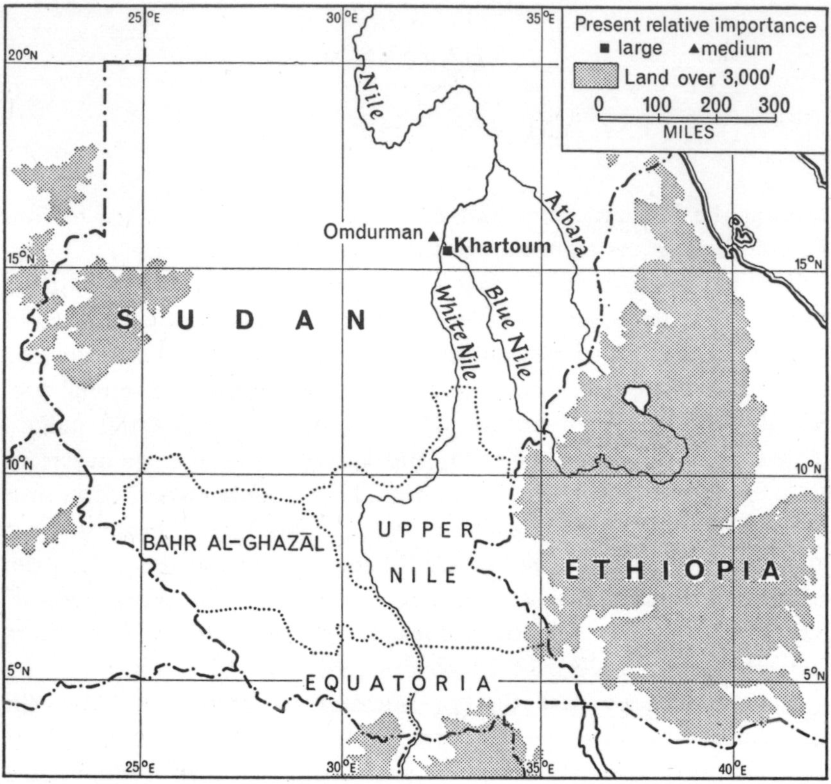

Sudan.

status and brought in Western codes of civil and criminal law. With the Condominium came an important novelty: for the first time since the disappearance of the last Christian kingdom in the Nile valley in the late Middle Ages the political direction fell to non-Muslim hands.

Up to 1914 the Condominium government was haunted by the spectre of a revival of militant Mahdism and was forced to repress, sometimes with bloodshed, a number of pseudo-Mahdīs and wild, apocalyptic figures who rose in their frenzy in various parts of the Muslim north. Government declared Mahdism a proscribed cult and they banned the Mahdī's *rātib*, his book of devotions. After 1918, however, Mahdism became politically respectable and its adherents, the *anṣār* came to be treated as another religious brotherhood. Government patronized the more influential religious leaders.

The fourth and most recent influence upon Sudanese Islam was that resulting from the declaration of national independence in 1956. Like the Anglo-Egyptian regime which it succeeded the new government maintained the relegation of the Islamic law to the area of private status, retained the secular laws for the remainder of the legal field and continued the Condominium political structure of the one-tier Western-type, secular state.

The paths which history has taken in Egypt and the Sudan have not led to convergence in the things of the spirit. The traveller from Egypt to the Sudan is continually faced by contrasts. In Egypt he may have been among a party of students who in 1964 heard a senior member of the government referring to the Muslim Brothers in terms of abusive jocularity. In the Sudan he will discover the *Ikhwān* among the most respected members of society. Muslim Egyptian public opinion dismisses the *ṭarīqas* (where they are noticed at all) as associations for cranks and fellahin, which educated, reputable Muslims do not join. In the Sudan the highest in the land may be members of one *ṭarīqa* or the other. The head of the former military government, General Ibrāhīm 'Abbūd, is himself a member of the brotherhood of the Khatmiyya.

The government of the United Arab Republic has of late pursued an enlightened religious policy. Muslim–Christian relations are cordial. In March 1965 Cardinal Koenig, Archbishop of Vienna, addressed the teachers and students of al-Azhar University on the theme of monotheism in the modern world while in the following summer President Jamāl 'Abd al-Nāṣir and the Coptic Orthodox Patriarch jointly laid the foundation stone of a new Coptic cathedral, when the President made a speech on Muslim–Christian co-operation. In the Sudan Muslim–Christian relations have never been worse.

A final contrast. In Egypt the traveller will have observed the disappearance of the old cosmopolitan ruling class and its replacement by the rule of the Egyptian petite bourgeoisie. In the Sudan he will find the class structure little changed since Condominium times. The cars are smarter, the buildings in the capital are higher and more numerous, new works are everywhere flourishing, more people chain-smoke cigarettes and those twin reminders of colonial rule, pith helmets and shorts, have gone for good. As for the mass of the people, the politicians talk of a national renaissance but the foreign visitor must bridle his pen for fear of indiscretion. The people seem to have been fundamentally unaffected by the change of rulers.

The barriers of mutual misunderstanding between Muslims and non-Muslims are not easily removed. To the historical barriers of mutual misrepresentation and ignorance are added the barriers of temperament. We in the West are often foolish in conversation when we labour to be bright. But we are careful to curb our writings and public utterances that may be reported. By contrast the Sudanese are habitually prudent in speech but their comparatively recent acquaintance with the printed word leads them to frequent irresponsibility in political writing. They are not obsessed as we are by the law of libel and they are not given to our Western vice of recalling past verbal excesses of an opponent for the purpose of discrediting him. Among the northern Sudanese public opinion is swifter to change and reaches greater sublimities and absurdities than among the more phlegmatic nations.

Sudanese Islam has many of the characteristics of a frontier religion. J. S. Trimingham in his *Islam in the Sudan* (1949) noticed how the Sudanese infused the warmth and colour of Africa into their religious life. There are no indigenous pockets of doctrinal deviation unless we include those few dozen souls, mostly Kināna tribesmen, who live in the Blue Nile basin and call themselves The People of Abū Jarīd (*jamā'at Abū Jarīd*) whose rites being secret are unknown. The foreign Shī'īs are limited to a handful of Persian, Pakistani and Indian traders, mainly Ithnā 'Ashariyya, Aḥmadiyya and Ismā'īliyya. Aḥmadiyya missionary zeal has provoked the same resentment among the Sunnite majority here as it has in Pakistan; neither the military government nor its successors has allowed them to open missions in the southern Sudan.

The day has long since passed when Arabic-speaking Muslims have regarded their Islam as inherently superior to the Islam of their non-Arabic-speaking Muslim neighbours. Yet there lingers a slight shadow of religious xenophobia when it comes to Urdu-speaking Muslims. It depends, an Indian Muslim told the writer, on how far you identify yourself with your Sudanese neighbours and, just as important, on how you pronounce your Arabic. A Pakistani tailor, popular with his Sudanese fellow-citizens, was sure that it was the *sunna*, not pronunciation, that counted for a happy life in Omdurman.

Few of the Sudanese who have won fame abroad have been men of Islamic learning. In recent years *'ulamā'* have been seconded to Nigeria and Shaykh Aḥmad al-'Ajīb was the first recorded Sudanese to preach in Malaya and Java. The only *'ālim* in the Sudan who attained importance outside the country was the *qāḍī al-quḍāt* Shaykh Muḥammad Muṣṭafā al-Marāghī, but he was an Egyptian.

In Khartoum the main mosque of the Turco-Egyptian period was allowed to fall into ruin after the Mahdī had transferred his capital over the river to Omdurman. The Condominium government cleared away the debris and built another, more imposing, mosque, while the Egyptians later presented yet a second mosque, named after the former King Fārūq. Today Khartoum, Khartoum North and Omdurman, three urban areas which together compose Greater Khartoum, have a spreading family of small suburban mosques to match the spectacular growth of the city. These stout, economically built structures of brick have low, squat minarets characteristic of Upper Egypt and the Sudan, the result not of architectural aesthetics but of untrustworthy subsoil which makes the cost of building slender minarets prohibitive.

At the moment the University of Khartoum is a secular university without an official mosque; a common room is set apart for worship. A proposal to build a university mosque is under consideration. There is however a strong feeling among senior members of the staff that the university should remain secular.

Mosque organization differs little from the Egyptian. In the smaller mosques, the unpaid *mu'adhdhin* works on a roster of voluntary service and there is no lack of volunteers. Muslim friends tell of the repetitive Friday sermons in old times and how the intellectual and literary level has since risen with the progress of education among preachers and congregations. Sermons today extend over a wider field than Qur'ānic exegesis into the whole range of social obligations. Radio Mecca is specially appreciated during the feasts. Attendances at the Friday congregational prayers fluctuate for the same reasons as they do in Christian churches. In the great mosques of Omdurman and Khartoum the visit of a foreign preacher of distinction is always a draw. The practice elsewhere in the Middle East of calling the *adhān* from the minaret by means of electrically amplified speech is now universally accepted by public opinion.

Facilities in the Sudan for printing and publishing Islamic literature are at present restricted. The Sudan has printing presses but the standard of printing and binding is still low. The normal printed work is the roughly printed pamphlet. The type of religious work printed in the Sudan is usually the *wird* and the *rātib*, the seasonal collects and devotional excerpts from the Qur'ān, for the use of members of the religious brotherhoods. All the religious bestsellers, such as Sulaymān Dā'ūd Mandīl's pocket lithographed edition of the *rātib* of the Mahdī, first printed in 1342/1924, have come from the Egyptian presses. Printed Qur'āns used in the Sudan are almost always copies of the so-called Fu'ād Qur'ān of 1925 noted for its clear *naskhī* fount. Manuscript Qur'āns are still highly prized and there are *faqīhs* who for a modest fee will write Qur'āns, generally in the *sūdānī* or *ṣaḥrāwī* hands, both having affinity with the Maghribī and both practised throughout the vast trans-Saharan region extending from the Nile to the Atlantic.

It is only to be expected that the spirit of nationalism would penetrate the religious and legal spheres, and the question was debated whether the judges, who administer the Ḥanafī code should not adopt the Mālikī code of the people of the Sudan. A prominent jurisconsult, Professor Muṣṭafā al-Zarqā' of the University of Damascus, was invited in 1964 to examine the matter and report. Professor al-Zarqā' strongly recommended the retention of the Ḥanafī code for the practical reason that it permitted the judges a greater latitude than did the Mālikī and this in his opinion outweighed all arguments to the contrary.

The trend towards the monogamous family observable among the more Europe-orientated men and women of the Sudan in no way indicates a decline of Islamic authority in the home. Islam is not hostile to monogamy. The trend is simply a response to what these men and women, good Muslims, have come to regard as the good life. Polygamy makes the good life in this sense harder to achieve. It is incorrect to write of the emancipation of Muslim women in the Sudan. The recent revolutionary change in the social status of women at the apex of Muslim urban society represents only the first stage of an evolution, still far from complete in Europe and America, to raise women to be in a real sense men's equal partners in the home, a conception of two parents equally in their different ways sharing the sovereignty over themselves and their children in one homogeneous group.

Muslim university women retain, with minor modifications, the traditional outer garment, the *tōb* (classical *thawb*) which, as it covers the body, satisfies respectatibility and, as it is distinctive, appeals to the sartorial side of nationalism. The *tōb*, in rich variety of material and colour, is worn with elegance by slow-moving wearers, but requires, as convention demands, from the wearer a continual and graceful fiddling with its folds as though the wearer were involved in constant battle against exposure. The *tōb* symbolizes a certain stage in

Sudanese women's development. It is for speculation whether it is likely to survive unmodified in the event of an appreciable acceleration in the tempo of life or an industrialization of Sudanese urban society.

The *'ulamā'* are not collectively opposed to the education of women in general though voices have been raised in criticism of what they consider to be the excessive freedom claimed by some. Indeed, the pioneer of girls' education under the Condominium was an *'ālim*, Shaykh Bābikr Badrī. The remarkable vogue in women's education is producing university graduates in small but steadily increasing numbers. From their ranks come women activists of all political parties from the Communists to the Muslim Sisters. Women students, with very few exceptions, are industrious, single-minded and as intent on careers as on husbands. Education gives them a standing in society which would be the envy of their English sisters. If some are blue stockings they are blue stockings in the most favourable circumstances, for the social arrangements of Sudanese life exempt them from the servitude to domestic chores. Many marry with the express intention of continuing their pre-marital professional careers and of leaving their children to the care of grandmothers and servants, a reminder that Sudanese society is not divided into age-groups but into family groups in which, as in Mediterranean Christian society, grandparents have an honoured and a useful place. The situation of the young married Sudanese Muslim woman in society is not far removed from that enjoyed by our middle class "career" women in the Suffragette age, but with two exceptions: the modern Sudanese male is on the whole less reluctant to work alongside able women than were his English counterparts in the era of H. G. Wells, and the Sudanese woman is not prepared to sacrifice motherhood in the interests of her career.

The closely-knit Sudanese Muslim family, with all its social excellences, has a weakness: the overweening influence of the least liberal member of the group, the grandmother, on social customs. The grandmothers of the Sudan are often cited as the greatest obstruction to the abolition of female circumcision of the barbarous kind commonly practised in the Sudan. Although this practice has been condemned in 1946 by a *fatwā* of Shaykh Aḥmad al-Ṭāhir b. al-Faqīh 'Abdallāh when *muftī* of the Sudan and has nothing to do with Islam, it is still practised even among families otherwise enlightened and humane, so powerful is the influence of custom.

The simple lives of traditional-living Muslims with their heavy preoccupation with social customs, religious obligations and family celebrations, have long been open to contamination from abroad. In the seventeenth century the *'ulamā'* of Constantinople fought a rear-guard action against the use of coffee and tobacco; in the twentieth the *'ulamā'* of the Sudan have capitulated to the cigarette. It is not easy for moralists to shift their ground from time to time in the pursuit of changing vices.

Though there are those in the Sudan who would like to see the national drink *marīsa* brewed and marketed under hygienic conditions, there is some resistance to the proposal on the ground that permission to brew would involve a Muslim government in condoning a scripturally forbidden practice. Others contend that this objection is illogical since government already licences a brewery and distilleries. So long as *marīsa* is brewed by women in private houses and by less savoury women in the *marīsa* quarters of the towns, official Islam has nothing to say. At the moment opinion is divided on the moral issue, between those who argue that alcohol has become a secondary vice and that tobacco has taken its place as the more dangerous enemy of society, and those who uphold the formal Muslim aversion to alcohol and smoke to their hearts' content. This is a fringe problem; on all the great problems which face them the Sudanese *'ulamā'* have deserved well of their people. Sudanese Islam remains the solid, non-intellectual Islam that Shaykh Muḥammad 'Abduh, fresh from al-Azhar, found on his visit to the Sudan in 1904–5. The *qāḍī al-quḍāt*, Shaykh Sirāj al-Dīn al-Amīn al-Baqūrī, whose recent death gave sorrow to his Christian friends, was himself the very embodiment of that homely simplicity.

For all the European pressures in secular education the Islamic literary tradition remains strong. A foreign teacher may be forgiven for concluding that, whatever the branch of his studies, the Sudanese student applies to it a literary frame of mind. The Muslim student who is also Arabic-speaking is more consciously proud of his literary heritage than the ordinary English student is of his. There are not in Khartoum as there are in British universities scientists of ability who cannot speak or write their own language with felicity. Nor are there to be seen enthusiastic parties of intermediate schoolboys crowding, pencil and paper in hand, round the latest diesel locomotive of the Sudan Railways. Sudanese students have an exalted respect for politics and a gloriously literary standpoint on problems which in the West would be considered technological or economic.

A minority view on Islam which cannot any longer be ignored is that of the Muslim Brothers and Muslim Sisters. These are still an intellectual pressure group rather than a political party. Their impact on educated people is at present greater than that of the official exponents of Islam since they present the more exciting picture of the role of Islam in the world. If an otherwise uncommitted Muslim university student, or in fact any educated Muslim, feels deeply in spiritual matters, the chances are that he will join the *Ikhwān*. Like Christian missionaries they are committed partisans and do not live comfortably in the presence of propagandists of other religions. Less immediately but as a long-term objective the *Ikhwān* would restore the *sharī'a* as the sole legal authority among Muslims. Their policy, set out in their political manifesto of 1964 contrasts in tone with the violent extremism of the followers of Ḥasan al-Bannā' of the prescribed Egyptian branch of the movement. Unlike the Egyptian *Ikhwān* they do not appeal to the mob but to educated Muslims. Their nearest approach to a slogan is the cry of the authoritarians before the battle of Ṣiffīn, *lā ḥukm illā li'llāh*, to be interpreted in a modern election campaign as "No social order unless it is based on God's rule". The Brothers and the Communists form the only portion of the educated minority who show an intense interest in the social implications of their programmes. The thesis of the *Ikhwān*, the championship of essential Islam with its positive social content, leans less towards the position of the Egyptian reformers of the Salafiyya movement who were not primarily interested in social questions, than towards the Wahhābite standpoint. Regarded historically the appeal is conservative: we have deserted Islam, let us return to it. Essential Islam has no time for the *ṭarīqa*. The *Ikhwān* say of the brotherhoods that they prefer their own devotional literature to the Qur'ān, that they put *dhikr* before the obligatory prayers, that they accord their *khalīfas* and saints a degree of veneration due to God alone and are thus guilty of *shirk*, of attributing partners to God. In brief the *ṭarīqa* is an unnecessary obstruction in the path between the worshipper and God, a position which at once aligns them, if only in this respect, with the Mahdists in a common dislike of the brotherhoods.

It goes without saying that the *Ikhwān* are opposed to the religious betrayal, as they term it, by the government of the United Arab Republic which has forced the wrong kind of reforms upon al-Azhar University, reforms designed to weaken rather than strengthen that institution. And they accuse Cairo of having goaded the Egyptian *Ikhwān* into the violent course which alone was open to them.

The fact remains that the great majority of simple Sudanese Muslims are not receptive to the puritan clarion call of the young men of the *Ikhwān*, and still adhere to the *ṭarīqas*. The social and, indirectly, the political influence of the great brotherhoods, particularly the Khatmiyya, seems as great as ever. And among the smaller brotherhoods, such as the Burhāniyya there are nuclei of highly educated members worshipping and thinking together who share an intellectual approach to their religion.

Opponents of the *Ikhwān* are inclined to attribute to them the wish to put the clock back and resurrect a dead Islamic polity. The criticism is over-literal. It is as unreasonable to expect a Muslim Brother to insist on restoring the three-tier state of classical Islam, with the *ahl al-bayt* enjoying the governance and the *ahl al-kitāb* paying the bill as it is to expect a Christian revivalist to insist on re-creating the *Civitas Dei* on earth down to the last sociological detail. Left to themselves the Sudanese are not given to pursuing logic to absurd conclusions.

The same fussy concentration on doctrinal nicety may lead to the misapprehension that there must be an unbridgeable gulf between those who accept the claim of Muḥammad Aḥmad to be the Expected Mahdī and those who do not. At the moment there is no such gulf. The authenticity or otherwise of the Mahdī's claim is no longer in dispute; it is left in abeyance, nobody is now interested in the debate. This does not mean that his memory is not venerated by thousands of devout *anṣār*, especially in the western provinces of Kordofan and Darfur, to whom he is the Mahdī indeed. For the mass of non-Mahdist Muslims, however, Muḥammad Aḥmad was a great and good man, a saint of Islam, and he was more. Politicians speak of him as a national hero worthy of inclusion in the same pantheon with Taharqa and ʻAlī ʻAbd al-Laṭīf, the hero of 1924. He, if not his descendants, stands above party politics.[1]

An *anṣārī* has no feeling of belonging to a sect, and no trace of holier-than-thou mentality mars his relations with his non-Mahdist Muslim neighbours. He will worship in the same mosque as they and join with

[1] A recent exposition of this view of the Mahdī is to be found in Mandour El-Mahdi, *A Short History of the Sudan* (1965), a translation from the Arabic original. The author is principal of the Institute of Education, Bakht al-Ruda, Sudan.

them in celebrating the Prophet's birthday. Between Mahdist and non-Mahdist there is none of the religious and social separation that occurs in Pakistan and India between the deviationist Aḥmadiyya and the Muslim majority.

The Sudan is not a cultural centre of Islam and the history of Sudanese religious education is interesting rather than impressive. It was not until 1911 that an approach to an organized school of Islamic learning was founded in Omdurman. Its courses combined the Islamic sciences with what were officially and euphemistically called "modern subjects": arithmetic, history and elementary Arabic literature. The quality of instruction was low, and the graduates, deprived of an education in Egypt, could look forward only to badly-paid careers in the *sharīʿa* legal hierarchy. Institutes of even lower standard grew numerous in the provinces. Nevertheless, with all its difficulties of financing and educational standards it was from the senior class of *al-Maʿhad al-ʿIlmī* of Omdurman that the first post-secondary students in the whole Sudan were produced.

Unhappily the achievement of parity of esteem has been, and still is, the stumbling-block of Islamic religious education, and it is not surprising that the graduates of *al-Maʿhad al-ʿIlmī* have shown some resentment at their poor material prospects compared with the rosy future ahead of graduates from the University of Khartoum. Resentment in religious seminaries engenders in its students a narrow, aggressive attitude to the secular world of learning. With Dr Kāmil al-Bāqir's appointment as director of *al-Maʿhad al-ʿIlmī* of Omdurman in 1965 the odious comparison of material prospects is likely to lose most of its sting as it is the intention of the Sudan government to raise the *Maʿhad* to the level of a university of Islamic studies, a junior Sudanese al-Azhar set on the high road between the old Middle East and the new Africa.

There is an element of tragic inevitability in the continuing tension between government and Christian missions in the southern provinces. The tension is not new, certainly not the outcome of Sudanese independence in 1956 or the replacement of British by Sudanese administrators in the south in 1954. These were contributory causes but the root of the trouble goes back to the beginning of the Condominium in 1899 and was the result of friction which must accompany the simultaneous presence in the same region of an expanding Christianity and an expanding Islam.

Up to the present time there has never been a Muslim–Christian dialogue in the Sudan though before independence there were few if any signs of overt hostility. A Catholic might speculate whether a dialogue would have been possible if the work of spreading the Gospel in the south had been given to the "leftish" Dominicans with their eminent *arabisants* and their tradition of Islamic scholarship instead of to the "rightish" Verona Fathers. A Muslim might just as well speculate whether Islam might have assisted the cause of toleration by opening intellectual windows in Khartoum. All that is necessary for a Muslim to know of the principles of Christianity is set out in the Qur'ān and the Traditions, the Muslim inquirer has no formal need to search elsewhere. The *'ulamā'* have not encouraged the study of comparative religion, neither for that matter have the Christians. If an infallible source gives all the knowledge that is required, why trouble to learn about a pseudo-religion scripturally proved to have been corrupted and whose missionaries preach that yours is false? The Marxist association of Christian missionaries with aggressive Western capitalism, a frequent ascription in the Sudanese Press, still further alienates the Muslim inquirer from the facts about Christianity.

Ignorance, the mother of misrepresentation, is not a Muslim monopoly. The long years of interreligious segregation in the southern Sudan have had the disastrous consequence of shielding the Christian missionaries, both Roman Catholic and Protestant, from the necessity of creating an adequate Christian apologetic based on a sound doctrinal knowledge of Islam and an appreciation of that which unites as well as that which divides the two faiths. Instead so much of Christian statement on Islam has been informed by ignorance.

Up to the last century the Christian communities living under Muslim rule in the Middle East were models of submissiveness to Caesar and treated their rulers with deference. Further these Christian *dhimmīs* scrupulously refrained (for they valued their heads) from attempting to convert the Muslims among whom they lived. With the nineteenth century came the arrival in the Middle East and in Africa of Christian missionaries quite unlike their subservient co-religionists of the Eastern Churches. Roman Catholic and Protestant societies established missions in the Sudan at different times after 1842. On the Anglo-Egyptian reconquest of the northern and central parts of the country, completed by 1899, the missionary bodies asked the British authorities for leave to begin or resume evangelization.

From the first the British officers and officials on whom fell the responsibility of carrying out the government missionary policy were caught in a dilemma. They were themselves Christians, for the most part Anglicans of the aristocratic and public school tradition, men of moral self-discipline, loyal, incorruptible, uninterested in Christian and Muslim theology and history, devoid of religious enthusiasm and the will to proselytize, contemptuous of fanaticism and acutely fearful lest the presence of zealous missionaries might lead to administrative trouble. The man at the top, Lord Cromer, British agent and consul general in Egypt, who made all the decisions in concert with his first two governors general of the Sudan, Lord Kitchener and Sir Reginald Wingate, had no noticeable religious bias. Wingate regarded himself, as he wrote to Bishop Ll. H. Gwynne, as representative of a Christian king and a Muslim khedive and was responsible for maintaining an even balance over all subjects whether Christian or Muslim.[1]

So much for the theory. In practice the missionary policy was its undoing. Under the missionary regulations first formulated in 1904 Christian evangelization was forbidden in the north but permitted in the south where missionary societies approved by the government might open stations each within a prescribed territory. As a financial economy, for the Sudan government was then desperately poor and dependent upon the charity of the Egyptian treasury, government handed over education to the missions which opened schools under modest state subsidy. In 1910 a grave step was taken: English was established as the lingua franca of the southern provinces.

To Muslims who thought at all on the matter this act would seem to have been devised for only one purpose: to split the Sudan into two linguistic, cultural and religious parts. Yet no evidence is forthcoming that this eventuality ever entered Wingate's mind when he approved the act. Though he nowhere discloses his motives on paper he may have been swayed by considerations of public security, by the fear of baleful consequences of Mahdist preachers on simple negro minds. But it is only supposition.

Whatever the reason, the establishment of a second common language in one territory appeared to later northern critics as a betrayal of trust. In the long run the subsequent application of what was called the

[1] Wingate to Gwynne, 17 May 1911, Sudan archive, School of Oriental Studies, University of Durham, 300/5.

southern policy between about 1929 and 1947, by which Islam and Arab influence were deliberately kept out of the southern provinces, was of no substantial help to the Christian missionaries. It was on the contrary a vicarious aggravation of Muslim frustration.

The exclusion of Muslim and of Arab influence could have succeeded only if the Sudan government had been wealthy enough to have made segregation complete. It had not the material means, nor had it the will. From the first, as is to be expected in an administration of normally intelligent men with flexible minds, there were those who doubted the government's ability to carry out the southern policy in its entirety; some even doubted the rightness of the policy. Doubts grew with the passing of time, and with the prospect of Sudanese independence, British self-criticism made an end of the policy.

We now see that the southern policy of segregation was utopian and bore hardest on the Christian missions who were identified, though incorrectly, with the Sudan government. Extremist Muslims in the north discerned the old Crusaders in new armour, the secular enemies of Islam.

The document which the military government issued in 1964 to justify its expulsion of the foreign missionaries is entitled "Memorandum on reasons that led to the expulsion of foreign missionaries and priests from the southern provinces of the Sudan". The text altogether fails to represent the government's drastic action as one motivated by rational considerations. The effect of the document outside the Sudan has therefore been the opposite of that intended. The number of persons found to be actively hostile to the government was shown in the document (which bears all the marks of honesty) to have been very small indeed, small enough to have been dealt with under existing law. The impression given by a reading of the document was that the then government was afraid to bring the two or three suspected missionary trouble-makers to court. One inference which can be drawn for that government's action was that it was attempting to repeat the procedure of Muslim potentates in the past of attempting the extirpation of non-Muslim faiths by cutting off their adherents from the source of theological training.

The official case against the missionaries overreached itself when it asserted that the separation of the south from the north was "a preconceived political plan drawn up since the beginning of the present century when the Sudan came under foreign domination" and that the principal political objective was "the dismemberment of the country and its division into antagonistic regions...various missionary organizations were introduced into the country to serve that end".[1] Even allowing for the caprices of translation, statements of this order read as though they were the work of some old *aghā* in the former military government who, whatever his expertise in soldiering, misrepresented or mistook or was ignorant of the government–missionary relationship under the Condominium.

It is a relief to turn to the scholarly collection of documents prepared for the use of the Round Table Conference held in Khartoum in March 1965 in the endeavour to make a peaceful settlement of the Southern problem. It was a tragedy that the delegates had no time to digest this objectively prepared dossier essential to an understanding of the complicated issues. A careful study of it might have provided the northern delegates with a more attractive case and softened what seemed at times to have been the irresponsible intransigence of some southern delegates. The conference might even have been saved. Here the whole story of the Southern problem is unfolded in copies from the Condominium central and provincial government files, technical papers, reports, a rich variety of documents. Here also the Condominium government's reasons for inaugurating its southern policy are set out. It should not be forgotten that the government of that day knew what it was doing and gave reasons for what it did in the light of its interpretation of the evidence before it. The administrative experience of the Arab presence in the south, the memory of the slave trade and the more recent experience of the swindling *jallābī* pedlar, were unfortunate, so government planned to eliminate what Arab and Muslim influence there was outside the relatively small Muslim communities in some of the towns, and to establish a culturally separate area with Christian leadership guided by Christian social ethics. What the planners of 1929 could not foresee was that their southern policy would end by transforming the south into a *dār al-ḥarb*.

Perhaps a university don, Muddaththir ʻAbd al-Raḥīm has come nearest to the truth in terms of history when he wrote:

...But history cannot be simply legislated out of existence and the impact on our present life of...the British administration in the Southern Sudan

[1] Statement by the government on the problem of the south, dated 30 August 1964 (dupl. typescr.).

between 1899 and 1947 is too obvious to require comment. Southern policy was by far the greatest failure of that administration and there can be no doubt that by implementing it the Condominium regime has landed the independent Sudan with its most intractable problem and the present generation of Sudanese people throughout the country with the greatest challenge in their post-independence history.[1]

[1] "The Development of British Policy in the Southern Sudan, 1899–1947" (dupl. typescr.).

CHAPTER 10

ISLAM IN EAST AFRICA

HISTORICAL BACKGROUND

The proximity of East Africa to the Arabian Peninsula has created, through the centuries of the history of these two regions, a constant link between them in all fields of human activity; so that it seems only natural that Islam from its beginnings should have become an important factor in the cultural and religious development of the East African peoples. The circumstances, however, have been different in Ethiopia and the countries bordering on the Red Sea and in the regions situated farther to the south on the shore of the Indian Ocean.

At first sight the link between the Indian sub-continent and Ethiopia may appear rather vague and uncertain. But, if we examine fully the historical documents, we can assert, beyond doubt, that, for the most part, the history of Ethiopia has been determined by its importance on the maritime route from the Mediterranean to the Indian Ocean. In ancient times the two Great Powers of that age, the Roman and the Persian empires, had fought their "cold war" on the field of the international trade with Middle and Far Eastern Asia; and while Persia supported the continental road to India and China, the Roman, and later on, the Byzantine empire favoured the sea route through the Red Sea and the Indian Ocean. This rivalry of the two empires obliged them to intervene in the countries situated on both routes to protect or to block and obstruct the trade, according to political circumstances. A typical example of that situation is the Ethiopian expedition to southern Arabia in the sixth century. The Ethiopian enterprise, helped and probably suggested by the Byzantine government during the reign of Justin I, culminated in the attempted raid by the Ethiopian chief, Abreha, against Mecca just before the birth of the Prophet Muḥammad; and the expedition is quoted in the Qur'ān (CV, *Sūrat al-Fīl*), as having been defeated by a divine miracle. According to the Islamic tradition, the Emperor (Ar. "*najjāshī*"), of Ethiopia was one of the princes and personalities who received a letter from Muḥammad himself; and Ethiopia granted its hospitality to some Muslim refugees during the first struggles against the new religion in Arabia. Later on when the

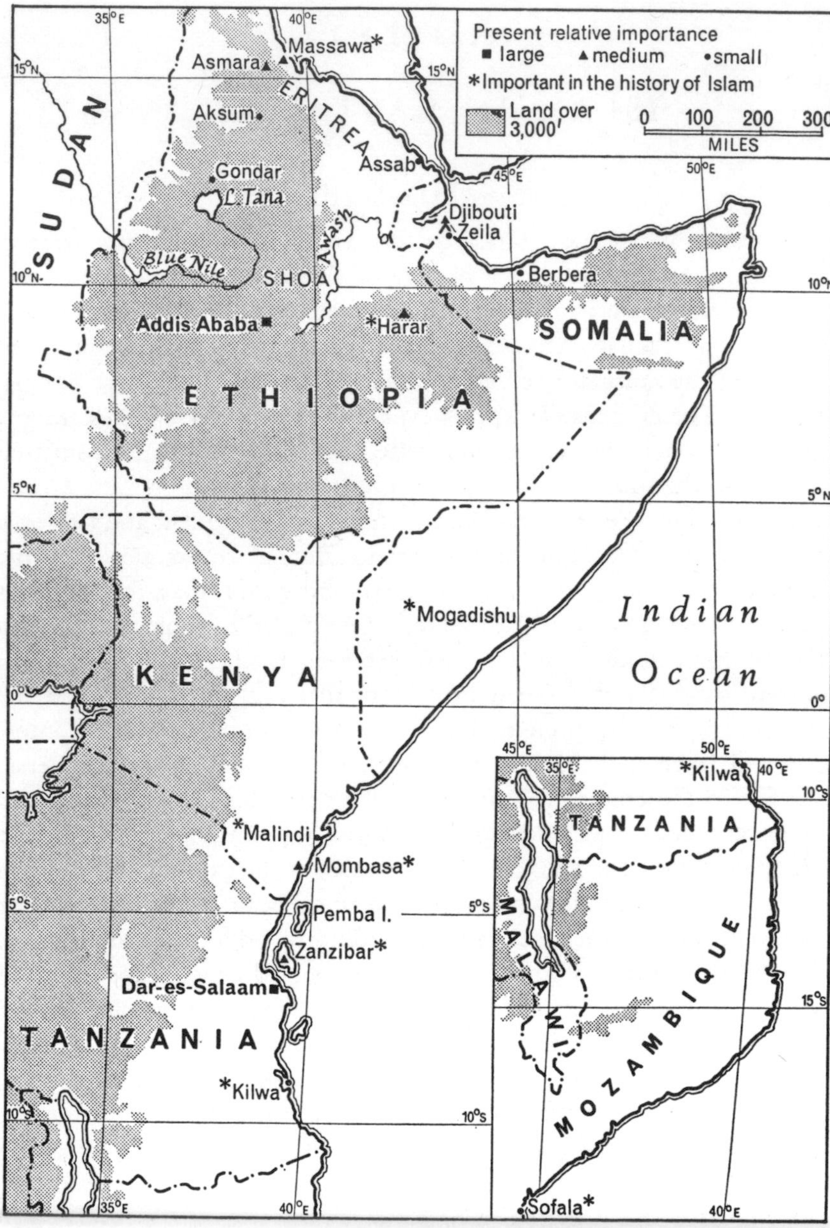
Present relative importance
■ large ▲medium •small
*Important in the history of Islam
Land over 3,000′
0 100 200 300
MILES
SUDAN
ERITREA
ETHIOPIA
SOMALIA
KENYA
TANZANIA
MALAWI
MOZAMBIQUE
Indian Ocean
Massawa*
Asmara
Aksum
Gondar
L. Tana
Blue Nile
Awash
SHOA
Assab
Djibouti
Zeila
Berbera
Addis Ababa
*Harar
*Mogadishu
*Malindi
Mombasa*
Pemba I.
Zanzibar*
Dar-es-Salaam
*Kilwa
Sofala*
35°E
40°E
45°E
50°E
15°N
10°N
5°N
0°
5°S
10°S
15°S

East Africa.

Islamic caliphate, after defeating both the Persian and the Byzantine empire, inherited the full control of the continental trade road to India, the maritime route, with the port of Qulzum in the Gulf of Suez as its starting-point, was not abandoned; still more, the defence of Arabia and the protection of the pilgrimage obliged the caliphs to assert practically their power on the African coast of the Red Sea. The islands of Dahlak, controlling the major Ethiopian port of Adulis, had already been occupied by the first Umayyad caliphs; and the caliphs Sulaymān b. ʻAbd al-Malik (715–17), and Yazīd b. ʻAbd al-Malik (720–4) exiled there the poet al-Aḥwaṣ and the jurist ʻArraq, according to the *Kitāb al-aghānī*. At the same time the Islamic faith was successfully beginning its preaching especially in southern Ethiopia, where the interior of the African plateau is more easily approached from the seashore along the valley of the river Ḥawāsh and where the local populations, ethnically Sidama and pagan in religion, were attracted to Islam as a new ideological force of resistance against the territorial expansion of the Christian Kingdom of northern Ethiopia. Small Muslim states were thus constituted in southern Ethiopia. Whereas, however, in the northern and central zones of Ethiopia the principalities established in each region by the chiefs of the immigrants from South Arabia were finally united in one state and the local princes and feudal chiefs accepted the sovereign power of the king (therefore called *Negusa Nagast*, "King of the Kings"); in the south the local Muslim states, however small and feeble, were not formally united. Only in particular conditions of crisis were they rather federated in temporary leagues; and, even if in practice the biggest of their sultanates or amirates had some paramount influence on the others, this leadership was not officially recognized. This lack of unity of the Muslim states was aggravated by internal quarrels which often damaged seriously their capacity for resistance to a foreign adversary. According to recent historical research, the paramount Muslim state in Ethiopia, at least in the thirteenth century, was the sultanate of Shoa under the Makhzūmī dynasty which claimed descent from the famous Makhzūmī tribe of Mecca, to which Khālid b. al-Walīd belonged. The Makhzūmī Sultans pretended to have ruled Shoa since the year 896/7, a chronology which indicates how early was the diffusion of Islam in southern Ethiopia. The sultanate of Shoa, after a sad series of civil wars between the rebellious Amirs and the Sultan, was conquered by the neighbouring Muslim state, the sultanate of Ifāt, which from that date (July/August 1285), acquired the leadership in Muslim Ethiopia and kept it for about three hundred years. The ruling dynasty of Ifāt was the Walasma', who also were connected by genealogical tradition with 'Aqīl b. Abī Ṭālib, the brother of the caliph 'Alī. The Walasma' Sultans of Ifāt are mentioned by many Arab historians, such as Ibn Khaldūn himself, al-'Umarī, who follows information brought to Cairo (in 1332–8) by Shaykh 'Abdallāh al-Zayla'ī; al-Taghrībirdī in his annals of Egypt and by al-Maqrīzī in his booklet *Kitāb al-ilmām*. The Royal Chronicles of Christian Ethiopia also record the wars waged by the Walasma' of Ifāt against the kingdom of Ethiopia, from the expedition directed by Sulṭān Ṣabr al-Dīn, in the year 1331, against the Christian King 'Amda Ṣeyon I, which ended with the surrender of Ṣabr al-Dīn, to the major enterprise of Sultan Badlāy b. Sa'd al-Dīn, who penetrated with his army to the very centre of the Christian kingdom, but was finally defeated and killed in the battle of Egubbā, in Shoa (26 December 1445), while his brother Khayr al-Dīn was pursued as far as the river Ḥawāsh and there massacred with his troops. The battle of Egubbā, which by a decree of the Christian King Zar'a Yā'qob was celebrated each year as a national feast, prevented any other Muslim enterprise for a long period; and moreover the Sultans of Ifāt were obliged to establish their new capital far from any danger of attack by the Ethiopian emperor. They took then the new title of Sultans of Adal; and in 1526, Harar was the new centre of the paramount Muslim state. But there too a new political organization was set up. The Sultans of the ancient Walasma' dynasty retained the formal title as sovereigns, but only as puppet kings, while the real power passed to the hands of the military chiefs who, as Amirs, ruled the country and frequently fought each other with disastrous effects. The Muslim state was again unified by a great chief, Aḥmad b. Ibrāhīm, who was nicknamed by the Ethiopians "*Gerāñ*" (the left handed), and honoured by the Muslims with the name *Ṣāḥib al-fatḥ* (the conqueror). Aḥmad b. Ibrāhīm, at the very beginning of his enterprises, assumed the title of *imām*; but it is typical that he did not depose the Sultans of the Walasma', so that the prestige of the legitimate sovereigns remained a strong card to be used in his favour. And, after all, this title of Imam was not easily accepted by all his subjects. An evidence of these doubts is the fact that in some MSS of Muslim Ethiopia we find copied on the margins of the pages a passage entitled *faṣl fī tasmiyat al-imām imāman* ("Chapter on the title of *imām* attributed to the Imam [Aḥmad b. Ibrāhīm]"), which explains how the title was rightly assumed. The invasion of Ethiopia under the leadership of Imam Aḥmad is one of the outstanding episodes of the history of East Africa. It seriously endangered the existence of the Christian Kingdom of Ethiopia and would possibly have succeeded completely but for the impact of the world situation. The Portuguese discovery of the new maritime route to India by the Cape of Good Hope had substantially modified the balance of power in Europe and the Near East. It became essential for Portugal, in order to guarantee her new acquisitions in India and her Indian trade, to block any initiative of her rivals, Egypt (and after 1517, the Turkish empire), and the Republic of Venice on the ancient route through the Red Sea. So it was that, after the voyages of Portuguese fleets to Bāb al-Mandab on the Red Sea from 1513 onwards and the occupation of the island of Kamaran near the coast of Arabia in 1513, a squadron commanded by Diogo Lopes de Sequeira arrived at Massawa in 1520 and friendly relations were established between Christian Ethiopia and Portugal. In these circumstances, if Ethiopia had been conquered by the Muslims of the Imam Aḥmad, Portugal would have been confronted on the Red Sea route by a strong military power like Turkey (after the conquest of Egypt by Sultan Selim I), and another Muslim power in Ethiopia. Therefore the Portuguese were easily persuaded to intervene in the Ethiopian war against the Imam Aḥmad. The Portuguese force, led by Cristovão da Gama, son of the navigator Vasco, fought gallantly at the side of the Ethiopians. Cristovão da Gama was taken prisoner and beheaded, but a Portuguese gunner killed the Imam Aḥmad in battle. The war was continued by the Amir Nūr b. Mujāhid (now venerated as a saint in Muslim Ethiopia) who defeated and killed the Ethiopian king Claudius in 1559. But this victory had no political consequences, because Nūr b. Mujāhid was obliged to go back to Harar which had been devastated by a terrible famine; and suddenly both the Christian and Muslim states of Ethiopia were attacked and invaded by the pagan tribes of the Galla. While the greatest Muslim attempt against Ethiopia ended thus, it is a remarkable fact that no Muslim state intervened to help Imam Aḥmad or Amir Nūr b. Mujāhid directly. Even Turkey remained virtually neutral and only afterwards tried to gain some territorial advantages by occupying the Ethiopian port of Massawa in 1557.

The invasion of the pagan Galla and their occupation of the greater part of western and southern Ethiopia reduced the Muslim state to Harar and the neighbouring region, where a local dynasty was established and reigned with the title of Amir from 1620/1, to the battle of Çallānqo, 27 January 1887, when Menilek II, then King of Shoa, defeated Amir 'Abdullāhi and conquered Harar, definitively unifying Christian and Muslim Ethiopia.

The first Muslim expedition to the African coast of the Indian Ocean recorded in the local chronicles is said to have been sent there by the Umayyad caliph 'Abd al-Malik b. Marwān (685–705), under the leadership of the Amir Mūsā al-Khath'amī; and was followed in 766/7 by a second expedition led by Yaḥyā b. 'Umar al-'Anazī, an officer of the 'Abbāsid caliph al-Manṣūr. As a result of these actions by the Arab empire, a chain of Muslim establishments was founded on the African seashore along the ancient road "of the monsoons" from the Gulf of Aden as far as Zanzibar; traditional Arab and Persian navigation opened up the African markets of slaves, ivory, tortoise shell and other local commercial products. These establishments, the so-called *banādir*, were also centres of Muslim religious propaganda among the African population: Somali (*Barābir* in the Arab documents), Galla, Bantu (*Zanj*). The Somali, who occupied in the early Middle Ages only the northern region from the Gulf of Tajūra as far as Ḥāfūn, were converted more easily to Islam because Muslim organizations from Muslim Ethiopia were also working among them. For instance their market town, Zayla', was annexed to the sultanate of Ifāt and shared the destinies of that state. On the contrary, the Galla were less disposed to accept Islam so that their national name was adopted in the Somali language as *Gālo*, to signify pagans. The Muslim *banādir* on the African coast became also the destination of groups of refugees who were obliged by political or religious crises to leave Arabia or southern Persia and tried to find a new field of activity far from danger. This fact explains also the composite formation of the Arabo-Persian population of the *banādir*, which has also given rise to interesting influences in culture and art. Thus the foundation or at least the beginning of the prosperity of Mogadishu was a consequence of the arrival there of Arab immigrants from al-Aḥsā' on the Persian Gulf, probably refugees during the repression of the Qarmaṭī movement in the tenth century; and the town of Merca has recorded in its traditions the fact that, before the arrival of the Somali in that region, the *bandar* had been inhabited by Persian immigrants from Sīrāf, the great medieval port of Fārs, which was finally destroyed in the second half of the tenth century. Some monuments in these towns on the coast of the Indian Ocean were built by Persian craftsmen and represent typically a kind of provincial art somewhat backward in comparison with the contemporary monuments of Persia itself.

In early times the market towns were ruled by a council of the chiefs of the different sections of the population; but in some of them local principalities succeeded to the ancient federative government. The best known of these small states are the sultanates of Mogadishu (Maqdishū), visited and described by Ibn Baṭṭūṭa in the early fourteenth century; the sultanate of Malindi on the seashore of Kenya, and the sultanate of Kilwa on the coast of Tanganyika. When the Portuguese, after the voyage of Vasco da Gama, arrived on the shores of the Indian Ocean, they found these Muslim potentates and were met by them in some cases with friendship, as happened at Malindi, and elsewhere with hostility, as at Mogadishu which Vasco da Gama bombarded, 3 January 1499. But the Portuguese soon realized the necessity of asserting their power along the new road to India by direct occupation and therefore the Viceroy Francisco d'Almeida in 1505 attacked and conquered Mombasa, which was permanently occupied in 1592; and two years later, in 1594, a fortress was built and garrisoned by order of the Viceroy Mattias de Albuquerque. Mombasa became the capital of the Portuguese possessions in East Africa. But, when the Portuguese power declined, the Imam of Oman, Sayf b. Sulṭān al-Yaʿrubī sent an expedition against Mombasa under the Amir Shahdād b. Shahdī, who besieged the fortress and finally occupied it in 1698. The control of the East Africa coast passed from the Portuguese to a Muslim power, the Ibāḍite Imamate of Oman; and therefore the *banādir* also and the small sultanates along the seashore accepted the paramount influence of Oman. However, it is remarkable that this situation did not in any way mean that the Ibāḍite faith of Oman was diffused in East Africa. The local population remained, on the whole, Sunnīs of the Shāfiʿī *madhhab*, while only the officers of the Imam and their garrisons were Ibāḍīs; so that there was no unity of belief between the Arabs and their East African Muslim subjects. The schism between the sons of the Imam Saʿīd b. Sulṭān was settled by the arbitration of the British Governor General of India, Lord Canning, on 2 April 1861; Zanzibar with the neighbouring African coast was constituted as an independent sultanate for Mājid b. Saʿīd, while Oman was assigned to his brother Thuwaynī b. Saʿīd. Thus began the new dynasty of Zanzibar which lasted until

1964 when a movement of the African native population of the island overthrew the sultanate and afterwards proclaimed federation with the Republic of Tanganyika under the new name of Tanzania. At that moment the sultanate, which had accepted a British protectorate in 1890, was reduced to the islands of Zanzibar and Pemba, because its possessions on the African coast had been ceded or leased to Great Britain (the coast of British East Africa, then Kenya, in 1895), to Germany (the seashore of Deutsch Ost-Afrika, afterwards Tanganyika, in 1890), to Italy (the Somali coast in 1893), and had followed, until full independence, the developments of these European colonies or mandates through both world wars.

GEOGRAPHICAL DISTRIBUTION

At present the Muslim population of Ethiopia is distributed in the western and southern regions of that country. In the districts of Eritrea between Keren and the Sudanese border, the Beja akin with the same nomadic tribes in Sudanese territory, the Māryā ("Red" and "Black"); the Bāryā and part of the Bogos are Muslim; on the Red Sea the port of Massawa and its district has been a centre of Islamic culture from the time of the Turkish occupation; and, south of Massawa, the Saho and Dankali tribes are all Muslim as far as the Somali boundary within the French Côte des Somalis. Then in western Ethiopia, the Banī Shangūl, south of the Blue Nile, are a section of the Sudanese Berta and therefore Muslim; an important group of Galla populations converted to Islam occupy the valley of the river Gibē; the Jimmā, Limmu, Gommā, Gērā, small former Galla kingdoms annexed to Ethiopia during the reign of Menilek in the second half of the nineteenth century; and this group is prolonged to the east by Sidama Muslim populations: the Hadiya, the Ṭambarō and Alabā as far as the rift of the Great Lakes. Also, the different tribes of the Gurāgie are partly Muslim and partly Christian. From there eastwards the territory of the former amirate of Harar and the region of Bali have a Muslim majority; and they again have a common border with the Somali country.

The central part of the Ethiopian plateau is therefore now encircled by two great strips of country inhabited by Muslims. It was the situation which Emperor Menilek described so well in one of his letters by calling his kingdom "a Christian island in an ocean of unbelievers". But in the interior of the Christian regions also there are some scattered groups of Muslims who are called, especially in the northern countries like Eritrea and Tigre, by the name of *Jabartī*. This is probably derived from Gabar, which according to al-Maqrīzī was an ancient southern Ethiopian state in the early Middle Ages. Within Muslim Ethiopia there are some cultural and religious centres of special prestige and importance, above all, Harar which has inherited the former tradition of its imamate and amirate, then Jimmā, whence the Islamization of western Ethiopia began, and, in the south, the Muslim establishment of Shaykh Ḥusayn, which is also the object of a famous pilgrimage, as we shall mention later.

On the coast of the Indian Ocean the Somali are all Muslims. South of Somalia the great majority of the population on the coast of Kenya and Tanganyika are Muslims, and their country, as we have already said, has been for two centuries and more under the sovereignty of the Imams of Oman and the Sultans of Zanzibar. The islands of the archipelago of Zanzibar are inhabited by Muslims: the Ibāḍites are Arab immigrants; the Sunnites are the African natives.

METHODS AND WAYS OF PREACHING ISLAM IN EAST AFRICA

The decline of the Christian and Muslim states in Ethiopia after their wars in the sixteenth century and the subsequent invasion of the Galla tribes obliged the Muslims to try at all costs to convert to Islam the Galla pagans who had just arrived in the regions bordering on the remnant of the Muslim amirate of Harar. Thus a small literature arose both in Arabic and in the Harari language, which has a special interest, both historical and linguistic. Harari, which is a Semitic language of the Ethiopian family, was tentatively written with the Arabic alphabet; and it would have been difficult for us to decipher it, since the Arabic script is not adapted to represent the sounds of Ethiopian languages, but for the happy circumstance that a Harari work, written probably in the seventeenth century, is recited till today during the month of Ramaḍān. This is the *Kitāb al-farā'iḍ* (The Book of Religious Duties), composed by the *faqīh* Ṭayyib al-Wanāgī. It shows us the method of preaching Islam in that epoch. The booklet deals with the five *'ibādāt* according to the usual order of the texts of *fiqh*; but the *'ibādāt* are explained by questions and replies as in a catechism (e.g.: "How many are the verities of the faith? They are four: to know that He is your

Creator; to know that He it is who lets you live; to know that He it is who will cause you to pass from the state of this life to the state of the other life; to know that He it is who will give you your retribution according to your merits".) The exposition of the Islamic faith, however, is accompanied by some moral precepts; and here the *Kitāb al-farā'iḍ* follows the pattern of a widely diffused model of local folk-literature: the "genre" called by the Somali *saddeḥliya* ("by three and three"). These are brief compositions, often humorous, consisting of threefold or fourfold propositions which make their point through comparison or contrast. Accordingly we find, for instance, in the *Kitāb al-farā'iḍ*: "Four things are jewels, but are spoiled by four other things. Understanding is a jewel, but it is spoiled by anger. Modesty is a jewel, but greed spoils it. Kindness is a jewel, but slander spoils it. Devotion is a jewel, but envy spoils it"; and again: "The behaviour to be adopted in human society has six elements: the silence of the serpent; the ambush of the cheetah; the jump of the leopard; the anger of the lion; the claws of the falcon, and to appreciate, when necessary, how to walk lowering the head as the wild boar." The insertion of these passages inspired by folklore is useful in keeping the attention of the reader of the *Kitāb al-farā'iḍ* and in making more accessible to him, as a prospective convert, Islamic notions of theology, even the most difficult propositions being very skilfully presented in this well-known popular form. Thus,

> If you ask what signifies "one" as an attribute to God, this signifies that: God is one who is singular in his being; that God is one of whom no one can say that anybody has perceived Him on any occasion or in any place; that God is one of whom nobody can say that He has had His cause in any cause; that God is one of whom no one can say that He is only on the earth or in the Heaven or on His throne or on any chair or in the high or in the low or standing or sitting or speaking or silent. God is one of whom no one can say that He is only in this world or anywhere else in the creation, or in union or in separation or near or far.

And in this way the first notions of Islamic theology are presented in mnemonic formulas to be easily retained and presented within the framework of the folk-literature which also makes them more agreeable.

A similar proceeding for Muslim propaganda is applied farther north in the Amharic-speaking countries. There popular poetry with its traditional rules and forms is employed to ridicule those Christian beliefs which appear least acceptable to Muslims.

And so, before all, the dogma of the Holy Trinity:

"Nine are the Gods", they say. Is there a whole village of Gods?
I am puzzled: of whom shall I ask hospitality among these Gods?,

and the veneration of the sacred images:

The question of the Christians: I do not understand it, no!
They hammer a piece of wood and dress it with silk.
O stupid Christians! O stupid Christians!
They hammer a piece of wood and then they say to it "Forgive me!",

and against the reality of the death of Christ:

Jesus, who was said to be "God's Spirit",[1] is himself a God and he himself was put in the Sepulchre: this is their lie.
Our Lord is not a dead being, He is always existing.
If He were dead, what would have happened to the universe?,

and alluding to the well-known beliefs of Islamic eschatology:

There is a tree which is called ṭūbā.
Its shadow occupies a thousand years of journeying by caravan;
and this even by the mule called Burāq
which to-morrow shall be given to the Prophet.
Such shadow is found in Paradise;
and the girls, that shall be married there, are splendour to the eyes.
The Lord will give us a great reward, if we are purified and guilty of no negligence to Him.

These songs again follow a popular vein and make Islamic ideas more accessible to the mind of local populations by a kind of mimetic attitude which is further evidence of the "souplesse" of the preaching of Islam in Africa.

ASSIMILATION OF ANCIENT LOCAL BELIEFS IN ISLAM

In Ethiopia as in Somalia Islam has easily assimilated some local ideas and practices of the paganism which was dominant in those countries before their conversion, in so far as they are not directly opposed to the basic tenets of the Islamic faith. Naturally we find today more examples of this assimilation in recently converted populations. Already the Imam Aḥmad b. Ibrāhīm said about the converts of his time (sixteenth century): "Their Islam is like a cloth, woven in Argubbā." The district of Argubbā, in Ifāt, was famous for its weavers of very thin

[1] Qur'ān IV. 169.

gauze. In southern Ethiopia the most striking instance of the Islamization of ancient rites is the pilgrimage to Shaykh Ḥusayn. The Galla tribes were socially and politically organized in a system of age groups, which regulated the gradual acquisition of juridical capacity by degrees of initiation. The highest grade reserved for a small minority, was conferred only by a personage having the title of Abbā Mudā ("Father of Unction"), who lived near Mount Walabō in the basin of the river Wēbi. The men, who deserved this supreme initiation, were obliged to go there on pilgrimage and perform complicated rites on the spot before being admitted to the grade. Now in the same region a Muslim saint of the past, Shaykh Nūr Ḥusayn, is venerated, and the Galla go there, from all the countries they inhabit in Ethiopia and in Kenya and Somalia, to perform certain rites of pilgrimage which have been modelled on the rites of the pilgrimage at Mecca. The pilgrimage has changed its character; and, even if the Abbā Mudā retains his former function and lives not so far from Shaykh Ḥusayn, the *qubba* of the Muslim saint appeals more and more to the Galla converts to Islam so that the Muslim pilgrimage in its new form is felt to be a satisfactory substitute for the ancient pagan rites in the same district.

Another ceremony which has been kept even in Muslim countries in Ethiopia as in Somalia is the rite of the *zār* (Somali: *sār*). The name *zār*, which etymologically derives from the name of the supreme God of the pagan Cushites (the vault of Heaven, whose eye is the sun), designates two different rites. The first rite is directed to procuring that a *zār*, one of the powerful genii or minor divine beings, should incarnate himself in the body of the officiating magician. This is done by special songs accompanied by music, often on drums, and by rhythmic blows on the breast which cause some congestion in the apex of the lungs. When the *zār* arrives, the man falls in a trance and frequently delivers oracles on particular questions or on the future of the tribe generally. This rite is used in western Ethiopia, where also some *zār* have the names of former pagan divinities. A second rite, widely diffused also on the coast of the Indian Ocean (Somalia, etc.), obliges the *zār*, who, because of particular circumstances (e.g. the excitement caused by the solemnity of the tribal assembly each year), has incarnated himself in a man or woman, to leave the possessed person and go away. Liberation from possession is also obtained by songs and special music, and the possessed man, when the *zār* is about to leave him, dances to the rhythm of the drums and, while dancing, gives evidence of the state of insensibility which the spirit has induced in him.

The *zār* or genii have each their favourite places where they usually remain and are invoked. Almost everywhere in western and southern Ethiopia and in Somalia, serpents are believed to be the preferred seat of the genii; so that particular formulae are employed to propitiate them and, when somebody kills a serpent especially in Galla countries, he is obliged to offer a symbolic gift to placate the *zār*. Similar ideas are widespread about some trees: about the sycamore, by the Galla tribes; about the *Poinciana elata*, by the Somali tribe of the Dīnla Mantān, etc.; and also running waters, that is, the rivers, torrents and especially thermal springs are considered as inhabited by *zār*, at least in western Ethiopia; and people going on the caravan roads usually present a small offering to the *zār* of the stream before crossing it.

In everyday life the distinction between lawful meat (*ḥalāl*), and forbidden meat (*ḥarām*), has been enlarged by adding—at least in Somalia—some other prohibitions according to local taboos. In fact it is forbidden to Somali men to eat the head (and all its contents), lungs, stomach and shins of animals. This prohibition has also been used to justify the rules against outcast groups of pariahs (hunters, tanners, potters, etc.), because they are said to eat forbidden meat and are therefore nicknamed *bakhti 'uno* ("eaters of carrion"), while *bakhti* (carrion) corresponds here to the Arabic *mayyita* and designates unclean meat.

CULTURAL CONDITION OF EAST AFRICAN ISLAM

The Islamic schools were fighting in different ways through the centuries against these remains of the former paganism. What has been and is now the state of Muslim cultural activity in East Africa? Again we must examine the question in Ethiopia and in Somalia separately.

In Ethiopia it is necessary, above all, to distinguish an early period when the upper classes had attained a high degree of culture, while the lower ranks of local society were attached to Islam more because of national opposition to the Christian Ethiopian Kingdom than because of religious knowledge. The thirteenth century brought, as far as we can gather from the documents, a remarkable flowering of that culture, and eventually its highest achievement. Exchanges of learned men between the schools of Arabia and Ethiopia are recorded in the chronicles: the *shaykh* Abu 'l-Rabīʿ Sulaymān, author of a commentary on the mystic poem *al-Khumarṭathiyya*, left his school in Zabīd (Yemen) and established himself in southern Ethiopia; while at the same period Ethiopian jurists ('Alī b. Abī Bakr al-'Aqīlī and Abū 'Abdallāh Muḥammad b. Abī Bakr al-Gidā'ī) founded schools of Islamic law in Arabia. In the Muslim sultanate of Shoa an Ethiopian *faqīh* had the title of *qāḍī al-quḍāt*, as supreme magistrate. In the subsequent period of the great wars between Christians and Muslims in Ethiopia, political feelings and the opportunities that the wars gave to less religious people are fully proved by the Muslim and Christian chronicles, which record numerous conversions of chiefs and soldiers from Christianity to Islam or vice versa according to the successes of the Christian Negus or the Muslim Imam. Thus an Ethiopian Christian chief named Takla Hāymānot passed to the Muslim camp and was appointed by Imam Aḥmad as governor of a district. Then, later on, when the Imam removed him from his office owing to the demands of the people, Takla Hāymānot left the Muslim side and again became Christian, so that the Negus appointed him feudal ruler of a frontier region. But that region was occupied, after some time, by the Muslim army, and finally Takla Hāymānot was captured and sold as a slave in Arabia. On the other side, the Muslim chief 'Uthmān b. 'Alī was taken prisoner in battle by the Christians. He was converted to Christianity, and the Negus gave him the military command in Ifāt. In that capacity 'Uthmān fought against the Muslims; but, when Imam Aḥmad personally attacked the Christian forces in Ifāt, 'Uthmān returned to Islam, brought all his soldiers to the camp of the Imam, and received as a reward the title of *amīr*. Later he fought again against the Christians, was killed in battle and honoured as a martyr of the Muslim faith.

But in Harar, which remained the capital of the Muslim state during the wars and until 1887, two small literatures flourished: in Arabic was written the "Conquests of Ethiopia" (*Futūḥ al-ḥabasha*), which is a narrative of the victories of Imam Aḥmad b. Ibrāhīm until the occupation of the islands in Lake Ṭānā in 1535. The author was Shihāb al-Dīn Aḥmad b. 'Abd al-Qādir, nicknamed (in Harari) 'Arab-faqīh, who wrote this history while he was living at Jizān in Yemen. A résumé of his book is found in the chronicles of Gujerat by al-Ulughkhānī, an Indian Muslim writer. Minor local chronicles and lists of important dates from the thirteenth century until the end of the amirate of Harar have also been found in the MSS. Later on, the need to keep alive Muslim religious culture and spread it among the pagan Gallas who had newly arrived on the Ethiopian plateau encouraged the use of the Harari language written in the Arabic alphabet. We have already discussed above the "Book of the (Religious) Duties" (*Kitāb al-farā'id*); but in addition there are some poetical works: hymns in praise of Amir Nūr Mujāhid, whose tomb is found in Harar; and the "Poem of the Four Caliphs" in 5,000 lines grouped in mono-rhymed strophes celebrating the four "orthodox" caliphs of Sunnite Islam. The strophes contain four lines, each one dedicated to a caliph.

In more recent times also the Galla language has been written in Arabic characters; for example, a song was composed for the Galla pilgrimage to Shaykh Ḥusayn, which begins:

When my soul shall be near to depart
And the Angel shall look at her
And "Go back to your home", he shall say;
And my reward shall be decided,
Be pitiful to me, O Nūr Ḥusayn!
When I shall be wrapped in my burial cloth
And on my bed I shall be carried away
And from my friends and family I shall be separated
And alone I shall be put away,
Be pitiful to me, O Nūr Ḥusayn!

We have already examined some Muslim songs in Amharic from central Ethiopia meant as propaganda against certain articles of the Christian faith. Other poems from that region are inspired by episodes of the life of the Prophet Muḥammad, like the following verses concerning his death:

'Azrā'īl was sent and came to the house of the Prophet.
"Peace be unto thee, O Prophet, and thy family!
I am here!", so said the Angel of Death.
By this salutation he was approaching the Prophet.
As the Prophet had tasted life, he could not escape death.
'Azrā'īl arrived and when he reached their door,
"There is a guest", said his daughter Fāṭima.
"Alas, Fāṭima, my daughter, what guest is he!
He is 'Azrā'īl who separates the fathers from their sons.
I pray thee, 'Azrā'īl, come back to me another day;
I would like to see previously my brother Jibrā'īl."
"Jibrā'īl thy brother, yes, I have just passed beside him;
All the angels were saying to him: Suffer this! Suffer this patiently!"
And the Angel of Death entered into the house.

On the coast of the Indian Ocean, too, similar Islamic literature has helped to spread the religion.

The Somali language has been used and written in the Arabic alphabet, for example, by the mystic poet Shaykh Uways b. Muḥammed, an adept of the Qādiriyya brotherhood (see below), who was killed in 1909. A long poem of his urges his countrymen to give back peace to the people of Somalia, while at that moment the struggles between the tribes, the movement led by the so-called Mad Mullah and the incidence of European intervention on the coast had deeply disturbed the prosperity of the population. Shaykh Uways again, in order to make his religious propaganda more accessible, composed other poems in different Somali dialects: three in the dialect of the Rahanwēn; one in Hawiyya dialect; one in Dārōd dialect; and thus he followed the general policy of Islam in Africa in adapting its methods to local cultures.

A small group of religious works in the Arabic language was composed by Somali authors. A collection made by Shaykh Qāsim Muḥyi 'l-Dīn al-Barāwī contains eight poems of various authors: Shaykh 'Abd al-Raḥmān al-Zayla'ī; Shaykh Ṣūfī of Mogadishu; Shaykh Uways himself (beside his poems in Somali), all poems inspired by the Qādiriyya brotherhood. Works in prose are: an interesting autobiography by Shaykh 'Alī Maye, of Merca; and the collection of polemic opuscules by Shaykh 'Abdallāh b. Mu'allim Yūsuf against the rival brotherhood of the Ṣālihiyya. This controversial book published at Cairo in 1919–20 caused serious repercussions in Somalia.

MUSLIM BROTHERHOODS

In the nineteenth century the activity of the Muslim brotherhoods (*ṭuruq*), in East Africa gave very efficient help to organized Islam, and not only in the field of religious culture. Some brotherhoods arrived in Ethiopia from the Sudan; the Mirghaniyya *ṭarīqa* which has its major establishments in Eritrea; the Tijāniyya, diffused in south-western Ethiopia (it was founded by Aḥmad al-Tijānī in Algeria, in the region of Oran); and the Sammāniyyah, established in the eighteenth century by Muḥammad al-Sammān, a mystic born in Medina who emigrated to the Sudan. Other powerful brotherhoods had entered Ethiopia from Arabia through Harar: e.g. the Qādiriyya *ṭarīqa*, one of the most ancient Islamic brotherhoods, founded by 'Abd al-Qādir al-Jīlānī in Baghdad; and the Aḥmadiyyah *ṭarīqa*, established by the Yemeni mystic Aḥmad b. Idrīs in the first half of the nineteenth century. These last two brotherhoods, Qādiriyya and Aḥmadiyya, also have their *zawāyā* in Somalia, where are found establishments of the Ṣālihiyyah *ṭarīqa*, a movement born within the Aḥmadiyya but a separate body with full independence, and Rifā'iyya, which is not widely diffused.

While in Ethiopia these brotherhoods were obliged to act with caution to avoid the mistrust of local governors and chiefs, so that they limited themselves to building religious schools and mosques as meeting places for their followers, in Somalia, and especially in the regions along both big rivers the Wēbi and Juba, they tried to acquire extensive landed property and thus asserted, wherever and whenever possible, a certain autonomy as against the local tribes and their chiefs.

CHAPTER II

ISLAM IN WEST AFRICA

West Africa is taken generally to be the area extending from Senegal in the west to Cameroun in the east, and from the southern Sahara to the Guinea and lower Niger coast. The oldest and most strongly Muslim areas are the Saharan and Sudanese belts running west to east and within these, as everywhere else in West Africa, there are many peoples of different language and race. In the western Sahara are Moorish tribes, called "whites" but including negro mixtures. They are linked with Berbers and Arabs of North Africa, and are important in the diffusion of Islam in West Africa. In the middle Niger regions and to the north of Nigeria are light-skinned and muffled Tuaregs, and round Lake Chad darker Teda; both of these became Muslim over the centuries though their social life follows traditional patterns.

In the vast extent of the western Sudan, from Senegal to Chad, are many diverse groups speaking forms of the Fulbe language (also called Fulani or Peul). The "red" Fulbe are herdsmen who are nomadic over a wide area and are only superficially Islamic. The negro Fulbe are farmers and the most solidly Muslim West Africans. Originally nomads, they settled, married negroes, then at the declaration of a *jihād* they subjugated negro pagans and founded states in which they were the ruling aristocracy, as in Jalon, Hausaland and Adamawa. Among the largest racial groups in Senegal are the Wolof and Tokolor who are wholly Muslim. To their south and east are the Mande peoples; of these the Soninke and Dyula are Muslim, Mandinka semi-Muslim, and Bambara pagan. The peoples of the upper Volta river area have mainly resisted Islam though some of them, like the Mossi, had powerful kingdoms in close contact with the Fulbe. Further north, along the Niger bend, the Songhay and Dendi are Muslim but with pagan minorities. In Northern Nigeria many of the Hausa-speaking farmers and traders were pagan till the Fulbe conquests in the nineteenth century, and conversion has continued so that most of them are now Muslim, though there are considerable elements of paganism. Similarly in the region towards Chad there is much Islam but many pagans.

In the Guinea and coastal areas of West Africa Islam has penetrated

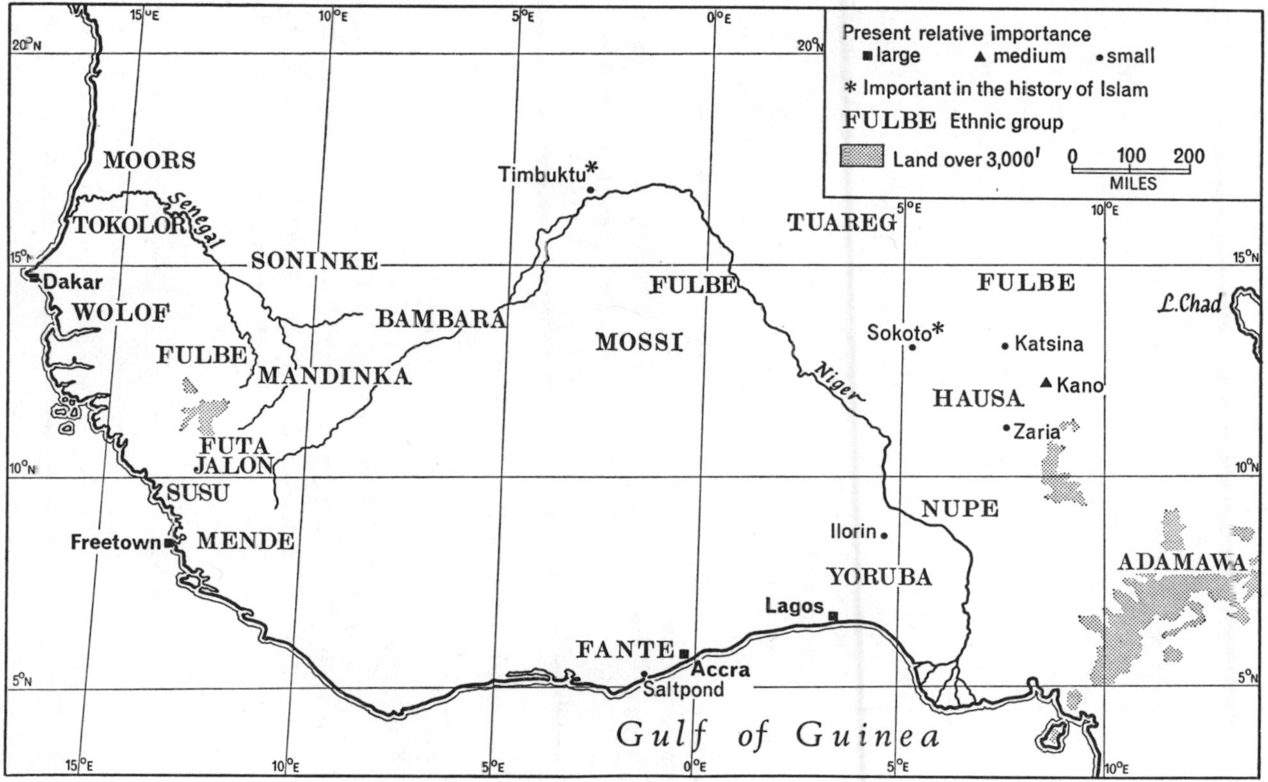
Present relative importance
large
medium
small
* Important in the history of Islam
FULBE Ethnic group
Land over 3,000′
0 100 200
MILES
MOORS
TOKOLOR
Senegal
SONINKE
Dakar
WOLOF
FULBE
BAMBARA
MANDINKA
FUTA JALON
SUSU
Freetown
MENDE
Timbuktu*
FULBE
MOSSI
FANTE
Accra
Saltpond
Lagos
YORUBA
Ilorin
NUPE
Niger
TUAREG
FULBE
Sokoto*
Katsina
Kano
HAUSA
Zaria
L.Chad
ADAMAWA
Gulf of Guinea
20°N
15°N
10°N
5°N
15°E
10°E
5°E
0°E

West Africa.

unevenly and much less extensively. In the west the Fulbe state in the mountains of Futa Jalon was the start of the diffusion of Islam in west Guinea; the Susu of Guinea are Muslim and about half of the Mende and Temne of Sierra Leone. Most of the coastal peoples of Liberia, Ivory Coast, Ghana, Togo and Dahomey are virtually untouched by Islam, though there are often Muslim ruling groups in towns in the north of these countries. Christianity, which came in from the sea, is strongest in the coastal regions and influential through education, though Islam is found in many towns because of Hausa traders and Aḥmadiyya missionaries. In southern Nigeria and Cameroun Christianity is strong and spreads into the interior. But in south-western Nigeria the Fulbe conquests took over the Ilorin region of the Yoruba people and extended their influence through other Yoruba down to the coast at Lagos. In the lower Niger region, the "middle belt" of Nigeria, the Nupe people also were conquered by Fulbe and are largely Muslim but with pagan and Christian minorities. In the plateau of north-east Nigeria a Fulbe dynasty was founded in Adamawa though many of the plateau peoples remain pagan.

Estimates of the numbers of Muslims in West Africa must be tentative in the absence of comprehensive statistics; there have been very few reliable censuses. The Saharan and north Sudanese areas are most firmly Muslim but least thickly populated. Senegal and Guinea to the west, and north and west Nigeria to the east, are the strongest Muslim regions of large population. In 1959 Trimingham, in his standard works on this subject,[1] estimated 24 million Muslims in West Africa out of an approximate total population of 64 million. Animists he reckoned at 24 million also and Christians at 3 million. But his figures were admittedly incomplete, as no details were given for the two populous regions of East and West Nigeria. There are hardly any Muslims in East Nigeria, and in the West Christians might claim up to half the population with Islam when paganism finally declined, giving Christianity more than half the population of these two regions reckoned in the 1964 census as 25 million. Census figures are being revised; the 1964 census gave Northern Nigeria nearly 30 million, and the whole federation of Nigeria always has been more thickly populated than all the rest of West Africa put together. But Islam can probably claim about half the population of West Africa. Other Africans

[1] J. S. Trimingham, *Islam in West Africa* (Oxford, 1959), Appendix v; also *A History of Islam in West Africa* (London, 1962).

come under the indirect influence of Islam, and modern life favours the universal religions at the expense of the old illiterate tribal rituals.

Islam entered West Africa slowly over the centuries, and nearly always from North Africa following the western routes. The coastal regions were cut off by unexplored sea and almost impenetrable forest, until modern roads and railways enabled Christianity to enter from the south and Islam to descend direct from the north.

The revival and expansion of Islam in West Africa in the nineteenth century was inspired by the Qādiriyya and Tijāniyya *ṭarīqas*. The Qādiriyya spread first and peacefully, teaching in Muslim and pagan regions. The Tijāniyya prospered in West Africa largely through the nineteenth-century *jihād*, which led both to conversion and to reaction to conquest when possible, for example, by the Bambara.

Already in the eighteenth century there had been a struggle for supremacy by the Fulbe of the mountains of Futa Jalon in western Guinea against the pagan natives, and this continued into the nineteenth century with the Fulbe dominating the hill and plateau regions. In the Futa area of Senegal and in many other places between there and the Niger Islam was spread by the astonishing conquests of the adventurer al-Ḥājj ʻUmar, from 1853 to his death in 1864.[1] ʻUmar b. Saʻīd Tal was born in Senegalese Futa, made the pilgrimage to Mecca, and was initiated *khalīfa* for the Sudan. In 1853, after forty days' retreat, he proclaimed the *jihād*, and sought to spread Islam among the pagan tribes and check European penetration of West Africa. His expeditions fed the slave trade to Central and South America which continued till the 1890s. French and British opposed slavery officially, though firearms were sold to ʻUmar, and slavery was not crushed till the full colonial occupation of West Africa at the end of the century. ʻUmar ranged across the western Sudan as far as Timbuktu, spreading the Tijānī way among Muslims and pagans. When he died his empire split and later fell in pieces to the French, but Islam had been widely extended and revived.

It was news of the successful Islamic advance in Futa Jalon that inspired the *jihād* of ʻUthmān dan Fodio in Hausaland, in what is now Northern Nigeria. In 1804 he was proclaimed by his Fulbe followers as *amīr*, or in Hausa *Sarkin Musulmi*, a title still held by the chief of Sokoto. He blessed flags and gave them to his disciples to proclaim the *jihād*. The Hausa rulers were alarmed and persecuted ʻUthmān's followers,

[1] Muḥammad ʻAlī Tyam, *La Vie d'El Hadj Omar*, tr. H. Gaden (Paris, 1935).

but this simply roused the Fulbe. Despite strong resistance 'Uthmān captured the Hausa towns of Zaria, Katsina and Kano by 1809. Hausa Muslims were forced to abandon pagan rites which many of them had continued, but even at the British occupation about 1900 many Hausa were pagan. After 'Uthmān's death in 1817 the Fulbe conquest was extended to the pagan regions of Adamawa in the east and Nupe and Yoruba to the south. Muslim success in Hausaland stimulated the growth of the religion to the east in Bornu and Waday. But the Hausa states were disorganized and only the religious authority of the chief of Sokoto was recognized. The establishment of European rule in West Africa did little to hinder, indeed it often helped, the fixing of Muslim allegiance and the process has continued with the return of political independence.[1]

In the coastal regions the establishment of Islam came late and slowly. Islam was observed by slaves and in secret in Lagos till 1840, and even after that there were few Yoruba Muslims till 1876 when a preacher came south from the Yoruba town of Ilorin. In the Gold Coast (modern Ghana) there were a few Muslims in Ashanti in 1817 and liberated slaves were landed in 1836, but the religion only progressed from 1872 onwards. The liberated slaves of Liberia and Sierra Leone were little touched by Islam, though the hinterland peoples were affected by the movements in the neighbouring Guinea and Senegal countries. With the opening of modern communications Islam has spread widely through the southern Yoruba of Nigeria, but much less in Ghana.

Significant in the propagation of Islam in West African coastal lands in modern times has been the arrival of Aḥmadiyya missionaries from India, of the majority sect from Qadian rather than from the Lahore Aḥmadīs. Fante Muslims in the Gold Coast wrote to Qadian requesting a missionary, and a man called Nayyar, a companion of Ghulām Aḥmad, was sent in 1921. He paid a passing visit to Freetown and went on to Nigeria, but his major success was among the Fante where he established his headquarters at Saltpond and converted nearly all the Muslim community to his views, with the exception of a few northerners. In Nigeria, despite initial success and the interest of the later chief of Lagos, there arose disputes and litigation for possession of mosques. A mosque built at the University of Ibadan in 1961 had not been used by 1963 because of the objection of northerners to Aḥmadi

[1] There is no full history of 'Uthmān dan Fodio and the Fulbe *jihād*; see Trimingham, *History*, pp. 193 ff.

contributions towards its building. There has been a great deal of Aḥmadiyya propaganda in West Africa, in English language newspapers and books, and in education. Aḥmadīs have been foremost in education in some coastal towns and have claimed to speak with the voice of Islam. But their numbers are not great. They are still strongest among the Fante but their capital at Saltpond is a backwater. Despite their claim to extend Islam very few Aḥmadīs come from pagan homes, nearly all are from Islam and Christianity. The exaggerated claims of Aḥmadīs make them suspect to the well educated, and orthodox Islam and the *ṭarīqas* have hardly yet come into contact with them. When they do the outlook will not be good for Aḥmadiyya.

It is generally agreed that, with some exceptions, the level of Islam in West Africa is low. Contact with the heartlands of Islam has always been difficult till quite recent times, and extension into much of West Africa awaited the nineteenth and twentieth centuries. But even in those parts of the Sudan where it is centuries old it was often inert and received little outside stimulus. The Saharan Tuareg are said to have apostasized fourteen times, and even today very few can read the Qur'ān, there are few religious leaders, and those who do perform their religious duties parade them ostentatiously under the impulse of the Tijāniyya.[1]

It has long been remarked that in the middle Niger towns, such as Timbuktu and Jenne, there is a numerous élite, well informed in Islam, but for most people Islam is superficial and many pagan ideas remain, though the significance of the outward profession of Islam should not be underestimated. J. Rouch has shown that while Islam spread among the Songhay since the thirteenth century with remarkable perseverance, the resistance of indigenous religion has also been persistent.[2] Islam played an important part both in the cohesion and in the fall of the negro Songhay empire, which was achieved in collaboration with the Moroccans. Islam is manifested in externals, and once having adopted the religion the Songhay never rejected it. There have been conversions of large pagan groups in recent years, owing to modern peace and ease of travel for marabout preachers. In the villages nearly all the men are to be seen at evening prayer. Yet there is unevenness of practice. At

[1] H. Lhote, *Les Touaregs du Hoggar* (Paris, 1944), p. 304 f.

[2] J. Rouch, *La Religion at la magie Songhay* (Paris, 1960), pp. 13 ff.; C. Monteil, *Djénné* (Paris, 1932), pp. 148 ff.; H. Miner, *The Primitive City of Timbuctoo* (Princeton, 1953), pp. 72 ff.

Timbuktu circumcision is practised with Islamic rites, but hardly anywhere else. Islam fills up certain gaps in pagan religion, such as ideas of a future life, and it demands outward conformity, but it is only one element in a complex religious life. The manifestations of Islam, daily and Friday prayers and Ramaḍān fast, made government administrators imagine that the people were all Muslims. But every Sunday at Niamey and Gao, and monthly in the villages, the beating of calabashes and the panting cries of ecstatics show that there are other levels of religion even among this long Islamized people. These are the cults of the *holey*, divinities of river, sky and other elements, and round them there is a ritual which receives great attention. A similar mixed religion is found among other people often thought of as thoroughly Muslim: Tokolor, Dyula, Soninke, Hausa and Kanuri. Others more recently influenced by Islam, such as Temne and Mende of Sierra Leone and Nupe and Yoruba of Nigeria, show many more pagan traits, yet they also reveal which elements of Islam are first adopted.

All West Africans believe in a Supreme Being or Creator who was the origin of gods and men; he is always associated with the sky though he often has the earth as partner. Yet he is rarely worshipped, whereas other gods and the earth spirit may receive much ritual attention.[1] The heavenly God was easily called Allāh by Muslim converts and he was now given greater attention in prayer. But even Muslim teachers say little about God except to declare his unity. The lesser gods might come to be regarded as angels or jinn, though in fact powerful spirit cults remain and the earth receives sacrifice in agricultural ritual. Angels may be thought of as personal guardians, like family and tutelary spirits in paganism.

African ideas of the soul have some similarities to Muslim belief, though African Muslim teachers have little knowledge of Arab teachings on the subject. An obvious difference is in various kinds of belief in the reincarnation of the soul which are held in Africa, in places the full rebirth of one element in the personality is held, elsewhere emphasis is simply placed on the maintenance of the family name and power through successive generations. There is a widespread belief in ghosts, which are spirits that have not received proper burial rites or are particularly restless. It is generally thought that the soul wanders about during sleep, when it is liable to be seized and eaten by witches.

[1] See *African Ideas of God*, ed. E. W. Smith and E. G. Parrinder (Edinburgh House Press, 3rd ed. 1966).

There are some ideas of judgment after death, and an afterlife either underground or in the sky. These are reinforced by Islam, with its much clearer ideas of heaven and hell and sleep till the resurrection.

African morality depended upon God and the spirit world, and especially upon the ancestors as makers and guardians of tradition. Their sanctions were group unity and fear: "no man is half as much afraid of the gods as of his own dead ancestors", said an anthropologist. The extent of moral obligation was limited to groups linked by kinship. Under Islam, morality stems from God, who rewards and punishes, and it has universal application; yet it is also more personal and brings in the concept of sin. Islamic taboos, such as against eating pork, are fairly easily adopted, though the same cannot be said of drinking wine or beer. But a double moral standard can be seen widely. This often seems to be followed without strain; but sometimes there is a direct conflict, as when possessed ecstatics give directions from the ancestors that conflict with Islamic law. The legalism of Islamic teachers is evident in the way in which they know the details of ablutions and prayers but have little to say on theological subjects.

Prayers are made in the old religion, in the morning and on family and agricultural occasions, at tiny shrines with or without images. There are few temples as large as a house and all are made of mud. Under Islam daily prayers are irregular; some perform them twice daily, or sandwich them together; few can do the ritual actions or recite the prayers without mistakes, and they are content that the clergy should do this for them properly. Friday midday prayer in the mosques is observed by most men. The type of mosque varies greatly. Nomads use a square marked out by branches or a straw fence, but even in towns many mosques are small and they may be only low mud walls into which the *imām* alone enters. However there are many large mosques, traditionally in the Sudan built of mud with projecting posts or battlements, and these are the best architecturally. Modern mosques, especially in the coastal regions, are often large enclosed buildings of concrete or brick, with corrugated iron roofs, and in incongruous styles. Only large mosques have minarets, and elsewhere the *mu'adhdhin* calls from the door.

Friday prayer is led by the *imām*, and responses are followed by the *mu'adhdhin* in a loud voice. Some mosques have pulpits, but few are well carved, and often there is only a block of wood on which the *imām* stands to preach a short sermon. Women are not allowed in the mosques at prayer time, though old women sweep up and may join in festival prayers. The Aḥmadiyya and some nomads allow women to pray in the mosques behind the men. Friday is not a rest day and most shops and offices close on Sunday instead, which is a time for drumming and dancing. The popularity of Friday prayer is its social and state character which reinforces group solidarity.

Almsgiving is no longer a state levy, as it was in the old Islamic states in pre-colonial days. But it is levied by mosque authorities for the support of teachers and is collected at the beginning of the year and the end of Ramaḍān. Voluntary alms are also given to the many beggars and deformed people who lie at the entrance to mosques, in streets and at railway stations, and cry for money "for the sake of the Prophet".

The new year festival of *'āshūrā'* is associated with some African agricultural practices, though as the date is always changing the link with the old solar year sacrifices has been broken. After a short fast there is a feast from sacrifices of rams, Islamic ablutions and, among the Songhay, a ceremony of purification by fire. Special prayers follow in the mosques, with reading of prophecies and sermons. Prayer is made for the dead and visits are paid to graves of ancestors and chiefs. The Prophet's birthday was not much observed in the past, but this has become more widespread with announcements of the date according to the western calendar.

Ramaḍān is observed fairly strictly, since it is a social custom breach of which would be noted and disapproved. Daily prayers are more diligently performed at this time, and it is believed that they bring forgiveness of sins. Special devotions are performed on the 27th day, and there are public processions in some places. At the new moon guns are fired, drums beat, and there is rejoicing. Morning prayer, about eight or nine o'clock, is held at special open air praying-places outside towns, with the *imām* leading prayers and reciting a homily standing on a wooden block or a whitewashed brick stand. In Guinea men rub their hands on his clothes to obtain power from it. There is feasting and dancing, at the same time.

At the pilgrimage festival, called *'īd al-kabīr* or *bayram*, the men gather again in great crowds at the praying-place, and the *imām* sacrifices a ram. Then the men return home to sacrifice their own rams before their houses, distributing the meat to family, teachers and poor. The skin of the ram is often kept as a prayer mat. There are three days' holiday but little dancing.

The pilgrimage routes to Mecca are still not easy, except for the rich. In 1956 Trimingham found that 2,483 pilgrims had travel certificates from Northern Nigeria of whom 2,420 were going by road. But nearly 1,500 booked air flights from the richer regions of south-west Nigeria. In Senegal Marty found that only twenty Muslim teachers out of 1,386 had made the pilgrimage.[1] The sea route may be taken, and can be fairly comfortable though long. But the great majority take the Sudan route eastwards, skirting the tropical forest and arriving eventually at the Nile. Formerly camels were the chief means of transport, but today lorries take pilgrims. However, many go on foot, with their families, and a donkey to carry their goods. Many stop on the way to earn money to pay railway and boat fares, and the pilgrims' expenses in the Ḥijāz. The journey may take seven years or longer, and as many are old they do not return home, dying or settling down on the way back. There are said to be 4,000 West Africans settled in Mecca. Although the pilgrim may not gain much renown from performance of the pilgrimage, and wears no distinctive dress, yet he takes the title *al-ḥājj* and has performed his religious duty. He has learnt more of Islam, both by travelling all the way to Mecca through Muslim lands and by seeing Islam in its home. Political ideas may also be picked up in the Near East and so strengthen Arab links.

Veneration of saints and their tombs, so prominent in the eastern Sudan and North Africa, is virtually absent in West Africa. This is probably because of the persistence of the spirit cults, the *holey* of the Songhay and *bōri* of the Hausa, which continue alongside Islam and provide a powerful lower level of dynamism in a complex religious structure. Marabouts from North Africa visit southern regions but return home again, and tales of saints performing miracles are rare and are told of few native leaders. Burial places are neglected and have no cult practices, nor do people visit them to pray for special needs. The only renowned tomb in Nigeria is that of 'Uthmān dan Fodio, which is dilapidated and visited by few people. Yet there have been some indigenous saints, of whom the most notable was Aḥmad Bamba of Senegal, who died in 1927 and was succeeded by his sons. Their way (*murīdiyya*) has had a powerful influence on the agricultural Wolof, has converted pagans, and transformed life by developing collective farming. The great mosque at Touba is the centre of the cult, and the tomb of

[1] Trimingham, *Islam in West Africa*, p. 87 n. 4; P. Marty in *Revue du Monde Musulman*, vol. XXVIII, no. 31.

Aḥmad Bamba has thousands of visitors in Muḥarram. Emphasis is laid on the holiness of the founder, personal submission, and dedication to communal life. This pattern of sanctified social life is comparable with others illustrated by some of the Christian separatist sects in Ivory Coast, Ghana and Nigeria. The *ṭarīqas*, Qādiriyya and Tijāniyya, might seem to approximate to saint cults, but for the layman adherence usually involves little more than the repetition of a few litanies and acceptance of some mutual obligations to fellow members. They have little connexion with mysticism, and stress negative morality such as avoidance of drinking and smoking, and repudiation of the spirit possession cults.

In personal and family life Islam has influenced West Africa irregularly; there is the same parallelism of new and old religion that is to be observed in the more strictly religious sphere. There is a widespread African custom of naming a child on the eighth day after birth. An Islamic name may be given, as well as a pagan name indicating which ancestor is reborn into or is protecting the child. When Islam is well established the local cleric comes to the home to announce the child's name, give amulets to protect it from jinn and witchcraft, kill a sacrificial sheep, and say prayers for the child and family. Pagan rites are often included by elders of the family: a libation to the earth spirit, lifting up the child to the moon, or carrying it round the house, shaving its head, and making tribal marks and excisions. Kola nuts and food are distributed to all present, everyone gives some gift and may utter a name or blessing. Many West Africans, though not all, practise circumcision of boys and some add clitoridectomy. This could be performed in infancy, though often it was left to be done in initiation schools in adolescence. Traditionally this was prescribed by the ancestors, but efforts are made to find justification for it in stories of Abraham and the Prophet.

Polygamy is permitted throughout West Africa and is one of the customs most resistant to change. Islam is welcomed because it allows polygamy, and there is little knowledge of changing marriage practices in North Africa and the rest of the Muslim world. Prohibited degrees of marriage vary, as do laws of inheritance. Some West African tribes are matrilineal, so that sons inherit from maternal uncles. The practice of dowry or bride-wealth makes marriage a contract between families rather than individuals and aims at ensuring stability, though it is widely complained today that dowries are too high and marriage is spoilt by mercenary motives. Concubinage is practised with descendants of former slaves; and that polygamy is no guarantee against prostitution and homosexuality is seen in the remarkable biography of Baba of Karo, a Muslim Hausa woman.[1] Inheritance of widows is common, since this is part of the family contract. Divorce was much less frequent under old African customs than under Islam; one of the commonest grounds of divorce was infertility which defeated the purpose of the marriage. Children belong to the father, in patrilineal societies, if the full dowry has been paid. Marriage is preceded by betrothal, which includes exchange of kola nuts by the families as the basic sign of contract, and libations to the ancestors. Dowry follows, and presents are given to many members of the family. The actual wedding may have little religious ceremonial, apart from offerings at ancestral graves, and the Muslim cleric may recite prayers. Widows usually do not remarry for several months or a year.

The position of women in the greater part of West Africa is one of considerable freedom and independence, both among nomadic tribes and among forest and farming peoples. One reason for polygamy was the need for workers in the fields, and this gave freedom of movement to women. Other women are great traders, and some amass personal fortunes quite independently of their husbands. The newly converted Nupe and Yoruba are unveiled, but some Sudanese women pull their head cloths over their faces if strange men are about. African Muslim women are rarely secluded; the Fulbe of Nigeria are fairly strict on seclusion but Fulbe in Futa Jalon are quite free. Richer women in towns in the interior may keep indoors in the daytime, but the spread of modern ways works against it.[2]

The strong social sense of African life finds an outlet in Islamic ceremonies, Friday prayers and annual fasting and festivals. To these are added agricultural rituals and ancestral memorials, for which Islam has not yet provided effective substitutes. Islam is mainly adapted to urban and trading peoples; many agricultural people have only been partially integrated into it or not at all. A grave disadvantage of pagan religion has been its local limitations, and here the brotherhood of Islam helps to overcome tribal enmity, especially important in the much freer and wider contacts of modern times. Where the chiefs in negro states became Muslim they continued to perform pagan rites

[1] M. Smith, *Baba of Karo* (Faber, 1954), pp. 63 ff.
[2] S. F. Nadel, *Nupe Religion* (Routledge, 1954), pp. 23 ff.

as before, for they were "divine" kings and the prosperity of society was thought to depend upon their performance of customary rituals. In course of time they might delegate their actions to accredited representatives, but it was of help to their prestige to retain the aura of sacred action and Islam added little to this in the eyes of the people. There was often no attempt at changing the religion of the ordinary folk, and as Islam was a private confession of faith there was no question of merely nominal adherence. Nevertheless the example of the ruler influences people, and many say that they are Muslims because their "father", the village chief, is a Muslim. Where chiefs were militant Muslims like the Fulbe, then this disturbed the balance which needed adjustment by careful growth, and deep-seated conflicts remain.

Although the French and British colonial governments recognized the chiefs as Muslim rulers, the election of chiefs proceeded according to traditional patterns. It was thought that law should be administered according to the *sharīʻa*, but in fact there is a wide measure of adaptation to African customary law. The colonial administrations introduced some of their own laws also, and these have been continued in the new independent states whose leaders are often modern politicians. Islamic law is of course applied in religious matters, but much less in family and inheritance affairs, and hardly at all in civil law except where it may be modified by adding Islamic regulations. Once again the villages are most resistant to any interference with ancestral custom and agricultural ritual, and the authorities here are chiefs and local councils rather than clerics.

Qur'ānic schools are to be found in many parts of West Africa, though in the villages they function irregularly owing to the demands of farming; a child or two from each Muslim village family may attend school in early morning or late evening. All towns where there is a sizable Islamic community have Qur'ānic schools where boys and girls recite the Qur'ān by heart in a monotone, and receive instruction in the elementary duties of Islam. The first Sūra is learnt and then the shorter Sūras beginning from the end of the Qur'ān. With the rapid growth of Western-style education children go to the Qur'ān school first for a year or two. There may be a special school building, in which more advanced lessons are taught later, or the class may meet in the teacher's house or under a tree, only rarely in a mosque. Pupils often work for their teacher, and may have to spend long hours in his fields; corporal punishment is freely administered. Teachers receive gifts rather than regular payment, in money and in kind. The Qur'ān is taught in small sections, and up to four years is taken in learning it all by heart. Relatively few children learn to write more than a few words or verses, since Arabic is little known and not spoken apart from the Qur'ān. Some of the Fulbe pupils are set to write out sections of the Qur'ān every day, and here there are examinations which are unknown in most parts of West Africa.

Religious leaders are educated clerks and heads of communities. The teacher is called *mālam* (Hausa), *modibbo* (Fulbe) or *alfa* (Songhay and Guinea). Through his knowledge of the Qur'ān and to a lesser extent of the *sharī'a* he teaches children, leads prayers, offers sacrifices, and officiates at namings, marriages and funerals. In a fully Muslim community he is present at all official functions. The chief cleric is the *imām*, appointed by the chief or council. He is elected for life and the office is often hereditary, as when held by Fulbe among Yoruba and Nupe. Distinctive clerical clans wearing white mufflers are found among Tuareg and Soninke. The clerics are trained in the Qur'ānic schools, first in the "tablet schools" where the Qur'ān is recited, and then in the "law schools" which include all other studies. These may be simply further details of prayer and occasional offices, and study of a law book. While there has been opposition to the translation of the Qur'ān it is translated orally for purposes of comment and preaching. African Muslims often have English and French translations of the Qur'ān which are available cheaply, and there are Fulbe, Yoruba and other translations in manuscript. Law proper is studied in Mālikite books, though the Indian Aḥmadiyya are Ḥanafiyya. There are West African compilations of laws, and al-Ḥājj 'Umar, 'Uthmān dan Fodio and his son Muḥammad Belo, were copious writers; but these works are mostly imitations and unoriginal. Some Arabic terms have found their way into West African languages but chiefly from the law books. Few of the clergy understand colloquial Arabic and in speaking the language they tend to use legal terms.

Some African languages have been written in Arabic characters: Tokolor, Wolof, Fulbe, Songhay and Hausa, and this proved a useful means of communication. But the clerics, with reverence for Arabic, opposed the use of Hausa religious poems; only in Futa have the masses been inspired by compositions in their own language fitted to an Arabic script. Many other African languages have been reduced to writing by

Christian missions, and a large new vocabulary has come from Europe for the new objects and needs of modern life.

Schools of higher Arabic studies have been founded and incorporated into the new universities. The Ahmadu Bello University of Northern Nigeria, opened in 1962 at Zaria, included a School of Arabic and a College of Arts, Science and Technology. But the Faculty of Arabic and Islamic Studies is small compared with the other faculties of arts, science, engineering, agriculture, architecture, veterinary science, law and public administration. In any case admission into universities demands at least a School Certificate of London University standards, and few would-be clerics could attain to this. Some West Africans go to al-Azhar in Egypt, where there are said to be a hundred of them at any one time.

The coming of Western culture and Christianity has posed problems which Muslim clerics were often unable to answer. Both French and British governments tried to keep Christian missions out of what they regarded as solidly Muslim areas. Yet they used Christian clerks from the coast to fill government posts which the northerners did not want and could not hold because of their inadequate education. For a long time the interior was more backward educationally than the coast, because missions were banned, but they provided schools in those places where they were allowed freedom. Some government schools were set up in the interior, but these were more expensive to run and difficult to staff than the mission schools. There are private Muslim primary and some secondary schools in the coastal areas. In the interior the government schools were given an Islamic air and time was allowed off for prayers, but the syllabus was European.

The attitude of Sudanese Muslims to the West and to Christianity has been largely negative. Where Christian missions have been established they have often been tolerated but have small success in conversion. In new areas, where the old paganism is breaking down, as among Yoruba and Nupe, there is free changing of religion; Muslim, Christian and pagan members may be found in the same family, and they may observe the festivals of the other religions which are regarded as social customs. Open opposition to Christianity is most evident among the prolific English publications of the Aḥmadiyya. Here there is criticism of the person of Jesus that is unknown to orthodox Muslims who revere the prophet 'Īsā. Christianity is sometimes called "the religion of the whites", but Islam also has been criticized by extreme nationalists as a foreign religion from Mecca. There has been occasional co-operation of Muslims and Christians in social matters, in opposition to interference with religious education or a proposal to establish a crematorium.

Modern Islam in West Africa is being subjected to influences from paganism, from Western culture and from Christianity. In its turn it is influencing all three as they exist in Africa. The growth of big new towns is favourable to the spread of an urban religion, and destructive of the old village cults which may become the concern of a few old people, with an occasional sacrifice by the representative of a chief. The old cults are bound to die despite artificial nationalistic revivals, for they have no literature, history, or universal doctrine and morality. Islam and Christianity have all these. Islam has the additional advantage of being propagated entirely by Africans who live at the same level as the people, though in the African churches the role of Europeans is rapidly declining. Much of West African Islam is at a low level and it is having to face education and secularism. But West Africa has and probably will continue to have a Muslim majority, with Christianity as a strong minority mainly in the coastal regions. Both religions will have to adjust themselves to each other, and they may even learn from each other, with that tolerance that has generally been characteristic of West African religious life.

CHAPTER 12

ISLAM IN THE BALKANS

An enduring legacy of the Ottoman empire is the presence today, in the European lands over which it ruled, of five million Muslims—some three million in five Balkan states and two million in European Turkey. Precise figures on the number of Muslims in the Balkans are not available. The dominant majorities do not care to reveal the exact numbers of potentially troublesome minorities. Furthermore, in Communist countries many persons of Muslim background have either renounced Islam or prefer not to declare their confessional affiliation. The following figures are estimates of the size of the principal Muslim communities based on official figures released at different times: Albania—800,000 Sunnite Muslims and 200,000 Bekṭāshīs; Yugoslavia—1,300,000 ethnic Muslims (Bosnia-Hercegovina and Macedonia), 900,000 Albanians, 180,000 Turks, and an undetermined number of Muslim Gypsies; Bulgaria—700,000 Turks, 180,000 Pomaks 120,000 Gypsies, and 5,000 Tatars; Greece—130,000 Turks; Rumania—21,000 Tatars, and 15,000 Turks.

No systematic study has been made of the Islamization and Ottomanization of the Balkans. It is generally agreed that few peoples have been so intransigently Muslim as the Ottomans, who took the missionary aspect of Islam seriously. Yet most historians have viewed the Ottoman policy of Islamization in the Balkans as essentially peaceful, with only a fraction of the conquered being forced to adopt Islam. Many of the initial converts accepted Islam for personal gain or out of fear of persecution. In the time of Ottoman expansion, the Christian world of Anatolia and the Balkans was in a state of anarchy precipitated by religious, national, and social conflicts. Islam seemed to offer a constructive alternative to chaos and misery; hence many Christians adopted it voluntarily.[1] Apostasy was far more extensive among the Christians than among the Turks, whose renegades were very few.

Conversion to Islam had its greatest success in the Albanian and Slavic regions. Many indigenous elements of various ethnic back-

[1] Many historians attribute the large number of Muslims in Bosnia-Hercegovina to the voluntary mass conversion of the Bogumils.

The Balkans.

grounds became Islamized and completely assimilated by the Ottomans. Today we divide the Balkan Muslims into two principal groups: the converted Christians (the Slavs of Bosnia–Hercegovina, Macedonia, and Bulgaria; and the Albanians), and the Muslim immigrants (Turks, Tatars, Cherkess [Circassians], Gypsies, Arabs, etc.). Nearly all Balkan Muslims are Sunnites of the Ḥanafite rite.

The Turks left a strong influence on the language of the Balkan peoples. The Turkish minorities have perpetuated archaic speech forms and developed minor local linguistic peculiarities. Other Muslims, as well as their Christian neighbours, borrowed many Turkish, Arabic, or Persian administrative, legal, religious, and professional words, as well as words for certain kinds of foods, vegetables, fruit, furnishings, tools, and utensils. The Turkish style of dress has been followed by

Christians as well as Muslims, with Christians in the backward villages still clinging to the traditional garb.

Examples of Ottoman architecture,[1] good and bad, can be found in many parts of the Balkans. The Ottoman touch survives in some of the arts and crafts, and the same is true of music. No Balkan popular lyrics are more beautiful and rich in oriental flavour than the *sevdalinka* of the Bosnian Muslims. Although not completely oriental, it betrays its Ottoman antecedents in language, music, and motif. The Turkish coffee house (*kahvehane*, *kafana*, *kaffeneion*) is one of the most cherished legacies, and Turkish influence on the Balkan cuisine is easily discerned.

On the other hand, certain undesirable features of Balkan life can be traced, in part at least, to Ottoman influence. Religious discrimination, coupled with constant exposure to a military atmosphere, produced negative traits in the Balkan peoples and a deep rift between Christians and Muslims. The Ottoman social system fostered such habits as bribery (*bakhshīsh*), distrust of government, fatalism (*kismet*), and the assignment of an inferior status to women.

In the eighteenth and nineteenth centuries the Muslims of Bosnia–Hercegovina developed a literature of their own, produced in Serbo-Croatian but modified in form to accord with Ottoman models. The Balkan Muslims showed a special fondness for folk songs and popular poetry, though their compositions are less heroic than those of the Christians and more in the tradition of the ballad. Particularly fascinating are the Bosnian Muslim epics,[2] but perhaps the best-known poem is the Bosnian *Hasanaganica*,[3] a popular story with a tragic motif about a certain Ḥasan Āghā and his wife (the origin of this poem is still disputed by native and foreign scholars). The story of the poem may be based on a family that actually lived or it may represent a synthesis of elements taken from various poems with similar themes.

Under Ottoman rule the Muslims of Yugoslavia were an integral part of the whole community of Islam. In the nineteenth century, as individual parts of the Yugoslav lands were liberated, Muslims organized separate Islamic religious communities (as in Bosnia–Hercegovina, Serbia, and Montenegro). On the basis of the Treaty of Berlin of 1878 and the Austro-Ottoman Convention of 1879, Vienna

[1] Ghazi Khusrev Bey mosque (1530) and medrese (1537) in Sarajevo, Aladža mosque in Foča (1550), Ferhad Pasha mosque in Banjaluka (1579), and Karadžoz Beg mosque in Mostar.

[2] Kosta Hermann, *Narodne pjesme Muslimana u Bosni i Hercegovini* (Sarajevo, 2nd ed. 1933).

[3] Tvrtko Cubelic, "Hasanaganica", *Enciklopedija Jugoslavije*, vol. III (1958), p. 662.

granted religious freedom to the Muslims in Bosnia and Hercegovina, but in practice this did not work out. A decree of 24 October 1882 provided for the designation of a chief of the *'ulamā'* (*ra'īs al-'ulamā'*) and a Council of the *'ulamā'*. The Habsburg monarchy assumed the right to designate and control these Muslim authorities, a development naturally resented by the Muslims. Finally, in 1909 a statute was approved by which the Muslims were permitted to elect their own leaders. The supreme authority was vested in the Council of the *'ulamā'*, presided over by the chief, who was chosen by a special religious college with the approval of the emperor and the Shaykh al-Islām in Istanbul.

By special decisions of 1868 and 1878 the government of Serbia granted its Muslims the right to full religious freedom. After the Second Balkan War, on 18 August 1913, these privileges were extended also to newly acquired Macedonia and the Sanjak of Novi Pazar, and the title of Mufti was raised to Grand Mufti. In effect, Islam was recognized as a religion, though it did not enjoy equality with the Orthodox Church. The offices of the Mufti were located in Niš. The Islamic community was permitted to maintain contact with representatives abroad under the supervision of the Minister of Education, and it received financial aid from the state.

After the wars of 1876–8 Montenegro acquired territories that included Muslims, to whom the government granted freedom of religion. According to Article 129 of the Constitution of 1905, the administration of the Islamic community was entrusted to the Mufti. The privileges and rights enjoyed by the Muslims of Montenegró were the same as those enjoyed by the Muslims of Serbia.

With the merger of the Yugoslav provinces into a single state in 1918, it became necessary to provide new regulations for the Islamic communities. For a while the organization of the religious communities remained as it was before the First World War. Article 12 of the Yugoslav Constitution of 1921 guaranteed freedom of religion and equality to all religions, and in 1919 and 1922 laws were adopted providing for the uniform administration of religious and *waqf* affairs under the supervision of the Ministry of Cults. The Muslims of Serbia (including Macedonia) and Montenegro were merged into a single community under the Chief Mufti, who resided in Belgrade, while the Muslims of Bosnia–Hercegovina and the rest of Yugoslavia constituted a community under the chief of the *'ulamā'* in Sarajevo.

By a law of 31 January 1930 the two separate Islamic communities were united under the Chief of the *'ulamā'* in Belgrade, who was appointed by the Crown. Councils of *'ulamā'* and *waqf* councils were based in Sarajevo and Skopje. The community was placed under state supervision, received some financial aid, and was permitted to maintain contact with religious representatives abroad. The administration of Muslim affairs was modified on 28 February 1936. The office of Mufti was abolished and the office of the chief of the *'ulamā'* moved to Sarajevo. There was much opposition to the abolition of the office of Mufti and the growing tendency of the government to interfere in Muslim affairs.

In 1919 the Yugoslav Muslim Organization (*Jugoslovenska Muslimanska Organizacija*) was founded with Mehmed Spaho as its head. This political party, representing the Muslims of Bosnia and Hercegovina, offered to support the government on condition that the proposed agrarian reform in the two provinces would grant generous compensation to the Muslim landlords, and that the administrative division of Yugoslavia would not tamper with the borders of Bosnia–Hercegovina. From 1935 until 1939 the Muslim party was closely allied with the Yugoslav Radical Union, then in power. But after the death of Spaho and the conclusion of the Serbo-Croat agreement of 1939—which did provide for the partition of Bosnia–Hercegovina—the Muslim party was reduced to impotence.[1]

Far less important in Yugoslav political life was the Džemijet (*Islam Muhafazaji Hukuk Džemijet*), the party of the Muslims of Macedonia and South Serbia, founded in August 1919. The Central Committee in charge of the party was chosen at an annual congress. The Džemijet published its own journal. Its principal leaders were the brothers Nedžib and Ferhad Draga. Divided over political tactics, and weakened by personality conflicts, the party had a short life. What is important however, is that in the interwar years the Muslims of Yugoslavia enjoyed significant freedom and were able to maintain their traditional institutions and religious practices.

The Second World War found the Yugoslav Muslims partitioned between Italy (Sanjak, Kossovo-Metohija, and Montenegro), Bulgaria (Macedonia), and Croatia (Bosnia–Hercegovina).[2] In each case the

[1] Smail Balić, "Die Muslims in Bosnia-Herzegowina", *Wissenschaftlicher Dienst Südosteuropas*, vol. XII (1963), pp. 158–61.

[2] Ettore Rossi, "I Musulmani della ex-Jugoslavia", *Oriente Moderno*, vol. XXII (1942), pp. 37–42.

Muslims accepted the new political order, and the Grand Mufti of Jerusalem, who visited Yugoslav territories during the war, encouraged them to back the Axis powers. The administrative apparatus for the conduct of Muslim religious and educational affairs largely remained as it had been before the war.

During the Second World War the Muslims of Yugoslavia, as well as those of Albania, were caught up in the ideological struggle between the Communist and nationalist resistance movements. As a minority, the Muslims everywhere chose to remain loyal to the governments in power. Those in Bosnia and Hercegovina recognized the Fascist (*Ustashi*) independent state of Croatia, and participated in the responsibility for the massacres of Serbs and Jews. The wholesale murder of Serbs evoked bloody reprisals by the Chetniks, a Serbian nationalist resistance movement led by General Draža Mihailović. With German help there was organized a special Muslim élite force (S.S. 13th Division of *Handjar*), which was used in an unsuccessful attempt to crush popular resistance to the Axis. Not all Muslims, of course, accepted collaboration. A handful joined the Chetniks and many the ranks of the National Liberation Front, a Communist resistance movement, led by Marshal Joseph Broz Tito.

When Yugoslavia collapsed in April 1941, Kosmet was merged with Albania. This was largely the work of Italy, which had conquered Albania in 1939 and espoused the cause of Albanian irredentism. Inspired first by the Italians and after 1943 by the Germans (who enrolled Albanians in S.S. Division Skanderbeg), the Albanians launched violent attacks against their Serbian neighbours. The efforts of the Yugoslav government to reduce the ratio of Muslim Albanians to Slavs in Kosmet through colonization by Serbs had come to naught. Co-operation between Yugoslav and Albanian Communist resistance forces finally made it possible to contain Albanian and Serbian passions in Kosmet.

Article 25 of the Yugoslav Constitution of 1946 and the fundamental laws of 1953 and 1964 guaranteed religious freedom to all Yugoslav citizens. The position of the Yugoslav state toward religious communities was defined by a special law of 27 May 1953, according to which state and church were separated, freedom of religion guaranteed, religious bigotry prohibited, the formation of religious communities within the existing legal order permitted, all religions put on an equal footing, schools divorced from churches (though religious instruction in churches and mosques was permitted), and state aid to religious communities envisaged. The state would not only make financial contributions to religious communities but would also provide social security for the clergy. In other words, religion and the clergy were subsidized so long as they served the state.

The organization of the Islamic religious community provided by the regulation of 1953 was a complex and cumbersome affair, consisting of three branches—administrative, religious, and financial. At the communal level there was still the traditional committee (*džemat*) elected by the faithful, and each commune had its *hodža* (*imām*), who was a member of the committee. Four republican *waqf* councils were elected by the Muslims of the respective republics (Bosnia–Hercegovina, which has jurisdiction over the Muslims in Croatia and Slovenia, Serbia, Macedonia, and Montenegro). The four councils in turn elected the supreme *waqf* council. Each of the four republics also had a council of *'ulamā'* to watch over religious and educational affairs. The highest Muslim authority in the country was the Supreme Religious Chancellery (*Vrhovno vjersko starešinstvo*), consisting of the chief of the *'ulamā'*, the spiritual head of the Yugoslav Muslims, and four other members.

The Muslims were permitted to have their traditional religious schools (*mektebs*), though, according to the law of 28 October 1955, these schools had to be located on the grounds of religious institutions. There were also two *medreses*—the Ghazi Khusrev Bey Medrese, founded in Sarajevo in 1537, with an eight-year programme of instruction, and the Priština Medrese with a four-year programme. The Islamic religious community published religious books and two periodicals.[1]

In time it was felt that the organization of the Islamic community should be modified in order to eliminate inefficiency and to provide closer control over the faithful. The result was the approval of a new constitution for the community by the Supreme Religious Chancellery on 13 July 1959. The communal committees (*džemats*) and *hodžas* were retained.[2]

On the republican level the Islamic council is the administrative authority. There are four such republican councils (Bosnia and Hercegovina with headquarters in Sarajevo, Serbia with headquarters in Priština, Macedonia with headquarters in Skopje, and Montenegro with

[1] For example, the official journal *Glasnik Vrhovnog Islamskog Starešinstva* and calendar (*Takvim*), intended for the general reader.

[2] Mehmed Begović, "Islamske verske zajednice", *Enciklopedija Jugoslavije*, vol. IV (1960), pp. 371–73; Rastko Vidić, *The Position of the Church in Yugoslavia* (Belgrade, 1962).

headquarters in Titograd). Each council appoints a board of trustees which supervises the local committees and appoints the local *hodžas* and the head *hodža* in the republic.

The Islamic councils of the republics also choose delegates to the country's Supreme Islamic Council, made up of thirty-five members (thirteen from Bosnia–Hercegovina, twelve from Serbia, seven from Macedonia, and three from Montenegro). The Supreme Council elects the Supreme Islamic Chancellery as its executive organ. On religious matters advice is tendered by a council of theologians.

The Supreme Islamic Chancellery is located in Sarajevo. Its members now comprise the chairman of the republican councils, six additional members, and the chief of the '*ulamā*', who is elected by the members of the Supreme Council, the members of the republican council, and the rectors of the religious schools. As the head of the Yugoslav Islamic religious community, the chief of the '*ulamā*' is chosen, on paper, for four years, though actually his incumbency tends to be good for life. He resides in Sarajevo. In 1965 the office was held by the highly regarded Muslim leader, Sulejman Kemura.

Albania is the only Balkan country in which the Muslims outnumber the Christians. Recognized as an independent state in 1913, Albania did not effectively become independent until after the First World War, and the religious organization of its Muslims was not elaborated until several years later. Before 1929 the head of the Sunnite Muslims was the Grand Mufti at Tirana. He was assisted by the Supreme Council of the *sharī'a*, made up of five members whose principal responsibility was the regulation of religious and *waqf* affairs. The Constitution of 1929 vested authority over the Muslim community in a General Council composed of the head of the community (at that time Rexhep Shapati), the four Grand Muftis (one for each of the four zones), and a lay delegate from each prefecture. The General Council elected the four Grand Muftis. In each prefecture there was a Mufti and in each sub-prefecture a deputy Mufti. The four administrative zones of the Muslim community were Shkodër (Scutari), Tirana, Korçë, and Gjirokastër. The leaders of the community outlawed veils and polygamy, an institution which had never taken deep root in Albania. The Muslim community had a *medrese* for the training of religious leaders and published a periodical (*Zani i Naltë*—"The Supreme Voice").[1]

[1] On Muslims in Albania and their religious organization, see Stavro Skendi, *Albania* (New York, 1956).

In 1922 the Dede (head of the Bekṭāshīs), an Albanian, moved to Tirana for political reasons. When the Turkish government abolished all dervish orders, the headquarters of the Bekṭāshīs was also moved to Tirana. The Bekṭāshīs were determined to win a separate organization for their group. At the Congress of Korçë in 1929 they demanded full independence from the Sunnite-dominated Muslim community, but they got no more than autonomy within the community. The Constitution of 1929 defined the role of the Bekṭāshī divines, both confirmed and ordinary. The Dede or *Kryegjysh* (Chief Grandfather) was the supreme leader, assisted by five *gjyshë* (Grandfathers), a number of *prindë* or *baballarë* (Fathers), and dervishes who lived in monasteries. In 1936 small groups of Qādirīs, Rifā'īs, Sa'dīs, and Tijānīs assembled in Tirana and formed their own organization called *Drita Hyjnore* ("The Divine Light").

The Second World War brought much harm to the Muslim community in Albania as a result of political, religious, and personality conflicts. Some of the faithful collaborated with the occupation authorities, and some backed various competing resistance movements. The Grand Mufti of the Sunnites, Rexhep Shapati, was removed by the Council of '*ulamā*' in 1941, and in January 1943 the leader of the Bekṭāshīs, Niazi Dede, was murdered.

In time the National Liberation Front, a Communist organization headed by Enver Hoxha, emerged as the strongest Albanian political and military force. Hoxha and the majority of his followers were of Muslim stock. The Bekṭāshīs, believing that the Front had much in common with their own social and economic program, offered generous support to Hoxha's partisans.

The Communist victory, however, brought with it an anti-religious drive. Stripped of independence and deprived of power through nationalization and secularization laws, the Albanian Muslims lost their importance as a political and cultural force.

According to the Constitution of 5 May 1945, the Muslims of Communist Albania were supposed to form a religious community, even though the Bekṭāshīs were not included. The head of the Sunnites is elected by the General Council, but the choice must be approved by the chief of the state, who also has the power to dismiss him. Until 1955 Hafëz Musa Hashi Ali served as the head, and since then Hafëz Sulejman Myrto. The General Council consists of the head (president of the community), the four Grand Muftis, and one lay representative from each prefecture. The community continues to be divided into the four zones already mentioned under the charge of the Grand Muftis, who are appointed by the General Council with the approval of the chief of the state. There are various other officials and agencies, including regional councils.

After the Second World War the Bekṭāshīs received a statute giving them independence. The intention of the government was to aggravate Bekṭāshī–Sunnite relations. The Bekṭāshī community still consists of initiated families (*ashikë* or *muhibë* degrees) and their religious leaders. The Chief Grandfather is Ahmet Myftar Dede. The community is divided into six zones (Krujë, Elbasan, Korçë, Gjirokastër, Prishtë, and Vlorë). Albanian has been made the religious language of the Bekṭāshīs. The community has its own school for training divines. The Bekṭāshīs have four monasteries (*tekkes*), located at Tirana, Akcahisar (the old centre), Berat, and on the Tomor Mountain. Like the Sunnite headquarters, that of the Bekṭāshīs is in Tirana. One of the most distinguished native poets and fighters for national independence, Naim Frasheri, was a Bekṭāshī. Today an award for literature and art bears his name.

The Khalwatī, Qādirī, and Saʿdī orders have also been given the status of independent religious communities.

According to Article 79 of the Bulgarian Constitution of 1947, all subjects are equal and have the right to use their own language and to profess their own faith so long as these privileges are not in conflict with the interests of the state. About 13 per cent of the country's population are Muslims, of whom 6 per cent are ethnic Turks and the rest Pomaks, Gypsies, and Tatars. The Muslims of Bulgaria have their own religious and educational organization, headed by a Grand Mufti, with subordinate Muftis in cities in which a substantial part of the population is Muslim. On 26 October 1964 Hasan Ademov succeeded Akif Osmanov as Grand Mufti. Each Muslim commune elects a council, which manages religious and charitable affairs and works closely with the local religious teacher (*imām*).

The Bulgarian government accentuates the difference between Turks and Muslims who are ethnic Bulgarians or Pomaks. The latter are encouraged among other things to adopt Bulgarian names, and they have their own religious organizations on communal and regional levels. The Mufti of the Pomak community is Isein Seferkov.

In 1940 the Muslim population of Rumania was reduced as a result of the cession of Bessarabia to the Soviet Union and southern Dobruja to Bulgaria. The census of 1956 gives 20,469 Tatars and 14,329 Turks in Rumania. These figures, however, are imprecise, since the census did not take into account the religious appurtenance of the population. On the assumption that the Turks and Tatars are Muslims, the number of Muslims in Rumania in 1956 may be estimated at about 35,000, though there is good reason to believe that the total may be considerably higher.

Articles 81 and 82 of the Constitution of 1952 guarantee all subjects of Rumania equality and the right to use their own language and to profess their own religion. All private schools, including those operated by the Muslims, are proscribed. The Rumanian Muslims have their own ecclesiastical organization and their own parishes, religious teachers, and mosques. The head of the community is Grand Mufti Jakub Septar Mehmed, with headquarters in Constanţa, which has the country's largest mosque.

As the result of a convention concluded in Lausanne in 1923, Greece and Turkey agreed on a compulsory exchange of minorities. Accordingly, some 400,000 Muslims were transferred from Greece to Turkey (1923–7) and over one million Greeks were moved from Turkey to Greece. Only about 100,000 Turks remained in Greece, located for the most part in Western Thrace. When Greece acquired the Dodecanese Islands in 1945, the number of Turks rose above 130,000.

The Muslims in Greece enjoy religious and cultural freedom and have their own religious and educational institutions and societies. They have endowments, mosques, and religious teachers. They have recently, however, suffered anxiety as a result of the conflict between the governments of Greece and Turkey over Cyprus.

The national consciousness of the Balkan Muslims was slow to develop. Religious feeling in the Islamic community was far stronger than social and ethnic awareness. Individual segments have reacted differently to the challenges of nationalism. Most of the Muslims of Bosnia and Hercegovina today identify themselves with Croat or Serbian nationalism. Yugoslavia's "ethnic democracy" and the founding of the Autonomous Region of Kosmet have contributed to the growth of Albanian nationalism there. Until the expulsion of Yugoslavia from the Cominform in 1948 there was a possibility that Kosmet and Albania, whose regime the Yugoslav Communist party helped bring to power, might be merged to form another republic in Yugoslavia's federal system. Since 1948 Albania has consistently pursued an anti-Yugoslav line, claiming Kosmet and other parts of Yugoslavia. As economic conditions in Albania are less favourable and the system of government more oppressive than in Yugoslavia, a number of Albanians have secretly left their homeland for Yugoslavia in recent years.

Under Yugoslav laws the Albanians in Yugoslavia are guaranteed equality. In Kosmet the Albanians enjoy cultural as well as political autonomy within the limits of the Communist constitution and laws. Priština, the capital of Kosmet, has grown from a small provincial town into a city of well over 40,000 inhabitants, with a university and other centres of learning, cultural institutions, and a radio station. Several publications appear in Albanian, which is also the language of instruction in schools. The Yugoslav government has invested large sums in the material and cultural development of Kosmet with the aim of making it a point of attraction for Albanians and thereby undermining Albania's irredentism.

The national consciousness of the Turks in Yugoslav Macedonia has also grown. Under a special arrangement with the Turkish government many of the Turks were permitted to emigrate to Turkey. Those who have remained in Yugoslavia have their own schools and enjoy religious freedom. These advantages, however, instead of satisfying them have intensified their sense of ethnic exclusiveness. As the Macedonian Turks live in an area some distance away from Turkey, they represent for Yugoslavia more of a social than a national problem.

If Enver Hoxha has given his people anything, it is a sense of national pride. In Albania proper the Muslims represent 70 per cent of the population. The state has adopted anti-religious measures, but the psychological implications of a minority cult are absent, the government being in the hands of men of Muslim background even if they are now self-proclaimed atheists.

In Bulgaria the Turks in the territories bordering on European Turkey behave as people oppressed both socially and nationally. The government's attack on religion and Islamic tradition is seen as an attack on nationality as well. The government's anti-religious campaign and policy of forced collectivization have made it difficult to control the Turkish minority. Between 1948 and 1951 the government unceremoniously expelled nearly 200,000 of its Turkish subjects into Turkey.

The Bulgarian government has been trying to convince the ethnic Muslims or Pomaks that they are first of all Bulgarians. The Tatars of both Bulgaria and Rumania frequently identify themselves with the Turks. The Muslim Gypsies, particularly numerous in Bulgaria, are a social rather than an ethnic problem, being looked down upon by all their neighbours. They live among other Muslims, with whom they try to identify themselves.

The Balkan Muslims are unevenly developed socially. In general they are considered to be among the most retarded elements of the population. How is it that these one-time rulers are now lagging behind their erstwhile subjects? Perhaps the answer is to be found in the stifling nature of the Ottoman state and its social system or in Islamic teachers who discouraged the faithful from accepting modernity. It is not without significance that the Muslim emigrants from the Balkans were the most affluent in the community, leaving behind the Muslim *rayah*—small landholders, landless peasants, and city poor. The patriarchal social organization (e.g. in Albanian tribalism and pastoralism) and the geographic location of certain provinces (e.g. Bosnia–Hercegovina, Macedonia, and Albania) have also impeded social progress. Where Ottoman rule lasted the longest, the signs of backwardness (primitive economy, illiteracy, and poor health conditions) are most pronounced. Until recently most Muslim groups constituted closed social entities, cocooned into a traditional Muslim way of life.

After the Second World War the state and religious establishment were separated, and the *sharīʿa* in the Balkan Islamic communities lost its force except in purely personal and religious matters. Religious rites and practices were permitted when not in conflict with secular laws. The aim has been to break down by legislative action and education Muslim isolation and the power of the *hodžas*, to secularize the Muslims, and to lift them socially and culturally to the level of the rest of the population. Muslim teachers and jurists have been stripped of all but their religious functions. Civil marriage ceremonies have been made obligatory, religious education drastically curtailed, particular garments (*fez*, *zar*) worn by Muslims prohibited, and the properties of Muslim religious institutions considered "excess" nationalized. After complying with the civil laws, the Muslim faithful are permitted to participate in certain religious services such as those involving marriage and burial.

In the sphere of cultural activity and education no other Muslim community in the Balkans compares with Bosnia and Hercegovina. Here pure learning has a longer tradition and modernity earlier roots, and a dynamic group of Muslim writers, artists, and political leaders has grown during the past century. Illiteracy among the Muslims of Bosnia–Hercegovina has been significantly reduced, and the social conditions under which they live much improved.

While discouraging the teaching of Islam, the Yugoslav government has been promoting the study of Muslim history and civilization. Oriental languages and history are taught at Sarajevo University, founded in 1949. One of Sarajevo's gymnasia provides work in Turkish and Arabic. The Oriental Institute in Sarajevo, founded in 1950, is the country's leading centre for the study of Ottoman and Muslim civilization; it publishes periodicals, documents, monographs, and symposia.

Among the prominent Muslims of Bosnia–Hercegovina are the writers Hamza Humo and Skender Kulenović, the caricaturist Zuko Džumur, the painter Ismet Mujezinović, and the historian Hamdija Kreševljaković. A number of other Muslim historians have published works of scholarly merit in recent years. Among the political leaders the best known are Osman Karabegović, Avdo Humo, Džemal Bijedić, Edhem Čamo, and Kemal Sejfula (a Macedonian Turk).

The Muslims of Kosmet, Montenegro, and Macedonia have also progressed materially and culturally, though their achievements have not been quite so impressive as those of the Muslims of Bosnia–Hercegovina. Since the end of the Second World War, there has appeared in Kosmet a small band of promising Albanian intellectuals and political leaders. Some of these Albanians favour Tito's brand of socialism, while others gravitate toward Hoxha's regime for nationalistic reasons, or like a number of their fellow intellectuals strive for a truly democratic society.

The Bulgarian government has paid close attention to the education of its Turkish and Muslim minorities. There are a score of elementary and secondary schools in which Turkish is the language of instruction, and in 1959 there were founded mixed schools, ostensibly to enable the Turkish children to learn Bulgarian and thereby qualify more easily for employment. The Turks have three schools for training religious teachers. A special department for Islamic studies has been established in the University of Sofia. In nearly every major centre of the Turkish population there are newspapers in Turkish. Periodicals and Communist party journals and guides in Turkish are published regularly, as well as handbooks for Communist agitators. There are radio stations which broadcast in Turkish, Turkish folk dancing troupes, and at least five Turkish theatres.

The Bulgarian government has been spreading anti-Islamic propaganda through lectures, brochures, and handbooks in an attempt to enlighten the faithful, especially the young, about the undesirable aspects of religion. There have been frequent warnings against the continuing practice of certain Muslim rites. Circumcision, for example, can be done only by qualified surgeons, yet this has been repeatedly violated by Muslims. Prohibited Muslim clothing, here as in other Muslim communities, is often seen. From time to time reports are published of the sale of female children into marriage and of *hodžas* who practice primitive forms of medicine and perform special religious rites for the ailing.

Nonetheless, even in the regions where the hold of Islam and tradition on the masses remains strong, Communism has made inroads in all phases of life. Many Muslims have ceased to attend mosques and have cast aside the dress and the practices which symbolized Muslim confessional exclusiveness. Marriages between Muslims and non-Muslims have become common. Everyday social intercourse, between Muslims and non-Muslims, is no longer frowned upon.

In Bulgaria an increasing number of Muslims are participating in the country's political and economic life. Many are chairmen of Communist associations and collective farms. Turks serve on the Central Committee of the Communist party, and several of them are secretaries of regional and district committees of the party. The Central Committee has a separate section for the Turkish minority, headed by a Turk. The Turks have their own party monthly, *Yeni Hayat*. The leading Turk in Bulgaria is Ali Rafiev, a member of the Central Committee.

In Albania there are elementary schools for religious education, and each of the Sunnite and Bekṭāshī communities has a seminary for training religious teachers. The Islamic community is allowed to publish its own journals and books. Albania, however, lacks a tradition for the advanced study of Islamic theology and law, so that religious training and studies there are simple in character.

In the less advanced regions where religion and nationalism are blended, Islam has shown a degree of resilience to Communism.

Much of the everyday life of the Albanians in Albania and in Yugoslavia is governed by Islamic principles and patriarchal customs. The powerful attachment of the Muslims to kin, religion, and community has impeded modernization. The Albanians, a vigorous and dynamic people, have resisted assimilation in Yugoslavia, where as migrant workers they travel far and wide, but almost always return to their Kosmet villages.

Communist successes in Albania since the Second World War would not have been possible without the backing of Muslims, many of whom have abandoned faith and tradition to take up the Communist tenets of secularism and materialism.

Even in Kosmet patriarchalism and religion have not been able to withstand the corroding influence of Communism. Secularization has made headway, and traditional life has been undermined. In 1961 there were about 20,000 Albanian members of the Communist party, with scores of them as chairmen of basic party organizations. Ten of them were members of the Central Committee of the Communist party of Serbia, and six of the Central Committee of the Macedonian Communist party.

In general the Balkan Communist governments have not waged a militant anti-religious campaign; they have been content to fight religion (not only Islam) by law and propaganda. By emasculating organized religion of economic, cultural, and political power, they hope to starve it out. If Communist governments give financial aid to religious institutions and provide social security to some of the divines, this is done in order to transform them into auxiliaries of the state, through whom human resources can be mobilized for Communist programmes and those opposed to the regime can be controlled.

Communist activities have had the effect of accelerating processes long at work: secularization of Muslim communities and de-Turkization of Balkan societies. These are natural corollaries of modernism, industrialization, and urbanization. The emigration of Muslims, begun in the nineteenth century, has been facilitated by the Communist governments, and everywhere, with the exception of Albania and Kosmet, the percentage of Muslims in the population in the Balkans has been decreasing. Unprecedented social mobility has tended to weaken the Islamic communities. Many Muslims from Bosnia and Hercegovina, for example, have moved to other parts of the country in quest of economic opportunity or education, or have been sent out as civilian or military officials. The movement of population from villages to urban centres and from smaller to larger towns has affected the

Muslims like the rest of the population, though in most cases to a lesser degree.

Yugoslavia has a special problem. The liberalization of the Communist system there has removed shackles that restrained nationalism. The devolution of central power and decentralization of economic management, relative economic prosperity, and the absence of major threats from abroad have turned the attention of Yugoslavs to local affairs. All this has served to awaken latent particularism and nationalist aspirations. As the national and confessional awareness of Yugoslavs has increased, the Muslims also have been stirred. A closing of the ranks in the Muslim community of Bosnia–Hercegovina can be observed. The schism caused by ideological squabbles has been largely healed, with considerable solidarity now existing between those who espoused the Yugoslav and Communist cause and those who once had thrown in their lot with the Croat Fascist movement.

Balkan societies are shedding the last vestiges of their oriental past. At work everywhere is a social and ethnic levelling. While Communist authorities endeavour with financial aid to preserve the Ottoman historical monuments, Islam in the Balkans has lost much of its vitality, and hope for its regeneration seems slim indeed.

CHAPTER 13

ṢŪFISM

The name *ṣūfī*, by which the mystics of Islam soon came to be known, means literally "wearer of wool", and there can be little doubt that already in pre-Islamic times woollen dress was associated with spirituality. It is significant that the Prophet had thought it worthy of mention that Moses was clothed entirely in wool when God spoke to him,[1] and the fact that Muḥammad himself died wearing a woollen garment must have added greatly to the spiritual associations that such dress already had. It is true that "the Ṣūfīs have not made an exclusive speciality of wearing wool",[2] but the mystics of Islam needed a name, and *ṣūfī* had the advantage of honourable associations and implications without being vainglorious. As often as not, however, they refer to themselves simply as "the folk", *al-qawm*, and also as "the poor (in spirit)" *al-fuqarā'*, plural of *faqīr*, in Persian *darvīsh*, whence the English fakir and dervish.

Inveighing against his times the tenth-century Ṣūfī al-Fushanjī said: "Today Ṣūfism is a name without a reality, but formerly it was a reality without a name." Commenting on this in the next century al-Hujwīrī adds: "In the time of the Companions of the Prophet and their successors this name did not exist, but the reality thereof was in everyone; now the name exists but not the reality."[3]

If this pronouncement be toned down slightly as regards its praise of the past as well as its blame of the present, it may be said to agree with the unanimous opinion of the Ṣūfīs themselves, who hold that although there have been many holy men and women scattered throughout the later generations of Islam, sanctity has never been so common as it was in the first generation; and apart from the fact that this thousand-year-old opinion cannot be lightly brushed aside, those Western scholars who still cling to the opinion that mysticism was a later development in Islam are forced to turn a blind eye to more than one powerful piece of evidence which corroborates the Ṣūfī view. An examination of the Qur'ān shows that from the very outset even before the law had been fully revealed, Islam was in principle a twofold

[1] Tirmidhī, *Libās*, 10. [2] al-Qushayrī, *Risāla*. [3] *Kashf al-maḥjūb*, ch. 3.

religion comprising an outward and an inward aspect, an exoterism and an esoterism or mysticism, a path of salvation and a path of sanctification. On three occasions in the earliest Meccan *sūras* the faithful are divided into two groups:[1] one is the group of those who are near to God and who drink directly from the fountains of Paradise; the other is the group of those who drink draughts which have merely been perfumed at the fountains. Moreover, when we read these earliest *sūras* we are conscious of an élite whose lives were utterly dedicated to God and whose intensity of worship clearly went far beyond the norm of human possibility. Such revelations as "Prostrate thyself and draw nigh (unto God)",[2] "Glorify Him the livelong night",[3] "Keep vigil all the night save a little",[4] "Flee unto God",[5] strike the keynote of this period. The path of Islam was, at its outset, the highly rigorous path of doing one's utmost, unalleviated as yet by the establishment of a legal minimum. A later verse,[6] revealed at Medina within the last ten years of Muḥammad's life, refers to a group—no doubt by this time more of a minority than it had been—who followed the Prophet in his extreme intensity of worship as opposed to the majority who did not. In general also, and quite apart from such direct Qur'ānic evidence of the existence of Ṣūfism—in all but name—at the outset of Islam, we may quote the following recent remark which, if it had been made at the beginning of this century, might have saved Western orientalism from many misunderstandings:

> One reason why Western people have difficulty in appreciating the Qur'ān and have even many times questioned whether this book does contain the premises of a spiritual life lies in the fact that they look in a text for a meaning that is fully expressed and immediately intelligible, whereas Semites, and Eastern peoples in general, are lovers of verbal symbolism and read "in depth"...But even without taking into consideration the sibylline structure of very many sacred sentences, we can say that the Oriental extracts much from a few words: when, for example, the Qur'ān recalls that "the world beyond is better for you than this lower world" or that "earthly life is but a play" or affirms: "In your wives and your children ye have an enemy" or "say: Allah! then leave them to their empty play", or, finally, when it promises Paradise to "him who has feared the station of his Lord and refused desire to his soul"—when the Qur'ān speaks thus, there emerges for the Moslem—we do not say "for every Moslem"—a whole ascetic and mystical doctrine, as penetrating and complete as no matter what other form of spirituality worthy the name.[7]

[1] LVI. 10–40; LXXVI. 5–6; LXXXIII. 18–28.
[2] XCVI. 19. [3] LXXVI. 26. [4] LXXIII. 2. [5] LI. 50. [6] LXXIII. 20.
[7] Frithjof Schuon, *Understanding Islam* (London, 1963), pp. 59–60.

The same principle can be applied also to many sayings of the Prophet such as: "Be in this world as a stranger or as a passer-by",[1] and his definition of the religion as having, in addition to a creed and a practice that are binding on everyone, an extra dimension, that of excellence (*iḥsān*), namely, "that thou shouldst worship God as if thou sawest Him".[2] The transcendent certainty of faith and the profound unwavering concentration of worship which this definition implies is clearly an ideal for an élite rather than an obligation for the whole community; and this particular dimension of Islam has always been considered as the special domain of the Ṣūfīs, just as it is the theologians and canonists who stand for the two obligatory aspects of the religion.

The basic doctrine of Islamic mysticism, which later came to be termed Oneness of Being (*waḥdat al-wujūd*) and which Western scholars term "monism", is implicit in the Divine Name *al-ḥaqq* (truth, reality). All Muslims must accept the doctrine that there is no absolute reality or truth but God, but it is only the Ṣūfīs who push this formulation to its full conclusion. If it be asked: "What is reality?", they reply: "That which *is* as opposed to that which is not". If God alone is absolutely real, God alone *is*, whence the term Oneness of Being. But this does not mean that God is the sum of all existing things as Massignon supposed it to mean. That would be pantheism, whereas on the contrary it is an essential aspect of the Islamic doctrine of Unity not only that God is the all-else-excluding Infinite, but also that He has no parts. The Name *Aḥad* (One) to do full justice to its meaning must be translated "the Indivisible One-and-Only". The doctrine of Oneness of Being means that appearances are deceptive and that each apparently separate object is, mysteriously, nothing other than the indivisible plenitude of the absolute, infinite and eternal truth.

"Wheresoe'er ye turn, there is the Face of God",[3] says the Qur'ān; and al-Ghazālī comments this verse as follows: "Each thing has two faces, a face of its own and a Face of its Lord; in respect of its own face it is nothingness, and in respect of the Face of God it is Being. Thus there is nothing in existence save only God and His Face."[4]

This passage of al-Ghazālī is also implicitly a commentary on the Divine Name "the Outwardly Manifest" mentioned in the verse *He is the First and the Last and the Outwardly Manifest and the Inwardly Hidden*,[5]

[1] Bukhārī, *Riqāq*, 3.
[2] Muslim, *Imān*, 1.
[3] II. 115.
[4] *Mishkāt al-anwār.*
[5] LVII. 3.

and on the saying of the Prophet: "Thou art the Outwardly Manifest, and there is nothing covering Thee."[1] Much quoted also by the Ṣūfīs is his saying: "God was, and there was naught with Him",[2] together with its anonymous commentary, attributed by some also to the Prophet: "He is now even as He was". This last is one of several Ṣūfī formulations which place exoterism in the dilemma of not daring to deny it and not daring to accept its inevitable implications. For the average theologian-jurist, this is a mere abstraction, and a dangerous one at that. But if the Ṣūfīs have always concentrated on the doctrine of Oneness of Being, it is not because they are addicted to abstract philosophy—they are in fact more directly responsible than any other section of the community for putting abstract philosophy outside the pale of Sunnī Islam—but because mysticism means piercing through the veil of appearances to the eternal truths that lie beyond. Moreover they are fully aware of the dangers of idle speculation. It is only by intellectual insight, that is, by transcendent, superhuman means and not by any power of the human mind, that these Truths can be glimpsed; and it sometimes happens that a novice is temporarily forbidden to meditate on Oneness of Being if he is judged to be intellectually too dormant.

This doctrine is also approached from a rather different and more subjective angle, which reveals it equally clearly as nothing other than an extension, along the dimension of depth, of what all Muslims are bound to believe. The belief in God's nearness is of catechismal importance in Islam. A verse of the Qur'ān, directly addressing the Prophet, says: "If my slaves ask thee of Me, say I am near. I answer the prayer of the pray-er when he prayeth."[3] And if it be asked: "How near is God?", the answer comes from another verse: "We (God) are nearer to him (man) than his jugular vein".[4] The question: "How can this nearness be perceived?" is answered indirectly by the verses: "All things perish but His Face",[5] and "All that is therein (in creation) passeth away; and there remaineth the Face of thy Lord in its majesty and bounty".[6] This last verse is the basis of the Ṣūfī doctrine of passing away (*fanā'*) and remaining (*baqā'*) or, as they are often translated, extinction and subsistence. The perishable is as an illusory veil over the imperishable. It is only through the extinction of the created subject, that is, the human ego, and the created object, the world, that the truth

[1] Muslim, *Da'wāt*, 16; Tirmidhī, *Da'wāt*, 19. [2] Bukhārī, *Khalq*, 1.
[3] II. 186. [4] L. 16. [5] XXVIII. 88. [6] LV. 26–7.

of things can be seen, for only the Divine can see the Divine: "Men's sight cannot reach Him."[1] Consequently if a Ṣūfī appears to speak of a man seeing God as when al-Ghazālī says: "The gnostics...see directly face to face that there is nothing in existence save only God",[2] one must remember that the term for gnostic (*ʿārif*, knower) is an abbreviation for *ʿārif billāh* (knower through God). The beatific vision is only possible because "God cometh in between a man and his own heart".[3] If finally it be asked: "How can the grace of this divine intervention be obtained?", the answer lies in the following holy Tradition (*ḥadīth qudusī*), so called because in it God speaks in the first person upon the tongue of the Prophet:

Nothing is more pleasing to Me, as a means for my slave to draw near unto Me, than the worship that I have made binding upon him; and My slave ceaseth not to draw near unto Me with added devotions of his free will until I love him; and when I love him I am the Hearing wherein he heareth and the Sight wherewith he seeth and the Hand wherewith he smiteth and the Foot whereon he walketh.[4]

The whole of Ṣūfism, as it has shown itself to be throughout the centuries, as regards both doctrine and practice, is summed up in this Tradition.

The Prophet, to whom it was addressed, and who is the beloved of God *par excellence* and therefore the gnostic *par excellence*, stands for the Ṣūfī as a mould into which the aspirant to gnosis must first pour himself. In this connexion it may be remarked that the source of the doctrine which places the spiritual nature of Muḥammad at the very summit of the created universe—with an opening on to uncreatedness—is unquestionably the Prophet's ascension (*miʿrāj*) to that summit, where grows the lote tree of the uttermost boundary,[5] and where the Divine Presence was revealed to him. This ascent, the inverse of the process of creation, was a reabsorption of his human nature into his spiritual nature. Therefore, since the path traced out by the *miʿrāj* passes through the spiritual nature of Muḥammad or, in other words, through that aspect of the Spirit which may be called "his", and since the *miʿrāj* is the prototype of the Ṣūfī path, it is natural that the term "Muḥammadan Spirit" (*al-rūḥ al-muḥammadī*) should stand as a doctrinal "signpost" to mark what is, for the Ṣūfī, the threshold of the end. The following Tradition is an example of the Prophet's identifying himself,

[1] VI. 103.
[2] *Mishkāt al-anwār*, p. 103.
[3] VIII. 24.
[4] Bukhārī, *Riqāq*, 37.
[5] Qur'ān LIII. 13–18.

not with Muḥammad the man, but with the Muḥammadan Spirit, though this actual term itself must have been a later development: "A man said to the Prophet: O Messenger of God, when wast thou made a Prophet? He said: When Adam was between spirit and body."[1]

As may be inferred from the already quoted all-embracing holy Tradition, the practices of the Ṣūfīs are of two kinds: rites which are binding on all Muslims, and additional voluntary rites. In the case of a new entrant into a Ṣūfī order, the shaykh will not as a rule undertake direct guidance until his subordinates have made sure that the novice is thoroughly well grounded in his legal obligations and unfailing in his practice of them, though in most cases this can be taken for granted, since a man who came short of the legal minimum would not normally presume to seek entrance to a *ṭarīqa*, as the orders are called. There is no need to dwell here on what the legal obligations are, since these "five pillars of Islam" have already been defined in a previous chapter. On the basis of his orthodoxy as regards these, the novice is instructed in the inward dimension of depth or of height which all sacred rites have in themselves, independently of the fact that they are performed by the vast majority of believers in a more or less "exoteric" way. Needless to say, a rite is always symbolic. A ritual ablution, for example, symbolizes the aspiration to an inward purity which each Muslim is free to define for himself. But unlike the majority, the Ṣūfī aspires by the ablution to absolute inward purity, that is, purity from "other than God". Analogously the rite of prostration, which for the majority is an expression of inward humility before God, means for the Ṣūfī that absolute humility which is no less than total extinction (*fanā'*) of the individuality in the Divine Presence.

As to the voluntary rites of Islam, these are performed by the Ṣūfīs as an extension of what is obligatory, and with the same profundity of purpose. This purpose is expressed by the general term *dhikr Allāh* (remembrance of God) which is used to comprise all the different spiritual practices, both obligatory and voluntary, on which the Ṣūfī path is based. But in particular *dhikr Allāh* refers to the invocation of the Divine Name *Allāh*, the word *dhikr* meaning "mention" as well as "remembrance". One of the first injunctions received by the Prophet was: "Invoke in remembrance the Name of thy Lord, and devote thyself to Him with an utter devotion";[2] and this form of

[1] Ibn Ḥanbal, IV. 66; Tirmidhī, *Manāqib*, I.

[2] Qur'ān LXXIII. 8.

dhikr, the continual invocation of the Divine Name, has always been considered by the mystics of Islam as an outstandingly direct means of approach to God.

Parallel in a sense to the invocation of the Name is the recitation of the Qur'ān. This *dhikr* is a general practice in Islam and not confined to the Ṣūfī orders. What may be said to distinguish them from others in this respect is the length and regularity of their recitations and, above all, their conscious aspiration to mysterious union with God through the uncreated Word. The doctrine of the uncreatedness of the Qur'ān —and therefore of the Divine Name which is the chief jewel of the Qur'ānic text—presents no problems for the Ṣūfīs, and most of their practices are in a sense grounded upon this doctrine.

Another marked feature of their practice is the recitation of litanies. The Traditions abound in recommendations to recite this or that formula a certain number of times. Here are some examples:

"God hath 99 Names; he that telleth them shall enter Paradise."[1]

"Verily each day there is a mist over my heart until I have asked forgiveness of God 100 times."[2]

"Whoso hath invoked most blessings upon me, he of all men hath most claim upon me on the Day of Resurrection."[3]

It is through litanies possibly more than anything else that Ṣūfism overflows as it were into the outer world of Islam, exerting there an incalculable influence. *Dalā'il al-khayrāt*, a manual of traditional litanies compiled by Muḥammad b. Sulaymān al-Jazūlī of the Shādhilī order, is perhaps, after the Qur'ān itself, the most widely distributed book in Islam. In the preface to her *Muslim Devotions*, Constance Padwick writes:

> In purchasing the books (prayer-manuals) it was my desire to avoid the more esoteric works for the inner life of the dervish orders, and enquiry was made as to what had a popular sale. Even so, the majority of the books proved to be linked with one or other of the orders that have played, and still in these days of their official submergence play, so great a part in the life of Islam. Indeed it seems almost impossible for a man seeking for instruction in prayer, beyond directions for the daily prayer rite, to avoid works connected with one or other of the orders. Since these became illegal in Turkey there is a dearth of devotional material in Istanbul, once so rich a centre.[4]

Almost every order has at its outer fringe a number of men who do not feel equal to entering it but who wish to do more than the average

[1] Muslim, *Dhikr*, 2.

[2] Bukhārī, *Da'wāt*, 2; Muslim, *Dhikr*, 12.

[3] Tirmidhī, *Witr*, 21.

[4] Constance Padwick, *Muslim Devotions* (London, 1961), pp. xi–xii.

Muslim does in the way of worship. The shaykh will sometimes consent to give limited spiritual guidance without formally initiating the seeker, and the transmission of a litany for regular recitation is nearly always part of such guidance.

Within the orders there is usually one litany of special obligation which is recited twice a day, after the dawn and sunset prayers. The three main formulae of what is perhaps the most widely practised of these litanies are, first asking forgiveness of God, secondly invoking blessings and peace upon the Prophet Muḥammad, and thirdly an affirmation of the oneness and glory of God. Each formula is repeated 100 times, nearly always on a rosary.

Apart from rites in the ordinary sense, the voluntary devotion of fasting, in addition to the obligatory fast of Ramaḍān, is widely practised among the Ṣūfīs. Many fast every Monday and Thursday, as was recommended by the Prophet. Also following the apostolic precedent —it was in one of his spiritual retreats that Muḥammad received the first Qur'ānic revelation—almost all the shaykhs lay stress on the importance of *khalwa*, solitude reinforced by fasting, as a support for concentration on the *dhikr*.

As a complement to *khalwa* the orders hold regular "sessions of *dhikr*" at which, all together, they recite the Qur'ān, chant litanies and invoke the Divine Name. Women are accepted regularly as disciples by the shaykhs of almost every order, but in most they are not allowed to attend the sessions of the men. Usually, they have their own sessions presided over by a woman, the wife of the shaykh or another. But it is normal for the sisters of an order to receive spiritual instruction direct from the shaykh himself, or from one of his representatives.

In many orders, at the sessions of *dhikr*, a kind of dance is performed of which the most famous is that which was given by Jalāl al-Dīn Rūmī (d. 1273) to his order the Mawlawī *ṭarīqa*, whose members are in consequence better known in Europe as "the whirling dervishes". Very different, though equally elaborate in its own way, is the much less known dance of the Siqallī *ṭarīqa* of Morocco. Some orders, on the other hand, confine themselves to very simple movements. But there is nearly always a singer, with or without a drum, to accompany the dance; and in a few orders the flute and the lute and other instruments are used also.

Although the Companions of the Prophet probably made some spontaneous rhythmic movements of the body while reciting litanies at their sessions of *dhikr*—the rhythmic repetition of a formula is extremely conducive to such things—there is no evidence that this had developed in their generation to anything like an organized collective movement. Consequently the sacred dance of the Ṣūfīs has been frowned upon by some jurists in almost every generation. The question also of music, whether or not it is permissible, has been hotly debated. The Ṣūfī point of view is that concentration in worship has a priority of importance. The Egyptian Saint Dhu'l-Nūn al-Miṣrī (d. 856) said: "The repentance of the generality is from sins, whereas the repentance of the elect is from heedlessness",[1] that is, from lack of concentration, and the Ṣūfīs hold that rhythmic movements of the body, with or without music, are fully justified if they can be an aid to overcoming the distractions to which the soul of man is subject. But the sacred dance is never more than an auxiliary. As regards the basic rites of Ṣūfism, it is not outwardly but inwardly, in the aspiration that lies behind the form, that they differ from those practised by the generality of Muslims.

By the time of the Prophet's death the religion as a whole including Ṣūfism (in all but name) had been endowed with a doctrine and a practice that were anchored in the Spirit to protect them from change. The great mystics of each generation could bequeath, in addition to the unchanging constants, their own particular spiritual counsels and formulations of spiritual truths; but it cannot be said that later generations, in virtue of a greater accumulation of such treasures, were better equipped for following the mystic path than were the earlier generations. On the contrary, these secondary assets have shown themselves to be no more than part compensations which tend to be outweighed by the general decrease in spiritual giftedness. Such, at any rate, is the unanimous opinion of the Ṣūfīs. On the other hand, "the fact that from the third generation of Islam onwards there is a gradual increase of outspokenness on the part of the mystics, makes it difficult [for Western scholars] not to see in this crescendo a kind of 'progress' despite what one may know, in theory, of the 'goldenness' of silence, and despite the opinions of the Ṣūfīs themselves".[2] But this remark is perhaps less true now than it was only a few years ago, for there are signs of a more general recognition that the history of Ṣūfī literature is by no means identical with the history of Ṣūfism itself, or in other words that mystical

[1] Qushayrī, *Risāla*.

[2] Abū Bakr Sirāj al-Dīn, "The Origins of Sufism", *Islamic Quarterly*, vol. III, no. 1 (1956).

treatises are no more than sparks from a fire, and that some fires do not throw out any sparks at all.

An obvious kind of secondary development which may truly be said to have taken place in Ṣūfism, as in Islam as a whole, is organization. Though it is unlikely that, in the reigns of the first four caliphs, there was any definite organization of groups, members of the second generation grouped themselves spontaneously round certain of the Companions, and according to tradition one of the chief mystic centres of such attraction was ʻAlī himself. The following remark attributed to him is typical of Islamic mysticism in more than one respect. In particular, it reveals its author as a personification of the general truth that "the repentance of the elect is from heedlessness". "I and my soul are as a shepherd of sheep. No sooner are they herded together, on one side than they break forth on the other."[1] Among the Companions it is Abū Bakr who has always shared with ʻAlī the special veneration of the Ṣūfīs. Junayd said: "the noblest utterance about realizing God's Oneness is the saying of Abū Bakr: Glory be to Him who has made for His creatures no means of attaining to knowledge of Him save through their impotence to attain (in themselves) to such knowledge."[2] But Abū Bakr only outlived the Prophet by two years. The second generation had therefore a greater direct debt to ʻAlī.

Among the many outstanding figures of the second generation special mention must be made of al-Ḥasan al-Baṣrī (A.D. 642–728) who as an adolescent sat at the feet of ʻAlī during the last years of ʻUthmān's reign, and lived to the age of 86, to within twenty-one years of the ʻAbbāsid caliphate. The following utterance of his throws light on the deep, sober and serene sadness which appears from all accounts to have settled on him like a cloak:

> God has slaves who have already seen the people of Paradise forever in Paradise and the people of the fire forever in the fire. The hearts of these slaves are saddened, yet their woes are sure of redress, their needs are light, their souls are continent. They know they have only to be patient for a few short days and that then a long repose will follow...The onlooker thinks that they are sick, but no sickness has smitten that folk. Or, if you will, they are smitten—overwhelmingly smitten by the remembrance of the Hereafter![3]

One of the greatest women saints of Islam, Rābiʻa al-ʻAdawiyya, was probably the disciple of one of al-Ḥasan's disciples. It was her vocation

[1] Sarrāj, *al-Lumaʻ*, p. 132. [2] *Ibid*, p. 124.
[3] Abū Nuʻaym al-Iṣbahānī, *Ḥilyat al-awliyāʼ*, pt. 2, p. 151.

to incarnate, as it were, the words of the Qur'ān "God's Beatitude is greater (than Paradise)"[1] and the utterance of the Prophet in which God is represented saying to the people of Paradise: "I will give you better than this. I will let down upon you my Beatitude."[2] Especially characteristic of Rābi'a is her insistence that the end of the path is not Paradise but God himself. It was in this sense that she once quoted the adage: "The neighbour first, then the house." Not unconnected with this, are her words to a man who claimed to be innocent of sin: "Alas, my son, your existence is a sin with which no other sin can be compared!" The words "your existence" may here be glossed "the illusion that you exist when in reality only One exists". This formulation, which would have been unthinkable in the first generation of Islam, is an example of another kind of secondary development that took place in Ṣūfism—secondary because there is no change in the doctrine itself. By the time of Rābi'a, who died in 801, the spiritual degeneration of the community as a whole, like a receding tide, had left the Ṣūfīs a much more distinct class than they had been before, and they for their part, acutely conscious of this ebb and struggling against its current, felt driven to go to lengths hitherto unknown in Islam both as regards asceticism and doctrinal formulations. Dā'ūd al-Ṭā'ī said: "Fast from the world and make death your breakfast and flee from men as you would flee from beasts of prey";[3] and Ḥātim al-Aṣamm said: "Every morning Satan says to me: What will you eat and what will you put on and where will you dwell? And I say to him: I will eat death and put on my shroud and dwell in the tomb."[4]

As regards doctrinal formulations, Rābi'a's definition of "sin" may be compared with al-Ḥallāj's paradox: "Who affirms that God is One is guilty of idolatry (by the intrusion of his own existence, manifested in his utterance)."[5] He also said "I am the Truth", for which he was put to death (in 922) though it is doubtful whether this would have happened but for an unfortunate combination of circumstances. Abū Yazīd al-Bisṭāmī had previously said with impunity: "Glory be to Me! How great is My Majesty!"; and others after al-Ḥallāj were no less outspoken. But the fate of al-Ḥallāj proved to be, in the long run, a blessing for the Ṣūfīs. *Vox populi vox Dei.* According to the ultimate judgment of Muslims upon him, in the light of writings he left and what tradition has handed down about his life, he was one of the greatest

[1] IX. 72.
[2] Bukhārī, *Riqāq*, 51; Tirmidhī, *Jannah*, 18.
[3] Qushayrī, *Risāla*.
[4] *Ibid.*
[5] *Akhbār*, no. 49.

saints of Islam, and guilty of no more than imprudence; and the disproportion between this offence and the frightful cruelty of his execution still horrifies the Muslim mind and serves to thrust home the fact that the Ṣūfīs sometimes utter inspired ejaculations (*shaṭaḥāt*) which are not to be judged in the same way as the sayings of other men.

Very different from such ejaculations are the mystical treatises which began to be written about this time. Yet both ejaculations and treatises may be considered as part of the same development in that both spring from the Ṣūfīs as a distinct class. But whereas the ejaculations cleave as it were a chasm between this class and the rest of the community, some of the treatises serve to bridge that chasm. Both chasm and bridge are necessary and in the nature of things. Junayd of Baghdad (d. 910) was once asked if Ṣūfism was an attribute of God, and he replied: "In its innermost reality it is an attribute of God, but in outward form it is an attribute of man."[1] To be true to itself Ṣūfism must be both transcendent and immanent, like the divine mysteries of which it is the embodiment. In his treatises Junayd formulated the doctrines of *tawḥīd* (realizing God's Oneness) and *fanā'* (extinction of the individual soul) with a sobriety which contrasts with the spiritual drunkenness of some of the ejaculations, but which sacrifices nothing in the dimension of depth. By his time the Ṣūfī orders had acquired a definitely organized form, and most of the later ones can trace a line of spiritual descent back to him, whence his title "the shaykh of the shaykhs".

The chasm between Ṣūfism and the rest of the Islamic community has been bridged, in most generations, by men who have been members of Ṣūfī orders and at the same time eminent authorities in one or more of the outer domains of Islam. One of the most famous of these "bridges" was al-Ghazālī (d. 1111) the great Shāfi'ī canonist and theologian who devoted his latter years to the mystic path and who wrote an autobiographical treatise, "The Saviour from Error" (*al-munqidh min al-ḍalāl*) in praise of Ṣūfism as the only sure antidote to scepticism and as the highest way of life. Quotations have already been made from his "Niche of Lights" (*mishkāt al-anwār*) which was written exclusively for Ṣūfīs and which is altogether uncompromising in its formulations. But he is better known for his longest work, "The Revival of the Sciences of the Religion" (*iḥyā' 'ulūm al-dīn*) which was addressed to the community as a whole, and which is an eloquent

[1] Hujwīrī, *Kashf al-Maḥjūb*, ch. 3 (in Nicholson's translation, p. 36).

reminder of the distinctly mystical bent which had characterized Islam in the time of the Prophet.

al-Ghazālī's vocation to ensure a general recognition of Ṣūfism as an integral part of Islam was carried on after his death, in a somewhat different mode, by his younger contemporary 'Abd al-Qādir al-Jīlānī (d. 1166) whose sermons, despite their eloquence, probably give no more than a faint suggestion of the radiance which must have emanated from his actual presence. He is known as "the sultan of the saints" and was the founder of the great Qādirī order which within only one generation after his death had spread to most parts of the Islamic empire.

His *ṭarīqa* is no doubt the most widely spread of all the Ṣūfī orders with the exception of the Shādhilī *ṭarīqa*, which was founded about a hundred years later by Abu 'l-Ḥasan al-Shādhilī. These two orders hold an even wider sway than they are generally credited with, for most of the variously named orders founded within the last 600 years are in fact branches of either the Qādiriyya or the Shādhiliyya.

Abu 'l-Ḥasan's slightly older contemporary, the Spanish born Muḥyi 'l-Dīn b. 'Arabī also founded an order, but in a sense he belongs to all the orders in virtue of his writings, a vast and much drawn on treasury of mystical prose and poetry. His longest work, the Meccan Revelations (*al-futūḥāt al-makkiyya*) "contains, in addition to the doctrines of Ṣūfism, much about the lives and sayings of the earlier Ṣūfīs, cosmological doctrines of hermetic and Neoplatonic origin integrated into Ṣūfī metaphysics, esoteric sciences like *jafr* (divination), alchemical and astrological symbolism, and practically everything else of an esoteric nature which in one way or another has found a place in the Islamic scheme of things".[1]

The following quotation is also relevant: "In every religion, some centuries after its foundation, one sees a fresh flowering or a kind of second youth, and this is due to the fact that the presence of a collective and material ambience realized by the religion itself creates conditions allowing, or requiring, an expansion of an apparently new kind: in the West, the Middle Ages...were the Christian Ages *par excellence*; they were so, moreover, in a manner different from the first centuries of Christianity which, from another point of view, clearly retain their superiority of original perfection. Similarly in Islam, the period of a saint like Ibn 'Arabī, the 'genius' of his time, coincides with a world

[1] Seyyed Hossein Nasr, *Three Muslim Sages* (Cambridge, Mass., 1964), p. 98.

elaborated in the course of several centuries of Islamic moulding, and displays, on the esoteric plane, a very ample and profound flowering which at times verges on the initial prophetic revelation."[1]

The great crystallization of the Ṣūfī orders in the twelfth and thirteenth centuries (which were, incidentally, the centuries of St Bernard, St Dominic and St Francis) was one of the remarkable features of this "second youth" of Islam, which was also, like its counterpart in Christianity, something of an "Indian summer" and not without a truly autumnal bounty. The Ṣūfism of this period has overflowed with extraordinary amplitude, through its dead, into the community of Islam as a whole. A living saint belongs above all to his disciples, but dead he belongs to everyone. The spirit of 'Abd al-Qādir al-Jīlānī still presides over Baghdad where his tomb is a place of pilgrimage from far and wide, and within easy walking distance of it is the tomb of "Shaykh 'Umar" as he is affectionately called, 'Umar al-Suhrawardī (d. 1234), disciple of 'Abd al-Qādir and founder of the Suhrawardī order. Over southern Iraq presides Aḥmad al-Rifā'ī (d. 1183), the founder of the Rifā'ī order; and before passing farther west, mention must be made of Rūzbahān al-Baqlī (d. 1209), a spiritual heir of al-Ḥallāj and patron saint of Shīrāz, and also of the founder of the Chishtī order, Mu'īn al-Dīn al-Chishtī (d. 1236), whose tomb at Ajmer in India is one of the great shrines of the sub-continent, revered by Hindus as well as Muslims.

It was four years after the death of this saint that Ibn 'Arabī himself died in Damascus. His tomb, over which a mosque has since been built, is just outside the town on the slopes of Mount Qāsiyūn. To the north lies the patron saint of Anatolia, greatest of Persian poets and founder of the "whirling dervishes", Jalāl al-Dīn al-Rūmī (d. 1273), whose much visited tomb at Konya is a serious threat to modern Turkish secularism. Going south, as the traveller approaches Alexandria from the sea, he cannot fail to be struck by the mosque which entombs Abu 'l-'Abbās al-Mursī, the successor of Abu 'l-Ḥasan al-Shādhilī. But it is Aḥmad al-Badawī, who died and was buried at Ṭanṭā in 1276, who must be considered as the patron saint of Lower Egypt. In Cairo, at the foot of the Muqaṭṭam hill, lies buried the greatest of Arab Ṣūfī poets, 'Umar b. al-Fāriḍ (d. 1235) who wrote, amongst other things:

> "We have drunk to the remembrance of the Beloved a wine
> Wherewith we were made drunk before the vine was created."

[1] Frithjof Schuon, *In the Tracks of Buddhism* (Allen and Unwin, 1968), ch. XVII.

Not far from Ibn al-Fāriḍ lies Ibn ʿAṭāʾ Allāh al-Iskandarī (d. 1309), who was a disciple of Abu ʾl-Ḥasan al-Shādhilī. Though his tomb is relatively unknown, his masterly collection of the sayings of his master and others, *al-Ḥikam*, is one of the most famous of all Ṣūfī treatises. Farther south, in the desert of Upper Egypt, lies the great Abu ʾl-Ḥasan himself who died there in 1258 on the way back from the Pilgrimage, having bought his winding-sheets in Mecca where he told his disciples who asked who was to be buried in them: "You will see." Abu ʾl-Ḥasan also in a sense presides over Tunis, for one of its holiest and most visited shrines is the cave where he used to make spiritual retreats, on the slopes of a hill that overlooks the town. The patron saint of Algeria is a disciple of the great ʿAbd al-Qādir, Shuʿayb Abū Madyan, who died and was buried near Tlemcen in 1197; and it is his spiritual heir ʿAbd al-Salām b. Mashīsh (d. 1228), the master of Abu ʾl-Ḥasan al-Shādhilī, who may be said to preside over all northern Morocco from his tomb on Mount ʿAlam overlooking Tangier and Taṭwān.

If "the greatest Shaykh" (*al-shaykh al-akbar*), as Ibn ʿArabī is named, may be said to represent something of a final stage in the written exposition of Islamic mystical doctrine this does not mean that the subject has been exhausted—for indeed it is inexhaustible—nor does it mean that his successors wrote nothing of importance. But his tremendous output made doctrinal exposition decidedly less necessary than it had been before. It must be admitted however that Abu ʾl-Karīm al-Jīlī's early fifteenth-century treatise "Universal Man" (*al-insān al-kāmil*) fulfilled a real need by presenting the whole of Ṣūfī doctrine in a remarkably clear and accessible form. This is in fact one of the most often consulted of all the mystical treatises of Islam, and it is to al-Jīlī that we owe, amongst other things, the illuminating symbolism of water and ice as representing respectively God and creation in their apparent difference and secret identity.

Needless to say, this summary section on the development of Ṣūfism does not claim to do more than single out one or two landmarks, which is all that the scope of this chapter as a whole will allow. As regards the much underestimated period of Ṣūfism from the fourteenth century until the present day, suffice it to point out here that mysticism is by definition the domain of religion which lies nearest the spirit and which is therefore most immune from the ravages of time. The rule *Corruptio optimi pessima* (corruption of the best is corruption at its worst), may be said to apply when, for example, part of an order breaks off from the rest and devotes itself to jugglery and sorcery as has happened more than once. But such deviations represent only a small fraction of the whole. Where Ṣūfism remains even remotely true to itself, it is far less liable to degenerate than the more outward sections of the community. There have continued to be truly great shaykhs throughout the Islamic world in each of the last six centuries. The Moroccan al-'Arabī al-Darqāwī, the Shādhilī founder of the Darqāwī order in the eighteenth century may also be counted among the very greatest, and the same may be said of his spiritual descendant, the Algerian Aḥmad al-'Alawī who founded the 'Alawī branch of the Darqāwā some fifty years ago. If such shaykhs are fewer in number than they used to be, and if there is a greater disparity between them and most of their followers than there would have been in earlier centuries, the orders still comprise thousands of deeply devout men and women in nearly every Islamic country.

In a quotation already made from Constance Padwick she refers to the present "official submergence" of the orders. But it is only in Turkey and Saudi Arabia that they are officially proscribed, in the one state because they are too conservative, and in the other because their conservatism is not sufficiently narrow. Moreover the Wahhābīs like to think that there is nothing in true religion which everyone cannot understand. Statements such as "there are no mysteries in Islam" are often upon their lips. Also they see the seeds of idolatry in the practice, so much encouraged by the Ṣūfīs, of visiting the tombs of saints. But the official ban does not prevent Mecca and Medina from being great meeting places for Ṣūfīs from all parts of the Islamic world; nor in Turkey have the orders ceased, in fact, to be operative. Elsewhere they are merely criticized, while being allowed full liberty. The particular criticisms against single individuals are often justified, except that it is unjust to make such criticisms an excuse for condemning the orders as a whole. As to the general criticisms, they really amount to a judgment of the community upon itself. Nearly all Islamic countries today are frantically bent on imitating the West, "on being progressive", "acquiring a sense of nationalism", "taking their place in the modern world", "raising the standard of living", and "throwing off the fetters of superstition". For none of these aims can Ṣūfism evince any enthusiasm; to most of them it is bound to be hostile. Being itself the science of progress on a higher plane—the progress of individual souls towards the absolute, the infinite and eternal—it cannot be anything but critical of a material progressism which has partly usurped even the place of religion, while tending to lead souls in the opposite direction. The most general criticism levelled against Ṣūfism is that it refuses to "move with the times". But from the point of view of the mystic this blame is really praise. The three phases of the Ṣūfī path are fear (*makhāfa*), love (*maḥabba*), and knowledge (*ma'rifa*); and the phase which comes first (though all three are partly simultaneous) has always been much concerned with the question, precisely, of how *not* to move with the times.

CHAPTER 14

THE WAHHĀBĪS

The name Wahhābī was given to the followers of shaykh Muḥammad b. ʻAbd al-Wahhāb by Muslim opponents who feared the revolutionary power of his appeal. The name was intended to suggest that the shaykh had founded a new sect whose spread should be resisted and whose doctrines should be suppressed. The people to whom the name was applied, convinced of the shaykh's orthodoxy, have scornfully rejected the opprobrious label. For them his call was and remains *al-daʻwa ila'l-tawḥīd*, summoning to belief in the unity of God, neither more nor less than a reaffirmation of the call of the Prophet Muḥammad at the beginning of Islam, a reaffirmation directed towards men who wilfully or unwittingly had drifted away from this early belief and the conduct it entails. Unitarianism is an accurate rendering of *al-daʻwa ila'l-tawḥīd*, but for Western readers Unitarianism has connotations which may be misleading. Western writers long ago borrowed the name Wahhābī and gave it currency, but they have not always used it pejoratively. Adopted in this work for the sake of clarity, it does not here carry the hostile implications given it by its originators.

The inaugurator of Wahhābism, Muḥammad b. ʻAbd al-Wahhāb of the ancient tribe of Tamīm, was born in the small town of al-ʻUyayna in Najd, the central region of Arabia, in 1703. His grandfather and father were Ḥanbalite *qāḍīs* (religious judges), he was brought up a Ḥanbalite, and such he remained until his death; he was prone to repeat, "We, praise be to God, are followers, not innovators, in the school of the Imam Aḥmad b. Ḥanbal". Ibn ʻAbd al-Wahhāb's theological studies, begun at home, were pursued at Medina, at Baṣra in southern Iraq, and in the eastern Arabian oasis of al-Aḥsā', where his teacher was a Shāfiʻite scholar. The young man was deeply troubled by the decay of the popular faith, both in his homeland and in the neighbouring countries. People calling themselves Muslims engaged in reprehensible practices which fell into the category of *shirk* (syntheism), the association of persons and things with God, who, in the common Muslim phrase, "has no associate". Ibn ʻAbd al-Wahhāb perceived syntheism in the excessive reverence paid to saints and their

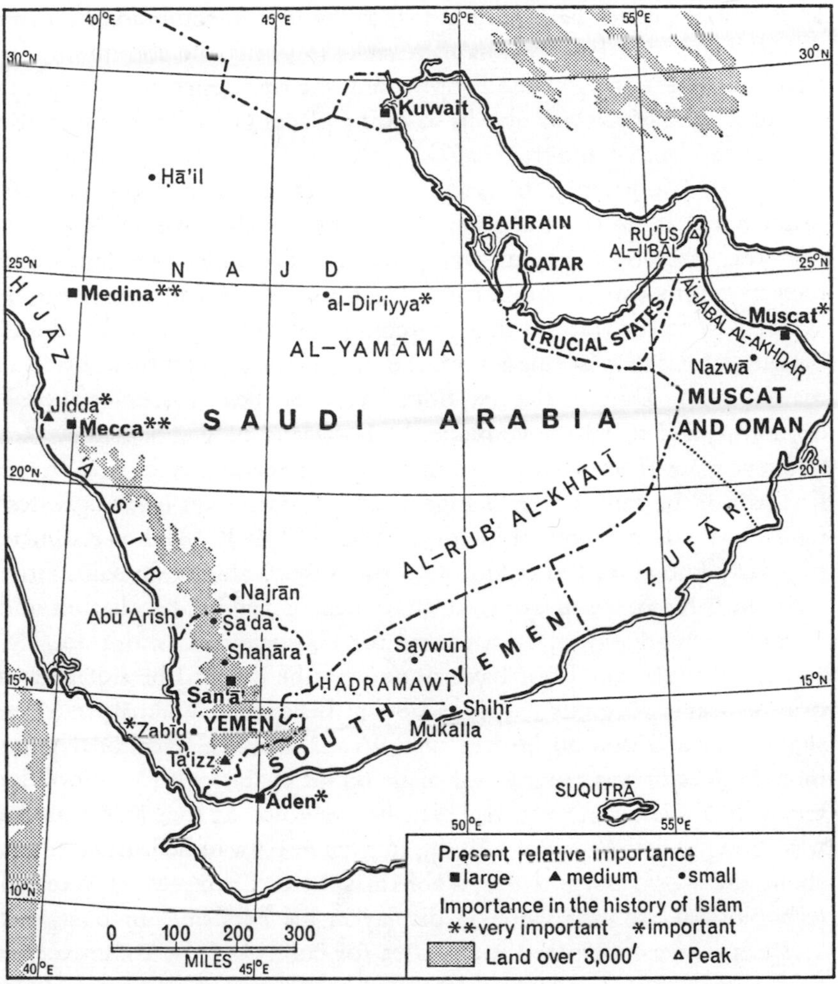

Arabia.

tombs, as well as in prayers addressed to sacred trees and stones. For him syntheism was the one sin God himself does not forgive, the one sin that justified branding self-styled Muslims as unbelievers.

In combating syntheism, Ibn 'Abd al-Wahhāb exalted the doctrine of *tawḥīd*. Wahhābī literature expounds at length the two principal aspects of *tawḥīd*, God's uniqueness as omnipotent lord of creation (*tawḥīd al-rubūbiyya*) and his uniqueness in deserving worship and the absolute devotion of his servants (*tawḥīd al-ulūhiyya*). Syntheism, the violation of the doctrine of God's oneness, proceeds from *bida*' (innovations), which have infiltrated into the Islamic community during the later ages of Islam. Wahhābism seeks to purify the community by returning to the ways of the Prophet and the first generations of pious Muslims (*al-salaf al-ṣāliḥ*), and in so doing places great emphasis on the texts of the Qur'ān and the *Ḥadīth*.

In 1744 Muḥammad b. ʿAbd al-Wahhāb made a compact with Muḥammad b. Saʿūd, the ruler of another small town in Najd, al-Dirʿiyya, whereby the ruler was promised dominion over lands and men in return for his supporting the cause of reform. Ibn ʿAbd al-Wahhāb won converts by his preaching and writing; Ibn Saʿūd and his successors, who as rulers bore the title of Imam, won them by their martial skill. During the twentieth century new forces—political, economic, and social—have made the homeland of Wahhābism a very different place from what it was in the two preceding centuries. In the first half of the century the changes were presided over by the greatest figure in modern Wahhābī history, ʿAbd al-ʿAzīz b. ʿAbd al-Raḥmān, popularly known as Ibn Saʿūd, who ruled the Wahhābī domains from 1902 until his death in 1953. A statesmen of genius, he charted and steered a remarkably smooth course for his society in transition.

ʿAbd al-ʿAzīz could not have done what he did had he not been a man of deeply religious nature, a devout believer in Wahhābism. The slight formal education he had was Wahhābī in the traditional vein; more important was the imprint made on his character and outlook by the Wahhābī environment in which he grew up. At the same time he was a pragmatist. As a youth living in exile in Kuwait he learned much about the world beyond the Wahhābī sphere. Examples of Western technological progress were on display in the Persian Gulf port, and Western powers competed in the area for control of the routes to the East. Laying plans for the re-establishment of the political power of the House of Saʿūd, ʿAbd al-ʿAzīz may have begun to realize while still in Kuwait that Wahhābism could not endure as an island sufficient unto itself and that the enmeshing of its life with the outside world would require adjustments on a broad scale. For the sincere Wahhābī, however, such adjustments would have to be restricted to externals; no compromise would be tolerated on matters of doctrine.

ʿAbd al-ʿAzīz, like his ancestors before him, became embroiled with the *sharīf* of Mecca. The reigning *sharīf*, al-Ḥusayn b. ʿAlī, aspired to leadership of the entire Arab world, as shown by his taking the title of King of the Arabs when he revolted against the Ottoman Empire in 1916. ʿAbd al-ʿAzīz would not recognize his primacy even in Arabia. Attempts by the new king to stem the spread of Wahhābism in the borderlands between the Ḥijāz and Najd caused friction, made worse by al-Ḥusayn's abortive bid for the caliphate when the Turks gave it up. In 1924 Saudi military pressure compelled al-Ḥusayn to abdicate, and in 1925 ʿAbd al-ʿAzīz erased the last vestige of the power of the Meccan *sharīfs* in Arabia by taking Jidda, whereupon the citizens of the Ḥijāz besought him in 1926 to become their king. A year later the sultanate of Najd was transformed into a kingdom linked with the Ḥijāz in a dual monarchy, and in 1932 the state was consolidated under the name of the kingdom of Saudi Arabia.

During the second and third decades of the twentieth century two new phenomena distinguished ʿAbd al-ʿAzīz's regime, a programme for settling Bedouins in *hijras* (agricultural colonies that also served as military cantonments) and the widespread adoption of mechanical devices of foreign origin, such as automobiles, the telegraph, and telephones. While settling the Bedouins represented an intensification of traditional Wahhābism, conservative Wahhābīs looked upon borrowing from abroad as a procedure to be condemned. The basic antithesis of the two phenomena at last provoked a clash, the outcome of which went far towards determining the future course of Wahhābism.

Throughout Wahhābī history the townsmen of Najd have proved a stauncher force on the battlefield than the mercurial Bedouins. By making townsmen out of the Bedouins, ʿAbd al-ʿAzīz increased his military potential. The Bedouins who took up the new mode of life were called *Ikhwān* (Brothers), and in the settlements they received more intensive indoctrination in the beliefs of Wahhābism than they had while roaming the desert. ʿAbd al-ʿAzīz thus acquired a legion of devoted and fanatical men, eager to impose by force their version of Islam on all who disagreed with them, whether in the peninsula or beyond its borders.

Valuable as the *Ikhwān* were to ʿAbd al-ʿAzīz in his campaigns inside Arabia, the time came when they began to embarrass him in his foreign relations. In 1922 raiding *Ikhwān* penetrated far into the territory of the new state of Transjordan, a British mandate. Aircraft and armoured cars of the Royal Air Force drove the intruders back. Trouble later developed beyond the newly established boundaries between the Saudi state and its northern neighbours, Iraq and Kuwait, where the *Ikhwān* again came up against the military machines of the

British. The *Ikhwān* resented attempts by 'Abd al-'Azīz to restrain them from the *jihād*, and they further charged him with religious laxity in the adoption of foreign contrivances unknown to early Islam, a charge the Wahhābī *'ulamā'*, who in general sided with their sovereign, declined to support.[1] In 1928 the *Ikhwān* rose in open revolt. The crushing of the revolt by January 1930 and the destruction of the principal *hijras* marked the end of militant Wahhābism. Since then Saudi Arabia has engaged in two wars—against the Yemen in 1934 and against Israel in 1948—but the moving sentiment on both occasions was more nationalistic than religious.

In the fourth and fifth decades of the twentieth century another phenomenon emphasized the originality of 'Abd al-'Azīz's reign in the annals of Wahhābism: a wider opening of the doors of the kingdom to ultramarine influences, paralleled by the kingdom's assumption of a larger place in the comity of nations, non-Islamic as well as Islamic. In the past religion had dominated the life of the country. The simple economy was based on oasis agriculture and pastoralism, and society differed little from what it had been in the time of the Prophet. The annual income of the government during the first ten years of 'Abd al-'Azīz's reign was estimated at about £50,000. The occupation of the Ḥijāz and the flow of revenue from the pilgrimage helped to raise the figure to four or five million a year, but the expectations of the people and the demands on the treasury kept pace. The world depression of the late 1920s brought about a serious curtailment of the pilgrim traffic, worsening the economic plight of the Saudi state and inducing the king to seek the collaboration of foreigners in a search for new resources. Oil and precious minerals were discovered in the 1930s, and during the next decade the production of oil in particular soared so amazingly that the government's income at the end of 'Abd al-'Azīz's reign rose to about £100 million a year. Expansion continued under 'Abd al-'Azīz's sons and successors, Sa'ūd (regn. 1953–64) and Fayṣal, and the government's budget for 1965 showed an income of about £250 million, some 80 per cent of which was derived from the oil industry.

[1] The Arabic text of the *fatwā* issued by the *'ulamā'* in February 1927 is given in Ḥāfiẓ Wahba, *Jazīrat al-'arab*, pp. 319–21; an Italian translation is furnished by C. A. Nallino, *L'Arabia sa'ūdiana*, pp. 119–122. The *fatwā* dodged the issue with respect to the legality of the wireless telegraph (*al-barq*), stating that judgment could not be passed as long as the true nature of the device was not revealed by the corpus of the *sharī'a*. 'Abd al-'Azīz consequently suspended the use of the telegraph for a brief period. 'Abd al-'Azīz, though he had already taken the title of King, is referred to throughout the *fatwā* as the *imām*.

Although Saudi Arabs are now participating actively in virtually every phase of the oil industry, the exploitation of Saudi Arabia's underground resources in the earlier stages was mainly the work of foreign technicians, most of whom were Christians. Geologists ranged far and wide over the land in motor vehicles. The oil fields with their complicated paraphernalia spread over large parts of the Eastern Province and out into the waters of the Persian Gulf. A great pipeline snaked its way across the desert, with pump stations at intervals along its course, to deliver oil to tankers in the Mediterranean port of Sidon. New communities, peopled largely by foreigners wedded to their own customs, grew up at formerly barren spots. In the beginning the foreigners and their towns were almost entirely cut off from the closed Wahhābī society surrounding them, but in time the newcomers and the natives got to know and respect each other, and their intermingling, professionally and socially, became easy and frequent. The exposure of Wahhābīs to Western ways was not limited to what was going on in Saudi Arabia. Government officials, military men, merchants, students, and others, once they had the means, took to travelling abroad for business or pleasure, their favourite resorts being Europe, the United States, and the cosmopolitan cities of the Arab world, Cairo and Beirut.

Since the humbling of the *Ikhwān*, many of the Wahhābīs of Saudi Arabia have shown a growing spirit of tolerance towards both non-Wahhābī Muslims and non-Muslims. Gone forever, it would seem, are the days of the Wahhābī *jihād* against "syntheists" and unbelievers. The Shī'ites of the Eastern Province, once unwelcome residents in the eyes of the government,[1] have seen their lot improve; the Wahhābī king has been an honoured guest at official functions in their towns. When the Ibāḍī Imam of Oman was forced to flee his homeland, the Wahhābī government gave him asylum. When the Zaydī ruler of the Yemen was driven from his throne by republican revolutionaries, the Wahhābī government came to his support with funds and equipment. The government, it is true, was moved by political considerations rather than by sympathy for the cause of Ibāḍism or Zaydism, but in former times a Wahhābī government would have been much less ready to let politics override religious hostility.

The spirit of tolerance has extended to Christian persons and powers as well. Numerous foreigners of Christian faith have been employed

[1] The *fatwā* of February 1927, cited in the preceding note called upon 'Abd al-'Azīz to use compulsion in converting the Shī'ites of the realm to Sunnism.

in recent years by the government and private concerns as advisers and technical experts. Several decades ago almost all such advisers and experts from abroad were Muslims or an occasional Druze who could pass as a Muslim in Arabia. The armed forces of Saudi Arabia have been trained in part first by a British military mission and more recently by one from the United States. When Saudi Arabia and the United Arab Republic came to the brink of war with each other after the revolution of 1962 in the Yemen, the Wahhābī government agreed to the participation of United States troops and aircraft in joint manoeuvres in Saudi Arabia to demonstrate the concern of the United States for the stability of the Saudi regime.

The spirit of tolerance has not, however, gone so far as to include the Jews, though it might have done so had it not been for the political complications arising out of the establishment of the state of Israel. Hatred and fear of Zionism and the suspicion that almost any Jew may be a Zionist sympathizer have led to the barring of all Jews save a few anti-Zionists from entry into Saudi Arabia. The one small Jewish community in the country, which had lived in Najrān for generations, though its members were on good terms with their Muslim neighbours and were not oppressed by the government, emigrated *in toto* to Israel.

The acquisition of wealth during the past twenty years has posed a serious problem for Wahhābī society. High moral standards and religious devotion seem to be easier to attain in a harsh and poor environment than in a land of plenty. Neither ʿAbd al-ʿAzīz in his declining years nor his first successor Saʿūd had the financial acumen needed for the wise spending of the large sums pouring in. Particularly under Saʿūd, extravagance and ostentation of a very un-Wahhābī-like character tainted the atmosphere of the Saudi court. More than a few princes of the royal house, government officials, and private citizens drifted away from the austere life of their predecessors. But the latest Wahhābī ruler, Fayṣal, has reversed the trend, beginning with his first assumption of full powers in 1958 as Prime Minister under his brother Saʿūd. A man whose own tastes are relatively modest, Fayṣal appreciates the importance of proper management of the state finances and the need to channel an ever-growing share of the revenue into economic and social development for the benefit of the whole people.

During the reigns of ʿAbd al-ʿAzīz and his successors the old system of education with its emphasis on theological studies and the Arabic language has been retained and expanded, but alongside it there has developed a new and comprehensive system. The progression from elementary school to university, the inclusion of scientific and technical subjects and foreign languages in the curriculum, the new types of classrooms and teaching aids and textbooks, the public instruction of girls—none of these things had been known in Wahhābīland before. Yet such a system is essential for training Saudi Arabs to play their part in the new society they are building. The government's concern lest the new system diverge too sharply from the old is indicated by the fact that the Minister of Education under King Fayṣal comes from the House of the shaykh.

The revolution in education has been accompanied by a revolution in communications. Ports have been modernized, roads and railroads built, transport mechanized, and air traffic extended to nearly every part of the kingdom. The press, the radio, and television carry words and pictures and ideas to thousands of citizens who once lived in isolation.

WAHHĀBISM TODAY

As the official form of Islam in the kingdom of Saudi Arabia, Wahhābism is supported by the power and wealth of the state. The firmness of the alliance between the House of Saʿūd and the House of the shaykh is personified in King Fayṣal, a direct descendant of both Muḥammad b. Saʿūd and Muḥammad b. ʿAbd al-Wahhāb. The royal family is thoroughly Wahhābī; the few princes who once dabbled in Arab socialism have confessed their errors and returned to the fold. The *muftī* and the chief *qāḍī* come from the House of the shaykh, and its members and their colleagues of long standing dominate the *ʿulamā*ʾ. The courts are largely Wahhābī in character, though not exclusively so (Mālikite judges, for example, are found in the Eastern Province). A preponderance of high positions in the central government is held by Najdīs, most of whom are Wahhābīs. Provincial governors are chosen either from the royal family or from the Sudayrī family, with which it is closely linked by marriage ties (King ʿAbd al-ʿAzīz's mother was a Sudayriyya, and his Sudayriyya wives bore him more than a dozen sons).

The spread of education and the improvement of the system of communications have made it easier to transmit the gospel to the population as a whole. Wahhābism is the prevailing faith among the townsmen of Najd and to a somewhat less degree among those of

'Asīr. In the towns, especially the larger ones, of the Ḥijāz and the Eastern Province, the adherents of Wahhābism are proportionately fewer, with many Shāfi'ites in the Ḥijāz and Mālikites and Shī'ites in the east. The Bedouins throughout the kingdom tend to be loyal to Wahhābism, even though they may have little knowledge of its doctrinal refinements. Ever since the crushing of the rebellion of the *Ikhwān*, the Bedouins have been submissive to the will of the king, and obedience to the king entails obedience to the religion of his state.

In the more remote towns and villages of Najd, the Wahhābism of the eighteenth century flourishes in virtually undiluted form. Its chief agents are the *qāḍīs* and *muṭawwa's* (preceptors of lower rank but not inferior in zeal) and the local Committees for the Commanding of Good and the Forbidding of Evil, and the authority of these agents in matters of dogma is rarely if ever questioned. Some of the larger cities show the same attachment to the ways of the past. The citizens of Burayda refused to have schools for girls in their midst long after they were sanctioned by the central government. In Riyāḍ, on the other hand, there is more scope for diversity, despite its closeness to the throne and its reputation as the citadel of orthodoxy. The old city walls have been torn down, and their disappearance is symbolic of a turning away from the former seclusion. Foreigners, Muslims and non-Muslims, throng the hotel lobbies—fora of discussion unknown in Wahhābiland until a few years ago—and some of the foreign ways they bring with them win acceptance. Riyāḍ sets the pace, which other parts of Najd follow as the influence of the capital reaches out and the country becomes more closely knit.

In borrowing from outside sources, the Wahhābīs are confronted with a dilemma. Wahhābism, as has been seen, vigorously rejects innovations. Yet even the early Wahhābī divines distinguished clearly between religious and worldly innovations. Coffee, though not known to the first generations of Muslims, was allowed as its use was not religiously harmful; the same was true of weapons such as the musket, long the standby of the Wahhābī hosts.[1] King 'Abd al-'Azīz advocated a liberal interpretation of this distinction against the objections of some of the *'ulamā'* and chiefs of the *Ikhwān*, and the liberal interpretation

[1] See the passage on *bida'* in the epistle written by 'Abdallāh, son of Muḥammad b. 'Abd al-Wahhāb, setting forth Wahhābī beliefs for the enlightenment of the people of Mecca just after the first occupation of their city by the Wahhābīs in 1803—*al-Hadiyya al-sunniyya*, pp. 46–50.

continues to gain ground. The old Wahhābī mosques were built without minarets; the *mu'adhdhin* gave the call to prayer from a slightly raised platform. The new congregational mosque in the heart of Riyāḍ has towering minarets. It can be argued that such an innovation, though it falls within the sphere of religion, is worldly in that it does not touch upon the essence of belief. Until recently illustrations showing the human form were taboo among Wahhābīs, but the Qur'ān itself contains no sweeping prohibition of representational art, and the press of Saudi Arabia is now replete with photographs and drawings. The attitude towards tobacco is also changing; no longer do all sincere Wahhābīs regard the use of the weed as a sign of moral laxity. On the other hand, the Qur'ānic injunction against *khamr*, interpreted as including all alcoholic beverages, stays in force, even though some Saudi Arabs yield on occasion to the lure of the grape.

Wahhābism with its goal of restoring the initial dominance of Islam gives religion mastery over the state. The Qur'ān is the constitution of the kingdom, supplemented by the other sources of the *sharī'a*, all binding on the king and his subjects. Yet the *sharī'a* with its elaborations has not proved ample enough to cope with the complexity of a modern state and its array of worldly innovations. On a plane lower than the *sharī'a*, the Saudi Arabian government has issued detailed regulations (usually designated as *niẓāms*) governing the use of motor-vehicles, the application of customs tariffs, the registration of trade marks, and so on. Liberal elements favour an even bolder departure from the past through the adoption of a constitution (*dustūr*), an instrument that has found a home in many other Islamic countries. Constitutional government implies popular elections. Islam is not hostile to the electoral principle, though it has customarily restricted the franchise to men of influence ("the people of loosing and binding"), and the ceremony of swearing allegiance (*bay'a*), which is linked with this principle, has been traditional in the Wahhābī state throughout its history. Many Wahhābīs, including the present king, feel that an immediate switch to a constitution and an electoral system modelled on Western procedures would be too abrupt a break with the past. Before becoming king, crown prince Fayṣal in November 1962 set forth a reform programme that would begin with consideration of the enactment of a fundamental law (*niẓām asāsī*, the term *dustūr* being carefully avoided). Dilatoriness in implementation has, however, left the modernists disappointed or even disillusioned.

The constitutional question in Saudi Arabia is not being dealt with in a vacuum; it has become an issue in the arena of Arab politics, where Arab socialists confront the monarchies of strongly Islamic stamp. Far from abjuring Islam, most Arab socialists maintain that their reverence for it distinguishes their variety of socialism from the socialism and Communism of Europe. At the same time, the Arab socialists with their republican and democratic doctrines stand clearly apart from the Arab monarchies, and friction between the two is hard to escape. The revolution in the Yemen in September 1962 overthrew an Islamic monarchy of far more ancient lineage than the House of Sa'ūd (the Zaydī Imamate was founded in the ninth century) and established in its place a socialist republic. The discord and troubles, however, that have plagued the Yemen Arab Republic since its inception have given at least some of the modernists in Saudi Arabia pause for thought.

A number of forward-looking Saudi Arabs feel that their government has a ready-made vehicle for broader popular representation in the Consultative Council (*majlis al-shūrā*), instituted in 1926 shortly after the Wahhābī occupation of the Ḥijāz. The Council, which takes its name from the title of Sūra XLII of the Qur'ān (*shūrā* = consultation or counsel), is designed to bring about closer collaboration between the sovereign and his subjects. Election instead of appointment of members should, in the view of modernists, make the Council far more effective than it has been in the past and should further the evolution of the government machinery within the traditional framework of Islam. In November 1962 Prince Fayṣal spoke out in favour of the "development" of the Council. Although it was commonly believed that he was indicating a willingness to consider elections for the Council, his subsequent inaction has undermined this belief. The fate of consultation in the Wahhābī state remains undecided.

The reform programme of 1962 contained two striking indications of the government's readiness to accommodate Wahhābī society to the new circumstances of the time. The first of these was the absolute abolition of slavery. Although slavery was not nearly as widespread in Arabia as ill-informed Westerners often charged, it was an institution of pre-Islamic origin which had been accepted in modified form by the Prophet and had flourished in the Islamic world for well over a millennium. The *'ulamā'* opposed any tinkering with an institution of such antiquity, but Prince Fayṣal showed courage in emancipating all slaves in the realm. The second sign of accommodation appeared in

Fayṣal's statement that the situation of the Committees for the Commanding of Good and the Forbidding of Evil would be improved. This was widely interpreted as meaning that the high-handedness of the committees in enforcing the observance of religious duties would be curbed. The government has in fact quietly taken steps to restrain the zealots, who at times still act arbitrarily.

An aspect of Wahhābī society that has received wide publicity in the West is the public carrying out of severe punishments decreed by the Qur'ān, such as cutting off the hand of a thief and beheading a murderer. In the eyes of the Wahhābīs, they are simply executing the commands of God, and they can point out that Saudi Arabia has a lower crime rate than countries where such punishments are criticized. Nevertheless, the Wahhābī authorities have again moved towards an accommodation by gradually reducing the number of public spectacles of this nature, though in view of the Qur'ānic texts they have shown no inclination to question the validity of the penalties.

How far can Wahhābism go along the path of adjustment without losing its essential character? Much depends on the quality of the leadership, and much also depends on the generality of Wahhābīs. Borrowing and adaptation from various sources, both Eastern and Western, will go on, but if the Wahhābīs can hold fast to their fundamental beliefs, they stand a good chance of preserving the state which their predecessors in the faith laboured to build.

Nowhere outside Saudi Arabia are the followers of Muḥammad b. ʿAbd al-Wahhāb very numerous. In the Yemen and southern Arabia Wahhābism appears only among the nomads along the edges of the Empty Quarter. Some of the tribes of Oman have been Wahhābī in their beliefs and sympathies since the early nineteenth century. Wahhābism has made considerable headway along the shores of the Persian Gulf, especially in the Arab principalities; many emigrants from Najd have settled in this region, even on the Persian side. The populations of Kuwait and the town of al-Zubayr in Iraq contain large Najdī elements, upon whom Wahhābism has often made an impression.

The militancy of Wahhābism in the past and its readiness to excommunicate other Muslims tended to raise up enemies rather than to win friends and converts. The wild mien of the desert warriors inspired fear in those they attacked, and their systematic destruction of the shrines of saints made their name a reproach. The way in which

Muslims often misapply the term Wahhābī as an epithet is indicated by the situation that once prevailed in Morocco:

...beaucoup de vieux turbans, pour dénigrer les jeunes Marocains à idées avancées, les traitent souvent de Wahhabites, alors que les doctrines du Wahhabisme sont au contraire absolument réactionnaires et opposées à toutes les innovations.[1]

In India the followers of Sayyid Aḥmad Shahīd of Bareli (1786–1831), in a movement which began with a *jihād* against the Sikhs and later turned against the Hindus and the British, were commonly called Wahhābīs by those who disliked their doctrines and conduct. Some historians maintain that Sayyid Aḥmad, who spent more than a year in Mecca early in his career, was converted to Arabian Wahhābism during this stay; others hold that his basic beliefs were formed before he went to Mecca, his chief inspiration being the teachings of Shāh Walī Allāh of Delhi (1703–62).[2] The reform movement of the Fara'iḍīs in Bengal exhibited Wahhābī tendencies that may have been directly derived from Arabian Wahhābism; the Wahhābī spirit appears in the refusal to observe the Friday congregational prayers on the grounds that India under British rule was infidel territory, not Islamic. The founder of Fara'iḍism, Ḥājj Sharī'at Allāh, made the pilgrimage to Mecca as a youth and lingered there for many years, and his son and successor, Dudhu Miyan, also went to Arabia. Towards the close of the nineteenth century the Ahl-i Ḥadīth (the People of the Prophetic Tradition) brought upon themselves the charge that they were Wahhābīs by attacking innovations and advancing other doctrines reminiscent of the Arabian movement.

The brotherhood of Wahhābīs is small, but the leaven of Wahhābism during the past two centuries has been pervasive and far reaching, penetrating into all quarters of the Islamic world. A Western authority, speaking of the first Islamic movements in the modern period, calls Wahhābism "the most major, still reverberatingly influential".[3]

Since Muḥammad b. 'Abd al-Wahhāb first began preaching, Islam has been stirred and revitalized by a number of movements resembling

[1] Ed. Michaux-Bellaire in *Renseignements Coloniaux*, p. 489, suppl. to *L'Afrique Française* (1928).

[2] W. W. Hunter, *The Indian Musulmans*, gave currency to the story of the conversion of Sayyid Aḥmad to Arabian Wahhābism. The authenticity of the story is challenged on the basis of extensive evidence by such scholars as Muhammad 'Abdul Bari, "The politics of Sayyid Ahmad Barelwi", and Mahmud Husain in *A History of the Freedom Movement*.

[3] Wilfred Cantwell Smith, *Islam in Modern History* (Princeton, 1957), p. 41.

Wahhābism in one or more of their aspects. The nature and extent of their debt to Wahhābism are often difficult to determine. Ibn 'Abd al-Wahhāb disclaimed any originality for his views, and the sources he drew upon—the Qur'ān, the *ḥadīth*, and the writings of Ibn Ḥanbal and Ḥanbalites such as Ibn Taymiyya—have been available to other reformers, who might themselves read them in the same way or might again rely on his reading.[1] From the eighteenth century on opportunities existed for the diffusion of Wahhābī beliefs. They were known and discussed in Mecca, to which Muslims came from near and distant places. At the same time the Wahhābīs sought to secure a better understanding of their doctrines by diligent correspondence with Muslims abroad.[2]

Muslim and Western scholars have discerned beliefs and practices that may derive from or through Wahhābism in lands even more remote, such as the East Indies, China, and Central Asia. In Africa the great *jihāds* of the nineteenth century, led by 'Uthmān dan Fodio, Ḥājj 'Umar Tal, and others, were marked by striking similarities to their Arabian counterparts. An investigator of the African *jihāds* says of Ḥājj 'Umar:

> His stay in the Holy Cities themselves was also a very important spiritual experience for him, and while there he can hardly have remained unaffected by the ferment of thought and activity which was accompanying the struggle between the Wahhabiyya and the Turks.[3]

Wahhābism in general disapproves of Ṣūfism and most of its trappings, but links or resemblances between the two movements are not lacking. One of the great Ṣūfī masters of the nineteenth century, Aḥmad b. Idrīs, lived in Arabia and died there in 1837, the year in which his pupil Muḥammad b. 'Alī al-Sanūsī established in Mecca the first chapter of his own order. The teachings of both the Idrīsiyya and the Sanūsiyya seem in various ways to hark back to Wahhābism. 'Abd Allah al-Maḥjūb al-Mīrghanī, grandfather of the founder of the Mīrghaniyya (popularly known as the Khatmiyya), was born in Arabia and died about the same time as Ibn 'Abd al-Wahhāb; members of the

[1] The development of Ḥanbalite doctrines from Ibn Ḥanbal through Ibn Taymiyya and Ibn 'Abd al-Wahhāb is surveyed in Henri Laoust, *Essai sur les doctrines sociales et politiques de Taḳī-d-Dīn Aḥmad b. Taimīya* (Cairo, 1939).

[2] See, for example, the letter sent by Imam Sa'ūd to the people of Tunis in the early years of the nineteenth century (Arabic text and German translation in E. Pröbster, "Die Wahhabiten und der Maġrib").

[3] H. F. C. Smith in *Historians in Tropical Africa* (Salisbury, 1962), p. 153.

order admit the closeness of the two contemporaries in their interpretation of *tawḥīd*. Students of the Mahdiyya in the Sudan find in it overtones of Wahhābism, and the same is true of the activity of Muḥammad ʿAbd Allāh Ḥasan, the so-called "Mad Mullah" of Somaliland.

The appeal of Wahhābism has not been limited to fighters for the faith; it has been heeded as well by scholarly reformers such as the Syrians and Egyptians and North Africans of the Salafiyya, among whom was Muḥammad Rashīd Riḍā (1865–1935), the journalistic champion of the cause of Wahhābism and the House of Saʿūd.

It is becoming clear to perceptive Western observers that Arab nationalism, the most powerful force in the public life of the Arab world today, draws its strength from native roots and concepts as well as imported ideas. For a true appreciation of its growth and the nature of the thematic variations now current, one must go back beyond the landing of Bonaparte in Egypt and explore the earlier development of Arab society. In conservative Islam religious reform calls for the remaking of all aspects of life. One of the objectives of Wahhābism, largely implied rather than openly proclaimed, was the expulsion of the Turks from Arabia and the rebuilding of a community within Islam in which the Arabs would be, as they were in the first generations of the pious, the essential element. Wahhābism does not forsake its orthodoxy by denying the equality of all Muslims, but at the same time it cannot escape the consequences of the thoroughgoing Arabness of its constituency.

CHAPTER 15

THE ZAYDĪS

Of all the numerous "legitimist" or Shīʿa sects in Islam, the most moderate is that of the Zaydīs, the followers of the Imam Zayd b. ʿAlī, so moderate indeed that the only remaining Zaydī community today, that of the Upper Yemen, sometimes describes itself as the "fifth school" (*al-madhhab al-khāmis*) of the four orthodox or Sunnī schools of the religion. The Zaydīs appear to represent in the early stages of their development a form of Islam closest to the original primitive theocratic shape of the faith, and at all stages this "legitimist" sect is remote from the extravagant beliefs of the *ghulāt*, the extremist Shīʿa.

"The disagreement between the Sunna and Zaidiyya", Friedlaender states, "is not one of deep-seated antagonism. In point of fact, the whole difference reduces itself to the question of the candidacy for the Imamate." The early geographers, al-Maqdisī and al-Masʿūdī, even account the Zaydiyya outside the Shīʿa group altogether because of their tolerant acceptance of the first three caliphs. As demonstrated earlier[1] the principal schisms in emergent Islam arose from the struggles to obtain supremacy in the theocratic state, created originally around the nucleus of the two sacred enclaves of the Ḥijāz, while differences of a theoretical theological nature are a secondary and considerably later development. In Yemen at the present day there seems to be virtually no conflict in law as between Shāfiʿīs and Zaydīs, and they worship in the same mosque, with a common *imām* leading the prayer. It can be fairly stated that geo-political factors really divide the two sects, not differences in religious matters, though these exist. The Imams have traditionally relied on the warlike Zaydī mountain tribes for their programmes of expansion into the Shāfiʿī Lower Yemen, employing Zaydī tribesmen as soldiers and tax-collectors, and subsidizing them from taxes collected, no doubt, *inter alia*, from Shāfiʿī districts. Minor ritual variations, such as that in the *adhān* or call to prayer, are naturally of far less moment than questions of taxation.

During the first century of the *hijra* the Umayyad branch of the holy house of Quṣayy had established itself in Damascus as heir to the

[1] Cf. pp. 17ff.

caliphate, but the Hāshimite branch, despite its reverses, had not abandoned its "legitimist" pretensions and aspired to grasp power through manipulating the Arab tribes, a small military aristocracy dominating the vast Islamic empire. The tribes for their part, far from abandoning their pre-Islamic rivalries, doubtless hoped to realize objectives of their own under the banner of an aspirant to the theocratic power.

ʿAlī b. Abī Ṭālib in the days of the Prophet's expansion in the Arabian peninsula had, in one day, induced the Yemenite confederation of Hamdān to accept Islam at his hands, and the rest of the Yemen followed.[1] As the extempore verse of a Hamdān shaykh at the battle of Ṣiffīn testifies, the Yemenite tribes garrisoning southern Iraq gave him support as caliph:

> O come to Bakīl's aid, Lakhm of it and Ḥāshid.
> My soul be your ransom, thrust with spear, slash with sword.[2]

Hamdān, let it be remarked, was opposed by ʿAkk of the Tihāma, and Ḥimyar, both confederations today being Shāfiʿī and opposed to the Zaydī tribes of the Yemen.

With the blood of the Umayyad ʿUthmān richly avenged by the death of Ḥusayn b. ʿAlī at Karbalāʾ, the score between Hāshim and Umayya may have seemed even—until the emergence of Zayd b. ʿAlī, grandson of the martyr of Karbalāʾ in opposition to the Umayyad caliph, backed by the Kūfan Arabs who had proved no very effective supporters of his forebears. Zayd was the first of ʿAlī's numerous posterity to rebel openly after the decisive encounter at Karbalāʾ, declaring for the Book of God, the customary law (*sunna*) of his Prophet, the preservation of this customary law, and the abolition of all innovations (*bidaʿ*) to the foregoing. The irresolute support of Kūfa coupled with his own hesitations brought about Zayd's defeat, death, and the public exposure of his corpse, while a little later, in 743, his son met a similar fate in Khurasan. Up to this point the relationship between the Umayyads and Hāshimites had remained relatively amicable, the Umayyads even liberally subsidizing the Hāshimites, but the death of the two Hāshimites seems to have opened the old wound

[1] al-Masʿūdī, *K. al-Tanbīh wa-ʾl-ishrāf*, ed. M. J. de Goeje, B.G.A., vol. VIII (Leiden, 1894), p. 274.

[2] al-Minqarī, *Waqʿat Ṣiffīn* (Cairo, 1382 H.), p. 434. Bakīl and Ḥāshid are descended from Hamdān through Jusham (Ibn Ḥazm, *Jamharat ansāb al-ʿArab*, ed. E. Lévi-Provençal (Cairo, 1948), p. 369). Lakhm, though a Yemenite tribe, does not seem to be descended from Hamdān, but may have been allied to Bakīl.

afresh, and to have aroused feeling even among the Khārijites who had no cause to be friendly to the house of 'Alī. The Umayyad caliph Hishām himself wrote to the 'Alids disclaiming responsibility for Zayd's death.

In a society of the Arab tribal type where parties at dispute repair to persons of repute and experience rather than to the courts, Zayd b. 'Alī, a prominent member of a holy house, would frequently be consulted to settle cases at issue, and he cannot but have been experienced in the *sunna* of Islam. Nor need the tradition that Abū Ḥanīfa and other jurists studied under him be doubted. On the other hand, though Zayd is credited with a large body of legal opinion, the *Majmū' al-fiqh*, preserved in two redactions, the content of these collections cannot all remount to Zayd and later Zaydī writers do in fact present Zaydī jurisprudence in much less sophisticated development. For this, and other reasons, no very certain opinion can be advanced as to his views on legal or theological questions, but he is probably justifiably to be credited with opposition to *taqiyya*, the dissimulation of one's religious views under circumstances where it would be dangerous to display them, a practice characteristic of the other Shī'ī sects. The Zaydīs however must overtly practise "the ordering of what is good, and the prohibition of what is reprehensible" (*al-amr bi 'l-ma'rūf wa-'l-nahy 'an al-munkar*) as they understand it, without regard to the consequences. Traditionally he is held to have been opposed to the doctrine of predestination (*qadar*), that of *badā'*, the intervention of a new set of circumstances in bringing about the alteration of an earlier divine determination, the concept of the advent of a *mahdī* (*raj'a*), and the attribution of miracles (*mu'jiza*) to Imams. On the question of the commission of a major sin by a Muslim, a political–theological question of the time, he took the intermediate position of the Mu'tazilites. Zayd is stated to have been the pupil of Wāṣil b. 'Aṭā', the reputed founder of Mu'tazilism, though only partially in accord with the latter's views. In contradistinction to the Sunnīs most Zaydīs hold, with the other Shī'a groups such as the Imāmīs, that the word of God, i.e. the Qur'ān, is created, thus following the Mu'tazilite reasoning, but, if controversy on this vexed issue were known at this period, Zayd's views are not. In jurisprudence he appears to have agreed largely with the Mu'tazilites in the application of reason (*'aql*), but later Zaydī law and theology are permeated by Mu'tazilite thinking, and it is difficult to distinguish Zayd b. 'Alī's own contribution.

In the late ninth century the Imam al-Hādī ila'l-Ḥaqq Yaḥyā considered that the distinguishing factor between the Islamic sects was their attitude on succession to the Prophet. Now Zayd b. 'Alī is credited with the view that 'Alī was the most worthy (*afḍal*) to succeed the Prophet and Abū Bakr "outworthied" (*mafḍūl*) by him, but that allegiance (*bay'a*) to the "two shaykhs", Abū Bakr and 'Umar was nevertheless valid. The very application of the term "*shaykhān*" to them is suggestive, however, of tribal leadership rather than of theocratic succession. So, in general, the Zaydīs regard the first two caliphs as legitimate rulers and take a moderate view of the caliphate of 'Uthmān—wherein they hardly differ from the Sunnīs, but are sharply marked off from the "Seven" and "Twelver" Shī'a, so hostile to 'Uthmān. The Zaydīs, moreover, dissent from other Shī'a in denying the existence of a written bequest (*naṣṣ*) from the Prophet designating 'Alī or his posterity as his successors, though they believe that Muḥammad indicated 'Alī by description. They maintain that the Imamate may legitimately be held by *any* descendant of 'Alī and Fāṭima, provided he has the appropriate qualities and summons the faithful to support him in it. In another respect also they diverge from the main Shī'a factions, namely in recognizing Zayd as the fifth Imam after 'Alī, followed by his son Yaḥyā. They admit the co-existence of two Imams, and unlike other Shī'a Imams, theirs have remained manifest in the world right up to the present day.

There is still much obscurity about the earliest Zaydī groups—the number of sects, their names and characteristics, which are diversely reported. Chronology is equally difficult to establish, but the attitudes of the various Zaydī sects developed after Zayd's martyrdom in the second century after the *hijra* when primitive Arabian Islam underwent its great modification, exposed to many currents of ideas but especially to Mu'tazilism. In its origins this would seem to have been simply a political movement, but in the course of time it developed into the rationalist scholasticism of early Islam.

To form some conception of the Zaydī trend of thought, however, it is sufficient to review the six sects distinguished by al-Ash'arī though other heresiologists may not entirely concur with him.

Of these the Jārūdiyya are accounted the extreme branch, for, in rejecting the Imamate of Abū Bakr and 'Umar and maintaining that 'Alī was designated Muḥammad's successor by bequest, they hold views counter to those of Zayd himself. The Sulaymāniyya (or Jarīriyya) and Butriyya[1] are the moderates. The Sulaymāniyya admit the Imamate of Abū Bakr and 'Umar, and defend the principle of conferment of the Imamate through a council (*shūrā*). They oppose the religious quietism (*taqiyya*) of the Imāmī Shī'a, and *badā'* (cf. p. 287). The Butriyya or Ṣāliḥiyya accept Abū Bakr and 'Umar, abstain from judgment on 'Uthmān, and acknowledge 'Alī only from the time of his proclamation as Imam. They were perhaps a pre-Zaydī Shī'a group, opposed to the Imāmīs, and later absorbed in the Zaydiyya. The Nu'aymiyya consider 'Alī was best qualified for the Imamate, and the conferment of the office on the first two caliphs a mistake on the part of the community, but not a sin—they reject 'Uthmān. A fifth group resembling the Jārūdiyya holds the doctrine of *raj'a*, the return of the *mahdī*, while, on the contrary, the Ya'qūbiyya, though recognizing the first two caliphs, do not consider those holding the opposite view as heretics, but those who defend the *raj'a* doctrine.

The sects do however agree on the superiority of 'Alī as a successor to Muḥammad and the rightness of his action in regard to arbitration after Ṣiffīn. They also concur on the duty of revolt against unjust Imams to abolish injustice and establish the right, and that only a leader of prayer who is not a man of evil ways (*fāsiq*) can be followed. In their day the Zaydīs seem to have had considerable influence on the development of Islam, perhaps among other reasons, because of the dispersal of Zayd b. 'Alī's pupils, and the author of the *Fihrist*,[2] for example, avers that the majority of Traditionists (*muḥaddithūn*) were of Zaydī opinion.

Strothmann maintains that "Zaydiyya only became a united community when 'Alid claimants themselves took over the spiritual leadership". In this he attributes a major role to al-Ḥasan b. Zayd who founded *c.* 864 a Zaydī state in Tabaristan, south of the Caspian Sea, and to al-Qāsim al-Rassī b. Ibrāhīm Ṭabāṭabā (d. 860) in the Ḥijāz, but, whereas al-Ḥasan's writings are known only in citation, al-Qāsim has left many treatises, as yet unpublished, and is known for his polemics against the Christians and Manichaeans.

The Imamate of Tabaristan, though founded earlier than that of the Yemen, endured only till *c.* 1126 during which period some twenty Imams and *dā'īs* appeared, but the last ruler was unable to prevail against

[1] Van Arendonk vocalizes this name as Batriyya but I have read it as above with Sprenger and Lees, *Dict. of the Technical Terms used in the Sciences of the Musalmāns* (Calcutta, 1862). Cf. Nashwān b. Sa'īd, *al-Ḥūr al-'Īn* (Cairo, 1948), p. 155.

[2] Ibn al-Nadīm, *K. al-Fihrist*, ed. G. Flügel (Leipzig, 1871), pp. 178–9.

the Assassins. In a very confused history, one of the most notable Imams was al-Nāṣir al-Uṭrūsh (d. 917) who combined intellectual capacity with political acumen, and availed himself of the discord and anarchy prevalent in Tabaristan. In pursuit of his political aims he conducted vigorous missions to islamize the Majūsī tribes of the Caspian coast, so that thousands were converted at his hands to Islam, according to the typical 'Alid Zaydī pattern, and became his supporters. Among about a hundred works (as attributed to him by the *Fihrist*) there survives what is perhaps the earliest manual of *ḥisba* known to Islam, a compendium of market and other regulations, for contemporary use. This manual contains much of interest—restraints on professional story-tellers (who seem from the earliest times to have been employed for political propaganda), injunctions that mosques must not be made like churches, contain pictures, be ornamented with gold, hung with curtains, or decorated with plaster-work. Minarets are not to be raised above the roof-level of the mosque; in Yemenite al-Shahāra to this day the minaret is only a few steps on the mosque roof. Weapons are not to be exported to non-Muslim countries, not even to anti-Zaydī Muslims (*ahl al-baghy*). Muslims must not wear polytheist dress, and many more rules of every sort. The manual continually quotes 'Alī's practice where perhaps Sunnī writers would quote other sources of authority. Al-Uṭrūsh differed on certain points relating to burial ritual, inheritance, and divorce from Yemenite Zaydīs, but the school called al-Nāṣiriyya after him eventually merged in al-Qāsimiyya[1] founded by one of his generals. This sect has become prominent in the Yemen and is now the only surviving school. There were close links between the Caspian and Yemeni Zaydīs for there is an allusion to a Ṭabarī contingent aiding the first Zaydī Imam of Ṣa'da. The Buwayhids of Baghdad coming from the same region appear to have come under Zaydī doctrinal influences allied with Mu'tazilite tendencies deriving from these Tabaristan Zaydīs.

In the Yemen, al-Hādī ila'l-Ḥaqq, founder of the Zaydī state there, went by invitation in 893–4 first to al-Sharafa of Nihm, a tribe which supports al-Badr today, but though they pledged him obedience they disliked his insistence on the *sharī'a*; he returned to the Ḥijāz for a short while until invited to return once more by the Khawlān of

[1] E. Griffini, "*Corpus iuris*" *di Zaid ibn 'Alī* (Milan, 1919), p. cxxiii, names the other schools Hādawiyya, Mu'ayyadiyya, Manṣūriyya, Imāmiyya.

Ṣa'da when many dissensions (*fitan*) had broken out following upon his departure.

The coming of the Zaydī Imams probably meant the beginning of the real islamization of the north, for Islam there may have been little more than a persisting tradition of allegiance to the Holy Family of Medina remounting to the days of 'Alī himself, and even today I have known tribes in South Arabia which retain their heathen practices and have virtually no knowledge of Islam. There were traces of a public sexual morality diametrically opposed to Islam for, apart from open indulgence in wine, al-Hādī's own tribal supporters engaged in unconcealed profligacy with males and females, while prostitution of a sort resembling that known in Dathīna today by the Ma'n gypsies, was not only publicly practised, but the lover's rights as against payment were upheld by tribal customary law. The honoured guest was provided with the hospitality of a woman to share his sleeping place in some districts—then as now. Indeed even in the seventeenth century it could be said of the Banū Mālik and Fayfā, "They neither pray, nor fast, nor give alms, nor go on pilgrimage, nor study the Qur'ān; in fact they are heathen though they call themselves Muslims. They know not the sacred law for they have no teacher. They have no marriage rite."[1] Consequently, we cannot immediately dismiss as malicious Sunnī fabrication the poem attributed to 'Alī b. al-Faḍl the Carmathian leader, attacking the pilgrimage and prayer, encouraging promiscuous sexual intercourse with males and females, and music—against which the Zaydīs have set their faces. This may represent among the Carmathians a revolt against Islam and a reversion to more ancient ways. Above all, however, it was probably also the ancient pre-Islamic customary law, the *ṭāghūt* which Ettore Rossi found still existing in north Yemen, that the tribes were averse to abandoning.[2]

On the pattern of his ancestor, the Prophet, at Medina, al-Hādī healed the dissension (*fitna*) between Khawlān of Ṣa'da, and proceeding to Najrān, he was welcomed by Wādi'a, Shākir, and Yām, on account

[1] A. S. Tritton, *The Rise of the Imams of Sanaa* (Madras, 1925), p. 82. Cf. Ibn al-Mujāwir, *Tārīkh al-mustabṣir*, ed. O. Löfgren; *Descriptio Arabiae Meridionalis* (Leiden, 1951–4) *passim*; and C. de Landberg, *Daṯînah* (Leiden, 1905–13), pp. 908, 1181; and *Arabica*, vol. LV (Leiden, 1891), pp. 28 ff.

[2] *L'Arabo parlato a San'â'* (Rome, 1939), p. 139. Cf. his valuable "Il diritto consuetudinario delle tribù arabe del Yemen", *Rivista degli Studi Orientali*, vol. XXIII (Rome, 1948), pp. 1–36 and G. Rathjens "Ṭâghût gegen scherîa", *Jahrbuch des Linden-Museums* (Stuttgart, 1951), pp. 172–87.

of the wars between them and the Bal-Ḥārith. He again put an end to dissension and induced them to give pledges (*mawāthīq*) and to end their differences, and they paid him allegiance. He also made a pact with the *dhimmī* Christians of Najrān.

During the reign of al-Hādī and those of his successors it was common for tribes to summon an Imam to them, pay him allegiance, revolt, and be brought back to the fold, often by force. In the case of al-Hādī his enforcement of the *ḥadd* punishments, and the rapacity of his representatives in tax-collection appear to have occasioned the revolts, for, although Islam prescribes precisely what taxation shall be levied, the justest of Imams throughout Zaydī history have been unable to control their tax-collectors adequately. Nevertheless the basic tribal need for an overlord of the Holy House, and not of their own kin, to judge impartially between them, has always led the tribes to return to an Imam. Nor was the Imam in any sense a monarch but the president of a theocracy, resembling the *umma* of Muḥammad, a form of constitution which has existed from long before Islam right into the mid-twentieth century. In the Yemen nowadays the institution whereby a descendant of the Prophet Muḥammad moves from his place to ask a particular tribe if he may live alongside it is entitled *hijra*, and the family in question is called *hijrat Ṣaʿda*, for example, or *hijrat Ḥūth*. This is only used amongst the Zaydī tribes, and there are laws governing its operation, it being of course a great honour to the chosen tribe. Though the specific term *hijra* does not seem to be used at this early period, this does essentially seem to be the process whereby al-Hādī settled in the Yemen.

Al-Hādī was a prolific writer and an important source of law. His answers to legal questions have been collected in a rather remarkable volume entitled *al-Muntakhab fi 'l-fiqh*. The three bases (*uṣūl*) of his opinion are said to be the Book of God, consensus (*ijmāʿ*) on the authority of the Apostle of God and his Family, and the evidence of God (*ḥujjat Allāh*) which God implanted in the breasts of the scholars (*ʿālim*). Like all Zaydī works it contains many Traditions not in Sunnī sources, the non-Shīʿa schools being called "the generality" *al-ʿāmma* as opposed to the scholars of the (Holy) House (*ʿulamāʾ ahl al-bayt*). Al-Hādi does not even mention the *Majmūʿ* of Zayd b. ʿAlī, and he sometimes rejects Traditions remounting to ʿAlī himself. This, says a later authority, he was entitled to do, because al-Hādī was a *mujtahid*[1]

[1] The *mujtahid* "exerts himself" to form an opinion in a case, or to form a rule of law by applying analogy (*qiyās*) to the Qur'ān and *sunna*.

and considered other traditions more sound. Qualification as a Zaydī *mujtahid* is conditional on knowing Arabic, the Qur'ān and what thereof has been abrogated (*nāsikh wa-mansūkh*), the *sunna*, where there is consensus (*ijmā'*) and variance of opinion, how analogy (*qiyās*) is applied, the intentions of the laws (*al-aḥkām al-shar'iyya*), understanding, and good judgment (*taqdīr*). *Ijtihād* can be applied only to the "branches" (*furū'*), not to the fundamentals (*uṣūl*) of law.

In his efforts to build up a Zaydī state al-Hādī met with limited success. For a time he occupied Ṣan'ā', but lost it to the Carmathians, Ismā'īlīs who appeared in the Yemen at almost exactly the same time as he did, and who have survived in pockets till today. Subsequent Zaydī Imams have enjoyed very varied fortune, but apart from occasional brief incursions southwards they have but rarely held territory beyond the confines of the northern Yemen. The intricate political history of the Imams would be wearisome to follow in any detail. Different branches of the house of 'Alī b. Abī Ṭālib have held office; some periods, especially in phases of anarchy, have seen rival Imams appear at the same time, and of course an unjust Imam can be deposed. In the early days of the Zaydīs of the Yemen the Imamate passed from the Rassid house of al-Qāsim (cf. p. 289) descended from al-Ḥasan son of 'Alī, but the present Imamic family, Bayt Ḥamīd al-Dīn, is of Rassid descent, its founder being the Imam al-Manṣūr al-Qāsim who appeared in 1597 and drove the Ottoman Turks out of the Yemen. The Zaydiyya are averse to the designation of an heir-apparent—Imam Aḥmad's designation of al-Badr is alleged to have been one of the causes of the 1955 revolt.

The consistent pattern of Zaydī politics is one of opposition to the series of foreign dynasties which have from time to time governed the lower Yemen, such as the Rasūlids, the Egyptians, and Ottoman Turks. Indeed it can be said that the Ottoman invasions of the sixteenth and nineteenth centuries, as also the Egyptian invasion of the twentieth century, have produced astonishingly similar reactions and results. The mountain strongholds al-Qāra, Ahnūm, Rāziḥ, al-Sūda, and al-Shahāra, the spiritual capital of the Bayt Ḥamīd al-Dīn which figure in today's news were vigorously contested with the Ottomans in both their invasions. The Zaydīs have always, of course, fought intermittently with other petty local states, and have never ceased their bitter struggle with the Ismā'īlīs of Najrān and Ḥarāz. Within the Yemen highlands themselves as has been stated, the tribes have been constant only in the way they accept an Imam, turn dissident, but come back to the fold, their actions often, as at the present moment, swayed by bribery.

It is characteristic that Yemenis should inform the Ottoman general Sinān Pasha that the Imam's tribal support would collapse when their enthusiasm for a prolonged war had begun to wane. The Ottomans made every effort to turn the inveterate hostility of the Ismā'īlīs for the Zaydīs against the Imam, and it is typical also that when the Imam escaped from the Turks to Najrān, some of the tribes should acknowledge him, but that the hatred of the Ismā'īlīs of the Yām tribe should oblige him to leave for Mount Baraṭ. The constantly changing pattern of allegiances at that time, political rather than religious, is evident in a battle at Ḥarāz in 1599/1600 when the Imam found Zaydīs, Shāfi'īs, Bāṭinīs (Ismā'īlīs) and foreigners in the ranks of his opponents.

The heyday of Zaydī territorial expansion, however, followed al-Manṣūr al-Qāsim's expulsion of the Ottoman Turks by 1636. Al-Jarmūzī's history, probably *al-Sīrat al-mutawakkiliyya*[1] narrates in detail the Zaydī invasion of the Shāfi'ī tribes of what later became the Aden Protectorate and the entry of the Imam al-Mu'ayyad into Saywūn, the capital of the Kathīrī Sultans of Ḥaḍramawt. In Ḥaḍramawt the Zaydīs came into conflict with the spiritual power of the Bū Bakr b. Sālim Sayyids of 'Īnāt over the tribes of the country. To them it was that the Kathīrī Sultan referred the Zaydī Imam's first letter with its exhortations on religious matters. The important western tribe of Yāfi' itself habitually repaired for decisions (*ḥukm*) in disputes to the *Manṣab* of 'Īnāt who claimed to perform marvels and who hated religious scholars (*ahl al-'ilm*)—the Zaydīs especially, says al-Jarmūzī, but others as well. These Sayyids, or Ashrāf, as al-Jarmūzī calls them, were Bedouin, i.e. tribal in temperament and anti-Sayyid. The Zaydīs accused the Ḥaḍramīs of tolerating music and musical instruments—it is true that Ṣūfī *nashīds* at a saint's *ḥaḍrah* are sung to this very day in mosques there, and no doubt the Zaydī anti-ṣufistic attitude occasioned their disapproval of such in Ḥaḍramawt. Muḥammad b. Hāshim says the Zaydīs put a stop to the litany (*rātib*) of the celebrated Ḥaḍramī Ṣūfī Sayyid 'Abdallāh al-Ḥaddād, and added to the call to prayer, *Ḥayya 'alā khayr al-'amal* which marks out Shī'ites from Sunnīs. Such sympathy as the Zaydīs found in Ḥaḍramawt arose from those Kathīrīs who

[1] Discussed in my *Portuguese off the South Coast of Arabia* (Oxford, 1963), pp. 112 ff. I now possess a Xerox copy of the MS.

sought their aid against the Yāfiʻī tribal mercenary element, but as the Imams grew weaker, Kathīrī power collapsed. In fact all the southern tribal confederations fell away from the Imams into their normal anarchy—Yāfiʻīs, Faḍlīṣ, Lower ʻAwlaqīs, Lahej and Aden, but to this day Zaydī forts from that period are still pointed out by people in the Wādī Yarāmis.

A divergence between the Shāfiʻī Sayyids and Zaydīs not unworthy of notice is their respective attitudes towards *kafāʼa*, equality of standing between two parties to a marriage. Ḥaḍramī Shāfiʻī law will scarcely permit a *sharīfa* of the Prophet's posterity to marry any but a Sayyid or *sharīf* under any but extreme circumstances—this being an attitude remounting to pre-Islamic times. The treatise of al-Ḥasan b. Isḥāq al-Mahdī on the contrary seems to indicate a far more lenient view—*kafāʼa* can be waived so that a woman may give herself in marriage to a man not her equal if her guardian consents, and both piety and lineage are considered in assessing equality. But an equal partner is a woman's entitlement, and she can choose not to marry a man not her equal even against her father's wishes.

In the mid-nineteenth century the Ottomans had once more gained a foothold in the Tihāma, and they reached Ṣanʻāʼ in 1872. Aḥmad Mukhtār, the Turkish Pasha, took over the fortresses around Ṣanʻāʼ and demanded from the Imam the tax-registers (*dafātir*) of the tithes (*ʻushūr*) which would reveal the fiscal structure of the country. He drove out the Yemeni officials whom he replaced by imported Turkish *maʼmūrs*, with the result that the Imam and the *ashrāf* were put to straits; nor were they allowed access to the leaders of the tribal confederations. Furthermore, the Yemenis disapproved of the irreligion of the Turks in not praying and their open profligacy including sodomy (*liwāṭ*) and wine-drinking, but they especially disliked their abandonment of the *sharīʻa* for the Turkish civil code. There were clashes over fraudulence in collecting the *ʻushūr* and the Yemenis reacted violently when Turkish soldiers came to their villages and attacked their women's honour. Turkish rule was by no means invariably bad, but corruption and changes of policy made it generally distrusted, and to crown all, the Turks, though almost infidels in Zaydī eyes, despised them and stigmatized them as heretics. Both Zaydīs and Shāfiʻīs considered the Turks as foreigners, oppressors, and bad Muslims—so the Yemenite historian al-Wāsiʻī sums up the Yemeni view.

The Imam al-Manṣūr who had taken refuge (*hājar*) in Ṣaʻda and constructed a fort (in which I stayed in 1964) at Ahnūm died in 1904, and his son Yaḥyā who adopted a title (as has been customary among the Zaydī Imams from the earliest times), took the style of al-Mutawakkil 'ala 'llāh. The '*ulamā*' of al-Shahāra and other places paid him allegiance, and his summons (*da'wa*) ran like fire through the country. From every district the tribes responded and in a swift campaign he took Ṣan'ā', though he later evacuated it. His main support lay in the two great tribal confederations of Ḥāshid and Bakīl which, as we have seen, fought for 'Alī b. Abī Ṭālib, over 1,200 years before, and today for the most part support al-Badr. The Ottoman Sultan sent a delegation of Meccan '*ulamā*' to advise the Imam but he countered by stating the Zaydī attitude that he was entitled to fight the Turks who had removed the "pillars" (*arkān*) of Islam. After a further siege of Ṣan'ā' the Imam and the Turks reached a *modus vivendi* which in effect divided the Yemen into Zaydī districts controlled by the Imam, and Shāfi'ī districts administered by the Turks. The arrangement withstood the stress of the Italo-Turkish war of 1912 and World War I, for, political considerations apart, the Zaydīs probably felt more sympathetic to an Islamic than to Christian powers.

On the departure of the Ottomans after the war, Imam Yaḥyā entered Ṣan'ā' to a triumphant welcome. Al-Wāsi'ī records that he sent teachers to all the villages and commanded that heresies, *bida'*, innovations, cease, and prayers be performed at their appointed times. The whole country (*sic*) obeyed him and he took hostages to guarantee good behaviour from the tribes. (The Bayt Ḥamīd al-Dīn has been severely taken to task for the hostage system, but this ancient and general practice is a deterrent to tribes all too ready to infringe public security.) In fact, extremely obscure though this period is, the Imam waged a series of campaigns to effect control over Zaydī and Shāfi'ī Yemen alike. His heir, Sayf al-Islām[1] Aḥmad won his right to the warrior's title, *mujāhid*, through suppressing the Zarānīq. Imam Yaḥyā also clashed with the Idrīsī Sanūsīs of 'Asīr, and later with the Wahhābīs, this arising from their political, not their religious differences. He claimed suzerainty over the Shāfi'ī tribal districts under British protection but the latter were strongly opposed to Zaydī rule.

Within the Yemen it appears that each great Sayyid family had its own *hijra* where it was protected and supported by the tribes—such as

[1] This title is applied in my recent Yemenite experience to all princes of Bayt Ḥamīd al-Dīn.

the Sayyids of *hijrat* Kibs, east of Ṣan'ā'. This immensely ancient mosaic of theocracies (the Zaydī *hijra* corresponding to the Shāfi'ī *ḥawṭa*), is found all over south-west Arabia. To centralize power in the Bayt Ḥamīd al-Dīn, Imam Yaḥyā is said to have followed the deliberate policy of sapping the power of the small theocracies of the Yemen, a measure which is believed to have redounded to the advantage of the 1962 secular revolution. In pursuance of the Zaydī policy of Islamizing the country, he substituted *sharī'a* law for the customary *ṭāghūt*; in his reign, I was told, merely to possess a book of *ṭāghūt* would be punished by death. Zaydī anti-Ṣūfī policy is apparent in the demolition of the domed tombs of Shāfi'ī saints such as Bin 'Alwān of Yifrus and they combat popular religious practices of a superstitious nature. The *ḥadd* punishments were enforced—beating for wine-bibbing, the stoning of adulterers, the amputation of a thief's hand. The sword was used for executions which were sometimes, at least, performed in public. Nevertheless where the law was concerned people often preferred to take their cases to mediators outside the courts. Imam Yaḥyā did take measures to extend education to some extent, and in 1964 I noticed a surprisingly high degree of literacy in north Yemen. Though Yaḥyā early made his anti-Zionist views known, Yemeni Jews were protected by him, paying the *jizya* poll-tax, not a very large sum. Jews and Baniyans, Hindu traders, have always been protected in South Arabia, though subordinate to the Islamic community. The Ismā'īlīs of Ḥarāz and Manākha on the other hand were forced by Yaḥyā to abandon certain of their religious practices contrary to *sharī'a* and he sent them upright *imāms* to instruct them in religion.

The Imams and the Holy House are generally popularly regarded throughout the Yemen with a respect that a true Zaydī must often consider superstitious. The kissing of their hands and knees is probably thought to confer *baraka*;[1] Rihani cites cases of the Imam's power to harm, and of the belief that he is proof against bullets. Indeed, the late Imam Aḥmad's several remarkable escapes from murder, and that of al-Badr from assassination in 1962, tend to confirm such popular beliefs. The Holy House is also credited widely with power to employ the *jinn* in their service.

Yaḥyā wished to preserve the Yemen as a medieval Islamic state. Rihani quotes him as declaring he would prefer his people to eat

[1] *Baraka* is a quality examined by E. Westermarck, *Pagan survivals in Mohammedan civilisation* (London, 1933).

millet-stalk rather than come under colonialist rule, but whether this report be true or not, he seems to have feared the effect on the Yemen of the current of Western ideas, the influence of which in Arab countries themselves he disliked. He managed to keep out radios, gramophones, and musical instruments, but he was obliged to come to terms with the West to some extent. A government newspaper and magazine used to appear monthly, and eventually, in 1947, Radio Ṣan'ā' was founded. The despatch of a "mission" of young students to Iraq early in World War II, the arrival of an Iraqi military mission in the Yemen in 1940, and the influence of Yemeni emigrants and diplomats abroad had however already had repercussions in the country itself.

There was circulating within and without the Yemen by 1940 a printed manifesto of the Yemenite Liberal party, composed of Zaydī and Shāfi'ī members, expressing dissatisfaction with the medieval conditions prevailing in the country. While orthodox in tone, it demanded "awakening of the Yemeni nation from its apathy, diffusion of education throughout all regions of the country, despatch of scientific missions abroad, and the composition of books and publications to stir the nation and take it by the hand". Its principal grievances were against the corrupt way in which taxation was levied, and revenues expended, but it demanded freedom for the *'ulamā'* to express their views, and reform of the law-courts. These proposals were moderate and reasonable, but while Yemenis disliked the governmental system which they rightly considered to be stagnant, corrupt, and oppressive, the impious assassination in early 1948 of Imam Yaḥyā, hero of the struggle with the Ottomans, profoundly shocked them. The vigorous reaction of Aḥmad, the heir-apparent, placed him in power and set back the liberal movement for fifteen years.

Imam Aḥmad, in his turn, however, caused much disaffection by his tyrannical though able rule, but foiled the military conspiracy supported by Egypt in 1962 by dying a few days before it was due to burst. He had already broken with Jamāl 'Abd al-Nāṣir in 1961—an uneasy alliance for secularist Egypt, with a ruler it dubbed "feudalist" (*iqṭā'ī*) and reactionary (*raj'ī*). In his famous poems Imam Aḥmad attacks "you who have no respect for Islam", commending unity in accordance with the *sharī'at al-Islām*. The poem also opposes the seizure of private property on the pretext of nationalization (*ta'mīm*) which Aḥmad maintains is contrary to the *sharī'a*. This brought a riposte[1] from Muḥammad Aḥmad Nu'mān, a younger member of the Yemeni Liberal party, cleverly playing on the word *ta'mīm* which could be construed to mean "Imamization", a diatribe against the evils of the taxation system which, he implies, is putting everything into the Imam's pocket. Nu'mān quotes a Hāshimī Yemenite *amīr*, Muḥammad b. Ismā'īl, as attacking the "unjust laws of the Hāshimite Imams" in regard to the *zakāt*, i.e. the tithes, but I have not yet traced this work stated to have been written about 800 years ago.

Of course Yemeni attitudes had greatly changed between 1948 and 1962. The flood of ideas released by the propaganda of post-revolution Egypt had permeated into Yemenite towns either directly by radio or through the floating labour returning from Aden. The presence of foreign aid missions in the Yemen and the despatch of missions to study abroad had broken down some of Yemenite isolation. The liberalizing policy of the heir apparent al-Badr gave positive encouragement to expect reforms. Younger members of the Bayt Ḥamīd al-Dīn and other noble houses sent abroad for education, had begun to ponder methods of reform of the Zaydī state, but it is important to observe that several of these latter while in Egypt had become opposed to Jamāl 'Abd al-Nāṣir; they now hold prominent posts in the Royalist organization.

One of al-Badr's first actions on becoming Imam was to declare his intention to initiate a programme of reform and of constitutional rule, but this would have stolen the thunder of the revolutionaries who, though temporarily dismayed by Imam Aḥmad's death, aimed at a secular state on the military pattern of Egypt and Iraq. 'Abdullāh al-Sallāl is reputed to have little care for religion, and his circumstances would not render him sympathetic to an aristocratic theocratic state. The anti-theocratic attitude can be perceived in Muḥammad Sa'īd al-'Aṭṭār's study on subdevelopment in the Yemen. Indeed the war was described to me as being, in a sense, that of Qaḥṭān against 'Adnān, i.e. anti-Holy House, the Prophet of course being of 'Adnān, and the obliteration of the Sayyid village of Kibs and aerial attacks on al-Shahāra,[2] both Sayyid *hijras* and centres of Zaydī learning, do seem to be a manifestation of this current of thought. The Imam al-Badr followed the Zaydī tradition of taking refuge with the tribes after his escape from the revolutionaries in Ṣan'ā'.

[1] *al-Ta'mīm fi 'l-Yaman*, publ. by al-Ittiḥād al-Yamanī; *Lajnat al-thaqāfa wa-'l nashr*, on 11 December 1961 (no place of publication given).

[2] For a description see Tritton, *The Rise of the Imams of Sanaa*, p. 120.

The Zaydīs on the other hand, feel they are fighting for a traditional, national, religious belief (*mu'taqad taqlīdī waṭanī dīnī*) and they object to the new traditions which, they say, the Egyptians attempt to impose on them without understanding them themselves; the reference is to Nāṣirite socialism. A Zaydī tribesman described the Imam to me as "an angel sent down from God" (*malak marsūl min Allāh*)![1] The tribes want prophetical Hāshimite rule (*ḥukm*), or else each tribe to rule itself (*kull qabīla taḥkum nafsa-hā*) but they do not like the rule of individuals not of the Hāshimite house, especially those at present ruling the Republic, because they consider them inferior persons (*safala*). Nāṣirite socialism, they believe, will lead to the communizing of their land and their wives. It is said that there have been small local theocratic revolts against the Republic, independently of the followers of the Imam al-Badr, for instance at al-Ḥaimatain, for they regard the Republic as the symbol of atheism and the pollution of Islam.

Given the archaic polity of the Yemen, Imamic theocratic rule seems the only solution to the present conflict, but when the phase of what the Zaydīs call "Pharaonic colonialism" (*al-isti'mār al-Fir'awnī*) has passed there will, as the Zaydīs themselves acknowledge, have to be far-reaching reforms, and even in their preoccupation with the war they have been attempting to work out the shape of the new state. The one unifying element in the multiplicity of disconnected tribal units and towns is tribal recognition of the superior virtue of the Holy House, and a certain willingness to submit to it—under conditions it is true, and to a limited extent. A constitutional Imamate, as envisaged by some, seems far from inconsistent with the constitution in Medina in the Prophet's day, but a balance must be struck between strong dealing with the tough Yemeni tribes and limitation of the Imam's powers. If the Yemen reaches the stage where the theocratic form of government becomes obsolete, a state of affairs of which it is at present difficult to conceive, no doubt the influence of the Holy House will diminish as it has already done in the Aden Protectorate where theocratic units have given way to larger secular states, but until now Ibn Khaldūn's dictum (cf. p. 3) still holds true. Politico-religious evolution should not be theoretically difficult for the Zaydīs since for them the door of *ijtihād* is still open, and it should not be difficult to give

[1] Ameen Rihani, *Arabian Peak and Desert* (London, 1930), p. 108, gives a list of fourteen conditions which must exist in an Imam: Strothmann, *Das Staatsrecht der Zaiditen* (Strasbourg, 1912), p. 80, gives a longer and more accurate list.

religious sanction to what practical considerations dictate. It is to be remarked that the Zaydīs in their *ijtihād* can draw on any of the tenets and practices of the four Sunnī schools, just as the Sunnīs are doing themselves at the present time.[1]

[1] In addition to the well-known catalogues of the libraries, reference should be made to E. Rossi, "La stampa nel Yemen", *Oriente Moderno* (Rome, 1938), vol. XVIII, pp. 568–80, for Zaydī works printed in the Yemen but extremely difficult to obtain; the *Fihrist kutub al-Khizānat al-Mutawakkiliyya*, the Ṣan'ā' Library of which a microfilm exists in the Library of the S.O.A.S., London University; Khalīl Yaḥyā Nāmī's report (*Taqrīr*) on the work of the Egyptian Mission to Photograph MSS in the Yemen, published by the Egyptian Ministry of Public Instruction in 1952; and Salahuddin El-Munajjed, *Catalogue des manuscrits arabes de l'Ambrosienne de Milan* (Cairo, 1960), incomplete but covering part of the previously uncatalogued section of Yemenite MSS.

CHAPTER 16

THE IBĀḌĪS

The Ibāḍīs are a moderate branch—and today the only survivors—of the Khārijīs, the oldest Islamic sect, which in the eyes of Sunnī or orthodox Muslims is heretical. At the present time they form the main part of the population in the oases of the Mīzāb (Mzab) in Algeria, of Zuwāra and Jabal Nafūsa in Tripolitania, of the island of Jarba (Tunisia) and of Oman, while small groups are also to be found in the island of Zanzibar.

At a time when the Khārijīs were increasing in numbers from day to day, a moderate trend made its appearance, which was opposed to armed insurrection and political assassinations (*isti'rād*). The chief representative of this trend was a leading Khārijī of Baṣra, Abū Bilāl Mirdās b. Udayya al-Tamīmī, who about the year 670 rallied around him the so-called *qa'ada*, or quietists, that is to say those Khārijīs who sanctioned the *qu'ūd*, the temporary abstention from holy wars. Abū Bilāl was murdered in 681 and was succeeded some time afterwards by Abdallāh b. Ibāḍ al-Murrī al-Tamīmī. Concerning this personage, from whom the Ibāḍīs derive their name, tradition tells us very little, but we know that he came from Najd and that in 683 he accompanied his father to Mecca, to help in the defence of the holy city which was threatened by the general Muslim b. 'Uqba, whom the Caliph Yazīd had sent to subdue his Meccan rival 'Abdallāh b. al-Zubayr. When the siege of Mecca was raised in November 683, 'Abdallāh b. Ibāḍ went to Baṣra, which had been occupied by the Khārijīs. In the course of the following year a meeting of the leaders was held in the mosque to decide whether they should take the field against Muslim b. 'Ubays who, at the head of an army dispatched from Mecca by 'Abdallāh b. al-Zubayr, was preparing to attack the city. The meeting decided in favour of a sortie (*khurūj*), whereupon the extremists, known as Azraqīs, from the name of their leader Nāfi' b. al-Azraq, left Baṣra, while the others repented and remained in the city, under the leadership of Ibn Ibāḍ. The Ibāḍī historian, al-Barrādī, explains this defection as due to psychological motives which throw light on the placid character and piety of Ibn Ibāḍ: "At nightfall he heard the voices of the *qurrā'*, aṣ they read the Qur'ān, the call of the *mu'adhdhin* and the invocations of the faithful, whereupon he turned to his companions and said: 'And must I go with those others and abandon these?' And he concealed (*katama*) his belief." Ibn Ibāḍ and a few companions therefore remained in Baṣra, mingling with the orthodox population while waiting for better times. Subsequently there was a further schism among the moderates themselves, when the Tamīmī 'Abdallāh b. al-Ṣaffār, in opposition to Ibn Ibāḍ, maintained that non-Khārijī Muslims ought to be considered polytheists (*mushrikūn*), and founded a group of his own, known as Ṣufrīs, who, like the Azraqīs before them, left Baṣra.

When the Khārijīs lost control of Baṣra, there began that period of Ibāḍī history known as the *kitmān*, or concealment. The sources frequently refer to 'Abdallāh b. Ibāḍ as the *imām al-taḥqīq* (Imam of the verification), or as the *imām al-muslimīn* (Imam of the Muslims, that is to say of the Ibāḍīs). The title of Imam shows that Ibn Ibāḍ was regarded as the head of a secret Ibāḍī government in Baṣra, the so-called *jamā'at al-muslimīn*, that is to say, the Muslim Ibāḍī community. He established friendly relations with the Sunnī authorities in the city, who under Muṣ'ab (from 684) were anti-Umayyad, and after his defeat (691) supported the Umayyads.

In Arabia after the collapse of the ephemeral Khārijī state in 692 a few centres of revolt remained, especially in the south-eastern portion of the peninsula, and towards the end of the Umayyad period the Ibāḍī propagandists in Baṣra, led by Abū 'Ubayda al-Tamīmī, took advantage of this situation.

In Oman the Ibāḍīs established themselves firmly and for over a century managed to beat off the expeditions sent against them by the 'Abbāsids. As a result the capital, Nazwā, became the spiritual centre of Ibāḍism, and the *mashā'ikh* (doctors of the faith) gradually migrated thither from Baṣra. Aḥmad b. Sa'īd (1749–83), founder of the reigning Āl Bū Sa'īd dynasty, abolished the title Imam, replacing it by those of Sayyid (lord) and Sultan, since the dynastic principle was incompatible with the system of election postulated by Ibāḍī doctrine. In 1898 and 1900 the sovereigns of Oman signed treaties with Britain and established such close relations that the country soon became to all intents and purposes a British protectorate. Thanks to British support, the rulers were able to maintain full control even of the interior of the country, until in 1913 a revolt headed by a learned Ibāḍī, 'Abdallāh b. Ḥumayd al-Sālimī, who was an opponent both of the dynastic principle and of

British influence, led to the formation of a small separate state in the Jabal Akhḍar with its capital at Nazwā and under the rule of an Ibāḍī Imam, though foreign powers refused to grant it recognition and still considered the sultanate of Oman, with its capital at Muscat, as forming one state, despite the fact that its authority was limited to the coastal regions and the territory of Ru'ūs al-Jibāl. Later, when huge oilfields were discovered in al-Aḥsā' and in Kuwait, and it was believed that there might be other deposits in Oman, the sultan tried to assert his sovereign rights over the interior, in which he had previously taken no interest because it was of practically no value. In December 1955 he reoccupied Nazwā and drove out the Imam. An attempt by the latter to regain control of the territory was unsuccessful.

In the island of Zanzibar, on the other hand, Ibāḍism was merely the religious cult of the reigning family and the ruling classes, and did not spread among the Africans, since the Ibāḍī conquerors made no attempt to convert the natives and allowed them to profess the Shāfiʿī Sunnī creed, which had been introduced by Arabs from the Ḥaḍramawt. Eventually, to escape from their isolation, the Ibāḍis themselves became Shāfiʿī Sunnīs. They had always shown great tolerance towards the Sunnīs and Richard Burton tells us that during the reign of Saʿīd b. Sulṭān Indian Twelver Shīʿīs were allowed to build an *imāmbārā* in which to commemorate their Imam, and he adds that "few Sunnī countries would have tolerated the abomination".

The spread of Khārijism in North Africa was a direct consequence of the collapse of the movement in the central portions of the empire. After being defeated by the Umayyads in the territory of Mosul, in Iraq and in central Arabia, the Khārijīs emigrated to North Africa, where the Ibāḍī branch succeeded in founding in 776 a stable state having its centre at Tāhart in modern Algeria.

Ibāḍī administration was the same as that of any other Muslim state except for the predominant rôle played in it by the *mashā'ikh*, or doctors of the faith, who alone had the right to criticize the Imam, to watch his behaviour and see that he kept within the limits prescribed by their religion, and to remove him if he overstepped them. The most important among them were called *ʿazzāba*, meaning those who lead a retired life, and they formed the *ḥalqa*, which were formerly schools but later became religious orders with their own rules.

In 908 the kingdom of Tāhart fell at the hands of the Fāṭimids, and the Ibāḍī survivors, not wishing to renounce their faith or submit to the conquerors, moved farther south. The invasion by the Banū Hilāl Bedouin tribes in 1051 drove them still farther into the interior of the Algerian Sahara, to the oasis of Wargla (Ouargla), where they founded a new centre at Sadrāta, which also achieved a certain renown in the realm of art, and to the Wādī Rīgh. From the latter, either for missionary reasons or because they hoped to escape persecution, they pushed southward to the region of Mīzāb, which at that time was sterile and uninhabited. There, during the eleventh and twelfth centuries they founded five centres which constituted the so-called Ibāḍī pentapolis (Ghardāya, Malīka, Banū Isjan, al-ʿAṭf and Bū Nūra)—to which the surviving Ibāḍīs later flocked from Wargla and the Wādī Rīgh. During the seventeenth century two other urban centres were founded at Garāra (Guerrara) and Baryān (Berriane), which with the five already existing formed the confederation of the Ibāḍī heptapolis. The constitution given to these towns by the *ʿazzāba* was based on the rules of the *ḥalqa*, adapted to meet the new political and social requirements. The Turks made no attempt to occupy the region, but in 1853 it became a French protectorate and in 1882 it was annexed to Algeria.

Farther east, after the occupation of southern Ifrīqiya by the Aghlabids, Ibāḍism survived in the island of Jarba, the population of which still follows this creed. At the time of the Banū Hilāl invasion the Ibāḍīs of Tripolitania withdrew to Jabal Nafūsa, where they preserved their own faith and their original Berber language throughout the Turkish domination. An Ibāḍī group remained in the coastal centre of the Zuwāra. When the Italians occupied Tripolitania in 1911, the Nafūsa at first adopted a hostile attitude and tried to set up an independent Ibāḍī principality, but they submitted after being defeated in 1913. Since 1953 they have formed part of the kingdom of Libya.

POLITICAL AND RELIGIOUS DOCTRINE

Our earliest information concerning Ibāḍī doctrine comes from two comparatively late sources. The earliest are the Sunnī heresiographers, beginning with al-Ashʿarī (d. 935), based mainly on polemical writings, which give merely a brief exposition of the points of dissension. On the Ibādī side, we find a few items of information in historical works, for example in the chronicle of Abū Zakariyyā' (eleventh century), but the first extended and organic treatise is the *ʿaqīda*, or profession of faith, of al-Jannāwunī (twelfth century), which may be an elaboration of a credo dating from the eighth century. Al-Jannāwunī's work, like others which followed it, was written in North Africa. There is no trace of any elaboration of the doctrine by the eastern Ibāḍīs, and it would seem that none was ever attempted on a large scale, for the historian al-Barrādī, already mentioned, tells us that in the early years of the thirteenth century eastern Ibāḍī doctors instructed their counterparts in the West to write treatises on their own account.

Characteristics of Ibāḍī doctrine which are common to all Khārijī sects are the peculiar political conception of the Imamate, as the Ibāḍīs prefer to call the caliphate, and the religious concept of the relationship between faith and works. These two concepts are interdependent and owe their origin to the same historical events.

Like the Sunnīs and the Shī'īs, the Ibāḍī community was under an obligation to elect an Imam, the obligation being based on the Qur'ānic precept of "promoting good and preventing evil" (*al-amr bi 'l-ma'rūf wa'l-nahy 'an al-munkar*; III. 100, 106, 110; VII. 156; IX. 72, 113; XXII. 42; XXXI. 16), to which the Ibāḍīs, like the Mu'tazilīs, attach great importance. This precept, which implies in particular the obligation to defend the true faith and ensure the reign of God on earth, could be fully realized only if there were one head to guide the faithful.

The Sunnīs restrict the caliphate to the descendants of the Quraysh and the Shī'īs choose a descendant of 'Alī, but the Khārijīs, and consequently the Ibāḍīs, support the principle that any Muslim can be elevated to the supreme dignity of the Imamate, even if he is "an Abyssinian slave whose nose has been cut off", provided always that he is of irreproachable character. They also maintain that there is an obligation to withdraw recognition from the Imam and depose him if he should diverge from the straight path. They therefore consider as legitimate Caliphs Abū Bakr and 'Umar, but 'Uthmān only until the seventh year of his caliphate, until, that is to say, in their opinion he prevaricated, and 'Alī until the arbitration, in which he sinned, while the Umayyads are considered to be usurpers.

As a result of the vicissitudes which befell the sect, the dogma defined four "states" in which the faithful might find themselves. In times of persecution, if it was impossible to triumph over the enemies of God they were in the state of *kitmān*, or concealment, and the obligation to appoint an Imam was waived, as actually happened in the days of Ibn Ibāḍ. During such periods the policy of *taqiyya* could be followed, according to which it was permissible to conceal one's own political and religious convictions, to dispense with the observance of rites and even to profess the forms of the prevailing religion to protect oneself and one's co-religionists. It was, however, necessary to preserve one's faith intact while awaiting the day when it could be imposed upon others.

If during the state of *kitmān* a grave danger threatened the community, a state of *al-difā'* (defence) was proclaimed, and a temporary *imām al-difā'* was appointed with the specific task of combating the enemies of God. The first Khārijī leader 'Abdallāh b. Wahb al-Rāsibī was one such Imam.

Members of the *ahl al-kitmān* (people of the *kitmān*) could individually elect to enter into the state of *al-shirā'* (achievement of Paradise) by sacrificing their own lives, as was the case with Abū Bilāl Mirdās.

In contrast to the state of *kitmān* was that of *al-ẓuhūr*, the "manifestation" or "declaration of the Imamate". This was proclaimed by the *mashā'ikh* when conditions were favourable for the open election of an Imam, that is to say when the Ibāḍīs had half as many men, arms, horses, provisions, etc., as the enemies of God.

The Imam was elected by a committee of which only doctors of the doctrine (*mashā'ikh*) could be members, and their decision was publicly proclaimed. An Imam elected in this way was called *imām al-bay'a*, and he had to exercise his office in conformity with the Qur'ān and the *sunna* of the Prophet, following the example set by the first two Imams, Abū Bakr and 'Umar. In addition to his religious functions he also fulfilled those of military commander, judge and theologian. His rule was absolute and no one could impose conditions (*sharṭ*) upon him, or oppose him so long as he acted in strict conformity with the religious law; should he deviate from it or introduce innovations, his authority would immediately come to an end, but even in such cases only the *mashā'ikh* who had elected him could decide to what extent he had in fact violated divine law, and they alone could depose him. Theoretically there could be only one Imam, but in practice it came about that there were often several at one and the same time in the various Ibāḍī countries, at Tāhart, in Oman and in the Ḥaḍramawt, and sometimes the functions of government were even exercised jointly.

As regards the religious conception of the relationship between faith and works, for the Ibāḍīs anyone who had committed capital sins (*kabā'ir*) was a *kāfir*, or infidel, and as such he was expelled from the Ibāḍī community. He was not, however, held to be a *mushrik* (polytheist) and hence no longer a Muslim, as he was by the Khārijī extremists such as the Azraqīs. For the Ibāḍīs, who looked upon themselves as the depositories of the true faith, there were two categories of infidels: (1) Muslims (that is, Ibāḍīs) who failed to obey the divine law, committed cardinal sins or introduced innovations. These were expelled and combated so long as they remained dissenters (*mukhālifūn*), but their property (with the exception of weapons) could not be confiscated, and it was not permissible to imprison their children, kill their wounded or pursue fugitives, while their right of inheritance and the state of matrimony were left intact. (2) The *mushrikūn* (or polytheists). These included not only idolaters (*ahl al-awthān*), but also the "possessors of the book" (*ahl al-kitāb*), that is to say the followers of the scriptures—Jews, Christians and Sabaeans—to whom were added the Magians (*Majūs*). Towards these the attitudes varied and corresponded to those laid down by the Sunnī schools. With idolaters there was a perpetual state of war which could terminate only with their conversion to Islam, but to followers of the scriptures who accepted Muslim rule and were willing to pay tribute (*jizya*) great tolerance was shown and they enjoyed the benefits of protection and public safety (*amān*).

Bulwarks of the true religion were the doctrines of *wilāya* and *barā'a*, that is to say the obligation of friendliness towards the followers of the true faith and of more or less militant hostility towards those who did not deserve to be considered as such. These doctrines, which have counterparts in orthodox belief only in so far as regards the general obligation of solidarity with the faithful and hostility towards infidels, were given great attention by the Ibāḍīs. The *wilāya* was obligatory towards (*a*) the faithful in general (*wilāyat al-jumla*); (*b*) those who are praised in the Qur'ān; (*c*) a righteous Imam; (*d*) individuals (*wilāyat al-ashkhāṣ*) who carry out the precepts of religion in a satisfactory manner. Conversely, the *barā'a* was obligatory against (*a*) infidels in general; (*b*) those blamed by the Qur'ān; (*c*) an unjust Imam; (*d*) individuals who do not deserve to be called believers. Both the *wilāya* and the *barā'a* remained in abeyance as regards those whose opinions were unknown.

To these basic precepts others were gradually added when fresh problems arose, these being in the main a reflexion of, or due to, Mu'tazilī influences. It is not easy to establish a logical or chronological sequence of the various points which arose, and we can only say that in the days of al-Ash'arī (d. 935) all the principles of Ibāḍī doctrine were already firmly established. In contrast with orthodox teaching it maintained:

(*a*) the essential character of the divine attributes;

(*b*) the creation of the Qur'ān;

(*c*) the eternity of punishment in hell for reprobate Muslims as well as for others;

(*d*) the inadmissibility of the vision of God in the life to come;

(*e*) the principle of intercession, but only in favour of repentant sinners;

(*f*) the symbolical value of certain eschatological details, for example the *mīzān* (scales) and the *ṣirāṭ* (the bridge over Hell);

(*g*) the rejection of all forms of anthropomorphism.

All these points of Ibāḍī doctrine are, as Goldziher and Nallino have noted, definitely of Mu'tazilī origin, but when and where this influence made itself felt is a question which has not yet been settled. It may have originated among the eastern Ibāḍīs in Baṣra, which was their spiritual home, and have been transmitted thence to the West as a result of the intellectual contact between eastern and western Ibāḍīs, but it is far more probable that Mu'tazilī influence was operative in North Africa, where it had penetrated towards the end of the eighth century and found ready acceptance among the Idrīsī Shī'īs.

The ethical principles reveal the same rigorous conception that we find in the Ibāḍī conception of the state and of faith. For example, sinful actions, whether those of the tongue (lying, evil-speaking, calumny or perjury), of the eyes (admiring the physical charms (*maḥāsin*) and sexual organs of women, or looking into houses without permission), of the ears (listening to gossip, spying out secrets or listening to musical instruments), or of touch (touching the hands of strange women or the genitals of animals, etc.) implied the loss of the state of purity and rendered the sinner unfit to participate in religious rites. This moral austerity even led the Ibāḍīs to attack the integrity of the Qur'ān and to exclude the twelfth Sūra (*sūrat Yūsuf*), since its mundane and frivolous contents seemed to them to be unworthy to be the word of God. Averse from any kind of innovation, laxity or modern ideas, they interpreted the ancient precepts in the most rigorous fashion and forbade anything that smacked of frivolity or luxury, such as the use of tobacco, the ornamentation of mosques, etc. In this way they earned for themselves the nickname of "Puritans of the desert", and the austerity of their customs, which bordered on asceticism, easily bridged the gap between it and mysticism. Though declaring themselves opposed to the exaggerations of the mystics and the confraternities, because these were novelties, they nevertheless accepted the principle of mysticism. Their theologians admired, and frequently quoted or plagiarized, the *Iḥyā'* of al-Ghazālī and expounded the art of intuition (*'ilm al-mukāshafa*), the mystical conception of the oneness of God (*tawḥīd*), and the doctrine of the pre-existence of the Prophet's soul (*nūr muḥammadī*), in addition to the *karāmāt* attributed to so many luminaries of the sect, who were venerated as saints.

The early definitions of the Khārijīs and the points they brought up for discussion may have provided the first impulse for the formation of the oldest juridical schools. What is certain is that in the legal field, as in that of dogma, the Ibāḍīs elaborated a system of their own, in concordance with the orthodox schools. When the political and religious importance of the sect declined in the eighth century, the activity of the Ibāḍīs in the legal field must certainly have declined as well, but this is not a sufficient reason for doubting a development of Ibāḍī doctrine parallel to that of the Sunnīs, or that the same problems were discussed, since the Ibāḍīs were in close contact with the orthodox community for a considerable period, especially during the eighth and ninth centuries. A proof that the juridical system of the Ibāḍīs was not—or at all events not preponderantly—merely a passive acceptance of the principles already laid down by orthodoxy, as some scholars have assumed, but was the outcome of their own opinions, can be seen in the fact that in numerous important respects, not necessarily connected with dogmatic positions, it differs from the orthodox system. For example, the banning of the *waqf ahlī*, or family *waqf* in favour of the descendants of the founder, the right of mothers to retain the *ḥaḍāna*, or custody of minors until they reached the age of discretion; the shortened prayers for travellers until they had established a permanent abode; the rule whereby those who were absent were deprived of the right of pre-emption (*shuf'a*); the forbidding of marriages between those guilty of adultery; the abolition of fasting in cases of impurity due to sexual intercourse, with the result that the *mujannab* had to wash before sunrise; the forbidding of *masḥ 'ala 'l-khuffayn*, that is to say rubbing shoes with the wet hand instead of washing the feet; the obligatory ablutions on conversion to Islam, etc.

The Ibāḍī legal system has much in common with the Mālikī school, because the latter always had a predominating influence in North

Africa. As regards points in which they differ, the Ibāḍī system coincides either with the Ḥanafī or with the Shāfi'ī school. This does not imply any eclecticism on the part of the Ibāḍīs, but proves that they deliberately contrived a system of their own. For example, the Ibāḍīs agree with the Ḥanafīs that in cases concerning property one witness and a sworn statement by the interested party are insufficient, and that there must always be two witnesses; that no final interrogation (*i'dhār*) by the *qāḍī* is necessary before sentence is promulgated; that the consent of a woman, whether a virgin or not, must be obtained before the *wālī* (registrar of marriages) can celebrate the wedding, unless she is both a virgin and under the age of puberty, etc. On the other hand Ibāḍīs and Shāfi'īs agree in considering the *basmala* (the words "In the name of God, the compassionate and merciful") as forming part of every *sūra* in the Qur'ān.

Religious unity among the Ibāḍīs was soon shattered by schism (*iftirāq*) and dissension (*khilāf*) which resulted in the formation of numerous sects. The largest and most important, and the only one effectively surviving today, is the Wahbiyya, to which the above-mentioned doctrines are ascribed. The name is derived from that of 'Abdallāh b. Wahb al-Rāsibī, the first Khārijī Imam, or else, though with less probability, from that of the Rustamid Imam 'Abd al-Wahhāb b. 'Abd al-Raḥmān. Regarding the beliefs of other sects we have only fragmentary information. The sect of the Nukkāriyya ("those who reject") owes its origin to the fact that some of the Ibāḍīs refused to recognize the second Imam of Tāhart, 'Abd al-Wahhāb b. 'Abd al-Raḥmān b. Rustam (784–5), who would not accept the conditions (*shurūṭ*) they wished to impose on him. A dissident Nukkāri Imamate was set up towards the end of the ninth century, and a few followers of this sect still survive in the Maghrib. A political question was also the cause of the formation of the Nafāthī sect, whose founder, Nafāth, accused the Rustamid Imam Aflaḥ of leading a life of luxury and neglecting the war against the Aghlabids; Nafāth withdrew with his followers to the Jabal Nafūsa, where a few remnants of his sect still survive. The Khalafī sect dates from the end of the eighth century and takes its name from Khalaf b. al-Samḥ, who had proclaimed himself Imam of Tripolitania. According to L. Massignon remnants of this sect are still to be found in Gharyān.

In the early days these sects were hostile to one another, but with the passage of time peaceful relations were established between many of them. The Ibāḍī historian al-Darjīnī tells us that in the first half of the tenth century the district of Zīzū in Tripolitania was governed by a council headed by a Wahbī, who entrusted the administration of justice to a Nukkārī, the Ramaḍān prayers to a Khalafī, and the call to prayer to a Nafāthī.

THE PRESENT SITUATION

At the present time the Ibāḍīs, once so numerous in the Muslim world, do not number more than half a million souls. Most of them are in Oman, where, according to L. Massignon, they represent about 70 per cent of the total Muslim population of 500,000, and are divided about equally between the faction of the Hināwī, who claim that they belong to the great South Arabian branch of the Qaḥṭānīs and that they are the oldest Arab element, and that of the Ghāfirī, who believe that they are an offshoot of the great North Arabian or Nizārī branch, supposedly descendants of Ishmael, the son of Abraham. The administration of the sultanate is approximately the same as that of other Muslim states at the present day. Each province has a governor (*wālī*), a judge of the *sharī'a* (*qāḍī*), and troops under the orders of a military commander (*qā'id*). The legal system, in the coastal districts as well as in the interior, is the *sharī'a*, but in the interior the Islamic criminal law is ruthlessly applied, and this may be because of either strict observance of the principles of the sect or the influence of Wahhābī austerity. Consequently, the hands of the thieves are amputated, murderers are killed, and fornicators are stoned if they are *muḥṣan* (legally married at least once) or flogged if they are not *muḥṣan*. The Qur'ānic penalty of flogging is also applicable to those who drink wine, while the use of tobacco is likewise punished, with the result that it can only be obtained clandestinely. Little information is available about religious practices and education. In conformity with the principles of the sect, membership of confraternities is forbidden.

In Zanzibar, according to J. S. Trimingham, the Ibāḍīs number now only about 6,000, and it is difficult to say how far recent events will accelerate the trend towards Shāfi'ism, nor is it possible to say whether their creed has remained immune from local influences. Unlike the other sects the Ibāḍīs have no congregational mosques, as they do not perform the common prayer because they maintain that this will only be possible when power is in the hands of a legitimate Imam elected by the whole community.

In North Africa, according to L. Massignon, Sunnism is making headway among the Ibāḍīs of the island of Jarba, of whom there are about 40,000, but on the contrary the 30,000 Ibāḍīs of the Jabal Nafūsa and the 12,000 Ibāḍīs of Zuwāra remain firmly attached to their own beliefs. It would appear that Sunnī preachers who recently visited some of the centres of the Jabal met with a hostile reception. In Jarba as well as in the Jabal Nafūsa the Ibāḍīs have mosques of their own, differing in certain architectural features from those of the Sunnīs. From the political and social point of view neither group has any organization peculiar to the sect.

On the other hand in the Mīzāb, where the Ibāḍīs have remained a marginal element untouched by modern developments, they have retained almost intact their ancient theocratic organization based on the *ḥalqa*, concerning the modern application of which we find full details in a recent Arabic work written by the Algerian Aḥmad Tawfīq al-Madanī. Each of the tribes forming the population in the various centres divides its members into two categories—the *ṭalaba*, who might be called the "religious" element, and the *'awāmm*, or laity. The former of these two categories consists of the *'azzāba*, the *talāmīdh* ("students"), and the *aṣḥāb al-maḥāḍir*, who are the teachers and pupils of the Qur'ānic schools.

The body of the *'azzāba* is normally composed of twelve members—in the capital, Ghardāya, there are also twelve substitutes—and has the authority that was once exercised by the Imam, though in practice this is naturally subject to the common law of the country. Its members wear a special dress, are obliged to shave their heads completely, and apparently still receive a formal investiture. To the category of the *'azzāba* belong the *shaykh*, who is their head; the *muftī*, a jurist who gives legal advice based on the *sharī'a*; the *imām*, who leads the prayers; the *mu'adhdhin*; the superintendent of *awqāf* property; the *mu'addib al-ṣibyān*, who acts as a kind of preceptor; and those whose duty it is to wash the bodies of the dead. The *'azzāba* controls all the religious life of the community, giving guidance, exhorting the faithful to do good and shun evil, and repressing all actions which are contrary to the *sharī'a*, as well as opposing innovations, instructing the laity in both religious and worldly matters, supervising the markets, preventing fraud and suppressing monopolies. If a layman rebels against a decision of the *'azzāba*, the members of the latter stop exercising their functions, abandon the mosques, no longer give the call to prayer (*adhān*), abstain from common prayer, etc., until the people as a whole implore their forgiveness and ask them to resume their functions. A committee of four is responsible for administrative matters, consisting of the shaykh, the *imām*, the *mu'adhdhin* and a fourth chosen from among the members of the *'azzāba*. The supreme power is vested in the shaykh, one of whose duties it is to make public announcements in the mosque of the excommunication (*tabri'a*) of guilty persons. The aim of this measure is not only to safeguard the doctrine, but also to raise the moral tone of the masses, and in the hands of the *'azzāba* it is definitely an instrument of power and is generally feared, to such an extent that the mere threat of its application is often sufficient to restore order. The injured party can claim his rights by the simple procedure of attending the Friday prayers and exclaiming in a loud voice: "Companions of the faith, I will not permit you to pray, to give *zakāt*, to fast or to make pilgrimages, until you have given me my rights." The guilty party is then summoned, and if he refuses to accept the verdict, he is excommunicated. This can have serious moral and material consequences, for a man who has been excommunicated is abandoned by his dependants, his friends and even his own family. He cannot eat, drink or sit with others; he cannot take part in festivals or banquets; he cannot purchase goods even at increased prices and cannot act as middleman, and no one will accept the meat of animals slaughtered by him. In short he suffers a civil death, and if he dies before having given public proof of repentance, his body will be washed by a layman, instead of by the *'azzāba*.

The feminine counterpart of the *'azzāba* is the association of women called *ghāsilāt*, or washers of corpses, who represent the families of the village and are responsible for settling all family questions. The *'azzāba* choose them from among the women who are known to be pious and experienced in religious questions concerning women. It is their duty to wash the corpses of women and children, to check whether they have reached the age of puberty or are pregnant, to see that the regulations laid down for menstruation and childbirth are observed, to proclaim a *barā'a* against any woman who fails to observe the *sharī'a*, to discourage novelties and excesses, and to report offenders to the *'azzāba*. The right of accepting penitence and granting pardon, however, is vested in the shaykh or the *imām*. The *ghāsilāt* live in special houses adjoining the mosque, and through windows giving on to the interior of the latter they can participate in the common prayers, and listen to edifying sermons or lessons on *fiqh*, which is to say on legal questions. Once a year they hold a public meeting called the *lā ilāha illā Allāh*, "there is no other God but Allah", because they repeat this formula a thousand times before beginning their discussions. They make suggestions as to the best way of averting evil from the families under their care, and these suggestions are subject to the approval of the *ʿazzāba*. Thanks to their activities women enjoy a more privileged position than in any other Muslim country. In the marriage contract, a husband must bind himself not to take other wives without the consent of the first wife, not to stay away from home for more than two years or at the most three, not to take his wife abroad, to abstain from fornication, gambling, drinking of wine and the use of tobacco, not to neglect his prayers, etc. If the husband violates any of these rules, the wife regains her freedom, but conversely, a woman who disobeys her husband loses her rights.

All those who have attended the Qur'ānic schools can become members of the body of "students", provided their principles are sound and their behaviour satisfactory. Candidates submit their applications through the headmaster of the school (*faqīh*) to the chief of the "students" (*ʿarīf*). They must prove that they know the Qur'ān by heart, though in some countries it is sufficient if they know a quarter of it. After passing the examinations they offer their colleagues a banquet, at which the *ʿazzāba* are also present. To the latter the candidates promise to conduct themselves in an exemplary manner, to avoid evildoers, to preserve their religion and to continue in their studies. The candidates then take their places next to the junior "student" and from that moment are officially known as "students". In a building reserved for this purpose they take courses in theology, law, grammar, mathematics and eloquence.

In the Qur'ānic schools (*maḥḍar*) the pupils study the Qur'ān and calligraphy. Each community has from two to four such schools, and each school is under an *ʿazzābī* who is called the *faqīh*, assisted by the older masters. Those who know the Qur'ān best collaborate with the *ʿazzāba* and the *talāmīdh* in supervising the ethical and religious activities of the community.

The laity, or *ʿawāmm*, have an organization of their own, comprising the *qā'id*, the *jamāʿa* and the *makārī*. Each community has a *qā'id* with administrative powers, who at one time was appointed by the elders from among themselves, but nowadays is chosen by the government.

The *qā'id* can inflict physical punishments, detention and fines, and he is responsible for the maintenance of public order and the observance of laws. He presides over the *jamā'a*, or assembly consisting of the elected heads of tribes, which discusses the budget, transmits the *qā'id*'s orders to the tribes, collects the taxes and remits them to the *qā'id*, and looks after local interests in general. Police duties in the case of a public emergency are carried out by the *makārī*, or guards, who are appointed by the *jamā'a*.

What one might call legislative functions are under the joint control of the *ḥalqa* of the *'azzāba* and the *jamā'a* of the *'awāmm*. Their joint decisions correspond to what the Sunnīs call the *ijmā'*, the *consensus populi*, the third source of Islamic law. Among the Ibāḍīs this system still preserves the same form as in the early days of Islam, while in other Muslim countries it has been discontinued. The decisions of the assembly are called *tifāqāt* (*ittifāqāt*), or conventions, and concern both civil and criminal law. They are transcribed in registers and together with the *Kitāb al-īḍāḥ* of Shaykh Abū Sākin 'Āmir b. 'Alī al-Shammākhī (d. 1390) and the *Kitāb al-nīl* of Shaykh 'Abd al-'Azīz al-Isjanī (b. 1718) constitute the *corpus juris* in force. Meetings are usually held in cemeteries, as if to symbolize the continuity of the sect's principles. At Ghardāya, in the mosque of 'Abd al-Raḥmān al-Kurthī or in that of 'Ammī Sa'īd b. 'Alī, a general assembly is held to deal with matters of general interest.

Judicial matters, once the prerogative of the *'azzāba*, are now in the hands of the *qāḍi*, who is appointed by the government. A court of appeal, called the *majlis*, sits at Ghardāya. Since 1890 there have also been Ibāḍī tribunals at Algiers, Constantine and Mu'askar (Mascara).

Respect for tradition is now tempered by the aspirations of the younger generation, and modern ideas, as J. Schacht was able to observe on the spot, are making headway, especially at Guerrara and Berriane, the most recently founded centres. This trend was started about 1920 by the Bayūḍī movement, which takes its name from its founder, Bayūḍ Ibrāhīm, shaykh of the Guerrara *ḥalqa*. On his initiative schools were founded at Guerrara (the *madrasat al-ḥayāt* and an institute of secondary studies called the *ma'had*), at Berriane (the *madrasat al-fatḥ*), at Bū Nūra (the *madrasat al-nūriyya*), and at Ghardāya (the *madrasat al-iṣlāḥ*). The Bayūḍī movement began with the programme of abolishing the veto on the emigration of women. Because of the modern tendency to emigrate abroad, the abolition of this veto would certainly have been detrimental to the integrity of the communities in the Mīzāb. The opposition of the elders and the *ṭalaba* is thus understandable, but it has not succeded in preventing the emigration of young couples from time to time. The distrust of change could also explain the hostile attitude which the *ṭalaba* are said to have adopted towards certain social reforms recently introduced by the government.

CHAPTER 17

THE ISMĀ'ĪLĪS

During the tenth century A.D. traditional Islam had already begun to show signs of that petrifaction which has become the subject of endless discussion in the last two centuries. The orthodox faith was challenged by at least three movements: by the Ṣūfīs who taught a direct approach to God; by the philosophers, who enthroned reason as the supreme instrument for the measurement of truth; and by Ismā'īlism, a doctrine which "expressed itself in an infinity of forms, both doctrinal and organisational".[1] The chief appeal of the Ismā'īlīs lay in putting forward the Imam as the leader of the Muslims, an infallible being several degrees higher than the Prophet of Islam,[2] who was descended from the Prophet's daughter Fāṭima, married to his cousin, 'Alī. Instead of the usual literal, grammatical and historical interpretation of the Qur'ān, it propounded an allegorical exegesis known as *ta'wīl*, which was the gate to the ultimate truth called *ḥaqīqa*, or more usually, the *ḥaqā'iq*, using the plural to designate the whole of the esoteric science. Its hierarchy of priests, the *ḥudūd* (singular, *ḥadd*), was derived in all probability from early Christian practices, as Zāhid 'Alī has shown. Historical truth was not one of its strong points; it confused fact with legend, and its exponents using *taqiyya* (dissimulation) employed arguments which do not stand the test of historical or logical demonstration. W. Ivanow justly observes that "as genuine Isma'ili literature was essentially religious in character, it completely ignored history".[3] On several important questions, contradictory statements will be found in the Ismā'īlī authorities, and they are justified by the fundamental principle of their faith, as expressed by Imam Ja'far al-Ṣādiq: "*Taqiyya* (dissimulation) is my religion (*dīn*) and the religion of my fathers."[4]

Ismā'īlism takes its name from the eldest of the sons of Imam Ja'far al-Ṣādiq. It appears that Ismā'īl was appointed the heir-apparent by the sixth Imam Ja'far, but later incurred the displeasure of his father. The

[1] Bernard Lewis, *Origins of Ismā'īlism* (Cambridge, 1940), p. 1.

[2] This doctrine, however, has been countered by Shīrāzī in his *Majālis* (Ivanow, *Ismaili Literature*, no. 160) in volume III *majlis* 39, where he clearly proclaims the absolute pre-eminence of the Prophet Muḥammad.

[3] *Rise of the Fatimids* (Bombay, 1942), p. 2.

[4] This is so, in all matters, except three specified cases. Qāḍī al-Nu'mān, *Da'ā'im al-Islām*, ed. Fyzee, vol. II, para. 464.

causes are not known; but it is suggested that he was addicted to drink, and that Jaʿfar being displeased appointed his younger son Mūsā Kāẓim to the Imamate in his last days. The Twelvers (*Ithnā ʿAshariyya*) believed in Mūsā Kāẓim, while the so-called "Seveners" adhered to the claims of Ismāʿīl and were known as the Ismāʿīlīs. There is, however, little doubt that Mūsā Kāẓim did have some sort of rank in the Ismāʿīlī hierarchy, for Zāhid ʿAlī, quoting ancient authorities, declares him to a *ḥijāb* (protector, veil) of the infant Imam Muḥammad b. Ismāʿīl,[1] who ultimately became a usurper. Such usurpations, as we shall see later, were a common feature of traditional Ismāʿīlī history. As Ismāʿīl died before his father, his son Muḥammad, the seventh Imam according to the Ismāʿīlī computation, was given a special status. Some historians identify Imam Muḥammad b. Ismāʿīl as the spiritual father of Maymūn al-Qaddāḥ;[2] while the sectarians declare him to be the seventh Imam, the seventh *waṣī*, the seventh *nāṭiq* and the seventh *rasūl*, who completely abrogated the *sharīʿa* of the Prophet Muḥammad.[3] These are large claims and are hardly compatible with any of the known forms of Islam.

The career of the seventh Imam Muḥammad b. Ismāʿīl raises the first of the historical puzzles. Who was this Maymūn al-Qaddāḥ and his son ʿAbdallāh? And what was their relationship with Imam Muḥammad b. Ismāʿīl? Here the historians differ vitally. That he was the younger contemporary of Imam Jaʿfar seems tolerably clear; and the majority of historians identify him (or one of them) as the real founder of Ismāʿīlism. Bernard Lewis, and above all Zāhid ʿAlī, accept the theory; while Ivanow rejects it and says that Maymūn and ʿAbdallāh are the twin myths created by unsympathetic historians. The matter cannot be said to be settled, but the weight of authority is on the side of Zāhid ʿAlī, a learned Dāʾūdī Bohora of priestly extraction, fully trained in Western methods of critical research, who produced two volumes of remarkable learning and critical acumen on the history and the tenets of the Western Ismāʿīlis.[4] After Muḥammad there followed three hidden Imams; and it

[1] Zāhid ʿAlī, *Madhhab* (Hyderabad, 1954), pp. 161–2.

[2] Bernard Lewis, *op. cit.* p. 49.

[3] Zāhid ʿAlī, *Tārīkh* (Hyderabad, 1948), pp. 538 ff., on the basis of *Kanz al-Walad* and *Anwār al-Laṭīfa*, two of the most secret and authoritative of the Mustaʿlian texts. This view has, however, been refuted by Ḥasan ʿAlī Sārangpūrī, *Dāmigh al-Buhtān* (a comprehensive but repetitive official refutation of Zāhid ʿAlī's works in three volumes, published by the Jāmiʿa Sayfiyya, Surat, no date), pp. 30, 115 ff., 154, and other places.

[4] Bernard Lewis, *Origins*, gives the Sunnite sources, pp. 54 ff.; Zāhid ʿAlī, *Tārīkh*, pp. 47, 502; *Madhhab*, pp. 148 ff., 183 ff., 198, 610. *Contra* W. Ivanow, *Ibn al-Qaddāḥ* (Bombay, 1957), and *Brief Survey of the Evolution of Ismailism* (Leiden, 1952), pp. 7 ff. and Index. He has repeated this in a number of other articles and books.

is impossible to be certain whether they were historical persons or fictitious Imams created by the founders of the movement.

With the foundation of the Fāṭimid Caliphate in Egypt we are on surer ground. 'Ubaydallāh, who assumed the title of al-Mahdī bi'llāh (d. 933) was the first of the fourteen Fāṭimid Caliphs and the eleventh Imam of the Ismā'īlīs, computing Ḥasan as the first Imam, not 'Alī, who was of higher rank, namely *waṣī*. Mahdī had a choice of establishing himself in the Yemen where Ibn Ḥawshab, his brilliant *dā'ī* had had a great success; or in the Maghrib, which was conquered by his able lieutenant 'Abdallāh al-Shī'ī. He rightly chose the latter, and by ability and enterprise established a large kingdom. However, as soon as his position was established, he got rid of his helper, al-Shī'ī, by the common and effective method of assassination.

The Fāṭimid extraction of al-Mahdī is not beyond doubt. At least nine different forms of his pedigree are known, of which W. Ivanow gives us three in his article on the Ismā'īliyya in the *Supplement* to the *Encyclopaedia of Islam*. This hardly convinces anyone but a devout Ismā'īlī, and there is a charming story related by Ibn Khallikān about al-Mu'izz (the fourth Fāṭimid caliph) who, when asked about his genealogy, unsheathed his sword and scattered gold to offer irrefragable proof of his pedigree and power.[1]

This story although apocryphal contains a great measure of truth. What after all does it matter whether the Mahdī was a descendant of the Prophet or not? The decisive fact was that the sectarians believed in his 'Alid descent implicitly as a matter of faith; and ancient historians like Ibn Khaldūn and some modern scholars such as Ivanow, are satisfied about his antecedents. The historical fact remains that the Fāṭimid Caliphs, or rather their able *wazīrs*, created a prosperous empire which lasted close upon two hundred years, produced a great civilization, described in detail by the traveller Nāṣir-i Khusraw among others, and finally left a valuable legacy in theological literature which combines Islamic thought with a variety of strands drawn from Pythagorean, Aristotelian and Plotinian sources. This *da'wa* literature is a fit object of study for understanding the theology produced in the Middle Ages.

Of the Fāṭimid caliphs, the most remarkable were al-Mu'izz and al-Ḥākim, deified later by the Druzes. Al-Mu'izz li-dīni'llāh, fourth Fāṭimid Caliph and fourteenth Imam (d. 975) may be compared with

[1] O'Leary, *A Short History of the Fatimid Khalifate* (London, 1923), p. 35.

Akbar the Great Mughal in some ways. After the kingdom was well established, he patronized learning and encouraged trade. Al-Mu'izz came from the north and, with the help of his great general Jawhar, conquered Egypt and laid the foundations of modern Cairo, al-Qāhirat al-Mu'izziyya. He built the mosque and *madrasa* of al-Azhar, the oldest existing university of Islamic learning. He was a man of impressive personality, and began the tradition of pomp and ceremony which was a characteristic of the Fāṭimid caliphate. He also encouraged his Chief Justice, Qāḍī al-Nu'mān to compose the authoritative corpus of Ismā'īlī law, *Da'ā'im al-Islām* in two volumes, which to this day applies to the sectarians.[1]

The death of the eighth Fāṭimid caliph al-Mustanṣir (d. 1095) after a long reign of fifty years, brings us to the division between the Western (Musta'lian) and the Eastern (Nizārian) branches of Ismā'īlism. The eldest surviving son of al-Mustanṣir was Nizār, aged fifty. He had already been declared heir apparent; but the youngest son Musta'lī, aged twenty-one, was the son-in-law of the Armenian general al-Afḍal, the commander-in-chief of the armed forces. Afḍal seized power and obtained for al-Musta'lī the allegiance of the nobles of the court, while Nizār was forced to flee for his life after a show of resistance. There are conflicting accounts of what happened; but both Ibn al-Athīr and Ibn Khaldūn agree that Nizār was the duly appointed heir apparent whose claims were overlooked by the energy and diplomacy of al-Afḍal.

The next Imam was al-Āmir who ruled till he was assassinated by a group of Nizārīs. He was succeeded by four other caliphs, until the Fāṭimid caliphate was destroyed by the Ayyūbids. These four caliphs were not descended from al-Āmir and were therefore not Imams in the true sense; and we must return to al-Āmir and his son al-Ṭayyib, the twenty-first and last of the Imams of the Western Ismā'īlīs. It is said by Ismā'īlī historians that al-Āmir, knowing that there would be political disturbances after his death, hid his infant son al-Ṭayyib, the future Imam, and made Ibn Madyan his guardian. This story is difficult to substantiate, but apparently Maqrīzī and the Musta'lian authority Idrīs 'Imād al-Dīn have no doubts as to the historicity of al-Ṭayyib. Ivanow, on the other hand, treats him almost as a fictitious person and his doubts are justifiable. Al-Ṭayyib, according to Musta'lian belief, was hidden (*mastūr*) and certain protectors were appointed, as the period of *satr*

[1] This work has been critically edited by me, in two volumes (Maaref Press, Cairo, 1951 and 1961).

(hiding) had commenced, and the period of *ẓuhūr* (manifestation) had terminated. In Western Ismā'īlī belief such Imams will go on living and handing down the Imamate from father to son till the day of Resurrection.

The Yemen, since the days of the tenth Imam Ḥusayn al-Mastūr, had been the stronghold of the Musta'lian Ismā'īlīs. Ḥusayn, one of the "hidden" ancestors of the Mahdī, had sent his *dā'ī* (chief propagandist) Ḥasan b. Faraḥ b. Ḥawshab to the Yemen in 881–2,[1] and ever since that time the *da'wa* had flourished there. After the extinction of the caliphate in Egypt, it was organized as a petty state in addition to its being the chief mission of the Musta'lians. The so-called Yemenite *da'wa* commenced with the first *dā'ī* Dhu'ayb b. Mūsā (d. 1151). After him there followed twenty-six *dā'īs* till the split between the Dā'ūdīs and the Sulaymānīs which occurred in 1589. Since then the *dā'īs* of the Sulaymānīs have reigned in the Yemen, and the *dā'īs* of the Dā'ūdīs have established themselves in Surat and Bombay. There have been fifty-one *dā'īs* in the Dā'ūdī branch, and forty-five in the Sulaymānī line.[2]

We must now turn our attention to the Eastern Ismā'īlīs, the followers of Nizār. If the pedigree of the Western Ismā'īlī Imams is weak, the Imams of the Eastern branch have even weaker claims to 'Alid ancestry. Nizār it is said had two sons, al-Hādī and al-Muhtadī; sometimes three are mentioned. Al-Hādī was murdered together with his father in prison, but the infant al-Muhtadī escaped and was brought up in great secrecy by Ḥasan b. Ṣabbāḥ, a man of talent and enterprise. Al-Muhtadī died in 1162 and his son Ḥasan al-Qāhir bi-Aḥkāmi'llāh, ascended the pontifical throne. This is the opinion of Ivanow, but his genealogy is uncertain. Now this al-Qāhir, or to give him his sonorous title Ḥasan *'alā dhikrihi 'l-salām*, made the well-known announcement of the *qiyāmat al-qiyāmāt*, the Resurrection of Resurrections, in 1164 (on the 17th of Ramaḍān, 559 A.H.), at Alamūt. This declaration is so remarkable that a few details may be of interest.[3]

Ḥasan (whose 'Alid descent is unproved)[4] collected a large number of his followers in Alamūt, and wearing a white garment and a white turban, greeted the gathering three times and sat down. Then he rose and baring his sword, he addressed not only the inhabitants of this

[1] Zāhid 'Alī, *Tārīkh*, p. 357.

[2] Asaf A. A. Fyzee, "A Chronological List of the Imāms and Dā'īs of the Musta'lian Ismailis", *Journal Bombay Branch of the Royal Asiatic Society* (1934), pp. 8–16.

[3] Hodgson, *The Order of the Assassins* (The Hague, 1955), pp. 148 ff. and Appendix 1.

[4] Hodgson, *Ency. of Islam* (2nd ed., 1960), s.v. "Alamut", vol. 1, p. 352.

world, but the *jinns* and angels as well. He proclaimed "The Imam of our time sends you his blessings and compassion, calling you his specially selected servants. He has lifted from you the burden of the obligation of the *sharī'a* ritual, and has brought you the *qiyāma* (Resurrection)...Ḥasan b. Muḥammad b. Buzurg Ummīd is our *dā'ī* and *ḥujja*; our *shī'a* must be submissive and obedient to him...considering his word to be Our word." He then came down from the pulpit and performed two *rak'as* (prostrations) of the prayer of *'īd*. Thereafter he set up a table and seated the people to break the fast; and they made merry and exulted in the manner of ritual festivals. After this declaration, the 17th of Ramaḍān was celebrated by the community as the festival of the *qiyāma*, and it is said that wine was freely used as part of the merriment.

Ten weeks later, Ḥasan made a second declaration and said that he, Ḥasan the Second, was the representative of God on earth, and the Ra'īs Muẓaffar was his agent in Kuhistan, and as such was to be obeyed in all things. He thus made three revolutionary declarations: he proclaimed himself not merely *dā'ī*, but the Imam, the final authority on earth; he ended the rule of *sharī'a*, not only by word but also by deed; and he proclaimed the resurrection of the dead, combining in himself the authority of the Imam of the time and the Messiah.

The history of the four *khudāwands* of Alamūt is well known and need not detain us. In Syria the Nizārians flourished under a talented leader, Rāshid al-Dīn Sinān, whose picturesque fortress at Maṣyaf is now in ruins. The son of Rukn al-Dīn, Shams al-Dīn was hidden as a child, and his descendants remained in complete seclusion and no details are available. From here on, the official genealogy is so mystifying that a student can well appreciate the wisdom of the Musta'lians who took refuge in *istitār* (seclusion of the Imam), rather than expose themselves to ridicule or obloquy.

Coming to the last century, the scene is Persia and India. Ḥasan 'Alī Shāh, the Imam of the time, married the daughter of Fatḥ 'Alī Shāh Qājār of Persia, and was duly appointed governor of Kirmān. Later, as a result of intrigues in Persia, he fled to India and died there in 1881. 'Alī Shāh succeeded him as the Āghā Khān, the title given by the British rulers of India to the Imam of the Isma'īlīs, known as *ḥāẓar imām*, among the Khojas. This is to distinguish him from the *imām-i ghā'ib* of the Ithnā 'Ashariyya and the *imām-i mastūr* of the Musta'lians. His son Sulṭān Muḥammad Shāh was a well-known public man and racehorse owner who died in 1957 and was succeeded by his grandson Prince Karīm Khān, the 49th Imam of the Eastern Ismā'īlīs.[1]

Having dealt with the history of the two branches, a word may be said about their religion. The religion of the Western Ismā'īlīs is older and differs in some respects from the religion of the Eastern branch. It is incomparably better documented than that of the Nizārian school, and a fair proportion of their texts are preserved. These have been described by W. Ivanow, in his indispensable *Guide to Ismaili Literature*. The fullest and most accurate account of the religion of the Musta'lians will be found in Zāhid 'Alī, *Hamārē Ismā'īlī Madhhab kī ḥaqīqat awr us kā Niẓām* (Hyderabad, 1954).[2]

The religious sciences are divided into three parts: *sharī'a*, the external law; *ta'wīl*, the allegorical interpretation of the Qur'ān and the ritual, leading to the third and final stage, *'ilm al-ḥaqīqa*, and more commonly, the *ḥaqā'iq*, the ultimate reality. The sciences are to be acquired gradually and with due regard to secrecy; for, the *sharī'a* is the *ẓāhir* (exoteric) and the *ḥaqā'iq* is the *bāṭin* (esoteric) part. A graduated mode of acquiring these sciences is laid down in the earlier texts, and the *bāṭin* works cannot be read without the permission of the religious hierarchy, the *ḥudūd* (sing. *ḥadd*).[3]

An early source for the study of the religious sciences of the Musta'lians is the *Rasā'il ikhwān al-ṣafā'*. According to the Fāṭimid authorities the tracts were composed by the ninth Imam Aḥmad al-Mastūr, one of the three "hidden" Imams; but even if this tradition is proved to be apocryphal the tracts are clearly of Isma'īlī origin; and all authorities, ancient and modern, are agreed that the *Rasā'il* constitute the most authoritative exposition of the early form of the Ismā'īlī religion.

The ultimate creator is called the *mubdi'*, who is unknown and unknowable. It has often been identified by modern scholars with the Plotinian One. The *mubdi'* created a large number of spiritual beings in

[1] Accounts of the Nizārian Imams and their communities will be found in J. N. Hollister, *The Shi'a of India* (London, 1953), pp. 300 ff., and S. C. Misra, *Muslim Communities in Gujarat* (Bombay, 1964), pp. 54 ff.

[2] A critical summary of Zāhid 'Alī's account will be found in his *Tārīkh*, pp. 469 ff.; see W. Ivanow, *Ency. of Islam*, Suppl. p. 98, who has also given us a translation of the later creed of Sayyidnā 'Alī b. Muḥammad b. Walīd (1215), in *The Creed of the Fatimids* (Bombay, 1936); shorter accounts will be found in J. N. Hollister, *op. cit.*, pp. 246 ff., and Henri Corbin, *Histoire de la philosophie islamique* (Paris, 1964), p. 110 and Index.

[3] An account of the course of studies is given by me in an article entitled "The Study of the Literature of the Fatimid *Da'wa*" in *Arabic and Islamic Studies in Honor of Hamilton A. R. Gibb*, ed. G. Makdisi (Leiden, 1965), pp. 232–49.

the *'ālam al-ibdā'* (the world of Primal Creation). This state is also called *al-kamāl al-awwal* (The First Perfection), possessed only by the *mubdi'*. One of the spiritual beings out of those that were created surpassed all others in knowing itself, and was thus named The First Intelligence (*al-'aql al-awwal*). It understood its relation with the One, testified to its power, and thus became first in rank. The First Intelligence thereupon acquired the Second Perfection (*al-kamāl al-thānī*), by which it acquired knowledge of the past, present and future.

Among the other spiritual beings created at the time of *al-kamāl al-awwal*, two in particular distinguished themselves by understanding the reason why the First Intelligence had acquired a position of primacy. They realized that they were created beings; and of the two, only one acknowledged that the First Intelligence was superior to it in excellence. By this knowledge and wisdom, it became the Second Intelligence and was admitted to the Second Perfection, and obtained the knowledge of past, present and future.

The other of these beings did not accept its inferiority to the First Intelligence and claimed equality with it. For this reason, it descended into spiritual darkness and ultimately became the Tenth, instead of becoming the Third, Intelligence. Similarly there were seven other spiritual beings, each of which realized its own limitations and became successively the Third to the Ninth Intelligence. The Tenth Intelligence seeing that it was the last in rank among these bodies, tried to improve its lot by contrition. It was told that the only way in which it could improve its position was to give proper guidance and instruction to those beings which had been misguided by its rebellious conduct. The Tenth Intelligence then began to give guidance to a number of spiritual beings, collectively designated as *al-hayūlā al-ūlā*, the Primal Substance. This guidance was not very satisfactory and the beings, being dissatisfied, made a supreme effort on their own; the first effort created Length; the second, Breadth; and the third, Depth. All these movements were the result of the will of the Tenth Intelligence. On this theory, the Tenth Intelligence is the actual creator of the world, the Allāh of the Qur'ān. After some 50,000 years, man was created, as we know him. The creation of man was preceded by the creation of other things such as water, earth, and life, both vegetable and animal.

Out of numberless human beings thus created, there appeared twenty-eight superior men in the most excellent part of the world, Ceylon (Sarandīb). Of these, only one reached perfection, and the

Tenth Intelligence gave him the title, *ṣāḥib juththat al-ibdā'iyya*. This is difficult to render, particularly as the Greek and Latin equivalents are unknown to me; tentatively, it may be rendered possessor of the perfect personality of man. He is above all men; his position among men is analogous to the rank of the First Intelligence among purely spiritual beings. He is also called Adam the First; he has knowledge of past, present and future. His spirit descends into the Imam of the time. He began to give instruction to his other companions, and each of them came up to a certain "limit" (*ḥadd*). This has now become a term of art and means the particular rank the individual gains in the *da'wa* (the mission), depending upon his capacity and faith. The *ḥadd* possessed a certain dignity and was to perform certain duties; later, the term came to be applied to the members of the spiritual hierarchy in their proper gradation.

The members of the hierarchy, the *ḥudūd*, gave instruction in their own turn and gained converts whom they initiated into the true faith. Those who accepted the true faith were called *mustajībs*. The *mustajīb*, if he is fit, progresses and becomes united in spirit with the Imam. The Imam in turn also progresses and unites with the Tenth Intelligence, and this process is called *ma'ād*, return. The leader, Imam, if he is manifest (*ẓāhir*), is called *mustaqarr* (confirmed, permanent); or else he may be hidden (*mastūr*). The period of manifestation (*ẓuhūr*) is the period of strength; the period of seclusion (*satr*) is the period of weakness. Accordingly there are three periods: *ẓuhūr*, manifestation; *fatrat*, an interregnum, a period of decline; and *satr*, seclusion, a period of weakness.

The Imam is thus the most perfect of human beings created by the Tenth Intelligence; faith is not perfect without knowing him; the world cannot exist without him. During a *satr*, the Imam is in hiding and appoints his assistants, namely the prophets, such as Adam, Noah, Abraham, Moses, Jesus and Muḥammad. Muḥammad the Prophet was therefore the *nāṭiq*, the outwardly manifest leader; while 'Alī b. Abī Ṭālib was the silent one, *ṣāmit*, the permanent Imam, the *waṣī*, who appointed the Prophet to his mission, and who was capable of forgiving his faults. For the Imam is sinless and infallible, *ma'ṣūm*; but not so the Prophet. 'Alī is, therefore, in the estimation of the Ismā'īlī thinkers of far higher rank than the Prophet of Islam.

The nomenclature of the hierarchy in Ismā'īlism shows certain variations; the one commonly received is as follows. (*a*) *Nabī* is the

Prophet who teaches the exoteric doctrine. (*b*) *Waṣī* is higher than Imam he is also called the *ṣāmit*, the Silent One, teaching the esoteric philosophy, and ranking higher than the Prophet. (*c*) Imam is the protector of the Imamate, an eternal institution. He may be either permanent or a mere protector of the true Imam. (*d*) *Ḥujjas of the Night* are special teachers of religion; they always accompany the Imam. (*e*) *Ḥujjas of the Day* teach the external doctrine in the twelve *jazīras* (divisions) of the world. (*f*) *Dāʿī al-balāgh* is the chief active missionary of the faith. (*g*) *Dāʿī al-muṭlaq* is the chief representative of the previous official. Sometimes there is a chief among the missionaries, and he is called *dāʿī al-duʿāt*. In the two chief Mustaʿlian communities, the Dāʾūdīs and Sulaymānīs, there is no one who claims to be of higher rank than the *muṭlaq*, although from time to time, higher rank has been claimed in smaller sects by petty officiants. (*h*) *Maʾdhūn* is the assistant of the *dāʿī* and is permitted to take initiates into the fold. (*i*) *Mukāsir* is the second assistant, who argues with the uninitiated and "breaks" the arguments of the opponents and refutes them.

There is no certainty about the founder of the movement known as Ismāʿīlism; probably it was an active group rather than a single individual. Zāhid ʿAlī in common with the generality of authors agrees that Maymūn al-Qaddāḥ was the *ḥujja* of Imam Muḥammad al-Mastūr (seventh Imam), and his son ʿAbdallāh b. Maymūn was the *ḥujja* of Imam ʿAbdallāh al-Mastūr (eighth Imam). These two, according to the Ismāʿīlī authorities themselves, were among the earliest of those who organized the Ismāʿīlī mission.[1]

The Eastern form of the faith is slightly different and even more radical, although there is a great deal in common. The books of the Eastern school have not come down to us in anything like the profusion and accuracy that is to be found in the Western branch; but much can be learnt from a text such as the *Kalām-i Pīr*, edited and translated from the Persian by W. Ivanow.

The Imam is the spiritual guide of the world. His absence from the world even for a moment would destroy it. And he who does not know the Imam of the time, dies the death of the Days of Ignorance, that is the death of an unbeliever. The Prophet, on the other hand, comes only from time to time. He is the proof of God's existence in the world, but the Imam, in a sense, partakes of the Divine Essence. The Imam is the hypostasis of the primal volition, called *amr*, *kalima* or logos. This

[1] Zāhid ʿAlī, *Tārīkh*, p. 502.

essence exists in the Imam and is transferred from father to son by *naṣṣ* (valid appointment). Among the Khojas of India, the *ḥāẓar imām* is a direct descendant of 'Alī, who is to be regarded as the Tenth *avatār* (incarnation) of the Hindu deity Vishnu.[1] All Imams are sinless, *ma'ṣūm*, and therefore infallible.

Ismā'īlīs generally deny belief in the theory of incarnation, *ḥulūl* or *tanāsukh*. It is difficult to define terms where the language is difficult of comprehension, and where sometimes the authorities differ, but *ḥulūl* is very nearly epiphany and *tanāsukh* refers to the transmigration of souls. None of these doctrines is accepted by the two forms of Ismā'īlism existing in India. What is transferred from father to son by an Imam is the Light of the Imamate (*nūr-i imāmat*).

It is not easy to determine the present distribution and the numerical extent of the two Ismā'īlī communities. A feature common to the missionaries of both groups is the tendency to inflate figures.

The Western Ismā'īlīs, disregarding microscopic groups, are represented by the Bohoras in India. They are divided into two groups, the larger being the Dā'ūdī, and the smaller the Sulaymānī. They are to be found chiefly in Western India, with a sprinkling in East Africa. The Sulaymānīs claim adherents in the Yemen as well, where their *dā'ī* resides. Their total figures are rightly estimated at about 200,000.

The Eastern Ismā'īlīs are represented by the Khojas in India. Smaller groups of whom we know very little are the Imāmshāhīs, Satpanthīs, and the followers of Pīr Mashā'ikh. A few scattered communities are also to be found in Syria, Khurasan, Kirmān, Badakhshan, Chitral, Hunza and Gilgit. An approximate total is 200,000.[2]

The main question in Ismā'īlism is historical: who was the founder of Ismā'īlism? How did he and his followers act? And what in point of fact were they able to achieve? When we begin the investigation, we are faced not so much with fact and history as with legend and myth; conjecture and hypothesis; the passions and prejudices of historians; the tales of the Old Man of the Mountain, of the daggers of the Assassins, and of the secret Path of Reality. And we are forcibly reminded of the words of Bernard Lewis: "the history of the Arabs has been written in Europe chiefly by historians who knew no Arabic,

[1] *Law in the Middle East*, ed. Majid Khadduri and H. J. Liebesny (Washington, D.C., 1955), vol. 1, p. 118.

[2] *Ency. of Islam*, Suppl. p. 99, and Asaf A. A. Fyzee, "Bohoras", *Ency. of Islam* (2nd ed.), vol. 1, p. 1254.

or by Arabists who knew no history".[1] And the history of the Ismā'īlīs has been written by historians who had no access to Ismā'īlī authorities, or by Ismā'īlīs who considered *taqiyya* (dissimulation) a religious duty. It is therefore not surprising that the majority of students should give up the quest as hopeless, after struggling with the subject for some time.

Ismā'īlism was a sect of the Shī'ites which developed an extreme doctrine of the Imamate; it placed 'Alī far above the Prophet; proposed an interpretation of the Qur'ān so radical and imaginative as to remove it basically from the received forms of Islam, and injected a curious mixture of Pythagorean, Plotinian, Manichaean and Indian elements in the blood-stream of Islamic theology.

There is no certainty about its founder; probably it was an energetic group rather than an individual. The majority of historians point to Maymūn al-Qaddāḥ and his son 'Abdallāh, but this is by no means certain, for Ivanow describes this as a myth, "A lie, however ridiculously absurd it may be, by constant repetition becomes the unassailable truth".[2] Zāhid 'Alī and Bernard Lewis hold the contrary view, and the perplexed student can leave it as an unsolved mystery, with the probabilities in favour of the majority.

Originally a conspiracy aimed at destroying the power of the Baghdad caliphate, the Ismā'īlīs became a powerful schism, producing some colourful leaders, holding several impregnable fortresses and claiming the allegiance of a group of energetic schismatics. Eventually Ismā'īlism has become practically extinct by endless branching, having a few survivors left in India, the Bohoras and the Khojas, and stragglers in Syria, the Yemen, Chitral, East Africa and elsewhere. Ismā'īlism, in its numerical strength and spiritual appeal, is neither an intellectual substitute for, nor a serious rival of, orthodox Islam; and it may well be doubted whether there is any future for the sectarians except gradual absorption into the broad highway of Islam in its modern environment.

[1] "Islam" in *Orientalism and History*, ed. Denis Sinor (Cambridge, 1954), p. 16.
[2] Preface, *Ibn al-Qaddāḥ* (Bombay, 1957).

CHAPTER 18

THE DRUZES

The number of Druzes in the Middle East is estimated at approximately 300,000. About half of them live in Syria, where the Ḥawrān mountain area has a Druze majority (88 per cent of the population) and is therefore known as Jabal Druze. The second largest concentration is in Lebanon.[1] Ten per cent live in the state of Israel, viz. in Galilee and on Mt Carmel, and 3 per cent in the kingdom of Jordan. Though fewer in number than other communities in the region akin to them in religious respects, viz. the Mutawālī and Nuṣayrī-ʿAlawī, the Druzes have come in for particular attention both from scholars and travellers and from European politicians.

It is difficult from the first to define the position of the Druzes among the peoples and communities of the present-day Middle East. Are they a nation, in the ethnic sense, professing *tawḥīd* (pure monotheism), as they call their religion? Or are they a religious community, *muwaḥḥidūn* (monotheists), as they call themselves, like the Mutawālī in Syria or the Maronites in Lebanon? Above all, they regard themselves as a secret sect, Ḥākimiyya, believers in the divinity of al-Ḥākim bi-amrihi, the ruler by his command (they do not call him al-Ḥākim bi-amri 'llāh). They are *ahl al-maʿrūf*, the people who submit to the will of Allāh; they believe in predestination—everything is preordained, man can change nothing and must accept everything humbly. As members of a secret sect, the Druzes are liable for one another; they must all help one another, especially against strangers, although only part of them—the *ʿuqqāl* or sages—know the principles of their religion and only very few know all the secrets.

The special character of the Druze community is discussed in the following under two headings: the Druze religion; and the history, structure and organization of Druze society.

[1] The estimated figure for Syria is 3–3·1% Druzes in a total population of 4·8–5 million, i.e. 144,000–155,000, including about 10,000 in the Aleppo District. In Lebanon, the estimate is 6·3% of a total population of 1·75 million, i.e. 110,000 (there has been no census in Lebanon for decades past). No reliable figures are available for Druzes throughout the world.

THE DRUZE RELIGION

Our information as to the origin of the religion asserting the divinity of al-Ḥākim is based on brief accounts by the founders of the community and on non-Druze authors. These two kinds of sources are utterly different in approach, and neither of them, evidently, is objective, although it should be noted that the Druze sources do not deny certain odd features of the inception of the community, but try to explain them in their own way. Another significant fact is that contemporary Jewish sources present al-Ḥākim in a very favourable light, especially as regards the first half of his reign. Muslim and Christian testimony on historical events should be treated with reserve, and their suggestions about Druze theology should certainly be received with caution. In the latter respect, the most authentic source is the Druze *Kitāb al-ḥikma*, the Book or Books of Wisdom (i.e. knowledge of God), which is shown to no non-Druze, but which has nevertheless found its way into European libraries. Already at the end of the eighteenth century, European scholars knew about 120 Druze manuscripts dealing with the community's religion. Some of them were written by, or are attributed to, al-Ḥākim, and most of them were written by his earliest disciples. Other writings acquired by Europeans include some whose authors are not known and some whose sanctity is not fully recognized.[1]

A special position within this literature is held by a popular tract on the Druze religion in the form of questions and answers—a kind of catechism, and as such we shall describe it. Its importance lies in the fact that its anonymous author tries to encompass most aspects of religious life: beliefs; ethics; commandments of a specifically religious character; relations between members of the community; attitude towards other religions and their adherents. He mentions several sacred writings on which he relies, viz. *Risālat al-taḥdhīr wa 'l-tanbīh* ("The Epistle of Warning and Reproof") by Ḥamza, in which the latter reveals the magnitude of his mission and the penalties awaiting unbelievers; *Risālat al-iʿdhār wa 'l-indhār*, similar in title and contents to the aforementioned; *Risālat al-nisā'* (Epistle to Women); *Kitāb al-mīthāq* (Book of the Covenant), according to which the believer

[1] S. de Sacy, *Exposé de la Religion des Druzes*, vol. 1, Introduction (Paris, 1838), pp. 454–517; M. Sprengling, "The Berlin Druze Lexicon", *Am. Journ. Sem. Lang. Lit.* vol. LVI (1939), pp. 388–414; C. Brockelmann, *GAL*, Suppl. 1, pp. 716–18.

accepts the authority of "the ruler of the period"; *Risālat al-riḍā wa al-taslīm* (The Tract of Resignation and Surrender) by Ḥamza; *al-Sijill 'l-mu'allaq*, the proclamation posted up in Cairo mosques after al-Ḥākim's disappearance; *Ḥaqā'iq al-mahdhal*, on the true significance of strange deeds done in al-Ḥākim's presence.

The last-mentioned tract, sometimes called *al-Ta'līm* (Instruction), is very widespread (in manuscript), and although different versions exist, it must be regarded as reflecting the views accepted by the Druze community.[1]

The Druze community originated in the reign of Manṣūr Abū 'Alī, known by his caliphal surname al-Ḥākim bi-amri 'llāh (the ruler by Allāh's command), the sixth caliph (996–1021) of the Ismā'īlī Fāṭimid dynasty. That dynasty emerged in the early tenth century (909) in North Africa and, after conquering Egypt (969), extended its rule over Palestine, Syria and wide areas of the Arabian peninsula.

The catechism mentions the years 1009–21 (400–411 A.H.) as decisive for the development of the faith:

Q. When and how did our Master al-Ḥākim appear?

A. In the year 400 of the Muslim *hijra*.

Q. And how did he appear and proclaim himself to be of Muḥammad's stock, concealing his divine nature, and why did he conceal it?

A. Those who believed in him were few, and those ready to defend him were not numerous.

Q. When did he appear and reveal his divine nature?

A. In the eighth year after the year 400.

Q. For how many years was his divine nature manifest?

A. During the whole of the eighth year (after 400 A.H.); and it was hidden in the ninth year, for that was a time of concealment; and he appeared in the tenth year, and in the eleventh year he disappeared, and he will not appear again until Judgment Day.[2]

Various sources permit us to conclude why 1009–10 (400 A.H.) was fixed as the year of al-Ḥākim's first appearance. That year saw decisive events in the history of his reign. It was then that he issued the decree abolishing taxes and charitable gifts based on the Qur'ān or on Ismā'īlī tradition, forbade the pilgrimage to Mecca, abrogated Ismā'īlī institu-

[1] De Sacy, *Exposé*, vol. I, p. 516: first published in Europe by J. G. C. Adler, "Monumentum Cuficum Druzorum", in *Museum Cuficum Borgianum* (Rome, 1782); and a year later in Eichhorn's *Repertorium für morgenländische und biblische Literatur*, vol. XII (1783). An English translation in *PEF*, Quart. Statem. (1886), pp. 35–43. I am using a MS. in the National and University Library in Jerusalem HU Ar 8° 185.

[2] *Catechism*, p. 2.

tions and customs and published the proclamation prohibiting the drinking of wine; in the same year, the harassment of the Christians, which had begun several years previously, was intensified, and the Church of the Sepulchre in Jerusalem was burnt down. According to Christian and Muslim sources, these persecutions included also the Jews, but, as already hinted above, part of these reports should be treated with caution. An "Egyptian scroll" of 1012 mentions al-Ḥākim as the protector of the Jews; the latter are said to have assembled in the Great Synagogue of Fusṭāṭ to thank God that the caliph had saved them from a rioting mob. Another version of the same scroll says:

> And it was in the days of the king called "the Ruler by Divine Command", who reigned over the land of Egypt and governed the corners of the earth, west, east, north and south; and his kingdom was exalted, powerful and firmly established, and his throne was higher than that of his ancestors. He was thirteen years old on becoming king, and he administered the whole realm generously and wisely, and he had no need of a deputy or adviser. Several plotters plotted against him, and several rebels rebelled against him, and God caused them to be trodden under his feet, for he loved justice and hated wickedness, and he appointed judges in the land to try cases justly and judge truly.

This favourable appraisal is confirmed by the letters of two heads of *yeshivot*, R. Yeshaya Gaon, head of the Palestinian Yeshiva, and R. Elḥanan b. Shemarya of Fusṭāṭ, who mention that al-Ḥākim subsidized their *yeshivot*.[1]

These sources carry weight as the objective testimony of a group which was not a party to the religious dispute between the various Muslim trends and the Druze, or to the communal tension between Muslims and Christians, attributable to the fact that the latter held positions of political and fiscal importance in the Fāṭimid administration. Of particular interest is the agreement between the reference to al-Ḥākim's enemies in the "Egyptian scroll" and the explanation of the concealment of his divinity in 1009–10, in the catechism, by the paucity of his adherents and their inability to protect him.

Jewish sources indeed show that after 1012 the persecution included the Jews also; synagogues were burnt, and there were instances of forced conversion to Islam. The tribulations ceased only in the last years of al-Ḥākim, who permitted the rebuilding of the places of

[1] J. Mann, *The Jews in Egypt and in Palestine under the Fatimids* (London, 1920–2); vol. II, pp. 35–6; 40, l. 31; 70, ll. 14–15.

worship; at the same time, the forced converts were allowed to return to their former religion. This was in the years 1017–20 (408–11 A.H.), i.e. at the time when the caliph openly appeared as the incarnation of the deity. The two events were undoubtedly interrelated.

Propaganda for the new religion began even before 1017. Ḥamza ibn 'Alī al-Zūzanī (i.e. of Zūzan in Persia) seems to have been the first disciple and missionary of al-Ḥākim, and it was he who persuaded the Shī'ite missionary (*dā'ī*) Muḥammad al-Darazī, called Neshtegīn (a Turkish word meaning the son of a Turk and a non-Turkish woman), to recognize al-Ḥākim's divinity and assume the task of spreading the new faith. In 1017 these two publicly proclaimed al-Ḥākim's divinity. That year is regarded as the first of the Druze Era (the year 1 of Ḥamza). The two missionaries eagerly competed for al-Ḥākim's favour. Muḥammad al-Darazī is said to have preached the new faith in Wādī al-Taym in the Lebanese plain, which was inhabited by extremist Shī'ite sects that might well be expected to provide neophytes for al-Ḥākim's religion. He is reported to have been killed shortly afterwards in a quarrel with some Turks. According to another version, he never left Cairo, where the proclamation of al-Ḥākim's divinity had aroused great anger, and was murdered there by a Turk, perhaps at the instigation of Ḥamza ibn 'Alī. Although Muḥammad al-Darazī gave the new religion its name, "Druze", he is hardly mentioned in its writings. His opponents reproached him for permitting the drinking of wine and indulging in sexual debauchery and other vices. A tract written in the year 2 of Ḥamza (1018) says that Neshtegīn al-Darazī and his disciple al-Bardha'ī rebelled against Ḥamza, so that al-Ḥākim was forced to hide him for a time.

At the beginning of 1021 al-Ḥākim disappeared, and it is believed that he was murdered. A rumour spread among his followers that he was hiding and would appear again in the fulness of time (after a thousand years).

The proclamation *al-Sijill al-mu'allaq*, which turned up at Muslim sanctuaries (*mashāhid*) after al-Ḥākim's disappearance, contained the warning: "Let everyone of you beware of trying to locate the Commander of the Faithful, and do not disclose any information concerning him."[1] There are those who attribute that proclamation to Ḥamza and regard this warning as warranting the suspicion that he was implicated in the death of his master. On the other hand, de Sacy

[1] De Sacy, *Chrestomathie arabe*, vol. II, pp. 77–8.

thinks that al-Ḥākim lived for several more years in hiding, exchanging letters with Muqtanā Bahā' al-Dīn ("the Splendour of Religion"), one of his most famous disciples.[1]

Al-Darazī's death (1019) left Ḥamza as the principal architect of the Ḥākimiyya, assisted by Ismā'īl b. Muḥammad al-Tamīmī, Muḥammad b. al-Wahb, Salāma b. 'Abd al-Wahhāb al-Samūrī and 'Alī b. Aḥmad, surnamed al-Muqtanā Bahā' al-Dīn. All these played important parts in the theological development of the Druze religion. Bahā' al-Dīn is known as the author of a series of basic sacred writings, the latest of which date from the year 26 of Ḥamza (1041). He concludes the formative period of the *tawḥīd*.[2]

Druze religious beliefs developed from the concepts of the Ismā'īlī sect. Ismā'īlī theology propounds a kind of historical counterpart of the Neoplatonic doctrine of cosmic emanations, establishing a system of periodical manifestations in which *'aql al-kull*, universal intelligence, reveals itself. The series begins with Adam, who is followed by Noah, Abraham, Moses, Jesus and Muḥammad; it is concluded by Muḥammad b. Ismā'īl, the seventh Shī'ite Imam. Each time, the divine spirit reveals itself more completely. As Ismā'īlism split up into extremist sects, its link with Islam became purely formal; the *sharī'a* was interpreted allegorically, and the binding character of its commands and prohibitions was denied. A system based on initiation and successive stages of mystical insight was very cleverly used in propagating the Ismā'īlī faith.

Among the Ismā'īlī sects, the adherents of the Ḥākimiyya are the most extreme, those who have moved furthest from the common origin. Their first article of faith is that al-Ḥākim was the last incarnation of the deity; he cannot have died, and his followers, therefore, are awaiting his return (*raj'a*). He was preceded by nine other incarnations of the deity. Such an incarnation is called *maqām* (place). Ḥamza explained that the bush out of which God called to Moses (Exod. iii. 4) was a *maqām*. Another incarnation is called *mukārī*, the Driver (of a 1,000 camels).[3]

From the light of the Creator (*al-bārī*) emanates Universal Intelligence (*'aql*), which contains all the elements of Creation. From Universal Intelligence emanates the Universal Soul (*al-nafs*), from which, in turn, emanates the Word (*al-kalima*). The Right Wing (*al-janāḥ al-ayman*),

[1] De Sacy, *Exposé*, vol. II, p. 364.

[2] On the dating of his writings, see de Sacy, *Exposé*, vol. I, Introd., pp. 496, 515.

[3] De Sacy, *Exposé*, vol. I, p. 18; N. Bouron, *Les Druzes*, p. 274. For an explanation of the term *mukārī*, see p. 340.

called also the Precedent (*al-sābiq*), is the fourth emanation, and the Left Wing (*al-janāḥ al-aysar*), called also the Successor (*al-tāliʿ*), the fifth. These five highest emanations are called *al-ḥudūd*. *Ḥudūd* (sing. *ḥadd*) means "boundaries", and in Qur'ānic metaphorical language, "laws"; in the terminology of the Druze sacred writings, *ḥudūd* are the five highest "ministers" in which the five emanations and all the tenets and precepts of the *tawḥīd* were incarnated.

The need for the emanation of *nafs* arose after *ḍudd* "darkness", i.e. the Adversary, who fights *ʿaql*, had split off from the latter. *Nafs* emanated from *ʿaql* as its female partner and helper. *Nafs*, in turn, has an adversary called *asās* "basis" and therefore requires the assistance of *kalima*, in relation to which it is the male element. In al-Ḥākim's time, the *ḥudūd* were represented by his five highest-ranking disciples, from Ḥamza to Bahā' al-Dīn (in the order in which they are mentioned on p. 335). The four ministers below Ḥamza are *ḥaram*, "women", in relation to him.[1]

As stated before, Ḥamza is the highest of al-Ḥākim bi-amrihi's ministers. He has several titles, which the people of the *tawḥīd* are supposed to know: *al-sirāṭ al-mustaqīm* (the straight road); *qā'im al-zamān* or *imām al-zamān* (the ruler or leader of the epoch); *qā'im al-ḥaqq* (the ruler of truth); *nuqṭat al-baykār* (the point of the compass (or the compasses)), i.e. the central, immovable point; *al-sābiq* (the precedent), i.e. the sublime prophet, the prime cause.

There were earlier incarnations of the *ḥudūd* similar to the earlier incarnations of the Deity. Before Ḥamza, Universal Intelligence was incarnated in Imams, leaders of their respective generations, such as Shuʿayb (Jethro) in the days of Moses; the Messiah of True Justice in the days of Jesus; and Salmān al-Fārisī in the days of Muḥammad, one of whose most famous companions he was. Adam, Noah, Abraham, Moses, Jesus, Muḥammad and Saʿīd were merely prophets whom "Our Master" (i.e. God—al-Ḥākim) removed from the *tawḥīd* religion, similar to the first of them, Adam the rebel, whom Allāh drove from Paradise. Knowledge of the five *ḥudūd* is obligatory on the Druze monotheist (*muwaḥḥid*).[2]

[1] De Sacy, *Exposé*, vol. II, pp. 8 ff. On the *ḥaram al-imām*, the women of the leader, see *Catechism*, p. 12; De Sacy, *Exposé*, vol. I, p. 187 n. 1; Sprengling, "The Berlin Druze Lexicon", pp. 403–4. The resemblance to terms used in the Kabbala for the mystery of sex is only formal; G. Scholem, *Major Trends in Jewish Mysticism* (New York, 1941), pp. 226–8.

[2] *Catechism*, pp. 7, 11. According to our source (comp. de Sacy, *Exposé*, vol. I, p. 36 n. 1) Saʿīd, and not, as stated by P. K. Hitti (*The Origin of the Druze* (New York, 1928), p. 37), Muḥammad b. Ismāʿīl, is the seventh prophet.

Below the ministers are three ranks of emissaries, one below another. As the Druze sacred writings put it: a rank is a female element in relation to the next higher and a male element in relation to the next lower.

The three ranks are: (1) *dā'ī* (missionary); (2) *ma'dhūn* (authorized agent); (3) *mukāsir* (one who breaks through, opens the way) or *naqīb* (one in charge of a district).[1]

The function of all these is to spread the knowledge of the *tawḥīd* among the believers. The names are borrowed from the *bāṭinī* Shī'a, who developed very efficient methods for the propagation of their teachings.

The duty of spreading the faith applies only within the community itself. It expressly encompasses women and the *juhhāl* (the ignorant), i.e. that great majority of members who do not belong to the *'uqqāl*, the religious scholars: "Our Master ordered them (women) to join the covenant and they accepted the message of al-Ḥākim, as is stated in the 'Epistle to Women' and the 'Epistle to Daughters'. The *juhhāl* not introduced to the mysteries of the religion will be condemned to eternal humiliation on Judgment Day."[2]

This strict exclusivity, a parallel to which we find with the Yazīdīs, is based on the belief—discussed on p. 335—that all souls were created from the light of Universal Intelligence. The number of all the souls of the believers, i.e. the Druzes, and of the unbelievers, i.e. the adherents of the other religions, is limited and fixed since the Creation. There was a short time, during the appearance of al-Ḥākim, when the *da'wa* was issued, i.e. the call to accept the Ḥākimiyya consciously and to penetrate its mysteries through the missionaries. But since then, it has been forbidden to reveal the *tawḥīd* to non-Druzes.

The reason why Ḥamza ordered the *ḥikma*, the Druze religious doctrine, to be kept secret is that it is considered an instrument of salvation and that the Druzes do not wish strangers to attain salvation. The *da'wa* ceased, the gate was closed, and since then believer remains believer and unbeliever remains unbeliever. The believer who embraces another religion will after death revert to his former faith, and so will the stranger who, by chance, becomes acquainted with al-Ḥākim's religion and adopts it.[3]

The catechism describes the ceremony by which a Druze is initiated

[1] De Sacy, *Exposé*, vol. II, pp. 18–19, 384 ff., 498.

[2] *Catechism*, pp. 5, 7.

[3] *Catechism*, pp. 14, 15. For an explanation of the term *da'wa* see de Sacy, *Exposé*, vol. II, p. 498 n. 1.

into the mysteries of the Ḥākimiyya. The novice signs the *mīthāq walī al-zamān*, the covenant with the leader of the generation, by which he assumes the obligations of a believer. Since everything connected with the Druze religion is shrouded in secrecy, and in times of persecution it is permitted to conceal one's affiliation to it (see below), there are special signs enabling members of the community to recognize one another.[1]

The first *dā'ī* was Bahā' Allāh, whose function was that of link between the first four emanations (called also *ḥujja*), to which he did not belong, and the lower ranks, of which he was in charge. These "inferior ministers", too, are incarnations of divine emanations. From the light of the Left Wing, the Successor (Bahā' Allāh), all corporeal forms in the world emanated.

The Druze concept of the deity combines almost all notions current at the time of its emergence. Besides Jewish and Christian beliefs, we find Gnostic, Neo-Platonist and Persian elements, and all this under the flag of strict monotheism.

Extreme Ismā'īlī doctrine interprets the practical commandments of the Qur'ān allegorically. Ḥamza went one step further. Denying Muḥammad's mission, he virtually abolished the first of the five fundamentals of Islam (*arkān*); and he also did away with the four others: prayer, charity, the fast of Ramaḍān and the pilgrimage to Mecca.

Instead of these five duties (to which may be added another two: the Holy War (*jihād*) and obedience to the authorities), Ḥamza proclaimed *al-shurūṭ al-sab'a*, the seven duties incumbent on the Druzes: (1) recognition of al-Ḥākim and strict adherence to monotheism; (2) negation of all non-Druze tenets; (3) rejection of Satan and unbelief; (4) acceptance of God's acts; (5) submission to God for good or ill; (6) truthfulness; (7) mutual help and solidarity between fellow Druzes.[2]

Recognition of al-Ḥākim includes also the belief in Ḥamza and the four ministers below him. The duty of truthfulness, in matters of religion, applies only to the relations of Druzes with each other. Towards non-Druzes strict secrecy is enjoined, and in times of mortal danger due to religious persecution it is even permitted to renege the faith outwardly (*taqiyya*, *kitmān*).

The duty of *taqiyya* is explained in the catechism as follows: "Our Master commanded us to hide under the wings of the majority religion.

[1] For the text of the *mīthāq* see de Sacy, *Chrestomathie*, vol. II, p. 83; *Catechism*, pp. 18–19: English translation *PEF*, QS (London, 1886), pp. 37–8; Hitti, *Origin*, pp. 58 f.

[2] The number and order of the duties vary in the different texts. Cf. de Sacy, *Exposé*, vol. II, pp. 647–51.

When among Christians, we should act like Christians, when among Muslims we should act like Muslims, and so on. For our Master, al-Ḥākim bi-amrihi, said: 'If any community prevails over you, follow its lead (ostensibly), and keep me in your hearts.'"

The question of how such behaviour fits in with the written promise to worship no one but the Master is answered by pointing out that it is outward behaviour (*ẓāhiran*), not inward behaviour (*bāṭinan*), like a garment a person puts on, which does not alter his body.[1]

The Druzes believe in *tanāsukh*, "metempsychosis", in connexion with the doctrine that the number of souls in the universe was fixed for ever at the time of the Creation. To the question when the souls were created, the answer is: after Intelligence, i.e. al-Ḥamza b. 'Alī, was created; after that the souls, whose number is fixed, never more, never less at any time, were created from his light. Accordingly, it is impossible that a person should join or leave the Druze community. Whenever a Druze dies, another Druze is born, i.e. the soul of the former enters the body of the latter.

Ḥamza sharply attacked the Nuṣayrī doctrine that a sinful soul may enter the body of a dog, monkey or pig. However, the catechism states that the adherents of 'Alī b. Abī Ṭālib will appear as donkeys on Judgment Day.[2]

Druze descriptions of the Last Judgment evoke apocalyptic visions of celestial and terrestrial signs which announce the appearance of al-Ḥākim and Judgment Day itself. Here is a very short version of this eschatology:

> The day on which he (al-Ḥākim) will appear in human shape (*nāsūt*) and judge the world sternly with the sword is not known. It will be announced by certain signs: Kings will act strangely, and the Christians will overpower Islam. After all the communities have been judged and have perished, they will be born again by way of metempsychosis, and al-Ḥākim will thereupon judge them a second time. There will then be four groups: Christians, Jews, Muslims and *muwaḥḥidūn*. The Christians will be divided into Nuṣayrī and Mutāwila (*sic*!). The *muwaḥḥidūn* will include also apostates, i.e. those who have been instructed in the religion of our Master, blessed be He (and left it). The righteous *muwaḥḥidūn* will obtain the power and the kingdom, property, gold and silver. They will be emirs, pashas and sultans.[3]

[1] *Catechism*, p. 20; *PEF*, p. 38. Cf. also *taḳīya* in *Shorter Ency. of Islam*; Hitti, *Origin*, pp. 46–8.

[2] *Catechism*, pp. 5, 9, 22; *PEF*, pp. 39–40. Sprengling, "The Berlin Druze Lexicon".

[3] *Catechism*, pp. 2–3; *PEF*, *loc. cit.*; cf. also Sprengling, pp. 406–7. We may mention a belief current among the Druzes that al-Ḥākim will reappear a thousand (*hijrī*) years after his first appearance, i.e. in the year 1987.

A harsh judgment awaits the Mutāwila (the adherents of 'Alī), the Muslims and the Christians. They will be punished for believing in Jesus, who changed the words of the just Messiah (i.e. Universal Intelligence) and of the four evangelists (who are the four ministers below Universal Intelligence). The latter had meant al-Ḥākim, but Jesus had represented their writings as referring to himself.

Comparatively lighter is the punishment of the Jews. They will be bath-house attendants (according to another version, book-keepers), go naked and will only be given food in return for their labours. The catechism deems it necessary to explain this by stating "that our prophet and ruler appeared at Mount Sinai in the shape of a driver (*mukārī*) of a thousand camels". He was called a Jew, one of the believers of the nation that stems from Moses, that is to say, the Jews. And as the Jews were vouchsafed to witness his appearance, he was not severe with them, as he was with those who came after them.[1]

This attitude towards other nations and their religions was undoubtedly influenced not a little by actual historical relationships. The Druzes suffered at the hands of the Muslims and (from the Crusades onwards) the Christians, while relations with the Jews were satisfactory—as attested by Benjamin of Tudela (see below)—because the latter were in no position to harm them.[2]

THE HISTORY AND STRUCTURE OF DRUZE SOCIETY

The tenets of the Druze sect found ready acceptance among the ethnically and religiously variegated population inhabiting the slopes and valleys of the Lebanon. The first testimony on the Druzes in non-Arab literature occurs in the Hebrew book of travels by Benjamin of Tudela, who toured Syria about 1167:

> Ten miles therefrom (Sidon) a people dwell who are at war with the men of Sidon; they are called Druzes, and are pagans of a lawless character. They inhabit the mountains and the clefts of the rocks; they have no king or ruler, but dwell independent in these high places, and their border extends to Mount Hermon, which is three days' journey. They are steeped in vice, brothers marrying their sisters, and fathers their daughters. They have one

[1] *Catechism*, pp. 21–3: The appearance of the *mukārī* at Mount Sinai may conceivably have been influenced by the Bible: Ps. lxviii. 18; Deut. xxx. 2; Judg. v. 4–6.

[2] Very interesting is the advice (in *Catechism*, pp. 19–20; *PEF*, *loc. cit.* p. 38) as to how to talk to people: meekly and with the utmost restraint (literally: with humming and hawing). Talking in this way to a Druze means blessing him, and to an unbeliever, cursing him.

feast-day in the year, when they all collect, both men and women, to eat and drink together, and then they interchange their wives.[1]

Benjamin adds that the Druzes are friendly towards the Jews who come to them as craftsmen and pedlars. Druze traditions tell of Druze rule over Beirut and the Lebanese coast, but these reports are not confirmed by other sources. In Crusader days, the Druzes seem to have inhabited Wādī al-Taym, near Baniyās and Beaufort. At the end of the thirteenth century, we find them in the Ṣafad District. An author who lived at Ṣafad about 1375 repeats Benjamin's accusations against them and concludes: "But their behaviour in commercial dealings is excellent and trustworthy; they do not go back on their pledged word."[2]

The more obscure phase of Druze history ends with the Ottoman conquest. On that occasion, the Amir Fakhr al-Dīn of the House of Ma'n, helped the Sultan Selim, who, in return, confirmed him as Amir of the Druzes. Fakhr al-Dīn's son, Qurqmāz, revolted against the Ottomans, and the revolt was quelled (1583). Nevertheless, a few years later, Fakhr al-Dīn, the son of the rebel, was recognized as *amīr*. The life-story and political methods of this young man make him the prototype of most of the subsequent Druze *amīrs*. From his centre of government, Ba'qlīn, and later Dayr al-Qamar, he began to expand his sphere of influence, and to this end used several means. In 1602, taking advantage of Turkey's preoccupation with a war against Persia, he conquered Ṣafad and certain areas in Transjordan. It was then that he first came into contact with the Grand Duke of Tuscany, who wished to increase his trade with Syria. It was then, too, that the idea of establishing an independent Crusader state in Syria, Palestine and Cyprus was conceived. When this became known to the Sublime Porte, the *wālī* of Damascus was ordered to march against the Amir, who preferred to flee to Italy rather than become involved in a war without prospects of easy victory. Fakhr al-Dīn returned to his country only in 1618, after spending several years at the courts of Italian princes. He

[1] M. N. Adler, *The Itinerary of Benjamin of Tudela* (London, 1907), Hebrew text p. 20, translation p. 18. The accusations of vice are based on ancient Persian marriage customs which survived in Islam; B. Spuler, *Iran in früh-islamischer Zeit* (Wiesbaden, 1952), pp. 199 n. 4, 200, 377–8, 382; N. Pigulevskaja, *Les Villes de l'état iranien* (Paris, 1963), pp. 134, 140–1, 211. According to P. Hitti, *Origins*, pp. 18–23, the earliest followers of al-Ḥākim included not a few Persians; but cf. Sprengling, "The Berlin Druze Lexicon", pp. 391–3.

[2] B. Lewis, "An Arabic Account of the Province of Safad", *BSOAS*, vol. xv (1953), p. 484; on the author, *ibid.* p. 477. Cf. also M. A. F. Mehren, *Cosmographie de Chems-ed-Din Abou Abdallah Mohammed ed-Dimichqui* (St Petersbourg, 1866), p. 211.

then again made use of favourable circumstances to extend the influence of his house, this time as far as Aleppo in the north and al-ʿArīsh in the south. Though in name his son, ʿAlī, was Amir, he, the father, was the actual ruler, and it was he who renewed the alliance with the Grand Duke of Tuscany against the Sublime Porte. The Grand Duke promised to provide the Amir with troops and experts on arms and fortifications in return for cities and harbours which he would obtain after victory. Fakhr al-Dīn reiterated his promise to become a Christian.

In view of the threat to the integrity of the Ottoman Empire, Turkey's land and sea forces were ordered to attack the Druzes and to impose a maritime blockade, so as to prevent outside assistance. Fakhr al-Dīn was routed at Ḥāṣbayyā and executed with his two sons in Constantinople (1635). The House of Maʿn nevertheless continued to rule until 1697. When the Amir Aḥmad died without issue, the amirate passed to a son of his daughter, who had married a member of the aristocratic Shihāb family.[1]

The position of the House of Shihāb grew stronger after the Battle of ʿAyn Dāra (1711), fought between two political factions among the Druzes, viz. the Qays and the Yaman (similar factions existed among the Arabs). The Yaman were beaten, and the power of their leaders, of the Houses of Arslān and ʿAlam al-Dīn, declined. The supporters of the Yaman then began to migrate to Ḥawrān, which became known as Jabal Druze. Eighty-eight per cent of the Jabal's inhabitants today are Druzes.

Outstanding among the Amirs of the House of Shihāb was Bashīr the Second (1788–1840), who rose to power after a struggle with his cousin. They were both Christians in name. Bashīr enjoyed the support of the British. Later he became the faithful ally of Muḥammad ʿAlī and his son Ibrāhīm and gave them valuable assistance during the occupation of Syria (1833–40). His policy was one of the causes of the rift that began to develop between Maronites and Druzes in the Lebanon. Upon the withdrawal of the Egyptians, the Sublime Porte deposed Bashīr. His son, officially a Maronite, who was appointed in his stead, was unseated a year later, and in order to ease the tension between Maronites and Druzes, two *qāʾim maqāms*, one Maronite and one Druze, were appointed.

[1] There exists a rich literature about Fakhr al-Din II, in European and oriental languages, which the present writer has used in the portrayal of this Amir in: I. Ben-Zvi, *Eretz-Israel under Ottoman Rule* (in Hebrew, Jerusalem, 1955), pp. 18–23.

The leadership (*ri'āsa*) now passed to the Junbalāṭ family. These were Kurds who had immigrated to the Lebanon from the Aleppo region and had joined the Druze sect. Meanwhile, tension increased between the Druzes, who enjoyed the support of the Sublime Porte and Britain, and the Christians, who leaned on France. In the war which broke out between the opponents in 1860, about 10,000 Christians fell in battle in the Lebanon (at ʻAyn Dāra, Dayr al-Qamar, Ḥāṣbayyā and Zaḥla) and in Syria (at Damascus). The French landing force which was sent to the Lebanon on the initiative of the European powers restored order without bloodshed. After lengthy negotiations, it was agreed between the Sublime Porte and the European powers (in 1864) that the autonomous administration of the Lebanon should be headed by a Catholic, but not Lebanese, governor.[1]

After the political defeat of the Druzes in the Lebanon, increased importance attached to the Jabal Druze, where the Aṭrash family rose to power. The eight sons of one of its heads, Ismāʻīl, as it were divided the mountain between them. The division of the area of the Fertile Crescent after the First World War into mandated territories gave Ismāʻīl's grandson Sulṭān al-Aṭrash, the hero and leader of the Jabal, wide possibilities for political manoeuvring. The four *shaykhs* of the spiritual leadership and the Shiblī branch of the al-Aṭrash family were prepared to co-operate with France, which in 1921 proclaimed the independence of the Jabal Druze within the framework of the French Mandate over Syria. Sulṭān al-Aṭrash, however, opened negotiations with the Amir of Transjordan, who acted under British inspiration. The first Amir of the Druzes, Salīm (of the Shiblī family) was compelled to resign; a French army officer, Carbillet, who was appointed governor pending the election of a new Amir, fell down on his job; the French High Commissioner in Damascus showed faulty judgment in handling the situation. The result was a revolt of the Druzes, which spread over Syria and part of the Lebanon. At the end of 1925, the rebels infiltrated into Damascus, moved on to Wādī al-Taym and occupied Ḥāṣbayyā. But they were unable to withstand the regular French forces, which shelled Damascus with heavy artillery, employed the air force in the Jabal and captured Suwayda and Ṣalḥad. The revolt began to subside because the Lebanese Druzes and the Mutawālī were deterred from giving assistance by the French successes.

[1] C. H. Churchill, *The Druzes and the Maronites under Turkish Rule*, pp. 178, 219; N. Bouron, *Les Druzes*, pp. 196–211; P. K. Hitti, *History of Syria* (New York, 1951), pp. 691–6.

Sulṭān al-Aṭrash was compelled to flee to Transjordan and was not permitted to return to his country until 1938.[1]

The Druzes in Palestine were almost without historical significance. Their settlements in Upper Galilee were indeed reinforced by immigration in the days of Fakhr al-Dīn, especially after the Battle of ʿAyn Dāra, and according to oral tradition, the number of villages inhabited by Druzes was almost twice as great as today. They were in part voluntarily abandoned and in part destroyed by their Muslim neighbours after the retreat of Ibrāhīm Pasha (1840). The first census taken by the British mandatory government in 1922 counted not more than 7,000 Druzes in Palestine.

The religion and history of the sect, as described above, have shaped Druze society and given it its peculiar character. One of its salient features is the division into *juhhāl* (sing. *jāhil*), the ignorant, who have not been initiated into the secrets of the religion, and the *ʿuqqāl* (sing. *ʿāqil*), the enlightened, who have been found worthy of knowing its principles after passing various tests. There are several grades of *ʿuqqāl*, and few are those who reach the higher grades after a period of study, meditation, mortification of the flesh and seclusion; they are called *ajāwīd* (sing. *jawwād*, *juwayyid*), i.e. the generous. Every village where Druze live has a *khilwa* (plur. *khilawāt*), a place for seclusion and prayer, usually outside the actual village, well away from its houses. It is an austere hall, without architectural embellishments and without furniture, except small lecterns to lay books on during meditation. Usually on Thursday nights, meetings are held at the *khilwa*, and while public affairs are discussed, even the *juhhāl* may attend, but they have to leave when prayer, study and meditation begin. On the other hand, these latter are participated in by women who have been initiated into the mysteries of the religion.

Though the spiritual leaders of the sect usually did not interfere in political matters, the position of the religious sages—collectively referred to as *mashā'ikh al-dīn* (religious elders)—was a highly respected one, especially in Palestine, where the secular leaders were less conspicuous. The *mashā'ikh al-dīn* were entrusted with the management of the *waqf*, a fact which enhanced their prestige.

The status of the sages found visible expression during rallies at,

[1] N. Bouron, *Les Druzes*, pp. 212–53; N. Nimri, "The Warrior People of Djebel Druze", *Journal of the Middle East Society*, vol. 1 (1946), pp. 58–60.

and pilgrimages to, famous *khilawāt*, where high-ranking shaykhs used to retire for prayer, mortification of the flesh and also for taking decisions. The *khilawāt* at Qanawāt near Suwayda (Jabal Druze), Bayyaḍā (near Ḥāṣbayyā) and Nabī Shu'ayb (near Khaṭṭīn in Israel) were erected over or near the graves of illustrious religious personalities. Qanawāt is the seat of the highest ranking *shaykh* in the Jabal Druze, of the al-Hajarī family, who has three colleagues in the spiritual leadership, belonging, respectively to the Jarbū', Ḥināwī and Abū Fakhr families (the al-Hajarī, Jarbū' and Ḥināwī hail from the Suwayda region). As we have already seen, the four *shaykhs* took a decidedly pro-French stand in 1921. In Lebanon, the spiritual leadership consists of two *shaykhs* who belong to the Ḥammāda and Ṭālib families, so as to satisfy the aspirations of the Shaqrāwiyya and Ṣamadiyya factions. In Palestine (and also now in Israel) the spiritual leadership consisted of members of the Ṭarīf, Khayr and Ma'addī families. Widely renowned is the pilgrimage to the traditional grave of Jethro (the Shu'ayb of the Qur'ān) between 23 and 25 April, which used to be attended by Druzes from Lebanon and Syria. The prayers and devotional exercises of the religious shaykhs on this occasion are followed by a mass pilgrimage and a great popular "fantasia".

The theocratic trend was counterbalanced by the political aspirations of certain members of the great families. These people were known as *mashā'ikh al-zamān*, i.e. temporal shaykhs. In regard to religion, they belonged to the *juhhāl* class (some of the Amirs were even Christian in name). We may describe them as feudal barons because of the large estates they possessed. Since until quite recently almost all the Druze lived in rural areas, it is easy to imagine how great the influence of the "temporal shaykhs" was in every sphere. Political activity provided influential and capable *juhhāl* with an outlet for their personal ambitions —and they did not come into conflict with the religious leaders, who belonged to the same families.

A third formative element in Druze society is the respected position of the women, in addition to their religious equality. Marriage is permitted only within the community, and as strict monogamy prevails, there is no room for all those features that weakened Muslim and even Oriental Christian society. Divorce is indeed possible, but a divorced woman can under no circumstances remarry her former husband—unlike Jewish law, which forbids this only if she has meanwhile been married to another man, and unlike Muslim law, which permits this only in the very same case. This finality is a deterrent against hasty divorces, which usually turn out to the detriment of the wife.

Religious law ordains sexual modesty and abstinence from wine and smoking, and these precepts are particularly strictly observed by women and *'uqqāl*. Any charges of debauchery and incest must be regarded as slander originating from hostile sources—a very common weapon used against religious minorities.

During the last generation, there have been increasing signs of profound changes in Druze society. The feudal families have been compelled to concede positions in communal life to wider strata. In Lebanon, besides Kamāl Junbalāṭ (member of Parliament) and Majīd Arslān (minister of Defence in 1964), we find new men such as Muḥammad 'Ali Nāṣir al-Dīn, editor of the Druze newspaper, *al-Ḍuḥā* (The Morning), which is published in Beirut, Amīn Abū Ismā'īl, Director of the Institute of Research on the Druze, and others.

The changes in Syria were largely determined by political trends in that country. The Ṭurshān faction (supporters of the al-Aṭrash family), which advocates political autonomy for the Druzes, was opposed by younger people organized in the al-Sha'biyya ("populists"), which supports the central government in Damascus and identifies itself with the aims of the Arabs. The conflict between the two trends led to a civil war (1947), in which Sulṭān al-Aṭrash scored a military victory.

On account of the internal struggles, many Druze left the Jabal for Jordan. This resulted in an increase of the number of Druzes in the Zarqā region (between the Jabal and Amman), where some 10,000 are reported to be living now. The Druzes living in Syria proper, viz. in the region bordering on Lebanon and in the Aleppo District, have become fully integrated in the political life of the country, including the recurrent *coups d'état*. Druzes hold top positions in the army (chief of staff), the national guard, the medical corps, the army's legal system, the civil service (radio and television) and, of course, the *Ba'th* (Rebirth) the political party now ruling the country.

In Israel, we note extraordinary demographic changes. Between 1922 and 1965, the number of Druzes increased more than fourfold. The rate of increase between 1922 (7,000) and 1949 (13,000) was 85 per cent, and between 1949 and 1965 (30,000) 130 per cent.[1]

[1] I. Ben-Zvi, "Druze Settlements in Israel" (in Hebrew), *Eretz-Israel*, vol. II (1953), p. 206; according to the census of the population of 22 May 1961, 24,282 Druzes were then living in Israel (Central Bureau of Statistics, Jerusalem, Israel, 1964, Publication No. 17, p. xxi). The figure given for December 1965 is based on an expert estimate.

Even more conspicuous is the change in the legal and social position of the Druzes. Under Turkish rule and during the Mandate, the Palestine Druzes were reckoned as part of the Muslim community and were subject to its religious authorities as regards both personal status and the management of *waqf* property (in so far as its existence was known). Great bitterness was caused among the Druzes by the Supreme Muslim Council's demand that the lands of Nabī Shuʿayb, which were most sacred to them, be registered in its name. This meant discrimination against the Palestine Druzes compared with those in Lebanon and Syria and with all the other religious communities in Syria and Palestine. Upon the establishment of the state of Israel (1948), the Israel provisional government recognized the autonomy of the Druze community *de facto*; the Spiritual Leadership, which in 1949 consisted of the Shaykhs Amīn Ṭarīf (of Jūlis), Yūsuf Khayr (of Abū Sinān) and Kamāl Maʿaddī (of Yirkā), at once obtained the management of religious affairs and control of all matters relating to the personal status of the Druzes. The next step (1957) was recognition under the Religious Communities Ordinance inherited from the mandatory government. According to the Druze Religious Courts Law of 1962, which confers on Druze *qāḍīs* the same powers as are wielded by the religious judges of other communities, the spiritual leadership is *ex officio* the religious Court of Appeal. Of the three *qāḍīs* who had already been serving de facto and who were now appointed under the law, only one (Shaykh Salmān Ṭarīf) is a representative of the conservative families, whereas two (Shaykhs Ḥusayn ʿAlyān and Labīb Abū Rukn) represent the younger forces. The material law applied by the Druze religious courts is the Law of Personal Status (of 1948) in force in Lebanon, which in 1953 was recognized as binding on Druze religious courts in Syria as well.

It must be admitted that not all the laws of the state at once commended themselves to the more conservative Druze religious leaders. They were sceptical of the effects of coeducation, which obtains in state schools—even with regard to the youngest age groups. They also anticipated unfavourable reactions in Arab countries to the conscription of young Druzes into the Israel Army. It was only after an internal struggle that the younger elements, led by the Druze members of the Knesset—at times there were two—and by the chairmen of the local councils, succeeded in overcoming that opposition.

The fermenting agents in Druze society are secondary school and university graduates—a novel feature in that society, which had been backward in this respect, too; some of them have been abroad for advanced study or on missions on behalf of their community. They find it extremely difficult to fall in with the ways of thought of the more conservative circles.[1]

Obviously, the Israeli Druzes have not been altogether unresponsive to events and trends in Syria. But it may be said that in their great majority they are sensible of the turn for the better that has occurred in their position as individuals, and as a social group and religious community.

[1] The young generation of the Druzes is very alert to events in both East and West, and especially in their own community in the three countries where Druzes live. This alertness has found its expression in several publications, such as: Maḥmūd Qāsim, *The Druzes and al-Shishaklī* (Arabic) (Nazareth, n.d. (1955?)); S. H. Fallah, *Kefar Sumayya, A Druze Village in Upper Galilee* (Hebrew) (Jerusalem, 1963).

CHAPTER 19

THE AḤMADĪS

The Aḥmadiyya Movement was founded by Mirzā Ghulām Aḥmad who was born about 1835 and died in 1908. The title Mirzā indicates Mughal ancestry, for his family had left Samarqand in the sixteenth century following Bābar and received lands about seventy miles from Lahore, their capital being Islampur, the modern Qadian. During the early years of Sikh rule they were expelled from their property, but some of it was restored by Ranjit Singh to Ghulām Aḥmad's father. Ghulām Aḥmad received a good conventional education, being specially well instructed in Persian and Arabic. In his late teens he was given a post in the office of the Deputy Commissioner at Sialkot, but after four years, during which he had entered into religious discussions with the Church of Scotland missionaries, he returned to Qadian. There he spent most of his time studying his own and other religions, showing great distaste for the legal disputes about property which his father urged him to undertake. He was an ardent Muslim who longed for the regeneration of Islam, and he began to have frequent dreams and visions in which he took a prominent part.

In 1889 he announced that he had received a divine revelation giving him the right to receive homage from others, and this was accepted by a few followers. During subsequent years he claimed to be the Messiah, the expected *mahdī*, the world teacher prophesied in the books of Zoroastrians, Hindus and Buddhists, and an avatar of Krishna. He also claimed to have come in the spirit of Muḥammad.

To prove that he was the Messiah he argued that this, the seventh millennium since Adam, was the millennium of God's reign, so the second Adam must have been born though not yet recognized. God put Adam in a garden eastward, so the second Adam should be born in the East. Adam was born on a Friday and a woman was born with him; Ghulām Aḥmad was born on a Friday and had a twin sister. Another argument was based on the relationship between Moses and Christ who were separated by twelve to fourteen centuries. Muḥammad, as predicted in Deuteronomy xviii. 18, was a prophet like unto Moses, so another prophet must come twelve to fourteen centuries after him, and must be Ghulām Aḥmad. He argued that the second coming of Christ was not to be in person, but in spirit and power. As John the Baptist had come in the spirit and power of Elijah, so he had come in the spirit and power of Jesus. The Qur'ān (LXI. 6) tells that Jesus predicted the coming of a messenger called Aḥmad, which is normally interpreted as referring to Muḥammad, but Ghulām Aḥmad claimed that he was the one foretold.[1] Although his name was Ghulām Aḥmad, his followers commonly called him Aḥmad. He held that his having come in the spirit and power of Jesus was strengthened by their similar circumstances. The Jews were under Roman rule, but Jesus refused to encourage rebellion; India was under British rule, but Ghulām Aḥmad was loyal to the government.[2]

Although he claimed to have come in the spirit and power of Jesus, Ghulām Aḥmad was inclined to ridicule or condemn aspects of the life of Jesus as recorded in the Gospels, which may be excused, for Muslims believe that the Gospels are corrupted. The editor of the *Review of Religions* has said, "The person of Jesus as described in the Gospels has been attacked in Ahmadiyya literature, not that of God's Great Prophet Jesus as described in the Quran".[3] But while this is understandable, one is surprised to find that Ghulām Aḥmad and his followers often base arguments on New Testament passages. A characteristic doctrine of Ghulām Aḥmad related to the death and resurrection of Jesus. The Qur'ān (IV. 156) says that Jesus was not crucified and that the Jews did not kill him. Ghulām Aḥmad, contrary to the normal teaching, held that Jesus was put on the Cross, but he argued that he was taken down before death and cured by an ointment called *marham-i 'Īsā* (ointment of Jesus) within forty days, after which he went to Afghanistan and Kashmir. He had said, "I am not sent but unto the lost sheep of the house of Israel", which clearly meant the lost ten tribes who had settled in those regions. As he had not gone to them before the crucifixion he must have gone afterwards, for he said, "Other sheep I have which are not of this fold...they shall hear my voice". Ghulām Aḥmad found a tomb at Srinagar said to be that of a prophet, Yūs Āsaf, who must have preceded Muḥammad, the final prophet, and he received a revelation that it was the tomb of Jesus who had died there aged 120. He explained Yūs as a corruption of Yasu

[1] H. Walter, *The Aḥmadīya Movement*, pp. 26 ff. But Aḥmadīs insist that they are called after the Prophet Muḥammad's other name Aḥmad. They object to being called Mirzā'īs.

[2] *Ibid.* p. 35.

[3] XXXVI (1937), p. 499.

which, he said, was the original name of Jesus. Āsaf was the Hebrew verb meaning "to gather", so the name represented Jesus who had gone to gather the lost ten tribes.[1]

Ghulām Aḥmad held that he was the expected *mahdī*, but he differed from the prevalent view that the *mahdī* would be a warrior. Islam is somewhat vague about the *mahdī*, but one tradition says there is no *mahdī* but Jesus, and Ghulām Aḥmad accepted this as the true account. He held that his work was spiritual, so he disapproved of any political affiliation. He said, "To believe in me as the promised Messiah and *mahdī* is to disbelieve in the popular doctrine of *jihād*".

Muslims commonly believe that a reformer is sent at the beginning of each century, and Ghulām Aḥmad appeared to some to be the reformer (*mujaddid*) of the fourteenth century.[2] He began to write a voluminous work, *Barāhīn-i Aḥmadiyya* (Aḥmadī proofs), the early parts of which were welcomed by Muslims who read them; but he was later denounced and branded as an infidel (*kāfir*) when he began to make high claims for himself. One such which always rouses hostility is that of being a prophet (*nabī*) and a messenger (*rasūl*), for Islam holds that Muḥammad was God's final prophet. Ghulām Aḥmad explained the use of these titles in a work entitled *Ek ghalaṭī kā izāla* (a misunderstanding removed), saying that no prophet can come after Muḥammad with an independent law, and that no one can attain to prophethood without having merged his whole being into that of Muḥammad. As he had done so completely he was both prophet and messenger without infringing the sense of the expression *khātam al-nabiyyīn* (seal of the prophets).[3]

He argued that his claims were proved by the signs he had performed, and he offered money to anyone who came to Qadian without seeing a sign. The signs included the high quality of his Arabic poetry, his wonderful discoveries regarding points of etymology, his discovery of *marham-i ʿĪsā* which he offered as a cure for bubonic plague, his cures and even his raising the dead. He also made predictions, but some of them caused trouble. For example, he predicted that Pandit Lekh Ram would die within six years, and when he was murdered four years later, members of the Ārya Samāj and others accused Ghulām Aḥmad

[1] See Nazīr Aḥmad, *Jesus in Heaven on Earth* (Woking, Lahore, 4th ed. 1956), which deals fully with the subject. The Pakistan government impounded all copies in 1953, but after appeal the order was set aside in 1956.

[2] The fourteenth century in Islam began on 2 November 1883.

[3] *Review of Religions* (hereafter R.R.), vol. XXXVI (1937), pp. 341 ff.

of being responsible. He was charged, and though acquitted, a government order made him promise to refrain from predictions involving anyone's disgrace, from challenging opponents to appeal to God to disgrace the losing party in a religious dispute, and from publishing anything purporting to be a divine revelation declaring someone to be an object of God's wrath.[1]

While he roused great hostility among *mullās* and the main Muslim community, to many he was an attractive personality, a persuasive speaker and writer with an appealing message. He held that he had been sent to recall mankind to orthodox Islam and when he found himself at variance with other Muslims he argued that they had gone astray. In many respects he was perfectly orthodox. He held that the Qur'ān was unique, much superior to the Bible which he called "a collection of myths and stories and fables and idle tales, fit for women only". Although not expressly stated, it would seem that he did not accept the orthodox Muslim doctrine that the Qur'ān is eternal and uncreated, for his followers evidently do not do so today.[2] He differed from the view that some Qur'ān verses abrogated others, holding that the abrogation mentioned in the Qur'ān refers to previous Scriptures. He insisted that revelation has not ceased with Muḥammad, but was careful to explain that his inspiration was not like that of the Qur'ān. Like modern Muslims he believed in the sinlessness of Muḥammad. He believed that Tradition was an important guide, but rejected traditions which did not agree with his point of view. He upheld the five pillars of practical religion (attestation of belief, prayer, almsgiving, fasting, pilgrimage), but considered a mechanical observance of them valueless. He strenuously opposed all rationalizing tendencies and disapproved of reforms influenced by Western ideas. He upheld polygamy and the *pardah* system, and opposed attempts to adapt Muslim teaching to the practice of Christian nations. He upheld the Qur'ānic prohibition of alcohol and also forbade tobacco. While he repudiated the doctrine of warlike *jihād*, he admitted that fighting was necessary in the early days of Islam, being defensive warfare which is always justifiable.

A long paper in Urdu was read at the Great Religious Conference in Lahore, 1896, presenting much of his characteristic teaching. A manifesto he issued before the conference says, "This paper derives

[1] Walter, *The Aḥmadīya Movement*, pp. 43 f. Cf. Phoenix, *His Holiness* (Lahore, 1958), p. 66.
[2] Based on a statement by the *imām* of the London mosque in the course of conversation with him, and on a reply to a query made to the secretary of the Lahore *Anjumān*.

from the Power which is not human. Indeed, it is one of the many signs of God, and has been written by His peculiar assistance. The thesis embodies certain truths and doctrines, inferred from the Holy Quran, which will make it clear that it is of divine origin...The God of all knowledge has informed me through revelation that my paper shall surpass the other papers to be read in the Conference."

He explains that his arguments are drawn from the Qur'ān, but insists that while in Muḥammad there is a perfect law, apostleship and prophecy, "access to the sacred fountain of revelation is not thereby barred". God speaks now as He did in the past. Dealing with spiritual development Ghulām Aḥmad declares that we have paradise in this life, not only in a future one. "In short, an earthly person becomes a heavenly being when illuminated by the heavenly light." He says Islam causes the death of the passions and true regeneration, which is the stage called union. He holds that in the after life man will make infinite progress, and argues that "according to the Islamic teachings" heaven and hell "are the images of the actions we perform here below". In discussing inspiration he says, "Islam is the only religion in which God draws His servant to Him and speaks to him and through him". He adds that "the mantle of divinity is cast upon the person who is thus favoured by God and he becomes a mirror for the image of the Divine Being". He declares that Muḥammad said, "Whoever has seen me has seen God", adding that this is the final stage of spiritual progress. Then he says, "I would be guilty of an injustice were I to conceal the fact that I have been raised to this spiritual eminence. Almighty God has favoured me with His certain Word and has chosen me that I may give sight to the blind, lead the seekers after truth to the object of their search, and give to the acceptors of truth the glad tidings of the pure fountain which is talked of by many but discovered by few." This paper was later translated into English by Muḥammad 'Alī, and editions of his translation are still published in Lahore and Rabwah.[1]

Ghulām Aḥmad had original explanations of some Islamic teachings. The traditions speak of the one-eyed *dajjāl* (anti-Christ) who is to appear before the end of the world, of the irruption of Gog and Magog, and of the sun rising in the west. As he was the promised Messiah the *dajjāl* must appear in his time. He taught that the *dajjāl* was the Christian missionaries who mix truth with falsehood; Gog and Magog were the

[1] The Rabwah edition (1959), entitled *The Philosophy of the Teachings of Islam,* gives the manifesto in an appendix.

prosperous western nations which have been victorious. The rising of the sun in the west meant that the western world which lay in darkness was to be illuminated by the light of Islam. In a dream he saw himself preaching in English on a pulpit in London, after which he caught a large number of white birds. This meant that, although he might not visit London personally, his writings would spread there, and many would accept the truth.

On 24 December 1905 Ghulām Aḥmad published his will in which he said God had revealed to him that his end was near. He directed that after his death new members should be admitted to the Movement by the righteous among his followers. Previously he had admitted new members personally. He also established a society called *Ṣadr Anjumān-i Aḥmadiyya* (Chief Aḥmadiyya Society) to administer the movement's affairs. When a dispute arose regarding the *Anjumān's* powers Ghulām Aḥmad was consulted, and declared that a majority of votes should settle a matter, but he desired to be informed about religious matters which had reference to his mission. After his lifetime the *Anjumān* was to have full authority.

He died on 26 May 1908 and Maulvī Nūr al-Dīn was appointed *khalīfa* (successor). He evidently tried to work in harmony with the *Anjumān*, and so unity was preserved during his brief period as leader; but after his death in 1914 a split took place. Muḥammad 'Alī speaks of differences of opinion even during his period regarding the relation of the *khalīfa* to the *Anjumān*, and the denunciation of non-Aḥmadī Muslims as unbelievers, adding that this second divergence was the final cause of the split.[1] Additional reasons probably lay in the objection of a section to the idea of a *khalīfa*, and disapproval of Bashīr al-Dīn Maḥmūd Aḥmad, Ghulām Aḥmad's son, who was felt to be trying to usurp authority. His father had disapproved of political entanglements, so when Khwājah Kamāl al-Dīn spoke against a government proposal in 1913 to remove an abutting part of a mosque in Cawnpore to realign a road, he criticized him in his journal *al-Faẓl*. Some Aḥmadīs resented his remarks. Others criticized Kamāl al-Dīn and others along with him who had joined the All-India Muslim League, a body which Ghulām Aḥmad had condemned. So dissension was growing, and when Bashīr al-Dīn was appointed *khalīfa* in Qadian after Nūr al-Dīn's death, a split took place. The party under the new *khalīfa* had its headquarters at Qadian, and the other party, two of whose most distinguished members

[1] *Mirza Ghulam Ahmad of Qadian* (Lahore, 1963), p. 34.

were Muḥammad 'Alī and Kamāl al-Dīn, made its headquarters at Lahore where a society called *Aḥmadiyya Anjumān Ishā'at-i Islām* (Aḥmadiyya Society for the Propagation of Islam) was founded.

THE QADIAN (LATER RABWAH) PARTY

The Qadian party has always held that Ghulām Aḥmad was a prophet. It has its own mosques and does not allow its members to take part in public prayers led by an outsider. Sir Muḥammad Ẓafrullāh Khān, a very distinguished member of this party, was severely criticized for not attending the funeral ceremonies for Mr Jinnah. He replied that as the leader of the prayers had publicly called Aḥmadīs *kāfirs* (infidels) and *murtadds* (apostates), he could not join prayers led by him. Ghulām Aḥmad is reported as saying that Aḥmadīs may join the funeral prayers of others who do not call him a liar and an infidel,[1] so one can understand the reason for the abstention. While they disapprove of being called *kāfirs*, Qadianīs apply this term to other Muslims; but when challenged they explain it in a manner which waters down the meaning. Bashīr al-Dīn has said, "Our calling other people *kāfirs* only means that we consider ourselves alone the true Muslims". He argues further that others mean by *kufr* (infidelity) denial of Islam and consign those they call *kāfir* to everlasting perdition, whereas the Aḥmadiyya idea of *kufr* does not involve this. By denial of a fundamental doctrine of Islam a person becomes a *kāfir*, for only belief in all the essentials makes one a true Muslim. He adds that the Aḥmadiyya call a person *kāfir* only when asked; they do not take the initiative.[2] When questioned after the Panjab riots of 1953, the reply given was that *kufr*, when applied to other Muslims, related to minor heresy which does not convey the idea that they are outside the pale of Islam.[3] Bashīr al-Dīn has said that all, even atheists, may go to heaven eventually, though dying in a state of *kufr*. Both branches of the movement teach that the punishment of hell is not eternal.

Since Bashīr al-Dīn's appointment as *khalīfa* in 1914 the Qadianī branch has developed a closely integrated system. A serious problem arose because of the division between India and Pakistan in 1947, for Qadian was on the Indian side of the Radcliffe Line. When removal to Pakistan became necessary a site near Chiniot in the Panjab, lying

[1] *Report on Panjab riots* (commonly called *Munir Report*), p. 199.
[2] R.R. vol. XXXIV (1935), pp. 247 ff. [3] *Munir Report*, p. 199.

between hills on the west side of the Chenab, was purchased and named Rabwah. Qur'ān XXIII. 52 says, "We made the son of Mary and his mother a sign and brought them for refuge to a height (*rabwa*) with a plain and running water". Ghulām Aḥmad had claimed a revelation in which he was addressed as Mary, and another in which he was addressed as Jesus. Later he said, "My name is Jesus Son of Mary, for my capacity of Jesus is an offspring of my capacity as Mary".[1] The name therefore has its appropriateness.

Among the Rabwah party Ghulām Aḥmad receives high praise. He is commonly called the Promised Messiah, sometimes His Holiness. His son says the Promised Messiah "was such a perfect follower of Islam that he attained to the stage of prophethood and God raised him to that stage of spiritual knowledge which had not been attained even by Abraham, Moses or Jesus (upon whom be peace)". He speaks of God clothing him in the mantle of His glory, and of his manifesting each attribute of God in his own person. He illustrates the attribute of knowledge by saying that when "God raised him to prophethood, He bestowed on him, during the course of a single night, such thorough knowledge of the Arabic language, that the learned men of Egypt and Arabia could not rival him in it". He wrote books in Arabic and challenged opponents to produce the like, but none dared to take up the challenge in India, Egypt, Syria, or Arabia.[2] He goes on to speak of predictions fulfilled and wonderful deeds of healing. A. R. Dard, speaking of Ghulām Aḥmad's birth, says, "There were great rejoicings at his birth. Those who looked at the babe were struck by the Divine halo that encircled the swaddling clothes and thanked God for the manifold blessings that he had brought to the whole family."[3]

Bashīr al-Dīn is also highly praised. Like his father, he is sometimes called His Holiness. As his birth was foretold he is called the Promised Son of the Promised Messiah. He tells how his father foretold that "a son would be born to him through whom many of the prophecies would be fulfilled and whose name would be carried to the ends of the earth. He would rapidly advance from success to success and would be blessed with the Holy Spirit."[4] He says further, "At each step He has blessed me with His guidance and on numerous occasions He has honoured me with His revelation. Then the day arrived when He

[1] Walter, *The Aḥmadīya Movement*, p. 32.
[2] *Ahmadiyyat or the True Islam* (Rabwah, 1959), pp. 74 f.
[3] R.R. vol. XXXVIII (1939), p. 223.
[4] *Introduction to the Study of the Holy Quran* (London, 1949), p. 436.

revealed to me that I was the Promised Son, the tidings of whose advent had been proclaimed by the Promised Messiah in 1884, five years before my birth...Whenever any teaching or doctrine contained in the Quran is made the target of criticism on the basis of some new scientific development, God reveals to me the true answer contained in the Quran."[1] Ghulām Farīd Mālik calls Bashīr al-Dīn a full-fledged *khalīfa* who enjoys the rights and privileges of the *khilāfa* exercised by the first four *khalīfas* of the Holy Prophet and the first Successor of the Promised Messiah. He has the additional distinction that "he is the Promised Son and the Promised *Khalīfa* of his blessed Father, the Prophet Ahmad".[2] He claims that Bashīr al-Dīn is the only *khalīfa* of the Holy Prophet in the world today and that "to call any other person now by the name of *khalīfa* is to defy God and His Prophet (peace be upon him)".[3]

Speaking of revelation Bashīr al-Dīn says God has not only made revelations to the Promised Messiah, but "more than half the Aḥmadis have been recipients of revelation in some form or other". Revelation may come in a dream or in *kashf* (vision). He says he "can confidently state on the basis of his own experience that revelation is conveyed in words and is not a mere idea of the mind".[4]

During his lifetime Ghulām Aḥmad conducted controversies with Christian missionaries, members of the Ārya Samāj, and Muslims who condemned him and his teachings. In some attacks against people of other religions he expressed himself strongly. This opposition to other religions, especially Christianity, has been characteristic of both branches of the movement. Bashīr al-Dīn, however, says no disrespectful language should be used of the founders of other religions. No religion is wholly false, and all nations have had prophets.[5] Elsewhere he says, "To find faults in other religions does not prove the truth of one's own religion". So missionaries should confine themselves to the fine qualities of their religion and the results arising from following its teaching.[6] This is most admirable, but the same irenic spirit is not shown in his *Introduction to the study of the Holy Quran*, where he finds much to criticize in the Bible and the Vedas.

The issuing of challenges to non-Muslim leaders has been characteristic. Ghulām Aḥmad had challenged people to come to Qadian and

[1] *Ibid.* p. 438. [2] R.R. vol. XXXVI (1937), p. 314. [3] *Ibid.* p. 320.
[4] *Ahmadiyyat*..., pp. 68 ff. Cf. H. J. Fisher, *Aḥmadiyyah* (Oxford, 1963), pp. 155 ff.
[5] *Ahmadiyyat*..., p. 202. [6] R.R. vol. XXXII (1933), p. 57.

leave without seeing a miracle. He had also issued challenges to Christian missionaries to see whether he or they could have prayer answered to heal the sick. His son, the present *khalīfa*, also issues challenges. The Secretary of the Home Department to His Holiness the Khalīfat al-Masīḥ, for example, sent an invitation to "The Most Right Reverend the Archbishop of Canterbury, London" to come to India to debate on differences between Islam and Christianity.[1] Bashīr al-Dīn says, "The world would be materially assisted in the search for truth if Christians could persuade the Pope or other high church dignitaries to put forward the revelations received by them as against those received by me for the purpose of determining which of them are true manifestations of God's power and knowledge". He adds, "The Pope and other ecclesiastics whose predecessors, in defiance of the pacific teachings of Jesus, were eager to incite Christendom to undertake Crusades against Muslim states, should be only too eager to embrace the opportunity of participating in this spiritual crusade".[2]

The movement has aroused great hostility among Muslims. Ghulām Aḥmad was branded as an infidel, and some of his followers have suffered death through their devotion to his teachings. Bashīr al-Dīn speaks of martyrs in Afghanistan, some of whom were stoned by order of the government, others being assassinated by "fanatic people of the country".[3] One of these was Mawlvī Niʿmat Allāh who was stoned to death on 31 August 1924. The *Islamic Review*,[4] while deploring the manner of the stoning, argues that this was not martyrdom, for Niʿmat Allāh "seems, unfortunately, to have interpreted his 'mission' as an obligation to create, stir up and foment disturbances in and around Kabul—and that at a time when the Afghan Government was facing a rebellion of very serious proportions". In 1953 there were serious riots in the Panjab when some Aḥmadīs were killed and many suffered injury and loss of property. This followed the rejection by the Prime Minister of Pakistan of an ultimatum by the *'ulamā'* presented in Karachi on 21 January. It threatened direct action if within a month the Qadianī Aḥmadīs were not declared a non-Muslim minority, and Chaudhri Ẓafrullāh Khān, the Foreign Minister, and other Aḥmadīs holding key posts in the state were not removed from office.[5]

The Rabwah party still maintains the *Ṣadr Anjumān-i Aḥmadiyya* which governs its general affairs, but is subject to the *khalīfa*. Another

[1] R.R. vol. xxx (1931), p. 190. [2] *Introduction to the Study of the Holy Quran*, p. 441.
[3] *Ahmadiyyat...*, pp. 228 ff. [4] Vol. xii (1924), pp. 371 ff. [5] *Munir Report*, pp. 137 f., 145.

body is the *Taḥrīk-i Jadīd* (New propaganda) which administers mission work, its treasury being separate from that of the *Ṣadr*. Bashīr al-Dīn speaks of members' regular contributions, recognizing property as a sacred trust from God. One sixteenth of income is contributed monthly for religious and charitable purposes, besides contributions to other funds, this being a minimum. He says, "Every member of the organized portion of the community contributes one tenth to one third of his income to the funds of the community according to the degree of his zeal and spirit of sacrifice". Many women sold jewellery and their best dresses to contribute to the building of a mosque in Germany.[1] Sir Muḥammad Ẓafrullāh Khān tells that the London mosque was built with funds contributed by the women of the movement.[2]

Rabwah has a missionary college where preparatory training is given to missionaries, emphasis being laid on proficiency in Arabic and English. Converts from foreign countries are received and given instruction. A young men's organization, *Khuddām al-Aḥmadiyya* (Servants of the Aḥmadiyya), has branches in many communities, its purpose being to encourage men to take an active share in the work. *Lajna Imāullāh* (Commission of God's handmaidens) is a similar organization for women of all ages. There is a boys' high school, *Ta'līm al-Islām*, and a college of the same name for male students which is affiliated to the Panjab University. Nuṣrat College for women is also affiliated. Faẓl-i 'Umar laboratory at Rabwah is engaged in chemical research, and various products are produced for sale. Great emphasis is laid on education, so much so that Bashīr al-Dīn claims their standard is higher than that of other communities.[3] Books and pamphlets are published in many languages, and journals are also published. The *Review of Religions*, the oldest established English journal, is still published at Rabwah. The *Muslim Herald* is an English journal published by the London Mosque. There are missions in various parts of Africa, in Europe and America, as well as in Asian countries and Australia. Sir Muḥammad Ẓafrullāh Khān says, "The purpose of the Movement is to review Islamic values drawn from the Quran and the example of the Prophet, in every sphere of life, and to carry far and wide the message of Islam, with particular emphasis on its application

[1] *Ahmadiyyat...*, p. 235 f. The *imām* of the London mosque has told me that the basic rate in England is one twentieth, the cause of the difference being that the rupee is divided into 16 annas and the pound into 20 shillings.

[2] *Islam, its Meaning for Modern Man* (London, 1962), p. 206.

[3] *Ahmadiyyat...*, p. 234.

to the present age". He speaks of encouraging success, particularly in East and West Africa, and of missions established in England, the Netherlands, the Scandinavian countries, Germany and Switzerland.[1] In the United States the headquarters are in Washington, D.C., where a mosque is maintained. There are also mosques and meeting places in several other cities of the United States.[2]

The movement has in Rabwah its own courts to which members may have recourse in civil cases. The lowest court has a single judge from whom appeal may be made to the *qaḍā'* (adjudication) board, and final appeal may be made to the *khalīfa*.

An annual conference is held at Rabwah, usually from 27 to 29 December. Large numbers gather and listen to lengthy speeches about the movement's work and teachings. A separate ladies' conference is also held at the same time.

It is difficult to estimate the number of members. The India Census Report for 1901, when Aḥmadīs were enumerated separately, gave 1,113 males in the Panjab, 913 in the United Provinces, and 11,087 in Bombay Presidency. In 1908 Ghulām Aḥmad claimed half a million throughout the world, but in the 1911 census the total in the Panjab was given as 18,695. Walter calculates that by 1918 there were not more than 70,000 all told.[3] The Munir Report of 1954 remarks that the number then in Pakistan was said to be near two million, in addition to others in other Muslim countries, and in India, Europe and America.[4] Fisher speaks of the difficulty of estimating the numbers in West Africa. He says Rabwah claims about 45,000 in Ghana, but the local Amir says there are between 18,000 and 28,000. Fisher guesses roughly that there may be 25,000 in Ghana, 7,000 in Nigeria, and about 3,000 in Sierra Leone.[5]

THE LAHORE PARTY

The Lahore party holds strongly that Ghulām Aḥmad never claimed to be a prophet. They speak of him as a *mujaddid* sent to revivify Islam which had become decadent. They insist that one cannot call any Muslim a *kāfir*, and accordingly they do not feel themselves separate

[1] The mission in Germany was established in 1949. Mosques were inaugurated in Hamburg in 1957 and in Frankfurt in 1959. The mission in Switzerland was established in 1948 and a mosque opened in Zurich in 1963. A mosque was opened in Copenhagen on 21 July 1967.

[2] *Islam...*, pp. 205 f. [3] *The Aḥmadīya Movement*, p. 112. [4] P. 10.

[5] *Ahmadiyyat...*, p. 155. Since this chapter was written Mirzā Bashīr al-Dīn Maḥmūd Aḥmad has died (8 November 1965). He was succeeded by his son, Ḥāfiẓ Mirzā Nāṣir Aḥmad.

from the main body of Islam, holding that all who accept the fundamentals of Islam are Muslims. They follow Ghulām Aḥmad's teaching about Jesus dying in Kashmir. They agree that *jihād* is not a warlike occupation but a spiritual struggle to establish the truth. They are ready to pray behind a non-Aḥmadī *imām*, and do not prevent their women from marrying non-Aḥmadī Muslims. But they follow a tradition which says that one who calls another Muslim a *kāfir* ceases to be a Muslim.[1]

This party has conducted a vigorous missionary and literary programme. Kamāl al-Dīn (d. 28 December 1932) came to England and was *imām* of the Woking mosque, editor of the *Islamic Review* and author of many books in which he waged a vigorous propaganda against Christianity. The Woking mosque and the *Islamic Review* now claim to be independent of the Aḥmadiyya Movement. In the *Islamic Review* of December 1964[2] the editor, in reply to a letter which quoted some people calling it a Mirzā'ī journal, said it receives some support from the Lahore *Anjumān* in the form of cash donations and advertisements of their books, and also from other organizations; but he insisted that such monetary help did not influence the review's policy. On the other hand, in a letter of 21 May 1965 received from the secretary of the Lahore *Anjumān*, he says that in 1948 the Woking Trust authorities were affiliated to the Lahore *Anjumān*, and that while the policy of the Woking mission remained strictly non-sectarian, one of the terms of affiliation lays down that the decisions of the Trust are subject to ratification by the *Anjumān*.[3]

There has been some decline in the missionary work. In Europe the only mission now is in Berlin. One which was conducted in the United States has been closed. There are still three missions in Africa,[1] and mission work has been carried on in Indonesia. The literary work, however, is active, and this fulfils a missionary purpose. Among the most notable publications are Muḥammad 'Alī's *The Holy Qur'ān, Arabic Text, English Translation and Commentary*, 5th ed. (1953) and his *The Religion of Islam*, 3rd ed. (1950).

The ideals of the party are stated to be the service of Islam, the unity, defence and propagation of Islam. Its work is establishing Islamic

[1] From a letter from the Lahore secretary, dated 8 February 1965. [2] Pp. 39 f.

[3] In a letter dated 23 June 1970, the Honorary Secretary of the Woking Mosque Trust pointed out that the Woking Mosque Trust Ltd was registered as a trust corporation in 1953 and subsequently was no longer affiliated to the *Anjumān* or any other body, and nor were its affairs subject to ratification by an external body.

missions, preparing Muslim missionaries, translating the Qur'ān into different languages, and broadcasting Islamic literature. Its beliefs are the finality of prophethood in Muḥammad, the Qur'ān as God's final and perfect book, "no portion of which has ever been or shall be abrogated", that all who profess belief in God and His messenger, whatever their school of thought in Islam, are Muslims, that Ghulām Aḥmad is the *mujaddid* of the fourteenth century, and that he stated he laid no claim to prophethood. Although not included in the statement of belief, it should be added that the Lahore party does not believe in the *khilāfa* as understood by the Rabwah party, and is governed by the *Aḥmadiyya Anjumān-i Ishā'at-i Islām*.

The membership of the Lahore party is comparatively small. The secretary, in his letter of 21 May 1965, says that neither government nor the *Anjumān* has made any serious effort to count numbers. He estimates that the Lahore Aḥmadīs in Pakistan "may be put at a maximum of about ten thousand, while a few thousands more may be present in other lands. But this is a very rough and crude estimation."

Both parties are very earnest and sincere in their mission. While they are quite distinct from one another, this difference is not always realized by other Muslims, one result of which was that members of the Lahore party suffered equally with members of the Rabwah party during the 1953 Panjab riots. The Rabwah party speaks at times of the hope that the Lahore party will return to the fold; but the Lahore party feel that the Rabwah party have misunderstood Ghulām Aḥmad's position and have gone astray in other matters. References in the Munir report to accusations of aggressiveness in missionary work apply more particularly to the Rabwah party. While there is no doubt about the vigour with which the publications of both parties attempt to refute and even ridicule Christian doctrine, the missionaries show great courtesy in personal relations. It should be added that the movement as a whole demands of its members a high moral standard.

PART 2

THE THREE RELIGIONS IN CONCORD AND CONFLICT

CHAPTER 20

DOCTRINE

> I know how to walk behind camels in the sands,
> How to carry upon my back a heavy hump of afflictions,
> And look out for the Messiah.
> And I also know how to stand among the many
> In the hollow in a quarry,
> How to cleave the rock primeval,
> And look out for the Messiah.[1]

Simple sentiments, and not profoundly expressed, but at once recognizable as the temper of a twentieth-century Palestinian. Sands and rocks, pilgrimages and toil, and the ever present mystery of the Messiah. The ordinary reader would immediately identify the lines as Jewish—and rightly. They are the composition of Abraham Braudes, a minor poet of the modern Hebrew renaissance. The whole thesis of this chapter, however, turns upon claiming them, or better their interior quality, for all three traditional faith-cultures of the Holy Land. There is about Judaism, Christianity and Islam in the Middle East, a common if admittedly diversified stake in the territorial concept. Each in their different ways involves a trinity of people, book and land: and this measure of identity is no small part of their discord and antagonism, both actual and abstract.

Since the whole concern in *Religion in the Middle East* is with the interplay of faith and place, it will be well on every count to take a point of departure from the emotions of geography and let the sacrament of territory introduce what will here be assumed as the definitive issue, namely universality. Where, with John Donne in a famous sermon, the expositor must say: "Be pleased in this exercise to give me leave to shift the scene thrice" it would be tedious to venture in catalogue style to summarize, in turn, the respective Jewish, Christian and Muslim accounts of God, man, creation, law, revelation, prophecy, history, sin, redemption, righteousness, prayer, ritual, behaviour and immortality, and other themes in their doctrinal affinity and tension. Rather, it is urgent to isolate and pursue a single, unifying clue

[1] Quoted in Simon Halkin, *Modern Hebrew Literature* (New York, 1950), p. 181.

which will lead into a just assessment of divergence within what is mutual.

It is precisely such a clue which the land affords in its centrality to all three faiths. Given the geographical intention of these volumes, it is proposed to let the doctrinal agreements and conflicts emerge in that context, and take universality, with its translation of the local significance, as the key to the discovery and elucidation of each religion. There are obvious practical, not to say poetical, advantages in such a procedure. Self-understanding and the rest of the world, community and humanity, may be said to constitute the largest and most searching equation within religious relevance and destiny. To belong within themselves and with mankind are the two dimensions of their integrity. From what local "mystery" does this vocation proceed? We begin with what teaches all else, namely the Hebraic.

THE HEBRAIC: LAND AND WORLD

"My name is 'Mugo' which in the language of my fathers means 'Man of God', I came from a long line of men who have borne this name, a line stretching far back into time."[1] But for the "shape" of the name, it could be any child of Israel speaking, though it is in fact a narrator from the Kikuyu telling his story of boyhood, "facing Mount Kenya".[2] We do not rightly understand the Old Testament's sense of place and people unless we know that it mirrors and educates the self-awareness of all lands and dwellers. The nationhood of Israel, the love of Zion, has its counterpart in every continent. Its uniqueness lies, not in the emotional experience, but the theological intensity.

> So while the light falls
> On a winter's afternoon, in a secluded chapel,
> History is now, and England...

is unmistakeably Eliot: yet the sense of the sacramental particular belongs in a like conviction to all the varieties of human continuity of habitation.

> So while the sun floods
> O'er the promised hills, on the river's further shore,
> History is now, and Canaan...

[1] R. Mugo Gatheru, *Child of Two Worlds* (London, 1964), p. 1.

[2] Title of Jomo Kenyatta's now celebrated study of Kenyan life and society, one of the earliest pieces of African anthropology from within. The potential parallel with "facing Mount Zion" is evident.

is the implicit poetry of the Old Testament, in both chronicle and psalm. The whole self-understanding of the Hebrews turns on "enlandisement" and habitation and then, centuries later, on "disenlandisement" and dispersion. Its two poles are Exodus and Exile, the twin themes of the old covenant. "He brought them out that he might bring them in..." "Here will I dwell, for I have a delight therein." The triangular relationship is that of God, people and territory. The land is the divine gift to the nation: the nation the custodians of the divine habitation: and God the Lord the architect of their dwelling place that "glory—the divine praise—may dwell in our land".

The Exile is the shattering of this destiny and represents at once the physical symbol and the proper retribution of the recalcitrance of the nation. "How shall we sing the Lord's song in a strange land?" is more than a plaintive lament of the homeless for their depopulated home. Its unconscious irony derives from the strange song their history had sung in the Lord's land; the refusal in their colonizing history in Canaan to render back the priestly oblations of thanksgiving properly due from their kingship over nature. They had declined the abiding invitation of the Torah to Divine human co-operation, to which their self-awareness as "a royal priesthood, a holy nation, a kingdom of priests" had summoned them, and of which their very habitation was the sacramental token. So the new mystery of exile had overtaken them, as the divinely decreed correction of their unrighteous tenancy through the fact and symbol of a painful interruption. Thus the Exodus into promise and the exodus from its physical means and privilege mark, in related crises, the single theme of "enlandisement" as the sign and pledge of the divine will and the human response. This, it may be said, is the nationhood to educate nations, the awareness of election and particularity that embraces a universal parable for all the segments of mankind and all the diversified economic and spiritual tenancies of terrestrial habitation by peoples and races in those interactions that make culture and history.

It is assumed, in this broad summary of the mind of the Old Testament, that we are dealing with history in its true quality as both event and meaning. This conviction is basic to the Judeo-Christian tradition, though for reasons which will appear it is largely absent from the Muslim scheme. For history, in its widest sense, is what happened and what is remembered and rehearsed. The former is mediated through the selecting and interpreting of the memory which in the latter perpetuates its significance. To ask for historical record free of all interpreting activity is to ask for what cannot be had, or had only in respect of what is essentially insignificant. The less things need the living mediation of memory the less likely they are to deserve or receive any record. But such interpretation need not distort or falsify what it relates. On the contrary, it often sees and takes that event in precisely the tenor which grasps its point and measure. When this happens, history, as event, has itself generated the interpretations by which history, as meaning, emerges and abides and so in turn perpetuates the authentic participation by which alone the event can be known. The biblical Exodus and Exile are of this nature, in what Martin Buber has called the "saga" of Israel, the corporate possession of historical meaning as the valid sense of what the event was when known, not simply as making a narrative but creating a nation, and ensuing not simply in a chronicle but in a destiny.

This recollected participation does not mean the "historization of myth", the falsification of actuality into legend or fantasy. Rather it should be more accurately described as the "mythization of history"—events reported from within the national memory of what they had meant in memorable experience. "History", Buber continues, "cannot be dissevered from historical wonder...The experience of the event as wonder is itself great history. Whether Sinai was a volcano cannot be determined historically, nor is it historically relevant. But that the tribes gathered at the burning mountain comprehended the words of their leader, Moses, as a message from their God, a message that simultaneously established a covenant between him and their community is essentially a historical process, historical in the deepest sense."[1]

Hebrew history, then, is inseparable from a fundamental philosophy of experienced Zion, in which it is told as the concrete shape of a metaphysical reality, where what happens is the pattern of the nature of what is. Territory and trust, election and law, liberation and covenant, Exodus and Sinai, tenancy and Torah, all belong together, not by idle or assertive association, but in the inward quality of each. In pondering what the historians believe, we learn what the history is. The destiny is there because the events have enabled and launched it: the events have received this interpretation because the destiny was there. "This history is in its character sacred history because the people who work

[1] Martin Buber, *Moses* (Oxford, 1946), pp. 16–17.

and suffer in it work and suffer as they do in virtue of their relationship with God."[1] The faith has become flesh in national history and the very flesh is constituted in that faith.

The biblical understanding of what happens in history cannot rightly be isolated from its setting in nature. If the human story is a drama, territory is the stage. History has its local habitation. It has become fashionable in some Christian quarters to find in the biblical view an exclusive emphasis on time, to the neglect of place, and to deny the Hebraic mind any metaphysical concern,[2] alleging that the prophetic awareness of God in history precludes or even denies the contemplation of God in nature.

The alert reader of the Old Testament has the surest corrective to these claims. "The place the Lord thy God doth choose, to cause His Name to dwell there" is the way it speaks. "A land of milk and honey ...a land whose stones are iron and out of whose hills thou mayest dig brass." These are not negligible as terrestrial things. They are the warp and woof of the economy of divine praise. There is doxology in ecology.

So the psalmist "lifts up his eyes unto the hills" not as an alternative, tried and wanting, to the "help which is in the Name of the Lord", but as the token of the quality, the abiding stability, of that guardianship of Israel which the hills proclaim. The Exile is not simply a "when" but a "where" and the yearning for return is wistful for a place as well as for a time. So the occupancy of the land, to which Exodus leads and which the covenant at Sinai inaugurates, involves a relationship with the natural order that is, in the fullest sense, sacramental. "The ploughman keeps the eternal creation alive" and with that active tenancy perpetuates also the national trusteeship under God. The "history festival" of the Passover has its counterpart in the festivals of first fruits and harvest. By these and the recurrent meal, corn and farmyard offerings, as well as the burnt sacrifice, there is what André Neher has called "a metaphysical intimacy"[3] between God and man, fulfilling itself in co-operation, the marriage of soul and soil, of land and labour, being the primary and always parabolic foundation of every other shape of duty and adoration.

[1] *Ibid.* p. 19.

[2] E.g. Harvey Cox, *The Secular City* (New York, 1965), which may be cited more for the popularity than the penetration of its thought.

[3] André Neher, *Moses and the Vocation of the Jewish People*, trans. by Irene Marinoff (London, 1959).

This quality of sanctity in the most prosaic of physical pursuits, the holiness one might almost say of sweat itself, which reappears most movingly in the literature of Zionism, not least the writings of Aaron David Gordon, is part of the truth that everything creaturely is material for sanctification, this being the comprehensive intention of God's "promising" the land. The land of promise is properly not merely a divine bestowal but human fulfilment. It is a land so conceived because it admits and invites a tenure which hallows its latent resources of hill and pasture in a covenantal awe and makes them actual in the labour that prays and the enjoyment that gives thanks. Thus the belief in the destiny of the nation is at once a philosophy of its wealth: the assurance of "enlandisement" is a theology of economics. Both belong in turn with what St James' Epistle calls "the poetry of the word" (James i. 22)—the transmuting of experience into art and art into praise.

Nowhere was this inner meaning of the Old Testament covenant of the land more splendidly vocal than in the Ḥasidism of late eighteenth- and early nineteenth-century Judaism, emerging from the traditional privations and introversions of the ghetto and not yet bitterly thrown into the political assertiveness of Zionism. As Simon Halkin has it:

> Its fundamental insistence was on the dignity of the human personality and the privilege of being alive, of thrilling to the glories of the God-given world ...It not only revealed the immanence of God in trees and water, in color and sound, in thought and feeling: it lighted up the worlds of nature and the soul with a sense of the divine which made physical nature and the human personality sources of endless ecstacy. It not only stressed worship; it stressed also the song and the dance. It venerated the unfolding of personality in action, speech, thought and feeling...Its main emphasis was on the sacredness of life.[1]

As such, it was the flowering, even in adversity, of the deepest implications of the Old Testament belief in the stake of every son of Zion in territorial right and his dignity as God's tenant–farmer–citizen. It was, and is, the first meaning of a faith about its own geography, a creed which declares that "the earth is the Lord's" and therein "*this* earth is ours" under Him. Hebraic agriculture harvests the footstool of God, and over all "the heavens declare His glory".

We turn in later sections to some corollaries of this Hebrew sense of the good earth, this ecological metaphysic which is the love of Zion.

[1] *Modern Hebrew Literature*, pp. 32–3.

It reaches out into the whole meaning of law and righteousness, of Messiahship and the kingdom. For the moment we stay only with its awareness of the territorial and the ethnic, for it is these which constitute its sorest temptation, despite their universal implications about all men and their habitats.

Territory, to be blunt, has first to be possessed and then in turn defended. If a Moses leads you out there must needs be a Joshua to lead you in. If there is emancipation, there is also dispossession. One cannot turn Canaan into Zion without ousting and disavowing the Canaanites. God's giving the land pre-supposes his expelling the former occupants. Whatever the ethnic and other migrations that lie within the traditional history, the particularism, with "the mythization of history" which hallows and perpetuates it, involves a theological "scandal". It has to do with an "election" which is in the last analysis racial and national and therefore, unlike the Church, has no necessity for an open door and every temptation to sustained exclusivism.

This "particularity" of Israel in the Old Testament, marching with "enlandisement", and both buffeted and confirmed in "disenlandisement", is the largest issue, as it is the sure focus, of all other doctrinal themes. Election is always properly conditioned by instrumentality. It is the Old Testament itself which most eloquently proclaims the universal intention of the chosen-ness. The pledge to Abraham is: "I will make of thee a great nation...and in thy seed shall all the nations of the earth be blessed." Isaiah, Micah, Zechariah and Malachi all foresee the attraction of the faith of Israel for humanity and its open welcome to the gathering nations. Among the tenderest hopes of the Deutero-Isaiah is the vision of the servant who effectuates the greater exodus of mankind. The Books of Ruth and Jonah in their characteristic ways proclaim the divine compassion and purpose in unlikely places.

Yet the instrumentality of election never overcomes the retention of privilege and the status-maintaining instincts of particularity. It is a Christian belief that the chosen-ness of Israel is both fulfilled and transmuted in the hospitality of grace and the Gospel and, further, that it cannot be fulfilled without being transcended. This conviction, to be summarized below, proceeds with, and is achieved through, the Messiahship of Jesus. The first great subsequent battle for its meaning comes in the conversion and career of Saul of Tarsus as apostle to the nations—a conversion which the New Testament Scriptures evidently take as the conversion to exemplify conversion, the mystery of an election to illuminate election. That conversion is clearly within an opposition to the alleged Messiahship of Jesus continuous with the original antagonism to his ministry—a ministry understood as having to do critically with the "opening" of the destiny of Israel.

Thus the continuing Jewish "quarrel" with the Christian version of their universalizing, of which Paul's biography remains the focus, serves to define the issue at the heart of Jewish identity, namely the fulfilment within the particular of the universal duty for which it exists. Disavowal of the Christian "answer" sharply perpetuates the question. But by the same token the enduring belief of Judaism in an unimpaired, never to be transcended, destiny creates an essential ambiguity for the Church, in that the very source of her criteria disclaims her appeal to them.

The theme of Jewry is painfully, indeed tragically, complicated by the enormities perpetrated against the Jewish identity by European and "Christian" antagonism—outrages which have made the burden of its mission to mankind wellnigh insupportable in the soul and unmanageable in the actual, without the still further alienating factor of statehood. On every count, then, of externally threatened extinction and interior political dynamism, the ultimate problem remains. If Jewry disapproves the universalizing of its human mission which has happened in the Church, how does it continue to reconcile its sense of privilege with the self-transcending obligation, confessed and prized, within that very identity?

There is, of course, the view espoused by Franz Rosenzweig (1886–1929) that Israel's mission to the nations is in fact taken up by the Church in Israel's stead. While Israel is the central incandescence, let the Church be the emanating rays of that star of David and let the Church, through her very mission, know the contamination as well as the accession of the heathen. Meanwhile, the synagogue, for all its brokenness and inward insulation, will continue to bear her own children. While Christianity is commissioned to preach, Judaism is summoned to suffer. "Nothing beyond its physical existence and the propagation of the holy seed of Abraham is necessary to assure the presence of God...By its very existence Israel bears witness to God in the world."[1]

For all its noble tenacity this answer, if taken as it stands, seems to

[1] Samuel Hugo Bergman, *Faith and Reason: Modern Jewish Thought*, trans. by Alfred Jospe (New York, 1961), p. 64.

make of Israel merely an ethnic continuity and to equate spiritual vocation with biological persistence. Can "the seed of Abraham" in any case be, in these times, a physically guaranteed notion? Is destiny identical with heredity and fidelity with birth?

Rosenzweig's concept of the churchly validities *vis-à-vis* Gentiles is echoed in Hans Joachim Schoeps' view that the grace of Christ is, for "the seed of Abraham", "an unnecessary detour". It is agreed that Christian "universality" has a complete extra-Jewish authenticity as truth for the heathen. But with Israel, birth makes it superfluous, indeed improper, since Jews are already ethnically within the divine covenant made "with one nation...in full physical reality".[1] There *is* a new covenant; but not for Israel. The heirs of privilege may not say, as did the apostle Peter, according to Acts xv.11: "We (a Jew speaking) believe that we shall be saved even as they" (the Gentiles). For then the privileged entity would have passed away in a larger whole. By its faith the Church may be seen as a sort of "Israel" universalized for the world. But for Dr Schoeps there is no "new Israel" abrogating the old in a new and equal unity of Jew and Gentile. Thus he continues to hold together an ethnic "inevitability" with a moral conditionality. "The covenant effects sanctification for the man who keeps it." Yet "whoever is born an Israelite is a member of the covenant by virtue of his birth".[2]

This problem of the uncovenanting, still covenanted, Jew of birth and disloyalty, is no more than the peculiar Jewish form of a perennial burden of religions as a whole. None can presume, least of all here, to trespass on another's inwardness. No one outside Israel knows its mystery from within. Nevertheless an ethnic interpretation of that mystery, incurring as it does these moral dilemmas, and assigning the task of universality to the Christian faith, seems to elude the real "answerability" of Jewry for its election under God. Can it either delegate its universal duty or realize it merely by the parentage of literal seed?

There is another view that has historically linked Diaspora with vocation. It lay behind the hopeful philosophy of assimilation and identity within the Gentile world, represented, among others, by the great Moses Mendelssohn (1729–86), Samuel Holdeim (1806–60), Abraham Geiger (1810–74) and Hermann Cohen (1842–1918), in the

[1] *The Jewish Christian Argument: A History of Theologies in Conflict*, trans. by D. E. Green (New York, 1963), p. 4.
[2] *Ibid.* pp. 163–4.

days when the ghetto had been left behind and the ominous shadows of late nineteenth- and twentieth-century pogroms and genocide had hardly begun to darken the scene. The theology that made the dispersion itself the missionary self-fulfilment of Judaism has been ably summarized by André Neher:

The *Shekinah* resides with every exiled fragment of the Jewish people. In every particle of land trodden by a Jew the presence of God is revealed. Far from being an outward road leading the chosen People farther and farther away from their election, the exile is for Israel a mission, each stage of which strengthens the bonds between the Jew and the God who accompanies him...The universe would be lacking in shape unless Israel were omnipresent, making the divine sap pulsate through the organism of the cosmos like the blood through the body...In each field of his exile the Jew places the seeds which will one day all bring forth together the divine harvest.[1]

In terms of this understanding, the call of Judaism was to an ardent "presence" within the world of non-Jewry, absorbing its values, using its languages and participating in its life, while casting off, sometimes almost in embarrassment, the distinctivenesses of its own history and cultic life.

Whatever may be said in debate about this posture it did at least confront the world and by virtue of its very compromises—if such they were—mitigated those isolating features which impeded Jewry's self-confessed obligation to mankind. Yet it tended also to diminish, or discount, the historic elements of dogma and sanctity within that obligation. As indicated elsewhere in this volume, the fates were in any event against the assimilationists at least in eastern and central Europe. There arose the dominating philosophy of Zionism, reasserting the ancient geographical *qibla*, invoking anew the territorial concept and fusing religion and nationality into a single impetus.

Theodore Herzl (1860–1904) insisted that the only valid fulfilment of Jewry lay in territorial statehood. "The Jewish State", he affirmed in a crucial pamphlet in 1896, "is essential to the world...It will therefore be created." Like the parallel statehood policy of Pakistan, the Zionist expression of the meaning of Jewry gathered to its banner many diverse, even critical, adherents. Its practical issue has been in large part secular and its price has all but bankrupted some of the concepts within its genesis. But, by all its ambiguities and its ardour and assurance, it posits in new and more incisive form the old question of universality.

[1] *Moses*, p. 162.

It was possible for Martin Buber to give reserved and apprehensive support to the statehood goal on the ground that a spiritual Israel would co-exist with the new physical Israel, that the opportunity of a new state would foster a new type of Jew and that its nationalism would be *sui generis*, nobly different from the perversities of ordinary states. Universalist Muslims, like Iqbāl in Pakistan, have had similar hopes relating to their statehood. Every one, indeed, is tempted to esteem his own nationalism as unique and potentially irenic—a means of contributing more robustly to the wholeness of mankind. The problem belongs, not with nationality and the political order—for these are plainly inseparable—but with the conjunction of the religious equation to either. It can be claimed that the inevitable asperities that go with state-making are the profanities that serve to fashion the holy of holies and that realism is the price idealism must pay for its opportunity.

Yet, for all the liberation of energies, the clear focus of objectives, the massively compassionate hospitality of the Zionist achievement to the decimated survivors of European Diaspora, there is still within it an ever sharper ambiguity about the final questions of the universal meaning and obligation of the chosen people. The means to preservation militate against its end. By its own deepest convictions Judaism is committed to the benediction of all peoples and without this loyalty its very particularity is disqualified. The age-long symbol of a Jewry renewed as the divine servant by the "Return" "as embodied in the state of Israel ... constitutes the most officially and organically secular and areligious element in the world Jewish community".[1]

The pathos and paradox of this conclusion bring us back where we began to the Hebraic understanding of land and people under God and the true significance of that triangular relationship. Has the new "enlandisement" betrayed the old? Was Diaspora the true symbol or the tragic negation of what vocation meant? Are chosen-ness and the law, identity as God's and duty to man, still proper and feasible clues to Jewish existence? Or is the land now no more than the territorial location of a secular nationality apostate from itself? Is the sacred soil still a sacrament of a divine purpose that embraces the world? Or has it become a religious asset, convenient to a statehood that has lost its hidden mystery?

These are the questions which belong with contemporary Jewry and,

[1] André Neher, *Religions and the Promise of the Twentieth Century*, ed. G. S. Métraux and F. Crouzet (New York, 1965), p. 141.

so doing, reach most deeply into its doctrinal heart. They merge into the issue of whether Messiah ever comes, where we shall encounter them anew. Meanwhile it is time to look at the Christian sentiment about Jerusalem.

THE CHRISTIAN: LAND, CHRIST AND WORLD

Christians are distinguished from the rest of men neither by country nor by language nor by customs. For nowhere do they dwell in cities of their own ...They dwell in both Greek and barbarian cities, each as his lot is cast... They live in fatherlands of their own but as aliens. They share all things as citizens and suffer all things as strangers. Every foreign land is their fatherland and every fatherland a foreign land.[1]

The familiar claim of the Epistle to Diognetus rings strangely through the major Christian centuries. But its paradox sets forth a primitive, and it is fair to say a definitive, conviction about Christianity and territorial connexion, even with the lands of the Bible. The sentiment which cherishes "enlandisement" is powerful but not imperative. The Church is heir to the theology about nature which the Old Testament proclaims and sees man, whether simple husbandman or subtle technologist, as king-priest, with an empire to explore and exploit and enjoy, in a temper of gratitude, responsibility and worship. Man, biblically understood, secularizes nature only because nature hallows man—a posture fully shared by the Islamic doctrine of mercy, "signs", thankfulness and submission.

But this terrestrial tenancy is for the Church an equal truth about all places and climes. In this primary sense of territorial man every homeland under God is its people's Zion. Every piece of earth with its potential fertilities actualized in the occupation of men is a house of prayer and privilege. For the rest, a Christian interest in the particular scene of the life and ministry of Jesus is purely sentimental, as the mother country of a proper and irreversible emigration. With that sentiment goes a quality of "sacrament"—the sanctity of association. Pilgrimage, however, has never been one of the necessary duties of the Church. "Next year", or indeed any year, "in Jerusalem" is not a cry of Christian anguish. Romance, penance, prestige, adventure, scholarship, affection, curiosity, all these have been motives within the urge of Europe towards Palestine, medieval and modern. In the Crusades

[1] *The Epistle to Diognetus*, para. v, trans. H. G. Meecham (Manchester, 1949), pp. 80–1.

these mixed motives bludgeoned into bitter militancy and angry zeal, served by massive ignorance and much-tried devotion and superstition. But in the final analysis those Crusades had as much to do with the means to pilgrimage as with its end, with the liberty more than the significance of access.

Tested, then, by its surest criteria from the New Testament onwards, there have been no Christian imperatives about Jerusalem, not correspondingly valid everywhere. The effective leadership of the Church quickly passed to other bases, beginning with Syrian Antioch. The concern of St Paul for Jerusalem in "the Gentile offering" was for human poverty not geographical tribute. That statesmanlike gesture, for which he staked and forfeited his freedom to itinerate, was meant as a token and sign of Jewish–Gentile unity. The sack of Jerusalem in A.D. 70 doubtless served in a cruel way to accelerate this loosening of the Church from its first Palestinian moorings but the process was already psychologically well under way and was doctrinally underwritten from the start in the universalizing of the Jewish destiny which the Church believed itself to constitute.

There are many evidences of inner struggle, but none of ambiguity, in the New Testament about this basic issue. The purpose and destiny of the old covenant are taken as realized in the new. "This is that which was spoken by the prophets" is an affirmation embracing more than the circumstances of "the day of Pentecost". In the person, ministry, death and resurrection of Jesus the hope of Israel has happened, concretely and inclusively, and by its own inner logic extends its hospitality to all men, conditionally as to repentance and faith, unconditionally as to race and reputation. What Jesus in his preaching had extended to publicans across the frontiers of the law's moral self-regard, his disciples extended to "foreigners" across the boundaries of the law's racial self-regard. They were part and parcel of the same movement of grace, the same implicit, then explicit, abrogation of privilege in its fulfilment. The word "Christian" itself (Acts xi. 26) seems to have been coined, in Antioch, to describe a unity which was neither Jewish, nor Gentile, nor Jewish proselyte, but new Jew–Gentile, in a different sort of equation and that, around the Christhood of Jesus. The wits of the Antioch market-place had a certain acumen.

It should be noted that this "Christian" community, incorporating the old contrasted communities in a new society, was different in one vital particular from the widespread "Judaization" of Greeks and others in the Mediterranean lands in the first century. Hospitable, as Zechariah had foreseen (viii. 23), Jewry certainly was and proselytism was a wide and in measure a gracious phenomenon. Yet it had about it an irreducible "imperialism" of the spirit: it welcomed on condition of provisional incorporation. It required a Judaized adherence. The ethnic element persisted in the spiritual transaction.

It was just at this point that the Church, through all its struggles and frailties, involved a fundamental contrast. When the decisive issue emerged from the tensions and stresses of its making, it was clear that the Christian faith was not some essentially Jewish thing which had graciously opened itself to non-Jewish participation, but rather an inherently universal thing which had found historical nurture in the bosom of Jewry and was to be understood not by the "whence?" of its origins, but the "what?" of its fullness. The course of history shapes but the climax defines. So the Church saw itself as a "new Israel" in this sense: an Israel that had become what the promise had always been and in the becoming had brought the promise, in both senses of the word, to its end.

The ongoing existence of "spiritual" Jewry is, therefore, both a puzzle and an "undoing" for the Church. A physical Jewry is entirely valid, indeed deeply admirable in its ethnic continuity, with all its cultural fecundity, and seen with a unique affection and wonder by the rest of mankind. But as a persistence in still unfulfilled chosen-ness it has, from the angle of these Christian criteria, missed the universality for which its specialness was meant. It wants to remain private with God, perpetuating a particular passover and relationship, in default of its mandate to inaugurate a universal table and communion. Christianity cannot acquiesce in this foregoing of destiny by Jewry without, in turn, disqualifying itself. As Buber has it, "the Jew is to the Christian the incomprehensibly obdurate man, who will not see what has happened".[1] The vitality, the greatness, the long-suffering, of that enduring spiritual Jewishness only make the Christian dilemma more acute.

Nevertheless, within Christian experience, the "newness" of Israel has occurred. "In Christ there is neither Jew nor Greek." "The same Lord over all is rich unto all that call upon him." There *is* a unity of faith which realizes the Old Testament vision and hope and liberates

[1] *Mamre, Essays in Religion*, trans. by Greta Hort (Melbourne, 1946), p. 31. "Incomprehensibly" is a word many Christians would want to question and for that reason "obdurate" tells only half the truth: "understandably reluctant" might get the point sufficiently.

them from the privacy of their matrix into a promise accessible to all. Thus the Church cannot be other than wistfully discontent, when Rosenzweig, Schoeps, Buber and others in their various ways validate Christian universality as in measure fulfilling "for the nations" the Jewish mission, so long as Jewry is exempt. For this, if the phrase may be borrowed, is "the wound of absence". In the Gospel, these thinkers seem to say, the Hebraic heritage is satisfactorily "gentilized". Are not the liturgies of Christendom in lineal descent from the synagogue? Are not the demands of Sinai and the sweet psalms of Israel transcribed by the Church into the vast audience of mankind? Truly the contentious setting of Jesus' ministry and the tragic arguments about his crucifixion have involved Christianity in an entail of anti-Jewish animus and an emotional predilection to hostility. Christendom has all too often believed about crucifiers so differently from the Crucified and so has betrayed the Cross in espousing it. Yet these massive obstacles can be surmounted and Christianity given a conditional acceptance as an appropriate, or at least an operative, universalizing of the Hebraic experience of God and his mercy, provided that the Gospel of that universality allows Jewry itself to persist in exemption from it in the name of both the Gospel and the Hebraic. The Church believes, however, that it can be loyal neither to Jewry nor itself if it accepts this exemption. For then the universality remains incomplete and "obduracy" forbids fulfilment, while chosen-ness remains an enigma.

To return, for a moment, to the land, to Palestine. The foregoing explains why, in the ultimate sense, it is incidental in Christian affection. Yet, for the historical reason, it is focal. If Jesus has, as we have yet to explore, a universal, messianic reach and achievement, the particular scene and setting of his life and death must always draw the scholar and the saint.

> ...those holy fields
> Over whose acres walked those blessed feet
> Which fourteen hundred years ago were nailed,
> For our advantage, on the bitter cross.

Yet, if they are rightly to be visited on pilgrimage by the Western Church, or cherished in local possession by the Eastern, they must always be seen, and sacramentally revered, as the point of incidence of a Divine Incarnation and the point of departure of an inherently universal, land-leaving, race-mingling community. The Jerusalem that fronts the Mount of Olives is to be encountered in the Jerusalem that is everywhere.

The related concepts we have studied between Jewry and the Christian Church find their crux in the theme of Messiahship, realized, or mis-identified (as the case may be), in Jesus of Nazareth. There is no space here to do more than ponder the heart of this issue, leaving aside the large documentary and conceptual problems that belong with it, and only noting later in the argument its necessary antecedents.

The definition of the "Christian" must be sought in the Messiah. For what "Messiah" is in (Anglicized) Hebrew "Christ" is in Greek. In Christian theology what it takes to be the Christ is manifest in Jesus and becomes the active clue to the meaning of God. What it means that Jesus is the Christ is the central criterion by which the Christian —faith and disciple—is constituted. Christology, rightly understood, is precisely this theme of "being the Messiah". As such, it must not be monopolized, as has sometimes been the case, by categories that care only about metaphysical status. These have been one of the saddest Christian preoccupations *vis-à-vis* Islam.[1]

For being Messiah has to do with action and achievement: it is, we may say, within history the answer to history's biggest question, an answer coming forth from faith's deepest assurance. The old covenant saw Messiah as the fulfilling of the divine responsibility for a world, made and shaped for man's dominion, but blighted by his self-will. Messianic action is seen as the integrity of a faithful Creator, who because, in the Qur'ān's fine phrase, he had not created the world in jest, took active cognisance of creation's goodness, the law's worth, sin's tragedy and yearning. God's partnerships of benediction, man had frustrated in obduracy and disorder. In the person of Messiah judgment and mercy would accomplish a divine salvaging of victory from history's defeat. Messiah was the central figure, the crucial necessity, one might almost say the divine in self-consistent action, within that recovery. By him the broken covenant would be renewed, the dishonoured law retrieved, the prostituted land restored and the people truly redeemed.

Such was the place for the answer that Messiah was to be. Here is the heart of the biblical understanding of man, called into divine patterns of well-being and wilfully preferring his own ruin. So clear-

[1] Debates about nature, person and Sonship have often obscured the fact that Christhood has to do with *being* the Christ, with Gethsemane and the crown of thorns. But this achievement must always be seen in the meaning of God and this brings us back to theology. What is here meant is not some "Man-for-others" Jesus, asserted in theological agnosticism. Christology in both senses is *within* theology: it is not a substitute for it.

sighted is the Hebraic-Christian account of man's high calling that it cannot but accuse the deep measure of his sin: yet so confident of God's sovereignty that it cannot believe the divine initiative frustrated or withdrawn. "Deep calleth unto deep." History, as men representatively shape it in the Old Testament, is a chronicle of defiance of good, in a setting of divine power and purpose whose goodness is invincible. History is, therefore, a place calling for a divine answer and Messiah is the shape of it.

Tragically this anticipation of divine fidelity to the divine nature, implicit in messianic action, came to be monopolized within the categories of nation, land and race within which the old covenant was set. This tragedy, expounded for the moment from the Christian angle (since Judaism does not acknowledge its tragic quality) arose, partly in innocence and partly in wilfulness, from the two central and quite valid factors in the messianic scheme, namely people and polity. The old covenant had somehow in its very nature, as Christianity sees it, the temptations calculated to divert its own vindication, and make for miscarriage in its very travail. Ideas of Messiah might become the most stubborn of the enemies Messiah would have to save and his own understanding the deepest struggle of his achievement. It is for these reasons that Christianity lives by the Cross: and for these reasons also that, in Judaism and Islam, Messiah crucified is a contradiction in terms, in that, for the former he cannot be said ever to have come, and, for the latter, ever to have suffered.

Yet race and nation seemed so clearly the hub of messianic action. Could "enlandisement" be the parable of Israel's destiny or Exile the shape of its disobedience, and restoration of the nation in independence and authority for the world *not* be the form and pledge of its redemption? Could alien tyranny and imperial servitude, Babylonian or Roman, be the form of defeat and statehood with liberation *not* be the themes of victory? Could Messiah's reign be other than popular, national, political restoration? Out of the very promise of Messiahship the misconceptions sprang. The people's hopes required a sharply nationalist fulfilment: the agent of God's reign must be majestic: the nation, for its own sake and in its full potential as the world's educator, must be the vital factor. Throughout the Similitudes of Enoch, the Psalms of Solomon, the Books of the Maccabees, and other mirrors of mind familiar to the generation of Jesus, there is no hint of humiliation, no darkness of tragedy, unless incidental to militant victory.

The issue can be summarily studied, so to speak, *sub judice*, in the New Testament and more particularly in the inter-play of Jesus and his disciples. On the face of it the very language of its hymnology seems to share these patterns. "That we being delivered from the hand of our enemies might serve Him without fear." Mary's own *Magnificat*, sweet hymn as it is of the reversal of values, could be taken, or mistaken, in the usual sense of the great hope: "He hath scattered the proud...He hath put down the mighty..." This is the ambiguity within the perplexity, evident from the Gospels, in the disciples' following of Jesus through his ministry. The common shape of hope fitted ill with the growing pattern of his ways and words. By this logic there was bewilderment at his apparent disinterest in building up an external following, his readiness for a career of diminishing returns and growing defection (cf. John vi. 66), which in the finale the disciples themselves were to share. His works of compassion were deliberately neutralized, as far as public acclaim was concerned, by repeated instructions to those involved to "say nothing to any man". Through all, the intent of Jesus to check idle enthusiasms is unmistakeable. Yet a popular Messiah needs all the enthusiasms he can muster, idle though they be.

Deepening the disciples' perplexity, according to the New Testament, was the fact that "Messiah" was a title he seemed anxious they should associate with him, yet one he was strangely reluctant to use. His own preferred description was "Son of Man". Does this tend to the conclusion, manifest elsewhere, that Jesus' concern was with the "how?" as much as the "who?" of Messiahship? It would be disastrous for men to think they knew who he was, unless they were clear how he meant to fulfil the identity they thought he had. Yet why, it may be asked, did the prophecies of a suffering Messiah have such little weight? Or why, relatedly to that question, did the disciples seemingly pay such scant heed to his own warnings about humiliation ahead?

The passion predictions were certainly emphatic (cf. the sequence in Mark viii. 31; ix. 33–5; x. 35 and 45). The disciples were plainly oppressed and baffled. At first they may have hoped to bring him to a better mind. Or they may have reasoned that the purpose was to steel their wills for adversities proper to disciples and which they would gladly shoulder so long as Messiah himself went unscathed. For such immunity was crucial: a Messiah unable, or unwilling, to secure himself, could save nothing. As it grew clearer that suffering was to be, precisely, messianic and inalienably so, dismay turned their loyalty into doggedness and their hope into confusion. Only in the sequel could they take the clue, that suffering, far from being a grim stage on the road to its revenge, was in fact and truth the very form of Messiah's authority and power to save.

Here was the hidden relevance, neglected by the popular mind, but, it would seem, compellingly authentic to Jesus, of the suffering servant of the Deutero-Isaiah. That picture of redemptive self-oblation appears to have been shrouded or concealed. Commentary, finding it strange and disturbing, transformed it altogether.[1] On every popular and exegetical count, it seems plain that the contemporaries of Jesus saw Messiahship in terms far different from those which the passion of Jesus took to be the counsel of God. Why then did Jesus, in this heroically solitary way, see these as he did? For Christians the answer lies in what may be called his openness to God and man which is the meaning of divine sonship. The reasons within Jesus' revolutionary Messiahship must be sought in the character of his whole ministry.

There was about his preaching and action a keen independence of mind as to Jewish tradition. This realism over the pride and temptations of the law and covenantal status left him with no illusions that Messiahship after the popular ideal would touch the ancient ills. It would likely merely dig a new pit, as a Nigerian proverb has it, in filling up an old. The evils of the human situation would simply have changed hands. Liberate Israel, as such, from the Romans and you have still saved neither Jews nor Romans from the tyranny of themselves. Exchange of dominion does not renew the creation or bring back the covenant. As long as it is "national" it does not bring to birth that chosen-ness of all peoples into God's design of which special vocation is no more than the pledge. Full and true Messiahship must break into these universal and radical reaches of God's purpose or it remains betrayed in the partial.

This does not mean that states and politics are in themselves invalid or that Rome has some eternal right to lord it over all races and zealots no business to be patriots. On the contrary, lands and people, married in freedom, are part of God's design. But if Messiah himself is imprisoned within these relatives he is no redeemer of the world. Rather by a patient sufferance under the pride of the chosen people, the

[1] See the translation of the Targum on Isaiah liii in W. Manson, *Jesus the Messiah* (London, 1946), pp. 229–32, where Messiah's sorrows are postulated of his foes.

injustice of the Romans, the national rejection, the disciples' failure, Messiah achieves for them all a salvation which leaves no element outside its reach of pardon and restoration. When Jesus had been Messiah in that redemptive encounter of love with sin his followers knew within themselves who Messiah was. And they knew how he was: for the two questions could only be answered together, in an answer which both constituted Christianity and gave Messiahship its hitherto hidden cruciformity. The Cross left no room for pride because it pardons, no room for monopoly because it is universal, no room for anger because it is forgiving, no room for despair because it has known and overcome the depths.

In all these respects, its "imitation", which is the vocation of Christianity, makes for that "de-territorialized" nature of the Christian community with which we began. The First Epistle of St Peter has this point very starkly in saluting "them that are scattered abroad" as "the elect of God" (i. 1–2), using the quality of Diaspora as the very token of oneness—a view which the old covenant and the new Zionism find a false reconciliation of opposites.

The historical emphasis of the foregoing study of Jesus' Messiahship as Christianity interprets its import has been deliberate. It justifies the earlier insistence that Messiahship is something to be accomplished. We do it wrong if we make it only a status to be asserted. Christology, that is, the art of being Messiah, is first a moral and actual, before it is a metaphysical, study. All too often Christian doctrine is improperly manoeuvred into a position where it seems to be doing battle for a divine status, whereas the very essence of that quality is an unconcern for status in itself, since the surest self-revelation lies in self-oblation. Christian Christology often ends up in hostile aggressiveness about the divine standing which, according to Philippians ii. 6, deliberately repudiates self-preserving canons of prestige.

At the same time the metaphysical Christology, properly disciplined, is a necessary part of the confession of "the deed of the Christ". In a revealing passage (Sūra IV. 172) the Qur'ān moves among the same terms as Philippians and the New Testament when it speaks of the servant and the son. But it finds them mutually exclusive. Since, as Christianity too agrees, "Messiah never scorns to be servant to God" Islam assumes and asserts he would, therefore, never claim to be a son. In this Qur'ānic reckoning, sonship, presumably for reasons of prestige, would disdain and exclude servanthood. "Scorning" means having in mind a "reputation"—precisely the realm of thought in Philippians, where, however, being willingly "of no reputation" is the quality and proof of sonship. So, for Christian faith, there is in this redemptive mission a quality of service which is divine not only in its source in will but its accomplishment in deed, a service which it takes God to achieve: and Christ is God undertaking it. Taking the Messiahship of Jesus as by character divine, the Christology of Christian faith is the movement of recognition from flesh to Word, from deed to nature, from Christ to God, but only because the movement of initiative flows the other way.

To the mind of continuing Jewry this "Messiahship" is contradicted by the persistent non-realization of its own cherished notion, namely redemption. The unrelieved "unredeemedness of the world" belies the assertion of Christian "Christhood". Admirable as its kinship with Jewish concepts must always be, in effect it betrays these by making them concrete. This is the core within all other pressing reasons for Jewish "outsideness" in respect of Christianity. Within this central decision, often in deep love of the Galilean Jesus, against the Church of his Christhood, belongs the Jewish refusal thus to be universalized which we have already pondered. By the same token, the Church's universalism and the Messiahship of Jesus are all of one piece. For Jewry, however, the world still has need, always will have need, both for an actual Israel and a prospective Messiah—and for the same reason. The rejection of the race-transcending Church is one with the inacceptability of a time-particularizing Messiah.

God's redeeming power is working everywhere at all times, yet "nowhere and at no time is there a state of redemption" writes Buber.[1] Only the pattern of redemption is clear: it is never inclusively fulfilled, nor is humanity decisively divided into saved and unsaved. "Messianic self-disclosure is the disruption of the Messiahship...the Messianic *mysterium* stands or falls with its seclusion; not because it is kept secret but because it is in itself a true and actual seclusion which penetrates to the innermost existence."[2]

There is an element in this rejection of the focus of man's redemption in the Cross with which the Christian could agree, in that there is in Christ crucified an unrealized condition. As "the perfect sacrament of the power whereby in the whole and in the end all evil is redeemed", it yet requires to be "imitated" and received. But, for the Christian,

[1] *Mamre, Essays in Religion*, p. 25. [2] *Ibid.* pp. 117–18.

that reproduction is the more surely wrought in man in time through the confidence that its prototype is veritably within history and divinely wrought in eternity. This sense of the prospective, through the definitive, Cross—man's fitting himself gratefully into the heavenly truth of this Christ—could gather to itself the wistful "pause" given to it by the Jewish sense, so tragically wrought all too often by Christian antipathy, of the abiding wrongness of the world. For the Cross is not manifest victory: but it is victory manifest. As such the Church takes it: here is at once the hidden and the disclosed Messiah.

Yet the cherished hiddenness of Jewry's Messiah continues and with it that *sui generis* quality of the Hebraic self-awareness. "The fulfilment of the Torah is entrusted to the Jewish people alone",[1] writes André Neher. "The narrow Jewish medium" remains the law's judicious policy as "a covenant community, completely distinct from all other nations...in full physical reality" from the Sinaitic occasion of grace.[2] Yet Hans Schoeps is ready, in an act of recognition not to be taken for an act of faith, to allow a divine origin to Christianity, on a different plane from "biological election",[3] as "Christian" truth for Christians. So then, "to Israel upon Sinai, to the world upon Golgotha",[4] and the issue—covenant perpetuated or completed, community unique or open.

The Christian verdict here involves a final paradox. Though nowhere private and everywhere at home its universality, being uncompulsive and "of grace", is everywhere selective. It invites but it does not insist. It is "a new Israel". Its pledge is never to refuse disciples yet never to grow by duress. That "whosoever will may come" is a charter at once of inclusion and of exclusion. Here, of course, is the brunt of Buber's concern about the "unredeemedness" of the redeemed world that neglects or declines or distrusts its own redemption. The "new Israel" is selective, not biologically, nor racially, nor meritoriously; but by the simple sanctities of will and its readiness for grace and penitence and compassion. The universalism is there, ambitious for all humanity. But its actuality, being beyond covenant from Sinai, turns upon grace and human will. Islam, in its unique fashion, has embraced the universality of the Church but proposed to make it actual by a return to its own account of law. To this third dimension of the Abrahamic triangle we must now pass, staying for the present with the kindred themes of place and people.

[1] Neher, *Moses*, p. 152. [2] Schoeps, p. 4. [3] His own phrase. [4] *Ibid.* p. 5.

THE ISLAMIC: "AN ARABIC QUR'ĀN" AND THE WORLD

Islam is "a harmony of idealism and positivism: and as a unity of eternal verities of freedom, equality and solidarity has no fatherland".[1] Thus Sa'īd Ḥalīm Pasha of Lahore, writing in 1921. "No fatherland" and a wide human dispersion, yet nevertheless a *qibla*, or geographical direction of prayer, an annual physical pilgrimage, "an Arabic Qur'ān", an Arab apostle of God and, for thirteen centuries, a caliphate of Arabian, that is, Meccan, descent.

Despite these unmistakable Arab denominators of Islamic genesis and history and the several emphatic Islamic nationalisms of the contemporary scene, this claim to a universalism of Islam belongs firmly within a Semitic sense of destiny. Yet it differs sharply from the universalizing temper of the Christian Church. For it goes back on the Christian idea of grace and the openness implicit in an abrogating fulfilment of the old covenant. It goes back, also, on the Christian diagnosis of man under law in rebellion and reasserts in vigorous extra-Jewish form the earlier ground of divine legislation. It centres its cohesion around the dominating idea of submission and adherence, rejecting both the Hebraic notion of vocation, with its ethnic particularity, and the Christian concept of the Church. Its universalism has the ambiguity of the specialness hinging on the Arabic Qur'ān. Where the Church offers Jewry the reasoned and grateful apologia about its own fulfilment, Islam offers it only the reproach of castigation and a re-education in which its unworthily held Scriptures take correction.

There is thus a profound contrast in the assumptions and temper of the development relating Christianity to Judaism and that relating Islam to either. Here is the right universality over against the privacy of Israel's chosen-ness: here is the simple finality of law-giving, without the covenantal mysteries of Moses, over against the new covenant of grace and regeneration that complicates the pretentious and precarious universality of the Church. Here is a posture simpler and more logical than Sinai, more robust and virile than Golgotha and for both reasons more assuredly and effectively bent towards the world.

Of necessity, it will be admitted, Islam has "a local habitation and a name". Its camel riders could claim to belong in their elusive way with the Palestinians of Braudes' poem.[2] For them 'Īsā (Jesus) is always *al-Masīḥ*, Messiah, Son of Mary, born under the date palm. When Islam

[1] *Reform of Muslim Society*, Eng. trans. (Lahore, 1921). [2] Quoted above, p. 365.

began, the *qibla* of its worship, like the expectation of its founder, was towards Jerusalem. Even when this direction was abandoned for the still idolatrous shrine at Mecca, so that the thoughts and aspirations of the new Muslim community might concentrate on its ultimate acquisition, the change was explained, not as a substitution of localities, but as a sign of the divine omnipresence. Jerusalem, it could be claimed was not abandoned but retentively enlarged.

The *hijra* itself, by which Yathrib became al-Madīna (Medina), and Mecca was for the time abandoned, became the symbol of Islamic venture. The community was constituted in migration. The initial date of the Muslim calendar is the definitive event in Muslim experience. Its founder community was a partnership of settlers and "receivers", *muhājirūn* and *anṣār*, goers-forth and takers-in. It is the reproduction of this hospitality which makes for universalism.

Aside, too, from the original *qibla* of Jerusalem, the heartlands of Semitic religion have their Islamic heirs. It is well not to forget the third party in the Palestinian scene, third in chronology but first in present circumstance and statistics. Muḥammad's Night Journey to the Masjid al-Aqṣā (Sūra XVII. 1), Abraham's associations with the Ḥaram al-Sharīf and with Hebron, other shrines and habitations of the patriarchs and the veneration given to Jesus, all involve Muslims in a deeply religious stake in territory. The Palestinian should not be lost to sight in the larger expanses that are Arabia, south and east.[1]

There is nothing of course sacramental in the Christian sense about that association, nor integral in the Hebraic manner. There is, however, the same Semitic theology of territorial tenancy. The tribes of men, as the Qur'ān sees them, are "installed in their habitations"—"caused to colonize" is the phrase[2] for the same purposes of "magnifying the Lord" that belong with the Hebrew sense of vocation to a God-fearing

[1] This is not to add the obvious sanctions of more recent political self-expression. A ready example would be Khalīl Mardam Bey's national anthem for Syria:

"Defenders of the Fatherland, all hail!
Your noble spirits cannot cringe or fail.
The Arab homeland is a shallowed shrine
None may assail this sanctuary divine.
The coasts of Syria are as stars on high,
Vieing in splendour the uplifted sky:
Not heaven's self is more sublimely grand
Than where our forbears glorified our land."

See A. J. Arberry, *Aspects of Islamic Civilization* (London, 1965), p. 394.

[2] The word is *ista'marakum* (Sūra XI. 61) which gives Arabic its most reproachful modern word, that for "imperialism".

husbandry and a God-confessing society. There is also the same intangible connexion between "people" and "Book", that describes all scriptures, and from which, as it would appear, the germ of Muḥammad's peculiarly Arabic vocation was drawn. This reception of a Holy Book fortifies the sense of "election" or perhaps better, in this context, of self-confidence, which characterizes Islamic experience. The possession of Scriptures develops an instinct to possess the earth. The immediate treasure of revelation confers a status which confronts all other places and peoples with a didactic authority—an authority which Islamic canons of state action quickly translated into suzerainty and government. From the beginning, in the *hijra* if not at Ḥirā', the mount of vision, the implications of Islamic prophethood were set towards territorial expansion and racial inclusion.

This destiny became indubitable, and over many areas irresistible, through the conviction of revelatory finality and scriptural supercession. It was not simply that Jewish and Christian "people of the Book" had afforded a germinal example. They had also merited a displacement on account of disloyalty. Thus Muḥammad's mission and Islam's claim gathered momentum by turning the flank of privilege, both abrogating and consummating earlier revelation.

This claim to finality was not solicitous of the feelings it violated or the beliefs it disqualified. The Qur'ān, in its main emphasis, pursues a vigorous polemic against Jews and Christians, takes their theological tensions as proof only of confusion or mischief and proceeds to inform them of the things about which they differ. This energetic downrightness misses the subtleties within the issues and rides roughshod over their complexity. It castigates Christians for preaching adoptionism, which is a contra-Christian heresy[1] and embraces docetism to the degree in which this sectarian deviation sought to spare Jesus the ignominy of actual crucifixion. Contentious themes are here. Of immediate relevance is the total neglect, within the Qur'ān's abrogation of the two other faiths, of the meaning of Messiahship.

The term "Messiah" is reverently used of Jesus in the general sense of "anointing", or possibly of "homelessness". But it falls squarely within the sense of prophethood, a ministry to teach and warn, which is not climactic in its nature but only didactic. The *Injīl*, or Gospel, by Jesus has, therefore, an educational constituency, its due time and place,

[1] This aspect is usefully presented in R. C. Zaehner, *At Sundry Times* (London, 1958), app. pp. 195–217: "The Qur'ān and Christ."

and no inherent universality except in its ultimate absorption into the Qur'ānic. Shorn of any redemptive role, and thus severed from all relevance to the Jewish–Christian debate about Christhood, the Qur'ānic *Masīḥ* remains subordinately within the divine economy of exhortation and guidance, and his own particular appointment.

The destined universality comes only with the final prophet, Muḥammad, who begins however with a specific audience and sphere. The Qur'ān is by its own insistence "an Arabic Qur'ān". As Sūra XVI. 38 observes, there is "to each nation a preacher". So, in Sūra XXVIII. 46 Muḥammad is reminded: "You were not on the side of the mountain when We called Moses: but you came through a mercy of your Lord that you might warn a people to whom no warner came." These were the Arabs, the *ummiyyūn*, the unscriptured. That initial calling widened into a "a mercy to all nations" (Sūra XXI. 107). "We have not sent you but universally to (all) men as a bringer of good tidings and a warner" (Sūra XXXIV. 27). When it did so, it did not reckon with what earlier criteria had taken "mercy for the world" to entail and intend. Nevertheless the Arabs in Islam adapted, in partial form, the specialness that had characterized Jewry as those who had heard the Word, and pursued an uninhibited universalism, in distinction from the Christian unities of grace, race and the Gospel.

That pursuit and the conscious authority that inspired it stemmed from the formative decision of the founder himself, a decision, nevertheless, proceeding out of a problem common to faiths in general, namely the duty of truth under adversity. What do vocations in truth do with hostility? Successive Hebrew prophets knew this dilemma, bearing the brunt of missions which they could neither forsake nor consummate in success. Jeremiah represents, in the deepest agony, the sharpest form of this prophetic burden. It recurs, of course, within the ministry of Jesus where the course of preaching and teaching is in steadily intensifying relation to opposition and rejection, the climax of which is the Cross, faced and inflicted.

Many of the same features emerge in the confrontation of Muḥammad and the Quraysh of Mecca. He too is greeted with obduracy and repudiation. Within the Meccan period before the *hijra*, his attitude to antagonism remains essentially "religious". He reacts in a sustained steadfastness of preaching, and warning, and in a consequent acceptance of risk and contumely. There is potentially in his situation, so borne, the shape and quality of a cross. In and by the *hijra*, which breaks out of the impasse, comes a new pattern of energetic assertion and a contrasted policy of statehood and physical sanction as a means of ensuring success and surmounting the adverse. There then occurs what is cumulatively a decisive change in the whole orientation of Muḥammad's career. What had been "religious" becomes now "politico-religious". Every interpreter has to assess whether to see this development as implicit from the outset and not operative before the *hijra* for lack of occasion, or whether to see it embraced as a new decision emerging from the anguish within the pre-*hijra* "Cross" of a valid and yet rejected mission. Be the alternative, historically, as it may, the outward contrast is clear in the two sets of circumstances, pre- and post-*hijra* and in the different temper of the Medinan sequel.

That invocation of the sanctions of power, the acquisition and employment of the civil arm and the city state, inevitably engendered an element of prudence and insincerity in human allegiance. One cannot successfully oppose one's enemies without attracting time-serving friends. The Qur'ān becomes increasingly aware of untrustworthiness in the context of the Medinan development. It frequently reproaches the *munāfiqūn*, the hypocrites, and warns against the pretenders. Submissions had to be questioned, in case they were only politic and not genuine. This necessity of suspicion tended to breed its own justification. The atmosphere took on a quality of intrigue and the reader has the distinct impression that the prophet is ringed around with subtle foes.

Clearly not all this malevolence is engendered by the political. We have already noted that hostility belonged in the "preaching" period. But, by the political measures, it was met, and thus accentuated, on its own level and in these post-*hijra* events, Islam itself moves into the instinct that identifies the cause with success and both with the imprint of God. Thus the note of self-criticism was muted and muffled, while the sense of mission became habituated to the reproach of exterior malice. *Fitna*, the operative word in the Qur'ān here, undergoes a significant progression of meaning from "trial" and "persecution" (which is what religious minorities face from majorities), to "intrigue" and "sedition" (which political majorities face from minorities). The inversion is complete from minority to majority status and from ill-will borne to ill-will suppressed, and each because of the other.

Closely relevant to this analysis is the Qur'ān's interest in the patriarchal histories. Its narratives belong mostly to the middle and late

Meccan period. Their presence in considerable length and frequency is explained from two related angles, namely the reminder of the fate of earlier recalcitrant people and the consequent encouragement of the prophet to tenacity in the face of opposition and attack. Vindication is the theme of both: warners were upheld and warnings came to pass. This motif undoubtedly buoyed up Muḥammad in his experience of adversity and justified, as God-intended and ordained, the measure which brought to pass the steady turn of the tide.

From this has followed the characteristic simplicity or forcefulness of Islamic expansion, untroubled by internal questions and sure in its sense of right and, what is no less important, its adversaries' wrong. It rarely produces Hamlets "sicklied o'er with the pale cast of thought", nor do the currents of its enterprises "turn awry and lose the name of action". The Qur'ān describes itself as "a Book with nothing dubious within it". A similar conviction fits the activity of historic Islam and derives from this initial history of antipathy confronted and subdued by forthright assurance. The point has been well noted by Maḥmud Mukhtar Katircioglu in his *Wisdom of the Qur'ān*.

> From its first appearance (Islam) was surrounded by enmity and treachery. Its earliest steps were taken past the ambushes of lurking foes. As it became older there grew up along with it suspicions, malice and hatred. When, in spite of all these it succeeded in reaching man's estate and becoming fully adult, it was still obliged to defend itself unceasingly against vehement attacks, to fight for its very existence and even take arms against its opponents whom it thought of starkly as enemies of the Divine Truth.[1]

Perhaps the best summary lies in the observation that Islam is a supreme iconoclasm.

From this legacy of its own immediate history another feature emerges, namely the absence, for the most part, of those historical attitudes of the biblical mind. The patriarchs are fulfilled in the lesson of vindication. The great Old Testament writing prophets are unknown to the Qur'ān, and despite the notion of prophetic succession from Adam to Muḥammad there is no cumulative meaning to the succession save the didactic repetition and enlargement. There is no development of the sort through which the parallel New Testament story of the vineyard and the husbandmen proceeds to its climax. Education sums up the divine relation to mankind: and prophecy itself climaxes its own

[1] *A selection of verses, with Introduction, conveying the moral, religious and social philosophy of Islam*, trans. by John Naish (London, 1937), p. vii.

sequence. "More than a prophet" finds no echo in the convictions of Islam. Its sense of ancient history is of a series of hortatory missions, issuing either in responsive obedience or in merited judgment. The call of Abraham is to repudiate idolatry rather than inaugurate a dispensation. The task of Jesus is to preach righteousness, not to bring all things into subjection that God may be all in all. Islam is the inveterate natural religion: time consists in the interventions and interludes of the messengers and the vicissitudes of the communities that hearken or refuse.

This incisive quality of Islam, thus summarized, set a vexing pattern of relationship for the earlier faiths, the entail of which remains to this present, embittered by reciprocal enmities which, from the other side, resented its psychology of finality, its rough assurance and the short shrift it made of the antecedent heirs of Abraham.

These communal estrangements and dogmatic contentions, however, must be resolutely held in proper perspective. Despite their sharpness they concern what unifies. Islam's unceremonious severity against synagogue and church is sometimes a militancy they themselves would share against notions that they do not hold. Doubtless when we have disentangled the senses in which actual Jewish or Christian doctrine is *not* being refuted in the text or sense of the Qur'ān, there remains a serious degree to which both are being disallowed. Yet even here the will to unify, to believe and know that "the Lord alone is our fear" and to be thus set free from all but this divine service—this is a religious intention which, for all their wounded susceptibilities, disciples from Sinai and Gethsemane can surely take in ready part. And doing so there lies the surer hope of untying the tangles of misconception which abide.

If both the insistent nature and the dismaying effect of Islam's controversies can be surmounted by mutual will, the themes of concord can take firmer control, gathering as they do around the acknowledgement of God. For here the positive achievement of Islam belongs.

Its central impulse is that God be acknowledged God, in the constant awareness, submission, "rightness", and worship of his world. "The exclusion of God"—a phrase the Qur'ān uses over eighty times[1] is its inner burden. People who disregard God, in thanklessness, in the tyranny or indulgence of false absolutes, arouse its reiterated surprise

[1] Thirty or more times with the word Allāh, thirty-six with the pronoun relating to him, and a few times with *al-Raḥmān*.

and dismay. In the idolater's world God is ousted from his due authority, while misdirected homage flouts man's true nature and his proper good. By this ignoring of God, which is the really damnable atheism, men miss the meaning of themselves. As Sūra LIX. 19 has it: "They have forgotten God and God caused them to forget themselves." As ever, the denial of God distorts and degrades the human. Hence the deep anxiety of Abraham, for example: "I will separate myself from you and from that on which you call to the exclusion of God" (Sūra XIX. 48). Their patrons, lords, intercessors, protectors, "other than God", not merely diversify as cults, but deceive the mind and disrupt the society. Only by this "demythologizing"[1]—not to be confused with disenchantment or deconsecration—can man find unity within himself and his communities.

This insistent, resolute Qur'ānic repudiation of idolatry and the concern that men should "esteem God a true esteeming" (Sūra VI. 91) is of so vital and central a religious significance as to outweigh, when viewed in patient Jewish–Christian perspective, those otherwise sad and provocative sources of conflict. It may be deplorable that the Qur'ān, in resisting the idolaters, extends the term and idea of *ittikhādh* (that God himself "pantheonizes") to the Christian account of Christ. This is tragically to include an equally urgent monotheism among the plural worships. Nevertheless, in disavowing what was done, Christians can learn to acknowledge what was meant and to find in the latter an intention within kinship.

The passion of Islam for the divine Unity brings it vitally within the most revealing of all theological mysteries where it finds both the antecedent faiths also utterly engaged, namely in the willingness of God to be ignored. The chorus of Qur'ānic repudiation of idols confronts us with the paradox that the inalienable worship is in fact alienated and the undeniable divine reality denied. The very relationship of God with men leaves room for the possibility of their idolatry. His being God does not depend upon men, but his recognition does. Here is a profoundly remarkable truth about the God the idolater ignores. His kingdom is a realm of the free and his worship uncompulsive. The more urgently we disown the perverted worships the more crucial becomes the shape and condition of their correction. By

[1] Cf. C. F. von Weizsäcker, *The Relevance of Science: Creation and Cosmology* (New York, 1965), who writes: "If mythology means that our thought is under the domination of the gods, it is precisely the faith in God which has demythologized our thinking from the time when the Old Testament was first written" (p. 50).

what means and through what cost shall men in their *islām* discern and allow the Godness of God? To have written that question into history is the supreme achievement of Islam and to have served it the kinship of its saints and common souls with the watchers for Messiah.

This threefold survey, set within the common terms of particular and universal, has, it is believed, disclosed the primary themes of concord and conflict belonging with the three faiths. It remains to take up certain corollaries of the foregoing and bring the picture nearer to completeness. It is proposed to do so by the clue of the *shekina*—the divine among men and a society lived in the realized consciousness of God. For this breathes the common air of the religions under review and makes their doctrinal dialogue. It is continuous with our territorial beginnings. Its mysteries shape the Old Testament world: its assurance informs the New and (though it only uses the word six times)[1] the Qur'ān stands for a quality of divine recognition, for the authority of the acknowledged Will, that mean, in its own imperative way, the dutiful awareness of God. Given a right imagination this pattern of argument will ensure a sense of concord and integrity, while readily disciplining the issues of conflict. It falls into three parts: theological, operative and institutional; and over all the responsive plea of the psalmist: "Arise, O Lord, into Thy dwelling place."

GOD

Hear, O Israel, The Lord our God is one Lord, and thou shalt love the Lord thy God with all thy heart, soul, mind and strength.

To us there is but one God, the Father, of Whom are all things, and we in Him and one Lord Jesus Christ, by Whom are all things and we by Him.

There is no god but God and Muḥammad is the apostle of God.

Here are the familiar confessions, each with their proper associated context of the truth of God, Israel, Christ, Muḥammad.

People in vocation for God: *shekina* and community.
Presence in action of God: *shekina* and the Son.
Prophet-spokesman for God: *shekina* in obedience.

[1] Sūras II. 248; IX. 29 and 40; XLVIII. 4, 18 and 26. In each case the general sense seems to be an assurance, or reassurance, as from God, of his presence and aid securing the truth. Arberry prefers to use the transliterated *Shechina*, rather than translate.

For all the sustained and intricate controversies between the three theologies here is their central concord in the unity of God. The conflicts lie, not in the fact, but the explanation, of the Unity. It is false to interpret the persistent Jewish particularism as a mitigation of the theological unity it has heroically confessed. While Christian theology, out of love for Judaism, must see that limitation as inconsistent with its theological vocation, there is no doubting its integrity. That association of the one Lord with the "exceptional" Israel has been the source of the very convictions whereby men question its continuing reservation.

There is, likewise, no proper ground for disqualifying the unity of God as the Christian dogma affirms it in the faith of Father, Son and Holy Spirit. Much Islamic thinking here has been ill-served by purely arithmetical debate. The Christian faith in Jesus as God the Son and in "the Holy Spirit proceeding from the Father and (or through) the Son" rests squarely within the Islamic confidence of God over all. If "let God be God" is the sum of Islam, it is the perfect expression also of the substance of Christian theology. "You believe in God, believe also in me." It is not a concern for unity but for unitariness which calls in question the New Testament and the Apostles' Creed. The theme of the Unity is a theme of unity.

Nor does conflict essentially fracture that concord in the third equation coming from the Islamic *shahāda* or Confession. Islam has always seen theology as being for the sake of law. Awareness of God's nature is for obedience to His will. It has become metaphysically discursive more for controversy than confession. True, the apostolate of Muḥammad, in history and emotion, has been the occasion of profound Jewish–Christian disquiet. Yet the inner objective, if not the pattern, of the Muḥammadan achievement belongs congenially within the Hebraic and Christian traditions. For these also declare the nonentity of the "gods many and lords many" and are set, either by denunciation or redemption, for the liquidation of idolatry. "Thou shalt not make to thyself any graven image" reverberates in the Decalogue. "Little children, keep yourselves from idols" are, likely, the last words penned in the New Testament. The undergirded kinship of the faiths about the divine Unity abides through and beyond all the quarrels about the associated claims.

Subtle differences of emotion and emphasis belong of course with the tensions already told. Ponder the classic summaries themselves. "There is no god but God", "Thou shalt have none other gods but

Me": "I believe in God..." The Islamic, in the given context of Arabian polydaemonism, is a negation prefacing an indicative: the Hebraic, within the given awareness of a people, is an imperative requiring an exclusion: the Christian, in the given setting of experienced fellowship, is a personal affirmation opening a long and careful confession.

To set these side by side is to see their triple bearing on the goal of each, as it might be quoted in the cry of the psalmist: "Whom have I in heaven but Thee?"..."There is none upon earth that I desire beside Thee." This means the negation of the false deities with forthrightness. It means the soul's liberation from the comforting, or haunting, false worships which persist in the heart when the propositions of unity have all been made and the commands trumpeted. It means the inward soul-commitment to the publicly witnessed convictions. The battle for divine unity is in the spirit as well as in the mind: it has to reject inner superstitions as well as outward denial. Its duty is not exhausted in assertions, nor in iconoclasm. "God dwells", said the old rabbi of Kotzk, "wherever man lets him in." In their characteristic and contentious ways, the three monotheisms are to be seen as caring for their own sense of that condition, namely in the ideal of the elect-people-sanctuary, in the new covenant of accomplished grace and in the insistent repudiation of rivals to the divine.

Earlier sections illustrated the shared sense of a hallowed nature, deriving from the common doctrine of creation. The goodness reiterated in the Genesis account of the world's elements makes creation the highway, not the obstacle, to human delight and divine communion. Christianity, from time to time, has faltered in that assurance under stress of its sense of evil and its intuitive affinity with suffering. But these, duly disciplined, belong with a grateful acceptance of the things of sense and desire. "Every creation of God is good", declares I Tim. iv. 4, "if it be received with thanksgiving". The Qur'ān has the same condition in its antithesis between *kufr* and *shukr*: unbelief is essentially ingratitude. In this appreciation of the natural world, the homilies of the Pentateuch, the praises of the psalmists, the appeals of the prophets, the parables of Jesus and the "signs" of the Qur'ān present a harmonious diversity.

Here we reach the Christian scandal of the Incarnation. For "scandal" it has always seemed to the Jew and the Muslim. Its implications ramify into every part of this discussion. It is within the sense of nature and creation that we may with hope shoulder its liabilities. The twin ideas of sovereignty and mercy within the doctrine of the Unity are its point of origin. The mystery, given affirmation in the Christian doctrine of God in Christ, gives intimations, perplexing and inviting, everywhere and certainly in those theologies which deem it unthinkable. Though the doctrine may be unique—and to them uniquely reprehensible—the secret within it finds relative anticipation in the sign-quality of the natural order, in the instrumentality of the prophets and the divine–human "associations" involved in all theological language.[1]

The biblical and Qur'ānic "signs" in the natural order are a rendezvous with the divine goodness in time. Revelation therein is perpetual. For Judaism, further, events in earthly history are taken as the locus of an experience in which God is known. "I will be there as He whom I there will be" is the sense of the exchange about the Exodus at the burning bush. The God of the Exodus is known only in the event, where "you shall find what I am and who I am and what I will".[2]

The doctrine of God Incarnate is boldly continuous with these convictions about the natural–historical–human sphere as expressing the divine name. It sees the divine "name-ability" (inseparable from all religion), not reluctantly, as Judaism and Islam, but confidently and specifically, in Christ. Its reasons for doing so are cognisant of the sources of that reluctance. The experience, it is well to remember, was defined from within monotheism. It could be claimed as within the whole Semitic insistence, not merely that what is not divine should never be worshipped, but also that what is recognizably so, always must be.

Christian theology would aver that the provisos by which the other two faiths withhold their minds from that crucial recognition of the worshipable might well, if pressed, jeopardize their own theisms. The Old Testament metaphor of the shepherd suggests that God stays in his heaven only by also leaving it. The total "dissociation" of the eternal and the temporal which, when consistent, denial of the possibility of the Incarnation involves, imperils the whole realm of law, prophecy, revelation and worship in which the mosque and the synagogue believe.

[1] More fully discussed by Kenneth Cragg in: *The Dome and the Rock* (London, 1964), ch. 8, "The Names of God" (pp. 83–93).

[2] Quoted, in fact, from a message of Staupitz to Luther, where the opening words are: "In Christ you shall find..." See P. S. Watson, *Let God be God* (London, 1948). (An intriguing "Muslim" title for a book about Luther's theology.)

Nevertheless, the steadfast Jewish–Muslim rejection of the belief about God the Son—for all its distressing insuperability from the standpoint of the Church—serves to keep always in view the transcendant mystery which that belief might seem to have impugned. It emphasizes the same will to unambiguous monotheism which is in fact the Christian intention of the phrase: "the only begotten Son". The conflict here is partly terminological. In Sūra CXII, and in Jewish dogma, God "neither begets nor is begotten". For he is *al-ṣamad*, the self-subsisting. In this passage, "begetting" is taken as meaning an alienation, and thus an alternative acquisition, of divinity, rather than, as in Christian terminology, an expression of it. This is an occasion in theological thought where the liabilities of a particular analogy have been acutely unfortunate.[1] The term which admits of unintended interpretation has a peculiar scriptural and credal centrality for Christians. Yet hope may be cherished that the Jewish–Muslim steadfastness for divine unity and the Christian sense of that divineness and unity as the doctrine of Christ enshrines them may yet find a concord that will do justice to the integrity of their controversial concern for each other.

That conjecture hinges upon more than the one question of the unity, even as the meaning of God in all three faiths lives with their whole understanding of man, law and sin.

MEN AND GOD

"As he came nigh to the camp and saw the calf...Moses' anger waxed hot and he cast the tables out of his hands and brake them beneath the mount" (Exodus xxxii. 19). The scene when Moses shattered the God-inscribed tablets of the Torah takes us all to the deepest heart of our religions. It is a drama of command and contradiction: there is the claim and the tumult, the law and the lawless, the rule and the unruly. Defiance, surging through the ranks of impatient, callous, gross and sceptical humanity, even while their seer is in rendezvous with their destiny on the mount, is too great to bear in the same hands with the divine invitation to partnership. The very tablets are impulsively destroyed in the overwhelming sense of their impossibility in the presence of a rejection already manifest at the foot of the very mountain

[1] See H. A. Wolfson, "The Muslim Attributes and the Christian Trinity", *Harvard Theological Review*, vol. XLIX, pt. 1 (1956), pp. 1–18.

and in the very moment of their heavenly *imprimatur*. Yet out of this dramatic disclosure of the enmities that wait for it, the law will be patiently renewed: the tablets will be inscribed anew. Turbulent humanity cannot be abandoned to its calves, its coward Aarons and profanities. The law has undaunted patience as well as unyielding authority. Moses will be recalled and will reascend the mount.

Yet the inner mystery persists: the unwelcome Deity and his unwanted claim. "The exclusion of God" it is the Qur'ān's fervent concern to reverse by entreaty, reminder and injunction. "Behold I stand at the door and knock" is the familiar word of Christ and characteristically divine. "God is wherever men admit him" said the rabbi—God, in that sense, "not of the philosophers", but of Abraham and Jacob.

> In beggar's part I will not cease to plead...
> I shall pursue my immemorial plan
> Past the low lintel of the human heart.

Judaism and Islam might find dismay at the language but the truth is implicit—this God whom men are free to neglect while they prefer their idols, this God who is in the desert where his people are—the desert of their own inhospitable absorption with themselves, the God who in human enterprise is met with crucifixion, the God who matches the enlandisement of men with his own abiding presence in the territory of their hearts and empires to make the home of his mercy in their wills, hinging not, mercifully, his right, but his reign, upon their willingness. This is, in their differing consensus, the God of Israel, of Christianity and of Islam, the God of law and prophet and Messiah. The *shekina* theology, it is true, comes, with that term, only in the inter-Testamental period. But it belongs integrally with the biblical themes. As we have been careful to note, the human adventure is accompanied by the divine: the "dwelling" in the Old Testament is to be mutual in the land. In the New it is in Christ that God dwells for, and so in, his people, while Islam's vigilance for his due, his solely due, honour is simply the practice of his omniscient and omnipotent presence.

Why, then, this mystery of recalcitrance in man—the golden calves, the wayward people, the unwanted Messiah, the broken prophets, the hypocrites and *ẓālimūn*, "wronging" in the Qur'ān's repeated phrase "their own souls"? Why the miscarriage in the enterprise of law? What and whence is the meaning of salvation? How are men justified before God and God in their justification? Should we call it righteousness, or submission, or redemption? How shall it be, this proper human relationship to the God whose purposes and nature have made that relationship so crucial to his being?

Islam, it might be said, would never pursue these queries to that final interrogative. For it carries a boldness unsuited to man and perhaps even takes the human situation too seriously. God is emphatically not harmed by men: sin brings him no damage. His impassibility is immune from consequences of our puny waywardness. Yet religion here is better than orthodoxy. If the impassibility of God is to hold in this form, the whole vehement anxiety of the Qur'ān about his "exclusion" becomes unreal. Submission from man cannot be both urgently sought and sublimely unwanted. Islam, by definition and its scripture, is irrevocably committed to the meaningfulness of evil and this cannot finally co-exist with an alleged indifference in God. It may be that here Jewish and Christian thought can encourage Islamic theology to a surer consistency with Islamic religion. For the latter has a latent depth of realism about man in sin.

"That religion may be wholly God's" is the objective of Islam, enjoined, with the final defeat of *fitna*, or unruliness, in Sūra VIII. 39. How is this rightness to be reached? Prophets indict the disobedience and its positive antithesis is found, in the Islamic realm, by their pleas and example, by the habituation of the religious duties, by the encouragement of human solidarity within the faith, by the sanction of proper fear and due exhortation, and with the support of overriding Islamic statehood. These are the factors in what may be described as doctrinal optimism in Islam. It does not normally use the word "salvation", still less "regeneration", though its saints and mystics know full well the mysteries of inward evil and its day-to-day devotions echo the plea for refuge.[1] In general Islam is content to draw back from the ultimate mysteries of evil, both in its dogmatic shape and its pastoral temper. It bids men fear the judgment, walk humbly, rely upon mercy, conform to the duties of *dīn* and be cast, without anguished inquiry, upon the compassion of God. It does not see that compassion pledged,

[1] Wilfred Cantwell Smith in "Some similarities and differences between Christianity and Islam" in *The World of Islam: Studies in honour of Philip K. Hitti* (London, 1960), pp. 47–59, makes the point that "righteousness" is "social salvation" in Islam and "faith in righteousness" the means to "personal salvation" (p. 53). It is well not to limit the concept of "salvation" to redemption. The final two Sūras of the Qur'ān are well known as "the Refuge Seekers". The deepest menace they mention is "the evil of an envier in his envy".

nor does it find it active, in any deliberate, recognizable, historical initiative where it may be dependably and crucially experienced. But it is there.

For this reason Islam remains inhospitable to Christian soteriology and rejects both the historical event, the moral quality and the divine necessity of the Cross of Christ. As Katircioglu puts it:

> The idea of a collective redemption, based on a definite historical event which took place at a fixed moment in the past, and the connected notion of a purchase of freedom for humanity at the price of the torture of a god, are both equally foreign to the thought of a devout Muslim.[1]

To this issue we must return. The form in which it is stated epitomizes both the misconceptions from which Islam assesses the Cross and the sanguine reliance it maintains in the remedial response of law, warning and education, to the world of God-excluders and forgetful worshippers. Man, after all, is too finite to be radically rebellious: it suffices that he be disciplined into peace with God and rightness within.

Jewry has its characteristic stake in the same mysteries. The Torah, we must be clear, is an invitation to divine–human co-operation. It is where and how God leaves room for man and where men, in their responsive loyalty, find room for God. It is, therefore, idle, as many Christians have done, to decry the mystery of the law as legalism and reproach it for being meticulous, formal, hypocritical and hidebound, making for pride, censoriousness and all unlovely things. These are its perversions, not its nature. The law itself repudiates them.

But it is no less idle, as some Jewish thinkers have done, to reprove and refuse Paul's anguished disqualification of the law, as if he had only seen it as such a legalism. Thus Hans Joachim Schoeps sees "the theology of the apostle Paul...as the theology of multiplied misunderstanding".[2] He (Paul) devalued the law by noting legalistic "righteousness" and on the basis of that accusation talked of a hardened heart and a forfeited covenant, whereas in fact "the law is not ruined by the disillusioning actuality of sin".[3] On the contrary it stands within a covenant that is above the vicissitudes of its reception. Paul's criticism, it is here alleged, points only to an intrinsic problem of Judaism: it

[1] *Wisdom of the Qur'ān*, p. xxiii.

[2] Hans Joachim Schoeps, *Paul*, trans. by Harold Knight (London, 1959), p. 262. A. Neher, *Moses*, rejects the view that Paul's strictures are merely an anti-legalism that has mistakenly questioned the whole law (p. 150).

[3] Schoeps, *ibid.* p. 282.

does not rightly raise the fundamental issue of whether the law is "fulfillable". All that it teaches is that Jews must beware of wanting "the will of God too quickly and rectilineally", and must look on always, as Paul might if his heresy were corrected, to "the eschatological power of the law's revealer".[1]

This does less than justice to Paul's agony of thought and to his autobiography. He does not degrade the law into legalism and then pillory the travesty, nor does his accusation of his heritage lie outside a lively sense of that covenant. Must "the eschatological power of the law's revealer" have only a future tense? May it not take action in a divine initiative that reaches to the problem, not merely of a legalistic righteousness, but of the law's own paradox? Here Paul's experience, as already suggested, links with the antagonism to Christ and the universal rebelliousness of which it is the "sign". "The good that I would I do not and the evil that I would not that I do." The law addresses at once an acknowledging obligation and an innate inability. Faced with my self-admitted failure—which is much more than superficial—the law must necessarily condemn. Yet I continue, even if so it be in my hypocrisy, to be the confessor of its right. I cannot deny its goodness, nor can I come by it in response to that recognition.

Here lies the core of the Christian diagnosis of man. Those who do not follow Paul from the Torah's school into his discovery of grace remain hopeful of the law, either along Islamic lines of a hortatory, communal and habituating sanction believed to be self-ensuring in the law itself, or in the deep assurance of Jewry that the law, somehow, has a prospective efficaciousness which will not in the end be wanting. Where either confidence exists the Pauline antithesis of law and faith is resented and rejected. The steadfast performance of the Jewish *mitzva* is a participation in Moses and with him in the covenantal relationship that neither formalism can distort nor unworthiness condemn. The point has been movingly put by André Neher:

> Performing a *Mitzva* means...by holiness restoring the unity of man who was created in the likeness of the unity of God. In this effort to achieve unity the commandments of the Torah soften their imperative character in favour of the imitative, and above all in favour of participation. The yoke is not arbitrarily laid on an unwilling neck. It is accepted freely, gladly, in the realization that on this acceptance or this refusal the fate of the Kingdom of God on earth depends.[2]

[1] *Ibid.* p. 293. [2] *Moses*, p. 149.

This, he adds, means a "sole reliance on the redemptive efficaciousness" of fidelity to the law, in response to its claim by obedience and to its communion by love.

On this Jewish ground it is misguided to ask with Paul about justification. The yoke and its acceptance, and the divine mercy, make the question pointless. If we insist on asking it, we shall end with a faith in faith rather than in God, or with an anxiety of conscience over the divine righteousness crudely out of touch with the eternally patient and competent author of the law. Moses' despair recalls him to Sinai, not to self-immolation in the multitude. Men are justified, not by the Messiah, who has other tasks, but by the law, if only they see it in its true grandeur and its everlasting fidelity. Here, then, lies the crux of the Jewish disapproval of Christianity in the age-old conflicts about law and faith, works and sin.

Christianity continues unpersuaded. It points to the radical self-centredness of man. "Imperative" or "imitative"—does our keeping fulfil the law? If we answer Yes, do we not degrade the law, reducing its demands to the measure of our attaining? And when we break it, do we not curry its approval, requiring and enjoying to be deceived, as Pascal put it, in our own favour? We want even our evil to be mistaken for good. Our very innocence has a way of being culpable. If we are ever to have a right justification must we not at all costs recognize and repudiate the false ones? And are not these the constant plague not only of our conscience but of our society? Are not too many of our goodnesses too cheaply so esteemed? Does not the law, in its very worth, point to a need beyond its own meeting, so that loyalty to its covenantal purpose means more than a lawgiver for God and other than merit in me?

To these questions—all but the first—Christian faith answers Yes. And thus it has, as it believes, at its heart an event which epitomizes "the sin of the world", which has in its very texture the whole sad truth of man. Christianity awaits no unknown lengths or depths of human perversity: in the Cross they have all been measured. This radicalness it finds reassuring. The central drama of man's redemption happens in the farthest reaches of his need.

The will to crucify Jesus—which the Qur'ānic denial of a climax to it in actual death still of necessity allows—is understood in Christianity as qualitatively incorporating in a representative deed the wrongness characteristic of all men. In the action of a particular place and time the evil of all places and times is identifiable. It is believed in the Gospel to have been carried—equally representatively—by a quality of forgiveness and love which Christianity recognizes as divine. In being carried, it is carried away. Out of an inclusive will to be forgiving in respect of "the sin of the world" comes an inclusive forgiven-ness for those who will to receive it. It is this which displaces merit, liberates love, co-operates with repentance and fulfils righteousness.

Nor, to return to Katircioglu, is this transaction properly seen as retributive or artificial. On the contrary, like all transactions between God and man, it is relational. It is not that evil is made arbitrarily to "torment a god" so that by some immoral calculus pardon can be dispensed. Our sins, as the Qur'ān insists, remain culpably our own: they are Christ's only as one who suffers what they do to him. Men in that doing are the only owners of their deeds. The Cross, rather, is seen and set forth in the Gospel as an encounter with ourselves in our sinful mirrored-ness. From the travail in Christ of what our rejection of him means we learn to take the reconciliation which in act it offers us and which in cosmic symbol it proclaims. It thus becomes our justification, through our readiness to acknowledge and repent our own identity and take its gesture of embrace as betokening the divine nature. Or in Paul's classic words: "God was in Christ reconciling the world unto Himself and has committed to us the word of reconciliation."

Often compassed about with an ill-service from theology, and having a foolish or scandalous character outside its own criteria of man and God, of law, merit, sin and suffering, this faith of the Cross remains the core of the Church's life: and the Jewish–Muslim patterns of *shekina* and submission also remain—divergent and unconvinced.

Our exposition still has certain doctrinal duties to the sanctities of Scripture and community in which the three faiths firmly and often contentiously differentiate themselves.

GOD AND MEN—AND US

"I know how...
...to stand among the many"

wrote the poet with whom we began. Throughout we have encountered the fact of community, within territory, around race, grace, language and tradition—the Hebrews' election, the Christians' "kingdom of (all) believers", the Arabs' Qur'ān—all of them in different ways conditioning, if not limiting, denominators, yet all in their insistent confession related to the entire world, by responsibility, hospitality or destiny. The psychological, and sometimes political, features of this communal identity are not our business here. But it reflects itself in doctrines relating to Scripture and to solidarity which have been implicit in all the foregoing. "God and men—and us" would certainly suit the essential temper of all three faiths.

The first element in this possessiveness of "ours" and "us" is the Scriptural. Despite their considerable kinship, the Hebrew, Christian and Islamic Scriptures have a controversial interrelationship, latent only in the first, explicit in the second and third. For Judaism, the Old Testament writings do not admit of their New Testament "development" in the vital particulars of Messiah, law and universality which we have studied. The Qur'ānic relation to them is that of explicit, even harsh, displacement, despite the common patriarchal histories. The New Testament, while evidently and gratefully deriving its being from the Old, disputes by its very existence the Jewish view of the precedent Pentateuch, Histories and Prophets. It also has, in the very texture of its Gospels and Epistles, a crucial controversy with "Jews". The Pharisees are the constant foil of the preaching of Jesus and the hostile synagogues the bane of Paul's evangelism. And over all, as we shall face below, looms the shadow of the Cross and the spectre of responsibility for it. Thus Christianity, for all its eager indebtedness to the Old, comes to birth in an inescapable conflict with the obduracy, as it sees it, the hardness, of Jewry.

Moreover, these circumstances are perpetuated in a definitive form in the sacrosanct status of the Scripture. One cannot have the teaching of Jesus without a context of reproach of the Pharisees. The lesson of the publican's penitence in the parable is inseparable from the Pharisee's pride about alms and fasting—though nothing is firmer in the story than the guilt of thanking God we are not as this Pharisee. Yet the association is there. The gist of Christianity, it seems, cannot be had either in the origins of the teaching ministry of Jesus, its fulness in his death on the Cross, its articulation in the apostles' thoughts and journeys, without an implicit temptation to associate with Jewry the enmity, prejudice and perversity that are its antithesis. The temptation is all too readily accepted, though it denies the fundamental forgivingness of the Gospel. Our immediate point is that controversy with Jews, if not with being Jewish, is within the very text of New Testament

Scripture, giving it both perpetual authority and definitive status. The reader has only to ponder St Matthew xxiii, St John viii or Acts xxiii to know the intensity of this theme, even though there is all the silent eloquence of Gethsemane to set against it.

When we turn to the Qur'ān we find more remonstrances against both antecedent monotheisms, while an even more absolute "Scriptural-ness" is given, on Qur'ānic theory, to their disqualification. The death of Jesus is denied both as an event and a Gospel. It is at once unhistorical, unthinkable and intolerable. There are other lesser issues of Jewish–Christian dismay about the Qur'ān—not least from its silences, its ignoring, for example, of Hosea and the Good Samaritan, the Suffering Servant and Saul of Tarsus. It redefines the *Injīl* or Gospel as simply a corpus of teaching. It has no place for the Epistles. Nor on the Qur'ān's assumptions about revelation could such documents of personal correspondence find any place in a sacred volume, though within a Christian doctrine of the Holy Spirit interpreting experience in definitive precedent they are most apposite. The Qur'ān's doctrine of abrogation hangs like a sword of Damocles over every part of the Old and New Testaments not Islamically acceptable. Its doctrine of its own authority makes it the touchstone of the valid beliefs and so of the proper contents of the earlier revelations. What is not Qur'ānically compatible is false, a claim which in so far as it is enforced, forecloses all discussion and eliminates all criteria uncongenial to Islam.

The "hard" orthodox Qur'ānic situation is, however, potentially moderated by the idea of previous Scriptures and their "confirmation", their commendation as proper sources of interpretation for the Arabic finality, and a kindred concern for the present and realized authority of God. The *shekina* in some ways awes even its own contestants.

There is no need in this context to explore the contrasted doctrines of revelation which belong with these competitively related Scriptures. The biblical understanding of Amos differs profoundly from the Qur'ānic concept of Muḥammad. Islamic Scripture is in the most strict sense a "scriptural" inspiration. The pen and the Book are its means. It is not a document derived from a personality to whom it gives dependable access as the essential locus of divine self-disclosure. Thus its status is in entire contrast with that of the New Testament which is to be seen as the documentary consequence of the Incarnate Son and only derivatively revelatory in terms of its service in portrait of him.

These fascinating differences do not, however, modify—they only underwrite—the point of present concern, namely the Scriptural source and authority of the inter-faith attitudes. The identity of communities is written controversially into the very charters by which they believe themselves ordained.

This possessiveness and incipient hostility ought, in all honesty, to be analysed in one particular direction, namely Anti-Semitism. Here are deep and painful reaches of emotion, tension and bigotry which defy doctrinal control. Yet their connexion with doctrine ought to be frankly faced and their utter perversity by test of that same doctrine urgently declared. It is plain that there was guilt in the crucifying of Jesus. The Cross is the last thing that ought to have happened by every count of justice or humanity. Nevertheless, as a matter of history and decision, it occurred. The worst we can say about the world is that it is the sort of place in which a cross could be the answer to the sermon on the mount. This, we might say, dramatizes the paradox of the rejected good more awfully than the breaking of the tablets of Sinai. Here the shattering mystery of the anticipated and implicit rejection in the people's deeds of the nascent covenant has found explicit shape in what is all mankind's epitome and all the more fearful for being open-eyed.

So the contemporary decision was taken, the verdict rendered and the Cross reared. It is possible, of course, to challenge the precise historicity of the New Testament narrative. Some have tried to transfer the focal responsibility to the Romans; others to suggest that Jesus merited or at least invited this fate because he had espoused the zealot line and incurred justifiable Roman wrath.[1] Muslims, save for Aḥmadiyyas, deny that there ever was any real crucifixion, but this notion, even so, allows necessarily the fact of a will to crucify. There seems no reasonable ground, in the perspective of the whole history before and beyond the Cross to question the broad outlines of the New Testament record. As such the crucifixion inculpates the actors in the drama, though it makes nonsense of time and intention to talk of

[1] R. C. Zaehner, *At Sundry Times* (London, 1958) has sought to read into the Qur'ānic denial "They did not kill him, they did not crucify him..." a sort of pronoun of emphasis meaning not *them*, the Jews, but *these*, the Romans. But the Arabic pronoun, which is "hidden", not emphatic, is unwarrantably strained by this exegesis. Two recent works from the Jewish side are Paul Winter, *On the Trial of Jesus* (Berlin, 1961), and Joel Carmichael, *On the Death of Jesus* (London, 1963). It is the latter who makes the "zealot" hypothesis. Both stress what they take to be the *animus* of the Gospels against the Jews, believing that it generates a diversion of the real onus from Pilate to the *sanhedrin*, whereas the correct account does the opposite.

"deicide". Nor is it congruent with the death of Jesus to take the bravado in their cry: "His blood be on us and on our children" out of the heat and vehemence of the moment and erect it into a principle of the divine economy, for that would be to invert the whole nature of redemption.

The truth is that the more urgently we blame the crucifiers the more falsely we exonerate ourselves. The sin of the Cross cannot rightly be arraigned unless the prosecution is universal. We have not understood it if we consider it a Jewish deed: it is the expression of a human decision in which all men share. To reproach it unilaterally is the worst form of hypocrisy. For it involves no guilt which is not of ecumenical order. It expresses "the sin of the world", and has no entail for Jews alone, or Romans. Caiaphas and Pilate, here, have no relevant nationality. We do not rightly diagnose what happened if we assign the responsibility, ecclesiastical, political, popular, outside ourselves. We are all inclusively the Jews of Good Friday.

Of equal importance is the inclusiveness of the forgiveness. "Father, hold it against them, we know well who they are", is no proper commentary on Gethsemane. The Church, while clear enough about the evil of the crucifying, is immediately in line with its Master in embracing perpetrators in the pardon. "Him you have taken and by wicked hands have crucified...the promise is to you" (Acts ii. 23 and 29). "You crucified the author of life...to you first God sent him to bless you..." (Acts ii. 15 and 26). The Christian paradox of guilt and reconciliation is in those earliest apostolic sermons and there is no proper exception from that inclusive quality, both of sin and grace, least of all the immediate participants.

There has, tragically, been a perpetual battle and frequent defeat for this truth within Christendom. Anti-Semitism is its foul denial and utter betrayal, the more damnably in that it draws false nurture from the Cross itself. It might almost be said that one of the clearest evidences of the radical perversity of men is the way their spirits have betrayed the very symbol and instrument of their salvation. From one angle this should hardly surprise us. There are no immunities for our doctrines from our travesties. By the same token it is those truths, fully acknowledged, which must purge their own traitors. Only so, in this sad territory, will the most pernicious of inter-religious attitudes be abated.

Other areas and aspects of community and doctrine in their mutuality need not detain us. There is the whole field of cult and liturgy, of institutional form and pattern, of architecture, music, hierarchy and order. There are the mystics in all three traditions, with their kindred attitudes and their contrasted orbits of thought and discipline, the variety of their masters and saints. All these evidently divide and unify. The mosque, the church and the synagogue set differing scenes and evoke their peculiar ethos. God is approached in the openness of domed colonnades and carpeted courts under the symbolic focus of *imām* and *miḥrāb* setting the radius of the circle around the Meccan centre. A pulpit stands for exhortation and calligraphy for its scriptural source and warrant. The church, in its variety of sanctuary and screen, houses, either in orthodox hiddenness or western access, the mystery of the divine hospitality, the holy bread and wine. Pulpits serve for proclamation, for *kerugma* and *didache*: art, in statuary, image or ikon, intends the sort of hallowing that derives from the Word itself made flesh. The synagogue, still precluded from the ancient sacrifices that require the Temple long destroyed, exalts the holy scroll, the sacred law, at once the symbol and the focus of God's will and presence, "the axis of the liturgy and the organ of the ritual".[1]

To these corporate places and forms must be joined the endless occasions of personal discipleship and private devotion. The ritual cycle of birth, circumcision, baptism, adolescence, marriage, home-making, travel, pilgrimage and death are a constant apprenticeship of the believer to his loyalty or simply sacramentalize existence as communal on the basis of shared heritage of belief and practice. There is no space here to compare the areas of concord and conflict that emerge from this triangular manifold. Custodianship and conformity stand in subtle relationship to the doctrinal setting out of which they grow. Their expression in the temper of rabbis, *shaykhs* and clergy and in the attitudes of "lay" allegiance constitutes a religious dialogue that distinguishes, within the common humanity that unites. Religions tend, thus, to be most apart where they are most at one.

Even the vast and intrusive new common denominators of twentieth-century change tend to sharpen, as well as anachronize, the emotions of particularity. The general theme of religions and technology is taken up in W. Montgomery Watt's chapter below. Here it suffices to observe how persistently self-consciousness remains despite the unifying impact of modernity and the over-all political recession of imperialism as a shared experience. The most striking single example is the

[1] A. Neher, *Moses*, p. 144.

formation of Pakistan in the name of Islam. Its decisive emphatic option for statehood as the indispensable sanction of religious security and fulfilment is echoed elsewhere throughout Islam. Zionism in Israel is parallel within Judaism. Identity here commands and requires statehood, since one cannot speak of the viability of religions, or even the equality of races, in any other terms than the political. In its deepest heart, of course, no religion can finally believe this enthronement of the political, for it disqualifies the sovereignty of God and the invincibility of the spirit—human and divine. But in so far as it is given strategic centrality in the reaction of religions to our time, it serves inevitably to intensify their competitive, or simply parallel, distinctiveness. For the political is the sharpest and most imperious, apart from chronic racialism, of all the sanctions of corporate behaviour and human division.

If Islam and Zionist Judaism, despite the large exemptions from the pattern in, for example, Indian Islam and assimilationist Judaism, have by statehood quickened their solidarity, Christianity has embarrassing identification in the minds of most peoples with the imperial order that has lately gone into history. It is also closely associated with the modern history of science. It is thus, for all its minority frailty in the Middle East, at the awkward psychological disadvantage of heavy involvement with the remembered enmities that infuse that present independence and with the ambiguous inevitability and disruptiveness of Western technocracy. Into this daunting complex we cannot here enter. It suffices to be reminded that the factors still undergirding religious distinctions, however effete or labouring their dogmas, have found immense political corroboration in our present situation. In that sense men are saying with communal incisiveness, if not with doctrinal argument: "Thy God shall not be my God." It is significant to remember that when Ruth so courageously reversed that negation she was also defying a territorial frontier. Religion in our time is in several senses again territorially expressed.

Territories, however, as Ruth may be prophetically interpreted to have sensed in her simple decision of fidelity, were always anachronisms to love, as they now have become to science and so, on both counts, to religion. Yet never was the ancient prayer: "that glory may dwell in our land" more urgent. It may be well then to turn in conclusion to the old patriarch whose stormy struggles and wanderings, in youth and age, are so vivid in the pages of Genesis and in the story of the hills and deserts of the Semites, the dreamer who learned how Bethel was "the very house of God" and whose rival sons became symbols of an age-long enmity. This was the Jacob who, years after the hallowing of Bethel, "wrestled with God" and emerged from one mysterious encounter both a prince and a cripple. In the myth of Peniel "the face of God" was truly seen. But the vision in its authenticity could not be entrusted to the old Jacob in his natural vigour, his self-willed powers, his urgent pride. Only in brokenness as a protagonist could he take his authority for God and his answer as a man. Was it not the stammerer Moses who was called to utter the defiant claim in the presence of Pharaoh and say the liberating word to the people?

"What is your name?", demands the voice. "Jew", "Christian", "Muslim", they reply, each claiming in his own sense the meaning of the name of the first of them. The "Jew" is one who ever glorifies the Eternal and so guarantees the holy indefeasibility of the law. Yet are they not all crippled witnesses?

The Jew insists on a private exemption from the universal inclusion belonging with those praises and this is his disjointedness. This reluctance to belong with a single humanity in grace notwithstanding, he abides in the glory of theophany.

Crippled, too, the law's other champion from Mecca and Medina. The Muslim echoes Sinai, free from particular covenant: he wills in universal community a full submission. But Islam is thwarted by the lawlessness of man, with which its prophetic exhortation has no redemptive reckoning. Its law-keeping limps within the halting measure of a natural religion. Yet it abides, splendid in its ardent unity and therein has power with God, whose will it treasures.

Between these in time and mediation is the Christian. The Gospel and the Church are a "seed" and a covenant, not exclusive but reconciling, not natural but regenerating. They too are crippled. Their preceding and generating society, in perpetuation of an "old" covenant, wills its exemption, while the subsequent and natural religion wills its own sufficiency. Each touches Christianity in the very sinew of its strength. The embrace of the Cross is deprived by those who set themselves beyond the need or reach of it.

The Christian is crippled most of all by his own compromise of the patterns of the grace of God in Christ, by broken instruments of his true doxology. Yet in that very crippling the Christian "Peniel" lives —the shape of the human crisis and experience of the face of God.

CHAPTER 21

LAW

It is not within the scope of the present work to make a detailed study of the relations which have, in the past, existed on the legal plane between the three religions and, in particular, the unquestionably inferior judicial condition imposed by Islam, at its beginning and in its subsequent predominance, on its Christian and Jewish subjects. The rigorous discriminatory statute applied to them throughout the Middle Ages became gradually less effective later on. Even under Turkish supremacy it had been distinctly alleviated, and the nineteenth century was to see not its death but its replacement by a kind of juridical-religious segregation confined to two or three fields of the law. Henceforward, all the humiliations, deprivations and disabilities which had for so long characterized the status of the "tributaries" were effectively to disappear, apart from a few exceptions like that of the Yemenite Jews.

However, the plan of the editors of *Religion in the Middle East* has been to limit the work specifically to the period from 1850 to the present day. What is required is a survey of existing conditions and one which, even better, looks ahead, in so far as it is possible to foresee, with the utmost caution, the conditions in which these three religions will continue their co-existence in the future. It might therefore seem unprofitable to revert to the distant past, so different from the present state of affairs. Nevertheless, in order to examine the rules still in force concerning the legal distinctions which, in the sphere of the personal status, characterize the exercise of certain rights—an examination which constitutes the principal object of this section—it is necessary to glance quickly at the original conditions, now obsolete, in which this kind of segregation came into being; it was not a racial segregation, since Islam has nearly always ignored racialism, but founded solely on the religious obedience of the persons concerned.

Moreover, the need for fixing the terminology of the subject-matter makes it necessary to refer briefly to certain historical conceptions regarding the legal position of the Christian and of the Jew, as formulated by medieval Islam.

A SHORT HISTORICAL SURVEY

From the beginning a basic distinction was drawn between, on the one hand, the Christian or the Jew *ḥarbī* and, on the other hand, the Christian or the Jew *dhimmī.*

The former was one who had settled in the *dār al-ḥarb*, in a country not ruled by Islam, a foreigner in the strict sense of the term and hence, according to the ideas of the time, a potential enemy, a *hostis*. In principle, the *ḥarbī* had no rights; neither his property nor his person was protected by Muslim law. Nevertheless, if this foreigner, whether Christian or Jew, obtained a safe-conduct (*amān*) which could be granted to him by any Muslim with full capacity, he became *musta'min* and henceforward protected from the arbitrary behaviour of any one; in virtue of this status he was able to exercise almost the same rights as his co-religionist who was the subject of a Muslim power.

Nevertheless, if he overstayed his sojourn in the quality of *musta'min* (as a general rule one year) in Muslim territory, the local authority certainly had the right to send him back to his country of origin; usually, however, he was regarded as a *dhimmī* and was subjected to all the obligations imposed on such people, whereas hitherto he had paid no taxes.

The *dhimmī* may be defined as the Jew or Christian who is the subject of a Muslim power. In the early days of the Islamic conquest, special pacts were signed between the Christian or Jewish populations who wished to retain their faith and the Muslim authorities. The content of these "treaties" varied considerably from one place to another. Disregarding any exceptional terms which may have been included in some of them, it may be said that, as a whole, they constituted both a recognition by the Christians and the Jews of the legality of the presence of the conquering power, and an undertaking to submit without reserve to the conqueror, the whole being substantiated by the payment of a capitation tax, the *jizya*, and a land tax, the *kharāj*, for land which remained in the hands of its former owners. In return the *dhimmīs* obtained not only the protection of their lives and property, but the right to practise their religion and to be governed by their own laws in matters of personal status (law of the family, of marriage and of succession) which were enforced by their own courts. This last prerogative, which at that time appeared quite natural, since it existed in every country in Europe or at any rate in those countries where the co-existence of different races imposed the system of applying the law appropriate to the particular individuals concerned, has continued to prevail throughout the centuries and still represents in most of the Muslim countries one of the few surviving traces of the former status of the *dhimmīs*.

Very soon, however, the agreed pact between victor and vanquished was superseded by a regulation which was imposed unilaterally by the Muslim authorities, although the fiction of agreement was officially maintained and the conventional form of a treaty recurred from time to time. This statute, inspired by the writings of the jurists and by "documents", *shurūṭ*, erroneously attributed to ʿUmar b. al-Khaṭṭāb, adopted the main provisions of the former treaties, with the addition of a series of discriminatory measures designed to humiliate the *dhimmī*. These measures, which have been called the "distinguishing marks", since their object was, according to the jurists, to make it possible to distinguish the *dhimmī* from the Muslim at sight, varied in number at different periods, according to the degree of fanaticism of the government in power. Historians are agreed in thinking that their strict enforcement occurred only sporadically, brief periods of severity being separated by years of considerable indulgence. Apart from the reign of the Fāṭimid paranoiac al-Ḥākim (A.D. 1004–20) under whom persecution reached a pitch never equalled before or afterwards, the "distinguishing marks", when they were really enforced, consisted in the obligation of the Christian or Jew to use a wooden framework instead of a saddle on his beast, which could be only a donkey or at best a mule; the requirement to wear a belt, *zunnār*, round their waists, to have their hair shaved above the forehead, not to bear arms, and to wear yellow or blue clothing (turban, robe, veil for women).

It is to be noted that there is no mention among these humiliating measures of the obligation to live in special districts, an omission which it is difficult to reconcile with the fact that, in the majority of Muslim cities in the East and West there were found, and still exist today, quarters for Jews and, more occasionally, for Christians. The phenomenon can be explained, however, without having recourse to the former regulations of the Muslim government. From the time when the *dhimmī* regarded himself as a member of a minority, which occurred not long after the Muslim conquest, he felt the need to live close to his co-religionists. Of their own free will, therefore, they formed themselves into a group around their spiritual leaders, their church or their synagogue, inspired by motives of convenience as well as caution. Historians make scarcely any mention of rescripts requiring *dhimmīs* to live apart from Muslims. It may even be considered that certain measures of discrimination relating to dwellings, such as the prohibition against having a house higher than its Muslim neighbour or against being able to look down on the latter from above, which in fact were very rarely enforced, prove *a contrario* that it would have been legal for *dhimmīs* to live side by side with Muslims had they so desired.

Finally, there existed on the judicial plane several disabilities and deprivations affecting Christians and Jews which were not, strictly speaking, consequences of the "contract" of the *dhimma*, but resulted from the application of the rules of the *fiqh* concerning infidels as a whole. The principle of juridical segregation, which will be considered later, is not at present under discussion, for that implies a mutual disability between members of groups governed by different laws to assume certain legal ties. The result was, and still is, that a Christian or a Jew, for example, cannot inherit from a Muslim, but that, in the same way, a Muslim has no right of inheritance from a Jew or a Christian. There is thus equality of treatment on both sides.

The disabilities now being considered concerned only Christians and Jews and conferred on them, under a law shared by all the communities, Muslim and non-Muslim alike, an inferior legal status. It is true that, since the early days of Islam, Christian and Jewish communities had enjoyed autonomy of jurisdiction, but this scarcely extended beyond what was later called the personal status, the law of family and inheritance. It is probable that the religious court (of the non-Muslim community) also heard disputes over the right to patrimony between two members of the same community, at least as a court of arbitration. Otherwise, all conflicts arising between members of different communities, and especially between Muslims and infidels, and all unlawful acts (various infringements, offences against public order, etc.) perpetrated by non-Muslims would certainly come within the sole jurisdiction of the Muslim judge. Moreover, according to the Ḥanafīs at least, the case would be brought before a Muslim judge who could be obliged to assume jurisdiction by agreement of the two parties, in spite of the fact that they belonged to the same community.

In such circumstances, the principle was that the litigants, whatever their religion, must be treated on a footing of strict equality, and their claims judged according to the provisions of Muslim law, which alone was applicable to the case, in exactly the same way as if the litigants had been Muslims. The few exceptions to this basic principle, which will be glanced at shortly, must not cause the principle itself to be obscured; it seems, even in the distant past, to have been respected not only in theory, but also in practical matters of daily life, to such an extent that perhaps the sole impairment to this principle has been the rescript of the Caliph Ḥākim (known to have been mad) which forbade all transactions between Muslims and *dhimmīs*—thus excluding the latter from the Muslim court.

Apart from several minor disabilities, which were of small importance, as, for example, the prohibition against infidels acquiring copies of the Qur'ān or Muslim slaves, and of which it may well be asked whether in fact they ever had any effect on the judicial plane, there were only two exceptions to the principle of equality between infidel and believer before the courts—one of them related to penal law and the other to the laws of evidence.

So far as concerned the *ḥudūd*, that is the fixed penalties for seven classes of offences (fornication, slanderous accusation of fornication, consumption of alcoholic beverages, robbery, theft, apostasy and sedition), the infidel found himself to some extent in a slightly better position that the Muslim. Although, in principle, the *ḥudūd* were to be applied to both alike without discrimination (blasphemy taking the place, for the Christian, of apostasy for the Muslim), the infidel would not in fact be punished for the simple offence of consuming alcohol, provided that he was not drunk in public; moreover, if he had been accused of fornication by his co-religionists—which was almost always the case in view of the self-contained character of the communities—he had only to be converted to Islam in order to escape paying the penalty, since the evidence of his co-religionists would then be invalid.

The law of retaliation did not apply to the Muslim who killed a *dhimmī* except under Ḥanafī law. Moreover the "blood money", the *diya* or pecuniary compensation payable by anyone guilty of bloodshed to the victim or to his heirs was appreciably lower when the victim was a *dhimmī*, except, again, under Ḥanafī law, where the *diya* was the same whatever might be the religion of the victim.

These inequalities in punishment rapidly disappeared at the same time as the penal law of Islam was falling into disuse, assuming that it had ever been enforced as a whole.

On the other hand, the regulations imposed by the *fiqh* regarding evidence before the courts were followed by Islam until a fairly recent date, in fact, up to the time when the Muslim states secularized their judicial administration by adopting codes of procedure which were no longer inspired by the rules of the *sharī'a*. In this sphere the inequality sanctioned by the *fiqh* was very evident and was in consequence resented by everyone, or at least by non-Muslims. It was contained in two rules: the evidence of a *dhimmī* was valueless, whether favourable or unfavourable to a Muslim, but a Muslim could always give evidence against a non-Muslim or, *a fortiori*, on his behalf. It was thus not a matter of juridical segregation, in the sense that the court would accept the evidence only of those who professed the same religion as the defendant, but of an actual disability deduced by Muslim legislators on logical grounds from the provisions of the Qur'ān which did not refer specifically to infidels but to witnesses in general, namely in verse 2 of Sūra LXV, which required that the witness should be "respectable", *'adl*. If, they argued, the Muslim who was not "respectable" must be debarred, how could unbelief, *kufr*, be admitted, as less serious and less culpable than the mere absence of respectability?

The status of *dhimmīs*, which is inscribed in the books of *fiqh* or in special treatises on the public law of Islam, has in theory remained unchanged. In fact, however, the legal and even the social position of Christians and Jews has been improving all the time, though usually not as a result of favourable decisions taken by the Muslim authorities, but rather incidentally, so to speak, as an indirect consequence of the legislative measures which have modified, in other spheres, the legal structure of most of the Muslim countries since the beginning of the nineteenth century.

The "distinguishing marks" were the first to disappear, having fallen into disuse very early; even the word *dhimmī* was replaced in everyday speech by *râya*, which also in turn disappeared. The two taxes, the *jizya* and the *kharāj*, lapsed automatically, the former when the Muslim states adopted a fiscal system modelled on those of the Western countries which do not include a poll-tax, and the latter as a result of land reforms into which it was quite impossible to incorporate land subject to *kharāj*.

From the time when the *qāḍī* abandoned his universal competence, with the result that he no longer judged any but Muslim cases in matters of personal status, the exasperation connected with the inadmissibility of the evidence of Christians and Jews lost its edge. It was in cases relating to commercial transactions or, more generally, to patrimonial matters, when the parties were frequently Muslims on one side and non-Muslims on the other, that this disability of Jews and Christians had been particularly vexatious. Otherwise, so far as concerned the personal status, the juridical gulf existing between the communities made it seldom necessary for the Muslim judge to hear non-Muslim evidence.

It has been seen earlier that inequalities of penalty imposed by the *fiqh* almost invariably remained a dead letter, just as the penal law of Islam usually constituted but a theoretical system which had in the past been enforced only in a very incomplete and limited way in some countries, such as the Ḥijāz and northern Nigeria.

With regard to the *ḥarbīs*, Christians or Jews subject to a foreign power, the transformation of their legal position was even more impressive than that of their *dhimmī* co-religionists. The Ottoman capitulations and even some earlier treaties guaranteed them, from Morocco to the frontiers of Iran, a singularly privileged regime, which in any case had little in common with the meagre concessions granted by early Islam, even to the most favoured among them, the *musta'min*.

At the present time the juridical relationships of the adherents of the three creeds (Muslim, Jew and Christian) are the same, generally speaking, as those which exist in all other countries between citizens of different religions: there is the right for each individual to practise his faith freely; the right to attain all ranks of public office, subject on occasions to a *numerus clausus* which, examined in the context appropriate to each country, does not in the majority of cases appear to be inequitable. There is unity of legislative and judicial competence for all, when there is no question of personal status, in the wide sense accorded to it by Islam, that is to say comprising testamentary and intestate succession.

No disability affects any individual because he is a Christian or a Jew, nor is there any restriction of his freedom of movement based on his religious affiliation. The prohibition of Jews and Christians from entering the two holy cities of Islam (*al-ḥaramayn*), Mecca and Medina, a prohibition limited by the Ḥanafī school (which is very liberal in this respect) to permanent settlement in these two cities, can hardly, if viewed objectively, be considered an exception, any more than there is evidence of legal discrimination in the repugnance of the Mālikī peoples of North Africa to allowing Jews and Christians to enter their mosques; the sociological and religious aspects of the question, however, go beyond the scope of this survey.

In spite of the present-day fusion—from the legal standpoint—of Christian and Jewish communities with the Muslim population, there remain even now several respects in which the former religious and legal segregation is still apparent. It must be emphasized that there is no question of racial segregation, since Islam has, on the whole, had no real experience of this pathological phenomenon.

Thus in the majority of Muslim countries included in that region of the Middle East which, in the cultural and social sense understood by the editors, extends from Morocco to India, Jews and Christians, when they are not foreigners, have generally retained their own courts of personal status, and are in the habit of applying their own religious law in this sphere; as regards marriage, the relationship between Muslim and non-Muslim communities has remained one-sided; as regards intestate succession and guardianship (*wilāya*) the former segregation still remains complete; finally, the Islamic conception of public policy which reappeared with the recent accession of these countries to full political independence has had the effect of giving Muslim law pre-eminence over other laws, though this is of course not apparent except in disputes between parties of different creeds and particularly when one of two non-Muslim marriage-partners is converted to Islam.

Each of these points will be made the subject of detailed study in the four succeeding sections.

THE LEGISLATIVE AND JUDICIAL AUTONOMY OF LOCAL JEWISH AND CHRISTIAN COMMUNITIES

From the time of the conquest the issue of legislative and judicial autonomy was fundamental to the negotiations between the Muslim conquerors and the *dhimmīs*. In return for all the subjection and vexation and for the burden of taxation, the latter demanded first the right to practise their religion freely and then the related privilege, which was customary at that period, of being tried by judges belonging to their own community and in accordance with the laws of the family and of succession which they had previously observed. Even in such documents as the "Edict of the Prophet" and the *shurūṭ* of 'Umar, which, although obviously not the work of Muḥammad nor of 'Umar b. al-Khaṭṭāb, are none the less contemporary with the first Islamic conquests, the major concession made by the conqueror to the conquered tributaries was the grant of this privilege, always combined with freedom of worship. Actually, in the texts which have come down to us, the word "privilege" never appears; it would not have occurred to a Muslim author to whom it was clearly no privilege to be exempt from the dominion of Islamic law.

In fact, however, for the Christian or the Jew, it was a genuine privilege to be granted, under cover of the *dhimma*, the right to "conduct his family life in accordance with his religious principles", a privilege which did not acquire its institutional character and was not extended to the whole of Ottoman Islam until after the fall of Constantinople in 1453.

At that time the Sultan Meḥmed III considered it advisable to recognize that the Greek and Armenian patriarchs and also the chief rabbi of the conquered city had complete authority over their former subjects, thus exempting them from Muslim jurisdiction and even from the sovereign power of the State, not only in matters of personal status, but also in all their civil and criminal cases. Never before had the non-Muslim communities' privilege of jurisdiction been extended so widely and this astonishing concession, which later came to be applied to the rest of the Empire, must be attributed in its origin to practical considerations, linked with the circumstances of the fall of Constantinople. The Turks, once settled in the city, constituted only a tiny submerged minority in the midst of the Christians, whose mass exodus towards the West, Meḥmed II had good reason to fear. Moreover, there was nothing *a priori* to exclude an alliance between the Churches of the East and of the West, which might, as he thought, have given the signal for a new series of Crusades. The granting of quasi-sovereign power within the Islamic state to Christians and Jews appeared to the conqueror to be the best means of holding them and of avoiding the worst. That the system should have come to be applied further and further afield was only to be expected. At all times and in all places privileges outlast the circumstances which have given rise to them and even tend to gain in strength as time obscures their original justification.

During the three centuries which followed, the constant preoccupation of the governors appointed by the Sublime Porte was to reduce, throughout the Empire, this excessive privilege to its original proportions as it was before the promises of Meḥmed II. The practical measures taken varied with their individual views of the problem, and were more or less successful according to the size and importance of the community with which they were dealing.

However that might be, and even when these retrograde measures were very restricted, they caused the resentment of the Jews and Christians, who had no very clear idea of the demarcation line between personal status, whose religious character it never occurred to anyone to dispute, and the other domains of the law which must, in every civilized state, be regulated by a uniform system of justice. The *dhimmīs* had always tended to regard themselves as deprived of their prerogatives by the slightest move towards unification taken by the Muslim authorities, however harmless it might be. It was in order to define precisely the extent of the privileged jurisdiction of the patriarchates and rabbinates and to please the Western Powers—particularly the Tsarist regime in Russia—all of whom were active in the defence of the local Christian and Jewish subjects (foreigners received adequate protection from the Capitulations) that the Sublime Porte took a series of legislative acts which have retained to the present day their moral force in many Muslim countries of the Orient. The most important of these enactments were the *khaṭṭ-i sherif* of Gülhane in 1839 and, particularly, the *khaṭṭ-i hümayun* of 18 February 1856, a veritable administrative charter for the courts of the respective communities. Both of them, as the result of having been expressly mentioned in the Treaty of Paris of 1856 and in the Treaty of Berlin of 1878, acquired an international significance which put them outside the range of the arbitrary whims of the Turkish authorities.

In point of fact, the *khaṭṭ-i hümayun* contained only some very broad generalizations. It could hardly have been otherwise, since it endeavoured to define in a relatively few words not only the rules of legislative competence, but also the rules governing the jurisdiction of numerous courts belonging to the different communities. For it must be remembered that in each of these countries composing the mosaic of the Ottoman Empire there was not, as is too often imagined, one single Christian community and one single Jewish community. The Christians were divided into Orthodox and Catholics, who were further subdivided amongst themselves into different rites, so that in Egypt, which furnishes the most striking example, there were four Orthodox communities, each of them endowed, until 1 January 1956, with its own jurisdiction, and six Catholic communities, each of them having (also until 1 January 1956) its own judicial organization. The Israelites, for their part, were divided into three rites, the Sephardi, the Ashkenazi and the Karaite, the last being regarded as heretic by the other two.

In most of the other countries of the Middle East there existed, and in many cases still exists today, a similar multiplicity of jurisdictions for the personal status, though to a lesser extent than in Egypt before 1956.

From 1850 until nearly the middle of the present century the judicial administration inspired by Ottoman principles, when considered in the light of the legal relations between the three communities, presented the following general characteristics. The whole of what has been called personal status fell outside the jurisdiction of the civil and secular courts which had just been established in the numerous countries of this area of the Middle East in the sense of the term understood by the present work. The *qāḍī* thus had jurisdiction over the Muslim, the patriarchal judge of his community over the native Christian and the rabbinical court over the local Jew; foreign Christians and Jews were tried, in such matters, by their consuls.

Included within the personal status (as is usual in most of the Muslim countries) were questions concerning the status and capacity of individuals, betrothal, marriage, the effects of marriage on dealings between the spouses and with regard to their children, the dissolution of marriage by any means: repudiation, divorce, separation by consent, separation *a toro*, cancellation and annulment. Also included within personal status was everything relating to affiliation, legitimation and, for non-Muslims, adoption. Custody, guardianship, trusteeship, deprivation of rights and emancipation also came within its scope, as well as parental and marital obligations to provide alimony. Finally, and this is what distinguishes the oriental conception of personal status, it included succession, under will and intestate; sometimes it was even extended to cover gifts during the lifetime of the donor. All other branches of the law: penal law, commercial law, the law of obligations and contracts, administrative law, etc., came within the province of the new courts, whose jurisdiction covered all nationals indiscriminately, whether they were Muslims, Christians or Jews, and in this respect they could be called courts of common law.[1]

[1] "Common Law" means here law applicable to all subjects of the state without regard to their religious affiliation.

To return to personal status as defined above, when a country had not established civil courts and the *qāḍī* in consequence retained very wide powers, these powers naturally allowed him to try his own co-religionists in matters coming within the scope of personal status, but not the local Christians and Jews in cases where both parties professed the same creed, or, more precisely, belonged to the same community, being of the same religion and the same rite. In that event it was necessary for the *qāḍī* to concede jurisdiction to the competent court of that community.

But what happened when the two parties belonged to two different rites (a Greek-Catholic and a Maronite, for example) or simply to two different religions (such as a Christian and a Jew)? For a whole century this question was the subject of protracted discussions. It was proposed to apply the principle *actor sequitur forum rei* and to give the court of the defendant jurisdiction, but to do so would have been to disregard the historical reasons which had contributed to the original granting of autonomous jurisdiction to the different communities, and also the spirit in which their powers of jurisdiction had been exercised.

The non-Muslim communities were exempt from Muslim jurisdiction only in matters concerning their "domestic affairs"; when therefore a party outside the particular community was involved, it was necessary to have recourse to the general principle by which all nationals of a country must be tried by a court deriving its authority from that Power. In the event, this could only be the court of the *qāḍī* and it was this trend which prevailed, in doctrine as in jurisprudence. Its advocates could invoke, apart from the historical arguments already mentioned, a provision of the *khaṭṭ-i hümayun* adopting this solution in matters of inheritance, and also a vizirial circular of 3 February 1891 which applied it to testamentary succession. It was a solution which had important consequences, for by giving the *qāḍī* jurisdiction it substituted Islamic law for the law belonging to each of the parties, since in any litigation the *qāḍī* was only able to apply the provisions of the *fiqh*.

The rules of legislative and judicial competence stated above were quite simple to apply, since the communities lived apart from one another. Moreover, the existence of the *Capitulations* in most of the countries included within this Middle East—extending in fact from Morocco to Iran—which conferred on foreign Christians and Jews jurisdictional privilege, made it difficult to deny the same privilege to their native co-religionists.

All these considerations have disappeared, one after another, during the first half of the twentieth century. Mixed marriages—in the sense of marriages between members of different communities, although of the same creed—which had for centuries been the exception, have tended to increase in number, aided by the intermingling of populations, since urban concentrations have brought the communities into closer contact and broadened the outlook of their respective religious groups. As a consequence of mixed marriages, there are bound to be frequent conflicts both of law and of jurisdiction, even though the difference in religion may often amount to very little, as in the case of two Oriental Catholics, both of them subject to the authority of the pope and consequently professing the same dogma and respecting the same canon law, but divided by a few details of purely liturgical significance. Moreover, after the 1914–18 war the *Capitulations*, which had maintained a system of privilege for foreign Christians and Jews, of indirect advantage to their native co-religionists, were abolished.

As a result of these changes, the Muslim states, which had meanwhile attained complete political independence, decided in general to revise the ancient conceptions of legislative and jurisdictional autonomy in relation to personal status which they had inherited from the Ottoman Empire. There were three courses open to them: to unify personal status law and make it applicable to all nationals whatever their religion, that is to say, whether they were Muslims, Christians or Jews; to abolish the various jurisdictions of personal status while preserving the principle that the court of common law ought to apply to each national the personal status law of his religion, just as the foreigner, in accordance with the principles of international private law, is subject to the personal status law of his own country; or the third choice and the most frequently adopted, to maintain the traditional system of legislative and jurisdictional autonomy while improving it in some points of detail, chiefly so as to apply a statute law, which would be free from the inconsistencies of custom and of jurisprudence, in settling disputes of the kind which had so often arisen in earlier decades.

Before examining the situation at the present time (1965) which has resulted from all these changes, most of them of comparatively recent date, a few observations may be made on two countries which are preponderantly, or at any rate largely, Muslim, but where, as a consequence of foreign political intervention, the influence of Ottoman principles did not make itself felt, or at least not later than 1850, the date which has been taken as the starting-point for this survey: they are India under British and Algeria under French rule.

In India the British abolished in 1864 the *qāḍīs* which had been instituted by the Muslim invaders some centuries earlier in all districts where the number of Muslims was sufficient to justify such a step. From 1864 onwards justice has been administered, even in matters relating to the personal status, by the same judges for all litigants, whatever may be their religion. At the same time, since there is no unified system of legislation in India, in matters of family law and of inheritance the common court regards each party as subject to the law of his own faith.

In Algeria, at the time of the conquest (1830–50) the French found no organized Christian communities; the few Christians living there were foreign traders. On the other hand, there existed in the large cities Jewish communities which were subject to the system generally in force at the time throughout the Ottoman Empire with regard to Jewish *dhimmīs*: Mosaic law administered by rabbinical courts, so far as the personal status of family and of succession was concerned. In 1870 the Crémieux Decree gave these Jews French citizenship and in consequence deprived them of their legislative autonomy; the rabbinical courts were already suppressed in 1841–42. The whole population was in principle to be governed for nearly a century by French law, except in matters of the personal status (law of family and succession) and with regard to certain institutions such as mortmain property (*ḥabīs*) in which Muslims were to be governed by Mālikī law and sometimes by Kabyl customary law; it should be emphasized however that in general French magistrates were to enforce the application of the personal status law. *Qāḍīs* existed only at the bottom of the judicial scale and their competence corresponded to that of a French justice of the peace; thus, it was necessary to raise the incompetence of the latter expressly to make him withdraw from a purely "Muslim affair".

Apart from these two countries whose judicial structure had for a long time been profoundly affected by a very high degree of colonization, the remainder of Middle Eastern Islam has attempted only recently to modify the Ottoman principle by virtue of which the Christian and Jewish communities enjoyed jurisdictional and legislative autonomy in all questions relating to personal status, parallel to that of the *qāḍī* who had jurisdiction of the same kind and extent over Muslims. These countries, as has already been stated, may be classified under three heads:

(1) Those who have unified their system of law in matters of personal status either by secularizing it completely, as Turkey has been doing since October 1926, in so far as she has adopted, as a whole, the regulations of the Swiss Civil Code, or by proclaiming, like Tunisia in 1956, a *Code of Personal Status* applicable to all Tunisian nationals (Law of 27 September 1957), which led to the abolition of the rabbinical courts and the legislative autonomy of the Jewish community. The same measure could not be extended to cover the national Christian communities, since they do not exist in Tunisia, nor in the rest of the Maghrib. It may be emphasized that, in these two countries, Turkey and Tunisia, the Muslim courts disappeared at the same time as the courts belonging to the different communities, since the actual basis of the law relating to personal status was unified.

(2) Egypt, whose judicial organization had in this respect remained unchanged for nearly a century, has, since 1 January 1956 (Law of 21 September 1955) abolished the Muslim courts for the personal status and *waqf*, the tribunal known as *al-maḥākim al-sharʿiyya* and the tribunals of the fourteen Christian and Jewish communities, whose jurisdiction in matters of personal status had been recognized by Turkish *fermans*, Egyptian laws or simply established custom, provided that the parties belonged to the same community.

But—and it is an important reservation—the civil court of common law which had inherited the jurisdiction of Muslim courts and patriarchal and rabbinical courts alike must, in principle, continue to apply to each Egyptian who comes before it the personal law to which he was previously subject in this sphere, that is to say, the Ḥanafī law for Muslims, the various canon laws for Christians of Egyptian nationality and Mosaic law for Egyptian Jews. As regards foreigners, they remain subject to the law indicated by the provisions of international private law, that is to say most frequently the law of their own country. Morocco did the same on 1 October 1965.

(3) The majority of these countries (Lebanon, Syria, Iraq, Jordan, Libya, etc.) have continued to administer the same system as in the past. All the courts of personal status law have been retained, applying the law appropriate to each community in everything relating to personal status in the broad sense of the term generally accepted in Islam, and where there are Shīʿī Muslims, their courts are completely independent of the courts of the Sunnīs.

The above classification is perhaps a little too generalized and requires some explanation. In all the countries mentioned the Muslim religious courts form part of the judicial organization of the State, and their judges are paid by the State, while the Jewish and Christian courts, although recognized by the State (Lebanese Law of 2 April 1951; Syrian Decree-Law of 17 September 1953, for example) remain, as in the past, outside the official framework of the Ministry of Justice. The courts are organized by the community and their members are paid by it, if they do not perform their office voluntarily. In the Sudan *al-maḥākim al-shar'iyya* exist at all levels of the judicial hierarchy, but community courts are not found there, not because they been have abolished, as in Egypt, but because they were never established. This does not prevent the "civil courts" from administering the law appropriate to the legally recognized communities, such as the Greek Orthodox and Greek Catholic, Roman Catholic, Jewish, Maronite and Evangelical Protestant.

Finally it may be mentioned that in the Lebanon the statute regarding inheritance has been unified, but only in so far as it affects non-Muslims, by the adoption of a system (Law of 23 June 1959) which owes nothing to Muslim law. The reform is interesting for two reasons. On the one hand, it takes Christians and Jews out of the range of the provisions of Muslim law which in many countries, such as Egypt and Tunisia, are imposed upon them, and on the other hand it marks the beginning of a unification of the law which might well inspire the legislative policy of other Muslim states in relation to their Christian and Jewish minorities.

MARRIAGE BETWEEN MUSLIMS AND NON-MUSLIMS

With regard to intermarriage, what has been called a one-sided discrimination comes into play. The principle, reduced to its most simple terms, as is follows: a Muslim has the right to marry a Christian or a Jewess whether she is *dhimmiyya* (and so has, in most cases, the same nationality as her husband) or *ḥarbiyya*, that is to say foreign; on the other hand a Muslim woman is not allowed in any circumstances to marry a Christian or a Jew.

Before examining the origin of these two rules, the reasons for the discrepancy between the rights of the man and of the woman, the reservations of certain schools concerning the marriage even of a Muslim to a non-Muslim woman, the extent of the absolute prohibition of the marriage of a Muslim woman with a non-Muslim and its active judicial sanction, it must be pointed out that this is not simply a prohibition formulated by the ancient classical law of Islam and allowed to fall more or less into disuse, but is a principle proclaimed in all the contemporary legislation of those Muslim countries which have passed laws in recent years dealing with personal status; it represents, moreover, the basic convictions of almost the entire Muslim population. All Muslims, whatever the juridical school to which they belong and whether they are Shīʿīs or Sunnīs, upper-class or plebeian, unreservedly condemn the marriage of a Muslim woman with a Christian or a Jew.

It may indeed be retorted that this reaction is dictated by the legal rule divesting such a marriage of all validity, which is in itself enough to discourage a Muslim woman from making the experiment, if we had not the test-case of Algeria where, in the opinion of all authoritative writers, French public policy could have been invoked in order to validate such a marriage and where, nevertheless, during more than 130 years of occupation scarcely any instances of it appeared in the judicial annals apart from a single isolated decision, and even that yielded to public opinion by annulling the marriage of a Muslim woman to a non-Muslim (Court of Guelma, 23 January 1907). Similarly in the Soviet Islamic republics, where of course there is no legal prohibition, a Muslim woman never marries a non-Muslim.

Recent evidence of the instinctive uneasiness, if it may be so called, felt by every Muslim at the idea of a Muslim woman marrying a Jew or a Christian is provided by the Law of 1951 on the organization of the family which applies to all Cypriot Turks. This law has completely discarded all the rules of Islamic law, with a single exception: in Cyprus the Muslim woman may not marry a non-Muslim. In these circumstances it is hardly surprising to find that the texts of laws relating to personal status enacted in recent years in Muslim countries explicitly recapitulate the prohibition contained in the classical law. The Moroccan Code of personal status law, which dates from 1958, states in Article 29, para. 4: "Marriage between a Muslim woman and a non-Muslim is prohibited." The Iraqi Code of personal status law of 30 December 1959 adopts a similar formula: "Marriage of a Muslim woman with a non-Muslim is not valid" (Article 17). The same formula is to be found in the Syrian Code of personal status law of 1953 (Art. 48, para. 2), in the Jordanian law of the organization of the family of 1951 and in the

Ottoman law on family status of 1917 (Art. 58); this last enactment is still in force in the Lebanon in relation to the Sunnīs and also in Israel where of course it applies only to Muslims.

In the countries of the Middle East which are predominantly Muslim and where the Islamic law has not been made the subject of new legislation, the rules of the *fiqh* are applicable, as interpreted by the jurists of each school, and there is accordingly an absolute prohibition of a marriage between a Muslim woman and a non-Muslim.

To return to contemporary legislation which follows more or less faithfully the principles of the classical *fiqh*, it is surprising to discover that the Tunisian Code of personal status (1956) is silent on this question. Some people have made this the ground for maintaining that the thousand-year old prohibition of Islam of the marriage of a Muslim woman with an infidel has lapsed by "preterition", but the majority of the interpreters of the Tunisian Code have rallied to the view of M. Es-Snoussi (al-Sanūsī), its official commentator, according to whom the maintenance of the prohibition is implicit, since the rule is derived from the general principles of Islamic law.[1]

To the legal and sociological observer, the course of events in Turkey would be of the greatest significance if it were possible to obtain information that should be objective and not based on vague hearsay. The prohibition of marriage between a Muslim woman and a non-Muslim was abolished there *indirectly*, as a consequence of the adoption in 1926 of a new Civil Code which, in so far as it followed the text of the Swiss Civil Code, could not retain a rule so inconsistent with the spirit of Swiss legislation. For the ensuing forty years it would, theoretically, have been possible for many marriages to have been concluded by Muslim women with non-Muslim men; it may be stated, however, that in actual fact such marriages have been practically non-existent, not so much on religious grounds, though the majority of Turks today are still very conscious of them, as in consequence of the exclusive nature of the different communities, which no legislation has the power to override.

It is true that instances are sometimes quoted, in the reports of travellers, of marriages of Muslim women with non-Muslims, but such examples must not be regarded as contradicting everything which has been stated above. Very frequently the narrator has omitted to mention that the non-Muslims in question has previously been con-

[1] *Code du Statut personnel annoté*, p. 13.

verted to Islam—an understandable omission, since the interested person would have undergone conversion without publicity and would have concealed it from his former co-religionists.

It is not correct to state, as is done too often, that the prohibition of marriage of a Muslim woman with a non-Muslim has no foundation in the Qur'ān. On the contrary, there are to be found in the Holy Book at least two statements specifically envisaging this hypothesis for the purpose of condemning it outright: "Do not marry (your daughters) to the polytheists" (II. 221, Egyptian edition). The polytheists or *mushrikūn* are those who associate other deities with the only God, as, in the opinion of Muslims, do Christians who believe in the Trinity. Still more specific is this verse: "When believing women in flight from infidels come to you...do not let them turn back to the infidels; it is not lawful that they should be with them, nor that the infidels should be their husbands" (LX. 10).

After the foundation of Islam this rule had been accepted unanimously by all Sunnī and Shīʿī jurists, to such an extent that it was scarcely discussed in the classical works, as though, being self-evident, it required no lengthy dissertation. Let us note in passing, that Christianity observed a similar rule at the same period: Jews and Christians might not intermarry, under the Byzantine Empire, on pain of death, and later on pain of excommunication for the Christian.

Marriage of a Muslim woman to a Christian or a Jew carries, under Islamic law, very severe sanctions. According to the Ḥanafīs, such a marriage in fact does not exist. Such a union "does not take place", state the scholars, that is to say it is *bāṭil* and may be dissolved without leaving any trace, even after consummation, except that, in the latter event, according to Abū Ḥanīfa, the woman has a right to recover her dowry, so as to avert the imposition of the penalties prescribed for fornication. In any case, if such a marriage should be entered in good faith (which would really be quite exceptional, since even the most ignorant are aware of this rule of law) it would be regarded by the four schools as equivalent to a union which was simply *fāsid*, that is, null and void for the future, though any children conceived or born before its dissolution would be considered legitimate. This is still the solution adopted by most of the contemporary legal enactments. However, the Ottoman law of the family of 1917 (Art. 58) and the Syrian Code of personal status law (Art. 48, para. 2), like the Indian and Sudanese systems of law, carry the prohibition much further, regarding the marriage of a Muslim woman with a non-Muslim as non-existent, *bāṭil*, in any circumstances, with the result that the children of such a union (which is considered to be simply a physical relationship) are rendered illegitimate and belong solely to their mother.

On the other hand, the Muslim has the right to marry a *kitābiyya*, that is a woman whose religious beliefs are contained in a book of revelation, which is the case with Christian women and Jewesses. Why should such toleration, for toleration it is, only be shown by the jurists, in view of the severity manifested by them when the religions of the parties are reversed?

The answer does not lie in the fact that the Prophet himself had a Jewish wife and a Christian wife, for this argument is by no means convincing. It is indeed known that Muḥammad, the Messenger of God, was endowed by the scholars of all the legal schools with a special status exempting him from the general rules applicable to the common run of human beings, even when such rules were set forth in the Qur'ān. By this means he was able to enjoy the privilege of having more than four wives at a time, which had from the beginning been forbidden to every adherent of the new religion; in the same way the Prophet, when he married, was not obliged to provide a dowry. It may therefore reasonably be conjectured that marriage to a Christian woman or a Jewess constituted one of the privileges which could not be claimed by believers in general.

In point of fact the doctrinal interpretation of the law has been more deeply affected by the example of the numerous companions of the Prophet, the *ṣaḥāba*, who married Christian women, and even Jewesses, without their wives being converted to Islam either before or after marriage, which was indeed to the credit of the wives, for, since the infidel cannot inherit from the Muslim, they would accordingly have been denied their share in the inheritance if their husbands predeceased them.

It is actually, however, a favourable interpretation of certain provisions of the Qur'ān which justify, on the legal plane, the marriage of a Muslim with a Christian woman or a Jewess.

The Qur'ān (v. 5 of the Egyptian edition) states quite explicitly: "You are permitted today to marry *respectable* daughters of believers and of those who have received the Scriptures before you." But it is also stated (IX. 30): "The Jews say: Ozair is the son of God. The Christians say: the Messiah is the Son of God...In so saying they resemble the infidels of former times."

"That man is an infidel (*kafara*) who says: God is the Messiah... He is an infidel who says: God is only the third member of the Trinity" (Qur'ān v. 73).

A small group of intransigents has maintained, on the strength of these verses, that Jewesses and Christian women whom a Muslim would have the right, in fact, to marry by virtue of Qur'ān v. 5, quoted above, ought not to believe in either Ozair or the Messiah as the Son of God, nor in the Trinity. By such an interpretation the verse (v. 5), which establishes in explicit terms the unconditional right of Muslims to marry a *kitābiyya*, would be divested of all substance, at least in so far as it concerns Christian women, and for this reason the *ijmā'* of the doctors of Islam has settled the meaning as follows: by verse v. 5 Christian women and Jewesses are excepted from the application of the verse revealed earlier in general terms (II. 221) which forbids Muslims to marry polytheists.

The marriage of a Muslim with a Christian woman or a Jewess, if it is not actually advised, is scarcely "reproved" (*makrūh*) by the Ḥanafī and Ḥanbalī schools. It is condemned by the other two schools, but only on moral grounds, and with some hesitation among the Mālikīs, when a *dhimmiyya* is concerned, that is a tributary woman, whether Christian or Jewess. Marriage with a *ḥarbiyya*, a foreign infidel, however, is subject to sterner censure. The reasons given for this "censure" by the Shāfi'ī and Mālikī schools are easy to understand. Although all the children of a Muslim, whether boys or girls, are automatically Muslims, they will still be exposed to the influence of their mother, at least during the first years of their lives. The Mālikīs in particular emphasize the pernicious influence of a woman who consumes wine and pork, possibly without moderation, and who goes to church. The Shāfi'īs pay more attention to the moral danger to which the husband may be exposed, affecting his religious principles and acts of devotion, by the "seductions" of a wife who does not share his faith in Islam.

However that may be, and even though the Shāfi'īs and Mālikīs are not generally much in favour of such unions, the marriage of a Muslim to a Christian woman or a Jewess is perfectly valid in the strictly legal sense, that is to say in the realm of law, and confers on the wife all the legal prerogatives enjoyed by a Muslim wife, with the exception of the right to inherit from her husband. Moreover, according to the doctrine of the Ḥanafī and Mālikī schools, the husband would not even have the right to forbid his Christian wife to eat pork, or to prevent a

Jewish or Christian wife from drinking wine and practising her religion openly.

Such is the unanimous doctrine, reproduced, of course, by all the contemporary legislative enactments, which it is not necessary to enumerate. Has it caused an increase in mixed marriages within Islam?

The situation as it was in the past lies outside the scope of this survey. In modern times a certain tendency may be observed among the upper classes to marry Christian women and Jewesses, more particularly those who in the past were called *ḥarbiyya* and today are foreigners, in preference to women belonging to the former class of *dhimmiyya*, who have now become simply nationals. It is done so frequently by students on missions abroad or by members of the diplomatic corps that certain Muslim countries (particularly the U.A.R., the Sudan and Iraq) have had to take steps—of a purely administrative nature—to combat this inclination to prefer foreign women to the girls of the country. Outside these circles, however, which are actually very small, mixed marriages do not often occur within Muslim populations as a whole. Moreover if, after several years of connubial life, such a marriage appears not to be threatened with repudiation, by the unilateral wish of the husband, the Christian or Jewish wife—sure that her marriage will last—is often converted to Islam in order, she maintains, to profess the same religion as her children, but in reality so as not to be deprived of the right to inherit from her husband.

The points outlined above apply particularly to countries which are largely Sunnī. The Shīʿīs, indeed, show even less eagerness to marry infidels than do their Sunnī co-religionists. It is doubtless the result of the doctrine of their scholars who have been more reticent than the Sunnīs on the subject of mixed marriages (in the sense of Muslim husband and Christian or Jewish wife). Even if such marriages are not forbidden among them—and how could they be in the face of the categorical statements of the Qur'ān—the Shīʿī jurists have attempted by all possible means to limit their numbers. One learned body of opinion maintains that a Shīʿī who wished to marry a Christian woman or a Jewess could do so only under the guise of a temporary marriage, *mutʿa*, recognized by them but regarded as a marriage of inferior status. For the rest it is particularly in the sphere of the relations of the spouses themselves, as determined by the *fuqahā'*, that their disapproval of such unions is expressed. The husband could object to his wife, Jewess or Christian, practising her religion openly or consuming wine or, if a Christian, pork.

It is chiefly the influence of such precepts, more moral than legal, concerning the daily life of married persons which has discredited mixed marriages in the opinion of the Shīʿī communities.

Regarding marriages between a Muslim husband and a Christian or a Jewish wife, the following question often occurs: should the Muslim judge appointed to decide the validity of a marriage, in which the wife is Christian or Jewish, take into consideration the rules of the latter's canon law, in case she is the subject of a Muslim country, or the law of her own country, if she is a foreigner?

To do so would be to apply a principle of private international law to a conflict of internal order. In a Muslim country nothing of this kind would be possible. Islamic public policy requires that in a conflict relating to personal status, if one of the parties is Muslim, only the *fiqh* may be administered. The same rule will be encountered later, with regard to conversions. Thus, since Islamic law determines that a Muslim is entitled to marry a Christian woman or a Jewess, the fact that the woman may be prohibited from marrying a Muslim by her own religious or national law will not constitute an impediment. This principle is being confirmed by the facts all the time. Mosaic law forbids the Jewish woman to marry a non-Jew; Coptic canon law contains similar provisions with regard to the Christian women of that community; nevertheless, everywhere in Islam there is evidence of Jewesses marrying Muslims, and, if the marriages of Coptic women in Egypt or the Sudan with Muslims are nowadays not very numerous, they are none the less regarded as perfectly valid within these two countries.

CASES OF COMPLETE JURIDICAL EXCLUSION

Marriage represents a very partial segregation, for, although the Muslim woman should never become absorbed into a non-Muslim society by way of marriage, the male Muslim, on the other hand, encounters no legal obstacle to marriage with a Christian woman or a Jewess.

There remains at the present time only very few Muslim institutions which impose, on the legal plane, an absolute separation between Muslims and non-Muslims. The *wilāya* or guardianship over person and property will be mentioned only briefly; on the other hand the incapacity to inherit, resulting from *ikhtilāf al-dīn*, that is, difference in religion, will be considered in some detail, followed by cursory notes on the *ikhtilāf al-dārayn*, difference in nationality, which has now fallen into disuse almost everywhere or has been abolished by legislation.

Under Islamic law there exists only one method of protecting a minor, whether he still has both parents living or is an orphan, which is called the *wilāya*. The protection of his person is guaranteed, successively, by the titular of the right of custody (*ḥaḍāna*) and then by his personal guardian, the *walī*, who always is a male through male kinship. This guardian must have the same religion as the minor under his protection, otherwise he is excluded from guardianship, even if he is the minor's own father.

The property of the minor is administered by the property trustee who, according to certain schools, may well not be the same as the guardian of his person. The persons invested with trusteeship over his property are the father and then, in his absence, but only according to Ḥanafī and Shāfi'ī law, the grandfather; subsequently this trusteeship devolves on any person whom the father (and under Ḥanafī and Shāfi'ī law the grandfather) may have nominated by will; he is the *waṣī*; in the absence of a *waṣī* it is the judge or his deputy who exercises the guardianship. But, except in this latter case, it is necessary for the guardian to have the same religion as the minor whose property he administers; the question arises chiefly in connexion with the *waṣī*, since the father usually has the same religion as his children. Accordingly, if the minor is a Muslim, the *waṣī* must be a Muslim; similarly, if he is Christian, the *waṣī* must be a Christian; if a Jew, the *waṣī* must be a Jew.

There can be no right of succession between Muslims, on the one hand, and Christians and Jews on the other, whether the deceased be Muslim or infidel; in other words, the prohibition operates in both directions—the Christian or Jew may not inherit from a Muslim any more than the Muslim may inherit from a Christian or a Jew. The rule in both its aspects was accepted very early in Islam and ratified by all the jurists of the Sunnī and Shī'ī schools together; it reappears at the present day in the positive legislation of all the Muslim countries.

It is a little surprising to find such unanimity and undeviating fidelity over the centuries to a principle for which there is extremely scant foundation in the scriptures.

There is practically nothing to be discovered on the subject in the Qur'ān; the *fuqahā'* who insist on finding a Qur'ānic justification for it have recourse to a verse of Holy Writ whose relevance to the absence of right of succession between Muslims and non-Muslims is not readily apparent: "Allāh will not give to the infidels any means of dominating believers" (iv. 141, Egyptian edition). It is true that they also adduce a *ḥadīth* which attributes to the Prophet the saying: "The Muslim does not inherit from the infidel, nor the infidel from the Muslim"; its terms correspond too well with the ideas of the early jurists for its authenticity not to be open to question.

It was in fact the first jurists, influenced no doubt by the refusal of Byzantine law to allow the heretic Christian the right to inherit from his Orthodox parents, who evolved the whole theory of what has been called in Arabic the *ikhtilāf al-dīn*. This may explain the fact that the prohibition is more absolute in character and is imposed more stringently when forbidding Christians and Jews to inherit from a Muslim than in the reverse direction. Ibn Qudāma, the great Ḥanbalī jurist, wrote in his *Mughnī*: "An *ijmā'* of all the scholars rules that the infidel shall not be able to inherit from the Muslim. Most of the companions (*ṣaḥāba*) and the *fuqahā'* are of opinion that the Muslim does not inherit from the infidel." This sentence contains more than one shade of meaning in its manner of reviewing the two sets of circumstances.

In respect of the structure of the family in Islam and the principles concerning mixed marriages (the impossibility of marriage between a Muslim woman and a non-Muslim), it is quite natural that infidels should be categorically forbidden to inherit from a Muslim. The rule will, almost invariably, affect only a Christian or a Jewish wife. It is rare, if not quite exceptional, for a Muslim, whether man or woman, to have a non-Muslim relative since the children are obliged to take the father's religion and the Muslim woman is only allowed to marry a Muslim. Assuming, therefore, that the rule applies almost exclusively to the Christian or Jewish wife, she could not logically have been allowed to inherit from her predeceased Muslim husband, for that would have had the effect of encouraging her to remain in her own faith; is it not known that the permission given to the Muslim to marry a Christian woman or a Jewess was dictated chiefly by considerations of religious proselytism? It is expected that, sooner or later, the wife will decide to embrace Islam. Hence it would be misguided not to exclude her from inheriting from her husband, since it is in fact the fear of such exclusion which is most often responsible for the wife's conversion. It is for this reason that the Ḥanbalīs and the

Shīʿīs will even allow the effectiveness of a conversion which takes place after the death but before the division of the property, an indulgence which is, however, rejected by the other schools on the logical grounds that the inheritance takes effect at death and belongs from that moment to the Muslim heirs, to the exclusion of infidels.

Conversely, the prohibition on a Muslim to inherit from an infidel has been more difficult to enforce because this prohibition concerns not only the husband of a wife who has remained Christian or Jewish, but also the children. Several companions of the Prophet and certain former *fuqahāʾ* were not able to see the justification for it. Has not the Muslim the right to marry an infidel? Why then should he not inherit from her? The arguments dictated by the religious policy designed to further the conversion of the wife to Islam do not operate in this eventuality, since, by definition, the husband is always Muslim. The Shīʿīs alone have conceded that a Muslim may inherit from an infidel. All the Sunnī schools have remained impervious to the arguments based on common sense which have been adduced in favour of this concession, and at the present time it is generally accepted that the *ikhtilāf al-dīn* operates in both directions, so that neither the Muslim nor the infidel can inherit from one another.

What are the reasons of social or religious expediency (since there is no scriptural authority) which have given the rule its secondary effect, the counterpart of the first with the positions of the parties reversed? It is difficult to believe that it was intended to discourage Muslims from marrying infidel women, in view of the fact that it is between married persons that the *ikhtilāf al-dīn* most often comes into play. Is it conceivable that at the time of his marriage a Muslim coldly contemplates the remote possibility of his Christian or Jewish wife predeceasing him and his own exclusion from the succession? Jurists explain the rule, in both its aspects, by the absence of common ground, juridically speaking, between believers and infidels in a realm (intestate succession) where the rights of the individual have been fixed intangibly by Holy Writ, without the intervention of the human will. The system of succession was revealed for the use of the Muslim world and it is separatist in character. It would have been neither logical nor indeed equitable to forbid the non-Muslim to inherit from a believer when, at the same time, the Muslim could inherit from a Christian or a Jew. It follows therefore that the impediment based on a difference in religion does not affect other ways of transmitting property gratuitously, whether as a legacy after death, or as a death-bed gift (treated in the same way as a bequest) or *waqf*. In these matters Christians, Jews and Muslims have exactly the same rights, a Muslim being able to bequeath the disposable third of his property to an infidel or to be a beneficiary under the will of a non-Muslim, because the will is a voluntary legal act, and it is well known that in the *mu'āmalāt*, the immense body of financial transactions, Islam has never discriminated between believers and infidels.

The *ikhtilāf al-dīn* is to be found today in the positive legislation of all Muslim countries (apart from Turkey). In India and particularly in Algeria before it became independent the basic principle underwent certain modifications to which it will be necessary to return, but first the position must be surveyed as it appears in the great majority of Muslim countries, extending from Pakistan to Morocco. In those countries that have not legislated on succession (Afghanistan, Libya, Sudan, etc.) the *fiqh* continues to be applied, unanimously for once, that is to say without any divergencies between the orthodox schools, since all are agreed in refusing to the infidel the least right of inheritance from a Muslim, and vice versa.

In Egypt (Law of 6 August 1943, Art. 6), in Syria (Code of personal status 1953, Art. 264, para. 2), in Morocco (Code of personal status 1958, Art. 228) Jews and Christians are expressly debarred from inheriting from a Muslim and the latter from inheriting from a Jew or a Christian. Iraq attempted (Code of personal status, 30 December 1959) to abandon the ancient Islamic law with regard to succession and, in consequence, the principle of *ikhtilāf al-dīn*. It is known that this attempt at secularization was of brief duration; it offended the deepest sensibilities of all levels of the population too gravely to have any chance of permanence. The law of 18 March 1963 substituted the Shī'ī law of succession for the bastard system which General Qāsim would have liked to impose arbitrarily, under pretext of unifying the laws. The new Article 90 of the Code of the personal status lays down that in all matters not dealt with by an express provision of the new law (18 March 1963) the courts will apply, with regard to succession, the law which was in force before the promulgation of the Code of personal status of 30 December 1959. The impediment to inherit when there is a difference of religion is accordingly reinstated; the prohibition which operates in both directions among the Sunnīs and only in one direction among the Shī'īs, according to whom the infidel is not able to inherit from a Muslim, although the reverse process is allowed.

The Tunisian Code of personal status of 1957 is silent on this question; its silence has been interpreted, like that relating to the prohibition on a Muslim woman marrying a non-Muslim, in the sense given above, namely that the Tunisian legislator considers it superfluous to mention a rule "which springs from the general principles of Muslim law".[1]

In former British India the application of the Islamic law on this particular point of the system of succession is open to argument. The authors state that "In the ancient Islamic law, a non-Muslim could not inherit from a Muslim, but in India this rule does not apply",[2] but these same writers declare, immediately afterwards, that the succession of a Muslim is controlled by Islamic law, which excludes the infidel from inheriting from him. In order to reconcile these two apparently contradictory statements, it may be considered that in India, when the *de cuius* was a Muslim and the succession subject to the rules of the *fiqh*, no Jew or Christian nor—*a fortiori*—Hindu should inherit, but, when the deceased was not a Muslim there was nothing to prevent a Muslim from inheriting if he was the heir in the order and the degree required by the law of *de cuius*.

The situation is thus almost the same as that which apparently exists at the present day in the Lebanon. A law of 23 June 1959 established a uniform system of succession there which is applied to all the non-Muslim communities; the Sunnī and Shīʿī Muslims continue to be subject to the *fiqh*. The new law has abolished the impediment to succession based on differences in religion; consequently a Muslim should be able to inherit from a Christian or a Jew, but not vice versa, since the succession of the Muslim is always subject to the rules of Islamic law.

It remains to discuss briefly the case of Algeria. For a long time the (French) courts had decided that the impediment based on differences in religion, which formed part of the "local statute", ought to apply when the *de cuius* was a Muslim. Then, at the beginning of the present century, there was a sudden reorientation in jurisprudence, after which the courts did in fact recognize the rights of Jews and Christians to inherit from a Muslim.[3] Such decisions, being few in number, were of

[1] Samaran, *Orientalisches Recht*, p. 399.

[2] A. Fyzee, *Outlines of Muhammadan Law*, 3rd ed. (London, 1964), p. 387.

[3] *Journal de Robe* (1921), p. 21; (1945), p. 47.

no great practical importance, but they revealed a lack of understanding of Muslim sensibilities; the price subsequently paid for it is well known.

If the Christian and the Jew are not able to inherit from a Muslim (any more than a Muslim can inherit from them), can they inherit from one another?

According to the Mālikīs and the Ḥanbalīs, the reply is certainly in the negative, at least when Jew and Christian are both subjects of the same Muslim power (*dhimmīs*), for there is no common ground of a religious and juridical nature between them. The Ḥanafīs, Shāfiʿīs and Shīʿīs take exactly the opposite view. In these schools there is no impediment to succession between Jews and Christians. The present argument will be based on the Ḥanafī doctrine, since it constituted the law which was applied throughout the Ottoman Empire, that is to say in the regions where both Christians and Jews were to be found in large numbers and where, in consequence, the problem of their claim to reciprocal succession was liable to occur.

The reader might well ask why an answer to the problem was not sought in the religious law of each of these communities from the time when the court of the community (whether patriarchal or rabbinical) of the deceased was empowered to say who was to inherit from him. The explanation, which will be stressed again later, is that the Muslim authorities always showed considerable reserve in recognizing that *dhimmīs* had the same legislative and judicial autonomy in matters of succession as they certainly enjoyed in matters concerning the law of the family, in the limited sense of the term; the policy usually followed tended to make the succession issues of the *dhimmī* subject to Muslim law and not to his own personal law.

According to the Ḥanafīs, therefore, Jews and Christians might inherit from one another, but their jurists (and also the Shāfiʿīs) made it a condition that both parties must be *dhimmīs* or both *ḥarbīs*, so that a Jew who had settled in the Ottoman Empire was not able to inherit from a relation, even though he was a Jew, who had died in a country of the *dār al-ḥarb*, that is to say not subject to a Muslim power. Conversely, the foreign *ḥarbī* could not inherit from his relation, whether Jew or Christian, if the latter was a *dhimmī*. It made no difference if the *ḥarbī* should have died in Islamic territory during the stay of one year to which the *amān* entitled him, for the *musta'min* was legally a *ḥarbī* and so his *dhimmī* relations found themselves excluded from his inheritance. His goods were placed under sequestration for distribution to his *ḥarbī* relations who had remained in the *dār al-ḥarb*, even though the latter were further remote in degree than the *dhimmī* relations; in the absence of *ḥarbī* heirs the succession passed to the Muslim public treasury. It was this doctrine which was reproduced in 1875 in the Code of personal status of Qadrī Pasha (Art. 588).

This *ikhtilāf al-dār* which prohibited *dhimmīs* from inheriting from *ḥarbīs* and vice versa, even when the heir was of the same creed as the deceased, may not have caused great inconvenience in the early days, when communications between the *dār-al-ḥarb* and the *dār al-Islām* were still very limited and the *ḥarbī musta'min* who extended his stay in Muslim territory was soon transformed into a *dhimmī*, but it became increasingly irksome and opposed to the most elementary rules of equity as the economic and cultural ties between Western and Oriental Jews, and even between European Christians and their Eastern co-religionists, increased in number and as marriages between them became less exceptional than in the past, while the change in status from *ḥarbī* to *dhimmī* no longer occurred automatically, since the *ḥarbī* had acquired the privileged status of a *capitulary* (that is a foreigner subject to foreign law) which, generally speaking, he had no intention of giving up.

Enlightened *muftīs*, in an attempt to escape from the bondage of an ancient doctrine, somewhat tainted with Byzantinism and, moreover, rejected by the Mālikī and Ḥanbalī schools, issued *fatāwā* (legal directives) which, like the jurisprudence of the secular courts when they were allowed to take decisions on these questions, tried to introduce improvements into the old Ḥanafī rule. They urged that, although in the early days of Islam the *ḥarbī* was, as the word suggests, an enemy, it would be irrational to include each and every foreigner under this heading today, especially if his country of origin was maintaining a friendly and co-operative relationship with the Muslim country of his *dhimmī* relations. The following extract from a judgment of the Mixed Court of Alexandria of 17 April 1928[1] indicates the progress of this gradual development which towards the 1930s and subsequently was to promote the juridical transformation of the conception of the *ikhtilāf al-dār* in the countries of the Ḥanafī school (while waiting for legislation to replace it by an entirely different principle, that of the impediment caused by the absence of reciprocal rights in the inheritance

[1] *Bulletin de Législation et de Jurisprudence*, 40th year, p. 308.

law of a foreigner who is called upon to inherit from a Christian or Jewish subject of a Muslim state):

> The principle by which a *ḥarbī* is incapable of inheriting from his *dhimmī* relation does not mean that a Christian who has given up his allegiance to a Muslim country is in consequence excluded from inheriting from another Christian who has remained the subject of such a country. Although in the early days of Islam the words "foreigner" and "enemy" were synonymous, just as at the time of the Twelve Tables it was said that *adversus hostem aeterna auctoritas est*, times have changed and the foreigner is no longer an enemy, under Roman or Islamic law, provided that a state of war does not exist to give him enemy status and curtail his civil rights accordingly. The prohibition contained in Article 588 (of the Code of Qadrī Pasha) does not apply to the subjects of two countries whose rulers are allied by treaties, whether of *wilāya* (protection), *ta'āwun* (support) or *tanāṣur* (aid). Thus an American citizen is a fit person to inherit from his Egyptian relation and the *ikhtilāf al-dār* cannot be invoked against him.

The rule has now fallen into disuse in those Ḥanafī countries which have not legislated on matters of succession; the others have, in general, followed the example of Egypt in giving the ancient impediment a different significance and application from those given to it by the Ḥanafī jurists. They have effectively abolished it, but without any flagrant contradiction of the teachings of these jurists. According to the Egyptian law of 6 August 1943 (Art. 6, last paragraph), "difference of nationality (*ikhtilāf al-dārayn*) is not an impediment to succession between Muslims. Between non-Muslims it is an impediment only if the foreign law excludes foreigners from succession rights." The Syrian Code of personal status of 1953 (Art. 264, last paragraph) more or less repeats the Egyptian provision: "The foreigner can inherit in Syria only if the laws of his own country recognize the same right for Syrian citizens." In Iraq two contradictory provisions of the Civil Code (Art. 22 and Art. 1.199) sanction, respectively, the new and the old versions of the *ikhtilāf al-dār*.

Sometimes the prohibition is abolished outright, in which case it must be understood that the legislator has not then thought it necessary to enact another rule to replace it, presumably allied to the former principle of *ikhtilāf al-dār*. This has occurred notably in the Lebanon: the law of 23 June 1959 imposed on all non-Muslim Lebanese a uniform inheritance law which contained no impediment based on differences of religion (this is consistent with the Ḥanafī *fiqh*, since the law is of interest only to non-Muslims) nor any prohibition resulting from a difference in allegiance, which is a relatively new conception.

With regard to the codes inspired by Mālikī law, the Tunisian Code of personal status of 1956 and the Moroccan code of 1958 are naturally silent on the question, since the Mālikī *fiqh* does not admit any impediment to succession which is based on the fact that the deceased and his heir, whether Christians or Jews, were the subjects of two different powers, one Muslim and the other non-Muslim.

So far as concerns the countries which adopted the principles of Ḥanafī law, but where, as in India (apart from Pakistan) the Muslim population was clearly in a minority, they naturally could not accept an impediment which depended on the distinction between the *dār al-ḥarb* and the *dār al-Islām*, for the *dār al-Islām* could exist only where the government, in all its aspects, was in the hands of Muslim authorities.

THE CONFLICT OF LAWS AND ISLAMIC PUBLIC POLICY

With the exception of Turkey, since 1926, and Tunisia, since 1957, all the countries of the Middle East have a plurilegislative system in matters relating to personal status which inevitably gives rise to conflicts of law of an internal nature, quite apart from conflicts in the international field. Such international conflicts are known to all civilized countries of the world in so far as they respect the universally accepted principle that in matters of personal status a foreigner should be governed by his own national law if it is not set aside by the requirements of the public policy appropriate to each state, varying, that is to say, not only according to place but according to the particular period of time.

Islamic public policy was for a long time not able to function or at best functioned only imperfectly in all these countries under consideration, owing to the presence of a non-Muslim occupying Power, whether such Power was unambiguously colonialist or merely exercising a so-called "protectorate", or simply because of the existence of a judicial and juridical framework inspired by Western laws in which it was difficult to incorporate this conception of Islamic public policy.

India, formerly British India, is still in this position; in spite of having attained political independence, she has not greatly modified the British judicial system and the regulation of the conflict of laws is still guided by the idea expressed in a legal decision in 1946: "British

India, as a whole, is neither governed by Hindu, Mahomedan, Sikh, Parsi, Christian, Jewish or any other law, except a law imposed by Great Britain, under which...all religions enjoy equal rights."[1] It is obvious that in such conditions there can be no question of the introduction of Islamic public policy. However, it may well be asked what principles must be invoked to resolve internal or international conflicts of laws arising from the multiplicity of laws applicable in the realm of personal status, and especially the serious difficulties connected with the conversion to Islam of one spouse, while the other remains Jewish or Christian (the present survey being restricted to the relations of these two communities with Islam).

Modern authors (Ameer Ali, Tyabji, Wilson, Fitzgerald and Asaf Fyzee) state unanimously that in India today the marriage of non-Muslims cannot, after the conversion of *one* spouse to Islam, be subject to Islamic law, although this is a fundamental principle of the Islamic legal system, and that even the conversion of both spouses would not subject them to Islamic law unless it had taken place in good faith. In other words, according to these authors, a Muslim married couple could, in certain circumstances, be subject to Christian or Jewish law, a situation which in Islam is literally unthinkable. Moreover, in the opinion of these same authors, the law which had prevailed before the conversion would continue to apply if *one* of the two Christian or Jewish spouses (even if it were the woman) were to be converted to Islam. It must be added, in the interests of truth, that the last of the above-mentioned authors reports a decision of the Calcutta Court of 1939 which went in exactly the opposite direction to that indicated.

However this may be, it is in fact desirable in every case to exclude former British India, since its peculiarities are, for historical reasons, very prounonced, and to confine the present explanatory notes to the other Muslim countries of this so-called Middle East extending from Pakistan to Morocco, apart from Tunisia, which is excepted for the reason given above.

All these countries, on attaining political independence, have attempted to recognize the claims of Islam, not only by such spectacular, if somewhat platonic, measures as the statement in the Constitution (of the U.A.R., Tunisia, Libya, Morocco, etc.) that Islam is the national religion, but more particularly by reintroducing into their juridical system the conception of Islamic public policy.

[1] Fyzee, *Muhammadan Law*, 3rd ed., p. 172.

Islamic public policy, regarded from the standpoint of the conflict of internal and international laws, may be defined in the following terms:

In all matters relating to personal status in its widest sense, that is to say including, as well as its usual content, inheritance by will and on intestacy, the Muslim can be subject only to Islamic law. The Christian or Jew who is converted to Islam is *ipso facto* subject to this law, and the effect of the conversion, which may even occur in the course of legal proceedings, cannot be countered by appeal, either to the concept of respect for vested rights (especially to the other spouse) or on grounds of equitable fraud.

There can be no question of vested rights; for if in most Western countries the mere change in the partner's nationality, provided it is not fraudulent, is enough to cause the loss of the benefit gained under the law of the marriage, how much more so is it, in the case of change of religion under a legal system in which faith is of paramount importance. With regard to the conception of equitable fraud, apart from the fact that it has been rejected by numerous Western countries, the necessity for investigating the private conscience of the individual has caused it to be rejected by the Muslim jurist. Besides, how could it be admitted that there was fraud involved in a conversion to Islam, even though it might have been effected without real conviction?

Finally, in the quite exceptional event of a Muslim judge (*qāḍī*) being called upon to settle a dispute between two parties, one or even both of whom are not Muslims, it will only be possible for him to apply Islamic law. There are no conflicts of laws before the *qāḍī* or, more precisely, the *qāḍī* eliminates such conflicts by always applying his own law.

By what practical measures has this conception of Islamic public policy been translated into action when Muslims, Christians and Jews are concerned in a dispute on a question of the personal status? What are the rules in the event of a conflict of international character?

In such a case the confessional factor seems *a priori* to be obscured and even to disappear completely. Most of the Muslim countries with which this survey is concerned have embodied, either in their Civil code (obligations, contracts and real rights) or in special enactments the rules which attempt to provide a legal solution for the various conflicts of law involving an extraneous element. Thus, the validity of the marriage of two foreigners, whatever their respective religion, will be judged by the secular courts, which will take into consideration the provisions of the national law of each of the parties. It is this rule which has hitherto been adopted by almost all the countries of the world. But —and this is the chief concern of the Muslim legislator—when in a mixed marriage one of the partners is a national of the country (Egyptian, Syrian, Iraqi, in the examples chosen), the only law applicable will be the law of that national (Art. 14 of the Egyptian Civil Code of 1948; Art. 15 of the Syrian Civil Code of 1949; Art. 19, para. 5 of the Iraqi Civil Code of 1951). This provision is the more surprising since an analogous provision is found in only one non-Muslim country—Hungary. It can hardly be imagined that the Muslim legislator intended to protect the Jew or the Christian of Egyptian, Syrian or Iraqi nationality. What would be his interest in deciding that the validity of the marriage of a local Jew with a French co-religionist would be decided by reference to the provisions of Mosaic law alone and without taking into account the substantive rules of French law? In fact, only those mixed marriages have been considered where one of the partners is not only a national, but also a Muslim (who, according to the principles of Islamic law, could only be the husband), and the other, whether Jewish or Christian, a foreigner. Such a marriage will be subject to Islamic law alone; it will be valid if Islamic law regards it as such, and invalid if this law condemns it, without any regard to the provisions of the national law of the foreign partner.

Nothing need be said of the conversion, regarded as apostasy, of a Muslim man or woman to Christianity or Judaism. So far as concerns the man, it is of very rare occurrence, for even though at the present day he no longer incurs the death penalty, the apostate is none the less cut off from his entire family, socially and juridically speaking. For the Muslim woman it was, until the recent adoption (between 1920 and 1960) by the Ḥanafī countries of the judicial divorce freely granted by the Mālikī school, a tempting if somewhat drastic method of obtaining the legal disruption of her marriage. Now that she is able to extricate herself on more favourable terms—it is, after all, possible for her to obtain a divorce today on grounds of mere incompatibility—she prefers not to meet general censure by apostasy.

To return to the conversion to Islam of a Jew or a Christian, it must be recognized that such conversion occurs quite frequently, even nowadays, especially with regard to Christians, a fact which is generally explained by the desire of the convert to evade what he regards as the excessively restrictive provisions of his former religious law. For example, Christian law imposes monogamy, the impossibility of dissolving a marriage by repudiation and the liability of the husband against whom divorce or legal separation has been pronounced to pay alimony to his former wife; all these restraints disappear if he announces his adherence to Islam, which is not concerned with them.

In order to become a Muslim it is certainly not enough, as it was in former times, to declare that there is only one God and that Muḥammad is his Prophet. The government and the judiciary in all countries with a Muslim majority have effective means of refusing anyone whose conversion to Islam has the sole object of enabling him to evade the legal consequences of his former personal law (whether Christian or Jewish); conversion must, indeed, be recorded in an authenticated instrument (called in Arab countries *ishhād*) which in theory is granted at the discretion of the government. The conditions in which this dispensation is effected vary from one country to another, to such an extent that it is impossible to discern any underlying principle observed by all Muslim countries. Some appear to be quite strict in the grant of this document, going so far (in Egypt) as to require the candidate to be interviewed by a representative of the religious authority to which he is subject. The object is clearly to foil the unduly self-interested schemes of a litigant at bay. In other countries, however, it is apparently enough for two witnesses to sign the statement of the convert for the public officer to feel obliged to grant him the *ishhād* in question.[1]

In any case, when conversion to Islam is official, even if it occurs in the course of legal proceedings, the former Christian or Jew is, henceforward, subject to the rules of Islamic law in all matters pertaining to personal status, understood in the widest sense of the term. This principle was always accepted without reservation in Muslim countries which had preserved their legislative autonomy. It disappeared in countries such as Algeria where the foreign occupying power had substituted for Islamic public policy another one which claimed to be more modern and was really inspired by the juridical conceptions current in its "metropolitan territory".

At the present time, since the acquisition of complete independence by many Muslim states, the principle that a local convert to Islam, of either sex, shall in future be solely subject to the *fiqh* in matters concerning the law of family and of inheritance is being all the time more

[1] Cf. for the Sudan, C. D'Olivier Farran, *Matrimonial Laws of the Sudan*, p. 227.

generally applied; some alleviations of the rule have, however, been introduced in certain countries, in a handsome but futile attempt not to jettison completely rights which had been acquired, under the authority of the former law, by the other partner who has remained a Christian or a Jew.

The principle which has just been formulated and which is regarded as a fundamental rule of Islam in all countries claiming to be Muslim, has not usually been expressly sanctioned by law, since it is considered unnecessary to formulate a truth which is self-evident. In recent years, however, in order to stop the restrictive interpretations prevalent in certain modernist societies obsessed by the idea of the secularization of personal status, the Muslim legislator has sometimes felt it necessary to recapitulate such a principle formally. Thus the Egyptian law of 24 September 1955, which abolished the courts of personal status, provides in Article 7 that conversion to Islam, even in the course of legal proceedings, entails *ipso facto* the application of Islamic Ḥanafī law. The Moroccan *ẓahīr* of 24 April 1959 goes further and brings under Muslim law, in matters affecting personal status, any individual, whether foreigner or national, who embraces Islam.

The Iraqi Code of personal status of 30 December 1959 (Art. 18) legislating in respect of marriage (though the principle is of general application) states: "If one of the two partners is converted to Islam before the other (that is to say, they are not converted at the same time), the rules of the *sharīʿa* will be followed to determine whether there are grounds for maintaining the marriage or for separating the parties."

The rule that the convert to Islam becomes immediately subject to Islamic law involves hardship (the attempted avoidance of which will be discussed later) specially in the matter of marriage, if the other spouse, whether Christian of Jew, should refuse to follow the convert into his new faith.

It is necessary to differentiate at the outset between the conversion of the husband and that of the wife.

When the husband embraces Islam and his wife remains Christian or Jewish, theoretically the marriage remains valid, since if he had been a Muslim *ab initio* he would have been able to marry a *kitabiyya*; if, however, there exists between the spouses an impediment which is recognized by the *fiqh* but disregarded by the canon law of the spouses before the conversion, this impediment will have the effect of annulling the union which had been valid until the time of the conversion. For example, Jewish law permits the marriage of uncle and niece, which is absolutely prohibited by Islamic law; hence, after the conversion to Islam of a Jewish husband who is the uncle of his Jewish wife, they will be severed. The consequences are the same in relation to a foster-mother: Jews and Christians, as such, have the right to marry the daughters and female relations of their foster-mother, but if they are converted to Islam the marriage will be dissolved.

Although it may be assumed that a marriage will remain in force because it does not contravene the basic rules imposed by Islamic law, the legal position of the married couple will nevertheless be completely upset by the conversion of the husband. If he is a Christian he can, as such, have only one wife and he is not allowed to repudiate her at his discretion; once having become a Muslim, he will be able to marry three other additional wives and to exercise at will the right of repudiation conferred on him by his new faith. Moreover, the right of succession which may have existed between husband and wife disappears.

If it is the Christian or Jewish wife who embraces Islam, the *fiqh* waits only long enough to urge the husband to follow his wife into her new faith. If he agrees, the marriage is not dissolved, but it must henceforward be subject to Islamic law. If the husband refuses to follow his wife's example, the marriage is annulled, for in no circumstances can a Muslim woman be the wife of a non-Muslim.

It may be admitted that these rulings are harsh, but it is difficult to imagine any others which will be consistent with the principle that a Muslim man or woman can only be subject in matters of personal status to the rules of the *fiqh*.

Before considering the alleviations which have been introduced here and there in the above rules, it must be remembered that the foregoing summary does not concern either Turkey and the Muslim countries of the Soviet Union, where the legal system, even in matters relating to personal status is no longer based on the *fiqh*, or, in a slighter degree, Tunisia, whose Code of personal status of 1957 applies to Muslims and non-Muslim nationals without discrimination: the conversion of one spouse to Islam is no longer allowed to have more than very limited consequences on the legal plane. Such a statement must be accepted with reserve, however, in the absence of any decisions of the Tunisian courts which are later in date than 1957.

The first alleviation of the rule by which conversion to Islam brings about the application of *fiqh* in matters related to family and to inheritance was believed by Anglo-Indian authors to be discernible in the conception that such an effect must necessarily be dependent on the *bona fide* conversion of *both* parties to Islam, and that one of the spouses was not enabled by conversion to change the legal status of the marriage from that which it had acquired at the time of its solemnization.

It is only necessary to look through the celebrated *Mahommedan Law* of Syed Ameer Ali, or the quite recent *Outlines of Muhammadan Law* of Asaf A. A. Fyzee, not to mention other similar works, to realize that the arguments of all these writers are not founded on judicial decisions —a fact which is, to say the least, surprising in works which are bristling with "cases"; their reasoning is based solely on grounds of juridical logic and on the opinion maintained by these jurists, who have been trained in the English school, that the relevant solution of Islamic law is not very equitable.

In the Sudan a slight modification has been introduced into the traditional system of the *fiqh*: while the conversion of the wife, Christian or Jewish, to Islam, when not followed by that of her husband, nullifies the marriage for the future—and only for the future, let it be understood, according to all the Islamic schools of law—if, on the other hand, it is the husband of a Christian woman or a Jewess who is converted to Islam, Sudanese law does not necessarily uphold this marriage, but recognizes that the wife has the right to secure its dissolution (Non-Mohammedan Marriage Ordinance, Art. 12). The decision appears to be a wise one. It would be impossible to continue to subject such a marriage to the Jewish or Christian law which governed it until the time of the husband's conversion, for it would be a juridical outrage under Islam. But, on the other hand, Sudanese legislation has taken the view that it would be inhumane to oblige the wife to live under a matrimonial system of a kind which she had not even contemplated as possible on her marriage, and it accordingly allows her to put an end to a union which is no longer what she intended when she consented to be married.

Finally it should be noted that in the Lebanon the Decree-Law of 3 February 1930, which established the grounds of competence of the religious jurisdictions, laid down in Article 36 that the competent judge in matters of personal status was the one representing the religious authority by whom the marriage was celebrated. This judge, whether Jew or Christian, would be obliged, nevertheless, to declare himself incompetent if both spouses had meanwhile been converted to Islam. The reverse decision would in fact be unthinkable, since it would result in litigants, all of the Muslim faith, being deprived of their natural judges.

In addition, the decree 146 LR of 18 November 1938 formally lays down that the conversion of *both* spouses gives jurisdiction to the court of their newly-acquired community.

When only one of the two Lebanese partners has embraced Islam, however, the judge who still has jurisdiction over the other partner will not be entitled to divest himself of it, for with regard to that partner, Islamic public policy does not come into operation; it is on the contrary incumbent on the judge to protect the existing rights of his co-religionist, who was married under the authority of that same law which the judge is required to administer, a law which in many cases was common in both spouses at the time of the marriage. Why should the non-converted partner suffer from changes of religious conviction in the other?

This Lebanese solution is quite exceptional and can be explained by the fact that in the Lebanon Muslims are in a minority, though Sunnīs and Shīʿīs together represent almost half of the population. Islamic public policy and the principle that a Muslim must be subject, in matters of personal status, only to the provisions of the *fiqh* do not apply, or are at any rate applied less stringently than in countries with a strong Muslim majority.

The above exposition is concerned with the situation which arises when all the parties are subject to an authority which is presumed to be Muslim, in which event, with rare exceptions, the thousand-year-old rule prevails which requires that when the male or female *dhimmī* is converted to Islam, his or her family life is thenceforward governed by the *fiqh*, irrespective of any contrary provisions of the religious law of the partner who has remained a *dhimmī*.

But what is to be the decision when the convert, although a Jew or a Christian, is not a "local subject"? The modern Muslim states have in general adopted the rules of international law relating to the conflict of laws which provide for the application of the "national" law of the foreigner in matters relating to personal status. Theoretically, the foreign "national" laws do not concern themselves with the religion of those to whom they apply, and it must be concluded that, when a Jew or a Christian non-national of a Muslim state is converted to Islam, his previous personal status ought not to be affected by the conversion.

The Egyptian courts, whose decisions are of particular importance in view of the very cosmopolitan character of Egyptian society in the large cities from the time of the abolition of the Consular courts (the problem now being considered not having arisen earlier) until the events of Suez, have had to find a solution to problems of this kind. From a somewhat confused case-law, which has not yet received very precise directives from the Court of Cassation, it seems to emerge that the personal law of the foreigner ought to be his "national" law and that the claim of certain litigants (usually Italians of the Jewish or Christian faith) petitioning the Egyptian courts to apply to their marriages the provisions of Islamic law, under pretext of their conversion to Islam, is unfounded, unless the intervention of Islamic public policy is invoked. But this invocation of public policy should have only a restrictive effect, excluding the application of certain provisions of the foreign law normally applicable but which appear to be contradictory to the fundamental principles of Islamic law. Thus, for example, the Egyptian judge will set aside, in the name of Islamic public policy, the rule allowed by Western legislatures under which disparity of religion is not considered an impediment to marriage or inheritance. To this limited extent the intervention of public policy is in conformity with the principles of private international law and is justified; but if the conception of public policy results in the total substitution of Islamic law for "national" law, under the pretext that the foreigner has been converted to Islam, then the entire functioning of the rules of international private law will be distorted. In this event public policy will no longer be a limited and exceptional obstacle to the application of the competent foreign law, but will actually destroy the very principle of the applicability of this law and, in consequence, the concept of the international conflict of laws. Thus certain Egyptian decisions, by a veritable abuse of the idea of public policy, have authorized a foreigner who has been converted to Islam to "repudiate" his wife without any legal proceedings. Repudiation, which is an indulgence or at least a licence granted to the husband, a licence moreover condemned by Muslim jurists themselves, can hardly constitute one of those fundamental principles of Islamic law which must be opposed to the application of foreign law.

The Moroccan *ẓahīr* of 24 April 1959 adopted a much more categorical, if not more juridical, attitude on this question. It does not appear to discriminate between Moroccan Jews or Christians (although there are very few of the latter in Morocco) and Jews or Christians of foreign nationality. All are subject to the Moroccan Code of personal status law of 1958 and therefore to the Islamic Mālikī law in all matters relating to personal status from the time of their conversion to Islam.

The inheritance of the Christian and the Jew is sometimes subject to the rules of Islamic law. This principle has always been maintained in the official doctrine of the Ḥanafī school. It was a rule which gave rise to much friction over the centuries between Jewish and Christian communities on the one hand and, on the other, the Ottoman government. Why should the latter have been concerned to apply the Islamic law of inheritance to the Jews and Christians under its jurisdiction? It has been alleged, not without an ulterior motive of denigration, that it was done with cases of escheat in view, so that the assets of the succession might go to the Muslim Public Treasury (*bayt al-māl*) and not to the religious community of the deceased. It goes without saying that the Ottoman authorities were regarding the problem presented by the inheritance of their Jewish and Christian subjects from a less sordid viewpoint, when they attempted to extend the application of the *fiqh* to all their Ottoman subjects.

In the first place it should be borne in mind that an inheritance does not concern exclusively the family of the deceased; creditors and legatees have their claims, even being given priority over the heirs, under the requirements of Islamic law. It is the business of the Muslim state to protect their interests, sometimes even by contravening the provisions of the confessional law of the deceased and imposing its own system of inheritance. Besides, more than in any other branch of personal status, as understood in the East that is to say in the broad sense of the term, the various persons interested, though they may not belong to different creeds (Jewish or Christian, which does not often occur) are likely to be members of different rites within the same creed. It may be remembered, incidentally, that there exist in Egypt (a typical example) six different rites for Catholics alone. However, one of the least questioned bases of the ancient jurisdictional and legislative autonomy of the Christian and Jewish communities has always been that litigants must belong to the same creed and the same rite. If therefore it were decided to apply the law of the deceased person's community, there would be a risk of imposing on certain heirs and on creditors and legatees, almost inevitably, a personal law other than their own, with which they would be scarcely familiar and the contents of which they would have considerable difficulty in discovering, in view of the more or less general lack of easily accessible information. It is for this reason that, apart from the effectively unrealizable eventuality whereby *all* the interested parties agree to settle an inheritance in conformity with the rules of the religious law of the deceased (a solution which was adopted by the Egyptian law of 23 March 1944) public interest, according to this argument, requires that Islamic law should govern the inheritance of a Christian or a Jew who is under the jurisdiction of a country with a Muslim majority.

It is indeed difficult to compile a definitive list of the encroachments of Islamic law in a field which, despite the reservations of the Ḥanafī writers, is traditionally connected with personal status and in which it is known that Christian and Jewish communities have always striven to be governed by their own laws, notwithstanding the practical difficulties involved in the application of such a privilege. In fact, though this does not simplify the problem, there exist in countries like Egypt and the Sudan numerous Christian communities (including the important Monophysite Copt community numbering three million adherents) which have for a long time adopted voluntarily, if it may be so described, or more precisely under force of circumstances, Islamic law, slightly modified in certain respects, as a system of inheritance.

Even today, in most of the countries outside Egypt which observe Ḥanafī law, non-Muslim inheritances are not governed by the *fiqh*, but by the religious law of the deceased, following an ancient practice which is not, for the most part, to be found expressed in any legislative document.

In recent years the question has assumed a more definite form in the countries which believe it to be their duty to give a legislative sanction to ancient practices, or which, on the other hand, wish to be rid of them. In Egypt, for example, the Civil Code of 1948 renders all Egyptians, whether Muslim or not, subject to the rules of Muslim jurisprudence and to the laws based upon it in all matters of *intestate* succession. Since the same Code also lays down rules regarding all Personal Rights and legal capacity, while under Article 914 testamentary succession is henceforward to be administered according to Islamic law, not very much remains in the realm of the personal status which is still subject to the confessional law of each community, especially now that the law of 21 September 1955 requires that canon law or Mosaic law can only be applied where there is unity of creed and unity of rite among all the persons concerned.

Some countries (Egypt, Syria, Libya, etc.) have introduced into their Civil Code (the code of obligations, contracts and real rights) provisions relating to the settlement and division of inheritances. These provisions which are alien to Islamic law properly so called, apply to all nationals, whatever their religion, and so constitute the first step in the unification of internal legislation with regard to inheritance, and are a protection to creditors against the unforeseen consequences of a religious law which might otherwise have been applicable to the case (see particularly Art. 876–914 of the Egyptian Civil Code and Art. 836–75 of the Syrian Civil Code).

The Lebanon (law of 23 June 1959) has put an end to all the former controversies, without making Jew and Christian subject to the inherit-law of the *fiqh*, by deciding that the inheritance of non-Muslims shall be governed by a uniform system, no longer derived in any way from Muslim law; the latter, in both the Ḥanafī and the Shīʿī versions, still continues to govern Muslim inheritance.

In Tunisia, despite its very large Mālikī majority, there has been the same reaction as in the Ḥanafī countries; by the law of 27 September 1957 Tunisian Jews (the number of Christians of Tunisian nationality being negligible) are made subject to Book IX of its Code of the personal status, which is however a very faithful copy of the classical law of the Mālikī school. It is noteworthy that Morocco, on the other hand, has allowed Moroccan Jews to keep their law of inheritance, in accordance with the Mālikī tradition.

Finally, mention should be made of a tendency, which in Arab countries at least is on the increase, to remove matters of testamentary succession from the religious legislation of the Christian and Jewish communities in order to submit them to the rules of Islamic law. Such a decision has been reached by the Egyptian, Syrian and Libyan Civil Codes and by the Tunisian Code of the personal status.

Is it possible, outside the plan which has just been outlined, to foresee in what direction legal relations between the three communities, Muslim, Christian and Jewish, in that region of the Middle East which extends, as has been said, from Morocco as far as Pakistan and India, will develop, in the near or distant future, regarding personal status?

Over the centuries an ever-increasing degree of association and unification has been achieved. Today on the legal plane, which is the only one at present being considered, there are few barriers between the three communities. There remain two absolute prohibitions, it is true—for a Muslim woman to marry a non-Muslim and for Christians and Jews to inherit from a Muslim and vice versa, there being no claim to succession in either direction. Certainly the conception of marriage differs greatly from one community to another, and around each view a law of the family has crystallized, with sometimes a complete personal status, which has been and still is a battlefield for clashes and misunderstandings. Time will do its work in this sphere even more rapidly than is generally expected, but these are matters which belong to sociology and custom rather than to law. In terms of legislation, what reforms, what changes can be forecast from the present position?

It is well known, alas, how dangerous such speculations are. When, in 1926, Turkey unified and secularized the law of the family and of inheritance, some people thought that her example would be imitated after a brief interval by other Muslim states. Forty years have passed and no state has followed in Turkey's footsteps, with the exception of the Soviet countries, but they are not free to choose their legislative policy, and that makes all the difference.

When, in 1955, Egypt abolished all the jurisdictions of personal status, Muslim, Christian and Jewish, it might have been inferred, with a fair degree of probability in view of the juridical influence which Egypt has in all the Arab countries, that many of them would have hastened to do the same. Tunisia alone abolished rabbinical jurisdiction two years later and unified her judicial system. Lately (1965) Morocco did the same towards rabbinical jurisdiction.

The jurist accordingly hesitates, having learned to regard the capricious "sense of history" with caution; nevertheless he is not prohibited from establishing an order of priorities.

It appears that the first sweeping reform would involve the abolition of all these jurisdictions of personal status, Muslim as well as Christian and rabbinical, which in many countries duplicate the jurisdiction of the common law. On this point the experience of Egypt and Tunisia has surely been conclusive. Such a multiplicity of jurisdictions, decayed and almost always badly organized, is difficult to accommodate within a modern state, whose judicial structure, having lost all its confessional character, offers a sufficient guarantee of impartiality to the litigants, whatever may be their religion.

Nevertheless, the legislator must proceed, even towards such a modest objective, with caution. He must not advance too far ahead of the social evolution of his country, otherwise he runs the risk of being obliged to retrace his steps and to return, crestfallen, to the system which he had pressed to abolish. Witness the case of Libya. The Libyan law of Judicial Organization of 20 September 1954 abolished there the jurisdiction of personal status and the civil courts became competent in all matters and with regard to all litigants, whatever might be their religion. The reform was premature. The people (especially the Muslim litigant) soon missed the simplicity of the *qāḍī*'s court, to which they had been accustomed and which seemed to them superior to the complexities of civil justice. In order, therefore, not to offend public opinion, the new law of Judicial Organization of 18 December 1958 re-established the duality of jurisdictions in all matters concerning personal status. The Libyan reform had lasted for exactly four years.

The second stage would be the unification of the law of the family and of inheritance applicable to non-Muslims (Jews and Christians), following the Lebanese example with regard to inheritance. Obviously this unified law, in a sphere where peculiar distinctions have prevailed for centuries, will not be evolved easily and will entail for each country a carefully selected intake of provisions borrowed from the various religious systems which this unifying state will be called upon to replace.

The third stage, which would involve the granting to all nationals of a Muslim country, whether Muslims or not, of a unified personal status including succession, generally inspired by the classical *fiqh*, would appear to be, at least for the majority of Muslim states and despite the Tunisian precedent, visionary if not pure fantasy. Even in Morocco, where there exist scarcely any Christian nationals and where the government, in its anxiety to unify the law, has contemplated extending the application of the new Code of personal status to all non-Israelites within its jurisdiction (the Israelites being still subject to Mosaic law), it has been found necessary to exempt Moroccans who are neither Muslims nor Israelites from the provisions of the Code relating to polygamy, to unilateral repudiation and to the impediment to marriage resulting from foster-motherhood (Art. 3 of the *ẓahīr* of 6 September 1950 on Moroccan nationality). Thus, in a particularly favourable set of circumstances, since there exist so few Christian Moroccans, there has been, it might be said, an inevitable return to the juridical pluralism which has characterized personal status in Muslim countries over the centuries.

CHAPTER 22

SOCIETY AND POLITICS

PREFATORY REMARKS

The religions of the Near East, their mutual attractions and repulsions, in harmony and in discord, constitute a subject whose adequate development would require bulky volumes covering many years of research.

It has been said more than once that the Near East is a mosaic of races and a patchwork of religions, but the comparison falls short of reality, for mosaic and patchwork are dead things which never alter, whereas races and religions are alive and active, always evolving, and in the Near East we find them inextricably mingled in a ceaseless flux of mutual action and reaction, hardly possible to follow in detail, and even less to explain.

The aim of the present work is to give in a limited compass a concise idea of the vicissitudes of the religious groups established in the Near East during the last hundred years. With this end in view the main field of inquiry must be confined to the realms of the old Ottoman empire outside Europe; but since certain of these religious groups have connexions which transcend shifting political frontiers, to make certain points clear brief notes on them have had to be included.

THE "MILLET" IN THE OTTOMAN EMPIRE

From the beginning of the nineteenth century the failure of the rickety bonds between its members threatened the destruction of the old Ottoman Empire. The passage of centuries had done nothing towards the fusion of the heterogeneous elements under the sultan's rule. No progress towards unity had been made in political, religious or ethnic fields. The state system itself prevented this. The Ottomans had always existed as a race apart from the peoples they dwelt among, and as their influence over them dwindled, political evolution naturally led to the dissolution of the empire. The Turks had never attempted to assimilate the ethnic elements of the peoples they conquered, not even those who, like themselves, were Muslims. Thus, the Turks were "foreigners" not only to the Christian inhabitants of the Balkans, but even to the Arabs of Syria and inhabitants of Egypt. The empire was a mosaic of races and a patchwork of religious sects.

Naturally, conquest led to the ascendency of Islam and the application of its canon law, *sharīʿa*. The special characteristic of the *sharīʿa* is that it has no territorial significance but is based on religious creed, and so is binding upon its followers, no matter where they might be living. Non-Muslim subjects were called *râya* (from Arabic *raʿāyā*, plural of *raʿiyya*, the herd). They were also known in Turkish as *ẓimmi*, from the Arabic *ahl al-dhimma*, the people of the covenant. In Muslim law the *dhimma* is a bilateral pact whereby the *ẓimmi* obtained a guarantee of domicile, tolerance of religion and protection of person and goods in exchange for a poll-tax, *jizya*, and a duty on lands, *kharāj*. This toleration did not extend to outward religious show, and in social life limitations were imposed on the *ẓimmi* which set them on a lower level than the Muslims, the upper class, who left to the *ẓimmi* those social functions less worthy of merit, reserving for themselves all matters of government, the carrying of arms, and offices in the administration and the state religion. The occupations left open to the *râya* allowed them to attain commercial, professional and technical positions which rendered them indispensable to their rulers.

With the capture of Constantinople in 1453 Meḥmed II became overlord of a numerous group of Christians at a time when the Orthodox Church was without a leader. The sultan ordered the election of a patriarch (he was to be Gennadios II) to the vacant seat, and by assuming the functions of the defeated *basileus* he presented in person the *dekanikion*, the patriarchial crozier to Gennadios II. This endowed the patriarch with an authority his predecessors had never enjoyed, for to the religious jurisdiction proper to his position the *padishah*, i.e. the sultan, added now civil power over all Christians in the Ottoman domains, which gave him much authority and equally great responsibilities.

What remained after this settlement, in line with the traditional Islamic policy of tolerance and live and let live under certain conditions, was an autonomous body, under the direct rule in religious and civil affairs of an authority dependent solely on the *padishah*, in effect a state within a state.

The generic name given to such systems was *millet*, from the Arabic *milla* in the sense of religious sect or creed, and from this sense by an easy semantic change, *millet* came to denote those religious groups recognized by the State.

Meḥmed II himself and his successors after him conferred the *berat* or instrument of investiture which granted recognition as *millet-bashï* or head of the *millet*, upon the Armenian patriarch, the chief rabbi of Constantinople and the leaders of the other religious groups, giving them civil authority over their followers. Among their assignments and responsibilities was the collection of the taxes owed by the *millet* to the exchequer. Provided these were paid regularly, and the *millet* aroused no suspicion of manoeuvres against the State or of dealings with foreign powers, the government rarely meddled with the internal affairs of the *millet*.

A result of the system outlined was that the *millet* was not confined to one region, for it often happened that its members were scattered over various parts of the empire. Another was that membership of different *millets* placed invisible yet effective barriers between neighbours, and established a coolness between them which began in the first days at school. Each *millet* had its own schools where the idea, and ideal, of separation and isolation were taught, thereby opening the door to mutual rivalries, quarrels, compromises and pacts within and without the empire. Fear of consequences which might prove worse than the *status quo* preserved a frigid peace between the members of different *millets* whose close daily life, far from knitting them together, led to friction and inflamed old racial and religious quarrels. Each *millet* clung to its customs and beliefs, convinced that only in this way had they been preserved through long years of affliction.

Such were the moulds in which the *millets* of the empire were cast, and the channels through which their social, political and religious life were to flow.

THE OTTOMAN EMPIRE

The decay of the empire early in the nineteenth century called urgently for reform. Selim III resolved to initiate it with the *niẓam-i jedid*, the New Order, and began where it seemed most urgent—the reform of the Janissaries. These mutinied and forced his abdication in 1807 in favour of Muṣṭafa IV. Selim was executed just as a successful reaction was about to restore him to the throne, and it was Maḥmud II who succeeded Muṣṭafa. With this exemplar before his eyes, the new Sultan proceeded cautiously and addressed himself to fortifying the central authority in the provinces, where it was practically unrecognized, above all in the distant ones. He solved the problem of the Janissaries, after careful preparation, by exterminating them to the number of 10,000 in June 1828. He was now more free to realize his plans of reform, stimulated as he was by what his nominal vassal Muḥammad 'Alī was doing in Egypt in the same way. The changes he introduced enabled his successors to go ahead with the programme of reforms. When he died he left a Sultanate with enhanced authority, but he could not leave his sons and successors his stubborn energy nor his hard-schooled prudence.

It fell to his son 'Abdülmejid to promulgate on 3 November 1839 the famous document known as *khaṭṭ-i sherif*, the Noble Decree of Gülhane whereby came into being the *tanẓimat*, the promised laws and reforms. The Sultan was anxious to do away with the inequalities which, above all in religious matters, divided the empire's subjects, and to guarantee to all without distinction of race or creed their life, honour and possessions. In Turkey and elsewhere the moral effect was great; in reality the *khaṭṭ-i sherif* had almost no material effect at all. Without due preparation it was impossible to overturn a secular order grounded on laws, customs and religion. The *râya* were tolerated in the sense that they were free from persecution and that within well-defined limits they might live in accordance with their religious precepts. But tolerance, meaning lack of discrimination, or equality before the law, there was not.

For their part the beneficiaries of the edict showed few signs of rejoicing. Centuries of experience had made them suspicious; they preferred the ills they knew to favours to come. As for the Muslims, their religious dignitaries and the mass of the people from whom they drew their support, and even many of the functionaries, were opposed to the reforms and the reformers, whose champion was Reshid Pasha.

The reformers could not, perhaps would not, go far in certain directions. In reply to pressure from the Powers to refrain from putting apostates to death, the Porte told the governments in Paris and London, 22 March 1844, that in future they would not execute apostates, i.e. Christians who had gone over to Islam and had subsequently returned to Christianity, but it was impossible to issue an order directly contrary to the *sharī'a*.

The Crimean War (1854) and the consequent participation of Turkey in what came to be called the "Concert" of Europe made it advisable to let the Powers believe that the empire was on the way to modernization. Current European opinion where Turkey was concerned was alert above all to the treatment meted out to the *millets*. So it was in May 1855 that a *ferman* abolished the *jizya*, tribute payable by the members of the *millet*, and declared them subject to military service, a privilege hitherto reserved for Muslims.

Soon afterwards, during the preliminaries of the Treaty of Paris (1856), a new decree, the *khaṭṭ-i hümayun*, Imperial Rescript, once more reaffirmed the *khaṭṭ-i sherif* and reiterated its guarantees. The privileges of the *millets* were to be respected and brought up to date. The office of patriarch would be held for life, and ecclesiastical fees would be replaced by fixed salaries, according to the rank of the holder. For economic affairs the *millets* would have elective assemblies composed of clergy and laity, entrusted with civil administration. All offensive references to *millets* in official documents would be cut out. There would be no discrimination in access to State offices and full liberty to profess any religion. Any man could bear witness before the tribunals, no matter his religion or race, and religious discrimination in the collection of taxes would go. And among other measures it was laid down that equality of rights implied equality of duties, and that all and sundry were liable for military service.

The mere fact that such intentions could be officially promulgated was more than remarkable in the Turkey of those days. In the East customs and traditions have an inconceivable influence. Notwithstanding all the edicts the general features of life in the *millets* continued without noticeable change until the close of the Ottoman regime. Christians and Jews remained on the margins of public life. They dared not raise their voices in the assemblies in which they had representation, and they bowed to the majority. Moreover there were difficulties in the *millets* over the application of the *khaṭṭ-i hümayun* in regard to military service. Continual warfare demanded a never-ending supply of recruits. The Christians felt no call to heroism for interests which were not their own, and the Muslims had no wish to associate with Christians whom it would be dangerous to arm. The solution was the payment of a sum, *bedel-i ʿaskerî*, in exchange for military service, and the gross return from this came to equal that from the revoked *jizya*.

In important centres of population the *râya* lived in separate quarters which were sometimes walled and approached by gates closed at night as a necessary safeguard. Under the cloak of religion and the defence of the *millet* quarrels were often due to economic, personal or political motives. Living in separate districts did something towards reducing opportunities of friction, but animosity smouldered like hot coals under ashes, and it needed but a puff of wind for the flames to break out.

It was towards this time that improvements in education had brought into being an intellectual class bent on solving the empire's problems. The reformers had made it a prior condition of 'Abdülḥamid's succession to the sultanate that he should agree to a form of constitution limiting the power of the sultan and ensuring the appointment of ministers responsible to a truly representative assembly. This constitutional assembly held its first session on 19 March 1877, but it was chosen so arbitrarily that neither representatives nor electors knew quite what was going on. It was a revelation to the elected members, when they met together, to realize that maladministration was a general ailment. Complaints turned to denunciations and demands for responsibility. In his displeasure the Sultan suspended the sessions on 14 February 1878, and henceforth governed absolutely. It has been said that the *tanẓimat* era ceased with 'Abdülḥamid II, but this is only true from a political point of view. The Sultan was not an enemy of progress. He encouraged it in education particularly, aiding existing institutions and creating new ones; but he had not foreseen that contact with modern culture would turn them into nurseries of ideas quite opposed to his policies. He also improved communications, notably in railways and telegraphs, at the same time easing the functioning of a centralized government. In the political field 'Abdülḥamid II was immovable. Alarmed by moves towards autonomy on the part of the Armenians, widely distributed as they were over the Russian frontier and within Anatolia, he tried at first to spread disunion among them, and when this failed stirred up Kurdish animosity, and there followed the terrible massacres of 1894–96. Disturbed by the spread of subversive ideas he organized a vast system of espionage and set up a rigid censorship of the Press. Yet these restraints did not impede the Press from taking an important part in the cultural growth of the country, and a new profession, journalism, came into being.

The schools, fertile grounds for the propagation of new ideas, nourished the first organized revolutionary movements. Common ground between the various opposition groups was lacking. Some, like the Armenians, divided even among themselves, looked for autonomy through foreign intervention. Some wanted a federation within the empire, a dangerous move in the opinion of others. In the course of years the cadets of the military schools who had suffered severely for their advanced opinions came to enjoy military command, and could now pass from ideas to action.

Outstanding among the secret societies which, within Turkey and without, opposed the Sultan's ways was that called *Ittiḥad ve-teraqqi jem'iyeti*, Committee of Union and Progress. Harassed in Turkey, it had its headquarters in Paris. A group of officers stationed in Salonica was in contact with the Committee, and it was they who started the rebellion which obliged 'Abdülḥamid II to restore the constitution he had suspended thirty years before. Still the Sultan did not give way, and with the help of reactionary groups organized an extensive reactionary movement which broke out in April 1909. In the capital this was soon quelled, though not so readily in various parts of Anatolia, where, especially in Adana, it degenerated into the massacre of thousands of Armenians.

The Committee of Union and Progress deposed 'Abdülḥamid II and replaced him by his brother Meḥmed Reshad, who was to be faced with hard days of fighting in the Balkans and the first World War of 1914–18.

THE TURKISH REPUBLIC

The advent of new Turkey was an event unparalleled in the history of post-war settlements. Although decimated by eight years of war, practically disarmed and with no recognized government, the country freed itself of its victors, some willingly, others by force of arms. The nationalists were now secured of power. In Ankara, on 1 November 1922, the *Kamutay*, National Assembly, stripped the last Ottoman sultan of his power, and proclaimed itself the sovereign authority. It permitted the existence of a caliphate divorced from the sultanate, in the person of a scion of Ottoman stock. Some feeling for the past led to a desire that a little authority be left to the caliphate but Mustafa Kemal was taking no risks, and by a decree of 3 March 1924, the Ottoman caliphate definitely receded into history.

Such far-reaching changes gave a new look to the religious situation in Turkey. The *millet* system was doomed to disappear. The Armenians had been almost entirely wiped out. At the close of the Greek war, by the terms of the Treaty of Lausanne of July 1923, the million Greeks living in Anatolia and Thrace were to be exchanged for the 400,000

Turks leaving Greek territory. Both states gained in homogeneity as a result of this drastic measure. The communities of Constantinople were privileged to forego this exchange. But, while the remaining *millets* scattered over the country were declining in importance, relations with Islam presented a grave problem to the new Turkish Republic, proclaimed on 29 October 1923, and to its first president, Mustafa Kemal.

A ministry of Religious Affairs had superceded the old organization governed by the *sheykh ül-Islâm*; on the proclamation of the Republic its function passed to two departments: *Diyanet işleri reisliği*, Presidency of Religious Affairs dependent on the presidency of the government, and *Evkaf umum müdürlüğü*, Directorate-general of *evkaf*, concerned with the administration of the property and religious buildings which had passed into State ownership. At the same time the *medreses* lost their identity *sui juris* and their property was made over to the Ministry of Public Instruction, which set up schools for the instruction of *imām* and *khaṭīb*, and appointed the *medrese* Süleymaniye for higher religious education. A professorial committee undertook to produce a report on the modernization of Islam.

The scheme on the schools was ineffective. They languished and in 1932 ceased to function. The Süleymaniye Faculty closed in the following year. Of the report on the modernization of Islam all that remained was a recommendation that Turkish should replace Arabic in Muslim religious rites. After lengthy preparation, in January 1932 and in the mosque of Aya Sofya before a throng which overflowed that roomy edifice, religious services were held for the first time in Turkish, broadcast by radio to the whole country. It has been said that this measure aroused a degree of public resentment never achieved by secularizing decrees of much greater importance. Faced by widespread opposition the government confined itself to urging that the law be obeyed in public places. The muezzins were taught the recitation of prayers in Turkish, and intoning the *adhān* in Arabic was declared an offence. Two years later the mosque of Aya Sofya was to become a museum.

In April 1924 the *maḥākim*, tribunals, of the *sharīʿa* were suppressed and their jurisdiction passed to the ordinary tribunals. Mustafa Kemal was face to face with his "greatest and most insidious enemies: laws in decay and their decrepit supporters".

The government's reaction against the dervishes was not unexpected. The *ṭuruq* were dissolved, their monasteries closed, their meetings forbidden. At the same time Mustafa Kemal began his campaign against the wearing of the fez and against traditional Turkish ways of dressing. The wearing of distinctive religious dress was also prohibited, no matter of what form of worship, though an exception was made for the head of any recognized religious group. Westerners can scarcely conceive the tremendous importance for the East of such summary measures. A rough idea may be gained by imagining a European country rapidly adopting Muslim laws, oriental display, veiled women, the lunar calendar, the Arabic alphabet, and covered heads and bare feet in the home.

In March 1926 the chief Muslim dignitaries in Egypt made energetic protest against practices "worthy of infidels". This would very likely have had the support of many in Turkey, but Mustafa Kemal as long ago as 31 October predicted that the movement would go on even if a few heads were to roll.

Close upon the exchange of peoples and with desires to weaken the authority of the ecumenical Orthodox patriarch, the Turkish government favoured the attempt to found an orthodox Turkish church. The prime mover was the *papaz* Eftym, or Euthymios Karahisarlioğlu, who in October 1923 tried to impose himself upon the synod of the Phanar. Undaunted by his excommunication in February 1924, with a few followers he founded the independent Turkish Orthodox Church, officiating in Turkish in the church of the Panagia in Galata. In March 1926 he assumed the title of archbishop and exarch of Turkish Orthodoxy, and despite his almost complete lack of followers did not cease to create difficulties for the Orthodox patriarch.

The regulations of the *sharīʿa* as regarding the civil state were abolished in March 1926 when the civil code and the code of obligations were promulgated. Polygamy, divorce and the prohibition of marriage with non-Muslims were banned. Finally in April 1928 the *Kamutay* voted the repeal of Article 2 of the Constitution which made Islam the official religion. Turkey, with its intensely Muslim population, perhaps the most Muslim of all, was officially declared a secular state. A law of 3 November forbade the public use of the Arabic alphabet after 1 January 1929, its place taken by the Roman. These measures invested the State with some show of secularization; but the soul of a people was not to be changed in a day, however intense the pressure. The new laws began to be observed in the big centres of population, but in remoter places life went on as before.

The second president of the republic was Ismet Inönü. These were difficult times, and worse were to come during the Second World War. To maintain its neutrality Turkey had to place itself on a war footing, at the expense of impoverishing the country. On the other hand Turkish products were selling at strategic prices and realized enormous fortunes, while the government was obliged to ration necessities. Two classes were enriched: landholders by the sale of agricultural products, and middlemen and merchants, above all in Constantinople. The former were nearly all Muslims. The latter mainly belonged to the *millets*. On 11 November 1942 the *Kamutay* passed the law *varlik vergisi*, a tax on capital. By this law farmers were limited to a tax of 5 per cent. For limited companies it was 50–75 per cent of the net profits in 1941. For all other categories, the tax was estimated by local commissions; no percentage was fixed, and no appeal was anticipated. Under the Ottoman empire the *millets* were taxed ten times more severely than the Muslim population, but now matters went much further. Confidential instructions went out to treat foreigner and Muslim alike, but through bureaucratic mismanagement some foreigners were grossly overburdened, and diplomatic protests followed. It was the old *muṣādara*, confiscation, a grievous discrimination between subjects of the same State, applied on a mass scale. Immediate payment was expected. For some the tax exceeded their possessions. Others had too short a notice to meet the demands. The Press had lengthy lists of "culprits" condemned to deportation and loss of all they had. The Powers, with victory in sight, were showing such an inconvenient and growing interest in the matter that on 15 March 1945 the freeing of prisoners and the cancellation of unsettled debts were decreed.

A strong current of opinion against dictatorial rule was gaining pace, as much in the political as in the social and religious fields. During May 1945 Ismet Inönü declared that it was time to return to normal ways, and very soon various parties were founded. In the field of religion new courses for *imām* and *khaṭīb* were established, Ankara got a Theological Faculty, elementary schools began special religious classes, and certain *turbas*, mausoleums, of special artistic or religious merit were opened again.

The 1950 elections cleared the way for the Democratic party, with Celal Bayar as president and Adnan Menderes as his prime minister. One new act of the government was once more to allow the recitation of the *adhān* in Arabic, repealing the law of 1933 which had forbidden it. The wish was to preserve the formula of a secular state, in the sense that religion should play no part in politics. Already several journals had begun to appear by 1947, and they played their part in starting the reaction of the following years which called for courses in Arabic for students of religion, the adjustment of civil law to popular feeling, and the return of the fez and the veil. Country people, out on the fringe of the law, went their wonted ways.

The diplomatic friendliness between Greece and Turkey clouded over on the Cyprus question. On 5 September a bomb went off close to the Turkish consulate in Salonica, causing material damage. Next day there were anti-Greek demonstrations in Constantinople, Izmir and Ankara. The Constantinople crowd destroyed churches and looted Greek premises while the police looked on.

To keep its hold on power the Democratic party had proceeded to govern less and less democratically, and in May 1960 the government collapsed before a military coup under General Cemal Gürsel.

During the Democratic party's management of affairs a marked return to Islamic practices became obvious. The study of Muslim religion became practically obligatory in primary and secondary schools, which grew in number parallel with the building of new mosques. According to the directorate of Religious Affairs, in the ten years from 1950, 5,000 mosques were built in Turkey, fifty of them in Ankara, as well as almost equally numerous schools. In the same period schools for *imām* and *khaṭīb* had grown from seven to nineteen, and in these the instruction had been sensibly modernized, so that ignorant *imāms* might be replaced by better educated ones. The secularizers resolutely opposed this, preferring an ignorant *imām* to one capable of exerting some intellectual influence over the people. They blamed the government for countenancing reaction, and the government knew it; but they could not afford to lose the popular vote, all in favour of religion. Atatürk had forced his views on the people. Now it was the turn of the people to bring force to bear on their governors.

THE ORTHODOX PATRIARCHATE OF CONSTANTINOPLE

The Ottoman conquest of Constantinople in 1453 at once placed its Orthodox Church on a new footing in relation to the civil power. On the one hand it entered a state of grievous servitude, on the other it acquired many privileges and considerable influence. In the eighteenth century the Phanar, that is the ecumenical Orthodox patriarch, so called from the name of his residence in Constantinople, had at his disposal all the important seats of Orthodoxy, excepting Russia alone.

The Greek rising in Morea in 1820 considerably diminished the influence of the Phanar in Constantinople. The news of the massacre of Muslims in Greece aroused deep feeling in the Ottoman capital, and since according to the rules governing the *millet* its leaders were held responsible for the acts of their followers, on Easter Day, 1821, the Greek Orthodox patriarch was hanged at the gate of the Phanar, along with some of his bishops, and his successor Eugenio II had to walk past the corpse on his way to be invested with the *berat* in the Seraglio. He died the following year and was succeeded by Anthemios III (1822–24) and Chrysanthos I (1824–26), both of whom were deposed by the Porte. His own followers got rid of Agathangelos I (1826–30), exasperated by his rapacity and greed. Constantios I (1830–4) was called from his chair in Sinai to govern the Phanar. As a good theologian, linguist and administrator he improved the financial situation, founded the commercial school of Halki and many primary schools. But his friendly relations with Russia aroused the suspicions of the Porte, and he had to return to Sinai and his studies.

Constantios II (1834–35) was forthwith dismissed for his immoral conduct. Quite otherwise was Gregory VI (1835–40), who proved to be energetic and prudent in his administration and reforms, and had the full support of the synod. In the Phanar he set up the church school which became the Theological School of Halki. He was firmly opposed to the missionary activities of the evangelical churches, and since the English ambassador had a preponderating influence with the Porte, the protestants succeeded in removing Gregory VI, alleging that he was opposed to the *khaṭṭ-i sherif* of Gülhane.

During the short reigns of the successors of Gregory VI the foundation in September 1842 of the Theological School of Halki by Germanus IV (1842–45) may be mentioned. The proclamation of the *khaṭṭ-i hümayun* in 1856 while Cyril VI was patriarch gave occasion for the orthodox Bulgarians to press their demands: for native prelates, the liturgical use of Slavonic, their own schools, and religious autonomy. In their own church of St Stephen in Galata, they did begin to use Slavonic, and, significantly, to omit the name of the ecumenical patriarch. The synod of the Phanar conceded nothing, and issued a sharply worded note in 1860 which made things worse. Russia intervened, and Joachim II (1860–64) offered the Bulgarians a sufficiently flexible programme, approved by the Porte. The Bulgarians would have none of it, for they aimed at becoming an independent *millet*, recognized by the Porte.

In March 1870 the grand vizier called the interested parties together and issued the imperial *ferman* establishing an independent Orthodox exarchate in Bulgaria. Despite Gregory VI's resolute opposition the riotous attitude of the Bulgarians gained the sultan's support. Gregory VI gave up office in June 1871. His place was taken by, in September, Anthemios VI, who also took energetic measures against the Bulgarian prelates. The Phanar called a general Orthodox council (somewhat misnamed, for only the Greek churches attended) which in September 1872 excommunicated the clergy and people of Bulgarian orthodoxy as schismatics. Athens was the only autocephalous church to approve the sentence, while the rest remained on friendly terms with the Bulgarian exarch.

Up to the middle of the nineteenth century the control of the Greek *millet* was almost entirely in the hands of the synod and the episcopate. Then the principles of the *tanẓimat* moved the lay members to demand a direct part in "national" affairs. Ignoring the opposition of the hierarchy to any reform, a decree of the Sultan (1858), forced acceptance of a regulation which came into force in 1862.

Joachim III (1878–84), by his disregard for the synod, won the sympathy of the lay members of the *majlis*. In his time the Serbian church, autonomous since 1832, became autocephalous in 1879, and so did the church of Bosnia–Herzegovina (in 1880). As well as being on bad terms with the Bulgarians, the Phanar had to face the demands of orthodox Rumanians for their rights. Although he had the backing of the Porte, Joachim III had to resign in 1884, accused of sacrificing the interests of his Church to the civil power. He retired to Mount Athos, planning to return with the help of his adherents. He had an implacable opponent in Germanus Kavokapoulos, metropolitan of Heraclea in 1884 and of Chalcedon in 1897, who had the backing of several prominent persons. Although the people tried to get Joachim back, Germanus managed to keep him at a distance until 1901.

Joachim IV (1884–86) made an attempt to improve relations between the Porte and the autocephalous churches, but his obvious cupidity brought about his retirement. Germanus managed to ensure the victory of his candidate Dionysios V (1887–89), who had Germanus as a close counsellor in his dealings with the Bulgarians, and with 'Abdülḥamid II.

When the sultan tried to cut out some old patriarchal privileges Germanus countermoved by closing all churches during the Easter celebrations. 'Abdülḥamid II feared popular uproar, and gave way. At the death of Dionysios V in 1891 Germanus was the obvious successor, but his recent opposition to the sultan's wishes stood in the way of his election. Yet his influence was still felt when Neofito VIII (1891–94) was elected. His tenure witnessed further friction with the Porte in the matter of schools and ecclesiastical immunity, for 'Abdülḥamid continued in his resolve to deprive the patriarchate of its privileges. Neofito VIII saw to the extension of the Theological School of Halki, and seemed to be seeking the support of an élite, and this Germanus did not agree with. In the end the patriarch got him removed, and to his cost, for Joachim III's allies took the opportunity to accuse him of feebleness in his dealings with the Bulgarians and the Porte, and he had to go. The influence of Germanus was still felt when Anthemios VII (1895–97) became patriarch. His resignation came when he surrendered the eparchy of Prizrend, a Serbian community, to the orthodox Serbs, in spite of a vigorous campaign against it in the Greek Press.

Once more Germanus successfully backed a candidate, Constantine V (1897–1901), but he ignored Germanus, and attempted to rule unswayed by sectional interests. In 1901 he introduced two of Joachim III's friends into the synod. These succeeded in getting a majority in the synod and tipped the balance in favour of the election of Joachim III (1901–12). He granted the church of Athens jurisdiction over the Greek Diaspora, Venice excepted, and would have liked to put an end to the Bulgarian schism.

The Young Turk revolution in 1908 stemmed from the disorders in Macedonia and from the dangers of serious consequences for Turkey if the Powers should intervene. With the revival of the constitution, the Committee of Union and Progress, *Ittiḥad ve-teraqqi jem'iyeti*, proclaimed universal equality and religious liberty. It was soon evident that this must be under Turkish hegemony. The Bulgarians seized the opportunity to occupy Thracian and Macedonian churches hitherto in Greek hands. They had Russian support, and the Turkish government ignored the protests of the Phanar and accepted the fact.

In 1912, with Joachim III dead and 'Abdülḥamid II dethroned, nothing stood in the way of the election of Germanus V (1912–18). He lost his majority in the synod in 1913. By the rules he should have resigned, but under lay pressure the synod waived the rules and the patriarch carried on until he was deposed at last in 1918, on the grounds of greed and collaboration with the Young Turks. The seat stood vacant for three years while Dorotheo, metropolitan of Bursa, acted as *topoteretes*. The regulations required the *topoteretes* to convene the electoral college within forty days, but the *megale idea* of a New Magna Graecia was in many minds, hoping for the end of Turkey and a great Hellenic renaissance. Dorotheo thought it better to wait.

The fall of Venizelos and the return of King Constantine in 1920 confronted the Greek Orthodox community of Constantinople with new problems. Meletios Metaxakis, primate of Athens and an ally of Venizelos, lost his seat and went to America, where he attempted to set up an autocephalous church. In Constantinople the Greeks were seriously divided, but mostly opting for Venizelos. While Allied troops occupied the city and Greek armies were pushing into Turkey, the synod came out in favour of the *megale idea*. When the *topoteretes* died in March 1921 his successor Nicholas of Cesarea decided to proceed at once with the election of a patriarch. Venizelos and his friends had a considerable hand in this, which gave the seat to Meletios IV Metaxakis in December of the same year. The Greek government had forbidden its prelates to take part in the election, the Turkish government had no desire to recognize a Greek occupant of the seat, and many churches regarded the election as null and void. Meletios arrived in triumph during February 1922, coming by way of London where he had declared his support for union with the Anglicans. He brought many plans for reform, among them the replacement of the synod by advisory councils of bishops, and the restraint of clerical finery. He preached a holy war against the Turks and called for aid to the campaigning Greek troops. The presence of Allied contingents restrained the exasperated Turks. The jurisdiction over the Greek Diaspora which Joachim III had made over to the Athenian church was once again assigned to the Phanar by Meletios. He created an exarchate in London, and made the synod recognize the validity of Anglican orders.

The rout of the Greeks in Asia Minor in September 1922 placed Meletios in a very critical position. Against this, now that King Constantine had abdicated, the movement in the Greek church against Meletios lost ground, and he was universally recognized as ecumenical patriarch. He continued his efforts on behalf of the fugitive Greeks, and summoned a Pan-Orthodox council, which was seriously disturbed by his opponents. He received rough handling on the stairs of the

Phanar, and only the intervention of a French patrol prevented his abduction. His position was becoming untenable. In July he recognized the autocephaly of Finland and Estonia and a month later retired to Mount Athos, leaving the synod to face the Turks.

With the signing of the Treaty of Lausanne on 23 July 1923 the ancient privileges of the *millets* disappeared, although the right of religious minorities to organize themselves in accordance with their own laws was conceded. Also an exchange of populations was envisaged which might solve the problem posed by the presence of an important minority within the State.

In September of the same year a *papaz*, an ordinary priest called Eftym, or Euthymios Karahisarlioğlu, "Baba Eftym", supported by Mustafa Kemal, proposed the foundation of a Turkish-Orthodox patriarchate as a countermove to the *megale idea*. On 2 October 1923 just as the last Allied troops were embarking to leave Constantinople, Baba Eftym broke into the Phanar, declared the seat vacant, expelled those prelates who held seats outside Turkey, and got himself nominated as delegate of the Phanar to the government of Ankara. When Meletios knew this he wanted the patriarchal seat transferred to Salonica, but as the Greek government was opposed to it he resigned in 1923.

The election of a new patriarch was permitted by the government on condition that it should devolve on a Turk. The manoeuvres of Baba Eftym and the intervention of the Turkish police led to more trouble. When Gregory VII won this election (6 December 1923), Baba Eftym invaded the Phanar to annul it, and had it removed by the Turkish police, on orders from Ankara. On his death-bed Gregory VII signed the document conferring autocephaly on the Polish Orthodox Church.

Meletios's old enemy Constantine VI was elected on 17 December 1923. Unfortunately he appeared in the exchange list of populations, and the Turkish police sent him off to Salonica. This aroused strong feelings, and protests were made to the United Nations and the Hague Tribunal, but Constantine VI had to resign after all. Basil III of Nicaea, enthroned 13 July 1925, had inclinations towards union with Rome, but his actions were limited, for the Turkish government allowed him no jurisdiction beyond Turkish frontiers, nor any relations with foreign powers. The Ankara government did everything possible to persuade the minorities to renounce those rights of self-government under their own laws which the Lausanne Treaty had authorized. On

27 November a meeting, said to represent the Turkish orthodox, declared willingness to give up such rights. The Phanar protested, but it was the Turks themselves who had inspired the decision.

After Basil III's death in September 1929 nothing impeded the succession of Photios II, who tried to raise the level of spiritual life in clergy and laity alike. But, as so often happens, this clashed with the apathy and even ill-will of those concerned. On the other hand the Turkish government made various excuses to meddle in church affairs, and vetoed preparations for the longed-for council. With the great political and social changes it was evident that old Ottoman regulations could no longer be applied, and in 1932 a commission was appointed to prepare for a new set of rules. Much as internal unity might be advisable in such troubled times, this never prevented quarrels between the prelates and between these and the patriarch.

When Basil III died Benjamin I (1936–46) took his place, and ruled for ten years in comparative calm. In 1937 Letonia became autocephalous. After the Second World War Russian pressure did much towards the election on 25 February 1946 of Maximos V; yet he refused the invitation of the patriarch in Moscow to attend a synod there in 1947. He fell out with other members of the synod and resigned in October 1948. Aimed at reducing Soviet influence, an agreement between Ankara and Athens, with support from the United States, paved the way for the election on 1 November 1948, of Athenagoras, head of the Orthodox Church in New York since 1930.

Outstanding among Athenagoras's activities were his efforts towards Christian reconciliation, within and without Orthodoxy. His visits to the patriarchs of Antioch, Jerusalem and Alexandria engaged general sympathy and helped to smooth out old differences. To him we owe the three Pan-Orthodox conferences which took place in Rhodes during 1961, 1963 and 1964, attended by representatives of all the Orthodox churches and by observers from other Christian bodies. Their principal conclusions were to affirm the unity and brotherhood of all Orthodox churches, to confirm the primacy of the Phanar, to express hope for eventual union with the Monophysites, to tighten relations with the Anglican and Episcopalian churches, and to initiate talks with Rome "hoping to become fellow-builders of universal unity". These trends were strengthened by the meetings in Jerusalem with Pope Paul IV during January 1964.

THE ORTHODOX PATRIARCHATE OF ALEXANDRIA

The Greek Orthodox patriarchate of Alexandria arose from the schism provoked in Egypt by the introduction of monophysite doctrines. Those who adopted these doctrines were called *copts* (Egyptians) and those faithful to the official religion had the name *melkites*. The bitter enmity between the two groups was long-lasting.

Early in the nineteenth century the Greek Orthodox patriarch was Theophilos II (1805–25). Following the Greek rising against the Ottomans in Morea he retired to Patmos, resisting Muḥammad ʿAlī's entreaties to return to his seat. The Porte stepped in and the Phanar had to decree his deposition and appointed his successor Hierotheos I (1825–45). In 1845 the community was composed of a patriarch, a bishop, some 50 clergy and about 1,750 members of the church. The Alexandrian flock nominated the archimandrite Hierotheos to succeed Hierotheos I, but the Phanar did not recognize his designation and appointed Artemios (1845–47). Muḥammad ʿAlī and the faithful protested against this intrusion by the Phanar. Artemios resigned, and finally the Phanar allowed that in future the election should take place in Egypt, and that, in the absence of a local synod, the representatives of the patriarchs of Constantinople, Antioch and Jerusalem should take part in the election. In this way the seat fell to Hierotheos II (1847–58) who worked hard to improve clerical education. The Phanar granted the community's demand for Callinicos of Salonica (1858–61) to succeed him.

The old enmity between Copts and Melkites had withered away, and relations were friendly enough to raise hopes of the union of the two communities. About this time the Russian archimandrite Porphyrios Uspenski made great efforts to this end. Callinicos, in Constantinople at the time, was inclined to give up his seat to the Coptic patriarch if he would accept the Orthodox feasts and canon law; but one of Uspenski's enemies, the Russian Orthodox bishop of Melitopolis and head of the Russian mission to Jerusalem, was so firmly opposed that Uspenski had to retire. Callinicos then resigned.

The split in the community occasioned a new appeal to the Phanar, which nominated Jacob, bishop of Cyzico (1861–65). When he died two bishops, 27 priests and some 17 laymen met in Cairo and ruled that the election of a patriarch should be the concern of clergy and people alone, free from outside interference, the synod to be the effective power. Thus, Nicanor of Thebes, who was in Moscow at the time, was elected. Righteous, but weak and incompetent, he soon displeased everybody. He put up some resistance, but was forced to accept a coadjutor who had the right of succession, with the approval of the synod, the government, the bishops and the majority of the church members. This coadjutor was the archimandrite Eugenio, appointed 19 June 1867. Nicanor withdrew to Alexandria, where he put himself under the protection of the French consul, gathered allies in the synod, denounced the intervention of the Phanar, excommunicated Eugenio and appointed Nilos as *topoteretes*. The Phanar retaliated by declaring Nicanor's synod illegal, upholding Eugenio and expelling Nilos. Nicanor gained the support of the patriarchs of Antioch and Jerusalem and the churches of Cyprus and Greece. While Eugenio was called away to Constantinople, Nicanor had his triumph in Cairo and Alexandria. Nilos received the episcopal *chirotonia* and Nicanor sent in his resignation on condition that Nilos should succeed him. The bishops agreed to this and sought confirmation by the Porte, but Gregory VI opposed this and intimated that Nilos—who after all was his subordinate—had better leave Egypt. Nilos refused as he reckoned on support of the patriarchs of Antioch and Jerusalem; but the Egyptian community was hostile, prevented him from presiding at the funeral of Nicanor, and asked the Phanar for another patriarch.

Nilos had to give way, and the ex-patriarch Sofronio III was elected as Sofronio IV of Alexandria (1870–99). The community prospered under his reign, but could not reach agreement with the government over a patriarchal electoral code.

Photios came next. Since 1880 he had opposed Russian plans for the Holy Places, and Russia had resisted his candidature for the patriarchate of Jerusalem, which fell to Nicodemos. Photios refused to recognize him, and spent seven years of exile in Sinai. He returned to Jerusalem in 1891, and to get rid of him Russia supported his accession to the patriarchate of Alexandria (1900–25). He showed considerable enterprise and persuaded many benefactors not only to supply the needs of the church but also to ensure the advancement of the numerous Greek community. In 1908 he set up the patriarchal press in Alexandria and founded two periodicals: *Pantainos* and *Ekklesiastikos Pharos*.

The Orthodox community, numbering but a few thousand members at the beginning of the century, had grown by now as the result of two waves of immigration, attracted by the atmosphere of order and prosperity which Egypt enjoyed. Some were Arabic speakers, mainly from Syria. Estimated at 35,000, they nearly all became naturalized Egyptians. Others were Greeks from the mainland. There were perhaps 100,000 in number, and they mostly preserved the Greek nationality. Their affairs came under the jurisdiction of the Greek consulate. As might be expected, misunderstanding and friction arose between different nationalities living in juxtaposition and speaking diverse tongues.

This introduced difficulties in the election of a patriarch. The Arabic-speaking Syrians wanted to participate, the Egyptian government claimed the prerogatives hitherto exercised by the Porte, the Greek consul wanted the seat for the Greeks and, behind the scenes, the English government showed some interest. The Arabic speakers were annoyed that no Arab appeared in the preliminary lists, while the Egyptian government favoured the idea of a national patriarch. Lengthy negotiations took place between synod, government and consul before Meletios Metaxakis took his seat on 21 May 1926.

To accept office Meletios had to become an Egyptian subject. The Arabic speakers, trusting to his promise of benevolence to both sides, did not oppose. He authorized the use of Arabic in their liturgy, and promised, among other things, the establishment of a school for clergy in which Arabic and Greek would be on equal terms.

To satisfy the Arabs the synod agreed that at least there should be an Arab metropolitan and nominated Nicolas ʿAbdallāh to the diocese of Axum. Meletios attended the Lambeth conference in 1930, and on his return announced that he would not in future confer the *chirotonia* upon Anglican clergy who went over to the Orthodox faith. After six years of preparation the statutes of the synod were settled in 1931, and the hierarchy put in order. The Greek inhabitants showed disgust when Meletios named the Syrian Nicolas ʿAbdallāh as his *epitropos* in Cairo, more so at his proposal in 1932 that establishments founded for the common good should pass to the patriarchate, and even more when it became known that the regulations for the election of a patriarch excluded laymen from participation. The Greeks put up a vigorous resistance, and when Meletios died on 28 August 1935, nothing had been settled.

Meletios had submitted two sets of statutes to the government. The Arabs wanted one, the Greeks the other. The Greeks, greater in number, were divided among themselves, and the government was inclined to favour the Arabs. The lay folk wanted Nicolas Evanghelidis of Hermopolis, the synod was for Christophoros of Leontopolis. The former won the election of Nicolas Evanghelidis (1936–39).

The Anglo-Egyptian Treaty of 1936 acknowledged the full sovereignty of the Egyptian kingdom, and this encouraged the Arabs to press their demands, to the dismay of the Greeks who feared the loss of advantages conferred by the agreements in force.

The appointment of Nicolas Evanghelidis's successor was without incident. Starting with good intentions the new patriarch Christophoros was soon at loggerheads with the synod to such a degree that for some years both sides had to call repeatedly on the civil authorities to settle their disputes. The patriarch maintained that the synod was a purely consultative body, while the synod insisted that its authority was superior to that of the patriarch.

Another source of trouble was that when Christophoros began his reign the majority of his flock were still Greek nationals, organized in communities responsible to the Greek government, which left out not only the Arabs but also those Greeks who had taken Egyptian nationality. Previously the lay leaders of the Greek colony had been very liberal towards the patriarchate, subsidizing churches, hospitals and schools out of their own pockets. Now they came out in opposition to the patriarch, and with the encouragement of the synod and the Greek government they withheld the customary contributions, to the extent that the patriarch had to bring them before the State tribunals. Preoccupied as he was with such matters, under the regime of 'Abd al-Nāṣir he faced growing demands by the Orthodox Arabs, who wanted further liturgical use of Arabic, participation in the mixed council, *al-majlis al-millī*, power to nominate bishops, and a share in the patriarchal election similar to that enjoyed by the Greek laymen.

In the early years of his administration Christophoros adopted a wary attitude to Russian Orthodox approaches, and took no part in the celebrations of the quincentenary of Russian Orthodox autocephaly, but in the summer of 1945 he did accept an invitation of the patriarch Alexis to visit Moscow, whence he returned with the promise of an annual contribution, payable at the Soviet embassy in Cairo. When illness forced him to give up in March 1956, the synod was able to have its own way again for a few months. In 1958 he was back in Moscow for the celebration of the fortieth anniversary of the restoration of its patriarchal seat.

Perhaps it was due to these travels that a change could be observed in the attitude of the Greek government, which now showed a disposition to assist the reconstruction of the patriarchate and advised the Greek communities in Egypt to settle their differences with the patriarch. There followed a reconciliation between patriarch and synod, whereby trials before State courts were given up and six vacant seats were filled.

The much-desired calm did not come. The laws of the Egyptian government on the *tamṣīr*, Egyptization, sowed panic among the Greek population and the non-naturalized Arabs. Now began a steady flow of families leaving the country to seek in Greece and other countries a sense of security lacking in Egypt.

In 1961 the now aged Christophoros withdrew to Kephesia, in the neighbourhood of Athens, still maintaining his hold in the patriarchate through delegates he had chosen without consulting the synod. A Greek journalist, C. N. Drosos, after a visit to the Orthodox patriarchates, described in *Ethnos* (July 1962) the sad condition of that of Alexandria, with its clergy recruited from the throw-outs of other professions. There was no theological school, nor any sign of one in the future. The few who might benefit would be well advised to seek instruction elsewhere. The 150,000 Greeks who had made up 80 per cent of Meletios's flock were reduced to 80,000 in 1953, and 40,000 by 1962. Religious indifference was widespread, and the young ceased to attend church. Christophoros stayed away in Kephisia, bitterly reproached by his prelates for his absence.

In 1964 Bishop Nicolas of Axum begged Christophoros in writing to retire for the good of the Orthodox community. In January 1966 *Pantainos*, the official organ of the patriarchate, congratulated the patriarch, still away in Kephisia, on his 91st birthday.

THE ORTHODOX PATRIARCHATE OF ANTIOCH

The privilege of civil jurisdiction over the entire Orthodox population of the Ottoman empire which belonged to the patriarch of Constantinople by virtue of his spiritual and temporal lordship of the *millet* of *Rum* enabled the Phanar to extend its authority over the historical patriarchates, particularly that of Antioch, the nearest. Up to the eighteenth century nearly all the Antioch patriarchs had been Syrians, but ever since 1724 the Phanar had been specifying Greeks for the seat of Antioch. Their main business was to counteract the efforts of the Latin missionaries, Franciscans, Carmelites, Capuchins and Jesuits, who from the seventeenth century had been encouraging Syrian Orthodox moves towards union with Rome.

Thus it is not strange that the patriarch Seraphim (1813–23) took upon himself the persecution of native Catholics, thereby incurring huge debts which had to be shouldered by his successor Metodio of Angora (1823–50), all the while carrying on his campaign against Latin missionary endeavour, and that of evangelicals who were finding their way into the region.

Hierotheo, *hagiotaphita*, i.e. a member of the Brotherhood of the Holy Sepulchre in Jerusalem, was the choice of the Phanar as patriarch. He had spent thirteen years in Russia collecting alms to wipe out the debt under which the Brotherhood was burdened. Not all the receipts had reached the coffers of the Brotherhood, and when he died in March 1885 he left the church chest empty, his own belongings to relations and friends, a seat without seminary and precious few schools, and a clergy and laity in a sad moral and material state.

The Arabs naturally wanted prelates of their own race and language, but had no means of obtaining this end, for they were at the mercy of the Phanar and could place no reliance on the Porte, fearful of Russian influence. So they accepted Gerasimo Propapas, hagiotaphita, during June 1885. He had once aspired to the patriarchate of Jerusalem, but a colleague Nicodemos won it, and proposed him for the seat of Antioch to get him out of the way.

Once in office Gerasimo adopted the same tactics as used by his hagiotaphite rivals in getting rid of him, describing Nicodemos to the Porte as a friend of Russia. He worked hard to eject him, and in March 1891 achieved his aim and occupied the seat of Jerusalem. He took with him all he could lay hands on, leaving behind recollections of avarice and misgovernment, and the hagiotaphita Spyridon to succeed him, to the disgust of the Arabs. Nevertheless Spyridon, by becoming the instrument of Russian influence, caused the Arabs to find themselves in a better position, with detriment to the Greeks.

From the mid-nineteenth century Russia had started a mission in Jerusalem, partly to deliver its numerous pilgrims from the extortions of the Greek clergy, but also as a base for its political plans. The imperial Russian Orthodox Society of Palestine was founded in 1882 with the task of countering Greek predominance by drawing attention to the ruthless exploitation of pilgrims by the Greeks and setting up schools and religious institutions in Palestine and Syria.

When Spyridon took over the seat of Antioch he found an empty treasury and no means of satisfying the demands of his people, who could see how other confessions were adding to the number of schools, churches and hospitals, and wanted the same for themselves. He accepted therefore aid from the Russian Society, which was willing to meet these demands on condition that it should retain control of those foundations. Nevertheless Spyridon was viewed with disfavour by the Syrians for being a Greek, and by the Greeks for lending himself to Russian penetration, and his foes accused him before the Porte. Spyridon retired to the monastery of Balamand where he summoned a synod, but of the fourteen prelates invited seven met in Damascus, where in accord with the *wālī* and the support of the Russian Society they deposed Spyridon in 1898 and elected a *topoteretes*, the Greek Germanus of Tarsus and Adana who was favourably known in Russia. The Phanar protested in vain, and followed this by adopting Germanus as their own candidate; but eight bishops of the Antioch patriarchate stuck to their rights to hold an election without the Phanar's interference. The thirteen prelates, gathered in the synod, were faced with the question of whether candidates outside the patriarchal jurisdiction could appear on the list, and eight bishops (some bribed with Russian gold) gave a negative answer.

With the seat still vacant, the *topoteretes* began the celebration of the offices of Holy Thursday in Greek, and was rudely interrupted by the metropolitan of Homs, demanding the use of Arabic. The Turkish police had to deal with the resulting affray. The eight bishops relieved Germanus of his office of *topoteretes* and appointed Meletios Dumani of Laodicea, finally making him patriarch in April 1899. The Greek churches refused to recognize one they regarded as a schismatic, but the Slav churches did. The Greek bishops under his control had withdrawn to Constantinople, so Meletios Dumani put Arab prelates in their place. Photios, the Alexandrian patriarch, gave the Greek bishops a hearty welcome, for he wanted them to make his synod up to strength, in furtherance of his plans for independence of the Phanar.

Meletios died in February 1906, to be followed in June by Gregory II (some lists make him Gregory IV), Ḥaddād of Homs (Ḥimṣ) (1908–28), without interference from the Phanar. Only the Slav churches looked with favour on his credentials, but during November 1908 Antioch and the Phanar were reconciled, and by the summer of 1909 the full independence of the Antioch patriarchate was recognized by the Greek churches. In 1913 the synod and the patriarch decided that all convents should come under the authority of the patriarchate and that their revenues should go to maintain the schools of the eparchies. This led to more trouble with the laity. The close of the First World War saw the end of the Russian institutions in Palestine and Syria, whose pupils had grown to 10,000 in number.

To decide who should succeed Gregory II (IV) on his death in 1928 was not easy. Antagonism between members of the synod, added to the demands of the laity, made agreement impossible. Some insisted on the *topoteretes* Arsenio Ḥaddād of Laodicea; others preferred Alexandros Ṭaḥḥān of Tripoli. For two years the wrangling went on over an empty seat. On 7 February 1931 the seven senior metropolitans elected Arsenio Ḥaddād, and next day the remaining metropolitans and the laity proclaimed Alexandros Ṭaḥḥān. The ecumenical patriarch sent an envoy to patch things up, with no success. The patriarchs of Alexandria and Jerusalem sent Alexandros a testimonial confirming the validity of his election. The death of Arsenio Ḥaddād in January 1933 put an end to the conflict. Divided they might be, but this serious crisis gave the laity a victory that was legitimized by other churches.

In March 1942 a law student, Georges Khodr (Khiḍr), with some of his friends, started the Movement of Orthodox Youth. The crisis in Orthodoxy, they said, had left them pained and confused. They called for a cultural, moral and social revival, a return to the practice of religion, a widening of educational opportunity, and the solution of social problems in a Christian spirit. They deplored communal rivalry, and sought fraternal relations with the Christian churches. The movement made headway, and in August 1945 the synod gave it its blessing as an official vehicle of Orthodox action in the patriarchate. Alexandros died in June 1958 on his way back from Moscow after attending the celebration of the fortieth anniversary of the restoration of the Muscovite seat. During his long reign Arabism was firmly established, many good works were undertaken, and relations between the Orthodox churches became more cordial.

The succession set a difficult task, for the internal dissentions of 1928–31 were not yet ironed out. Indeed, an Orthodox group in the Lebanon had petitioned the mandatory government to secure the independence of the Orthodox Church within the confines of the

Lebanese Republic, and this idea was still prevalent after Syria and the Lebanon had each reached independence. To add to the difficulties existing between these two states, civil war broke out in the Lebanon which made it impossible for Lebanese prelates to cross to Damascus. There was no way of appointing a *topoteretes* in the regular manner, so a committee of four was elected by the council of the community. Personal interests and ambitions, political and social hostility, differences between the Lebanon and Syria, the intrigues of Russian agents —all these were significant of a divided community.

At last, on 14 November 1958, the choice fell on Theodosios Aburgeli. On this occasion Pitirim, metropolitan of Minsk, gave a banquet in the name of Patriarch Alexis attended by the diplomatic representatives of the Soviet Union and the satellite countries. A Russian archimandrite was appointed to represent Alexis in Damascus and a Russian church with liturgy in Arabic was opened.

In February 1960 a full meeting of the mixed council attempted a revision of the statutes of the patriarchate. The prelates were bent on excluding the laity from activities they regarded as proper to the hierarchy, certainly that of choosing a patriarch, but seeing the firm resistance of the laity the patriarch cut the proceedings short, with a promise of a new scheme to be submitted for general consideration. It was estimated that in 1962 the patriarchate had 285,000 church members.

THE ORTHODOX PATRIARCHATE OF JERUSALEM

From ancient times the Orthodox patriarchate of Jerusalem had been a fief of the Greek Church which governed it through the Brotherhood of the Holy Sepulchre, until the nineteenth century when Russian infiltration began and the Orthodox Arabs were clamouring for their own prelates in a community whose only Greeks were those of the Brotherhood.

During the rule of Athanasius V (1927–44), evangelical missionary activity in Palestine began. In 1841 the patriarch refused to give way to a Russian request to acquire the Convent of the Holy Cross and two others as residences for the archimandrite and his clergy for the entertainment of the growing number of Russian pilgrims. The archimandrite Porphyrios Uspenski arrived in 1842 to "defend the Greek Church against Western propaganda". He was to represent himself as a pilgrim, win over the native clergy, demonstrate how the Greeks were enslaving them, and to inquire after the destination of the flow of alms pouring in from Russia. In 1844 Uspenski made a report in which the Greek clergy made a very poor showing, and advised that an educated bishop and clergy be sent, for only Russia could save the Church of Jerusalem.

On the death of Athanasius V, the Russian embassy made certain of the election of a new patriarch in Jerusalem—Cyril II (1845–72). Porphyrios Uspenski had been given the task of implementing the reforms proposed in his report, but the serious outcome of a trivial incident put an end to this. In 1847 a metallic star was missing from the altar of the Holy Nativity in Bethlehem. By 1852 the Porte had to step in to stop the disputes that for this reason arose between Latins and Greeks, with a *ferman* of 1852, saying that the Armenian, Greek and Latin communities should have the care of the Holy Places in perpetuity, either in common, or in an exclusive way—an order later confirmed by the Treaty of Paris, 1856, and of Berlin, 1878. This was the occasion for rival nations to become involved. The Porte, sensible of French and English backing, refused point-blank the Russian claim to protect, not only its own Orthodox pilgrims to the Holy Land, but all the Orthodox living in the Ottoman Empire. The Crimean War followed.

In 1878 Russia sent Bishop Cyril Naumov to lead the mission in Jerusalem and the first stone of the Muscovite church was laid in the following year. Cyril II governed with zeal and sought to improve the education of his people, but fell out with the hagiotaphites over the Bulgarian question. Whilst the synod was meeting to condemn the phyletists of the Bulgarian church he was in Constantinople, but at a hint from the Russians he did not take part in it himself. After his return to Jerusalem, the synod tried repeatedly to get him to join in the condemnation of the Bulgarians, but as he would not agree, the synod deposed him. Russia's reaction was to requisition the property held by the hagiotaphite Brotherhood in that country. The people as well were against the synod, but Cyril II was ordered to Constantinople.

Before they would appoint Procopios (1873–75), the synod made him swear to accept statutes which would deprive him of all authority. Russia refused recognition and incited the Arabs against the hagiotaphites. The people and minor clergy, emboldened by Russian promises, broke relations with the Brotherhood and left the churches deserted. Procopios appealed to the Porte, but the Sultan had no wish to approve a rule which went against the powers bestowed by the *berat*. At last, after negotiations which suffered many interruptions, the Porte gave heed to the contending parties, and in 1875 framed a constitution of 17 Articles. Procopios himself had previously resigned in February of the same year.

Hierotheo (1875–82) tried to conciliate the Arabs, and as the poor state of the finances told against the charitable institutions of the patriarchate he appealed to the Tsar to cancel the sequestration of the hagiotaphite Brotherhood's belongings in Russia, and this was done in 1881. In 1882 the Imperial Russian Society of Palestine was founded. It operated under the cover of charity and culture, but with such a marked anti-Greek bias that the patriarchate in 1895 sent an official protest to Russia.

Hierotheo died in 1882. The synod appointed a known enemy of Russian influence, Photios, but the Porte refused him, and the seat fell to Nicodemos (1883–90), who was in Russia representing the hagiotaphite Brotherhood. He made a wise choice of associates, and built the sanctuaries of the Ascension and the Assumption. He resisted all missionary efforts, Catholic and Protestant alike, but remained on good terms with the Armenians and Franciscans. He transferred the manuscripts from the convents of St Sabas and the Holy Cross to the library of the Holy Sepulchre and catalogued them. The autocratic Nicodemos antagonized the hagiotaphites; an attempted assassination by a monk left him wounded, and he relinquished his seat soon after.

Gerasimos (1891–97) had achieved his aim at last, and had to resort to Russia and Greece for funds to carry on. Damianos Kassiotis (1897–1931) found a large patriarchate upset by the political situation, strife between the Arab laity and Greek monks, and shortage of money. With the Turkish revolution of 1908 came new demands by the Arabs. The patriarch should no longer be a Greek and the mixed council must have a lay majority. To Damianos's vague promises the Arabs, egged on by Russia, replied with a campaign which went so far as the occupation of churches and street brawls. Damianos did grant them the administration of the patriarchal possessions under a council of six monks and six laymen, but of course the hagiotaphites protested, and the synod deposed Damianos. But he had the people behind him, and did not budge despite the efforts of Joachim III of Constantinople, Photios of Alexandria and Spyridon of Antioch who got from the Turks an expulsion order, for the Russian consul and the people backed him up and the government suspended the order. A commission was nominated and reached a settlement between the patriarch and the Greek party.

It has been said that had it not been for the war in 1914 Russia would have eliminated Hellenism in the Eastern patriarchates. In 1918 the Imperial Russian Society had 100 schools in Syria and Palestine with 12,000 pupils, besides other institutions.

In 1917, while the war was on, and Allenby's troops were closing in on Jerusalem, the Turks interned Damianos and the synod in Damascus. Once the war was over the synod tried again to depose Damianos, and the New British authority set up the Bertram Luke Commission to iron out the difficulties between Damianos and the synod.

At the end of 1921 the British High Commission pressed Damianos to restore the mixed council. He said he would do so when his debts were settled, to do which liquidators had been appointed. The Arabs were not appeased. Meeting in Haifa they propounded a memorandum demanding a mixed council with two thirds laymen, Arabic-based seminaries, ordination solely of Arabs, and Arab prelates. Some of these demands were set too high, and a group broke away to draw up more moderate proposals.

For his part, Damianos, in a memorandum of October 1923, pointed out to the authorities that the monastic character of the patriarchate precluded the laity from sharing the prerogatives enjoyed by other churches. The High Commissioner then set up the Bertram Young Commission. Damianos manifested his surprise that the High Commissioner should take any hand in the business and made it clear that he was not disposed to co-operate, because the *Rum millet* was the real owner, without whose consent nothing could be done, and by their conduct the Arabs had placed themselves outside the *millet*.

The Bertram Young Commission made a thorough examination of the case and showed that it was one episode in a vast movement which for generations had led the peoples of the Orthodox Church to assert their national and racial position; that it was not possible to separate the hagiotaphite Brotherhood from the local church; that the Holy Places were the heritage of the local church; and that the Brotherhood must no longer remain as a mere monastery separate from the rest of the church people. It suggested the prompt reopening of the Holy Cross seminary. It admitted the legitimacy of Arab demands and advised their immediate satisfaction. All this the patriarchate ignored.

A long crisis followed Damianos's death on 14 August 1931. During September 1931 the executive Arab committee met in Jerusalem to put before the High Commission a memorandum asking that the Bertram Young recommendations be put into operation before the election. The synod sat in December without the Arab members and elected a *topoteretes*, Keladion of Tolemaida, and prepared a list of twelve candidates. The High Commission gave assent on 6 January, and ordered the election to be held. But the Arabs appealed to the Supreme Tribunal against the legality of the proceedings. The Tribunal ruled against the synod, because the approval of the British Colonial Secretary was lacking (25 January).

The synod tried in vain to evade the ruling and in revenge closed the patriarchal schools in Palestine and Jordan. The Arab laity held a second congress in Jaffa during November 1932 to press for proportional representation; as things were they commanded only twelve votes to the Greeks' forty. To this the synod countered that nothing could be done while the seat was vacant. The civil authorities set up a mixed commission in June 1933, consisting of four hagiotaphites and four from the Arab committee but there was no agreement. In April 1934 each party received a sealed packet with the law governing the election and which was made public on 19 April. This transferred the prerogatives of the sultan to the sovereign, and those of the former grand vizier to the colonial secretary.

In July 1935 Timothy I Themelis became patriarch. The government deferred his recognition hoping for a settlement that the tense political situation in Palestine rendered more and more doubtful. When the government threatened that no settlement meant no *exequatur* the synod showed signs of yielding. On 21 July 1938 the government issued a plan for the organization of the Orthodox patriarchate of Jerusalem, and in the next year Timothy I Themelis was acknowledged patriarch.

After the gap caused by the Second World War the Arabs held their third congress in 1944.

Timothy I died on 31 December 1955. Once again the problems of a vacant seat and another election were complicated, this time by there being two civil jurisdictions, Israeli and Jordanian—for each contained part of the patriarchal territory. The synod made Athenagoras *topoteretes*. Before the election the Jordanian government had to signify its *placet* to the roll of candidates, knowing that many of the Orthodox were living in Israel. There were some less extremist groups, both

Greek and Arab. The fourth congress of the Orthodox Arab community took place in Jerusalem on 24 March 1956, the first to be held under an Arab sovereign. Nine from Palestine and nine from Jordan formed a committee. The synod, counting on Greek government support, replied to the reformist proposals that no decision could be made without a patriarch, and that an election under the 1875 rules must come first, and then they could give satisfaction to the Arabs. But the Arabs knew from past experience that they must insist on the new regulations, so both sides appealed to the Jordanian government for permits which when granted were rendered ineffectual by warring interests.

The Jordanian government had treated the Christians benevolently in many ways. In 1956 they made the Nativity an official feast in Jordan. On 23 December they assumed the sole right of confirming the election of a *topoteretes* and of authorizing the appointment of a patriarch; they recognized Athenagoras as *topoteretes*, and approved new patriarchal regulations, which satisfied most of the Arab demands. The election was held on 21 January 1957. Benediktos took the seat, and the very same day denounced the new regulations and proposed another set. The Jordanian government remained silent for a year and then devised yet another statute to replace that of 1875, and this was passed by the Chamber. Under its terms the Arabs would be able to see that the resources of the patriarchate were justly apportioned. In return, the patriarch and synod had the right to approve the estimates.

According to a Greek journalist, the reign of Ḥusayn of Jordan has been a blessing for the Orthodox Church of Jerusalem. Moscow was restrained from interference with White Russian monasteries. Officially dependent on the Russian Church of New York, in practice they come under Benediktos. He regards Latins and Lutherans as dangerous, by reason of the proselytizing activities of their agents, much superior in culture to his own Orthodox clergy.

Early in 1964 Pope Paul VI made his historic pilgrimage to the Holy Land, welcomed in Amman by King Ḥusayn. Religious communities of all denominations showed sympathy and enthusiasm, and in Jerusalem he engaged in cordial exchanges with the Ecumenical patriarch Athenagoras and other church leaders. Joint communiqués expressed a desire for closer co-operation and eventual unity.

In 1962 there were some 47,000 Orthodox Christians in Jordan, and 13,000 in Israel.

THE RUSSIAN ORTHODOX CHURCH

The Russian Orthodox Church is not reckoned among the Orthodox Churches of the Near East, but its influence there has been such that a rapid sketch of the vicissitudes of the "Third Rome" will help to a better understanding of Russian Church politics in the Near East.

The interest taken in the Orthodox Church of the Near East is attested by the institutions connected with the Imperial Society of the Russian Church in Palestine with its numerous and flourishing works of culture and charity. The Crimean War indeed owed its outbreak to the Russian resolve to extend its sway over all the Orthodox Christians of the Turkish empire.

The liberality of the Russians to the Orthodox hierarchy ensured their subservience. Everything witnessed to the power, piety and vitality of the Russian Church. Everything tended to represent Russia as the leader of Orthodoxy in the Near East, and Russia profited by all this in her plans for hegemony.

The independent patriarchate of Moscow had been established in 1589 by the ecumenical patriarch, Jeremy II, with the style of "Moscow and All Russia". In 1700 Peter the Great suppressed the patriarchate, replacing it by the Holy Synod, which remained under the emperor's thumb. The Church was at the disposal of the Tsars, and the Russians regarded themselves as heirs of a bygone Byzantium which it was their duty to reconquer. Byzantium was the goal of Russian politics, materially and spiritually. Moscow was the "Third Rome" destined to save Orthodoxy.

The Russian Revolution of 1917 made an end of the imperial government and gave the Orthodox Church an opportunity—immediately grasped—to reinstate the patriarchate. A pan-Russian synod met in August to elect the anti-communist Tychon Belavin as the first patriarch. But the October Revolution let loose a wave of atheistical persecution in which, not counting those imprisoned or exiled, some 120 bishops and 25,000 clergy perished and all church property was confiscated. Patriarch Tychon denounced these excesses and was imprisoned in May 1922. Set free a year later, perhaps "brain-washed", he shocked the faithful by forbidding any opposition to the government, which he now looked on as legitimate.

Tychon died in semi-captivity in April 1925 and a new patriarch could not be elected. A patriarchal vicar was appointed but he was soon arrested for "anti-revolutionary plotting" and his place was filled by a vice-vicar, Archbishop Sergius Starogrodskij. Both had sworn loyalty to the Soviet government, but this was no obstacle to religious persecution which was particularly severe in the periods 1927–32 and 1937–39. Many of the Orthodox got out of the country and formed the church of the Diaspora. In 1936 Article 124 of the new Russian Constitution made religious liberty a private and individual matter, and forbade any religious teaching to those under 18 years of age.

The Second World War made it imperative to enlist all the effective forces of Russia. In 1943 Stalin permitted the restoration of the patriarchate, the opening of some seminaries and monasteries and the issue of a bulletin by the patriarchate. A synod of seventeen bishops met in Moscow in September 1943 to elect a patriarchal vicar, Sergius, whose death occurred in February 1945. A council attended by representatives of other churches chose Alexis, metropolitan of Leningrad, to succeed him.

The changed attitude of the Soviet regime restored the liberty of the Church, so long as it upheld the State. Now the Soviet government were treading the old path of Imperial politics in their efforts to recover their lost influence over the Eastern Christian world. The Antioch patriarchate, an old sphere of influence, would make a good bridgehead, for it had its own church, and resources in Moscow, and the two churches had remained on good terms. Alexandros III Ṭaḥḥān and other prelates from Antioch took part in the synodal meeting which elected Patriarch Alexis. In return he paid visits to the Eastern churches, although he avoided Constantinople. One of his objectives was to regain control over the Russian Orthodox community of Jerusalem, but here he had no success.

For the Autumn of 1946 he had invited the churches to a pan-Orthodox congress in Moscow. The Phanar objected that such a project was a matter for the ecumenical patriarch to decide, so Alexis gave up the idea "for lack of time". The invitation was renewed next year in 1948 on the occasion of the quincentenary of the City of Moscow. Antioch sent delegates, who represented Alexandria as well. The rest of the Greek churches abstained.

In September 1952 Alexis asked Timothy of Jerusalem to cut off relations with the "dissenting" members of the Russian Church, especially those in Jordan who accepted the jurisdiction of the metropolitan Anastasius in America. This occasioned attacks in the Greek Press, accusing Moscow of trying to displace the Greeks there. Moscow replied that it was merely proferring brotherly aid. Under these circumstances the conduct of Christophoros of Alexandria caused some surprise. His difficult economic situation had led him to get in touch with the Russian ambassador in Cairo endeavouring to get back a *metochion* which belonged to the patriarchate in the old Russian empire, and had been confiscated. Alexis invited him to Russia, and there he went, in spite of his synod, and returned with what he went for.

In contrast with Jordan, the Russian Orthodox clergy in Israel came under Moscow. In 1960 predictably lengthy and difficult negotiations began with Israel over several properties which Russian societies had been acquiring since the mid-nineteenth century, above all in the quarter of Jerusalem round about the Muscovite Church, to which the Russian government laid claim. Under the British Mandate these had been rebutted and a manager placed in charge of them. Israel has now recognized the rights of the Russian government in principle.

THE ARMENIAN ORTHODOX (OR GREGORIAN) CHURCH

From ancient times the Orthodox Armenian Church has been linked with a people with an extremely chequered history, assailed at all times and from all points of the compass by powerful neighbours.

It was in one of these contests when the Seljuk Turks won the battle of Malazgirt (Manzikert) in 1071 that the Byzantines ceased to dominate Armenia. Most of the population remained behind under their new lords, although many Armenians took themselves to the part of Cilicia called New Armenia, in the lands between the Taurus mountains and the Levantine coast. The Armenian catholicos followed and established his seat in Sīs, an inland town north of the Gulf of Alexandretta. The kingdom of New Armenia, founded towards the end of the eleventh century, lasted until it was overthrown by the Mamlūks who seized Sīs in 1375.

In Sīs, Krikor IX Mussabeghian was elected catholicos in 1440. Four bishops from the north of Armenia who had taken no part in the election desired him to remove the seat to Echmiadzin. As Krikor would not hear of this they nominated another Catholicos in 1441, who in time came to be looked on as the supreme head of the Armenian Orthodox, in spite of his illegal election.

Before this there had been two secessions of less importance. In 1113

David, metropolitan of Aghtamar, an island in Lake Van, refused to accept the election of a catholicos, and proclaimed himself catholicos of Aghtamar and the surrounding district. This relatively unimportant seat suffered by the creation of the Armenian patriarchate of Constantinople in 1461. Aghtamar kept its titularies until 1895 when it came to be administered by a prelate. During the war of 1914–18 its 95,000 members perished or were scattered under Turkish persecution. In 1307 a council in Sīs had taken decisions that Armenian monks in Jerusalem refused to accept; and in 1311 they announced their independence of Sīs and formed the Armenian patriarchate of Jerusalem.

THE ARMENIAN ORTHODOX PATRIARCHATE OF CONSTANTINOPLE

The patriarchate of Constantinople dates from 1461 when Meḥmed II the Conqueror conquered the city and instituted the Armenian *millet* under its first patriarch, Joachim, bishop of Bursa.

Many Armenians took the opportunity of settling in the Ottoman capital, where their diligence and economies brought them to prosperity, power and influence. Its rulers, the *umarā'*, behaved generously towards the people, building churches and endowing schools; but some with ambitious designs, tried to impose on the patriarchate, and provoked the reaction of the *aṣnāf*, workmen and craftsmen. The patriarchate represented his "nation" throughout the empire, with a civil power added to his ecclesiastical authority. His civil authority extended over the whole Ottoman empire including Armenian catholics as well, who had a bishop in Constantinople since 1758. Relations between these and Kum Kapu (the name of the patriarch's residence in Constantinople) were uneasy, for Kum Kapu viewed with displeasure the sight of influential families crossing over to the Catholic community.

Under Patriarch Paul Gregorian (1815–23), hatred of deserters to Catholicism increased. Alleging the Catholics to be traitors in the service of foreign powers, the disorganization of their community was attempted by exiling the principal clergy and laity, under such conditions that many of them perished.

Nevertheless the demands of foreign policy obliged the Sultan to look to Austria and France for help against a victorious Russia; so under the Treaty of Edirne (1829), he had to grant the civil emancipation of the Armenian Catholics, on 3 January 1831. The head of the new Armenian-Catholic *millet* was given jurisdiction over the Catholics within the empire of all observances, save the Latins. This was the occasion for the institution of an Armenian-Catholic archbishopric of Constantinople. He had authority in spiritual matters only, temporal affairs being dealt with by an ecclesiastic called *patrik*, the only civil head recognized by the Ottomans.

The Protestants reached Constantinople in 1831, and at first were well received. Goodell worked with the Armenians and others with the Jews. The idea of converting Muslims was abandoned. In 1834 they opened a secondary school in Pera and had to close it in 1837 after fierce opposition from the Armenian Orthodox clergy. Patriarch Stephen proved too easy-going with the Protestants, and had to go. Under the new patriarch, Seropian, the Protestant parsons were locked in the patriarchal prisons. Sentence of excommunication was pronounced against their abettors, the Greek Orthodox patriarch joined in the anathema, and the sultan closed the affair with an expulsion order.

New political complications cropped up again. The Sultan Maḥmud II died on 1 July 1839, the Powers had checked Muḥammad 'Alī's victorious advance in Anatolia; British influence on the Ottoman court was growing; and Protestants recovered their lost ground. Stephen became patriarch again, but did not last long. In 1844 the new patriarch Matthew advised the Protestants to leave. They replied by opening a girls' boarding school. The blow of excommunication struck again, this time against Armenians who had embraced Protestantism, making them virtual outlaws. Canning, the British Ambassador, came to their aid, and persuaded the Porte, in 1850, to recognize the *millet prote*, thus freeing the Protestants, who numbered about 1,000, from the civil domination of the Armenian patriarch.

Troubles of a different kind disturbed the social life of the *millet*. The *aṣnāf* organizations had come out in opposition to the Kum Kapu administration which, influenced by the *umarā'*, had left the schools almost destitute. The Sultan gave them a favourable hearing and replaced the *umarā'* by the *aṣnāf* in the Armenian National Council. Even this did not solve their financial difficulties. The *umarā'* managed to replace the patriarch, too liberal in their view, by Matthew II, who devised a council in which the numbers of *aṣnāf* and *umarā'* were equal (1844).

The ideas behind the *tanẓimat* were taking effect, and the laity was gaining control of the Kum Kapu. It was becoming clear that the people intended to be the deciding factor where the temporal affairs of the "nation" were in question. In 1853 a constitution was drawn up that took ten years to gain the Sultan's approval, laying down that "any national action without majority approval is neither just nor legitimate". Without lands or liberty, the Armenians had assumed the constitution of a free people.

The Armenians had hoped that the Russo-Turkish War of 1877–78 would have destroyed the Ottoman empire and opened the door to freedom, as had happened in the Balkans. The Treaty of Berlin disillusioned them.

The uncertainty of life and property and the arbitrary ways of Ottoman officials had produced an atmosphere favourable to hostility and rebellion, reprisals and appeals to foreign powers, the flourishing of secret societies, and the retaliation of the police by a regime severer than ever. Many Armenians emigrated to Europe and America. Nationalist papers printed abroad kept the agitation going. Many of the groups formed at the time had a fleeting existence, but a few endured, such as the Hunchak or Hintchak, started during 1887 by a few students in Geneva. Another was the Dachnak or Tashnak, when various Armenian groups joined forces in Tiflis in 1890. It included Russian subjects inclined towards atheism and violence. 'Abdülḥamid II was so alarmed that he tried to sow dissension among the Armenians, and failing in this, resorted to extreme measures, with the terrible slaughter of 1894–96, in which he spared only Catholics who had had no part in revolutionary activities.

Matthew III Izmirlean was removed from the Kum Kapu in 1896, to be replaced by the ambitious ex-Catholic Malachi Ormanean, who incurred the hatred of the extremists by currying favour with the Sultan. He shared the Sultan's dismissal by the committee *Ittiḥad ve-teraqqi*, in 1909.

The unbelievable news that 'Abdülḥamid II had restored the Constitution led to an outburst of rejoicing, from the Christians most of all. The Armenians who had endured so much because of the revolutionary tactics of the Tashnak party were in the forefront of the jubilation. Unfortunately the unexpected reaction of the Sultan's supporters led to more dreadful massacres of Christians in Constantinople, and in Cilicia above all. The Tashnak party continued to collaborate with the *Ittiḥad ve-teraqqi*—with some forebodings, for it showed signs of hardening against the Armenians.

The results of the 1914–18 war were terrifying. It is sufficient to quote Mustafa Kemal (Atatürk) before the Military Tribunal constituted in January 1919. The pashas had committed "unheard-of crimes...organized deportations and massacres...had ordered town criers to announce that non-Muslims, in order to remain loyal to the government, must deny their faith and embrace Islam". An estimated 600,000 perished and as many again fled the country. Years afterwards, even under the republic, the Armenians, again like all other non-Muslims, were mulcted under the assessments of the *varlik vergisi.*

At the end of the war there were no Armenians left in the eastern Turkish provinces, the land of the Armenians. There were a few in Cilicia and Anatolia where once they had been so numerous. Almost all who remained in Turkey were in Istanbul: Gregorians, Catholics and Protestants.

THE CATHOLICOS OF SIS

The jurisdiction of the Armenian Orthodox catholicos when he left Armenia to settle in Sīs extended over all the Armenian Orthodox. This was later reduced by two schisms of little importance: Aghtamar in 1113 and Jerusalem in 1311. But with the defection of Echmiadzin in 1441, and the formation of the Armenian Orthodox patriarchate of Constantinople in 1461, the scope of his jurisdiction became severely limited.

Although every Armenian in the Ottoman empire came under the Armenian Orthodox patriarch of Constantinople in Kum Kapu for civil affairs, and because the provinces had few contacts with the capital, the catholicos of Sīs was almost autonomous until the *tanẓimat* centralized the administration and thereby enabled the Kum Kapu to regain his control. The resistance of Sīs found unexpected support from the Porte's policy of splitting the Armenians. It recognized his independence and, ignoring the Kum Kapu, assigned the vacant seat to Mighirditch Keyfsizian in 1871. Mighirditch, being short of funds, sought to restore them by smoothing the way for Anglican propaganda. The displeasure of the Porte placed Mighirditch in an awkward position which he tried to improve by making a bargain with Kum Kapu and renouncing his civil rights. After his death in 1894 the Cilician bishops and the Porte objected to Kum Kapu's nomination of his favourite Aladjian, and it was annulled.

For many years the seat of Sīs remained vacant on account of the

Porte's refusal to allow Kum Kapu to interfere, until Sahak II Khabayan became catholicos of Sīs in 1902. Exiled in Jerusalem, Sahak II escaped the massacre of Adana in 1908 in which 20,000 Armenians died, and the slaughter of the 1914–18 war. Fugitive from Turkey, he found asylum in the Lebanon and in 1921 established his seat in Antelias (Inṭilyās), where he built a cathedral and a seminary. Since so many of the Orthodox had found refuge in Syria, the Lebanon and Cyprus, Sahak II persuaded the patriarch of Jerusalem to grant him jurisdiction over all these lands. When he died in November 1939 Bedros Saradjian followed him in May 1940, but died in September of the same year.

To find a successor it was necessary to wait until Echmiadzin had an incumbent, and in 1943 the electoral assembly elected Karekin Khatchadurian.

The death of Karekin in 1952 provoked another crisis. Khat, the *locum tenens*, could not cope with the violent differences of opinion between all parties and resigned in October 1955. A new *locum tenens*, Zareh, planned the election for February 1956. A few days before the appointed date Vazken, catholicos of Echmiadzin, announced his arrival to take part in the election. He was received with all honours, but the majority of the council of prelates and laymen would not agree to his proposal to postpone the election, and notwithstanding many protests and the abstention of the electors on the side of the catholicos, the council proceeded to the noisy election of Zareh, under police protection. It was then observed that Zareh was a sympathizer of the anti-communist Tashnak, and that Vazken was a Soviet subject. In fact, France, the United States and the Vatican hastened to the support of the new catholicos, and so did the Lebanon. Not so Vazken, who continued to voice his protest against the illegality of the election.

Now Zareh had to face his enemies. The opposition gathered around Khat, as the "Rassemblement des Arméniens Indépendents pour la Défense du Siège de Cilicie". Although Khat had notified the constitution of the Rassemblement to the Lebanese government, they refused to recognize his faction. On the other hand Syria did acknowledge him as head of the *millet*. So the schism was complete.

When Zareh I died the Archbishop of Beirut, Khoren I Paroyan became *locum tenens* and on 5 May 1963 a council of two thirds laity and one third clergy elected him by 83 votes out of 85, and he was enthroned on 12 May.

In October 1963 Vazken, catholicos of Echmiadzin, went to Jerusalem in a conciliatory mood at Khoren's invitation, and both catholicos attended a solemn service at which Yeghishe Derderian, Armenian Orthodox patriarch of Jerusalem, officiated.

THE ARMENIAN ORTHODOX PATRIARCHATE OF JERUSALEM

During the nineteenth century the Armenian Orthodox patriachate led a quiet existence apart from a few disputes with Greeks and Latins. Until the end of Ottoman rule the patriarch was chosen in Constantinople from lists submitted by Jerusalem.

Elias Turian had been proposed in 1909 to follow Ormanian as Armenian Orthodox patriarch, but he retired in 1910 and devoted himself to study and teaching. In 1921 he received a call to the seat of Jerusalem, where he continued to teach in the seminary of Santiago. He was on the best of terms with the other Christian churches until his death in 1930.

After the end of Ottoman rule the monks of the monastery of Santiago began to elect their own prelates and patriarchs, who received the *chirotonia* at the hands of the catholicos of Echmiadzin.

When Nesrob Nechanian died in July 1944 there was some dispute over his successor, Kevork Israelian, consecrated in Echmiadzin in July, and who died in Beirut in October 1949 during the difficult period of the war between Arabs and Jews. The members of the Brotherhood of Santiago elected a *locum tenens*, Yeghishe Derderian. As a result of the war the Santiago convent was crowded with Armenian families while most of their resources were blockaded in the zone under Jewish occupation. In 1956 nine members of the Brotherhood of Santiago arrived from the United States, including Tiran Nesroyan, who had given up his diocese there. The Brothers from overseas brought with them new opinions, and some serious clashes took place. An order of expulsion against Tiran was obtained from the government of Jordan, annulled and confirmed time and time again at the instance of warring factions, and tension increased in the Armenian community, with meetings lawful and unlawful. Yeghishe unexpectedly disappeared, leaving a substitute no one would recognize. The police were called in, and the government were asked to intervene. More than once Tiran was expelled and let in again. Yeghishe was dismissed by his opponents, who then nominated Tiran as a *locum tenens*, *in absentia*. Tiran returned in triumph, got the government to recognize him as *locum tenens* and was elected in March 1957. Still, Yeghishe did oppose a petition against the election, which had not yet been confirmed by the government. Finally Tiran was put on an aeroplane for Beirut. Yeghishe came back at the end of March 1960, made himself *locum tenens*, he in turn obtained government recognition through a royal decree, and was at last elected in June 1960. In May 1961 the Israeli ministry of Religions recognized him as well.

THE ORTHODOX ARMENIANS IN RUSSIA

The 1828 Treaty of Turkmanchay with Persia handed over to Russia a large portion of Armenian territory, including the patriarchal seat at Echmiadzin. Russia's fine promises before the treaty aroused among the Armenians hopes for better times. But Tsarism was not going to permit a church so national and so independent as the Armenian Orthodox to remain long beyond its control. In 1836 Russia imposed a constitution framed on that of the imperial church. The election of a catholicos, formerly free, was now to be restricted to a choice between two candidates, nominated by the Tsar.

Russia adopted a fluid policy towards the Armenians so long as they could act as a spring-board for their plans against Turkey, but after the Treaty of Berlin (1878) a programme of Russification was taken in hand. The Armenians had advanced in prosperity and culture. Armenian intellectuals were in close contact with their Russian colleagues and were adopting their advanced ideas—as indeed were many Armenian countrymen, who were leaving their oppressive landlords for the cities.

So secret societies began to flourish in Tiflis and Yerevan, whose revolutionary aims soon led to the persecution of their affiliates. They were long-suffering, but when in 1903 the confiscation of church property was ordered, the people violently resisted attempts by the Cossacks to carry out the order. In 1905, when the new Constitution was proclaimed, ultrareactionary elements headed crowds of fanatics in attacks on the Armenian quarters, leaving murder, looting and fires in their wake. Then the government's attitude towards the Armenians took a turn for the better, and they conceived the notion of forming a national Armenian delegation which, with a mandate from the catholicos of Echmiadzin would represent the Armenians in the chancelleries of Europe. But the war of 1914–18 put an end to this.

During the war many Armenians, in flight from the Turks, had sought protection behind the Russian lines, and now the imperial rule was over, set up the short-lived Armenian Republic in 1918, only to succumb before the combined attacks of Turks and Russian Communists. By 1922 they were helpless in the hands of Soviet Russia, and their church shared in the persecution which fell on all religious confessions.

Kevork V (1912–30), catholicos of Echmiadzin, in 1912 put Ormanian, the Armenian Orthodox ex-patriarch of Istanbul, in charge of the Armenian Diaspora in Europe. Kevork V was succeeded by Khoren Muradbeguian, who died in 1938.

After the Second World War the changed attitude in the relations between the Soviet government and the Russian Orthodox Church was paralleled in the treatment of the catholicos of Echmiadzin. The difficulties he had in keeping in touch with the dioceses of the Diaspora, and the predominance of certain political trends, meant that Armenians living outside Soviet influence were turning towards the catholicos of Sīs, in Antelias. But from 1945 the new catholicos Kevork VI Ţchorekdjian, encouraged by the Soviet government to follow the new political line, had some success in restoring the authority of the seat of Echmiadzin over all Orthodox Armenians; but the unfortunate attempt of his successor Vazken I to impose his views during the election of the catholicos of Sīs-Antelias, Zareh I, broke the links between Antelias (Inṭilyās) and Echmiadzin. The strain lasted until the death of Zareh I.

The General Assembly of the Ecumenical Council of Churches, held in Paris (1962) invited delegates from both Antelias and Echmiadzin, but no reconciliation came of it. In October of the same year Vazken called a national ecclesiastical synod, which had the good offices of the Soviet government. It advised Vazken to compose his differences with Antelias. He went to Jerusalem in October 1963 and his conversations with Khoren I, Zareh's successor in Antelias, led to better relations.

THE SYRIAN OR NESTORIAN CHURCH

The Syrians or Nestorians call themselves the "Eastern Church". From the sixteenth century it has been usual to refer to the Nestorians, in relations with Rome, as "Chaldeans" and to the others as "Syrians".

In accordance with a celibate patriarchate the Syrian seat has been filled since 1450 by a peculiar hereditary system, collateral from uncle to nephew or brother to brother. All Syrian patriarchs have taken the name Mār Shim'ūn (Simon Peter).

There were occasional short-lived relations between the Syrian patriarch and Rome. The Syrians in their refuge among the steep mountain slopes of the Hakkārī region (where the seat of Kuchanis was), surrounded as they were by Turkish and Kurdish enemies, had to stick close together to survive.

The Nestorians looked outward to the major churches for protection against the Kurds. In 1841 C. A. Rassam, of the Society for Promoting Christian Knowledge, reported that the patriarch would welcome help from the Church of England in its resistance. The same year Dominican missionaries arrived in Mesopotamia and settled in Mosul, but avoided the mountains. American Presbyterians worked there and in Urmia, and Canterbury had missionaries in Kuchanis. Russian Orthodoxy also took a lively interest in Urmia.

In 1891 Mār Shim'ūn XVIII (1861–1903) approached the Dominicans with the object of obtaining papal assistance in building schools and seminaries, but his fellow churchmen gave him no encouragement. However, two nephews of the patriarch, Abraham, bishop of Hakkārī, and his brother Nemrud, had some leanings towards Catholicism and in 1902 Pope Leo XIII asked the new Chaldean patriarch, Manuel II Thomas to open discussions. The death of Mār Shim'ūn XVIII in 1903 while his two nephews were in Mosul gave the opposition party an excuse to elect the 19-year-old Benjamin as patriarch as Mār Shim'ūn XIX (1903–19), and with Russian and Anglican assistance stopped the drift towards Rome. While the 1914–18 war was in progress the Syrians lent a ready ear to the promises of the Allied Powers, and the patriarch led them away from the mountains, abandoning their lands and homes in the assurance that they would one day return—while Nemrud and the Catholics remained loyal to the Ottoman government. Shim'ūn XIX contrived the assassination of Nemrud and some of his relations before leaving for Persia.

When the Ottoman forces, fighting the Russians, arrived on the land, the Christians fell back behind the Russian lines. With the collapse of the Russian front (1917) they found themselves surrounded by enemies. For a year they defended their positions, then some of them made their way into Russia and Persia. Perhaps 70,000 sought refuge in the occupied parts of Mesopotamia, and many joined the British forces. Mār

Shim'ūn XIX himself had been assassinated in Persia in 1918, to be succeeded by his 24-year-old brother Paul, who made his entry into Mosul in 1919 as Mār Shim'ūn XX. He died of consumption and his brother Isaias was consecrated in Ba'qūba, Iraq, as Mār Shim'ūn XXI. He was sent to Oxford while the government of the "nation" rested in the hands of his father and his aunt Surma, who with her English upbringing was the virtual regent. Back from Oxford Mār Shim'ūn was regarded by the Iraqi government as civil leader of the Nestorians in their country; he was also the religious head of all those in Russia and India. In January 1923 the Syrians presented an ineffective petition to the Lausanne Conference, and in 1925 the League of Nations assigned to Turkey the Mount Hakkārī region, the ancient Syrian homeland. With the withdrawal of the British administration in 1931 Mār Shim'ūn lost his only ally. The guarantees made by Iraq to the minorities, to ease their way into the League of Nations, appeared extremely feeble to Mār Shim'ūn, and he protested against the treatment of his people. He pursued these protests in Baghdad, and as he opposed the plans for the settlement of the Syrians, and refused to promise loyalty to King Fayṣal, he was arrested, lost his Iraqi nationality, and was deported to Cyprus in August 1933. Meanwhile the governor of Mosul ordered the Syrians to lay down their arms. Some groups refused and after crossing the Tigris in Syria were ordered back again by the French military. Under attack by regular and irregular forces they and the rest of the Syrians underwent severe and bloody repression in July–August 1933. The case was submitted to the League of Nations. Some settled in Syria by the upper waters of the Khābūr, in the al-Ḥasaka and al-Qāmishlī regions.

The agreement between Mār Shim'ūn XXI and the Anglicans, who permit bishops to marry, divided the Syrians. The malcontents gathered around Timothy, bishop of Malabar, and a certain priest, Joseph, set up a school in Mosul in opposition to the one Mār Shim'ūn had placed in the charge of an Anglican.

Meanwhile some Syrians had migrated to Beirut and started a vigorous campaign against the position adopted by Mār Shim'ūn XXI, 1949–50, in which they were joined by those of the Khābūr. In March 1960 Mār Thomas Darnos, metropolitan of the Syrians in India wrote a pamphlet on the "Eastern Church" dealing with the canonical question posed by the legality of the patriarchal election in its traditional form.

THE SYRIAN JACOBITE CHURCH

This Church came into being in the patriarchate of Antioch through the adoption of Monophysite doctrines, simultaneously with the Coptic Church's similar action within the Alexandrian patriarchate.

From the sixteenth century onwards the history of this Church can be summarized as a struggle between a Romanizing party and one opposed to all union. It has been asserted that of all the Eastern Churches the Syrio-Jacobite is in doctrine nearest to Rome.

The heads of the Church took the name of Mār Ignatius, numbered according to their order of succession, though their own names were also used. Mār Ignatius XXX (George V) (1819–36) reacted sharply against the Roman party, one of them his own secretary and coadjutor with right of succession, Anthony Samharī. Mār Ignatius XXXI (Elias II) (1838–47) went even further in this hostility, going so far as to obtain injunctions from the Sultan against the Roman party. Mār Ignatius XXXII (Jacob II) (1847–72) tried to improve the economic status of his church. Mār Ignatius XXXIII (Peter IV) (1872–95) went by way of London to Malabar and, in 1892, in a letter to the Apostolic delegate made his submission to Rome.

A dispute over the succession arose between 'Abd al-Masīḥ and Sadda. The former won and became Mār Ignatius XXXIV (1895–1905) and Sadda betook himself to Diyarbakīr and turned Catholic. He went on to Sharfa in the Lebanon, continued to Rome, returned to Ḥimṣ and became again a Monophysite. Mār Ignatius resigned on account of differences between him and some of his clergy and laity. It was now the turn of Sadda to occupy the seat, as Mār Ignatius XXXV, or 'Abdallāh II (1906–16). 'Abd al-Masīḥ had retired to a monastery after his resignation. He was invited in 1912 to Malabar by the Syrio-Jacobites there, where he consecrated a number of bishops. He returned by way of Jerusalem, met the Latin patriarch Camassei and made his profession of faith in the Catholic Church. Later, in Rome, he was received by Pope Pius X.

Meanwhile Mār Ignatius XXXV ('Abdallāh II) had his troubles with the clergy. Some rebelled, one of them going over to Greek Orthodoxy and two to the Roman discipline.

When the 1914–18 war began the patriarchal seat of Mardin was transferred to Dayr Za'farān. The survivors of the Christian massacres left the Mardin, Diyarbakīr and Urfa areas for asylum in Syria and the Lebanon.

'Abdallāh II was succeeded by Mār Ignatius XXXVI (Elias III Shākir) (1917–32), during whose reign the synod of Mār Matthā was held, the first for many years. One Jacobite peculiarity was that their service books were written by hand, each ordinand writing his own missal, and using the anaphoras of his own preference. One resolution was to unify the liturgical books; and others were to reorganize the eparchies and inaugurate a seminary. Elias III was forced to go to India to deal with the growing demands for independence for the Malabar Syrio-Jacobites, and there he died in February 1932.

After him came Mār Ignatius XXXVII (Efren Bar Sauma) who made his seat in Ḥimṣ. He made a series of compromises with the Syrio-Jacobites of Malabar, while his successor Mār Ignatius XXXVIII (Jacob III Severios) (1957) achieved a precarious unity by granting the Syrio-Jacobites of India some degree of autonomy. The new patriarch made his seat in Damascus (1959). At this date the Church possessed eleven eparchies and 130,000 members, 115,000 of them in the Near East.

THE COPTIC ORTHODOX CHURCH

Copts, the most numerous Christian minority in Arabic-speaking lands, give a remarkable instance of survival. The Coptic *millet* survived the threat of destructive elements within and outside the community—the loss of their own language, lack of help from foreign sources, the steady drain of many apostasies.

Etymologically "Copt" is equivalent to "Egyptian", but what distinguishes the Copts is not their being Egyptians but their Christian faith. They are marked by surprising resilience, frugality, bright intellect and a capacity for hard work. A withdrawn community, marrying within the clan (frequently between cousins) it usually drew slighting references from consuls and travellers.

With better orientation to modern ideas than his Ottoman rivals, Muḥammad 'Alī's policy of rejuvenation bore favourably on Christian and Jewish immigrants. He guaranteed their rights, protected their commercial interests, and respected their religious liberty, and under his and successive governments the situation of the Copts gradually improved.

Towards the end of his life Muḥammad 'Alī let the reins of government fall into the hands of his son Ibrāhīm. On his death in the early months of 1848 the Porte appointed 'Abbās I as Pasha of Egypt; he died in 1854 and was succeeded by his uncle Sa'īd, a son of Muḥammad 'Alī, about the time when Cyril IV, the reformer, alive to the new ideas, behaved warily towards the government and occupied himself with educational matters, providing schools for boys and girls. Thereby the Copts began to surpass the Muslims in general culture, enabling them to occupy places in the administration. Cyril also set up a theological faculty, and established *al-majlis al-millī* with lay councillors to ensure representation of the laity in matters relating to the church.

Sa'īd in his endeavours to rid the country of Turkish influence took advantage of the current reformist and egalitarian movements to favour the Copts. In December 1855 he cancelled the *jizya*, a capital tax which weighed on the Copts, and in his desire to lessen distances between Copt and Muslim, he called them to the army on equal footing (January 1856). Sa'īd declared the right of Christian soldiers to observe their religion in public. It has been said—perhaps with some exaggeration—that he mended the split which religious differences had made between Egyptians.

Ibrāhīm's son, Ismā'īl, succeeded Sa'īd on his death in 1863. Educated in Vienna and Paris, he did not want religious differences to be a source of discord. His relations with the Coptic patriarch were cordial. He gave his land for building churches and 1,500 feddans of land as a source of revenue towards schools and teachers' salaries. He looked on Protestant proselytizers as intruders, and lent the patriarch a steam launch for his pastoral visits. Article 2 of the Constitutional Statute of November 1866 removed all distinctions between Egyptians, and the Assembly proclaimed that government schools *must* admit Christians and Muslims alike.

A sign of the patriotic solidarity between Christians and Muslims was the acceptance of fiscal impositions by both sides at the time of the financial crisis which preceded the abdication of Ismā'īl in 1879. All observers agree upon the friendly spirit shown by both groups up to the revolt of 'Urābī in 1882.

As a result of internal disputes the seat stood vacant for four and a half years until a new patriarch, Cyril V, was elected in November 1874, conditionally on his promising the *al-majlis al-millī* an increased share in church government. However, he did not keep his promise. There were two trends in community opinion: one conservative, the other progressive. Violent disputes provoked by the modern party brought down a decree of exile on the patriarch's head at the hands of the Khedive in 1892. The patriarch then laid the Coptic Church under an interdict, creating an impossible position in which the lay party lost ground, facilitating the patriarch's return in 1893. He pursued his own way, even if he did show some readiness to compromise; but this brought no settlement, and his long reign witnessed quarrels between old and new, between priests and laity, and appeals to the civil power until his death in 1927.

Ismā'īl was succeeded by his son Tawfīq. Until now the country, rich and open to civilizing influences, had offered ample opportunities for employment in the administration and for long the Copts had had a monopoly in departments of finance. Now, many appointments disappeared during the economic crisis and the British occupation. The embittered Copts entered politics and joined forces with Muṣṭafā Kāmil, the nationalist leader who pledged to work for the independence of Egypt. Buṭrus Ghālī, the first Copt to head the government, signed the agreement about the Sudan with England, and was soon afterwards assassinated by a nationalist in November 1906. This fact, and tactless behaviour by the successor to Muṣṭafā Kāmil (who died in 1908) influenced the nationalist party towards pan-Islamism and alienated the Copts.

The Copts met in Asyūṭ during 1911 to adopt resolutions similar to those they had already submitted to the British High Commissioner, Lord Cromer. Amongst other demands they asked for equal treatment in accession to state employment, religious instruction to Coptic pupils in State schools, and a Sunday holiday. A year later a few Copts took part in a Muslim congress in Heliopolis which denounced these resolutions.

The 1914–18 war imposed a truce on the antagonists, though these congresses had left an undercurrent of uneasy relations. All Egyptians looked forward to independence after the war, to be deeply disappointed. Zaghlūl headed a *wafd*, delegation, to the British. Warmed by patriotic emotion, Christians and Muslims fraternized in churches and mosques and raised the symbols of Cross and Crescent on high.

In 1922 the British government proceeded to replace its protectorate by some show of independence. While the laws of the new government were being framed King Fu'ād opposed proportional representation in the different communities, preferring to leave the affair to the electorate at large.

The political situation had led to better relations between Copts and

Muslims, but internal disputes were still eroding the Church when Cyril V died in August 1927 at the age of 105, with 53 years of patriarchal rule behind him.

The throne, in 1928, was now occupied by John IX of Dayr Ṭāsā, bishop of Alexandria for the past 40 years. He had worked with the late patriarch and now followed the same courses. After his death in 1942 the seat was left vacant until 1944, when it was filled by Anba Makarios, bishop of Asyūṭ, who had been president of the Coptic Congress in 1911. Dedicated to prayer and work, he attempted to reform the convents, and met with opposition not only from the monks themselves but also from the laity who preferred their own methods of administration. So there were further disputes between the synod and the *majlis*. He registered his protest by retiring to the convent of St Anthony. The prime minister Māhir Pasha intervened and the patriarch returned in triumph, but this had little effect on the deep disagreement between the laity and the hierarchy.

On his death in 1945, Anba Yussab II, bishop of the recently formed diocese of Girga, was enthroned. Discontent latent in certain Coptic circles, the atmosphere of revolution and renovation created by the fall of the monarchy in 1952, agitation against the British in Egypt, and the incompetence of patriarchal rule were among the factors which did nothing to alleviate the critical situation in which the community was placed.

The Egyptian revolution, late in July 1952, aroused scenes of enthusiasm and more fraternization between Muslims and Christians. Once more the slogan of 1919 "Religion belongs to God—the fatherland to all" was heard everywhere.

The year 1955 was fixed for the renewal of the Coptic *majlis millī*. The lists of opposing candidates were drawn up amid mounting excitement when on the eve of the election the government ordered its postponement, and nominated a provisional *majlis* which began to sit in August. It led to no appeasement. In September a gathering of prelates signified its readiness to depose the patriarch; sixteen out of twenty-four members of the *majlis* gave their support, and on 21 September the government removed Anba Yussab II, who then retired to a monastery. On the same day the government decreed the suppression of confessional tribunals as from the following January. Such a move on the part of the government threatened in the same way all the Christian hierarchies. They joined forces and made their reasoned protests to the head of the government, ʿAbd al-Nāṣir, who made no response. The hierarchies made up their minds to celebrate the next Nativity in mourning. A pastoral letter was read in the churches lamenting the damage done to religious observance, and to Christian marriage rites in particular. The government acted at once. The police arrested the Melkite-Catholic vicar general, the Roman vicar apostolic and two other priests. On Christmas Eve the ministry of Cults expressed the desire of the government for Christmas to be celebrated in the usual way, and was met by a refusal. However he took advantage of the activities of the contentious Copts to win over their hierarchy, who now refused to take part in the "Christmas strike of Christians in Egypt".

In January 1956 a new Constitution was published which by Article 3 made Islam the state religion. In April of that year the Ministry of Education decided that the free schools must teach each child his own religion—and these schools had 500,000 pupils. The American Mission in Cairo was the first to complain. There was no direct reply; the indirect response was a tightening of similar measures.

The deposition of Anba Yussab II had been effected without the knowledge or consent of the Ethiopian Church. The synod of Addis Ababa and the emperor demanded his reinstatement. Against the opposition of the *majlis* sixteen Coptic and fourteen Ethiopian bishops disputed the validity of the deposition; but the *majlis* itself was not unanimous, and confusion reigned. The patriarch had made his way back to Cairo to live in the Coptic hospital, close to the patriarchal palace. He was allowed entry to the patriarchal palace when he fell ill, and there he died the next day, on 13 November 1956.

In July 1956 ʿAbd al-Nāṣir nationalized the Suez canal, followed in the autumn by the occupation by Anglo-French forces. The Egyptian Christians were again desirous of displaying their patriotism, always in doubt. Once more there was the unusual sight of high officials of all creeds extolling national solidarity.

The national crisis may have ended, but not so the religious crisis in the Christian communities. In May 1957 ʿAbd al-Nāṣir maintained that no discrimination in religious affairs would be tolerated. In August, the Coptic, Catholic and Evangelical hierarchies were sending a collective note to ʿAbd al-Nāṣir deploring the discriminatory measures against Egyptian Christians.

Failure to agree among the Copts was worse when the question of a new patriarch came up. When the election was finally fixed for 17 April 1957, Ethiopia refused to take part and reserved the right to protest to the new patriarch, who this time was chosen from the monks, with the title of Cyril VI. His relations with the Church in Ethiopia were cordially started, and on 25 June 1959 agreement was reached on the following points: the patriarch of Alexandria to be supreme head of the two Churches; representatives of the Church in Ethiopia to take part in his election; the patriarch to be a Copt, of Egyptian parentage; the archbishop of the Church in Ethiopia, successor to St Takla Hāymānot, to be raised to the dignity of patriarch catholicos as chief of the Church of Ethiopia; this office to be filled by election among the Ethiopian clergy; and Anba Basilios to be the first patriarch catholicos of Ethiopia.

Hopes for a new era of reconstruction and reform raised by the election of Cyril VI proved vain. Disagreement between laity and hierarchy was endemic. The patriarch wrote to the *majlis* reminding them that it was he who had the right to call meetings of the *majlis* and approve its decisions. The laity replied by censorious articles in the Press.

THE MARONITE CHURCH

The mountains of Lebanon were sparsely populated until the Arabs seized the Syrian provinces from Byzantium in the seventh century. Its slopes and crags promised a safe refuge to the religious groups which resorted to them to escape from the nominal lords of the country.

The Maronites came into Lebanon from the north in the seventh century in search of asylum, and with the same object the Druzes entered from the south in the eleventh century; it was not long before powerful Druze families set up a semi-feudal system. Neither external political changes nor a succession of nominal Lebanese rulers affected the rough tribal liberty of the inhabitants. Although rule over the mountain was in the hands of the amirs, the patriarch's people looked to him as their supreme authority.

During the sixteenth and seventeenth centuries Lebanon enjoyed lengthy periods of prosperity and near-independence under Druze and Sunnī Muslim Amirs. The fabric of Lebanese history is shot with strands of political and economic rivalry. Complete equality and mutual respect were the rule between Druzes and Maronites in their religious and social affairs. The last of the great Lebanese Amirs,

Bashīr II, defied the Porte and assisted Egypt in its occupation of Syria in 1830. When, nine years later, the Powers forced the withdrawal of Egypt, Bashīr was deported and the Porte obtained a sovereignty it had long striven for.

The Maronites considerably outnumbered the Druzes, and were responsible for most of the agriculture. The Amir counted on the Maronites if he was to keep his power, so he countenanced their infiltration southward into Druze territory. The Druzes resented this, and the Porte took advantage of this to sow dissention. Now that England had had such diplomatic success at the Porte, she began to take an interest in the Druzes, as a likely base for operations against France's long-standing influence on the Maronites. They fomented religious differences, which up to then had never led to serious trouble.

The Porte took the opportunity, furnished by the first clashes between the Druzes and Maronites, to divide Lebanon into two parts, North and South; so that many Maronites stayed in the South, and a few Druzes in the North. These Druzes felt sure of Turkish protection and soon became involved in incidents which culminated in the massacres of 1860; the Damascus Muslims also attacked the Christians, killing and looting. A bright spot in this dreadful business is the magnanimous behaviour of the Amir, 'Abd al-Qādir, who, having been banished by the French from Algeria, resided in Damascus. His timely intervention saved 1,500 Christian lives.

Feelings ran high in Europe at this time and a French expedition landed in Lebanon. A conference of the Powers drew up a settlement which was the rule in Lebanon until 1914. It gave Lebanon a half-century of peace and prosperity never before experienced until the 1914 war brought Lebanon and Syria under Turkish military government.

The "Maronite patriarch of Antioch and all the East", since 6 January 1899, had been Ilyās Buṭrus al-Ḥuwayyik (Elias Hoyek). He defended the interests of his Church under the Turks, and while the war was on he was distinguished for his concern for the poor and needy.

When the war ended the Maronite patriarch begged the Peace Conference to create an independent Lebanon. France got the mandate for Syria and Lebanon and joined the populations of the coast, the plain of al-Biqā' and a part of Syria to form Great Lebanon. Its economic viability had been explored, but no one seems to have considered the effect on Lebanese political and social life of an influx of Sunnī Muslims parted without their consent from their native Syria. Ilyās al-Ḥuwayyik died when he was 88 on 23 December 1931, to be succeeded by Anṭūn ʻArīḍa. Both he and the Maronite Archbishop of Beirut were quite clear in their opposition to any proposal for merging Lebanon with the State of Syria, and their dislike of the policy of the mandatory Power. The latter produced, on 13 March 1936, a new statute for the religious communities of Syria and Lebanon, whereupon the Christian hierarchies, the *muftī* of Beirut, the Jews and the Druzes all joined to protest against most of its recommendations. The order prescribed the *status quo* of the religious bodies. Its Annex number 1 gave the "List of Communities enjoying recognition in law or in fact". It included the following bodies: Maronite, Greek Orthodox, Catholic, Melkite-Gregorian Orthodox, Armeno-Catholic, Syrian Orthodox, Syrian Catholic, Syrian-Chaldean-Nestorian, Chaldeo-Catholic, Latin, Muslim-Sunnī, Muslim-Shīʻī, ʻAlawī, Ismāʻīlī, Druze, and the synagogues of Aleppo, Damascus and Beirut.

Towards the end of April 1936 ʻArīḍa issued a Green Book with the title, *Lebanon and France, Documents published by the Maronite Patriarch* (Beirut, n.d.)—a summary of memoranda presented to the French government. It recapitulated the wrongs and aspirations of the Maronites. Lebanon had always shown its loyalty to France. Back in 1840 the patriarch Ḥubaysh had countered British proposals by affirming this loyalty and from then onwards "Lebanese independence had ceased to interest England". The Statute of 1861–64 may have given internal autonomy but not the real independence they sought, and from then onwards "Lebanon was putting its trust in France, as Israel did in the Messiah". Lebanon remained Francophile during the First World War, and suffered for it when the Turks allowed 200,000 to die of starvation. The French occupation was welcomed with joy. On 10 July 1919 the Great Lebanese Council in agreement with the High Commissioner issued the celebrated Order of the Day: "The Independence of Lebanon is proclaimed. The presence of France will in no way imperil the independence." Patriarch al-Ḥuwayyik was invited to the Peace Conference. His first talks with Clemenceau and Pichon were a forthright demand for independence. After much argument he accepted the mandatory regime, but with such decided reservations as would in fact give Lebanon full religious liberty. These were accepted by Clemenceau and were included in the Ḥuwayyik–Clemenceau pact by which the organization and administration of justice would be in the hands of the Lebanese. During the fifty-five years of the Statute of Agreement Lebanon had had eight governors only, with full administrative, legislative and executive powers; the Turkish sovereign had never allowed Ottoman interference; Article 14 of the 1861 agreement had guaranteed their right to maintain public order throughout the whole land. It contrasted this with the powers of the Mandate, under which everyone would be at the mercy of the High Commission, sustained by French forces, and concluded by insisting that the pact be put into operation.

When at last Lebanon achieved its long desired independence, the government's first task was to ensure internal stability, endangered by religious and feudal contention, and safeguard their external security, presented with the difficult task of remaining neutral as much between opposing Arab states as between East and West.

Thus in 1943 a "National Pact" was reached, never committed to writing, between the Muslim prime minister Riyāḍ al-Ṣulḥ and the president of the Republic Bishāra al-Khūrī, a Christian. On behalf of their respective communities they undertook jointly to uphold the integrity and independence of Lebanon, the Christians renouncing any attempt to get help from the West and the Muslims giving up any scheme for union with the other Arab countries. The Christians would still be the major influence, and the existing structure of the State would persist. Lebanese policy was henceforth to be based on this agreement.

Now that Lebanon was a collection of various sects on equal footing, the old *millets* of the Ottoman empire had to be joined by new creations. The Druze *millet* did exist in fact, though not lawfully admitted by the Ottomans. The Shīʿa welcomed the recognition of their *millet* as a positive advance, while the Sunnīs lost their former predominance.

Lebanon has eleven Christian *millets*, two Muslim and one Druze. The Maronite *millet* comes first in virtue of its history and its numbers, although it has only 8 per cent of the population in Beirut. Its Western contacts have provided it with a numerous class of persons of European or American upbringing well-fitted to take an advantageous part in social and political life. An increasing population in a small country and the persistence of old political attitudes have led to much emigration, especially by the Christians (in 1960 there were 470,000 Maronites in patriarchal territory, and 380,000 in the Diaspora).

There were about 150,000 Greek Orthodox in Lebanon in 1960, split into two fairly well defined groups: the proletariat of the North and the well-to-do of Beirut, where it made up 10 per cent of the population, with a growing middle class in between. With a patriarch away in Damascus, and the persistence of old traditions, the laity tend to take a predominant part in community affairs; while the clergy still dominate the lower classes, in Beirut it is the laity who manage communal business.

The Uniate Melkites, perhaps 100,000 in number, are the most advanced in culture; they inhabit mainly the central and southern regions. Many of its numerous middle class are found in the liberal professions. Its clergy, of Roman education, are considered to be the most learned and worthy in any of the Eastern Churches; devoted to their ministry, they leave political activity to the laity.

The last of the groups to find a refuge in Lebanon are the Armenians: Orthodox, Catholic and Protestant. The first were part of the tragic exodus consequent on the 1914–18 war. Next came the flight from the sanjak of Alexandretta when the Turks took it in 1939. In 1943 there were an estimated 70,000 Armenians in Lebanon, united by a strong national sentiment, overriding their religious differences, but hopelessly divided by communal questions that sometimes ended in bloodshed. They mostly settled in the suburbs of Beirut to form 20 per cent of the population. Hardworking and thrifty, they rose from poverty to comfort, and joined the professions. Compared with the other *millets*, their clergy have a minor influence in politics.

The remaining Christian minorities hardly reached 3 per cent of the Lebanese population in 1960. The Syrians or Nestorians, the Syro-Jacobites, the Chaldeans—weak in numbers and social influence, they were in the lower classes; in all cases their upper clergy lived outside the country.

In contrast the Syro-Catholics, the Latins and the Protestants wielded a greater influence than their small numbers would warrant. The Syro-Catholics were a worthy section of the middle class in Beirut, where their patriarch, the first Syrian cardinal, Mār Ignatius Gabriel Tappuni, had his residence in 1935. The American University and the University of St Joseph are old and esteemed seats of learning, for the Near East as well as Lebanon. The superior culture of these three groups has made them an important section of the upper middle class of Beirut, where most of them are congregated.

The 90,000 Druzes are found partly in Syria in the region called after the Jabal Druze and partly in the central zone of Mount Lebanon.

The feudal structure that once gave them control of the land has not altered. In Beirut they are only 1 per cent of the population. They are for the most part small folk mainly settled in the mountains. The authority of the heads of most influential Druze families is greater among them than that of their religious supreme *shaykh*, who resides in Beirut.

Muslim Sunnīs belong mostly to the class of "new" Lebanese. In former times they were only 4 per cent of the total population in Lebanon. Now they are 36 per cent in Beirut, and 78 per cent in Tripoli. Thrust willy-nilly into union with Lebanon they long to return to Syria. They had no official representation until 1936. Only for convenience can the term *millet* be applied to the Lebanese communities, particularly the Muslim ones; but the state was so constituted that it was necessary to bring the organization of these communities into line with that of the other *millets*, not only in their internal affairs but also to enable them to take part as a body in public life, social and political. Thus in 1936 a "*muftī* of the Lebanese Republic" was created, to "place him on equality with the leaders of the Christian communities for the defence of Muslim rights".

Most of the 250,000 Shī'īs of Lebanon belong to the "Twelver" (*ithnā 'asharī*) sect. Isolated from their fellow worshippers in Iraq and Persia, and harassed by the Sunnīs of Syria, they found a refuge in the southern parts of Lebanon in times past. More than 90 per cent are poor *fallāḥīn* under powerful feudal lords; 79 per cent are illiterate.

The patriarch Anṭūn 'Arīḍa died on 19 May 1955. His successor, at the request of the Vatican, was Peter al-Ma'ūshī (Meuchi), former bishop of Tyre, enthroned 29 May 1955.

A modern democracy with its opposing parties so delicately balanced might be expected to be short lived. Not so: the system was elastic enough to survive a crisis like that of 1958. The opponents took up arms and fought in the streets. That Christians were most prominent in one band, and Muslims in the other had nothing to do with religious questions. The Maronite patriarch condemned the former group, which also had Druzes and Muslims in its ranks. To avoid bloodshed among brothers the army commander, General Shihāb, remained neutral. After a summer spent in fighting with advantage to neither side, the leaders had second thoughts and concluded a peace.

THE MELKITE CATHOLIC CHURCH

The name "melkite" originally applied to all Christians of the Byzantine rite in the historical patriarchates of Alexandria, Antioch and Jerusalem. Nowadays it refers to the Byzantine Catholics in those patriarchates who use Arabic in their liturgy.

Towards the end of the sixteenth century Michael VIII, Orthodox patriarch of Antioch, retired to Aleppo when he resigned. While in Aleppo he accepted Roman allegiance and formed a nucleus of Uniates. From 1724 onwards Cyril VI, elected by the Damascus Uniates, headed an uninterrupted line of Melkite patriarchs of Antioch.

The first years of the nineteenth century brought persecution to these Uniates of Aleppo and Damascus, incited by the Orthodox Greeks, which did not affect the Melkites of Lebanon under the protection of the Amir Shihāb. The Orthodox prelates took these desperate remedies because they had not succeeded in preventing wholesale conversions to Catholicism—a relatively easy matter since the converts were still subjects of their *millet*. The Catholic Emancipation Act of 1831 put an end to the persecution, and after Muḥammad 'Alī's occupation of Syria the lot of the Christians of the country took a turn for the better.

The Basilian, Salvatorian and Chueirite orders provided the core of the Melkite Church owing to the scarcity of secular clergy. The most outstanding individual in the Melkite church in those days was Maximos Maẓlūm. Made bishop of Aleppo in 1810, his election was quashed in Rome. He went to Rome, and there he was forced to remain from 1813 to 1831. When the Eastern Uniates asked for the restoration of the Jesuit missions, Maẓlūm offered himself to the new Pope Gregory XVI as their guide. Gregory XVI was agreeable, and Maẓlūm accompanied Fathers Ricadonna and Planchet to Syria. Rome ordered the meeting of a synod in Zūq in 1831 to sort out the difficulties facing the Melkites. Maẓlūm was present and tried in vain to persuade the old patriarch Ignatius V Qaṭṭān to appoint him as vicar; but after the patriarch's death in Kisrawān in 1833, Maximos V Mazlūm stepped into the patriarchate. He was regarded as intelligent, diplomatic and sincere in his faith. Egyptian rule made it possible for Maximos to make his solemn entry into Damascus in 1834 and visit many dioceses. On 31 October 1837 he was invested with the *berat*, which now gave him civil jurisdiction over all his people in the Ottoman empire.

As long as the Orthodox clergy had power over the Uniates they would never allow them to copy Orthodox dress, above all the *kalummaukion* or *qallus*, black in colour and cylindrical in shape, which the Orthodox clergy wore on their heads (this prohibition did not affect the more independent Uniates of Lebanon). But when emancipation came to the Uniates they adopted the custom, and this angered the Orthodox and began a series of heated arguments, with frequent appeals to the Porte which exercised French and Russian diplomacy from 1838 to 1848. The Porte would give its *ferman* to the highest bidder. A trivial incident to be sure, but one of great moment in the East.

In 1836 Maẓlūm had gone to Egypt, to find himself involved in the struggle between Muḥammad ʻAlī and the Porte, so he wisely withdrew to Rome and afterwards to France, until in 1843 he was able to return to Constantinople where he stayed five years and contrived to obtain the complete independence and recognition of the Melkite *millet*.

With the object of reorganizing his Church he arranged for a council, which took place in Jerusalem from May to June in 1849. After his schemes were passed by the council, he proposed to promulgate them without reference to Rome, against the advice of his prelates. During this council he had some trouble with the metropolitan of Beirut, Agapios Riyāshī.

After the council Maẓlūm had moved to Aleppo, but when a Muslim revolt degenerated into a Christian massacre he fled to Damascus, where he stayed from 1851 till 1854. In 1852 Pius IX ordered him to Rome with Agapios Riyāshī. He refused to go. He set out for Egypt in November 1854 with the object of building a cathedral and palace, but death overtook him in August 1855. His patriarchate is conspicuous for the increase in membership of his Church which from 50,000 in 1833 had grown to 70,000 by 1855. He had brushes with his bishops when he meddled with their affairs, and occasionally with the laity. He laid the foundations of a regular celibate clergy as a nursery for future bishops. There were eight of these when he became patriarch, and thirteen when he died. To promote this education the Jesuits had founded the seminary at Bikfayyā in 1833; this was moved to Ghazīr in 1845 and later to Beirut in 1875. Until then he had had to rely on the monks for parochial duties, but extra-conventual life proved fatal to monastic discipline, and the brotherhoods became a battle-ground of monks, fighting for bishoprics and benefices.

Rome had appointed the metropolitan of Tyre as *topoteretes* but he died in 1854 and had not been replaced. When Maẓlūm died the Apostolic Delegate Brunoni convoked and presided over a synod which elected the Salvatorian bishop of Acre, Clement Bahuth (1856–64), a prelate who had kept outside church politics. He implemented the wishes of Rome to adopt the Gregorian calendar, hitherto accepted by Maronites and Chaldeans alone; Maẓlūm himself had given thought to this, but considered that some preliminary preparation was advisable. The new patriarch's decision had few objectors to begin with, but Agapios of Beirut, embittered against Rome among other things by his rejection as candidate for the patriarchate, secretly organized a movement of resistance. He befriended two clerical groups in Egypt and Damascus, refused to obey the pope and won over the bishops of Zaḥla, Sidon and Ba'labakk to his side. Without a word to Rome or the synod, Clement resigned and retired to his convent; but Pius IX would not hear of it, so he took his seat once more. Agapios ignored a summons to Rome, consulted his three allies in Zaḥla in 1859, intimated that he took Clement's resignation for granted, and put himself at the head of the *millet*. Rome condemned Agapios and advised Clement to appeal to the Porte, but the Porte, on the eve of the massacres in Lebanon, was not interested in Christian reconciliation. These massacres in Lebanon and Damascus hit the Melkites almost as hard as they hit the Maronites.

The three dissenting bishops yielded to the patriarch after the massacres, but Agapios, encouraged by Russian agents, still held out in company with other dissidents who had built their own chapels in Damascus and Alexandria, calling themselves *sharqiyyūn*, "orientals". However in the end most of them gave in.

Clement Bahuth again sent in his resignation which this time Pius IX accepted, on 24 September 1864. In his place, the Salvatorian Gregory II Yusuf of Acre, an alumnus of Ghazīr and Rome, received the title of the triple patriarchate. A zealous defender of the rites and privileges of his Church, he kept things going with a somewhat inferior body of clergy. He founded two patriarchal colleges, in Beirut in 1865 and in Damascus in 1874. In 1886 he re-established the seats of Paneas and Tripoli, as well as the 'Ayn Ṭirāz seminary. In 1887 he gave the charge of the ancient seminary of St Anne in Jerusalem to Lavigerie and the White Fathers, and at the pope's suggestion it was opened as a purely Melkite seminary, with complete respect for their rites. Gregory II died in Damascus, in July 1897.

The next election gave a lot of trouble, while Cyril Geha of Aleppo was *topoteretes*. Only by a majority vote after an election punctuated by unfortunate incidents was Peter IV Jaraigiry of Zaḥla elected. The unrest attending the election lasted for the duration of the patriarchate. His attitude during diocesan visits occasioned protests to Rome, and only at his death did they cease.

Cyril Geha, *topoteretes* once more, was elected unanimously at 'Ayn Ṭirāz on 28 June 1902. His peaceful disposition induced calm after five years of storm. Cyril VIII did not look forward to the conciliatory council suggested by Leo XIII, but it took place at last at 'Ayn Ṭirāz, lasting from 30 May to 8 July 1909—a sad spectacle of antagonism between reformers and monastics. The monastics hated the secular clergy from St Anne's, and the patriarch dared not interfere. They were in the majority, and removed any hope of an agreeable settlement. He escaped this difficult situation by removing himself to Alexandria, where he died on 10 January 1916.

The terrible war of 1914–18 with its sequel of hunger, executions and banishment made an election ordered by the Porte impossible. Basil Ḥajjār of Sidon only lasted a short while as *topoteretes*, for he died soon after he received the *ferman*. In March 1916 Dimitri Qāḍī, of Aleppo, was confirmed as *topoteretes* by Rome until the interned bishops could return to their seats in 1919 to elect him unanimously as Dimitri I. The new patriarch resolutely refused the laity any part in episcopal elections; he undertook to repair the damages of war, and began many charitable and cultural movements. He died in 1925.

Next in line was Cyril IX Mughabghab of Zaḥla, a sworn enemy of masonry. In 1932 he created the eparchies of Petra and Philadelphia in Jordan which progress towards union there during the twentieth century had made imperative. In 1936 and the years following various religious congregations were founded, many churches built, and schools in Cairo, Alexandria and other Egyptian cities were built or enlarged, to meet the demands of the growing streams of immigrants, to which the First World War had largely contributed. Then the Egyptian Melkites numbered 30,000, but from 1956 their numbers started falling off rapidly.

Cyril IX died on 8 September 1947, and on 30 October Maximos IV Ṣā'igh, metropolitan of Beirut, was elected. In 1944 the Melkite church had 550,000 members.

THE ARMENIAN UNIATE CHURCH

The establishment of the Uniate Armenian hierarchy in the Near East dates from the eighteenth century when Abraham Ardzivean of Aleppo was elected catholicos of Sis in March 1740, and was confirmed in his office by Benedict XIV in November 1742. He assumed the style of Peter, as did those who succeeded him, but he could not take up his seat as it was occupied by a catholicos of the Armenian Orthodox Church, so he installed himself at Kuraym in Lebanon, 1743–9. His successor moved it to Bzummār, 1749–1867, then to Constantinople, 1867–1928, and finally to Beirut. The state of confusion as a result of the *tanẓimat* in which the Christians in Turkey found themselves was shared by the Uniate Armenians who, like their Orthodox compatriots wanted their share in church administration, and looked to a possible union with them.

The treaty of Edirne in 1829 had obliged the Porte to concede *millet* status on the Uniate Armenians, freeing them from the persecution they had suffered during the past years. In 1830 Pius VIII gave Constantinople an Armeno-Catholic primatial archbishop. The first archbishop to be nominated, Anthony Nuridjean, was unacceptable by the Porte because he was an Austrian subject. When the Pope took it upon himself to present another candidate, Peter Maruche (1838–46), there were loud protests from those who wanted their share in church administration and the election of prelates. To avoid trouble in the next election, Rome (in 1842) proposed Anthony Ḥassūn, who, as the archbishop's coadjutor, had a right to the succession. He was made *patrik* in 1845, and in 1846 when the archbishop died he assumed both spiritual and civil authority, but gave way before the prevailing ideas and in 1848 relinquished his office of *patrik*.

The ever-growing numbers of the faithful persuaded Pius IX to create, in 1850, six new episcopal seats, without consulting the minor clergy or the laity. On the day fixed for the *chirotonia* a crowd assaulted the archbishop's palace and had to be dispersed by the police. The *chirotonia* did take place behind locked doors, but there were difficulties in persuading the Porte, bombarded by objections to Rome's interference, to recognize the new prelates.

The numbers of the community did not justify the existence of two primatial seats. Further, conflicts of jurisdiction between the two primates made unification advisable. On the death of Peter VIII, patriarch of Cilicia, in 1865, the synod unanimously voted for Ḥassūn, who became Peter IX (1866–81). The papal bull "Reversurus" ratified the election and established a united hierarchy with headquarters in Constantinople keeping the title of "patriarch of Cilicia of the Armenians". It prohibited absolutely any participation by the laity in patriarchal elections. Under the bull the restricted power of nomination which had hitherto affected only the seat of Constantinople was now to apply to the whole patriarchate. But centralization ran counter to the tendency of Orientals to cling tightly to their ancient privileges. Ḥassūn accepted the scheme, not without drawing the attention of the pope to its drawbacks. During his provincial visits he was well received, though in Bzummār he became aware of unrest among the monks, and decided to hold a synod in Constantinople.

This began its sittings on 4 July 1869. When disciplinary matters were being discussed a section of the assembly accused the patriarch of giving up his secular rights to the pope, and demanded his resignation. Ḥassūn suspended the sessions and proceeded to Rome, leaving the archbishop of Cyprus, Basil Gasparean, to act as vicar. The expected storm soon broke out. Basil Gasparean headed the opponents of the papal bull in an appeal to the Porte. Ḥassūn condemned the rebels and named Arakial, bishop of Ankara, to replace Gasparean, and it was his arrival in Constantinople which sparked off the revolt. His adversaries seized the patriarchal church, burned the papal bull, dismissed Ḥassūn, and elected Hakob Bahtiarean archbishop of Diyarbakir, on 25 February 1871.

The grand vizier favoured the rebels, and on 13 May 1871 pronounced the expulsion and banishment of Ḥassūn, and proposed an election. There were two: that of Filkian which the Porte rejected, and of Kupelian, who did become patriarch of Cilicia, even though the rebels still regarded the one they had elected, Bahtiarean, as their head. A struggle began between the factions for ownership of church property, churches and schools. The Catholics, with the French behind them, acquired recognition as a distinct community, and Ḥassūn was able to return to Constantinople. When Pius IX died, his successor, Leo XIII, conceded the synod of bishops its ancient right to proceed directly to an election, leaving it to Rome to verify its canonical legality. With this the aiders and abettors of schism gradually gave in. Ḥassūn was made a cardinal in 1880 and died in Rome in 1884.

During the patriarchate of Stephen Azarean (1881–99) the breach was finally closed. He had the good sense to warn his followers against joining Armenian secret societies, and so he won the favour of ʿAbdülḥamid, saving many of his flock from the massacres of 1894–96, and earning for himself the name of traitor to the national cause. He built a lycée in Pera, restored churches and induced the Mechitarists of Venice to prepare an edition of liturgical works which he presented to the Church. In 1890 he summoned a synod in Chalcedon (Kadîköy) which drew up a legislative code which was not approved by Rome, although the election of his two successors under the new code, Peter XI (Boghos Emmanuelean), 1899, and Peter XII (Boghos Sabbaghean), 1904, was sanctioned by Rome. Peter XII proved a skilful administrator and was generally well liked. The new libertarian movements stirred the laity to demand a larger share in the administration. The patriarch, ill and too weary to hold out, granted their wishes and retired.

Peter XIII Terzean, considered to be unsympathetic to Rome, had been, prior to his election, reluctant to sign the new regulations so advantageous to the laity. Now there was more trouble. He called a synod in Rome in August 1911 attended by sixteen bishops, during which the laity in Constantinople met in a national assembly to sue for his deposition, and forwarded a memorandum to the pope to that effect.

The prelates in council in Rome were unanimous in sending synodal letters to the communities, asserting the exclusive right of the Church to elect prelates, with some allowance *ex privilegio* for participation by the people; and exclusive rights over purely ecclesiastical property. On his return he was met by hostile demonstrations and a violent campaign in the Press. His enemies forced the government to dismiss him. He went to Rome, where Pius X would not countenance his resignation, and he continued to govern the Church through an apostolic visitor until after the war. This time the schism failed as it lacked spiritual leaders.

Dismembered by the ravages of war, reduced by the decline of many dioceses in Turkey, put out by the encroachment of the Constantinople laity, who actually gave a layman the title of patriarch, and this with *Kamutay* approval—the patriarchate was in sore need of reorganization.

The patriarchal seat was transferred to Beirut, and Constantinople got back its archbishopric. Of the eighteen pre-war dioceses there only remained Alexandria, Iṣfahān, Constantinople and Beirut. The numbers 100,000 in 1911, were in 1960 about 52,000 in patriarchal territory and 45,000 in the Diaspora.

Peter XIV Arpiarean followed Terzean on his death in 1931, with the task of rebuilding his Church. Many of his followers had emigrated to Syria and Lebanon. The next patriarch was Peter XV Agagianian (1937), a native of the Caucasus. He had studied in Rome, and was made a cardinal by Pius XII. The seats of Baghdad and al-Qāmishlī were founded in 1954. At last the Uniate Armenians, their disagreements at an end, found peace. Of their number are the celebrated Mechitarist order, whose two branches, of Venice and Vienna, are renowned for their philological and literary researches.

THE UNIATE CHALDEAN CHURCH

The expression "Chaldean Church" was coined in the West in the fifteenth century when the Western and Eastern branches of the Syriac language were called Chaldean. The word is still applied to those Christians of the ancient Sāsānid empire who in 486 adopted Nestorianism and became united to Rome in 1552 when John Sulāqā (Simeon VIII) went to the City. On his return the Nestorians assassinated him. His successors had seats in various places. There were some defections to the Nestorian camp, though a nucleus in Diyarbakîr remained obedient to Rome. The metropolitan Joseph of Diyarbakîr crossed over to Rome in 1672, and in June 1681 became the first of a second line of Uniate patriarchs (all under the name of Joseph) until Joseph IV gave up his office in 1780, and went to Rome to die, after naming his nephew Agustin Hindī as his successor. He was no more than a priest at the time, nor was he consecrated as bishop until 1804, when he claimed and assumed the title of patriarch.

Another claimant was John Hormizd, a Syro-Nestorian who had been consecrated bishop by his uncle when he was 16; he also had embraced the Roman doctrine in 1778 while he was metropolitan of Mosul. Rome would recognize him only as metropolitan of Mosul with authority over the southern parts of the patriarchate. This led to skirmishes between the pretenders and disputes over the vacant seats. Rome suspended the jurisdiction of John Hormizd until he should make peace with Hindī. Although this did not give Hindī the jurisdiction he sought, he did ordain Joseph ʻAwdū (Audo) as metropolitan of Mosul. Mār Yuḥannan Hormizd adhered firmly to Rome and had striven to extend Catholic influence. When Agustin Hindī died in 1828 the Congregation of the Propaganda wanted Mār Yuḥannan Hormizd for the seat, but Joseph 'Awdū was there already, and the monks of Rabban Hormizd and many of the Church were on his side. Mār Yuḥannan forced an entry into Rabban Hormizd and imprisoned 'Awdū in a monastery. The Propaganda, after listening to a series of conflicting reports, decided in March 1830 that Mār Yuḥannan should not receive the *pallium* until he had restored the convent and set free its Superior and 'Awdū. The latter was to be transferred to the seat of 'Amādiyya.

This was the moment when the sultan was granting civil liberty to the Uniate communities within the empire, while the Chaldeans were still being governed by the Uniate Armenian *patrik*. And it was in the same year—1830—that Pius VIII made Mār Yuḥannan Hormizd patriarch of the Chaldeans, with the additional title "of Babylonia", and invested him with the *pallium*. He took his residence in Mosul and feelings ran so high that Rome had to order visitations in 1835 and 1839. The aged Mār Yuḥannan made up his mind to retire, on 13 October 1837, and nominated Gregory Peter, bishop of al-Jazīra, as coadjutor and "guardian of the throne", no doubt with the idea of keeping some of his nephews out. On 25 September 1838 Rome nominated Nicholas Ḍiyā' (Zeya), bishop of Salmas, as coadjutor with the right of succession. Mār Yuḥannan had died on 16 August of that year. This nomination gave no pleasure to the prelates, deprived of their election rights. Ḍiyā' went to Constantinople to be invested with the *berat*, and returned to run into such unexpected trouble that he resigned and left for Persia, where he died in 1855.

During the vacancy Rome appointed Joseph 'Awdū as *locum tenens* and his election by the synod in December 1847 was unanimous. His long rule of thirty years witnessed many conversions; his community grew from 45,000 to 70,000. Monks from Rabbān Hormizd and Latin missionaries undertook parochial duties. In 1853 a synod held in Rabbān Hormizd made certain decisions: converts were to be confirmed, since this rite had no part in Nestorian observance; the Gregorian calendar was to be adopted; liturgical books were to be revised; and a seminary was to be founded. However, the Malabar incident put a stop to these reforms.

The "Christians of St Thomas", of Malabar, followed the Chaldean rite under Carmelite prelates, and naturally enough preferred prelates of their own rite. There had already been incidents while 'Awdū was *locum tenens* that he had reported to Rome. Then in 1856 priests arrived from Malabar and demanded a national bishop. 'Awdū applied to

Propaganda and proposed a visitation. They replied that Malabar was not his business. After further pressure from Malabar he consented to consecrate Thomas Rokos as bishop, to be his vicar in Malabar, against the veto of the Dominican apostolic delegate to Mosul, who censured both parties, although it appears that the delegate had exceeded his duties. 'Awdū was summoned to Rome while Rokos left for Malabar where he behaved like a schismatic, performed ordinations and was excommunicated by Rome. Meanwhile it was suggested to 'Awdū in Rome that he should submit and recall Rokos. This he did. He summoned Rokos, came to terms, and Rokos returned in 1862. 'Awdū did submit but was embittered against the Dominicans and the apostolic delegate, and determined to make things difficult for them.

1867 was the year of the bull "Reversurus" which was meant to solve the difficulties attending the election of Eastern prelates, and on 31 August 1869 Pius IX extended its provisions to the Chaldean Church after a favourable report by 'Awdū. Two bishops had just died and 'Awdū was asked to submit a double list of candidates. About this time the Vatican Council met, and 'Awdū attended. Most of the Eastern prelates opposed the bull and came very near to adopting the minority opinion on the question of infallibility.

'Awdū hesitated to consecrate the two bishops recommended by Propaganda until Pius IX ordered him to do so. Before giving way he did not scruple to beg the Porte to withhold the *berat* from the two concerned. Further, he was showing signs of partiality towards the Uniate Armenians who had deserted their patriarch Ḥassūn. In 1872 'Awdū requested the pope to restore to the Uniate Chaldeans the ancient jurisdiction of the catholicos of Seleucia–Ctesiphon over the Christians in India. Rome did not answer at once, but 'Awdū did not wait and sent John Elias Mallūs (Mellus) as visitor to Malabar, and he, in spite of the opposition of the apostolic delegate of Verapoly, began to ordain priests and to form a dissident church. At the same time 'Awdū consecrated four prelates without consulting Rome. Rome ordered him to recall Mallūs and to reduce the prelates to the rank of priests. 'Awdū objected and announced his intention of summoning a synod to debate the matter. Thereupon Pius IX addressed the encyclical "Quae in Patriarcatu" to the Chaldeans, giving 'Awdū 40 days in which to submit. This he did in a letter of 1 March 1877. He died a year later in March 1878. Mallūs left Malabar in 1882 for Mosul where he continued his schismatic activities, but he too submitted in the end. His successor, Elias XIV, Peter Abolonyan (1878–94), saw a gradual return to unity and the accretion to his ranks of Nestorian deserters.

After the short reign of Jorge Khayyāṭ who took the name of Abdisho (Ebed Jesus) (1894–9), Mār Emmanuel II Thomas was elected on 9 July 1900. A product of the Ghazīr school, he began a long reign notable for the number of converts he attracted. The war of 1914–18 hit the community hard; out of 100,000 in 1913, only 43,000 survived the slaughter. The religious congregations began to grow in number, and under the patriarch's judicious management the people settled down as a stable religious community, mainly in Iraq. The patriarch was then the only Christian member of the Iraqi Senate, and when he died in 1957 at the age of 95 he left Joseph VII with a community of 176,000 souls and a well-trained clergy. There was difficulty with a few priests in 1956. Administrative reforms resulted in the founding of the archbishopric of Baṣra in 1954, the dioceses of Aleppo and Beirut in 1957 and in 1960 the eparchies of Mosul and al-Qūsh. Many of the Nestorian refugees in Iraq, notably those in Baghdad, took the path to Rome in such numbers that the Uniate Chaldeans, whom war had reduced to barely 50,000, rose to 200,000. In Baghdad alone there are 75,000 (1964), which has led to the transference of the seat from Mosul to Baghdad. When Joseph VII died on 8 July 1958 he was succeeded by Paul II on 16 December, still enthroned in Baghdad.

THE UNIATE SYRIAN CHURCH

During the wars waged in the provinces of the Byzantine empire by Monophysite against official Orthodox doctrine, the Monophysites, called also Copts in Egypt and Syro-Jacobites in Syria, looked with disdain upon the emperor's subjects, calling them Melkites, from the root *mlk*, king or sovereign. So there were two patriarchates, the Melkite and the Syro-Jacobite, and each eparchy had two hierarchies. There were two million Jacobites and as many Melkites.

For ages there had been attempts at union with Rome, hampered by poor communications and the hostility of the Muslims and the Greek Orthodox. Aleppo had long been a great centre of commercial traffic and from the early seventeenth century had been the seat of Jesuit and Capuchin missions. In 1656 the Uniate party felt strong enough to elect as their patriarch an old pupil of the Propaganda, though the opposition was fierce. In 1781 the Jacobite archbishop of

Aleppo, Michael Jarwa, who had been a Uniate since 1774, was elected to succeed the Jacobite patriarch and on 4 January 1782 was enthroned in Dayr Za'farān near Mardin, which was the patriarchal residence. A Jacobite competitor was soon on the scene, and he moved to Lebanon and went on governing his community from there. Here the line of Uniate Syrian patriarchs begins.

Peter Jarwa, patriarch since 1820 and confirmed by Rome in 1828, ruled an extensive patriarchate. With the emancipation of the Uniates in 1831 he was able to go to his native city of Aleppo and, as all the Jacobites there joined him, he found himself the possessor of a fine Church. In 1850 the Muslims burned down the residence, and he only just managed to escape in time.

Anthony Samharī, a Jacobite bishop whose conversion came when he discovered in the Jacobite patriarchal library a number of professions of faith made by previous patriarchs, was his successor. He met George V (Mār Ignatius XXX) and urged union with Rome. George V feared the consequences, but Samharī faced them. He proceeded to Mardin to preach his new faith. He attracted prelates, clergy and some 150 families and together they made submission to Rome in 1827. It was not long before the Jacobite archbishop of Damascus followed suit, and in 1832 the archbishop of Mosul did likewise.

Annoyed and afraid, the Jacobite patriarch issued threats and appealed to the Porte, but Samharī was able to reach Constantinople where, with French help, he obtained a *ferman* allowing him to continue his propaganda.

Mār Ignatius XXXI, Elias II, carried on the campaign against Samharī as far as contriving his imprisonment, and only the death of Elias II put an end to the persecution.

When Peter Jarwa died in 1851, Rome had appointed Samharī as administrator during the vacancy of the seat. Now in 1854 the synod in Sharfa made him patriarch and the first council of the Uniate Syrian Church was held. Samhārī settled upon Mardin as his residence, and he built a cathedral there. The Jacobite bishop Zaytūn went over to Rome also during this period. When the patriarch died in June 1864 the synod could not meet in Sharfa owing to the cholera epidemic, which ravaged vast areas of the country. Only six out of ten prelates succeeded in reaching Aleppo to elect Arqus, who went to Rome in April 1866. He died in 1874.

Under George Shalḥūd (Chelhod) (1874–92) the numbers were increased by 8,000, including three Jacobite prelates. He presided over the synod in Sharfa and built a church there. His Rome-educated successor Behman Benni (1893) was in continual conflict with the Jacobite archbishop of Mosul over which of the two archbishops should own the property belonging to the seat. He went to Rome on his appointment as patriarch, where he was much esteemed for his wisdom and generosity.

Mār Efrem Raḥmānī, who became the new patriarch on 9 October 1896, attracted many Jacobites to the fold. For personal reasons he obtained permission to reside in Beirut, and the permission has held ever since. He died in 1929 and the Sharfa synod elected Gabriel Tappuni, an old pupil of the Dominicans. Tappuni became the first cardinal of the Uniate Syrian Church, on 16 December 1935. Under him a reorganized Church has attracted many Jacobites, especially those living in Lebanon, including their archbishop, Mār Ḥannā Dandūr, who died in 1961.

The faithful are spread over Syria, Lebanon and Iraq, with considerable groups in Jordan, Egypt and the Americas. As a rule they speak Arabic, though in such parts as Ṭūr ʿAbdīn and around Mosul a Syriac dialect is still spoken.

THE UNIATE COPTIC CHURCH

From 1742 on the Uniate Copts were ruled by apostolic vicars. Since for civil affairs they came under the Coptic Orthodox patriarch they had no churches of their own until the Sultan Maḥmud II granted them emancipation. Late in the nineteenth century Pope Leo XIII realized the time had come to set up a Uniate Coptic hierarchy, and on 15 March 1895 the priest George Makarios became its first patriarch, as Cyril II. (The first Cyril was of Alexandria, who died in 444.) At the same time Rome nominated bishops for Upper Egypt.

Events did not turn out as expected. Cyril II had disputes with Rome, gave way in 1912, and died in Beirut in 1922. For forty years the seat remained unoccupied until it was filled again in 1947 by the promotion of the apostolic vicar Mark II Khuzām. The bishopric of Asyūṭ was created at the same time, and at King Fārūq's request diplomatic relations were assumed between Egypt and the Vatican. Mark II died in 1948 to be succeeded by Stephen I Sīdārūs. The adherents, about 5,000 in 1900, reached 14,576 by 1907, and 35,365 by 1931.

Egypt is perhaps the only country in the world where the seven rites recognized by the Roman Church co-exist. Leaving aside the Uniate Copts and the Latins, the other five rites add up to about 50,000 followers.

THE LATIN CHURCH IN EGYPT

Muḥammad 'Alī had thrown open the doors of Egypt to Western culture. Technicians came, and Latin and Evangelical missionaries in their train. The first religious orders arrived in 1847; Daughters of Charity, Brothers of the Good Shepherd, Brothers of the Christian Schools and over the years perhaps forty more orders of both sexes, devoted mainly to education and charity.

Muḥammad 'Alī's successors showed equal consideration to the Latins and this induced a feeling of security which led to a spate of building, yet with no joint planning. The fluctuations of Egyptian politics hardly touched the Latins. The hierarchy was restored in 1839 with the nomination of an apostolic vicar in Alexandria whose jurisdiction extended over the whole of Egypt. In 1909 Rome partitioned off the Delta and part of Cairo, and in 1926 the Canal company asked for a vicariate which lasted until the nationalization of the Suez Canal.

The security and prosperity enjoyed by Egypt, so different from that of the provinces of the Ottoman empire, induced a flow of Lebanese, Syrian, Palestinian and Armenian immigrants, particularly in times of persecution. Although all these groups started schools, most families sent their children to schools run by the Latin Churches. These groups have much in common. With their Oriental characteristics, sharing two cultures, they serve as a link between the Europeans and the native population. Mainly city-dwellers, they are increasingly discriminated against and denied State employment. Immigration has ceased, the birthrate has fallen, life is not easy for them, and there are many who consider the feasibility of going away for good.

In 1956 of the estimated 22,000,000 inhabitants of Egypt, 2,500,000 were Orthodox Copts, 200,000 Protestants, 100,000 Orthodox Greeks, and 200,000 Catholics. Since then mass emigration has cut these numbers considerably. Many schools unable to comply with new regulations have had to close down.

The opposite is the case with the Uniate Copts. Their numbers have grown, especially in Upper Egypt, and they now have a patriarch, five bishops and a national seminary. The community is made up of a large rural block in Upper Egypt and groups which have left there to settle in the poorer quarters of the large towns. From a social point of view this is the weakest of the Uniate communities, yet it is the most compact group in the country. Its peculiar situation makes it very dependent on the moral and material support of its brother communities. Uniates have never held many high offices of state, and now they hold none.

THE EVANGELICAL CHURCHES IN TURKEY

Evangelical missionaries began to enter Ottoman territory early in the nineteenth century. The welcome they had in Lebanon soon changed to open hostility from Orthodox and Maronites alike. Schools had to close their doors and adverse political circumstances—the Morea revolt, the battle of Navarino in 1827—made it prudent for them to fall back on Malta.

In 1830 Smith and Dwight went to Constantinople and on to Russian Armenia. Received with good grace by the senior Armenian clergy, they soon ran into the difficulties inherent in a mission to the countries of the Near East since they aroused animosity by their opposition to ancient ways and traditions of the people.

Giving up the original intention of a mission to the Muslims, reckoning it to be an impossible task, they began a similar campaign in other directions by distributing bibles, establishing schools, making useful contacts, and by works of charity. They opened a school in Pera in 1834 and had to close it in 1837 after the Gregorian Armenian clergy had protested in strong terms. Patriarch Stephen was regarded as too tolerant with the missionaries, and was replaced (1839) by Seropian who hurled anathemas at the Protestants and their well-wishers. It must be observed that excommunication was a serious matter under the *millet* system, for its effects extended throughout the whole empire. All Armenians were subject in civil matters to the patriarch; anyone excommunicated was outlawed from the *millet*, and lost his "nationality". Then at once the situation changed. In that year the sultan died, and the British ambassador, Canning, acquired his great influence on the Porte. His efforts procured the Protestants a license to found the Armenian Protestant Church with 2,000 members well outside the reach of the Gregorian Armenian patriarch; it was granted by the *ferman* of November 1850, which created the *millet prote*. This was an effective solution but not quite satisfactory, for it seemed to follow that the converts would no longer count as Armenians if they belonged to the Protestant "nation".

Under the *khaṭṭ-i hümayun* the missionaries felt that they had won their freedom, and now was the time to tackle the Muslims. A few were won over, but hopes were soon dashed by the events of 1860 and the foolish behaviour of some agents of the CMS. The CMS ceased its efforts in Istanbul, although the mission did not definitely close down until 1877.

In 1856 the American Board's mission, to facilitate its activities, divided into two sections, for North and South Turkey respectively; in 1860 they made another division into three parts: West Turkey with headquarters in Constantinople, Central Turkey operating from Gaziantep, and Eastern Turkey centred on Harput. From then on to 1890 the numbers of their pupils increased considerably.

The medical mission in Sivas went well under the direction of E. West, and doctors and nurses trained there were a great asset to the mission. The same may be said of the printed propaganda in many languages, especially in Turkish and Armenian.

In the year of the first Armenian massacres, 1894, the American Board had 152 missionaries, 802 native assistants (teachers, ministers, catechists) working in the mission, 12,000 converts and 25,000 pupils in the schools. The mission suffered grave losses during the massacres: 10,000 victims including 25 missionaries and 160 assistants. These horrible events aroused the compassion of Christians irrespective of creed and the Protestant societies channelled their aid through the American Board. By 1910 the mission possessed 20 principal stations, 269 secondary ones, 7 hospitals, 11 dispensaries, 185 American Board missionaries and 92 native ministers, 830 assistants, 16,000 communicants and 42,000 affiliates, 1,250 students in 8 colleges, and 21,000 pupils of both sexes in 352 elementary schools, and 30,000 in the Sunday Schools.

The domestic life of the missions was troubled for twenty-five years (1858–83) by administrative disputes between natives and missioners who, affected by a common Western superiority complex, wanted to spend their money how they liked, while the Orientals wanted a taste of the promised responsibility

Relations with the Gregorian Armenian Church improved as time went by. In the come and go of everyday life the presence of the new community was accepted as an irreversible fact; both had shared persecution and assistance alike. In dogma they were divided, and neither side would budge.

In 1909 the United States ambassador persuaded the Young Turks to remit the taxes of the Armenian Board and allow them to build schools and hospitals. But in that very year the massacres in Cilicia struck them a heavy blow: twenty-five pastors and preachers perished in Adana. Even worse were the consequences of the war of 1914–18. At the end of the war missionaries held a conference in Gaziantep, which was under French occupation. When the French retired the Armenians retired with them, leaving behind all they possessed.

Missionary work found no favour with the secular Turkish Republic. As the schools were forced to close, charitable endeavour intensified. Hopes of converting Muslims proved more and more chimerical. Just a few parishes held on in Istanbul and around Mardin, but the Armenian Evangelical Church was now the Church of the Diaspora, well outside Turkey.

THE EVANGELICAL MISSIONS IN SYRIA

The first missionaries of the American Board landed on the shores of Syria in 1823, the Presbyterians to work in Syria and the Congregationalists in Armenia. They were joined in 1843 by Presbyterians from the Free Church of Scotland and in 1856 the Reformed Presbyterian Church in North America. In 1876 came the missionaries of the Irish and Scottish Reformed Presbyterian Church who had stations in Alexandretta and Aleppo. The most important of all was the mission of the American Presbyterians who after working in isolation joined up with the American Board in 1870.

The Maronite massacres of 1860 stirred many Protestant organizations to action. In that year Mrs Bowen Thompson was largely instrumental in founding the British Syrian Mission to care for orphaned children. (It still operates (1946) in Damascus and Lebanon.) Medical missions began to arrive, and hospitals were erected. In 1861 the Prussian Order of the Hospitaller of St John founded one in Beirut, served by the Deaconesses of Kaiserswerth. In 1864 the Syrian Protestant College (it became the American University in 1926) opened a Medical Faculty which in course of time has developed into the American University Hospitals in Beirut. Quakers from the United Kingdom came to Syria to erect hospitals in 1869. In 1864 the Edinburgh Medical Missionary Society did the same, in Damascus. Other organizations founded their establishments, and in 1925 and 1927 during the French mandate came the Mission Médicale Evangélique du Levant and the Œuvres Protestantes Françaises. Also during the mandate missions were sent by Danish and Norwegian bodies, certain American sects such as the Nazarenes (1920), the Memnonites (1923) and the Christian Missions in many lands. The Armenian Evangelical Union of Syria and Lebanon was made up of Armenian Protestant refugees. There were also interdenominational organizations such as the Near East Christian Council, the Near East College Association, and the Christian Medical Association of Syria and Palestine.

THE PRESBYTERIAN MISSION IN LEBANON AND SYRIA

The Syrian missions began when the American Board of Commissioners for Foreign Missions sent one to Syria in 1823. Among the first converts in Lebanon were the brothers Shidyāq. The Maronite patriarch anathematized them and all who had dealing with the Protestants, the Greek Catholic patriarch copied his example, and the friendly attitude of the Greek Orthodox clergy changed to one of alarm. Patriarch Methodius wrote to Bird and Goodell on 27 March 1827 expressing thanks for their provision of schools of great benefit to all, but pointing out that these schools were a source of friction. The bishop of Tripoli supported the mission, but others "by the order of the patriarch and the wish of the people" caused the schools to be closed.

The political results of the Greek revolt against the Ottomans and its repercussions in Beirut made it advisable to withdraw to Malta. The unrest continued for two years. In 1933 founts of Oriental type were sent to Beirut to set up the American Press. The most important publication was the Bible in Arabic, to replace the one in use issued by the Propaganda in 1671. Much help was given by Buṭrus al-Bustānī, and the reviser Nāṣīf al-Yāzijī, officially a Uniate Melkite, spent his whole life working for the American Mission.

The Maronite hierarchy, with the Jesuit Fr. Planchet, renewed their attacks when the missionaries returned to Beirut; the letters they exchanged with Bird were the reverse of friendly on either side. Few conversions were made. The first chapel was opened in 1839.

During this period Muḥammad 'Alī's Egyptians had mastered Syria and imposed a military levy on the inhabitants. To avoid the scorn poured on the *millets* the Druzes had passed for Muslims, but when they discovered that they were liable to be levied, they tried turning Protestant. But the missionaries did not welcome mass conversions, and what the Druzes wanted was schools and protection, not conversion. Still, relations with the missionaries remained friendly.

In 1826–27 they had kept a flourishing school in Ḥāṣbayyā at the foot of Mount Hermon. In February 1844 about fifty men from Ḥāṣbayyā—Orthodox Greeks—turned up in Beirut with the object of turning Protestant. But their motives were far from spiritual—they were trying to avoid a tax they thought exorbitant. They were advised to pay up and make their peace with the community: then preachers would be sent. Early in July some 200 came over to Protestantism, but in the middle of the month word came that an armed party and five priests from Zḥaltā were coming to persuade them to re-enter the Orthodox fold. The British consul in Beirut persuaded them to go back, but there was a remaining group there who rose up and called on the Protestants to abjure or get out of the town. The men took refuge in the mountain. The Greek Orthodox patriarch went in person from Damascus to entice them back. It was not until July 1851 that things settled down.

The Druzes made an assault on the Maronites in May 1845 and the Protestant missionaries, surrounded by slaughter, were on sufficiently good terms with the Druzes to save several hundred Maronites and get them away to Beirut. The Maronite and Uniate Melkite patriarchs made public acknowledgement of their gratitude to the American Mission.

The missionaries had been in Aleppo in 1848 and witnessed the terrible scenes of the Muslim revolt in October–November 1850, but the mission among the refugee Armenians was not properly on its feet until after the First World War. Other stations opened about that time were Tripoli (1848), Sidon and Dayr al-Qamar (1855), complete with their schools.

At the end of May 1860 the widespread massacre of Maronites began. The missionaries of Dayr al-Qamar managed to save a hundred people on 25 June, but in Ḥāṣbayyā, in spite of the promises of the commander of the Turkish garrison, the Protestants and the other Christians were beheaded on 11 June.

After the massacre more help arrived, and more stations were established. The native Protestants started their own missionary societies, but as one missionary said, one had to proceed with caution: "in Syria and above all with Maronites, the threat of turning Protestant or Jew or Muslim is the usual way to bully its own clergy without the slightest intention of doing so".

In 1866 the Syrian Protestant College opened its doors to sixteen students. Next year there was a medical school, and gradually the numbers of buildings and pupils increased. In 1870 the American Board handed over the Syrian and Persian missions to the Presbyterian Board. This had little consequence, for they retained the same missionary equipment. Then the number of native consistories was increasing, from the first formation at Sidon (Ṣaydā) in 1883.

The promulgation of the Turkish Constitution in 1908 aroused great expectations, as witness the call from the World Missionary Conference in Edinburgh to go out and evangelize the Muslims of Syria and Palestine. Hopes were once more dashed by the Balkan War and the First World War. Sufferings in Lebanon during the war were acute. The Turks banned all civilian aid, and the mission had to smuggle money from the refugees to their families.

After the war things looked better. Till then the Presbyterian Board had been content to restrict its activities to the coastal cities, but as communication improved and the Ottoman empire disappeared, the missions reached the Euphrates and opened stations in Aleppo, Dayr al-Zūr and other places, with the object of converting Islam. But the psychological barrier to converting a Muslim made any advance practically impossible.

In 1924 the three consistories of Sidon (1883), Tripoli (1890) and Beirut (1894) joined to form the synod of the Syrian Evangelical Church, a name later changed to the Protestant Synod of Syria and Lebanon. Their evangelical activities are directed towards conversion, schools, charity and the press.

The Syrian Protestant College was raised to university rank governed by the Board of the Trustees of the American University of Beirut; in 1960 it had 3,500 students.

On 28 January 1958 the Presbyterian Board closed the mission as such and merged it with the National Evangelical Church of Syria, without implying any break in personnel or supplies.

THE ANGLICAN DIOCESE OF JERUSALEM

Christians have never ceased to be attracted to Jerusalem and most rites and creeds are represented in the Holy City. The first Protestants in Palestine were those sent by the American Board, working from

1821 to 1844 among the Jews and Eastern Christians. Jerusalem was its first centre, whence they went on to Beirut in 1844 to confine their activities to Syria and Armenia.

It was the London Society for promoting Christianity among the Jews, founded in 1809, which paved the way for the Anglo-Prussian diocese of Jerusalem. Their principal agent was Nicolayson who worked there from 1826 until his death in 1856.

Frederick William IV of Prussia, the Anglican Church, and the British government all had a share in founding the diocese. Their object was to regenerate the "fossil and degenerate" Eastern Churches, give some sense of purpose to the *millet prote*, and assist Nicolayson's efforts to build up a diocese, with and for the Jews. There were many obstacles to be surmounted and a good deal of opposition to overcome before the British government approved the foundation of the bishopric in 1841. The bishop was to be Lutheran and Anglican in turn, and he had to subscribe to the 39 Articles and be consecrated by an Anglican bishop. His rule would extend over Palestine, Syria, Mesopotamia, Egypt and the Sudan. His main purpose was to convert the Jews and maintain friendly relations with the other Churches, especially the Greek Orthodox.

The first bishop was Salomon Alexander, a Polish Jew consecrated in 1841, who came to Jerusalem in January 1842 and began to work on the lines indicated. He had no trouble with the Orthodox, and died while visiting Egypt in 1845.

Samuel Gobat, a Swiss who had previously been sent to Abyssinia and then to Malta, was consecrated in 1846, and in Jerusalem found a small community of no more than fifty members. To add to these was a problem: his Jews were scarce, and he had little hope of finding more. He did get some proselytes from the Orthodox Greeks, and these were promptly excommunicated by their hierarchy. Voices were raised in England: the bishopric, they said, had not been founded to turn Orthodox Greeks into Anglicans. Gobat went on trying and called German missionaries to his aid, and when he died in 1876 the diocese possessed a seminary, various churches and stations, and thirty-three schools with 1,300 pupils.

Bishop Barclay, next in line, spent only two years in office, before his death in 1881. It was now the turn of the Prussian government to appoint a successor, but instead it denounced the pact and withdrew its annual subsidy. This left the Anglicans to proceed to the election alone. To avoid difficulties with the Anglo-Catholics it was decided to change the title from bishop *of* Jerusalem to bishop *in* Jerusalem, and to call the church of St George not "cathedral" but "collegiate church", so as to recognize the Orthodox patriarch of Jerusalem as the sole bishop, and the Church of the Holy Sepulchre as the only cathedral.

The next bishop was G. F. Popham Blyth. In 1891 he voiced several complaints against the Church Missionary Society, one being that they were still trying to capture Greek Orthodox converts. These complaints were examined by a commission of five Anglican bishops, and their verdict gave implicit freedom to the CMS, and relations between the bishop and the Society became very strained. In contrast, the Greek Orthodox were sympathetic, and their patriarch gave him the use of a chapel in the Church of the Holy Sepulchre as a token of his esteem. The London Jews Society was more to Blyth's liking, and with them he founded the Jerusalem and Eastern Mission.

R. MacInnes succeeded Blyth when he died in 1914. During his tenure Palestine came under the British mandate. He got on well enough with the Orthodox, even if his exertions with the Muslims and Jews came to very little. In 1920 he lost control of Egypt and the Sudan, which became a separate diocese. The Newman School of Mission was opened in 1928 for the training of missionaries, and the same year saw the erection of a large building for the YMCA.

Graham Brown followed MacInnes in 1942. By now a host of evangelical bodies had a foot in Palestine: the American Quakers, the United Free Church of Scotland, the Baptists, the Evangelical Society of Jerusalem, the Tabitha Kumi school, the Deaconesses of Kaiserswerth, the Pentecostals, the Christian Missionary Alliance, the Palestine Village Mission, and others from Germany, Sweden and Finland.

THE EVANGELICAL CHURCHES IN EGYPT

By 1825 the agents of the Church Missionary Society had reached Egypt. The patriarch and clergy of the Coptic Orthodox Church were friendly enough, but not the Orthodox Greeks. Its directives were to win the approval of the Eastern clergy and through them induce some reform into their Church. In Cairo a boarding school was opened which later (1942) became a seminary for Coptic Clergy. The mission had much to contend with, and Gobat, the second Bishop of the Jerusalem diocese paid them a visit in 1849, for Egypt was then in his diocese. He reported that results had not come up to expectation. The CMS at its annnal conference (May 1851) decided to restrict its activities, and they were finally abandoned in 1862.

When the British occupied Egypt the CMS renewed its activities, this time not directed primarily towards the Copts, but to the Muslims. In 1920 Egypt and the Sudan were separated from the Jerusalem diocese to form an independent one, a step taken on account of the great number of British subjects residing in Egypt and the Sudan. The CMS still had charge of propaganda.

The United Presbyterian Church of North America aimed to cover a wider field (they are not to be confused with the Presbyterian Church of the United States of America, which confined its operations to Syria). This mission had been started by the Associated Reformed Presbyterian Church in 1854, and the United Presbyterian Church took over its activities. Like most Protestant missions in these countries, they began with the object of winning over Muslims as much as Christian and Jews, but since other bodies were dealing with the Jews, and as Muslims would not be converted anyway, they directed their efforts at the Christians. The United Presbyterian Church mission expanded without much difficulty under the patriarch Cyril X (1854–61) and the Khedive Sa'īd (1854–63). It was less easy to counter the hostility of the Coptic patriarch Demetrius II (1861–73) and the Khedive Ismā'īl (1863–80), until the time of the British occupation in 1882. This mission did much to provide educational facilities, and their Women's General Missionary Society helped with their colleges for women in Alexandria and Luxor, a hospital in Ṭanṭā, an orphanage and their work in child welfare.

All these endeavours led to the formation of the Evangelical Church of Egypt (also known as the Synod of the Nile) with three presbyteries in Egypt, three in the Sudan, and 139 communities of 20,000 souls.

Many other groups of various denominations have worked or are working in Egypt: the Pentecostals, the Assemblies of God, the Canadian Holiness Mission, the Pentecostal Faith Mission, the Peniel Missionary Society, the Apostelstrasse, the North African Mission. Some had the Jews as their object, such as the London Jews Society. Others were aimed at the Muslims: the Egypt Salaam Mission, the Evangelische Mohammedaner Mission, the Egypt General Mission, the Central Literature Committee for Muslims. It remains to mention: the Church of God, the Standard Church of America, the Deaconesses of

Kaiserswerth, the Seventh Day Adventists, the YMCA and YWCA with centres in Cairo and Alexandria, and last but not least the American University of Cairo, an interdenominational institution which since its foundation in 1920 has exercised a great influence on the culture of the country.

THE JEWS

"A nation neither alive nor dead." Thus Leo Pinsker, an Odessan doctor of the nineteenth century. As a people with its own land, language and institutions, it had no existence. It was a nation with foreign countries for a fatherland, united only in its dispersion. But a race which had borne centuries of adversity was not as dead as might appear. It was a phantom nation inspiring terror, and therefore, hate.

Their talent for adaptation to, and adoption of, the ways of their neighbours, a resort always open to the downtrodden, makes it difficult to form a just estimate of the condition of the Jews in the ancient Ottoman empire. To begin with we must distinguish between the lot of the majority and the easier life of groups like the sephardim of Salonika and the well-to-do families in Constantinople.

As for the bulk of the people all over the empire, the reports of consuls and travellers are in close agreement. Lane, in his well-known book on the Egyptians of his time, says that in Cairo there were 5,000 Jews in a poverty-stricken ghetto, well penned-in against any possible disturbances. The Muslims hated and harassed them. The women were dressed like the rest. Even the wealthy dressed meanly when they walked abroad. Many were *ṣarrāfs*, lenders or changers of money; others kept shops or worked in metal. All avoided any appearance of prosperity.

Similar accounts were written of the Jews in Iraq, in those days mainly congregated in the large towns. They claimed (and so to this day do those few still there) to be the descendants of the Babylonian exile. Monopolizing banking and commerce, their wealth occasioned much animosity, for the officials, high and low, seized any pretext to relieve them of their gains; but they had to proceed with caution, for the wealthy Jews had protectors at the Porte; moreover from the late nineteenth century they could count on the support of the Universal Israelitish Alliance, as more than one governor found to his cost.

The Jews in Palestine were most numerous in Jerusalem and Tiberias, marked by their grim appearance and reserved disposition, and careless of their attire.

In Izmir and Edirne, and even more in Salonica and Constantinople, there were small groups socially and intellectually superior to the majority of Jews in Turkey. The *ḥakham bashî*, chief rabbi, was the head of the Jewish *millet*. 30,000 Jews lived in Constantinople, mainly near the Golden Horn, with others close to the Bosphorus; the wealthier preferred Pera. The Sephardim of Salonica were the most important element in the commerce of the city and still spoke an archaic form of Spanish. In all, there must have been 300,000 Jews in the empire. They were regarded with disdain, but their activities were little restricted. The Ottomans were not backward when it came to taxing Jews, but these had their own ways of circumvention. The State schools were open to them and quite a number arrived at positions of importance in the professions. During the hard times of 'Abdülḥamid's regime their condition was better than that of other *millets* more mistrusted by the sultan. Authors are agreed that the Jews were better off in the Ottoman empire than in Russia or Rumania, and a constant stream left these countries for Turkey to find their fellow Turkish Jews living under much better conditions.

With the accession of Alexander III to the Russian throne the Jews in Russia fell a prey to the methodical persecutions called *pogrom*: assaults, looting, assassinations, all in full view of the indifferent authorities. The only escape was emigration. Thus was born the movement BILU (*Beyṯ Ya'aqoḇ lēkhu we-nelkha*: "House of Jacob, let us depart", Isaiah ii. 5). It was founded by students who went to Palestine, whose 350,000 inhabitants included 30,000 Jews, about equally divided between Ashkenazim and Sephardim who had come between 1850 and 1880; many of them were living on supplies received from the Diaspora, *galuth*. With the *'aliyah* of Russian fugitives, organized and directed by the BILU, 300 families reached Palestine in 1882. They continued to come, fired by the ideas of the new Zionism. They acquired land and started agricultural colonies. The Turkish government paid no attention at first, then took alarm at the rapid growth of these colonies, and in 1890, new entrants were prohibited. "Temporary visitors" were allowed in, but once inside the authorities were powerless, protected as the visitors were by the foreign consuls.

Meanwhile the "Friends of Zion" was moving in the direction of political Zionism, and its ideas were stirring and gaining ground in the *galuth*, under the influence of Herzl. He believed that progressive colonization was not viable without some political impulse from the great Powers.

The Russian crisis of 1905 brought with it more pogroms, and an *'aliyah* of immigrants imbued with new social aspirations; these groups under the name of *poale Zion* were socialists who saw that the real solution of the Jewish problem lay in Palestine.

There were dissensions enough in the communities. Many rabbis who had been drawn into the movement had insisted from the first that life in the Palestine colonies must have a religious basis, with wardens under their direction. Others opposed, saying that the colonists were not a religious body but a national advance guard, and religion was a purely private concern. Herzl was all for religious liberty.

These liberal and modernist ideas had not touched Eastern Judaism. They were first introduced by the Russian *'aliyah* of 1904 and the following years. But there were plenty of Near Eastern Jews, and even some of the newcomers from Russia and Poland, whose prejudice against these ideas and against modern education went so far as the excommunication of those who sent their children to the numerous schools which the Israelite Alliance had established in Turkey.

In 1906 there were 450,000 Jews in the Ottoman empire, in scattered groups which had little to do with each other. The year 1911 saw the foundation of modern Tel Aviv south of Jaffa. By 1914 it was the centre of a tough and active population, quite distinct from the Arabs and Muslims. Modern Hebrew was gaining ground, in the schools and in everyday life. The war (1914) brought this to a halt.

During the war the Zionists had obtained the Balfour Declaration, 1917. After the war, the twenty-five years of British Mandate over Palestine was passed in attempts to reconcile the irreconcilable, with protests from the Arabs, more or less violent or legal as mandatory policies went from one extreme to another, with the corresponding Jewish reactions.

With the coming of the Second World War all sides hoped to recover what had been lost, but when the major conflicts ceased local ones began with ever increasing fury, with the Jews in an advantageous position. The proposals of the United Nations came to nothing before the negative and intransigent attitude of the antagonists. Then the British government announced its decision to give up the Mandate on 15 May 1948, and on that day the National Zionist Council, assembled in Tel Aviv, proclaimed the foundation of the State of Israel.

Officially Israel is a secular state; freedom of conscience is guaranteed by the State. In 1963 it ruled about two million Jews, 175,000 Muslims, 53,000 Christians and 24,000 Druzes.

In Jewry one can trace every shade of religious attitude from extreme orthodoxy to atheism. The Orthodox Jews make up 10 per cent of the Jewish population. Their ideal is a theocratic state based on the Torah, and theirs is no mere abstract principle, but a stern reality. Since their votes in the Chamber are vital to the government's precarious majority, they have an importance out of all proportion to their numbers.

The State, though secular in principle, has its own religious problems. Not only does it have its own differences with the synagogue and the chief rabbinate, it has to cope with disputes between believers and non-believers, and between the moderates and extremists. There are the Karaites who put their faith in the Scriptures, and nothing else, and the Rabbanites who accord equal authority to the Talmud. The hostility has reached such a pitch that the Rabbanites refuse to recognize their opponents as Jews. After all, there are only 15,000 of them in Israel.

Another splinter group is the Reformed Synagogue, which was first formed in Germany during the nineteenth century. One third of United States Jews belong to this movement. The World Order for Progressive Judaism was anxious to introduce this movement into Israel, where there were many Jews who did not take kindly to rigid orthodoxy and were very ready to join a moderate movement. As usual, the orthodox opposition was violent, but in 1955 the prime minister, Ben Gurion urged them to come: "Israel must reform itself. Set up your liberal synagogue. Liberty of conscience and of religion must cease to be mere words. Let the young people see that there are other kinds of Jews. I know those. Most of them have not God in their hearts." On the other hand, Ben Gurion did not understand why people should need religion.

Sabbath observance has been a bone of contention from the foundation of Israel. It is not regulated by State law, although there are some municipal regulations (1964). In Jerusalem these are stringent: there is no public transport on the Sabbath day from Friday night to Saturday night; private vehicles are not prohibited and often orthodox bands do their utmost to prevent their circulation, not always refraining from violence which leads to clashes with the police and such opposition groups as the "League against Religious Coercion".

There are also the *neturei karta*, so firmly opposed to Zionism that they will not recognize the State, to the extent of refusing to carry identity cards. They comprise some 300 families, almost all in one

Jerusalem quarter. The present State is to them a figment; the restoration of the Jewish State must await the coming of the Messiah. Their ideology is shared by many Orthodox Jews, as for instance those of the Agudat Israel.

Different again is the Mizrachi group, who court the lay organizations, hoping to bring them to a fuller religious life, ultimately to accept a theocracy.

This fragmentation and the passions it arouses, plus a freedom of speech and publication which sometimes verges on licence, set the rulers of the country a difficult and delicate task. No one yet, not even the administration, has been able to say precisely who is, or can be called, a Jew. In 1946 Moshe Sharett defined it: a Jew is one who in good faith declares himself to be a Jew. Officials of the registration in 1958 were told to take on trust any declarations relative to personal status or marriage, and that the word "Jew" must be interpreted in its civil and not its religious sense. These instructions called forth strong protests from religious quarters, and another government crisis arose over arguments with the Rabbinate as to who should decide the question.

It is not easy to reconcile the theoretically democratic and practically Jewish characters of the new State. The case of P. Daniel, a Polish Jew converted to Catholicism, is only one of many. He entered Israel in 1959, and under the law whereby any Jewish immigrant automatically takes on Jewish nationality he claimed this right. When this was denied him, he took his case to the Cabinet, which decided that a Jew who adopts another religion ceases to be a Jew: a confusion (or distinction?) between ethnic group and religious creed. In Israel, a secular state, a baptized Jew finds life impossible. There are many families of mixed religion who find themselves in a tragic situation, tormented by their neighbours and with their children taunted at school. Since the birth of the new State the orthodox party has begun an active Press campaign against the "Mission", a name which embraces all Christian schools, and implies their obedience to some mythical international entity or organization. The chief rabbinate has attacked the "Mission" through the Merkaz association, and has on occasion taken direct and illegal action. In 1955 the *Keren Yaldena* was founded to wage the same war under the aegis of the Mizrachi party of the grand rabbinate, and under the not unkindly eye of the ministry of Cults. All Jews dislike missionaries, even if they are not prepared to use violence or overstep the law. To them apostasy is treason. They admit that one born into another religion can be loyal to the State, but an apostate Jew never. Propaganda was particularly directed at keeping Jewish children out of Christian schools, and this is still going on. The ministry gave some figures for 1960: 10,822 pupils in Christian schools, of whom 1,458 were Jewish. It allowed that the mission schools were protected by international laws and agreements, but that attendance at such schools was not likely to turn young Jews into good Jews and Hebrews; nevertheless the liberty of parents must be respected. By 1964 there were only 900 Jewish scholars in those schools, and a mere hundred in missionary schools properly so called. The Catholics taught about 600 Jews. Since 1950 eleven Jewish children and about 200 adults have become Christians or Muslims, while 407 non-Jews have embraced Judaism.

It must be stressed that this is not an anti-Christian movement. It is directed against the "Mission", seen as an active agent of proselytism. If life can be made impossible for the missionaries, they will have to go. The freedom-thinkers, on the other hand, see no reason why anyone should not practise any religion he chooses, and deplore that a State calling itself secular should impose religious restrictions, and its opposition to rigid orthodoxy is growing.

In July 1958 the Latin patriarch sent the government a memorandum maintaining that the decision as to whether a man was a Jew or not should relate to his civil and national standing and not to his religion, and pointing out that the problem of mixed families had not found an equitable solution, that the minister's agents were bringing pressure to bear on the Christian party of mixed families to accept Judaism with threats that a Christian child had no future in Israel, and that in social and working life there was religious discrimination.

As in other countries of the Near East, in Israel the *status quo* of the recognized creeds was still maintained, for the legislation in force during the British Mandate had been accepted wholesale. This had recognized in 1932 these Churches: Greek Orthodox, Armenian Orthodox, Syrian Orthodox, Greek Catholic, Armenian Catholic, Syrian Catholic, Chaldean Catholic, Jewish, Maronite, and Latin. The Muslims did not appear in the list because it had up till then been the official religion, nor did the Druzes, for the Ottoman empire had never recognized them at all. There are some 20,000 Druzes in Israel, on good terms with the State. A law of 21 April 1957 put an end to their anomalous position by placing them on equality with the other Churches.

The announcement of the Vatican Council aroused great interest in Jewish circles. The World Conference of Jewish Organizations sent a note to Pope John XXIII on the desirability of certain changes in church doctrine. Cardinal Bea's declaration that the death of Jesus was only attributed to a minority of the Jewish race since some were Christians and many more had been ignorant of the event was received favourably on the whole. The visit of Pope Paul VI to the Holy Places early in 1964 and the findings of the Vatican Council on the Jews gave rise to less favourable comments.

CHAPTER 23

THE CULTURAL ASPECT
WITH SPECIAL REFERENCE TO EGYPT AND SYRIA

(1)

The co-existence today of Judaism, Christianity and Islam in the lands of their origin is due in no small measure to a tolerant Islam. As the last and most militant of the three it did not seek, in an age of intolerance, to eliminate its predecessors and rivals. Not only had it no positive policy of suppression when it was at the height of its political power, it had in fact a positive one of co-existence.

From the beginning caliphs and military commanders made special allowance for the protection of their Jewish and Christian subjects, and contrary to popular belief Islam was not imposed upon them at the point of the sword or indeed by any systematic means. On the contrary, Jews and Christians were immediately recognized as *ahl al-kitāb* (the people of the book), to whom earlier divine messages had been sent through God's prophets. Although according to the Muslim view these messages had been corrupted, there was still a residue of truth which deserved respect.

But as the final divine message to mankind, Islam came to correct and perfect these previous messages. Hence there was no question of absolute equality with its predecessors. At any rate the notion of religious equality is of fairly recent origin, and even in our own times it is still an ideal which is seldom attained. But barring concession of equality to other religions Islam was tolerant of them, both in theory and in practice. It is true that practice had occasionally fallen below the standards of theory, but its validity was irrevocable because it is enshrined in the divine revelation itself.

It is clear then that the doctrine of religious tolerance in Islam has an idealistic origin. When it was first proclaimed and practised in the seventh century A.D. it must have appeared in sharp contrast to the contemporary fanaticism, interdenominational strife and persecution amongst the Christians themselves in the Byzantine Empire. As a measure of practical politics the Islamic doctrine of religious tolerance was amply vindicated by the ready welcome of the Muslim armies by the Christians and Jews in Syria and elsewhere in the Near East.

Hence it is fallacious to allege, as it has recently become fashionable to allege, that "the people of the book" were treated by the Islamic state as "second-class citizens". The allegation is fallacious not only because it projects into the distant and different past the comparatively modern notion of equality of all citizens irrespective of their religious beliefs, but also because it ignores the view which non-Muslims *at the time* held of their status under Muslim rule. Could they have had a better status elsewhere?

Their status was of course regulated by mutual agreement. Jews and Christians were allowed a wide measure of communal autonomy under their spiritual leaders. They were guaranteed freedom of worship, possession of their places of worship, and safety of person and property. No duties were imposed other than payment of poll-tax. Those who nowadays argue that this tax itself is, according to the Qur'ān, a mark of inferiority, must not forget that the tax was in theory as well as in practice in return for the privileges mentioned and in lieu of military service. Muslims paid a comparable tax but had to serve in the army.

Such, in very broad outline, is the relationship established between the first Islamic state and its Jewish and Christian subjects. It is on the whole to their advantage. Lapses of intolerant times are undeniable, but for our present purpose it is more important to note that the early tolerant policy contributed to a gradual and voluntary assimilation of the bulk of the indigenous population in the Near East by the Muslim conquerors.

The process of assimilation was in the main linguistic and religious: the Arabic language and the Muslim faith were slowly but surely adopted by the native non-Arab and non-Muslim population of the Near East. No doubt the process was aided by the racial and general cultural affinity between the conquerors and their subjects. The consequences of assimilation were of immense significance. It left its permanent mark on the Islamic civilization that emerged.

Partly therefore because of the essential tolerance of Islam, and partly because of the broad basis of the civilization that grew under its aegis, there was room in the Islamic state for minorities: religious, racial and linguistic. Not only were such minorities allowed to exist, but they were encouraged to take part in shaping the Islamic civilization. Jewish and Christian names in its history are indeed numerous, but on account of its different background and numerical strength the Christian element was more amenable to assimilation.

The form and degree of assimilation naturally varied, but barring the acceptance of Islam, its most effective means was the adoption of the Arabic language for cultural expression, be it in speech or in literary production. Those who accepted both Islam and Arabic were of course more completely assimilated in the predominant community. Those who chose to remain faithful to their religion but adopted only the Arabic language constituted the bulk of the religious minorities. The process in both directions was gradual, but before the eclipse of the historic caliphate the religious and linguistic character of the Near East was fairly determined.

This is in brief the historic origin of the religious mosaic in Arab Asia which was inherited by the Ottoman Empire. It remained substantially the same till internal and external forces began to stir the peoples of the area a little before the dawn of the nineteenth century. There was then a predominant Arab Muslim majority; there were also important Arab Christian minorities, and apart from certain racial and religious groups there were small Jewish minorities. With but a few notable exceptions the Jewish minorities in the Near East did not participate in the stream of modern Arab cultural history as important Jewish minorities did in earlier times, for example in Spain. They chose to live apart with their essentially exclusive Hebrew culture, and when in recent times political Zionism was introduced among them, the Jews may be considered to have turned their back on cultural, let alone political, collaboration with the Arabs.

On the other hand the Christians showed from an early date a desire to share a common cultural, and political destiny with the Muslims. The most potent force that drew the two sides together was, of course, the common heritage of the Arabic language and Arabic literature. But there were also forces working in the other direction. From the early sixteenth century the Arab lands, the central heritage of the historic caliphate, formed part of the Ottoman Empire. Its administrative system, based largely on precedents set by the early Arab Muslim conquerors, provided for autonomous religious communities. Under this system each community (*millet*) in the Ottoman Empire led a separate life of its own which minimized intercommunal contact and co-operation. Thus Jews and Christians, even those whose speech and literary expression was Arabic, had till the last century very little direct contact with the Arab Muslims. Even in large cities Jews, Christians and Muslims lived in separate quarters, their children went to different schools, and even the crafts and professions which members of each community followed were different.

(2)

Some change in this social order began to take place in the eighteenth century and more perceptibly in the nineteenth. It was brought about by internal and external forces. Details need not detain us, but suffice it for our purpose to isolate for some consideration those forces that tended to break communal barriers and to bring Arab Christians and Arab Muslims closer together in Egypt and Syria. This study will primarily concentrate on the two countries.

It is little recognized that the revivalist movements among the Muslim Arabs had, even before the dawn of the nineteenth century, their parallels among the Christian Arabs, with one essential difference: while the former were of native origin, the latter was on the whole the work of foreign agencies. The rise of the Wahhābī and Sanūsī and other movements in the bosom of Islam require no elaboration here, but one of its products was a renewal of interest in the Islamic heritage, chiefly religious and Arabic studies. The foreign agencies among the Christian Arabs were principally religious missions, first Catholic but later also Protestant, whose activities produced similar interest in religious and Arabic studies. It must, however, be acknowledged that missionary work tended to sharpen denominational strife, and actually did upset the Christian communal equilibrium by the creation of new sects.

Nor is it sufficiently recognized that the efforts of the Ottoman statesmen at introducing reform or reorganization had as one of its products the breaking of some of the communal barriers by admitting Christians and Jews to office and to membership of local councils and state schools. Although introduced partly with the object of satisfying European criticism of the Ottoman system, the reforms were primarily intended to arrest the decline of the Empire and to restore vitality to its system. These measures were neither a conscious attempt to alter the substance of the system nor to change its underlying principles. Nevertheless their operation was destined to produce these very results.

The reform or reorganization was prompted originally by military consideration. The Ottoman armies, once invincible and the terror of Europe, began to suffer humiliating defeat when confronted by European forces using new weapons and new technical skills, the product of a profound scientific and industrial revolution. The disparity was partly educational and the need to remove it was recognized by thoughtful statesmen. But they had to contend with opposition from a powerful corps of *'ulamā'*, often in alliance with the notorious corps of the janissaries. The first genuinely feared that the social order of the community would be harmed, the second selfishly desired to perpetuate their vested interest in the profession of arms.

In the end the *'ulamā'* acquiesced in a compromise. The traditional system of education under their care was preserved intact, but a new state system was introduced to train army officers and civil servants. Thus the seeds of future doom were sown with the tacit approval of the *'ulamā'* who could not anticipate the consequences. Never did they realize that in learning the use of European weapons the young Muslims would also have to learn the language of the infidel, and through it his alien ideas. Nor did they realize that technical military education was only the first opening of the flood gates.

Tentative experiments on these lines were followed in 1839 by an imperial decree which laid down principles for future action. Commonly known as the Noble Rescript of the Rose Chamber, the *khaṭṭ-i sherif* of Gülhane, paid tribute to the old familiar order only to usher in measures for an unknown new order. It formally inaugurated the *tanẓimat* or reorganization by which gradually, and under different guises, legal, administrative, financial and educational innovations were grafted on to the traditional system. The origin of these innovations was Christian Europe. But those who presided over the process took precautions to declare, at times sincerely, at others perhaps cynically, and on the whole recklessly, that they were in conformity with the spirit of Islamic tradition.

It has ultimately become common knowledge that these innovations had the effect of undermining the tradition and what was based thereon. One of the new measures deserves closer examination here: the equality of all Ottoman subjects irrespective of religion. It was conceded in principle, and to a certain extent in practice, largely to satisfy European criticism. What was the outcome? Muslim public opinion remained against it, but the Christian subjects of the sultan were also against it—

in a different way and for different reasons. Although some of them accepted office and sat on central and local government councils side by side with Muslims, they generally kept their children away from state schools legally open to them. More indicative of their attitude was their evasion of the newly imposed duty of military service. Non-Muslims invariably bought their exemption with money, thus themselves restoring the payment of the "humiliating" poll-tax which under the new dispensation was abolished both to placate Europe and to conciliate the Christian subjects. In practice, therefore, the Christian subjects of the sultan, encouraged no doubt by European interests, desired to enjoy privileges but to assume no duties; equality without responsibility.

This attitude has its origin in habits of communal isolation formed over many centuries, and was moreover fostered by the potent agency of education. Native Christian schools naturally stressed the separate communal identity of their pupils. Foreign schools promoted in addition the religious and cultural ideology of their country of origin. Both types of schools cultivated, whether by chance or design, virtual disloyalty to both the legitimate government and the common fatherland. Such contradictions between theory and practice were never broken till the advent of secular nationalism.

(3)

Before that stage was reached, however, political and religious developments of great importance took place which tended to emphasize, rather than neutralize, communal separation and to jeopardize the little advance made towards religious equality under the reform measures. The measures which had been adopted for achieving such an equality were, as already mentioned, inspired, or rather prompted, by the European powers. But by their action in annexing Muslim territory in Europe, Asia and Africa they aroused grave suspicion and intense resentment which lost them the moral strength of their assumed role of mentors. European aggression was indeed a major factor in rekindling religious polemics and fanning the flames of dormant antagonism.

Small wonder if these feelings were soon embraced by powerful elements among the '*ulamā*', the intellectuals and politicians. But all of them were really powerless to do more than offer negative, defensive resistance. In the process they tended to reassert the Islamic character of the Empire, and from this position they moved towards staking a claim for the sultan to be counted as the caliph of all Muslims, whether they were his own subjects or subjects of other sovereigns. The *raison d'être* of the pan-Islamic movement was thus formed, and the birth of the movement may be seen, in a sense, as a response to Christian challenge.

For a generation or two the Arab Muslim was naturally drawn to the movement while the Arab Christian must have viewed it either with indifference or with disapproval. If he was definitely hostile, his hostility may be traced to attitudes built up over centuries as well as to European influence which confirmed the Christians in asserting their communal identity.

Since the Greek revolt against Ottoman rule which won the open sympathy of the major Christian powers, other Christian subjects hoped to achieve their national independence in the same way with some European help. Only the Arabic-speaking Christians did not entertain such ambitions. They did so only when they joined forces with their Muslim brethren in the Arab national movement in the twentieth century. Before that they were torn between loyalties to foreign patrons and ties of language and domicile with their Muslim compatriots. Ottoman loyalty they had practically none; and if anything, the pan-Islamic movement aroused their fears and suspicions. Those of them who were educated in schools sponsored by French organizations desired some form of French protection; others for similar reasons wanted English or Russian protection. Thus sectarian education, under European control, played a great part in maintaining, nay aggravating, the communal separatism.

And yet European influence contributed to the ultimate co-operation of Christian with Muslim, and led the former to his destiny perhaps more by chance than by design. The kind of influence meant here is cultural. Needless to say, that European cultural penetration was easier to accomplish among the Christians. The process had an earlier start than is commonly recognized. Outside the spheres of commerce and diplomacy its earliest significant manifestation was perhaps the re-establishment of the connexion, first begun during the Crusades, between the Church of Rome and the Maronites in Lebanon. Then early in the eighteenth century this connexion was formalized in a concordat, and the way was open for Catholic religious and educational missions, especially those of the Jesuits.

As the great Catholic power, France took early interest in the cultural penetration of the Near East, and used her capitulatory rights to enhance French prestige and influence. Almost all Catholic religious and cultural establishments in the Ottoman Empire claimed and received French protection. In Rome itself the Pope established institutions for the education of the clergy of the Eastern churches which accepted his supremacy. Several Maronite prelates received their education in these institutions. Not only they, but also to a lesser degree, those of their flocks who enjoyed humbler education at the hands of Catholic missionaries in Syria, acquired a new world view, more in sympathy with Christian Europe than with the Muslim East.

But despite this disqualification many Christian Arabs in the Near East were sometimes found by virtue of their special educational qualifications more useful than Muslims for employment in such departments as customs and finance. Not only Muḥammad 'Alī but also other provincial governors in Syria were quite ready to employ Christian Arabs in various capacities as secretaries, accountants, tax-collectors or customs officials. At the same time many other Christian Arabs found employment as dragomans or agents in European consulates in Syria and Egypt. They fitted themselves for these tasks not merely by their rudimentary knowledge of European methods but also by their skill in the use of languages, including their native Arabic.

For parallel with European influence there grew among certain Christian Arabs an assiduous cultivation of Arabic. Partly inspired by the need for educated clergy, partly by a utilitarian desire to acquire secretarial qualifications, this Christian Arab interest in the native tongue coincided with a less restricted and more vigorous revival of the traditional learning among the Muslim Arabs. To the historian the two movements appear separate and communal, but a closer look extending over several decades reveals increasing interaction, at first imperceptible but later unmistakable. Increasing use of the printing press in Egypt and Syria, the rise of a modest venture in Arabic journalism and a general spread of education through native private schools, Ottoman state schools and foreign mission schools, all contributed their share to the revival.

(4)

Gradually hazy ideas of common interests began to be formed. The Christian Arab and Muslim Arab had long found in the Arabic heritage an object of love and pride. For the former the seminaries in Aleppo and Lebanon and for the latter al-Azhar in Cairo and similar and smaller institutions in Jerusalem, Damascus and elsewhere produced the religious leaders whose education included a mastery of the Arabic language. The employment of the printing press in Egypt and Syria made the task of teacher, pupil and general reader much easier.

Parallel to the cultivation of the mother tongue the Arabs were gradually introduced to a vague notion of love of the fatherland (*al-waṭan*). Two of its first advocates deserve to be mentioned here by name, Rifāʿa al-Ṭahṭāwī in Egypt and Buṭrus al-Bustānī in Syria. The former may be considered as a prime creator in Arabic of the double idea that what is good in the European system is to be found in the Islamic tradition, and that there is no contradiction between the spirit of the Islamic sacred law and the principles of the European secular or "natural" law.

The idea of regional, territorial patriotism was among Ṭahṭāwī's acquisitions from Europe. Love of the limited fatherland (*patrie*) as distinct from loyalty to the universal Muslim community is not entirely novel but it led in the space of some half century to novel consequences. A generation later, Bustānī preached the gospel of love of the fatherland at a time of communal strife in his native Lebanon. He called upon his compatriots to forget that they were Maronite or Druze, Christians or Muslim and to work for reconciliation in their own interest and for the welfare of their common fatherland.

Ṭahṭāwī's fatherland was Egypt and Bustānī's Syria. But whereas the former as a Muslim took into account the larger community of Islam and made reflexions on the functions of government in modern times, the latter as a Christian was more limited both in his political interests and in the scope of thought. His immediate concern, after the end of the communal war of 1860, was the reconciliation, within the Ottoman system, of the religious communities in the interests of a common fatherland. It is doubtful whether these early expounders of regional loyalties foresaw the implication or the ultimate outcome. For we now see more clearly that the trend toward the national, secular state had been started by these early essays.

Muslim as well as Christian thinkers made their contributions towards this unforeseen end. Thus when the difficulties inherent in establishing religious equality and in diverting the appeal to men's loyalties from religion to the fatherland, were first comprehended perplexing and unanswerable questions began to be raised. Let us take one of them. Hitherto the fighter for the Islamic state had been a Muslim upon whom his Muslim officer could call for supreme sacrifice in the cause of Islam. But since the introduction of equality between all Ottoman subjects irrespective of faith and on the supposition that non-Muslims were enlisted in the national army, for which cause could an officer appeal to a Christian soldier to shed his blood in battle, probably fighting fellow Christians?

This is not to suggest that the attempt at religious equality was not sincerely conceived. Indeed, this sincerity is clear in a well-known argument by Namîk Kemal. He explained away the weakness of a multi-racial and multi-religious empire by pointing out that the racial and religious groups were so hopelessly intermingled that none of them could form a homogeneous independent entity. Their interests were in remaining within a large unit, loyal to the Ottoman throne which had made so many concessions designed to promote the freedom and welfare of its non-Muslim subjects.

Namîk Kemal was aware that his argument did not apply to the Arabs who possessed racial and territorial homogeneity. But here he relied on the ties of Islamic brotherhood which united Arab and Turk in a common allegiance to the sultan-caliph. This allegiance was deemed a sufficient deterrent against any separatist tendencies among the Arab Muslims. How mistaken was this assumption, and indeed the whole argument was clearly and quickly demonstrated by historical events.

Various racial and religious groups had long been thinking of themselves as Bulgars, Greeks and Serbs. In Asiatic Turkey the Armenians began the centrifugal movement which the Arab, despite Islam and the caliphate, did not take long to adopt. Religious ties, loyalty to a dynasty and love of a huge "fatherland" were all disappearing. Ties of race, language and love of a smaller, comprehensible fatherland were capturing men's imagination.

In the Arab lands Christian Arabs anticipated the break at least by their mental attitudes. To them the Ottoman Empire and what it stood for was an alien entity. European encroachment on it was not to the Christian Arab what it was to the Muslim Arab. The former not only welcomed it but hoped to reap advantages from it. For not a few Christian Arabs felt a vague cultural attraction to Europe, due in part to its inherent Christian character. Not a few of them were educated to entertain hopes of some identification with this or that European nation. They were thus the first to seek patronage and employment in Muslim countries newly occupied by European powers, such as Egypt. They were also the first to break away by emigrating to Christian countries overseas, such as America. Finally they were the first to answer the call of English and American missionaries by breaking away from their native churches and forming a new Protestant community. All these ventures had their repercussions in Arabic literature and political thought as we shall point out.

As for the Muslim Arabs they were for some time torn between a universal religious loyalty represented by the sultan-caliph and emergent regional loyalties which at first seemed in harmony with the former. In both the larger and smaller units, Muslims had to face the realities of modernization which had in the second half of the nineteenth century reached a crisis of orientation. Was it safe for the Islamic tradition and way of life to continue imitating Europe? Even a man of the stature of Muḥammad ʿAbduh had no hesitation in declaring that Islam and European civilization were not incompatible. But he and his followers after him were baffled by details. To them Islam was the true and superior faith and the ideal way of life. What agrees with its spirit in European civilization may be adopted and what does not, rejected. But how does one apply the test in practice, and who is the final judge?

(5)

These were for some time unanswerable questions. Their answers were eventually imposed by the force of circumstances and were not evolved by the speculations of theorists whose function was merely to rationalize the adoption of what was impossible to resist. Thus they argued that Europe outstripped the Islamic East in civilization not because it was Christian but because it made better use of science. If, therefore, the East could only learn European science and apply it to its resources there was no reason why it should not be a match for Europe. Nor was it undignified to do so, for science was originally handed down by the Greeks to the Muslims who passed it on, much enhanced, to Europe.

Implied in this reasoning is an acceptance of an alien idea to the Islamic system, the divorce of civilization from religion. Once this idea gained wide enough acceptance the next step was inevitable: that state and religion were two departments of human life which for their mutual prosperity are best kept apart. That was not what Muḥammad 'Abduh wanted or expected, but that is what has been deduced from his teachings as well as from those of his followers.

Nor was this an isolated deduction, for others not less significant were in the making. We mentioned that the Ottoman statesmen tried to give an Islamic Empire a façade of equality between its component religious communities and that the attempt was not very successful. Despite the efforts of statesmen non-Muslim communities continued to consider themselves "religious" or "ethnic" or "national" groups. Whatever the Islamic state was prepared to do, it was not enough to neutralize such tendencies among the various groups. Since the Greek revolt in the 1820s these tendencies were towards the formation from religious and ethnic communities of new national states, independent of the empire.

Transition from religious to ethnic or national loyalty was easy enough for the non-Arab Christian communities. It was difficult for the Arabs. Apart from a strong native element in their culture, rudiments of national consciousness began to reach the Arabs from Europe through two major channels, intellectual and practical. Large numbers of students, diplomatists, merchants and travellers became more and more acquainted with European thought and institutions. At the same time and a little later, thoughtful leaders in the Arab Near East became awed by the political dominance of Europe, itself a manifestation of vigorous national states. Most of these leaders were convinced that salvation and progress lay in some emulation of Europe.

However in adopting European ideas, including that of nationalism, it was inevitable that they should give them some local colouring. Thus some thought "religious nationalism" was possible, others "regional nationalism" and still others "ethnic nationalism". There was then no clear-cut distinction between these brands, and it may even be argued that there is none as yet at the present time.

The impracticability of putting into practice the principle of religious equality in a large Muslim empire had thus tempted some non-Muslims to seek it in the smaller regional units where Jews and Christians could share with the predominant Muslim community a loyalty which each community could understand. This local loyalty did little to eliminate religious or ethnic loyalties. Thus the Jews remained a race apart, whose religion, and later political Zionism, put them either outside the Christian–Muslim affiliation or in an ambiguous situation permitting little scope for outright alinement with either Zionism or Arab nationalism. This was particularly the dilemma of native Arabic-speaking Jews in Iraq, Egypt and Syria. Here again the dilemma was resolved more by the march of events than by cool speculation.

On the other hand the Christian Arabs took part by identifying themselves with the general sentiments of the Muslims, in changing the traditional Islamic view of the state, in gaining wider support for the idea of separating religion from politics and on the whole insinuating the secularism in modern Arabic thought. Not that these changes were made without Muslim participation and approval. Far fom it. The number of Muslims who embraced such ideas was comparatively large and they came both from those who had had European education and from those whose education combined the Islamic with the European.

Thus by two not dissimilar processes the Muslim Arabs and the Christian Arabs arrived at a working basis for their common destiny in the twentieth century. But it was no more than a basis. Tensions inside the Christian–Muslim front, the product of centuries of history, cannot be removed within a generation or two. For in the last analysis the spirit of Arab nationalism is really Islamic. Indeed the Arabic language, the glories of the Arab past, and the general Arab culture are very strongly permeated by Islam. There is thus no escaping the conclusion that even today it is much easier for a Muslim to be a sincere Arab nationalist than for a Christian unless he has mastered the Islamic and Arab tradition to a degree which at least equals that of the Muslim. For the latter has its essence in his veins, so to speak, while the former has only elements of it in his veins and he must assiduously cultivate the rest.

Hence those Christian Arabs who at one time tried to formulate an Arab nationalist philosophy without reference to Islam failed even more than those Muslim Arabs who tried to formulate it as a means of an Islamic revival. The former alienated the dominant majority and the latter failed to gain the confidence of indispensable minorities. A middle way was found in national philosophy which did not exclude religion from the life of the community and took into account the Islamic character of the Arabic tradition. This is partly the explanation of the persistence, underneath national unity, of religious reservations. Thus the Muslim Arab has certain reservations about the assertion of its Christian character by the Lebanese Republic, and the Republic itself has certain reservations both concerning the loyalty of its Muslim subjects and its place in its Muslim surroundings.

(6)

It was, however, for the predominant Muslim majority to give a lead. The efforts of its early thinkers may not always be consistent but they point to the same direction. The defenders of the "spirit" of Islam among them were themselves the authority for identifying such European concepts as freedom, democracy and parliamentary government with true Islam. They were quick to quote the Qur'ān and to point to the practice of the early Muslim community in support of their deductions. By the same process of thought they lent their support to national movements within the Muslim community, ignoring that these were essentially based on regional or ethnic loyalties even when paying formal tribute to Islam. In the Arab lands the first drift in the direction of secular nationalism was experienced in Egypt, and the example set by the foremost Arabic-speaking Muslim country was followed by the others almost without question.

Let us now illustrate the faltering steps that led Arab thinkers, both Muslims and Christians from a tacit acceptance of the universal Islamic state to a vague attachment to fragmentary national entities. Those Arab thinkers whose reflexions are quoted below were clearly experimenting with new ideas, and hence their formulation is not always clear-cut. But there is no mistaking the gradual re-shaping of traditional ideas to suit new situations. The first thinker is Rifā'a al-Ṭahṭāwī.[1]

He was an Azharī *shaykh* who was for five years from 1826 the official *imām* of the Egyptian students in Paris. He learned French and read some of the literature of the Enlightenment. In his writing he commends some French ideas and institutions to his fellow Muslims in a manner which became the model for all like-minded thinkers that followed him: The roots of what is good in the European system are to be found in Islam. Hence he says: "Let it be known that I did not find commendable [in Europe] what is contrary to the explicit text of the Muḥammadan *sharī'a*."

[1] *Takhlīṣ al-ibrīz* (Būlāq, 1365), pp. 4, 5, 7, 8 (in this order for the texts translated).

Despite its civilization France was to him "a land of infidelity". Even the specialists in Arabic whom he met, such as De Sacy, were not accepted without reserve. "Some Frenchmen", he says, "have a kind of participation in some Arabic sciences and succeeded in understanding their fine points and secrets...but they did not find the straight path and did not take the way to salvation..."

In the servile style of the age he sings Muḥammad 'Alī's praise and defends him against criticism. He was censored in Egypt and outside it by Muslim public opinion for his employment of the "Franks" in his various establishments. But quite correctly Ṭahṭāwī explains that they were thus employed because Muḥammad 'Alī needed their scientific skill and technical knowledge, not because they were Christians.

There were to Ṭahṭāwī two principal means of attaining and perfecting civilization:[1]

First, religion is the strongest basis for the virtuous and upright life. It guides man to justice and good deeds. In obedience to its law (*sharī'a*) duties are performed and through state policy (*siyāsa*) civilization is created. Both the obedience and the creation of civilization are the outcome of justice (*'adl*) which is [the guarantor of] the safety of the state...

Secondly, public utilities which create the wealth and well-being of society and uplift it from its primitive state. [Only] the civilization which comes through these two means is considered of universal benefit, through which men may realize the true meaning of happiness...

Ṭahṭāwī was mainly concerned with Egypt, but he sought examples from Islamic history to emphasize his point. He saw that Egypt contained a minority of native Christians and a smaller minority of Jews He recalled the early practice of the caliphate allowing such minorities to remain faithful to their religions. He clinched the argument by quoting the practice of modern states in Europe:

After the spread of Islam men were free to choose. This practice of permitting adherence to various religions is [now] accepted by all nations, even though the chosen religion is different from the state religion. This is allowed on condition that no harm is caused thereby to the state, as it is recognized in international law...

From religious tolerance Ṭahṭāwī advances towards co-operation and brotherhood in the interests of the common fatherland (*al-waṭan*):

The desire to see the fatherland civilized is the outcome of love. This love is enjoined by the law-giver, and hence the *ḥadīth*: "Love of the fatherland

[1] *Manāhij al-albāb* (Cairo, 1286), pp. 5, 6, 7, 66 (in this order for the texts translated).

is part of the faith", and hence the saying of the Commander of the Faithful 'Umar b. al-Khaṭṭāb: "God has made the land (*bilād*) prosperous through [men's] love of the abodes (*awṭān*)..." There is nothing in good morals to prevent the extension of the mutual obligations existing between a believer and his brother believer to [non-believers] who share the same fatherland because of the bond of patriotic brotherhood (*al-ukhuwwa al-waṭaniyya*)...It is therefore morally incumbent upon those united in one fatherland to co-operate towards its improvement and perfection of its system...

The second thinker was a soldier and statesman who served the ruler of Tunis and then the Ottoman Empire in high office. Khayr al-Dīn Pasha published a book in Arabic in 1867, later partly translated as *Réformes nécessaires aux États musulmans*. He stood for the rule of law and consultative government. He quotes Ibn Khaldūn in support of his contention that oppression was the cause of the decay and destruction of civilization. He cites as examples the past practice of European monarchs and the contemporary practice of Muslim monarchs. He then concludes:[1]

Nothing brought the Kingdoms [of the former] to the verge of disintegration and loss of independence except their misdeeds which were the product of their absolute rule, whereas the conduct of their Muslim neighbours was exemplary because their rulers were limited by the canons of the sacred law, both in religious and worldly affairs. One of the accepted principles of this law is protection of God's servant against his own passions as well as the protection of the rights of the subjects of the state, whether they were Muslims or not...

Khayr al-Dīn, too, mentions *al-waṭan* quite frequently but it meant to him Muslim lands as a whole rather than a particular region. He was preoccupied with the more concrete problem of how to reform the Islamic state while preserving its character, and how to raise its standards to the level of Europe. He, too, supports his prescription with extensive quotations from the precept and practice of the early Islamic community. He writes:

There is no reason [for the disparity between the Islamic state and Europe] except the advance of the Europeans in science (*ma'ārif*) which is the product of [political] organizations based on justice (*'adl*) and freedom (*ḥurriyya*)... Is it possible for us nowadays [to match Europe in military preparedness and strength] without advance in science and the means of civilization (*'umrān*)...and is that progress possible without introducing political

[1] *Aqwam al-masālik* (Tunis, 1284), pp. 15, 8, 9, 10 (in this order for the texts translated).

organization to match those of the others based on the two pillars of justice and freedom (these two being two fundamentals in our own sacred law)...?

Let it not be imagined that the people of Europe have reached such a stage of civilization because of their fertile soil or temperate climate...or that it is the influence of their religion, for although Christianity enjoins justice and equality...it does not interfere in political action...No, the people of Europe have reached that high degree of progress in science and industry only through organizations based on political justice, promotion of the means of acquiring wealth and exploitation of the treasures of the earth with the aid of the sciences of agriculture and commerce. The key to all this advance is the security (*amn*) and justice which are so well-established in the European countries...

(7)

We now turn to Syria in order to single out one or two illustrations of Arab thought on these subjects. Much has been said about the influence of foreign schools in shaping this thought, but none of those who wrote on the subject ever tried to study the aims and curricula of these schools. Hence their conclusions are largely speculation with little or no support from the facts.

This remark is made after years of close study of the sources, both native and foreign. On that basis I maintain that foreign schools began to influence the Arab mind in Syria on an appreciable scale only in the second half of the nineteenth century, and reliable evidence of this influence is available only for the closing decades. Nor is it a tenable assertion that Syria, and in particular Lebanon, and more precisely the Christians of Lebanon were the pioneers of the Arab revival. This assertion also does not bear close examination.

Nevertheless there were a few individuals whose native education was enriched by their contact with Western educational agencies about the middle of the century. Buṭrus al-Bustānī is such an individual. Educated at a leading native Maronite school in Lebanon, he came in contact with the American mission in Beirut, adopted the Protestant faith, served the mission as teacher and co-translator of the Bible into Arabic before embarking on an independent literary career of marked distinction.

He showed his independence even while still in the pay of the American mission. They did not find his theological views close enough to theirs to warrant his appointment as a native pastor. His preface to *Miṣbāh al-ṭālib*, a textbook intended for use in missionary schools quotes verbatim not from the Bible but the Qur'ān. He was instrumental in forming a literary society which specifically excluded "politics and religious controversy". He led the native Protestant community in their demand for a native Protestant church independent of the American mission.

His proficiency in foreign languages and his experience in translation opened for him the wide expanse of Western literature. He began to adapt and use in his teaching and public lectures, and later in his journals and encyclopedia, such facts and ideas as he thought were useful and relevant. From the beginning his writing breathes a zeal for literary revival and strong patriotism. He called for more schools, libraries, journals and printing presses, and he preached love of the regional fatherland (*waṭan*) but within the framework of the Ottoman state. His was a double loyalty to the larger political unit and to the smaller territory of Syria or Lebanon.

The measure of Bustānī's spirit was the 1860 civil war in Syria. In the midst of fanaticism and strife he preached the gospel of peace and conciliation. For this purpose he published an occasional sheet called *Nafīr sūriyya* in which he signed himself as the "lover of the fatherland". He called upon his compatriots of all communities to remember that they were still bound together by the common fatherland, language customs and interests. Three years later he established in Beirut *al-Madrasa al-waṭaniyya*, a non-sectarian school which cultivated the love of the fatherland and the mother tongue. It was not a "national" school, however, for it was strictly an inter-denominational Christian school which stressed no particular creed.

The following is reproduced from the first issue of the *Nafīr* dated Beirut, 29 September 1860:

O sons of the fatherland! The news of the abominations and the actions disapproved by God which the wicked among us have committed this year within a short time has reached the farthest ends of the earth...

O sons of the fatherland! You drink the same water and you breathe the same air. You speak the same language and you tread the same soil. Your customs and your interests are one. If you are still intoxicated through drinking the blood of your brethren in the fatherland, or if you are still dazed from the calamities that befell you, you must soon awake from this state of insensibility and realize the meaning of this counsel and your common good. This is what I desire to say to you now, and I hope to address you again. I pray God to guide you to the realization of your interests and the welfare of your country, and I pray Him to move your hearts to respect the principles of the religion you embrace...

It is clear that this address is not directed to the Christians exclusively; it obviously includes the Muslims and the Druzes. By rising above the sectarian strife and seeing beyond the calamities it inflicted on all the communities, Bustānī was the true patriot, the good Christian and the liberal man of letters all in one.

His work on the Arabic dictionary, in periodical journalism and the encyclopedic dictionary were all offered as from the same "lover of the fatherland" who had completely accepted the Ottoman system, and sought and received the patronage of men in high office from the sultan and the grand vizier to the khedive of Egypt. With politics as such, he had nothing to do, and there is no record of any consistent political views in his numerous writings—even though his periodicals included some political news which was at any rate very close to official policy. His connexion with the Syrian Scientific Society had no political significance, if the Society itself ever had any.

Bustānī's true service was in the literary and social fields. He was one of the earliest voices in the Arab world that called for the education of women. He summed up a public lecture given about 1849 as follows:[1]

If we try to reform a nation, the education of women should be the first step...Those who educate males and leave females aside...usually fail in this endeavour because their effort would hardly be enough to repair what [ignorant] mothers would spoil...Perhaps what I have said is enough as an introduction to a subject none of the writers in this country has treated before me...

Finally we reproduce Bustānī's view of the Arab renaissance in Syria in the nineteenth century and the place of Europeans in it:

They began to repay the East what they had learned from it...even though they do so most of the time in a spirit of haughtiness and contempt for the Easterners. We had handed them the sciences...by one way, and they are now beginning to return them to us by many ways. We must give credit to the American missionaries and the Latin missionaries and of the latter especially the Jesuits and the Lazarists. Their initiative and service in schools and printing presses are quite obvious...

But Bustānī was too impartial an observer to forget native initiative which antedates at least the American work and much of the Latin, both of which were at any rate restricted to Christian communities

[1] *al-Mu'allim Buṭrus al-Bustānī*, selections by F. A. Bustānī (Beirut, 1950) pp. 23, 35–6 for this and the following translated passages.

and did not reach the Muslim majority. Here is what Bustānī writes of Muḥammad ʻAlī's role:

He adopted in this age an attitude to the books of the Franks similar to that adopted in his age by Charles the Great to the books of the Arabs. He ordered the translation into Arabic of the best of them, and had these translations, together with many old Arabic books, printed at the excellent press at Būlāq...and thus there issued from it various books in Arabic on medicine, physics, history, etc. In this way he provided the Arabic language with the entire range (*sic*) of Arabic and Frankish arts and sciences.

But few of the ordinary Syrian and Lebanese Arabs shared Bustānī's support of the Ottoman government. Most of them had in fact no sympathy with it at all and would have preferred its replacement by some European control or protection. Some individual thinkers among them, however, would have been satisfied with the achievement of genuine equality with the ruling Muslim majority as laid down in the edicts of reforms. The Christian Arab was truly coming closer to the Muslim Arab, at least in literary and scientific pursuits. But such assertions as had been made by the late George Antonius of a positive union for national independence around 1880 are too sweeping and require re-examination in the light of the available evidence.

(8)

There is no convincing evidence that such early literary societies as were established in Syria in 1846 and in the next thirty years had any political aims, open or secret. The first concrete evidence of the existence of a small group of men with political aims was provided by anonymous handwritten placards which were posted up in Beirut, Sidon, Tripoli and Damascus in 1880. We owe the preservation of one of the placards in original and copies of two others to the British consul in Beirut. While the vice-consul in Damascus also reported the appearance of the placards he neglected to preserve any of them although one of them was fixed on his own door.

The first writer to call attention to the placard was George Antonius who, however, was extremely selective in using the evidence. I now wish to correct some of his conclusions. Before doing so I offer, for the first time, full translations of the three surviving placards, together with an analysis of the evidence of three contemporary eye-witnesses, two English and the third a Lebanese Christian. The first placard is a copy and it describes itself as a notice or proclamation (*iʻlān*). Under this word there is a sketch of a drawn sword and under the sketch there is one line of poetry which is followed by the text of the notice:

> By the sword lofty aims are attained,
> Then use it if you are to succeed!

O Sons of Syria! Moses rose as a reformer (*muṣliḥ*) but the Egyptians said he was possessed by the evil spirit; Socrates rose as a reformer but the Greeks killed him; Jesus rose as a reformer but the Jews said he was possessed by Satan; Muḥammad rose as a reformer but the pre-Islamic Arabs said he was mad. You may say that the writer (or rather writers) of this notice is intoxicated and that his words are delirium. But if he is mindful of your affairs then he is better than your rulers (lit. friend in the singular *ṣāḥib*) who do not care about your welfare nor uphold your honour (this rather than law for *nāmūs*). Would that you were all intoxicated [like the writer.]

We [the writers] spend the night awake with thought and the day with diligence in understanding events and news. But for our moribund condition we would not be the slaves of the degraded Turks; but for our dissension the Franks would not consider us insensible. Where is your Arab pride (*nakhwa*)? Where is your Syrian zeal (*ḥamiyya*)? O people! Return [to your past glory] while it is opportune! Do not despair of the mercy of your Lord! The [light of the] moon cannot be obscured, and he who lives will see.

The second placard, preserved in the original, also has a sketch of a drawn sword coloured with red ink, contrasting with the black ink of the circular itself which reads:

O sons of Syria! Reform of [or at the hands of] the Turks is impossible. Otherwise why did they not reform [or introduce any reforms]? They have given countless pledges of honour to their subjects concerning reform [but did nothing]. So what do you expect from them?

Despite their deep-rooted corruption, extreme ignorance and effeminacy, the Turks have continued till now to rule, with two millions of their number, over thirty-five millions of the servants of God. Are there not among our wise men, sons of our fatherland and guardians of our pride some men who are able to assume management of our affairs, who are jealous of our honour and [mindful] of uplifting our fatherland, though we are only two millions, sons of one fatherland? Does your great understanding prevent you from doing that?

As for ourselves we have dedicated our possessions and our lives for the redemption of the fatherland neither belong to us any longer, but to the fatherland. By the Great God we shall awaken you from your present repose of death even if we meet our death [in the attempt]. And he who lives will see.

The third preserved placard is a copy. It has the word woe (*al-wayl*) written between two drawn swords pointing downwards to the text which reads:

O people of the fatherland! You are aware of the injustice and oppression of the Turks. With a small number of themselves they have ruled over you and enslaved you. They have abolished your sacred law (*sharīʿa*) and despised the sanctity of your revered books (? possibly singular in the original and then the meaning would be "your revered Qur'ān"). They have even passed regulations to destroy your noble language. They have closed before you the doors of success. They have taken you as slaves and as if you were devoid of human feelings. But you were the rulers in the past. Among you were raised the men of learning and virtue. With you the lands [of Islam] were populated and through you the wide [Islamic] conquests were achieved. And your language contains the principles of the caliphate which the Turks had stolen from you. Look how [at present] your men are sent to the battle field and exposed to death and what [ill-]treatment they receive. Then look at your religious foundations (*awqāf*) how they are managed and in what manner [their income] is spent.

But now, and after consultation with our brethren in all parts of the country it was resolved and decided to make the following demands before calling the sword as an arbiter. If your demands are met we will turn to manage our [own] affairs. Otherwise,

Our aims by the sword we shall seek,
By it none of our aims can fail.
And we shall leave the uncouth Turk
To bewail the punishment of iniquity.

The demands which our council decided to make are as follows:

First, autonomy [not independence here for the Arabic *istiqlāl*] which we share with our Lebanese brethren, while our common interests bring us all closer together. Secondly, recognition of the Arabic language as official (*rasmiyya*) in the country and of the right of those who speak it to complete freedom in publishing their thoughts, books and newspapers, in accordance with the demands of humanity, progress and civilization. Thirdly, the employment of soldiers recruited from among us in the service of [their] fatherland only and to rid them of servitude to Turkish officers.

Then there are other indispensable improvements and concessions the discussion of which we leave for another occasion.

Awake ye Arabs and recover!
For you are knee-deep in adversity.
Why entertain vain hopes
While you are captives of armed force?
You have neither government to give you strength
Nor a helper upon whom to lean in distress.
Have you not blood to boil one day,
And remove this shame when it does boil?
He who lives will in future days see
And glean wonders in their events.

The dispatches from the British consulates in Beirut and Damascus on the subject of the placards are obviously an important contemporary source, containing as they do assessments by Dickson in Beirut, Abcarius the native dragoman of the consulate, and Jago the vice-consul in Damascus. Let us take Abcarius first. He was instructed to make inquiries among the native Christians and Muslims and report. The result was a lengthy memorandum clearly written with the complete freedom of one assured of diplomatic secrecy. Here is a striking passage from it:

> It is difficult, not to say impossible, to believe that the outcry, as set forth in the placards, is one of a joint combination between Muslims and Christians throughout Syria, because no earthly power can bring these two elements into union. Besides the end of the one is totally at variance with the object of the other—the one may be struggling to overthrow the Turks and establish an Arab caliphate, while the other may be working for a Christian Kingdom...

The memorandum rejects one by one the then current theories—that the outcry was purely Muslim or purely Christian or even one animated by "a spirit of patriotism or love of freedom". Instead Abcarius discerned either the personal interest of "one or two Beirut Muslims" or the personal ambition of Midḥat Pasha, the former grand vizier and governor of Syria at the time of the first placards, to be responsible for their issue. Consul Dickson confirms that Muslims and Christians alike suspected the Pasha of ambitious schemes for an autonomous Syria with himself as ruler. Although in the opinion of the Consul the placards "had very little effect on the minds of the people of Beirut", he gives a most significant piece of information to the effect that "for the last five years a secret society had existed in Syria" with branches in Baghdad and Constantinople with the aim of achieving autonomy for the Arabs.

Consul Dickson's assessment of the third preserved placard, containing as it does the most explicit grievances and the most positive demands, deserves notice. He wrote on 3 January 1881:

> A certain amount of discontent manifests itself amongst a class of persons connected probably with some secret society. A few days ago placards of a revolutionary nature, similar to what had been published in the spring of last year, appeared in Sidon on the 31st ultimo during the night, [and] two were posted in the streets of Beirut.
>
> At Sidon a little apprehension, especially amongst the Christians, was

created, and a few persons supposed to be implicated have been arrested by the authorities and imprisoned at Beirut, but in the latter place no effect whatever has been produced, and these placards are looked upon as the result of the discontent with the existing government that prevails amongst a small minority...

Not less perceptive, if less careful in preserving at least copies of the placards, Jago, the British vice-consul in Damascus writes:

During the last few days revolutionary placards have been posted up in Damascus, one of which I found on my door. It is written evidently by one of the ulema class, part of it being couched in koranic language; is addressed to the people as if by an outsider, and exhorts them to rise and shake off the rule of those who set the precepts of the Koran at naught, act as infidels, and have brought misery and ruin upon the true believers of Syria. Little or no notice has been taken of these appeals, there being, so far as I can judge, no party or individuals in Syria to take the initiative in any overt act against the government...

But neither the bare texts of the placards, nor the assessments of two British diplomatists, nor again the observations of a native dragoman in a foreign consulate are enough for a full understanding of the identity and aims of the authors of the revolutionary placards. George Antonius had published a thesis that the movement was inspired by Christian Arabs educated at foreign schools, and created the impression that Muslims became only later associated with it. This thesis must now be rejected and rather its opposite maintained.

The grievances voiced in such graceful Arabic style, especially in the third placard, can only be made by Muslims; Christians had little or nothing to complain of the fate of the *sharīʿa* at the hands of the Turks, nor of the latter's usurpation of the caliphate, nor again of their mismanagement of the *awqāf*. This is not to say that the Christians had nothing to do with the placards; what is maintained here is that they played only a secondary part.

The action taken by the Ottoman authorities confirms the theory that the prime movers were Muslims. Thus while two Christian suspects were arrested in Damascus and later banished from the country, the Turkish authorities paid more heed to a Christian theory that the placards were the work of a Muslim voluntary society called *Jamʿiyyat al-maqāṣid al-khayriyya* (Association of Benevolent Intentions) whose overt aims were philanthropic and educational. This society was greatly encouraged by Midhat Pasha. It seems that either it was infiltrated by members of a subversive society, or that this subversive society itself promoted the formation of a philanthropic branch as a cover.

Be that as it may, the Turkish authorities, who had no desire to magnify the affair unduly, proscribed the Muslim society and its branches and transferred its functions to the local official education boards in Beirut and other centres. I hope to deal more fully with the placards in a separate article. But now I will close this section by referring to Muḥammad 'Abduh's comment on the Turkish action cited more fully in the next section. He came to reside in Beirut soon after the agitation of the placards, and he deplored in very strong terms the proscription of the Muslim society as "harmful to the Muslims".

(9)

Much more profound and widespread were the ideas generated by Jamāl al-Dīn al-Afghānī and his disciple and associate, Muḥammad 'Abduh, in the Muslim World in the last three decades of the nineteenth century. The fortunes of Islam were then in very bad shape. Within four years major onslaughts on the last of the Islamic empires were launched by Christian Europe. Russian armies penetrated deep into the Balkans almost to the gates of Constantinople. France pounced upon Tunis and England occupied Egypt.

Concurrently with these shocks Ottoman statesmen proclaimed a liberal constitution in Constantinople as the culmination of the reform movement begun some forty years earlier. And exploiting the upsurge of Islamic sympathy for him as the victim of Christian aggression, the sultan staked a claim to be the caliph of all Muslims. Little did he or his advisers suspect that, pushed to its logical end, the claim meant recognition of the separation of the spiritual from the political powers of the ruler, and ultimately the separation of religion from state. But both the proclamation of the constitution and the espousal of a pan-Islamic policy were partly intended as checks against European encroachments.

The apostle of the pan-Islamic movement was, of course, Afghānī. The recent quibbling about his early antecedents, based in part on the vilification of his political enemies, must not be allowed to obscure his dedicated zeal in the cause of the unity and revival of Islam both as a state and as a faith. This is not the place to dilute upon his lasting influence on modern Islamic thought. Suffice it to say that he inspired the more systematic reformer, Muḥammad 'Abduh, who, through a school of followers, left even more marked influence on modern Islamic thought. A complete account of Afghānī's and 'Abduh's thought is out of the question here. What follows is merely a representation of their ideas on selected subjects relevant to the themes of this essay.

An essential part of Afghānī's thought was his insistence that the Muslim community would remain mighty and civilized so long as it correctly understood its religion and applied its principles. The subsequent weakness of the Muslims was due to a distortion of Islam or deviation from its straight path. Thus in the modern world[1]

neither progress nor civilization will be of avail unless we can base them on our faith. Nor can we overcome our present backwardness [without doing so]...What you see now of apparent improvement in our conditions is retrogression itself. For our civilization is an imitation of European nations, and it is to be feared that in consequence we might after a short time submit to the humiliation of foreign rule or the essence of Islam might be changed. [For real civilization and genuine equality with Europeans] we must have a religious movement...This movement should concentrate on propagation of the true creed and its correct and suitable interpretation with a view to leading men to the good in this world as well as in the next. It is also necessary to revise our sciences and make them intelligible so that they [will be conducive to] reform in the homeland (*waṭan*), prestige for the faith (*dīn*) and might for the nation (*umma*).

Afghānī had clearly reconciled himself to the fact that the Islamic community had split into separate states and that Muslims had different homelands. But he still advocated a common Islamic bond between the peoples and mutual assistance between states for their mutual benefit and for repelling external aggression. But the guiding principles of all government and personal conduct was Islam itself. He wrote under "Islamic unity":

I do not mean that the ruler in all [these separate states] should be a single person, for this is perhaps difficult, but I hope that the [common] ruler (*sulṭān*) over them all will be the Qur'ān, and the guide to their unity will be religion. Every sovereign in his domain must do his best to sustain the other, for the survival of the one is dependent upon that of the other. Apart from being the basis of their religion this [mutual assistance] is a practical necessity demanded by the requirement of the times (Riḍā, I, 306).

[1] Muḥammad Rashīd Riḍā, *Tārīkh al-ustādh al-imām* (Cairo, 1350/1931), vol. I, pp. 82–3, 306, 289 for this and the next two translated passages. Henceforth quotations from this work are abbreviated in the text as "Riḍā", followed by the number of volume and page.

When some concern was expressed at the purely Islamic tone of Afghānī's propaganda especially in *al-'Urwa al-Wuthqā*, and when its voice was compared with voices calling for love of the fatherland which Muslims and non-Muslims could share, both Afghānī and 'Abduh saw the justice of such criticism. In 1884 they published in their journal this statement:

Let no one conclude from our journal's special mention of the Muslims on occasion and its defence of their rights that it seeks to sow dissension between the Muslims and their neighbours in their [different] fatherlands, for the interests of the two sides in the same country are identical and their mutual benefits have been shared for many generations. This is neither our purpose nor inclination and it is not permissible in our religion and our sacred law. Our purpose is rather to warn the people of the East in general and the Muslims in particular against the encroachment of foreigners and the dissension they cause in their lands. If we address ourselves specially to the Muslims it is because they are the predominant element in the countries... (Riḍā, I, 289).

There is no reason to doubt the sincerity of this announcement. The two thinkers do not appear to have considered religion and patriotism incompatible, nor pan-Islamic and regional loyalties, nor again was the movement of Islamic revival conceived on a limited scale that neglected the place of Eastern Christians and Jews. Rashīd Riḍā's exposition of 'Abduh's thought on these matters is illustrated in the following passage:

He considered patriotism, which is the co-operation of all the inhabitants of a single fatherland (*waṭan*) of different faiths for all that promotes its civilization and the reform of its government, not contrary to Islam in any way... [Afghānī likewise] used to instruct his pupils, his followers and his political party in the necessity of unity and co-operation among the people of every Eastern country in national, political and cultural pursuits. His party was formed of the intelligentsia of different communities. But at the same time he used to call the Muslims to a self-reformation peculiar to themselves concerning the understanding of religion and the strengthening of the bonds of brotherhood with all the Muslims irrespective of their rites... (Riḍā, I, 917–18).

'Abduh's thought on the role of Islam in the modern world, its relation to science and the relationship between government and governed may be gathered from a striking autobiographical fragment in which he said that he called

first, for the liberation of thought from the shackles of blind obedience to tradition (*taqlīd*), for the understanding of religion in accordance with the methods of the first community before the appearance of dissension, for the return in its understanding to the first sources, for the consideration [of religion] as one of the scales of human reason which God created as a check against reason's error, confusion and recklessness, so that His wisdom may be fulfilled in the preservation of order in human society, and for seeing religion in this light as a friend of science... In making this call I have gone contrary to the opinion of the two great groups now forming the substance of the Islamic community, namely students of religious sciences and their followers and students of sciences (*funūn*) of the modern age and their followers...

I was also among the advocates of another matter while all the people were blind to it and far removed from reflecting on it. This matter is however the basis of their society, and their weakness and humiliation are due to its absence from their minds. This matter is the distinction between the rights of the government (*ḥukūma*) to obedience from the people (*sha'b*) and the rights of the people to justice (*'adāla*) from the government... (Riḍā, I, 11, 12).

'Abduh's methods differed in one important particular from those of Afghānī. The latter was essentially a political agitator whose weapon was religion, while 'Abduh was more of the religious revivalist who finally comes to terms with political reality. One of his most significant (and except concerning al-Azhar one of the least studied) ideas is the stipulation for the uplifting of the Ottoman state and the Egyptian nation through reforms in their educational systems. His ideas on this subject are preserved in carefully written memoranda which deserve more notice from those who attempt to chronicle modern Arabic thought.

One memorandum (Riḍā, II, 505–22) was addressed to the *sheyhk ül-Islâm* in Istanbul in 1304 on the occasion of the formation by an imperial *irade* of a commission for the reform of education. In this memorandum 'Abduh wrote:

Every zealous Muslim will see that the preservation of the Ottoman state must be, after belief in God and His Messenger, the third article of faith, for it alone is the guardian of religion... The one who thinks that the slogans concerning the fatherland (*waṭan*), interest of [one's] country (*bilād*) and such like high-sounding terms can replace religion (*dīn*) as incentive to effort and achievement, is wrong.

Ignorance of the principles of their faith has weakened the Muslims, led to their moral decadence and opened the way for the fiends among foreigners to reach the hearts of many Muslims... Thus foreign missions had spread their agents in the lands of Islam including the Ottoman dominions in order to misguide the Muslims, on such a scale that we hardly know of any area without a school for the Americans or the Jesuits or the Lazarists or the Frères or other European religious societies. Muslims do not shrink from sending their children to these schools in expectation of learning sciences or European languages which they imagine would be of profit for their livelihood and future.

This sad laxity is not confined to the common people and the ignorant; it includes those known for their zeal for the faith and even some who hold high religious office. Muslim children enter foreign schools at a tender age and become exposed to what contradicts the Islamic beliefs and the principles of Islamic law...By the end of their schooling their hearts become void of every Islamic bond and pass out as infidels under the cover of the name of Islam. Love of the foreigner becomes rooted in their hearts, and they become more inclined to follow the foreigners and execute their wishes...

[Ottoman state] schools (*makātib*) and traditional Islamic schools either give no religious instruction at all or so little of it that it hardly goes beyond the brief order of ritual in a mechanical way, restricted to memorizing the words without understanding their meaning and symbols. Hence we see that many of those who studied in the state military and other schools are devoid of religion and ignorant of its beliefs...

Three levels of education are then prescribed for three social classes. First, the common people who engage in agriculture, trade and crafts. Secondly, state officials in the law courts, administration, the army and schools. Thirdly, the '*ulamā*' to whom the guidance of the community is entrusted. But these groups are not mutually exclusive. 'Abduh specifically says that by merit and effort individuals could rise from one group to another.

Children of the first group must receive, apart from the essential three R's, sound religious instruction. A new textbook on the creed must be specially compiled for this purpose and should include a brief account of the differences between Christianity and Islam "in order to prepare the minds for rebutting the whispers of the Bible missionaries spread in every land". Another book on morals and a third on Islamic history completes the prescribed amount. These books should be in Arabic for Arab children and in Turkish for Turkish children.

It was assumed in prescribing for schools of the next level—military, legal, and administrative, that the student had passed through schools of the lower level and received that essential minimum of religious education. But he had now to cover the same syllabus more thoroughly and deeply, with the addition of logic as a new subject.

The syllabus for those who passed by selection to schools of the top level included, (*a*) *tafsīr* (exegesis) of the Qur'ān, "so that it could be read with understanding and in search of the secrets and wisdom which God had embodied in it, for the Qur'ān is the secret of the success of the [early] Muslims, and there is no remedy for their [present] condition, except by returning to it. The best method of understanding it is the direct way in accordance with the methods of the Arabic language..."; (*b*) the sciences of the Arabic language such as grammar, rhetoric and pre-Islamic history; (*c*) the prophetic tradition (*ḥadīth*) on condition that it is taken as a commentary on the Qur'ān; (*d*) moral education such as is to be found in al-Ghazālī's *Iḥyā'*; (*e*) jurisprudence which should be restricted to higher schools of religious law; (*f*) ancient and modern history, including Islamic and Ottoman history; (*g*) oratory and the art of argument; and (*h*) scholastic theology. As to the other sciences such as languages, mathematics, physics, etc., they must be pursued as prescribed by the Ottoman government "and there is nothing in them harmful to religion".

The second memorandum by Muḥammad 'Abduh (Riḍā, II, 523–32) was submitted to the governor of the province of Beirut. In an introductory note 'Abduh writes of Syria as a whole:

> Some of the previous Ottoman officials have surmised that its inhabitants had an inclination to independence and an ambition to sever their relation with the caliphate (we seek refuge in God [from such an idea]!). This is speculation without any foundation in fact...But even should such a vague concept pass through the mind of one who is in contact with foreigners it would be no more than an impossible aspiration...It is true that such an impression was gained from the words issued by some simple, low people with no standing among the community during the tenure of a former governor, because of his tolerance of such words and his paying no attention to them...And it is regretted that some of the officials who formed such an impression have taken such words so seriously that their reaction was harmful to the Muslims...The action of these officials in closing down the Islamic benevolent societies made it easy for others [i.e. Christian communities] to surpass the Muslims in this field.

The action of the Ottoman authorities is ascribed to the intrigues and jealousies of the Christians who convinced the authorities that these societies had political aims. Thus the famous *Jam'iyyat al-maqāṣid al-khayriyya* which aimed at the education of Muslim children, was, like other societies, compulsorily amalgamated with official school boards and their character was lost. The Muslim loss was a Christian gain, for many Muslim children had to go to French, English or German schools, all established to make converts to Christianity and to foster loyalty to the state sponsoring them. Muslim pupils come out of such schools "either Christian in belief and Muslim in name, or materialists (*dahriyyūn*) with no beliefs".

To counteract sectarian and foreign schools among the Christian communities 'Abduh recommended the opening of Ottoman state schools. As a first step towards counteracting the influence of foreign missionary schools on Muslims, he recommended the establishment of a boarding state high school in Beirut to teach first through the medium of Arabic, and then Turkish, and also to teach French as a foreign language. The school should be based on "the revival of religion and love of the [Ottoman] state". Then state elementary schools should be established on this basis in all parts of the two provinces of Beirut and Syria. Finally 'Abduh calls attention to the education of bedouins but he makes no concrete proposals for this purpose.

His loyalty to the Ottoman Empire and abhorrence of the idea of Arab secession, expressed at the beginning of this second memorandum are clearly prompted by loyalty to Muslim unity and not inspired by any political expediency. This is confirmed by his disciple, Rashīd Riḍā who writes (I, 913–14):

> I learned from conversation with him that he considered the Arabs the people most worthy of independence and civilization...on account of their heritage, history and language, and because of the Qur'ān, the prime spirit of perfect reform, in that language...But the Turks had robbed them of everything...and ignorance had overcome them. They should begin [the revival] by the acquisition of true learning, reconciliation of their differences and increasing their wealth. Then they should await their opportunity, but on no account would it be proper for them to rebel against the Ottoman state...

On his return from exile in Syria, 'Abduh formulated even more detailed ideas concerning education in Egypt which his disciple Rashīd Riḍā found among his papers (Riḍā, II, 533–53). After a long introduction in which 'Abduh points out that when he speaks of religion he means only Islam, although he knew there were non-Muslims in Egypt with whom true Islam enjoins co-operation in the common interest. He writes: "The Qur'ān which is the fountain of religion brings the Muslims so close to the people of the book that he who reads it with contemplation would think that there is no difference between the two sides except in certain rules (*aḥkām*)..."

Then he mentions the following types of schools in Egypt: (*a*) those state schools begun by Muḥammad ʻAli for utilitarian, and ultimately military or administrative purposes, "contain nothing of real knowledge or true education"; (*b*) foreign schools of different religious affiliations and they "are prejudicial to the harmony and love [among the Egyptians] despite the protest of their sponsors to the contrary"; (*c*) the Muslim religious schools culminating in al-Azhar, which needed radical reform in their curricula, methods of teaching, staff and, above all, moral tone.

This third memorandum contains in its introductory part a dictum which may seem commonplace now but, considered against the background of its time, must seem progressive, even verging on the subversive:

> The notion implanted in the imagination of some people in the East, as well as in the imagination of those Europeans who mingled with them and were deceived by their condition, that the power of the ruler (*ṣāḥib as-sulṭān*) is divine (*ʻulwiyya*), that the nature of the subjects is base (*sufliyya*), that there is no relationship between them except that the one is the subduer and the other the subdued, that the welfare of the second depends upon the virtue (*ṣalāḥ*) of the first so that he would treat him with mercy [but] that the first does not depend upon the well-being (*ṣalāḥ*) of the second who is at his mercy anyhow. The origin of this notion is conceit and ignorance of the nature of human society...

(10)

To the influence of ʻAbduh's disciples we shall refer again. Now we deem it necessary, for a proper balance in the treatment of the subject, to turn to the Christian Arab side and examine the contributions of two writers who, despite some intellectual ambivalence, may be considered representative of the last decades of the nineteenth century, namely Adīb Isḥāq and Faraḥ Anṭūn.

Isḥāq learned French at the Lazarist school in Damascus and Turkish as a clerk in the customs. His formal education ended at the age of eleven and his life at twenty-nine. He made his reputation as a journalist and orator after migrating to Egypt and visiting Paris. While in Cairo he attached himself to the circle of Afghānī. His ideas are often concealed beneath the forced assurance of his prose or obscured by frequent translation from French. Like some other Christian Arab writers in the second half of the nineteenth century he displays practically all shades of opinion. Thus he was like Bustāni before him, for Ottoman legitimacy. Even while in Cairo, where he was beyond any official

Ottoman pressure, his support of the sultan's government was outspoken. In the newspaper *Miṣr*, which he established in Cairo in 1877 he wrote of the Russo-Turkish war which was then raging:[1]

...The Ottoman and the Khedivial governments have made themselves consultative. Their only motive in doing so is their concern for the welfare of the state and its subjects...Consultative government is, of course, no innovation (*bid'a*) since the evidence of tradition (*naql*), supported by mental deduction (*'aql*) proves its antiquity...Consultative governments have prevailed in all civilized states except Russia, if it is correct to call an absolute despotism a civilized state. Not only had Russia remained a despotism...for some time it prevented the Ottoman government from completing what it began in the way of internal reforms and the organization of parliamentary government by [causing] this violent war...

Then after quoting the Sultan's assurances to a correspondent of an English paper that the prosecution of reforms and the constitution of a consultative government would be resumed after the conclusion of peace, Isḥāq writes:

all this confirms the nation's (*umma*) confidence in its sultan...and revives in its hearts the love of the fatherland (*al-waṭan*)...He who considers [the nation's sacrifice in war] as due to mere religious zeal is mistaken, for all Ottomans of all the different faiths have sacrificed themselves and their riches for the defence of their fathlerland...Armenian, Greek and other Ottoman [Christian] volunteers in the Ottoman army...were neither forced to do so nor were they religious fanatics. Rather they were prompted by their patriotic zeal which was rekindled by what they had witnessed of the good intentions of their government. On the other hand we do not deny that this war has also stirred up storms of fanaticism particularly among the ignorant ...but it is not difficult for the prudent among us to remove all traces of fanaticism from the minds of the ignorant, so that we may all be one nation which knows no fanaticism except for the fatherland...Long live the nation! Long live the fatherland!

Less precise is another piece of Isḥāq's rhetoric. He sings of the glory of the Arab past, laments the subsequent decline and deplores the contemporary decadence in Ḥijāz, Yemen, Syria, Egypt, Iraq, Tunis and al-Maghrib. Then he asks whether there was no small number of zealous leaders who would work to unite the Arabs (*jam' al-kalima al-'arabiyya*). For that purpose he suggests a conference of the leaders which would call in one voice (p. 202):

Let us search for the lost sheep and seek the plundered [? rights]; let us not take orders from one party to the exclusion of others, nor be zealous in the

[1] *al-Durar* (Beirut, 1909), pp. 94–7.

cause of one religion to the exclusion of the other. For we are brothers in the fatherland, our unity is that of the [Arabic] tongue and we are, though numerous, as one man...Such a gathering, if freed from religious aims and content to base itself on racial (*jinsiyya*) and national (*waṭaniyya*) unity (*ʿuṣba*) and is representative of the majority of Arab communities, is bound to shake the earth...[and] restore to the Arabs the rights they demand...

Not strictly consistent with the previous pronouncements is Isḥāq's definition of his terms. Thus he defines nation (*umma*) as a group of people adopting a single common racial characteristic despite different racial origins and languages. The fatherland (*waṭan*) is the territory (*bilād*) which the greater part of the nation inhabit. Love of the fatherland (*ḥubb al-waṭan*) is in the last analysis self-interest. This is in itself a virtue because it prompts men to serve the land (*al-arḍ*) which gives him sustenance and humanity (*al-insāniyya*) which places him in a society of men (pp. 101–2).

But he was not always satisfied with the rate or quality of progress:

Some of the rulers of the Ottoman nation have ignored the laws and canons ...They interpreted what bears interpretation and set aside what does not ...so that if God provides us with him who would guide us aright they would fail him or banish him...We sought the remedy...in personal judgement (*ijtihād*) but we were not equal to the task owing to weak hearts and insufficient preparation. Then we turned to imitation (*taqlīd*)...without moderation, and our excesses misled us while we in our ignorance imagine that we were on the right path...until we fell into the most dismal abyss... (pp. 111–12).

In a more explicit passage (p. 461) Isḥāq agrees that freedom is the aim of political life, and although the science of politics is connected with ethics this connexion does not mean that virtue is necessarily the aim of government. Then he goes on:

The purpose of the state (*dawla*) is justice (*ʿadl*), but there can be no justice without freedom (*ḥurriyya*). Excess of freedom is however harmful, unless the patriot (*al-waṭanī*) exercises it in the correct way, recognizing the rights of his compatriots and those of the state, without forgetting those of the fatherland...

Anṭūn learned French at the Frères school in his native Tripoli and later on taught at the Orthodox community school in the city before emigrating to Egypt in 1897. Another emigrant from Tripoli to Egypt who happened to travel by the same boat was Rashīd Riḍā. Both took up journalism, Riḍā founding *al-Manār* in Cairo a year after arrival and Anṭūn founding *al-Jāmiʿa* in Alexandria two years after arrival.

Riḍā was a devout Muslim who immediately became a close disciple of Muḥammad 'Abduh and devoted the new journal to the propagation of the ideas of the master. Anṭūn was yet another Syrian Christian who tried his hand at journalism in Egypt, but he was neither by educational attainment nor by experience of the calibre of the Syrian editors of the famous *al-Muqtaṭaf*. His journal was devoted mainly to adaptations from standard Arabic works and translations from French authors.

There is nothing in its early issues nor in the novels which Anṭūn wrote or adapted from French to betray the political thinker we are now led to believe he was. It was indeed a fortuitous piece on Ibn Rushd freely translated from Ernest Renan and published in *al-Jāmi'a*, which brought Anṭūn the honour of a retort from 'Abduh, at the instigation of Riḍā, which was first published anonymously in the latter's journal.

That in 'Abduh's view Anṭūn misunderstood Islamic scholasticism and Ibn Rushd's philosophy was of secondary importance. What seemed to 'Abduh much more objectionable was the accusation that Islam persecuted science and philosophy. The offending passage was, according to its writer, "a random digression" and reads as follows:

> And here we bring to mind an inevitable comparison between the Christian religion and the Islamic religion as regards the persecution of scientists (*al-'ulamā'*)... This comparison raises one question: which was more tolerant and less fanatic concerning science and scientists, the Christian religion or the Islamic religion?... Because in Islam the civil authority is combined with the religious, and the ruler is in accordance with the *sharī'a* also the caliph, tolerance in the Muslim way [of life] is more difficult than in the Christian, for Christianity has separated the two authorities, the one from the other, in an extraordinary way which opened for mankind the road to true civilization ... Then there is another consideration: science and philosophy were until now successful in overcoming Christian persecution, and therefore they grew and flourished in the soil of Europe and bore the fruit of modern civilization. But they failed to overcome Muslim persecution, and that is an objective proof that Christianity was more tolerant [than Islam] of philosophy.[1]

It is doubtful whether Anṭūn did at first realize the full implications of his "random digression" on such a delicate subject in the Egypt of his time. If such controversial matters raised by men like Renan did not

[1] *al-Jāmi'a*, vol. III/8, reprinted in *Ibn Rushd wa falsafatuhu* (Alexandria, 1903), pp. 124–5.

pass unchallenged they were less likely to be accepted from a native Christian Arab. Anṭūn probably found himself in this difficulty more as a result of his incomplete educational equipment than by a deliberate intention to offend or to provoke controversy. He was indeed little fitted to withstand the subtlety and seduction of an accomplished polemicist as Renan. The "digression" in question is not much more than an adaptation of the "*avertissement*" of Renan's *Averroès et l'Averroïsme*, 3rd edition (Paris, 1866), which reads:

Arab philosophy...was almost instantly suppressed...by the people who created it. In this case Islam revealed an irremediable narrowness inherent in its nature. Christianity was little favourable to the development of science; it succeeded in arresting it in Spain and hindering it in Italy. But it did not stifle it, and the more developed Christian nations were finally reconciled to it. On the other hand, Islam failed to transform itself and to admit into its system any secular element and divested itself of every germ of rational culture.

In his replies ʿAbduh attempted to correct what he considered were wrong notions about Islam, the nature of the Islamic state, Islamic theology, philosophy and science, but he took special care to show that Islam in history was more favourable than Christianity to the growth of science and philosophy. This latter part was published by Riḍā in book form under the title of *al-Islām wa 'l-naṣrāniyya maʿa 'l-ʿilm wa 'l-madaniyya* (Islam and Christianity *vis-à-vis* science and civilization). Alarmed by the emphasis on religion by such a high authority and frankly anxious to defend the interests of his journal (Ibn Rushd, VII, 87), Anṭūn desperately sought to correct the impression he created.

Stripped of its rambling details his defence has one single idea; the necessity in modern times to separate religious from worldly affairs. But this single idea was not really Anṭūn's, for here again he appears to have merely adapted one of Renan's judgments. Here is the original in translation from *L'Islamisme et la science* (Paris, 1883), pp. 16–17:

Islam in reality has always persecuted science and philosophy and in the end suffocated them...came the reign of dogma in which there was no possible separation between the spiritual and temporal, and which used coercion and corporal chastisement against those who did not conform.

In adopting Renan's idea in the heat of argument Anṭūn was clearly a man struggling for survival, not one engaged in the propagation of political philosophy. For had he had any he would have expressed it more calmly and spontaneously on the pages of his own journal over the past three years. It is hardly a philosophy that comes forth only in the heat of argument. Nor can scraps, clues, random sentences gathered from such an argument be stitched together by a modern writer and offered as one, still less as an expression of the "advanced" European thought at the time.

Anṭūn's essay on Ibn Rushd is his testament. Only its first part deals directly with its subject, and it is more Renan's than Anṭūn's. The second and larger part is a record of the argument, in which 'Abduh's writing is much abridged by Anṭūn while the latter gives himself a free run. As for the journal it had to cease publication and its editor had to seek his fortune and its re-issue in distant New York.

His exit was preceded by the publication of the essay on Ibn Rushd with its sequels. Apparently it failed to restore the writer's position, for few people were then interested in abstract discussion, but most were very sensitive to any semblance of attack on Islam. Anṭūn's disappointment, mingled with bitter attacks on Riḍā, are discernible in, though cut out from, the following belated declaration of his aim in publishing a journal and in writing on Arab philosophy. It was, Anṭūn says, for

> bridging the gaps between the peoples of the East, cleansing the hearts and reconciling the differences (*jam' al-kalima*)...We very firmly believe that this reconciliation cannot be achieved by one group proving its religion superior to that of another group...The reconciliation possible in this age, the age of science and philosophy, should rest on mutual respect of the opinion and beliefs of others. For truth and virtue is not a monopoly of one group to the exclusion of another, and God the most high is the God of all, not of one group to the exclusion of other groups...Our aim is then to break the sharpness and fanaticism in each of the two sister religions, Islam and Christianity... so that each will see the true way to this reconciliation upon which depends the revival of the East and the advance of its different peoples.

(11)

More than reconciliation was being forced by historical circumstances on Muslims and Christians in Syria and Egypt. Indeed, vocal Christian Arab opinion had, since the inauguration of the *tanẓimat*, been imperceptibly veering towards the general Muslim Arab loyalty to the Ottoman state which was tempered by insistence on certain internal reforms. Such was the attitude upheld in Syria and Egypt by men like Buṭrus al-Bustānī and Adīb Isḥāq. The change of attitude by the Syrian Arabs in general and their striving for complete national independence of the Ottoman Empire was a later development which strictly belongs to the first two decades of the twentieth century.

In Egypt the tolerance of Muḥammad 'Abduh and his disciples had in the long run brought the small Christian minority closer to the Muslim majority. It ultimately opened to the Copts the door of participation with the Muslims in the Egyptian national movements. For though Muṣṭafā Kāmil's patriotism was a mixture of loyalty to the Ottoman Empire and the smaller unity of Egypt, the struggle for Egyptian independence had a special character in that it sought to shake off Christian European domination, not merely to improve conditions under a Muslim state.

Thus by the last decades of the nineteenth century there were signs that, outside certain reserved religious interests pertaining specifically to Muslims alone or to Christians alone, thoughtful leaders of the two communities moved in the same direction, though not always following the same paths. The idea of equality with the Christian was slowly forced upon the Muslim, not so much by state laws as by the exigencies of daily life in a changed world. If the Christian had at the beginning of the nineteenth century little in common with the Muslim other than language, he had acquired by its end some notions about a common fatherland which Muslims and Christians together had either to seek to liberate from foreign control or to improve under the existing order.

We have shown above that contrary to popular belief the first to foster the idea of a territorial fatherland were Muslims, not Christians. But the latter seem to have been more enthusiastic promoters of the idea of a substitute for the universal Islamic state. Nor were the first practical steps towards separating religion from state promoted by Eastern Christian thought, for they were in fact taken, as indicated above, by the unconscious action of Muslim statesmen. But here again the idea suited the Christians and they were naturally more assiduous in cultivating it than Muslims from the turn of the century to our own days.

It was likewise through the unconscious action of the '*ulamā*' that the state was ultimately secularized. For they supported the national movements believing them to be essentially religious or at least more religious than secular. Like their earlier support of a new system of education outside their control this step too was a fatal compromise. Fatal because compromises on principles seldom work to the advantage of both sides. Ultimately the *'ulamā'* and what they stood for were the losers on both occasions.

Such were the means, whether adopted with that object in view or not, which gradually raised the Christian Arabs from the status of a minority to that of an equal partner with the Muslim Arabs. But this equality is still, even in our time, far from being absolute. Its seeds were first sown in Ottoman soil by the *tanẓimat* which remained, at least to the European cynic little more than reform by decree. But this era of reform did in fact culminate in a constitution and some form of representative government.

Muslims and Christians were at last hopeful of a fair deal under a professedly liberal system. But their hopes were soon dashed when the ruling party began to stress the Turkish as distinct from the Ottoman character of the Empire. The rulers could have scarcely been surprised at the reaction to this policy among the various races and nationalities under their rule. The Arab pride in race and nation has its roots deep in classical times. Nor did it lack exponents in modern times, even at the height of pan-Islamism and in opposition to Ottoman unity. 'Abd al-Raḥmān al-Kawākibī was only one in a line of distinguished exponents of the right of the Arabs to national independence and also to the recovery of the caliphate.

But this is not the place even to summarize the history of the Arab national movement. Suffice it for our purpose to point out that in Syria it had, before 1915, one major aim: administrative decentralization which would give the Arab provinces internal autonomy and established the primacy of Arabic in education and local government business. Then came the First World War and with it the repressive measures of the Turkish military administration, measures which contributed to the outbreak of the Arab Revolt under the Sharīf of Mecca. Although he protested against the irreligious measures of the Turkish rules, he was careful to stress also the Arab character of his movement. For despite his noble descent from the Prophet and his ambitions to recover the caliphate from the Turks, his call was primarily national not religious, to the Arabs not to the Muslims. It was all the more novel because it was proclaimed in alliance with a Christian power against the legitimate caliph, the sultan of Turkey.

By 1920, however, it was clear that the Arab objective in Syria was frustrated by Great Britain and France. The whole area was, after a brief interlude of an Arab government in Damascus, divided into two spheres of influence, the English taking the southern part, Palestine, in which they were pledged to further the establishment of a Jewish national home, and the French taking the northern part including Lebanon where they sought to establish permanent French influence. With the possible exception of Lebanon, vocal Christian Arab opinion was as outraged as Muslim Arab opinion. The Arab national struggle against the British and the French, as well as against Zionist ambitions in Palestine, was now a unified Christian–Muslim movement.

Meanwhile Egyptian nationalism was following its own course. The separate autonomous existence of Egypt throughout the nineteenth century, and other factors, gave its national movement a special stamp. From 1882 it was preoccupied with its own struggle against the British occupation, a struggle which antedated by some forty years that of the Syrian Arabs against European Christian domination and Zionist ambitions. And yet while the Arabs in Ḥijāz and Syria were active during the war, the Egyptians were held down by a British occupation which was converted into a protectorate and assumed the character of a rigorous colonial administration. Soon after the end of the war, however, the volcano erupted, and Egypt restarted, under Sa'd Zaghlūl, the fight against British control. The new leader was a disciple of Afghānī and 'Abduh and under his leadership the union between Muslim and Copt became an accomplished fact.

The Arab struggle against British and French domination and against Zionism was outwardly political, but it was also a deep ideological reaction. The Arab World had for nearly a century been assimilating Western liberal thought and incorporating such aspects of that thought into its system as were believed to agree with Islamic and Arabic norms. Therefore Arab intellectuals, perhaps even more than politicians, were naturally shocked by Western conduct in the Near East from 1882 onwards. They saw that all the liberal principles which they admired in Western civilization were being flouted by Western action. Not only was the right of nations to liberty and self-determination arbitrarily disregarded but attempts to assert them were suppressed by brutal force. Worst of all the Arab had discovered that the European did not honour his pledges.

But ultimately Britain had to recognize Egyptian independence and France that of Syria and Lebanon. Britain, however, clung long to the policy of forcing Jewish immigration on the Arabs of Palestine until the Jews and world Zionism became too strong for Britain and the Arabs. The loss of their homeland and national existence in Palestine had produced a profound revolution in the Arabs which was at once political and intellectual. For one thing it arabicized Egyptian nationalism, for another it compelled the Arab to undergo what he is usually reluctant to do, self-examination. For yet another, it deepened Arab suspicion of the West to a degree which now amounts to almost total alienation. And lastly it placed the Eastern Christian Arabs finally in line with the Eastern Muslim Arabs against the Christian West and Jewish nationalism. Religion has practically ceased to operate as a major factor drawing Eastern Christians to Europe, and this applies equally to political and religious leaders.

Thus, to take a recent example, the stand which Eastern prelates took concerning the Roman Catholic Church's attempt to exonerate the Jews from responsibility for the Crucifixion is in direct opposition to the stand of the German Cardinal Bea and his followers. The attitude of the Eastern prelates has drawn the following comment from the Jordanian paper *al-Manār*:

> Their stand reveals a fundamental though self-evident fact: the Eastern Christians are different from Western Christians in their understanding of Eastern problems...To acknowledge this fact in a practical manner, the people of the East must distinguish clearly between the Christian Arabs and the Christians of the West. The former are Arab citizens...belonging to their nation organically, spiritually and psychologically...They are the sons of these countries...and they constitute inseparable parts of the past as well as the future of these countries.
>
> Our memories and experiences of the Christians of the West are completely different. They include the memory of the Crusades with all its ugly horrors. They include the memory of Lord Allenby planting his sword in the Mount of Olives in Jerusalem and boasting "Now end the Crusades!" They include the memory of General Gouraud putting his foot on the tomb and exclaiming "We have returned, O Saladin!"[1]

The Western Christian record in the Near East, and more particularly in Palestine, not only alienated the Arabs, Muslims and Christians alike; it has, moreover, aroused in the minds of some Christian Arabs serious questioning of fundamental Christian teachings. In a poem entitled "The Hymn of Hate", a Palestinian Christian Arab,

[1] Reproduced from *al-'Arabī* (November 1964), p. 23.

himself a university graduate, was capable of writing of occupied Palestine:

> If Jesus could see it now,
> He would preach *jihād* with the sword!
> The land in which He grew
> Has given birth to a million slaves.
> Why does He not revolt,
> Settle the account, tooth for tooth and eye for eye?
> In spite of all His teachings,
> The West's dagger is red with blood.
> O apostle of forgiveness!
> Dazed by calamity, I do not know the answer:
> Is it true you lived to suffer?
> Is it true you came to redeem?
> O apostle of forgiveness! In our misfortune
> Neither forgiveness nor love avail.[1]

(12)

We will now retrace our steps to portray, against this broad political background, cultural developments from the times of Muḥammad 'Abduh down to the present. Clearly this is a very ambitious attempt within the limits of a single essay. I have therefore singled out one or two aspects for closer examination, and of these I consider education, religious and secular, and the Arabic language and literature the most relevant to the subject in hand.

The traditional facilities for education in Egypt and Syria in the last decades of the nineteenth century down to the end of the First World War were partly continuations of the medieval system of Muslim education and partly legacies of the reforms introduced by Muḥammad 'Alī and the Ottoman government respectively. This applies of course to the Muslim majority, but the Christian communities also had their own traditional school system as well as schools provided by foreign missionary agencies of different denominations. There was no national system of education in the strict meaning of the term. Even the Ottoman public education system, which was legally open to all Ottoman subjects of all races and religions, remained in practice largely for Muslims.

Briefly, the traditional Islamic system was based first on the *kuttāb* or primary school for teaching reading, writing and arithmetic with

[1] Kamāl Nāṣir, *Jirāḥ tughannī* (Beirut, 1960), pp. 196–7.

emphasis on the Qur'ān, and secondly on the *madrasa* which was devoted to religious sciences and Arabic studies. The traditional Christian system was similarly based, first on the parish school and then on the seminary with functions at both levels analogous to those of the schools in the Islamic system. These two native systems continued from about the middle of the nineteenth century to be eroded by rivals.

The Ottoman public system modelled on European lines and run parallel to the traditional Islamic system, was of course never intended to undermine the latter. But it did, largely because the state failed to establish parity of esteem between the two systems and because it failed to establish some equality of opportunity between their products. Thus in a material world it was soon apparent that a village *imām* earned less than a minor clerk in a government office, and consequently pulled less weight in society. In a similar way, native parish schools and seminaries suffered loss of prestige through the competition of foreign missionary schools. For here again a village priest earned less than an accountant in a shipping firm, with corresponding social consequences.

State schools and foreign missionary schools had an important part to play in the development of society, but their unsettling and disruptive influence is undeniable. This influence was due to a new attitude to religious education. Thus while in the traditional Islamic school religion was the matter and spirit of the whole curriculum, it became in the new schools a mere school subject among many. Students who passed through state schools to higher education, at colleges and universities controlled by the national states or foreign agencies, and finally to positions of responsibility in society had less and less of religious education and more and more of secular knowledge. Much of this tended to foster in immature minds either scepticism or false liberalism. They were branded by students in the traditional schools and by the conservative majority as "naturalists", *ṭabīʿiyyūn*, which is not much different in the public mind of the time from "atheists". The resultant tension between the new learning and the old was mounting and continued to do so till our own day.

Missionary educational institutions and those including two or three colleges which are now fully-fledged universities, produced similar tensions largely among the Christian communities. In the first place, and this is true of Anglo-American missions in particular, Eastern

Christians were considered no more than "normal Christians", and accordingly many of their children who attended missionary schools were deliberately converted to Protestantism. This action aroused the anger of the Eastern Churches, increased sectarian divisions and sharpened religious controversy. In the second place, the Muslim majority were considered "the followers of the false prophet", and the state religion, Islam, was subjected to polemic attacks which not only earned the missions the hostility of their hosts but also occasionally embittered relations between the native Christians and their compatriots the Muslims.

But native Christian Arab schools in Syria as well as foreign missionary schools designed for Christian Arab children had an advantage over the Ottoman state schools which only the traditional Muslim schools had. They taught through the medium of Arabic while state schools, to which the majority of Muslim Arab children went, taught through the medium of Turkish. There were loud protests against this extraordinary measure till in 1913 the Turkish authorities were compelled to concede the Arab case.

The educational set-up in Egypt was similar to that in Syria and the Ottoman Empire as a whole. There was first the traditional Islamic system the apex of which was the great *madrasa* of al-Azhar. There were secondly native communal schools for the Copts and other minorities. There was thirdly a new state system established by the government according to French models. But unlike Syria there were fewer foreign schools which at any rate originated rather later than in Syria. But the autonomy of Egypt and the prestige which al-Azhar and similar institutions had, distinguished the Egyptian educational system in one important respect. Arabic was without question the language of instruction, and Arabic studies were pursued at al-Azhar and Dār al-ʿUlūm at a level second to none in the Arab world. Thus for example, while Muḥammad ʿAbduh was before 1880 teaching the *Prolegomena* of Ibn Khaldūn at the latter institution, and *Kitāb tahdhīb al-akhlāq* of Ibn Miskawayh at his own house, lesser Syrian teachers were content to use indifferent elementary grammar books or at best Nāṣīf al-Yāzijī's *Majmaʿ al-baḥrayn*, an artificial composition in the style of al-Ḥarīrī.

But both Egypt and Syria had still to bide their time. Changes in their political status after the First World War brought about corresponding change in education. The relaxation of British control over Egypt was followed by the restoration of Arabic as the language of instruction in state schools which had to adopt English after the British occupation. In Syria at least two different policies were followed. The French sought, especially in Lebanon, to promote their own system and language, even at the expense of Arabic. In Palestine the English were far less assertive. But while they were content with nominal control over the education of the Jewish minority, they assumed full control over the education of the Arab majority. Their policy was to allow the languages of the two races, not English, to be used as the media of instruction in their respective schools. Thus in the educational system under direct British control, the schools were patronized by Christians and Muslims equally, almost in exact proportion to their relative numerical strength.

With the exception of Palestine, where the homeland of the majority was lost to the minority, all the Arab countries covered in the above discussion, were emancipated soon after the Second World War, and for the first time in their modern history Arab national governments were in full control of Arab education. They have, however, perpetuated the duality or rather multiplicity which the Ottoman government had tolerated: state schools had now to develop side by side with the traditional Islamic educational institutions and the communal Christian institutions. And these two or rather three systems had to exist side by side with foreign systems ranging from the primary school to college and university.

But excluding professedly religious institutions which have to submit to some state supervision, native education is now in the hands of the state. The education provided in institutions under state control is essentially secular whether in departments of science or departments of arts. The schools are designed for Muslims and Christians alike. They have in fact been accepted as such by the majority in each of the two communities.

Official pronouncements may sometimes be empty rhetoric but not apparently those issued by the educational authorities in the Arab states and the Arab League in recent years. For official policy is on the whole being put into practice by teachers who are in full sympathy with it. In the resolutions adopted by the first Arab cultural conference, endorsed by the council of the Arab League, there is strong emphasis upon the importance of the Arabic language as "the pillar of national culture" as well as upon the necessity to couple loyalty to the local homeland (*al-waṭan al-maḥallī*) with one to the larger Arab homeland embracing all the Arab countries. Under "national education" there is a striking passage which deserves to be reproduced:

It must be emphasized [in the course of instruction in the schools] that Arabism (*'urūba*) was never in the past nor is it in the present a monopoly of [the followers of] one sect or religion to the exclusion of others, that co-operation between Arab patriots, despite their different faiths, was strong in the past and during the modern Arab renaissance, and that difference in religion did not divide the Arabs except during foreign rule. Care must therefore be taken to spread a spirit of solidarity and co-operation between all sects to make them feel that they are brothers and that it is their duty to place the national objectives above sectarian considerations.[1]

But this does not mean the complete neutralization of religion or the silencing of all conservative opinion either among Muslims or among Christians. For there remained in both camps powerful elements who did not reconcile themselves to the idea that nationalism and the national state were above everything. Thus just before their association was proscribed, the Muslim Brotherhood issued a statement on educational reconstruction in which religion naturally comes before patriotism and in which Islamic history was more important than regional history. Among the aims of the educational reconstruction envisaged by the Brotherhood were

the training of new generations imbued with a religious, moral and patriotic spirit, and the re-writing of our Islamic and Egyptian history with a view to cleansing them from what the biased imperialists and orientalists have implanted in them.

Christian criticism was raised by a well-known Jesuit journal issued by the Université St Joseph in Beirut. It takes issue with national governments in Syria over history textbooks used in state schools. Its objections to the treatment of the Middle Ages and the papacy are standard Catholic objections applicable anywhere in the world, and need not detain us. But the objection to the emphasis laid upon Islam in books intended for use by all pupils, Muslim and Christians, cannot be ignored. The following is a translation of a trenchant passage:

If the teacher has to bring up a new generation in the principles of true patriotism, then let him abstain from spreading propaganda for Islam, and let him distinguish between Islam and Arabism as he distinguishes between Islam and Christianity...The cause of our complaint is the "nationalized"

[1] Sāṭi' al-Ḥuṣri, *Ḥawliyyat al-thaqāfa al-'arabiyya* (Cairo, 1364/1949), vol. 1, p. 581.

textbooks and our oppressors are its authors. For these books are the nightmare of Christian children in that they challenge their beliefs, plague the atmosphere in which the Christian pupils live, fight their freedom of conscience, and create tension between Christian and non-Christian pupils in the same school...[1]

A generation earlier, when Syria was under French control, Henri Lammens, also from the Université St Joseph, issued, with official French encouragement *La Syrie, précis historique*, which would have been used in schools, but for the intervention of the president of the Arab Academy in Damascus, Muḥammad Kurd 'Alī who wrote of the book:

I was very much pained to read Lammens's book, for I saw how unjust he was to the Arabs and the Muslims, and how much he distorted history and facts... This is a book which will make a Muslim pupil hate his co-religionists and despise Islam, and will make a Christian pupil hate the Muslims and Islam the Arabs and the Arabic language.[2]

But despite such sectional interests, the nationalists have been trying since independence to make state schools agencies of unity, and they employ Arab history and Arabic literature to achieve this end. They know how hard it is to divest "Arabism", as the Jesuit writer seems to demand, of its Islamic undertones, harder still to strip Arab history and Arabic literature of their Islamic content. Any attempt in this direction will not only be doomed to failure, but it will also tend to isolate the Christian Arab from the Muslim Arab. It will, from a national point of view, be a retrogressive step which may revive the now discredited adage: *abat al-naṣrāniyya an tata'arrab* (Christianity refuses to be arabicized).

If education is to be a unifying agency, and if the Christian Arab is to be completely integrated with the Muslim Arab, there is no going back to the Ottoman *millet* system. In the national states the system is virtually secularized and that is largely through the action of the Muslim majority and in an effort to bring the Christian minority in. There are signs that their thoughtful leaders recognize the need for reciprocal tolerance in the interests of the future generations of young Arabs from both communities.

[1] See the article by Père F. Taoutel on "Le mouvement intellectuel en Syrie" in *al-Mashriq*, vol. LVIII/3 (1964), p. 372.

[2] *al-Mudhakkirāt* (Damascus, 1367/1948), vol. I, p. 207.

(13)

The adage: *abat al-ʿarabiyya an tatanaṣṣar* (the Arabic language refuses to be christianized) is even more discredited now than its parallel cited above. Of course this second adage has no validity in history, since the Arabic heritage is enriched by Christian Arab and Muslim Arab alike. The maxim was probably invented by Muslim purists in the last century as a protest against the flood of foreign words and expressions, shaky style of writing and lax grammar of which Christian Arabs were the principal guilty party.

No one has deplored these lapses more authoritatively than Muḥammad ʿAbduh. It will be recalled that he reckoned among his objectives "the reform of the method of Arabic composition". But though his disapproval was mainly provoked by Christians, he was equally critical of Muslims. Indeed his disapproval covered the language used in government departments, in the newspapers and in general correspondence, and his stricture covers the pedantry of Azharite *shaykhs* as well as the slovenliness of Coptic clerks. But he considered journalistic Arabic particularly objectionable:

> Lately we have witnessed another strange style of [Arabic] expression. It comes to us from Syria through *al-Janna* and *al-Jinān*, two journals established by Buṭrus al-Bustānī. The same style was employed by *al-Ahrām* on its inauguration, but thank God this strange style has now disappeared (Riḍā, I, 11–12).

Before it did, however, a period of experimentation had to be endured, during which Christian Arabs indulged in experimentation almost to the point of recklessness. They were of course more proficient than their Muslim compatriots in foreign languages, more exposed through foreign schools to non-Arabic influences, and on the whole less steeped in a comprehensive Arabic literature, much of which was purely Islamic. For these reasons it was Christians more than Muslims who began experimenting with the writing of plain, almost conversational, Arabic. It took some time before the ill-effects of translation, imitation and adaptation disappeared, and in the end a smooth idiomatic Arabic was more or less achieved both by journalists and professional writers.

Meanwhile under the influence of Muḥammad ʿAbduh and his disciples in Egypt, and under the educational revival inaugurated by men like Ḥusayn al-Jisr and Ṭāhir al-Jazā'irī in Syria, the sterile, ornate style of the closing decades of the nineteenth century gradually gave way to a new graceful Arabic among Muslims. The new style was at once classical in obeying the rules of grammar, and modern in adapting itself to new themes and needs, including subjects touching on Western civilization and general culture.

There are three main themes, among others, bearing on our subject which recur in this new Arabic literature in Egypt and Syria during the last fifty years ending with the proclamation of the Arab Revolt in 1916. These three themes are: loyalty to the Ottoman rulers which was not confined to Muslim writers and poets; concern for the purity of the Arabic language as a symbol of Arab identity; and insistence on religious tolerance.

It would be mere simplification to dismiss the strong tone of loyalty to the Ottoman sultans in the Arabic poetry of the last three decades of the nineteenth century as subservience and flattery. It is of course easy to explain on grounds of honest belief what Aḥmad Shawqī wrote in 1897, addressing Sultan 'Abdülḥamid on the occasion of a Turkish victory over the Greeks:

> With your sword justice conquers and reigns supreme,
> And the religion of God is victorious where you strike.

But can any imputation of dishonesty be assigned to what Nāṣīf al-Yāzijī wrote some twenty-five years earlier of Sultan 'Abdülaziz?

> Caliph of God, His shadow over His creatures,
> May the world remain guarded and shielded by him!

No, there is no reason to doubt the honesty of either poet, or to deny that it represented fairly accurately the mood of the occasion or the times. I have seen no evidence of the kind acceptable to the historian that pressure was brought to bear on poets, least of all Christian poets, to sing the praise of the sultan. Yāzijī's line may be less spontaneous than that of Shawqī, but it does not seem to be less genuine.

Concern for the Arabic language was expressed by several writers and poets. A poem by Ḥāfiẓ Ibrāhīm may be taken as representative. It extols the richness of the language and its past glories, laments the dangers it was exposed to through modern journalistic style and usage and through the hankering of the modern generation after foreign languages to the neglect of their own. Thus the poet made his mother tongue speak:

> I am like a sea in whose depth pearls lie
> Have you asked the diver about my pearls?
> Every day newspapers push me on a slippery way
> To the grave it brings me nearer every day.
> Will my people—God forgive them!—foresake me
> And adopt language[s] foreign to their tradition?

The voices that spoke for tolerance were likewise numerous. Their message has since been translated into a slogan: *al-dīn li'llāh wa'l-waṭan li'l-jamī'*. Like most terse slogans it has to be paraphrased to be fully appreciated. Its first part proclaims an essentially Christian Protestant maxim that religion is a personal relation between the individual and God. Its second part is also, though to a lesser degree, a Christian conception imported from Europe. The fatherland, it adds, is a national possession belonging to all individuals of all religions living on its soil. The following lines from a poem by Anīs al-Khūrī al-Maqdisī published in 1910 bring out these ideas fairly clearly:

> If religion has divided us into separate groups
> Then our Arabic tongue is the best unifier.
> Leave me alone to worship [God] how I choose
> And you, too, worship as you please.
> But how long shall we suffer blind fanaticism to destroy us,
> How long shall ignorance reign over us like a tyrant?[1]

On fanaticism the prevalence of which these lines by a Syrian Christian Arab seem to take for granted, a well-known Egyptian writer, Shaykh 'Alī Yūsuf cites numerous illustrations that a spirit of tolerance rather than fanaticism has always animated the Muslims towards the Christians in Egypt. How else, he asks, could the Copts survive? How else could foreigners of all sects and nations live, work and prosper in Egypt under Muḥammad 'Ali and his successors? Can the Egyptian Muslims be accused of religious fanaticism when they suffer their children to be taught by foreigners and non-Muslims at that? Which Christian country would accept a Muslim prime minister to match Egypt's acceptance of the Christian Nūbār Pasha? "Fanaticism", he writes, "in the sense ascribed in the West to people of the East, namely the

[1] *al-Mukhtārāt al-sā'ira* (Beirut, 1946), p. 284.

harbouring by Muslims of a spirit of animosity and hatred towards Christians...is a vice abhorrent to Islam..."[1]

A similar note was struck by Muḥammad Kurd ʿAlī in Syria. Speaking of the relief work organized during the First World War by Gregorius Ḥaddād, the Orthodox Patriarch of Antioch, he applauds his humanity in not restricting relief to his own community. Gregorius was of course an Arab, the second in modern times to ascend the patriarchal throne of Antioch, but his seat was traditionally in Damascus. When he died, Kurd ʿAlī testifies, his funeral was attended by the Muslims in force. Kurd ʿAlī himself explained the reason to a foreign observer in these words:

> This great man was loved by all communities, for while truly faithful to his religion he never neglected his duties to his fatherland and his patriotism. He was the most beloved among the [Muslim] majority of the population who loved him as they loved the most popular of their own men. They often called him "the Patriarch of the Muslims, Muḥammad Gregorius".[2]

(14)

The half century which has elapsed since the Sharīf's revolt against the sultan-caliph has witnessed revolutionary changes in the Arab Near East in general and in Egypt and greater Syria in particular. In the political field the swift termination of Ottoman rule was followed by the gradual and often violent elimination of British and French domination, the success of which was marred only by the loss of Palestine to Zionism. In the social field great advance was made in education at all levels and the emergence of women from their seclusion. Thus a tradition of literary education has been balanced by the introduction of modern science and technology in school and university, and women are increasingly taking part in practically every walk of life.

Economic advance went hand in hand with these political and social changes. Various schemes of general development and industrialization were undertaken, and nationalization of the means of production in Egypt and, to a lesser degree, in Syria was put into force. All these measures are inspired by a new Arab socialism which aims at raising the standard of living of the masses and overcoming the great social disabilities of poverty, ignorance and disease. These measures are of

[1] Ṭāhā Ḥusayn and others, *al-Muntakhab min adab al-ʿarab* (Cairo, 1353/1934), vol. II, pp. 563–5.

[2] *al-Mudhakkirat*, vol. I, pp. 137–8.

course long-term and take time to bear fruit, but there is no mistaking the shape of things to come even to the casual visitor to Arab cities and the Arab countryside.

Stemming from these political, social and economic changes, or simply accompanying them, is perhaps a more profound change, with many facets, which involves the essence of the Islamic and Arabic tradition. First, the Arab national states have gone even further than the Ottoman Empire in transforming Islamic law and in limiting the jurisdiction of the Islamic religious courts. Even where a constitution names Islam as the state religion it is in practice shorn of its legislative powers. Secondly, on the theoretical level, the traditional Islamic view of the state has been challenged by an Egyptian author, himself educated at al-Azhar but who later studied also in Europe. This assault on tradition coincided with another, also by an Egyptian scholar with a similar educational background. In a book on pre-Islamic Arabic poetry he questioned, at least by implication, certain stories in the Qur'ān. Thirdly, the gradual invasion of Arabic literature by Western methods and themes has increased in almost direct proportion to Arab political disenchantment with the West.

Fourthly, the daring departure from tradition by the erection of statues of members of the ruling family in Egypt, matched by early precedents in the field of painting both in Shī'ī Persia and Sunnī Turkey, opened the way for the development and also the teaching, of art in schools on European as well as on Muslim lines. Fifthly, the development on European lines of a native theatre, under official patronage to start with, and the revival of the ancient Arab art of singing and music, in alliance with poets and men of letters. Sixthly, the increase of at least theoretical examination of European nationalist and other movements, such as Fascism, Nazism and Communism, which has culminated in recent years in a "theoretical rationalization" of Arab nationalism.

What is the place of religion, Christianity or Islam, in this cultural tangle? Except in powerful seats of learning, in purely religious institutions and in very conservative quarters, religion has been in practice edged out of the public life of the modern states. No doubt Christianity and Islam live and thrive in the hearts of believers. But if the former has a special position in Lebanon and the latter in Saudi Arabia, it cannot be claimed, even with support of certain paper provisions, that religion is now a major factor in state policy in Egypt or in Syria.

Thus in the end the Western Christian concept of Church separated from State has prevailed at least in practice. The Muslim majority has itself presided over the acceptance and implementation of this idea—during the Ottoman period in a vain effort to reconcile all Christians, and during the Arab national period in a more successful attempt to integrate the Christian Arabs. It is unnecessary to assess the losses and gains: they are writ large on the previous pages and larger still in the history of the last hundred years.

Nor is it necessary or possible to supply full illustration of all these developments covering the crowded history of the last sixty years. However, parts of the above discussion might remain abstract without some illustrations. I have accordingly chosen to illustrate the Sharif's revolt against the Turks and the rise of a new Arabic style among the Arab Christian immigrants in America, not because the two subjects are related or are of equal importance, but simply as further demonstration of the closer association between Muslim Arab and Christian Arab. Consider what Rashīd Ayyūb in distant America made of the Revolt:

> With the early morning breeze,
> From foreign lands we offer greetings.
> O wielder of the polished sword,
> Dreaded in grim combat.
> You have waged war on the oppressor
> With iron-clad lion-hearted men,
> And made the wicked Turk
> An example for future tyrants.
> Let [at last] in those lands rise
> A glorious Arab dominion.

Fu'ād al-Khaṭīb was himself an early convert and is reputed to have been acclaimed as the "poet of the Arab Revolt". The following lines come from a long poem, indicating that the Revolt, like Islam itself, began in the Hijaz and later expanded to Syria, Iraq and other countries:

> From this House, from these valleys,
> Along that road your ancestors marched.
> You are unworthy sons and descendants
> Unless you march in their footsteps—
> To Syria, to Iraq, to the farthest land,
> March forward with your standard high!

On the other hand, Shawqī was still wavering. He had not yet liberated himself from Ottoman loyalties nor had he espoused the cause of Arab nationalism as preached from the Ḥijāz. But on the capture of Jerusalem in 1917 by General Allenby he wrote what must be contrasted with his sentiments expressed some twenty years earlier on the occasion of the Greco-Turkish war. The emphasis is now on right, not on might:

> Rest your sword awhile, o conqueror of Jerusalem!
> (The Cross was of wood not of steel made.)
> No matter how far reaching its sway
> Even to regions beyond the pole-star—
> Might is still concealed beneath weakness
> And right, not might, is the [ultimate victor].

Might and right indeed did soon clash. The political shocks that awaited the Arabs after the war, the frustration of their hopes of independence and their despair of Western fair play are so frequently and copiously reflected in Arabic literature that it is difficult for any illustration to be brief and representative at the same time. But the spirit which animated the Arab struggle for independence from British and French control and Arab grievances against Western diplomacy are discernible even in the three instances given below. The first is by Khayr al-Dīn al-Zirkillī:

> Awake, the Syrian homelands are being dismembered
> And covenants and promises are all dishonoured!

Ma'rūf al-Ruṣāfī's lines are not as cynical as they appear at first. They do satirize what the Arabs could not comprehend in the post-war actions of their allies who turned out to be their masters. How, it was often asked in prose and poetry from the pulpit, could liberal minds be capable of illiberal action?

> How often Western statesmen make claims
> Which Truth holds up to ridicule?
> They have forbidden enslavement by capture
> But allowed themselves to enslave whole nations!

Arab frustration after the establishment of British and French control over their lands was profound. Patient remonstrations and negotiations were often followed by civil disturbances and even armed rebellion. For example in 1936 the Arabs of Palestine rose in arms against British rule and Zionist colonization. The rebellion lasted three years, and was interrupted for some time at the behest of the rulers of the neighbouring Arab states who were in varying degrees of dependence on Britain.

Their intervention was thus suspect, at least to the Palestinian poet Abū Salmā who thus addressed the rulers in a long poem:

Let my verse convey the woes
Of the oppressed to the depressed.
Rise and hearken in every home
The blood of martyrs cries.
Behold Farḥān on whose forehead
Marks of prostration in prayer clear
Keeping the fast and with a lion's heart
To the scaffold of martyrdom he goes.
Full seventy years he was,
True servant of God and justice.
Behold the nation lost
Between threats and promises.
Verily man's liberty is bought
With blood not promises.

Similar quotations may be cited concerning developments in Egypt. But the above must suffice, with the reminder that on our subject the main sentiment of literary Arabic was now more national than religious. The participation of the Christians in the national movement has contributed to the relaxation of the Muslim stricture of "Christian Arabic". However, some reservation remained, particularly concerning the less conventional prose and poetry produced by a handful of Christian Arabs in North America. They and the more conventional writers and poets in South America and in the home lands were of course neutral in the debate among Muslims concerning the caliphate and other purely religious matters. But the Arabic language, and particularly its use in modern times, was a legitimate concern to the Christian Arab whether at home or abroad.

An early assessment of the product of Christian Arab writers in America made by a modern Egyptian writer deserves notice, if only because it provides some answer to the question whether there was any advance since Muḥammad 'Abduh sneered at Bustānī's style. In 1922 a collection of contributions by Christian Arab writers and poets living in America was published in Cairo. It was welcomed by 'Abbās Maḥmūd al-'Aqqād for the modernist propensity of the authors and their revolt against tradition. But he added that their product suffered from such serious defects as "laxity in observing the rules of Arabic grammar and weakness in the use of Arabic as a medium of literary expression".

This has sometimes been ascribed to their presumed Anglo-Saxon education and to the influence of English literature. That is not so, for with three exceptions, the writers and poets concerned were acquainted with little or no English literature, and some of them did not even know enough English for literary appreciation. Their inspiration was, under a veneer of Western form, still oriental with nostalgic undertones for the fatherland, not infatuation with America. They were of course Syrians, or rather Lebanese, who never ceased to show concern and longing for the mother country. On the day the armistice was signed in 1918, Jubrān Khalīl Jubrān sketched a young maiden, representing "liberated Syria" holding up an unfurled flag bearing this legend: "On the ruins of our past we shall build the glory of our future."

Jubrān and Mīkhā'īl Nu'ayma were the most prominent among the founders in 1920 of an association of the Arab writers and poets in America known as *al-Rābiṭa al-qalamiyya*. The aims of the association as drafted by Nu'ayma may be deduced from the following:

> Not everything written with ink on paper is literature, nor is every one who composes an essay or a poem a man of letters. For literature in our view derives its nourishment from the soil of life and from its light and air... The man of letters we honour is he who is endowed with refined feeling, exact thinking and deep insight into the vicissitudes of life, and with an ability to express the impressions life makes on his soul...
>
> The new spirit aims at leading our literature out of a stage of stagnation and imitation to a stage of invention, both in style and meaning. On the other hand, the spirit which attempts with all its might to confine the Arabic language and literature within the limits of imitating the ancients in style and meaning is in our view like a woodworm which eats up the body of our language and literature. If this spirit is not resisted it will lead to where neither renaissance nor renewal is possible.
>
> But in endeavouring to encourage the new literary spirit we do not intend thereby to cut off all connexions with the ancients. For there are among them great poets and thinkers whose product will remain a source of inspiration for many in the near and distant future. But we see nothing in imitating them except death to our literature. Therefore our desire to preserve our literary identity compels us to leave the ancients alone and to turn to what we need in the present and the future...[1]

Nu'ayma is one of those Arab writers, Christians as well as Muslims, who had received a good measure of Western education and lived for long periods in Western countries and yet were angered by Western aggression and arrogance. Let it be remembered that Nu'ayma received

[1] From Nu'ayma's autobiography *Sab'ūn* (Beirut, 1960), vol. II, p. 171.

his formative education in Russian institutions both in Nazareth and in Poltava seminary before emigrating to America and obtaining the first degree of an American university. In 1922 he wrote the following in a poem:

> Who are you and what are you to rule over mankind,
> As if even the sun and the moon were under your control?
> Are you the light of heaven, or are you its creator
> Who directs the celestial spheres and controls destiny?
> Who are you and what are you, o son of the West, to order me about
> And I to find no power to resist your order?
> You say that I am weak and ignorant
> But I myself have proclaimed to the world what you say
> For many an ignorant man knew what the learned knew not,
> And many a feeble [subject] has his ruler vanquished!
> Abandon the task of enlightening and elevating me
> To him whose eye sees what yours sees not!

Jubrān was more the cosmopolitan poet and artist who used, with equal facility, pen and brush to pour out dreamy sentimentality. Perhaps he was at the beginning more successful in English than in Arabic, but there is no doubt now of his influence on lesser modern Arabic writers, both Christians and Muslims, of the so-called poetic prose. I have chosen as an illustration of this style one of the least known of Jubrān's pieces entitled "To you your thought and to me my thought" which is clearly an adaptation of the Qur'ān CIX. 5 substituting the word "thought" for "religion":

> To you your thought: a rigid tree whose roots cling to the earth of tradition and whose branches grow through the power of inertia—and to me my thought: a cloud hovering in the sky which then descends as rain, then flows as a stream to the sea and then rises as mist to the sky.
> To you your thought: a strong firm tower which neither tempests shake nor storms move—and to me my thought: tender grass which moves in every direction and finds pleasure in doing so.
> To you your thought: an old system which neither changes you nor changes itself—and to me my thought: an innovation which sifts me and I sift it every morning and every evening.[1]

There is no space to quote from Amīn al-Riḥāni, the third pillar of Christian Arab literature in America. He paid more attention than the others to the problems of the larger Arab fatherland by personal visits, study and writing. Perhaps because of this he was the most nationalistic

[1] Published in *al-Hilāl*, vol. XXXIII/1 (October 1924), pp. 21–4.

among the Christian writers in America, and he among them came nearest to identifying himself with the sentiments and aspirations of the Muslim majority. His style of writing Arabic is likewise modernist, but not as "cloudy" as that of Jubrān, nor as "bare" as that of Nu'ayma. He was more influenced than any of the American Arabs by the style of the Qur'ān and classical prose writers.

And yet this new style, especially in poetry, was destined, perhaps because of its very imperfections, to find many imitators, both among Christians and Muslims in the period between the two wars. It has since made so many converts that its acceptance is no longer questioned effectively by the purists. No voices like Muḥammad 'Abduh's are heard in protest, and voices like al-'Aqqād's are not echoed. It became almost unpatriotic to protest or even to grumble: the Christian–Muslim solidarity in the national movement must not be weakened. Thus "Christian Arabic" has in the end won tacit recognition, not through the translations of the Bible, but through the discrediting of classical style and usage which opened the door to the unworthy and ignorant as well as to the gifted and instructed.

Critical examination of this silent revolution is beyond the scope of this essay, but I may be permitted a word on the cruder forms which are now offered as "modern poetry". Of course one main reason why great poetry excites us is that it celebrates some of our own feelings. We recall the thrill and exultation at hearing it recited, and some of us experience the joy of guessing words and phrases, in an entirely new poem, even before they are uttered. Why is it that we seldom experience similar feelings at reading or hearing some modern poetry? Speaking for myself I often fail to hear a symphony and feel instead at sea in an open boat when reading some modern poetry.

(15)

The literary development we have just mentioned must not be taken too lightly. If we consider its implications it will appear to us as yet another concession, not less vital than the secularization of the state and national education. These concessions were clearly made by the Muslim majority in favour of the Christian minority. Among their conscious or unconscious aims was surely the necessity of integrating the two communities in one nation, if not in one state.

Those who even in the face of such vital change still accuse the

Islamic system of rigidity might reflect upon the deep significance of the changes which have taken place in an orderly and gradual manner. Such reflexion is bound to prove that the system has never lost its capacity for adaptation and assimilation. From its first contact with Greek philosophy and science in classical times to its latest confrontation with Western nationalism and technology it never refused the challenge nor did it fail to adapt itself to meet it.

So profound has been the resultant change that it cuts across religious boundaries. For thanks to an accommodating Islamic system, the Eastern Christians are now irrevocably ranged on the side of the Muslims at one and the same time against the West, against Zionism and against certain Islamic countries whose policies are considered inimical to Arab national interests. The transformation from separate religious communities to one Arab nation, cutting through state boundaries and religious affiliation has had a long history. We have seen that the idea was non-existent in the first half of the nineteenth century, and a mere mirage in the second half. Then from a dream early this century it was rapidly converted into the reality that it is now.

How is this reality now understood? Its historical development will show that it was largely without an initial and preconceived philosophy. Its philosophy is only now being written, obviously *ex post facto*. But this writing tends on the whole to rationalize what had actually happened. It seeks to confirm Christian–Muslim unity. It insists on their common pride in Arab history. But it generally underestimates the religious element, if it does not exclude it altogether.

The most prolific publicist of the ideas of Arab nationalism is paradoxically not strictly Arab. Sāṭiʿ al-Ḥuṣri does indeed hail from Aleppo, but he was brought up and educated in Constantinople. He served first in the Ottoman ministry of education, later became Fayṣal's minister of Education in Damascus and finally director of the cultural department of the Arab League. It was after this varied experience that he began to write extensively on the theory of Arab nationalism. He still writes Arabic with an admixture of some Turkish idiom and construction, with the result that careless readers or those with insufficient command of Arabic tend to misunderstand him. His very definition of nation and nationalism was thus misunderstood, and he had to explain it more than once and in more than one book:

The most important element (*uss al-asās*) in the formation of a nation (*umma*) and the building up of nationalism (*qawmiyya*) is the unity of language and history...But neither religion, nor state, nor economic interests, nor geographical unity is basic among the fundamental props of the nation...I never said that language was the sole prop. What I did say was that it is the most important prop but coupled always with history.[1]

Ḥuṣri appears to be the first and only Muslim to exclude Islam by not naming it as an essential element of Arab nationalism. So far as could be discovered no Christian Arab has done so. Ḥuṣri's opinion is not of course acceptable to the majority of Muslims, but its significance lies in the future rather than in the present. Like many concessions made by Muslims it cannot fail to make a completely secularized Arab nationalism more acceptable to all shades of Christian opinion.

Thus in the course of a hundred years or so all the obstacles to complete and equal partnership between the Christian Arabs and the Muslim Arabs have been removed one by one. The heritage, the language, the fatherland and the state are now common property shared equally by the two communities. Christianity remains a personal concern for the Christian and Islam for the Muslim.

[1] *Ḥawla 'l-qawmiyya al-'arabiyya* (Beirut, 1961), pp. 94, 154; *Mā hiya 'l-qawmiyya?* (Beirut, 2nd ed., 1963), p. 259.

CHAPTER 24

RELIGION AND ANTI-RELIGION

FORMS OF ANTI-RELIGION

Many persons would agree that religion today, both in the Middle East and elsewhere, is opposed by powerful forces. Some would say that the threat to religion is more serious today than it has been for centuries, perhaps more serious than it has ever been at any time in the past. This does not necessarily mean that the present crisis of mankind is any more serious than past crises, but only that it takes a different form. A crisis such as the Reformation in Europe was a crisis *within* religion, whereas the present crisis may be described as an attack on religion by anti-religious forces. In part this is a matter of definition. There is a sense in which humanism and Marxism may be called religions, but they are at least anti-theistic. Since the chief religions of the Middle East are theistic, it is convenient in the present work to regard hostile and anti-theistic movements as "anti-religion". The anti-theistic trends are indeed to be found chiefly in Europe and America, but, since many of the problems of the Middle East are due to the impact of Europe, it is helpful to look briefly at the phenomena of European anti-religion.

There is a tendency for Christian preachers to ascribe the present difficulties of organized religion to the lack of zeal and fervour among its practitioners, and to suggest that things can be put right by greater efforts. This tendency arises mainly from the Anglo-Saxon proneness to the heresy of Pelagianism or the exaggeration of human power. There is indeed a modicum of truth in the contention of the preachers, for the Christian community as a whole has probably slipped into false attitudes. The root of the trouble, however, is much deeper; and the trouble is not to be put right by greater efforts. It is above all necessary to achieve a more profound understanding of what is happening.

Human life can be conceived as a process of adjustment to the situations in which men find themselves. This applies both to single individuals and to the largest human societies. My present situation—the situation in which I have now to act—is something given to me, something which is fixed and which I am bound to accept. Much of this present situation is due to factors over which I never had any control. Even if the situation is partly due to my own past actions, yet as past they are beyond my control, and therefore in respect of my present and future activity belong to what is determinate and given. The same is true of societies. In particular the European society has had to act in situations partly created by its own scientific discoveries and the application of these in technology. Among such factors have been: the development of transoceanic navigation and the consequent discovery of America and of the sea-route to India; the harnessing of the power of steam, oil and electricity, together with the invention of elaborate machines to produce all kinds of goods; the speeding-up of communications; the establishment of mass-producing industry seeking a world market. Because of the values held by Europeans there was an inevitability about the whole development of European culture during the last four or five centuries. In other words there was a givenness about the situations in which Europeans found themselves and in which they had to act.

These inevitable factors are often economic, but this is not always so. The Roman conquest of Palestine was an inevitable factor in the situation from which Christianity emerged, but the inevitability was of a military character rather than economic. The basic and inevitable nature of economic factors is due to their being concerned with food, drink, clothing and shelter—the basic necessities of human life; and the maintenance of life is a prior condition of all human activity. All such inevitable factors, economic or other, are parts of the given situation in which men have to act.

The appearance of a new or modified "inevitable factor"—for example, as the result of some invention or discovery—sets in motion a process of social adjustment. Thus the change-over from subsistence agriculture to production for world markets requires a new social class of middlemen. In social adjustment there is sometimes an element of choice. Two or more ways of adjusting to a certain situation are conceivable. Sometimes the different forms of adjustment may be tried out in practice before one is definitely chosen. Once a choice has been made, however, this creates the inevitable or given situation which has to be faced by the next generation.

It is as a necessary complement of the processes of social adjustment that ideas are found. In some cases social adjustment may be achieved by simply removing the causes of discontent, and this may follow on a largely unconscious process of trial and error. Usually, however, social malaise has more complex causes, and can only be remedied when a whole community comes to share a positive aim and to devote itself to the achieving of this aim. The conscious adoption of a positive aim requires that this aim should be formulated in terms of ideas. In this way a set of ideas, especially religious or political ideas, becomes the complement of a process of social adjustment. The complementary character of the social factors and the ideas must be insisted on. Social malaise and discontent without any adequate ideas to express the positive aim are unlikely to achieve lasting success. On the other hand, ideas, however excellent in themselves, have no dynamic unless when linked to social motives.[1]

European humanism[2] or scientific materialism seems to arise chiefly from a belief in science; but social factors are also involved. When empirical science began to develop in the fifteenth and sixteenth centuries, it encountered much opposition, and had to fight hard to be acknowledged as a discipline comparable to the traditional university disciplines of the Middle Ages. This opposition was chiefly found in the "religious institution", for this comprised nearly all the European intellectuals of pre-Reformation times. The case of Galileo is notorious. After the Reformation the picture is not so clear. Many of the early members of the Royal Society in London had ecclesiastical connexions, but it was only with difficulty that the natural sciences gained a foothold in the universities. In the nineteenth century the publication of Charles Darwin's *Origin of Species* led to renewed hostility between empirical science and the "religious institution"—hostility which has not yet been completely resolved, though the sound and fury have died away. In the nineteenth century the reaction to the obscurantist conservatism of religious people was largely negative and the appropriate sets of ideas were correspondingly described as agnosticism and atheism. In recent years it has been more fashionable to speak of humanism, perhaps to indicate an interest in the organization of society apart from religion. Only a small number of men, the scientists, have been directly affected by clerical opposition. Nowadays, however, there are many admirers

[1] A fuller exposition of this view of the nature of religion will be found in Watt, *Truth in the Religions* (Edinburgh, 1963), esp. ch. 2.

[2] "Humanism" is here used in the sense common nowadays in which it is an alternative to theism. This must be distinguished from the older sense in which a humanist was a student of the humanities: cf. Arnold Hottinger, *The Arabs* (1963), p. 178, "The Humanists of Beirut"; on p. 307 the author distinguishes the traditional Islamic "theocentric humanism" from the "anthropocentric humanism" of Europe.

of science for its achievements; and these also tend to regard the "religious institution" as of negligible importance in the national life.

Socialism and Marxism are among the sets of ideas corresponding to the need for social adjustment that arose after the development of mass-producing industry with its potentially world-wide expansion. An immediate consequence of the development was the growth of the urban industrial proletariat; and this social phenomenon had a whole series of repercussions in social life. The various brands of socialism were so many attempts to deal with the problem. They differed in the particular social mechanisms suggested as remedies; but the chief difference was between a socialism which was prepared to co-operate with religion, and one which assumed that all religious institutions were bound to be hostile to socialism. Of the latter type Marxism is the outstanding example.

Specially relevant to a study of the Middle East is another feature found in most European religion. This is its "individualism", that is, its concentration on personal morality and personal piety to the neglect of other aspects of religion. This individualism facilitates the combination of adherence to a religion with the adoption of socialistic programmes in politics. It is probably also linked with a revulsion against religion which seemed to come over European intellectuals about the end of the seventeenth century, possibly because of the unscrupulous way in which religion had been used to support political movements during the "wars of religion". Some intellectuals turned right away and ceased all practice of religion. A more general reaction, however, among the leaders of society was to maintain religion but to restrict its scope to the domain of the private and personal. This "individualism"—regarding religion as a purely personal affair—is exceptional in world history, and indeed peculiar to Europe and America during the last three centuries. Elsewhere religion has always been taken to be relevant to the life of society as a whole.

The Islamic conception of religion, which is shared in some measure by other religious communities in the Middle East, is at the other extreme from the European. The Arabic word *dīn* signifies the total way of life of the whole community. It is not merely a world-view, together with some cult practices (which may indeed have social or public effects, as in the case of *zakāt* or "legal alms"). It also includes civil and criminal law, personal ethics, matters of etiquette and hygiene (like the use of the tooth-stick, which is the ancestor of our toothbrush), and even social customs. Originally the Islamic religion or *dīn* had also a political bearing. Apart from recent developments, religion continued to determine the conception of the aims of the state, though it ceased to have much influence over details of policy; the idea of the *jihād* or "holy war", for example, though very important during the period of Arab expansion, was not in general a suitable policy for a large empire. The contrast between this Islamic conception of religion and the common Anglo-Saxon or European one is obscured by the fact that in certain Christian circles in Britain there is much talk of the application of religion to social and political affairs (without a realization that such talk can have little practical effect). The contrast might be pointed by saying that, according to the Islamic conception, one of the distinguishing marks of being a Christian was the eating of pork.

This Islamic conception of religion, then, is nearer to what religion has in fact been through most of the course of human history. We must not restrict ourselves to the past, however, but should consider what may be expected of religion in the future. Is there something that only religion can do, or that it can best do? Is the future function of religion likely to be more in accordance with the European or the Islamic conception? The difference in the conceptions is relevant to a discussion of the process of secularization, for secularization is the most obvious phenomenon in the religious sphere in the recent history of the Islamic countries of the Middle East.

THE PROCESS OF SECULARIZATION

By "secularization" is to be understood the process by which activities formerly controlled explicitly by the religious institution come to be controlled by a non-religious body. If one looks only at the Middle East, the secularization that has taken place there may seem to be a substitution of the European conception of religion for the Islamic. Yet there has also been secularization in Europe (as in the withdrawal from ecclesiastical supervision of education and the care of the poor); and a more balanced view would be that both in Europe and in the Middle East there have been internal forces moving in this direction. This process of secularization is to be distinguished from secularism, which is an attitude of mind or set of beliefs with its focus in the assertion that there is nothing beyond this world. Scientific materialism, humanism (in the sense here given), naturalism and positivism are all forms of secularism. Secularism is characteristic of Europe and America, but in the Middle East, though it has appeared, is has not had any elaborate philosophical or literary expression. The chief example of it has been the laicism of the Turkish Republic.

The acceptance of a measure of secularism in the Middle East is only to be understood by looking at it in the light of the total European impact. Yet it is no mere mechanical result of that impact, but a conscious human response to the situations which arose, and one with an element of choice. Certain aspects of the European impact were indeed inevitable, and these went to constitute the successive situations in which Middle East men found themselves. Some of the earliest social repercussions to the impact might almost be classified as inevitable, since choices or decisions had been irrevocably made before men realized what was happening. In other respects, however, there was an element of choice in social matters, and intellectual views were only adopted when they suited the needs of those exposed to the European impact.

THE IMPACT OF EUROPE

In the modern period the impact of Europe on the Middle East (as on other parts of the world) has been a manifold one. Nothing need be said here about early contacts such as the Crusades and the Spanish Reconquista. The impact of modern Europe may be said to begin with the discovery of the techniques of long-distance transoceanic navigation which—given the necessary qualities of character in the mariners—made possible the discovery of America in 1492 and of the route round Africa to India in 1498. In particular the latter discovery led to the development of European trade with the Indies and a reduction of the volume of merchandise passing through the ports of the Eastern Mediterranean. It also led to the presence of Europeans in the Persian Gulf. This was the beginning of the commercial aspect of the impact of Europe.

Later, especially with the introduction of new factory techniques in Europe at the end of the eighteenth century, and then the invention of the steamship in the nineteenth, this economic aspect of the European impact became more extensive. The Middle East (like other parts of the world) came to be regarded as a market for the cheap mass-produced goods of European industry and also as a source of its raw materials. To enable the Middle East to buy European luxuries, loans were made, and before long most Middle East countries were staggering under a burden of financial indebtedness. To secure the payment of the money owed to it and for other reasons (or excuses) Europe interfered politically in the Middle East, even in the internal affairs of nominally independent states like the Ottoman empire.

This commercial, financial and political impact, developing and increasing through many decades, forms a series of factors constitutive of the ever-changing situation in which Middle East men found themselves. More obvious to them, however, was the military factor—the growing pressure of Europe on the Ottoman empire beginning in the late seventeenth century. In successive treaties the Ottoman ruling institution had to make concession after concession: Carlowitz, 1699; Passarovitz, 1718; Küchük Kaynarja, 1774; Jassy, 1791; Bucharest, 1812; London, 1827; Adrianople, 1829; Paris, 1856; Berlin, 1878. As they saw their territory shrinking, the rulers of the Empire were forced to realize their relative weakness and the emptiness of their pretensions to imperial dignity. The blow which first goaded them to action was the invasion of Egypt by Napoleon in 1798, because here they not merely had to submit to European military power but had an opportunity of seeing European administrative efficiency operating in their own territories.

THE RESPONSE TO THE EUROPEAN IMPACT

The inevitability of this impact of Europe—the powerlessness of the Ottomans to avoid being dictated to in many respects by the Europeans—constituted the givenness or determinate character of the situation in which the inhabitants of the Ottoman Empire had to live and act. Yet the givenness of the situation did not imply that the responses were wholly determined. The given situation was, as it were, the frame within which a picture had to be painted; but what the picture was would depend on the painters—on the ideas with which they came to the work of painting, and still more on the interests by which they were moved.

By 1800, as a result of the European impact, many members of the Ottoman ruling class were eager to make superficial changes in their polity, refashioning it, at least in outward appearance, on European models. Their motive was a desire to restore the Ottoman state and society to something like its former position of prestige; but they failed to realize that they were unconsciously accepting current European views of the reasons for the weakness of the Ottoman Empire—views which we now see to be erroneous and based on prejudice, as well as lacking in depth. Consequently these Ottoman rulers supposed they could take over certain features of the European polities without changing their own polity in any radical way. In particular they thought they could have a European-type army and give an officer a training in the natural sciences and in the languages of the Europeans without altering his intellectual outlook in other ways. They failed to realize that even these innocent-looking changes were bound to have profound repercussions.

There was indeed some justification for thinking that the young Muslims who were to receive some elements of European education would not be greatly affected by the theological and philosophical aspects of the European outlook. From its beginnings Islam had largely immunized itself against Christian thought. It had been forced to do this when it conquered Syria, Egypt and Iraq, where there was a superior culture linked with the Christian religion. The Arabs from the Hijaz and other parts of the Arabian peninsula, with no cultural heritage beyond the Qur'ān and pre-Islamic poetry and rhetoric, had to mix with much better-educated Christians. To defend them the doctrine of "corruption (*taḥrīf*) of the scriptures" was elaborated, and this enabled the Muslim to reject all Christian arguments on the ground that the scriptures on which they were based were corrupt. In early days a few Muslim scholars had studied the Bible seriously, but mostly they passed it by in complete neglect. Through the centuries this suspicion of all Christian thought had persisted, even in spheres (like political science) which had no close connexion with religion. The political ideas of the French revolution were among the first European ideas to be looked on with favour by Muslims, and this was due to the "secular" or anti-religious attitude of those who held them. In addition Muslim pride made it hard for Muslims to admit that in this sphere they had anything to learn from infidels. Nevertheless, once young men had learnt French or English and travelled to Western Europe, there was no way of limiting the subject-matter of their reading and of their conversation.

While certain members of the Ottoman ruling class, zealous to improve the condition of the empire, were the first to become enthusiastic about things European, there was a counter-balancing force in what has been called the "religious institution", namely, the '*ulamā*' or

Islamic intellectuals as a corporate body. The religious institution controlled the law, the administration of justice, education and the religious cult. (1) Islamic polities and societies are in theory governed by the *sharīʿa* or divine law which, because it is divinely given, cannot be altered. Yet authorized persons (the *ʿulamāʾ*) have authority to state the interpretation of the law, and this means in effect that they decide how the law is to be applied in particular cases. To this extent they control legislation. (It should be noted, of course, that in what are regarded as questions of administration the ruler is entitled to make decrees, but these are not considered as legislation in any sense.) (2) The religious institution controlled the administration of justice in that the judges came from the ranks of the *ʿulamāʾ* and had to conform to the standards corporately accepted. (3) They controlled education because they were the only educated people, and the only higher education available (before 1800 and apart from the practical training given in some cases on the job) was what they provided. (4) They controlled the practice of religion in daily life, because this depended on the *sharīʿa*, of which they were interpreters.

The *ʿulamāʾ* were thus a body of great power and privilege. They had won their position over the centuries in a series of struggles with the rulers; and some scholars consider that in the Ottoman empire in the eighteenth century they were stronger than the actual rulers. Their victory over the rulers, however, had been won at the cost of accepting rigidity. It had come to be held that the "gate of *ijtihād* (personal interpretation)" was closed; in other words, a judge pressed by a ruler or governor to give the decision the latter wanted, could say that such a decison was beyond his competence. This rigidity, however, though it prevented the divine law from being abused by political power, unfortunately also produced a certain rigidity of mind. To admit change of any kind was to risk throwing away some of their hardly-gained power. So they tended to be unintelligently conservative, to insist on keeping the Islamic social structure exactly as it was, to hide their heads like ostriches and deny or neglect the vast changes in the world around, and consequently to fail to take the lead in adapting the empire to the contemporary situation.

There was also a strong attachment to Islam among the masses, but the special nature of this attachment must be understood. The nomadic Arabs before Islam had as their "golden rule" the punctilious following of custom and precedent, and something of their attitude had been inherited by Islam as a whole. For Muslims "innovation" (*bid'a*) came to connote heresy. Thus popular Islam was strongly conservative, ready to fight to the death for what they conceived to be the unchanging substance of Islam, and ready to oppose with violence anyone accused of trying to alter this unchanging Islam. The attachment of the masses to Islam was thus a factor to be reckoned with, but one which operated in a negative way. It prevented any obvious alteration to Islamic practice, but was unable to support any move to apply the essential principles of the *sharī'a* to current problems, unless this could be presented as a return to the true pristine Islam. For example, the masses could be called out against supporters of the political ideas of the French Revolution on the ground that these ideas were inextricably bound up with atheism, although it would have been possible to give a good Islamic justification for at least the ideas of equality and fraternity.

THE FIRST REFORMS IN THE OTTOMAN EMPIRE

This was the set-up in which the first reforms took place in the Ottoman Empire. The rulers were worried at their obvious weakness compared with the Europeans, and some thought the weakness could be removed by adopting various European practices. In their reforms, however, it was necessary that they would not come into conflict with the religious institution by reducing its privileges or acting in any way obviously in disagreement with Islamic principles. Many reforms were in fact achieved, sometimes—as in the case of education—with bizarre effects because of the need for compromise. What has not always been observed by historians is that the ruling class were, in the process of reform, also promoting their own interests as a class. While claiming that they were eliminating features shown by European experience to be unsatisfactory or "uncivilized", they were in fact removing secondary and local sources of authority and so strengthening the position of the Sultan in Constantinople and of themselves as part of the central administrative machine. In this way the rulers also facilitated the adoption by themselves of a number of measures which gradually whittled away the power of the *'ulamā'*.[1]

[1] Cf. Bernard Lewis, *The Emergence of Modern Turkey* (London, 1961), pp. 77, 123 f., 167 etc. Documentation for most of the statements about the Ottoman empire will be found in this work. Cf. also N. Berkes, *The Development of Secularism in Turkey* (London, 1964).

The case of education is a most instructive illustration of this relation of the ruling élite to the religious institution. In 1805 Muhammad 'Ali, an Albanian officer in the Ottoman army, seized supreme power in Egypt, which had recently been evacuated by the Europeans, and managed to secure a ratification of his "appointment" from the Sultan. He was one of those men thoroughly convinced of the paramount need for a European-type army, and, once he was firmly in the saddle in Egypt, proceeded to create one. For his army he required officers with some elements of European education, and to train men in this way he imported European teachers and had textbooks translated. The '*ulamā*' hardly considered this "education", and did not object. Yet from the beginning there grew up a system of education parallel to that controlled by the religious institution but complete in itself. Young Egyptians were also sent to Europe to study, at first only selected individuals, but afterwards larger numbers. In 1827 a medical school was opened to train doctors for the army. By the end of the century there was a full system of primary and secondary schools of a European type. This educational edifice was crowned by the opening of the University of Cairo in 1906.

While for a time at the beginning of the nineteenth century most initiative in developing European education was shown in Egypt, before the middle of the century the centre of the Ottoman empire had caught up. Attempts in 1807 and 1808 to create a new army were thwarted by the Janissaries, and it was only in 1826 after the massacre of the Janissaries that the new army was definitely established; the Janissaries here offer a typical example of conservative opposition by vested interests. After 1826 existing army schools were developed in a European direction; the first students were sent to Europe in 1827; and in the same year a medical school was opened. By 1845 a governmental committee was proposing a complete system of primary and secondary education with a "modern" university, and after considerable delays this was achieved. The University of Istanbul (originally Darülfünun) was opened in 1900. This had been preceded by over a score of higher schools and professional institutes specializing in some branch of the studies required for the running of a modern state. Here again there was an entire and self-contained system of "modern" education under the secular control of a minister of Education (first appointed in 1857). Most of the traditional Islamic system of education continued to exist side by side with the modern system, though the number and importance of the posts open to those trained in the old way was diminishing.

In the creation of these "modern" systems of education useful contributions were made by Christian missionaries from Europe and America. Outstanding institutions were Robert College, Istanbul, founded in 1863, and the Syrian Protestant College, Beirut, founded in 1866, which later became the American University of Beirut. From one point of view the educational work of Christian missionaries is part of the impact of Europe on the Middle East; but in this sphere it is clear that the developments could not have taken place without a strong desire for "modern" education among an increasing proportion of the population. Such a desire is indeed part of the response of Middle Easterners to the impact of Europe, and was a factor leading the missionaries to devote so much of their effort to education. The obvious fact was that as the various countries became Europeanized, there would be many good jobs open to those with an appropriate education; and some parents quickly realized this. The appointment of the Ottoman committee in 1846 shows that the importance of education was also understood by the Ottoman ruling élite. Thus the individual or class interests of various groups were a component in this movement to develop education which was at the same time a secularization of education.

It is instructive to notice how secularization was effected. There was no frontal attack on the educational work of the religious institution. The *'ulamā'* continued to do what they had been doing for centuries. Meanwhile, however, the rulers were setting up what was in effect a rival system of education which in course of time would supplant traditional education in many spheres. This procedure had the advantage of avoiding a head-on clash, but it had also serious disadvantages. It produced a cleavage within the intellectual class, or one might almost say two distinct intellectual classes, those with a traditional education and those with a modern education. The two classes, moreover, because they lived in different intellectual worlds, had no real communication with one another. In many of the modern schools there was no Islamic religious instruction, because traditional jurisprudence and theology seemed irrelevant to the work of a modern army officer, and in any case the *'ulamā'* were not in a position to co-operate. The Christian schools, of course, gave Christian religious instruction. In the first half of the twentieth century a little instruction in Islam was sometimes given, but only at a fairly elementary level. Thus secularization came about through the by-passing of the *'ulamā'* by the rulers, so that the *'ulamā'* remained supreme in an enclave of diminishing extent remote from the rushing stream of contemporary life.

There was a somewhat similar process of secularization in the field of legislation. The old was allowed to continue, but something new was created alongside it, and in the end the new overshadowed and supplanted the old. In the Ottoman Empire the beginnings of this process may be dated to 1840. In that year a committee, usually known as the Council of Justice, produced a new penal code. This code was given the name of *kanun*, a term which had previously been used for codifications of some aspect of law in accordance with the provisions of the *sharī'a*. In this particular case the provisions, though influenced by French law, were not obviously opposed to the *sharī'a*, and the *kanun* was accepted without protest by the *'ulamā'*. In the following year, however, they secured the rejection of a commercial code dealing with partnerships, bankruptcies, bills of exchange and such matters. The precedent set by the *kanun* of 1840, however, eventually opened the way to wide changes. In 1850 a Commercial Code was adopted, followed by other codes between 1858 and 1863. Fresh courts of various kinds were set up to apply the new codes. The judges in these courts came to have so much business that it was assumed they would have no time for traditional legal studies and would be unable to apply traditional law as found in the manuals. Between 1869 and 1876, therefore, the basic law of obligations, according to the form of the *sharī'a* recognized in the Ottoman Empire, was codified in European fashion in a work known as the *mejelle*. Thus in the sphere of legislation as in that of education the nineteenth century saw the area controlled by the religious institution circumscribed and reduced, while alien control was established over large tracts.[1]

These developments further led to the religious institution losing some of its control over the judicature. To judges applying the new codes in new courts the traditional legal training was of little value. The appreciation of this point led to the compilation of the *mejelle*; and it is not surprising that the minister ultimately responsible for the *mejelle* also instituted courses of training for judges under the auspices

[1] Cf. Lewis, *Emergence*, pp. 106 f., 112, 116, 174 f., etc.; also N. J. Coulson, *A History of Islamic Law* (Edinburgh, 1964), pp. 151 f.

of his ministry. The appointment of judges was, of course, always in the hands of the sultan, but so long as the training was traditional and the judges members of the corps of *'ulamā'*, the religious institution may be said to have had some control over them.

THE KEMALIST POLICY OF LAICISM

This process of secularization continued throughout the nineteenth century in the Ottoman Empire. The old religious institution lost ground, and alternative non-religious institutions advanced. Finally after the First World War under Mustafa Kemal there was an all-out offensive against the religious institution and indeed against religion in general. Why should Turkey have been the scene of an anti-religious explosion of this violence?

The last quarter of the nineteenth century and the first eight years of the present one constitute the period known as that of the Ḥamidian despotism, a period of autocratic, near-tyrannical rule, reposing on an all-pervasive net of espionage. This political form seems to be a sign of a division within the ruling élite, presumably between those who wanted to retain their political privileges and those who realized that the process of modernization required some further sharing out of political power. Whatever the precise situation in this respect, there was certainly no reversal of the process of secularization. Yet, though the *'ulamā'* remained as they were, the Sultan and his immediate associates came to use religion to gain support and maintain their power. It was emphasized that the Sultan was also caliph, the successor of the Prophet, and in some sense (not clearly defined) the religious head of the whole Islamic world. The conception of Pan-Islamism or the unity of all Muslims was also employed to support the policies of the Sultan in the international sphere.

The persistent failure of the *'ulamā'* to realize the need for radical readjustment in the process of adaptation to radically changed circumstances brought its harvest of disaster after the defeat of the Ottoman Empire in the First World War. This defeat was much more serious for the centre of the empire than for provinces such as Egypt (which had not in fact been defeated) and Iraq. The provinces were gaining independence, but the centre of the empire had to accept its reduction from being centre of an empire to being a small state. Even this state was gravely threatened with dismemberment. To be viable at all it had to find a new basis for its existence, and this it did in Turkism or Turkish national feeling. Turkism was relatively new, for the ruling élite of the empire, until late in the nineteenth century, had thought of themselves as Ottomans and not Turks. These Ottoman rulers were often not from any branch of the Turkish race, and in their minds the word "Turk" was usually associated with some of the more backward peoples of the empire. Turkish national feeling had only made its appearance late in the nineteenth century when it became clear that the policy of Ottomanism and a multi-racial state was going to fail, and, though Turkism was still a tender plant in 1919 it was the chief hope of salvaging something from the wreck of the empire.

What led to the policy of laicism and the complete break with religion was the failure of the Sultan to understand what was happening in the years 1919 and 1920, and his opposition to the nationalist movement. The first move was purely political—the abolition of the sultanate in November 1922, or rather the declaration that the sultanate had ceased to exist on 16 March 1920 (the date on which British troops had occupied Istanbul). Meḥmed VI was thus removed from the sultanate, and at the same time it was decreed that the caliphate had passed from him to another member of the Ottoman house, ʻAbdülmejid. The *ʻulamāʼ*, however, had sided with the Sultan in opposing the nationalists, and as the new regime became stronger the religious institution was also attacked. In March 1924 Mustafa Kemal felt himself sufficiently strong to propose the abolition of the caliphate, and this was decreed by the National Assembly. By the appointment in 1922 of a caliph without political power his connexion with the religious institution was emphasized, and therefore this blow was all the more serious to the upholders of religion. Much worse was yet to come, however.

The process of secularization of education, begun in the nineteenth century, was carried to a logical conclusion. All traces of the traditional instruction were swept away. The old schools or *medreses* were closed so that there was no longer anywhere where Islamic law or Islamic religion might be taught. From this time onwards there was only one system of "modern" Euro-American education. The triumph of the new system and of secularization was dramatically asserted in 1928 by the change-over from Arabic to Latin script. This was a more fundamental step than is commonly realized. It was made to seem no more than a technique of modernization, and was linked with a campaign for universal literacy—a very laudable aim. But much more than this was involved. The religious aspects of Ottoman culture depended not merely on books in Ottoman Turkish written in the Arabic script but also on books in Arabic. The most basic of all, the Qur'ān, was studied and recited in Arabic. Since Ottoman Turkish contained a high proportion of Arabic words, especially in its religious and legal vocabulary, it was easy for someone who read Ottoman Turkish to learn to read Arabic. The adoption of the Latin script, coupled with some replacement of Arabic words by purely Turkish ones, altered all this. Henceforward only a few specialist intellectuals or some of the very devout were going to learn Arabic. The ordinary educated man, besides receiving no religious teaching, was going to be cut off from the possibility of learning directly (by reading) something of the Islamic religious and cultural tradition. Secularization was dominant.

Much the same happened in the sphere of legislation. Some aspects of law, notably those concerned with personal status, had been left to traditional jurisprudence despite the proliferation of "modern" codes in the nineteenth century. This remnant was now swept away. In 1926 a complete new code, an adaptation of the Swiss civil code, was voted by the National Assembly. This virtually meant the end of the *'ulamā'*. The traditional courts had been abolished in 1924, but in questions of personal status traditionally-trained judges had continued in the "modern" courts to judge according to the *sharī'a*. The promulgation of the new comprehensive code made the traditional training irrelevant and those with nothing but this training incompetent.

The earlier process of secularization had not touched matters of religion in the narrow European sense, but the new policy of laicism took the offensive even here. An attempt was made to have the Qur'ān translated into Turkish for use in public prayers, but the task was not completed. The one measure that was carried out was to have the call to prayer made in Turkish, and this proved highly unpopular with the ordinary people. Also attacked were the religious orders which had played a large part in religious life, and which are known as *tarikats* (*ṭarīqas*) or Dervish orders. These, besides their full members or Dervishes, who lived a kind of monastic life, had many adherents among the common people; and indeed the Dervishes were the real spiritual guides of ordinary men and had more influence with them than the *'ulamā'*. They were thus a potential source of great danger to the republic, and in 1925 laws were passed dissolving the orders, forbidding their special forms of worship and closing their convents or *tekkes*. This was in some ways the most serious part of the attack on religion in the name of laicism.

The recent authoritative study of *The Emergence of Modern Turkey* by Bernard Lewis adopts the view (p. 406) that the policy of laicism did not aim at the destruction of Islam but only at its disestablishment. This seems to be a debatable view on this particular matter. Mustafa Kemal and many of his chief associates would appear to have adopted a form of secularism as a creed, and not merely a policy of secularization; though they were prepared to tolerate the Islamic religion as a private matter in the citizens, their own belief was that religion was outdated and should be replaced by a philosophical outlook based on science. Men with such beliefs would naturally act in ways which would lead to the extirpation of religion, even if they had to profess that they were merely disestablishing it and reducing the power of the "men of religion" to interfere in politics. At the same time others among the associates of Mustafa Kemal definitely wanted to retain religion but to modernize it. It is the existence of these two bodies of opinion within the ruling institution that justifies Bernard Lewis's assertion that the policy was merely one of disestablishment, and was "anti-clerical" rather than anti-religious.

What may be called the pro-religious trend in the policy of laicism manifests itself in the attempts to maintain at least a skeleton of religious education. When the institutions for traditional religious education, the *medreses*, were closed in 1924, a faculty of divinity was established in the University of Istanbul. In 1928 this faculty appointed a committee to make recommendations for the modernization of the Islamic religion, and these were published in due course. Their effect would have been "to turn the mosque into a Muslim church, with pews, organ and an imam-precentor", and it is not surprising that they achieved nothing. Rather the situation became worse. The faculty of divinity was clearly failing to attain its aims, and was closed in 1933. Before this schools which had been set up to train *imāms* and preachers had also had to close. With the negligible exception of some schools for Qur'ān-readers, this was the end of formal religious instruction in Turkey for some time; "the attempt to form a new class of modern religious guides was completely abandoned".[1]

While the Kemalist policy of laicism was largely effective in destroying the political power of the "men of religion", both *'ulamā'* and

[1] Lewis, *Emergence*, p. 409.

Dervish leaders, it utterly failed to eradicate the Islamic religion from the hearts of the Turkish people. The death of Mustafa Kemal Atatürk in 1938 did not lead to any immediate changes of policy, though he was probably the chief upholder of secularism as a belief in contrast to the essentially administrative reform of secularization. The exigencies of the Second World War and the need for maintaining the morale of the troops led to the appointment of Muslim army chaplains. Religious journals also began to appear and indeed became numerous. In 1949 optional instruction in the Islamic religion was introduced into the schools. The same year saw a new faculty of divinity in the University of Ankara, and this continues to function, though it cannot as yet be said to have made any notable contribution to the religious life of Turkey.[1] In Istanbul a voluntary society is working towards a conservative modernization of Islamic religion. In many quarters there are signs of a ferment of thought, and this is specially noticeable among writers. Yet nothing has so far emerged which looks like becoming significant for the Turkish people as a whole.

The politicians are aware of the resurgence of Islam, and of its potentialities at least as a negative force in politics, that is to say, they are aware of the dangers of giving one's opponents any ground for saying that one is attacking Islam. This has not, however, prevented legal proceedings against Dervish leaders suspected of building up political power for themselves. The *tarikats* had maintained an underground existence after their proscription, and with the increasing toleration for religion came more into the open again; but their leadership tends to be reactionary. Despite secularization, however, religion is still very much alive in Turkey. Bernard Lewis's conclusion (p. 418) is that "the deepest Islamic roots of Turkish life and culture are still alive, and the ultimate identity of Turk and Muslim in Turkey is still unchallenged". It may be that secularization has prevented the formation of an adequate leadership. Yet even on this point the same authority is not unhopeful and thinks that "a true revival of religious faith on the level of modern thought and life is within the bounds of possibility" (*ibid.*).

[1] Cf. Howard Reed, "The Faculty of Divinity at Ankara", *Muslim World*, vols. XLVI (1956), pp. 295–312; XLVII (1957), pp. 22–35.

SECULARIZATION IN OTHER PARTS OF THE MIDDLE EAST

It seemed useful to go into some detail in describing the process of secularization in Turkey, since this was the country in which the process has been carried furthest. Turkey shows in an extreme form what has in some measure been happening everywhere. Even in the state of Israel there has been something comparable in the struggle between secularizing politicians and the traditional "men of religion".

In the sphere of education the common phenomenon in the Arabic-speaking countries and Persia has been the appearance of a "modern" or secular system of education alongside the traditional religious system. In the lands from Egypt to Iraq the secular system of education included Arabic language and literature as a main subject, and this slightly lessened the gulf between the two systems. In French North Africa, notably Algeria, the aim was to educate the Arabs into becoming Frenchmen, and Arabic was not taught in the "modern" schools; and this has produced a situation not unlike that in Turkey after the change of script, where there were no persons with a modern education who were engaging in higher religious studies. The tendency of the secular educational system to foster secularism or irreligion has been fortified by the fact that, when Muslim students came to Europe, they read attacks on religion by men like Bertrand Russell, but, because of their inherited suspicion of Christianity, would not read the attempts of Christian thinkers to reply to the attacks.

At this point it is appropriate to notice that, despite the bifurcation in the educational system, one of the *'ulamā'* managed to begin the task of *aggiornamento* in the sphere of theology. This was the Egyptian scholar Muḥammad 'Abduh (d. 1905). Although educated in the traditional way up to the highest level (at the university of the Azhar in Cairo), he also gained an introduction to European thought through the lectures of a wandering intellectual and reformer, Jamāl al-Dīn al-Afghānī; and subsequently he spent a year in Paris working along with al-Afghānī. He became a skilful orator and lecturer, and, when asked to give lectures on theology, broke away from the old methods of commenting on texts, and instead, as we might say, argued from first principles. The substance of his theological lectures was published in 1897 under the title of *Risālat al-tawḥīd* ("Epistle on the Unity, sc. of God"). In this work essential doctrine is unchanged, and occidental readers of today may not at once notice any great advance on the author's predecessors.[1] Yet it was a real beginning of change and as such noteworthy. Although he became head of the university of the Azhar, and initiated reforms in its teaching, he failed to start a new theological movement, though he had one or two immediate pupils. A thorough-going reform of the Azhar had to wait until Ṭāhā Ḥusayn became minister of education after the Second World War.

The recent reform of the Azhar has hardly had time yet to bear fruit. Until about 1950 the professors there did not have an adequate knowledge of European languages, and consequently their knowledge of European thought was confined to secondary works in Arabic and to such of the main texts as had been translated. Realizing that an attempt must be made to come to grips with philosophy, they turned to the study (in Arabic, of course) of Ibn Rushd or Averroes, who before the reform would have been avoided as a heretic. More has in fact been achieved by those who approached theological questions from a purely literary angle. Though there are several important works here, one may be selected for mention since it has been translated into English—*City of Wrong* by Kāmil Ḥusayn (Amsterdam and London, 1959). This is a study of the relation of communal to individual guilt based on an imaginative reconstruction of the events leading to the crucifixion of Jesus. At the present moment interesting developments are also taking place in Damascus, where one of the leading figures is Professor Muḥammad al-Mubārak. The Muslims of India under the British Raj were about a generation ahead of the Arabic-speaking world in their reactions to European thought. The outstanding figure was Sir Muḥammad Iqbāl.[2] In recent times there have been a number of writers who explain Islam in modern terms, such as Mawdūdī in Pakistan and Abu 'l-Kalām Azad in India.[3]

In matters of legislation and the judicature the Arabic-speaking countries have pursued a course similar to that of Turkey, but without going to extremes. There have been secular codes of law, usually based on French or Swiss models. These have in many cases dealt with personal status, but more in accordance with the Islamic outlook than in Turkey, though Tunisia has abandoned the traditional permission for a Muslim man to have four wives and has insisted on monogamy.

[1] Cf. Charles C. Adams, *Islam and Modernism in Egypt, a Study of the Religious Movement inaugurated by Muḥammad 'Abduh* (London, 1933).

[2] Esp. *The Reconstruction of Religious Thought in Islam* (London, 1934).

[3] E.g. Sayyid Abu 'l-A'lā Mawdūdī, *Towards understanding Islam*, trans. by Khurshid Ahmed (Lahore, 1960); Abu 'l-Kalām Azad, *The Tarjumān al-Qur'ān*, ed. and trans. by Syed Abdul-Latif (London, 1962).

Since the changes have not usually been so abrupt as in Turkey, the *'ulamā'* have tended to retain a measure of influence, varying from country to country. The position in the Sudan is interesting since there for a time (1885–98) the ruler of the country, the Mahdī or his successor, was also head of a religious movement and so not subject to the decisions of the *'ulamā'*; and the dominant political party at the moment is the *Umma* party, which continues the tradition of the Mahdī and has at its head one of his descendants, Ṣādiq al-Mahdī. It remains to be seen whether the relative weakness of the *'ulamā'* in the Sudan will make reforms there any easier.

Finally it may be noticed that among ordinary men, especially among those who have prospered, there is much secularism and materialism. Much of this is simply the result of exposure to the new possibilities of material luxury, and only means that men are so engrossed in the material aspects of life that they see nothing else. This is comparable to what has happened elsewhere, and is unlikely to be a permanent state of affairs. It is difficult to estimate how wide and how deep is the acceptance of secularism as a creed. Among those with a Euro-American education a number will argue on behalf of a secularistic outlook. It is often found in practice, however, that the same men retain a definite if tenuous religious attachment. For the last third of the twentieth century few are likely to adopt mere secularism as distinct from allegiance to some form of Marxism. On the whole it would seem that the wave of secularism and materialism is receding. Most serious-minded men in the Middle East realize the gravity of the problems of the present time, and are therefore aware of the need for a religion that will enable them to cope with the situations that arise from the impingement of these problems on their personal lives.[1]

In Turkey, doubtless because of the success of the process of secularization, a resurgence of Islam was slow in appearing. In the other countries of the Middle East, however, this resurgence came earlier, and often, notably in Egypt, attained a high degree of organization. It was in 1928 that Ḥasan al-Bannā' began to address meetings and to form the Muslim Brethren (*al-ikhwān al-muslimīn*), and by 1948 there were probably half a million members. In a profound and penetrating study of the political movements of the Middle East, including their intellectual and religious aspects, Manfred Halpern speaks of the Muslim

[1] The various intellectual trends are discussed by Kenneth Cragg in *Counsels in Contemporary Islam* (Edinburgh, 1965).

Brethren in Egypt, Syria and elsewhere, together with movements like *Fidā'iyān-i Islām* in Persia and the *Khāksārs* and *Jamā'at-i Islām* in Pakistan, as neo-Islamic totalitarianism, and points out their resemblances to fascism, including the National Socialism of Germany under Adolf Hitler.[1] From a purely political point of view this may be justified, and the resemblances certainly exist. Yet in a wider perspective this characterization is misleading. It is true that these movements sometimes "concentrate on mobilizing passion and violence to enlarge the power of their charismatic leader and the solidarity of the movement...", and that "they champion the values and emotions of a heroic past, but repress all free critical analysis of either past roots or present problems".[2] Yet political ineptitude and even failure do not outweigh their positive significance as marking a resurgence of religion.

From the present perspective a movement like the Muslim Brethren in Egypt is to be seen as primarily a revival of religion in reaction to the widespread secularization of political and social life. Many of those who felt unsettled and insecure because of the changes turned to religion. When the religious revival movement realized its strength, it began to use its influence in the political field. Yet just because it was a return to religious roots, it had no political programme relevant to contemporary needs. It resorted to one of the common shifts of politicians in the Middle East—the appeal to trust a new leader, coupled with the suggestion that a change of government will set everything right. This was not the whole programme of the Muslim Brethren, however, for they also insisted on a return to the Qur'ān and the Traditions (or *sunna*) of the Prophet. This is what one was bound to expect in a predominantly Sunnī country. The essential distinction between the two main forms of Islam, the Sunnī and the Shī'ī, is that the Sunnīs are primarily attached to a programme, namely, that contained in Qur'ān and Traditions, while the Shī'īs are primarily attached to a person, usually called the *imām*, and consider that he, because he is divinely inspired, is most likely to guide the community aright. In short we have in the Muslim Brethren a religious movement seeking a political programme, but primarily concerned with purely religious objectives (in the narrow sense).

There is an important difference, too, between the neo-Islamic mass

[1] *The Politics of Social Change in the Middle East and North Africa* (Princeton, 1963), esp. pp. 134–55.

[2] *Op. cit.* pp. 135 f.

1 Students in a courtyard of al-Azhar University, Cairo.

2 *Jabal Raḥma*, the Mountain of Mercy, during the Pilgrimage.

3 The *Maḥmal* or Holy Carpet carried in procession through Mecca.

4 Pilgrims round the Ka'ba, Mecca.

5 The Sultan Ahmed Mosque, Istanbul.

6 Interior of the Selimiye Mosque, Edirne, showing the *minbar*.

7 Self-mutilation among Shīʿīs near Shushtar.

8 The Shāh Chirāgh Mosque, Shīrāz.

9 *a* The Jāmiʿ Masjid, Delhi, at the time of prayer.

9 *b* Muslim prayer on the *maydān*, Bombay.

10 *a* Teaching the Qur'ān, Ahmedabad, Gujerat.

10 *b* Man dressed as a tiger during the Muḥarram Festival to represent the lion said to have guarded the body of al-Ḥusayn. An example of a Hindu practice given an Islamic interpretation.

11 Religious teaching, Islamabad.

12 *a* Fifteenth-century mosques, Samarkand.

12 *b* A Marabout.

13 Begova Mosque, Sarajevo.

14 *a* Mosque in Asmara, Eritrea.

14 *b* Mosque in Zaria, Northern Nigeria.

15 *a* The Ruins of Dir'iyya, Saudi Arabia.

15 *b* The Mutawakkil Mosque, Ṣan'ā'.

16 *a* The Āghā Khān accepting loyal addresses from an Ismāʿīlī leader, at Dar-es-Salaam.

16 *b* A Druze bride.

movements and fascism. Fascism has normally been confined to a single nation. The political leaders of the nation would naturally put the interests of the nation above those of other nations. They would even be inclined to sacrifice the interests of the individual to those of the nation. Because the conception of the nation was not associated with any statement of the rights of the individual over against the nation, opportunities for the abuse of power would be numerous. In the case of Islam, however, the community is potentially universal or world-wide. More importantly, Islam has in the Qur'ān (with or without the Traditions) a paradigm of just relations within a community, and this in the long run must almost certainly curb the ruthless and unprincipled exercise of power by those who happen to have seized it. In this way the neo-Islamic mass movements, far from being tantamount to national socialism or fascism, are likely to be an important barrier against such a development.

THE IMPACT OF MARXIST COMMUNISM

In considering "religion and anti-religion" a new phase of the impact of Euro-America on the Middle East may be said to have begun with the Russian Revolution of 1917 and the emergence of the USSR as a world power, though it was only slowly that the new features appeared. For one thing the USSR was to some extent a Muslim power. In 1939 it was reckoned that, out of a population of 170 millions, some twenty millions were traditionally Muslims, mostly living in Russian Central Asia. Some of these were already in revolt against the Tsar when the Revolution broke out, and most Muslims supported the Revolution. In return the Soviet regime encouraged Pan-Islamic congresses. The process of "communizing" the Muslims which began about 1921 was in fact comparable to the process of secularization elsewhere. There was no direct attack on Islam, and indeed the government tried to get *fatwās* or "legal opinions" from the *'ulamā'* stating that their measures were permissible according to the *sharī'a*. In 1928, however, with the policy of sovietization, Islam was openly persecuted, and this continued until just before the outbreak of war in 1939, when it was realized that to obtain a maximum war effort the support of religious bodies would be required. In recent years the attack on Islam has been renewed.

Once the Soviet government had properly established its control of the country after the revolution of 1917, it was able to consider the expansion of its influence in various parts of the world, including the Middle East. Russian interest in the Middle East was no new thing. Already in the eighteenth century the Tsars had claimed to be the protectors of all the Christians in the Ottoman empire. By the nineteenth century their official protégés were limited to the Orthodox Christians, but they made the most of this contact. Russian monasteries were established in Palestine with buildings sufficient to give at least a roof to the pilgrims who were encouraged to go in large numbers to the Holy Places. Various forms of help were given to other branches of the Orthodox Church, and there were facilities for Orthodox Christian Arabs, men and women, to study in Russia.

For the renewal of Russian influence in the Middle East the new rulers had at hand a new creed, Marxism, which already had many adherents in the region. As early as 1922 a Communist party of Egypt was admitted to membership of the Comintern. There were Communist groups in Turkey about the same time, but Communism never obtained much hold in Turkey, presumably because Russia was the traditional arch-enemy. There was a Syrian Communist party in 1930, and an Iraqi one a few years later. These early Communist groups tended to consist of intellectuals, who had few contacts with either workers or peasants. Attention was given, however, to the formation of trade unions and to the infiltration of trade unions which had already sprung up independently. In this way there was slowly built up a body of partly organized, politically conscious people. Most of them, however, were far from understanding, still less accepting the full Marxist doctrine.

There were indeed grave difficulties in the way of would-be Marxists in the Middle East. The politicians in Moscow who directed the activities of Communist parties elsewhere had no backing from intellectuals who had made a study of Middle East conditions. The directives issued to Communist leaders in the Middle East were based partly on the needs of Russia's international policies at a given moment, and partly to a doctrinaire application to the Middle East of the Marxist theories which had been worked out for European conditions. The results were frequent inexplicable changes in the party line, and consequent difficulties in arousing and retaining local interest, since nothing was done about particular local grievances. The greatest obstacles were found in Palestine. The Jewish intellectuals interested in Marxism were forced to accept the view that Zionism was reactionary; since this removed their reason for being in Palestine, many of them left. Later, in 1924, they were told that they must support the struggle of the Arab workers and peasants against the imperialists, and in fact became an Arab mass party. Since the creation of the state of Israel in 1948, things have been easier for Jewish Communists, but the Israeli Communist party (MAKI), though its membership is two thirds Jewish, has not lived down its reputation for anti-Zionism, and is relatively more important as an expression of the feelings of the Arab minority in Israel.

After 1941 Russian propaganda was helped by military successes, which Middle East peoples have always tended to admire perhaps more than others. After the end of the war, too, there was increasing awareness of the success of Communist governments in modernizing and industrializing a relatively backward country. This was thought to show what was possible in the Middle East, given proper organization. The directives to the local parties, too, became much more realistic. The line was now to co-operate with nationalists, even when not proletarian, in their efforts to expel the imperialists and gain independence. At the same time financial support was given in various forms, and large numbers of Middle East students received scholarships and subventions to enable them to attend universities and technical colleges in Russia and other Communist countries. This comprehensive policy has paid good dividends to the Russians, but they have not been as successful as at one time seemed likely. No Middle East country has so far wholly identified itself with Russia or with Communism. Even at the intellectual level there are very few convinced and instructed Marxists.[1]

REACTIONS TO MARXISM

A recent writer, Walter Z. Laqueur, who speaks with some authority at the political level of the growth of Communism in the Middle East, has argued that the "bulwark" theory is untenable. This is the theory that, since most of the inhabitants of the Middle East are believing and practising Muslims, atheistic and materialistic Communism would find little foothold among them. He even goes so far as to say that "Islam has gradually ceased to a be serious competitor of Communism

[1] Political aspects up to 1955 are fully treated by Walter Z. Laqueur in *Communism and Nationalism in the Middle East* (London, 1956).

in the struggle for the soul of the present and potential *élites* in the countries of the Middle East".[1] This judgment—now at the time of writing some ten years old—is not altogether sound.

While the growth of Communism and the increase in the number of Communist sympathizers in the Middle East is impressive when the facts are massed together, yet a comparison with other regions shows important differences. In Burma and China, we are told, there has been synthesis or syncretism between Marxist ideas and those of Buddhism and Confucianism respectively. This has not happened in the Middle East, and indeed is unthinkable. Marxist atheism has been generally rejected. Even where a Communist political programme has been acceptable—and this is not always the case—those promoting it have usually claimed to be good Muslims. The near-Communist Revolutionary Council that came to power in Zanzibar in 1964 continued or increased its religious practice; the president, Abeid Karume, dressed as a Muslim on public occasions and used the title of *shaykh*. The same is true in most of the Arabic-speaking countries. All politicians know that, as indicated above, Islam is a powerful negative force in politics in the sense that any man suspected of attacking Islam or being anti-religious will lose a vast amount of popular support; and there are always opponents ready to make the most of small pieces of evidence. If word got about that any plan or programme was anti-Islamic, and if this could not be refuted, the plan might well be rejected. In many people's eyes the charge of "being anti-Islamic" would justify the rejection of an otherwise good proposal.

This strong negative influence of Islam in most parts of the Islamic world still leaves a power vacuum in various respects. In particular there is a vacuum of positive ideas to direct the development of the Islamic countries as modern states. This vacuum of ideas Marxism does not quite manage to fill. There does not appear to have been any deep Marxist analysis of the special problems of the Islamic Middle East. Before the Second World War it was usually taken for granted that the Middle East could be put in the strait-jacket of classical Marxism, though it did not require much objective observation of the Middle East to realize that the Marxist theory of social classes just did not fit. Attempts to apply Marxist theory to the interpretation of the career of Muḥammad and the origins of Islam have achieved little more than offending Muslims. Indeed one might say that Marxist political

[1] *Op. cit.* p. 6.

scientists are at a serious disadvantage in studying the Islamic world, since they start from a general conception of religion which makes it virtually impossible for them to account for the continuing importance of Islam in the contemporary scene.

There are also signs of positive Islamic reactions to the presence of Marxist Communism. The more thoughtful Muslim politicians realize that it is futile merely to denounce the Communists as atheists, and that they must devise positive programmes to deal with the problems which the Communists attempt to tackle. There are a few leaders who would claim to be "Muslim socialists", but on the whole there has been less talk of Islamic socialism, than there has been, for example, of African socialism. By way of exception the idea of "Arab socialism" has been prominent in Egypt in the propaganda of Jamāl 'Abd al-Nāṣir (Nasser). Arab nationalism or Arabism (*'urūba*) has always been closely linked with Islam,[1] and thus it is not surprising to find a close link between Islam and Arab socialism. A semi-official Egyptian writer speaks of Islam as "the religion of justice and equality" and considers it synonymous with a "revolution which first laid down the socialist principles of justice and equality".[2] A notable document, showing how a responsible political group with a definitely religious basis elaborates a policy for the present situation, is *Barnāmaj ḥizb al-umma* ("Programme of the Umma party"); this was published at Khartoum in 1965 under the name of the leader of the party, Ṣādiq al-Mahdī, and contains detailed policies in the fields of education, health, justice and the economy generally.

There are, then, a few pieces of evidence to show that the Islamic giant is awakening out of sleep. So far is it from being true that Islam is no longer a serious rival to Communism that it would be more correct to say that Communism up till now has failed to dislodge Islam from its position of dominance.

FUTURE PROSPECTS

Talk of a vacuum of some sort in the Middle East—whether political or politico-religious or sheerly intellectual—prompts the question how this vacuum is likely to be filled, and so to a consideration of the future.

[1] G. E. von Grunebaum, *Modern Islam* (Berkeley, 1962), ch. IX, esp. p. 216; Sylvia Haim (ed.), *Arab Nationalism* (Berkeley, 1962).

[2] M. I. Hamza, *Ishtirākiyyat al-islām wa 'l-ishtirākiyya al-gharbiyya* ["The Socialisms of Islam and Western Socialism"] (Cairo, 1961), quoted from *Islam and International Relations*, ed. J. Harris Proctor (London, 1965), pp. 122 f., 152.

It is at once apparent that the usual European conception of religion as a purely individual matter is inadequate even as a description of the phenomena of Middle East religion. The attachment of most men in the Middle East to their religious convictions is so intense that it is nearly always a factor of which politicians are bound to take account. In western Europe and America, on the other hand, there are a few occasions when a politician has to pay much attention to religious factors. In part this may be due to the lack of intensity of religious feelings, but probably it is more the result of the indefiniteness of the religious convictions which have always to be respected. "Men of religion" are therefore forced to take part in politics by the need to prevent their religious feelings being exploited by politicians. Intensity, it would seem, comes to man's religious feelings when they meet some of his deepest needs. Definiteness often arises from controversy, and is not necessarily connected with essentials.

Is it possible for there to be once again in the Middle East religious convictions which, besides being definite and held with intensity, are relevant to the present situation? Can there be a sufficient revival of any of the old religions, or must we look for something new? Comparison of this situation with similar phases of various religions throughout the world suggests that, while there must be some break with the old, there is a power which works within the great religions for their revival and renewal. Such a renewal cannot be directly planned for by man, but we can state some of the conditions which such a new or renewed religion must fulfil. In the modern Middle East a religious movement able to contribute to the new growth of society and culture in the region would have to have a set of ideas which, though in some respects new, yet were basically in harmony with the essentials of the existing dominant ideas, especially the Islamic. If this condition was fulfilled, the set of ideas would probably also be capable of sustaining individual piety; and this is a point where Marxism tends to fail. Again, the set of ideas would have to be in accordance with the contemporary scientific outlook. Most important of all, it ought to be capable of giving at least general guidance in respect of political decisions.

The scholar-observer may point to these conditions but his contribution to their fulfilment is of necessity minimal. Even the self-conscious Middle Eastern intellectual can do little so long as he remains at the purely intellectual level. The advance can only come from a man immersed in the life of the region, out of whose inner being there emerge new ideas or new forms of old ideas. There will probably be a whole series of such persons influencing one another. The emergence of the ideas does not happen without much spiritual travail, yet mere effort will not produce ideas that are really dynamic. It is only when they spontaneously emerge from the deeps of a man—call it "collective unconscious" if you like—that they touch the deeps in other men, and so lead to a fundamental renewal not merely of religion but of life.

In the competition to supply the ideas for the renewal of the life of the Middle East, there are some entrants besides the world religions and Marxism, and these should be looked at briefly. So far no really new body of ideas specially relevant to the Middle East has appeared in Marxism, secularism or the great religions. On the fringe of Islam however, there have been new ideas, notably in Wahhābism, Aḥmadiyya and Bahā'ism. Wahhābism developed in central Arabia in the middle of the eighteenth century and is fundamentally a reassertion of traditional Islam. It is difficult to demonstrate that it is a response to the impact of Europe, and yet it is not unreasonable to look on it as somehow a result of the pressures of Europe on the Ottoman Empire as felt on the frontiers of that empire (as at Baṣra and Baghdad) and even beyond; one would expect that, as men felt their existing way of life to be threatened, they would turn to an older and "purer" form of their religion. In the course of time Wahhābism has had some influence in the great cities of Islam.

The response to the European impact is seen more clearly in the Aḥmadiyya movement which began at Qadian in the Panjab (now in India) towards the end of the nineteenth century. While claiming to return to the past and to be the true Islam, it also has features which show it reacting to some aspects of the impact. Thus Mīrzā Ghulām Aḥmad, the founder, claimed to be the "promised messiah" of the Christians, doubtless because he lived in a world which included European Christians, often in positions of superiority. He also copied Christian missionary methods to a great extent in the organization of his movement.

Bahā'ism also shows a reaction to Europe, but in a different way. Whether in its origin reaction to pressures ultimately due to Europe is prominent is a question difficult to answer, since its early social context has not been adequately studied. In its later phases, however, it has adopted to a great extent the outlook and ideas of Euro-American liberalism—an idealistic attitude to life without any complex metaphysical dogmas. Both the Aḥmadī and the Bahā'ī movements by their novelty have a chance of creating the new set of ideas required in the present situation, but their relative failure so far suggests that they are unlikely to do much better in the future and that neither is therefore likely to become *the* religion of the Middle East. This failure may be due to the fact that they have both taken over too much of the mistaken European assumptions that religion is an individual matter, that it consists chiefly of ideas and that it influences men through ideas rationally apprehended.

In the quest for the new ideas that are required two processes are discernible: a drawing closer together of the three great religions and their acceptance of ideas and practices from one another.

The coming closer together of separate religious groups is a universal feature in the history of religions and is not confined to the contemporary Middle East. In the latter case it would seem to be the result of social pressures which arise ultimately from the growth of large-scale organization in the economic sphere, though the persons being drawn together may not be fully aware of the economic factors involved. The same process is seen throughout the world in the Christian ecumenical movement. It may also be seen in the drawing together of formerly hostile Islamic communities. In East Africa the Ismā'īlīs—who are mostly Asians and see the possibility of expulsion by independent African governments—have emphasized their solidarity with the African Muslims by forming an East African Muslim Welfare Association and working for the welfare of Sunnī African Muslims. In other respects also there have been moves towards overcoming the age-old schisms in the Islamic community.

A still more interesting example of the way in which separate groups are drawing together is the tendency for Christian Arabs to come closer to Muslim Arabs and even to regard Arab nationalism as involving some degree of acceptance of Islam. Through the centuries there have always been Christian Arabs who became Muslims. The new feature is that they now proclaim a change of allegiance as something admirable, a fulfilment of their Arabism. There are some interesting materials on this point in Sylvia Haim, *Arab Nationalism*, especially in connexion with a writer called Khalīl Iskandar Qubruṣī.[1] This whole tendency is most noticeable among Christian Arabs from Palestine and may be due to the strains caused by Zionism, which may be regarded as one

[1] *Op. cit.* pp. 57–61.

of the latest forms of the Euro-American impact. Actually the immediate cause of Qubruṣī's change of allegiance seems to be the attitude towards Orthodox Christian Arabs adopted by the ecclesiastical hierarchy, which was almost wholly of Greek nationality; but this matter may merely have served to exacerbate the general tensions caused by the impact of Europe.

At the present time any general drawing together of the three great religions may seem to be unlikely. Yet in view of the completely unexpected acceleration in the tempo of the Christian ecumenical movement in recent years, it is conceivable that there might be some comparable and unforeseeable acceleration of the rapprochement between Judaism, Christianity and Islam. The possibility of rapprochement exists in the case of all the great world religions, but, because of the common origin of the three Middle East religions, it should be easier for them than say for Judaism and Buddhism. Thus it is by no means impossible that by the end of this century some spectacular change of this kind may have taken place.

Meanwhile there have been a number of conscious but limited attempts to bring the religions closer to one another and to increase their mutual understanding and sympathy. Between Christians and Jews closer relations have been relatively easy where both parties shared in Euro-American culture in addition to their common acceptance of the Old Testament. Such relationships have been given a degree of organization in the Council of Christians and Jews, which is an international body but is not of course specially concerned with the Middle East. Muslim–Christian relationships have been more difficult, yet here also something has been achieved. About 1941 a small group of Christian and Muslim theologians in Cairo began to meet to discuss topics of common interest such as religious toleration and prayer. They took the name of a group of early Muslim philosophers, "the Brethren of Purity" (*ikhwān al-ṣafā'*).[1] Rather more ambitious was the conference at Bhamdoun in the Lebanon in 1954, arranged by the American Friends of the Middle East; this brought together some seventy-four religious leaders, ecclesiastics and laymen, half Muslim and half Christian.[2] A continuation committee was formed, but, perhaps because of the death of the initiator, Garland Evans Hopkins, the original vigour seems gradually to have died away.

[1] Cf. *International Review of Missions*, vol. XXXVI (1947), pp. 74 f.

[2] Cf. *Muslim World*, vol. XLV (1955), pp. 37–44.

Most remarkable in this connexion is the personal contribution of the great French orientalist, Louis Massignon, both by his own activity and by the way he inspired others. When he discovered a chapel in Britanny dedicated to the Seven Sleepers of Ephesus, who also appear in the Qur'ān (Sūra XVIII) as "the men of the cave", he made use of this fact to bring Muslims and Christians together in worship in the chapel. Although he was a Christian priest of the Greek Catholic rite, he had so many friends among Muslims who knew his profound appreciation of their religion, that what he himself achieved to bring the two religions closer cannot yet begin to be estimated. The present writer has heard a highly-placed Muslim judge say of him that "he was both a Christian and a Muslim".

Among the conceptions disseminated by Louis Massignon and his associates was that of "the religion of Abraham" as a general term to cover Judaism, Christianity and Islam. This is an excellent way of putting the three religions on a footing of equality—the kind of equality that is, as it were, the external form of courtesy required if joint meetings are to run smoothly, but which does not necessarily imply an ultimate judgment. If you are to have amicable conversations with an adherent of another religion, you must in some sense accept the account he gives of himself, though such acceptance does not prevent you disagreeing and expressing your disagreement. Thus to say that "Islam belongs to the Judeo-Christian tradition" is a discourteous way of expressing a fact, for it appears to place Islam on a lower level than the other two religions. To say that all three religions are manifestations of "the religion of Abraham" is both more courteous and more accurate. All three do in some sense make this claim. The Jews worship the God of Abraham, Isaac and Jacob, while an important strand in New Testament theology emphasizes that Christian faith is one with the faith of Abraham. Muslims accepted the (Old Testament) genealogy which made them descendants of Abraham through Ishmael, and they connected Abraham with their central shrine, the Kaʿba at Mecca. So in a world in which we are learning that there are more kinds of truth than "literal", the conception of "the religion of Abraham" contains a deep symbolic truth, and its use is a contribution to the bringing together of the three religions.[1]

The fashionable term today for the conscious coming together of

[1] An eirenic study in this direction is Youakim Moubarac's *Abraham dans le Coran* (Paris, 1957).

religions is "dialogue". By this is meant a deliberate mutual confrontation of representatives of two religions in order to reach a fuller and more sympathetic understanding of the other religion. It usually comes about through oral or written communication. Here it is chiefly important to notice that dialogue has certain presuppositions. Not merely must the participants be ready to speak courteously and listen charitably, but they must be sufficiently open-minded to be prepared to learn, and if necessary to revise their own previous ideas.[1] Normally, too, any discussion must take place at the highest level of modern thought, so that there is bound also to be some accommodation to modern scientific thought, especially to modern sociological and psychological theories of religion. Thus dialogue, when fully entered into, is a most searching process for all taking part. All will require to examine some very fundamental questions about their own religion and indeed their whole scheme of thought. They will have to consider how they are to meet the criticisms that religion is an opiate and that belief in God is a projection. They will have to consider how symbolic or mythic truth is really truth, and what the place of history (and modern historical methodology) is in a religion.

Such a process should not mean that any of the religions has to discard a truth which is essential for it, but it may mean that a religion has to distinguish more carefully between essentials and non-essentials and even to reformulate its essentials. So we may expect that Christians will have to consider how to formulate the doctrine of the Trinity so as to restore the emphasis on monotheism which many Christians have lost, but which is retained in Islam. They will also have to consider how to give a positive interpretation to the life and career of Muḥammad which will be in accordance with the esssentials of Christianity. Similarly Muslims will have to find a positive interpretation of the life and teaching of Jesus which does not contradict their basic monotheism. Something like this will also be true of the Jews.

There is evidence that the influence of the non-Christian religions on Christianity has already begun. In *World Cultures and World Religions* (London, 1960), Hendrik Kraemer has a notable chapter (pp. 228–71) on "the Western Response to Eastern Cultures and Religions". This is indeed the second process mentioned above (p. 634). What has come about so far has doubtless occurred unconsciously, but from now onwards much will happen consciously. Whether new insights are

[1] Cf. *Truth in the Religions*, pp. 161–74.

attained consciously by dialogue or merely grow unconsciously, their incorporation on one's religion has a similar end-result. There is a sense in which that religion will be successful which is best at including the truths of other religions in its own body of ideas. Since external practices can be included more easily than ideas, an increasing external similarity between the religions is to be expected.

This whole discussion may seem to have avoided the fundamental aspect of religion, the personal. Yet this is omnipresent. It is at the personal level that Marxism as a quasi-religion is weakest. Above all we must not forget that current religion is the religion of men and women who live in the contemporary world with all its pressures, economic and social. When people think the personal is being neglected, their difficulty is perhaps due to the fact that men react to social and economic pressures without realizing that they are doing so. A man wrestling with a problem may think that his solution is purely religious, and yet an observer may see clearly that he has been reacting to social and economic aspects of the situation in which he is. Consequently, a social and economic approach to religion is not contrary to a personal one but complementary.

The personal side of religion, then, is not being over-looked when it is said that there are various pressures towards a rapprochement or even unification of religions in the Middle East and in the world generally. If a revised form of one of the old religions becomes dominant, it will be because it meets the personal needs of men living amid social and economic pressures. It must give them a set of ideas which will be a basis for a satisfying general attitude to the world and its problems. Among these ideas will be some which evoke a strong response—dynamic ideas or images—and public worship must be such as to strengthen these ideas and to bring the circumstances of daily life into relation to them. The same should be true of private devotions. One of the dangers present in the movement towards uniformity is that a religion may be induced to surrender some of its dynamic images and replace them by ideas which do not evoke the same response; it is usually in the distinctive or peculiar features of a religion that its strength lies.

From the standpoint of personal religion some of the assertions made earlier may be reinforced. The new forms of religion in the Middle East, which we envisage and hope for, cannot be discovered by any merely logical or intellectual process. They must be allowed to emerge of themselves from the unconscious; and this emerging usually takes place, if not in the course of public or private worship, at least as a result of engaging in worship. The scholar and observer may form some notion of the general direction in which events are moving, but he cannot say in advance which new formulation of ideas is going to lead to a mass response, still less (except when he is also a participant) do anything to produce the formula. The new formulation, when it comes from someone's unconscious, will be unexpected, and may be violently disturbing. Typical is the experience of Abraham who heard an inner voice commanding him, contrary to all human prudence, to sacrifice his son. A vital renewal of religion in the Middle East will come about when men rediscover the capacity for hearing the voice that speaks in the inner silence, and when, having heard, they are ready to obey however high the cost.

GLOSSARY

GLOSSARY

In this glossary of foreign words appearing in the text, the following abbreviations are used:

A:	Arabic.	P:	Persian.
Eth:	Ethiopic.	Serb:	Serbo-Croatian.
Gr:	Greek.	T:	Turkish.
H:	Hebrew.	U:	Urdu.

'abhōdhāh (*avodah*) H: physical labour; (divine) service.

abuna Eth: title meaning "His Paternity"; in Ethiopia, head of the Church of Ethiopia. In the Coptic Church the title now used for all bishops and metropolitans and for the patriarch.

'āda A: custom, habit.

adhān A: Muslim call to prayer.

'adl, *'adāla* A: justice.

aggādāh (or *haggādāh*) H: non-legal part of rabbinic literature in Talmud and Midrash, especially tales, stories and legends.

aḥādīth—see *ḥadīth*.

'ahd 'Umar—see *shurūṭ 'Umar*.

ahl al-bayt A, *ahl-i bayt* P: members of the household of the Prophet; they are particularly revered among the Shī'a.

ahl al-dhimma A: protected people—see also *dhimmī*.

ahl al-kitāb A: "people of the book", i.e. people whose religious beliefs are contained in a revealed book, as in the case of Jews and Christians.

aḥyā' A: keeping awake at night to perform religious duties, especially during the nights of Ramaḍān.

'ālim—see *'ulamā'*.

'aliyah (*'alīyāh*) H: "going up", Jewish immigration to Palestine.

amān A: a safe conduct; hence, public security in general.

amīr (pl. *umarā'*) A: leader, military leader, prince.

anba Coptic: ecclesiastical title for a saint, patriarch, metropolitan or bishop.

anjumān P, U: society.

anṣār A: helpers, notably the helpers of Muḥammad at Medina and of the Mahdī in the Sudan.

'āqil—see *'uqqāl*.

'aql A: reason; Universal Intelligence.

ashikë Albanian: "Lovers", a grade in the Bekṭāshī order. From Arabic *'āshiq* through Turkish *âşik*.

'āshūrā' A: Muslim voluntary fast-day on the tenth of Muḥarram, adopted from the Jews by Muḥammad. For the Shī'a of much greater significance than this, for on this day the third Shī'ite Imam, al-Ḥusayn, was killed at Karbalā'.

aṣnāf (pl. of *ṣinf*) A: although now used often with reference to unions, term denotes the guilds of craftsmen whose members are united by a spiritual as well as professional bond. The whole organization is often connected to a Ṣūfī order.

atse Eth: traditional title for Ethiopian king.

avodah—see *'abhōdāh*.

'awāmm A: the common people.

'awāriḍ A: extraordinary taxes not foreseen by the *sharī'a*.

awqāf—see *waqf*.

'azzāba A: "those who lead a retired life"; a group of individuals who together form a *ḥalqa* (ruling body) of a North African Ibāḍī community.

baballarë Albanian: "Fathers", a clerical rank in the Bekṭāshī order. From Turkish *babalar*.

badā' A: intervention of circumstances causing alteration of an earlier divine determination.

bakhshīsh P: bribery, a tip.

barā'a A: disavowal; the Ibāḍī doctrine of *barā'a* is the obligation of militancy towards those who are not followers of the true faith.

baraka A: "divine influx" or "grace" that reaches man in those actions and objects that have a religious and spiritual content.

basileus Gr: title of the Byzantine emperor.

basmala A: invocation of God's name.

bāṭil A: null or non-existent, as contravening a basic rule.

bāṭin A: esoteric.

bay'a A: act of swearing allegiance to new sovereign performed by notables of the realm on behalf of the community as a whole.

bayt al-māl A: treasury.

bedel-i 'askerî T: sum paid for exemption from military service.

beglerbeg, *beylerbey* T: Turkish provincial governor of highest rank.

berat T: letter of appointment; diploma of title.

bey T: lord, title of the former rulers in Tunisia.

be(y)th dīn H: religious court of law.

be(y)th dīn gādhōl H: high court of law.

bid'a (pl. *bida'*) A: an innovation; Wahhābism condemns and rejects all *bid'as* in religious belief and practice that have appeared since the time of *al-salaf al-ṣāliḥ*.

bismillāh A: "in the name of God".

büyük T: great.

chirotonia Gr: moment when prelate extends his hands over head of ordainee, during the ceremony of conferring holy orders.

daftar (pl. *dafātir*) P: (tax) register.

ḍahīr—see *ẓahīr*.

dahriyyūn A: materialists.

dā'ī A: (Shī'ī) missionary, propagandist.

dajjāl A: Antichrist.

dār A: house, building, abode, area.

darād'āh—see *dör de'ō.*
dār al-ḥarb A: lit. war-territory; any country not under Muslim domination.
darvīsh P—see *faqīr.*
da'wa A: propaganda, missionary activity of a *dā'ī.*
dawla A: state.
dayr A: monastery or church.
dayyān (pl. *dayyānīm*) H: religious judge.
debtera Eth: cantor, precentor or lay clerk.
dekanikion Gr: patriarchal staff, the sign of his authority.
derekh ereṣ H: good manners, lit. "way of the land".
devshirme T: levies of the unmarried male children of Orthodox subjects, reducing them to the status of slaves and training them for military and civil service.
dey T: maternal uncle; title of the former rulers in Algeria.
dhikr A: invocation of God's name; frequent repetition of God's name or of certain words and formulae in praise of God.
dhimma A: protection extended to "possessors of a book" (*ahl al-kitāb*), e.g. Jews or Christians, living under Muslim rule.
dhimmī A, *ẕimmi* T: protected, enjoying *dhimma*; second-class citizen of Muslim state.
dīn A: religion.
dīwān A, *dīvān* P: register; administration.
dör de'ō H: Yemenite for classical Hebrew *dōr dē'āh* = age of reason, with Arabic plural *darād'āh* = rationalists.
du'ā' A: prayer.
dustūr A: the common word for constitution in the modern Arab world, for which the term *niẓām asāsī* is often substituted in Saudi Arabia.
džemat Serb: a gathering, society, community. From Arabic *jamā'a* through Turkish *cemaat.*
džemijet Serb: a society, association, organization. From Arabic *jam'iyya* through Turkish *cemiyet.*
echege Eth: the premier monk of Ethiopia and, until 1950, the premier indigenous cleric.
epitropos Gr: procurator, controller, overseer.
Ermeni milleti T: Armenian community.
evkaf—see *waqf.*
faḍl A: virtue.
fallāḥ (pl. *fallāḥīn*) A: peasant.
faqīh—see *fuqahā'*
faqīr (pl. *fuqarā'*) A: literally the poor, but referring to those who participate in voluntary poverty and thereby follow the spiritual path as contained in Ṣūfism.
farā'iḍ A: religious duties.
fāsid A: an act which is null and void but which leaves certain lasting effects after annulment.
al-fātiḥa A: the opening Sūra of the Qur'ān.

fatwā (pl. *fatāwā*) A: a juridical opinion given by a *muftī* on a question relating to the *sharī'a*.

ferman T: order issued from the Ottoman chancery. From Persian *farmān*.

fiqh A: Islamic jurisprudence.

fitna A: dissension.

fiṭr, *ifṭār* A: fast breaking.

funūn A: sciences, knowledge.

fuqahā' (pl. of *faqīh*) A: those who teach the *fiqh*; jurists in general.

fuqarā'—see *faqīr*.

futuwwāt A: the Islamic brotherhoods based on chivalry and nobility which were popular and powerful in the Middle Ages.

galuth H: Diaspora.

gā'ōn (pl. *ge'ōnīm*) H: head of Talmudic academy in Palestine and Babylonia (Iraq) during the Middle Ages.

genīzā H: = "hidden", storage chamber in old synagogues for disused books and documents; most famous *genīzā* was in Cairo.

ghiyār A: discriminatory signs of Jews and Christians.

gjushë Albanian: "Grandfathers", a clerical rank in the Bekṭāshī order.

göbek adî T: name given to a Turkish child at birth.

haḍāna A: custody of minors.

ḥadarīm—see *ḥēder*.

ḥadd—see *ḥudūd*.

ḥadīth A: the corpus of Islamic tradition going back to Muḥammad; any single such tradition (pl. *aḥādīth*).

ḥāfiẓ (pl. *ḥuffāẓ*) A: one who has memorized the Qur'ān.

haggādāh—see *aggādāh*.

ḥā'ik A: cloak, mantle.

ḥājj A, *ḥājī* P: title accorded a Muslim who has made the *ḥajj* or pilgrimage to Mecca.

ḥākhām H: "sage, wise man", title of the rabbi of Sephardi (Spanish and Portuguese) and oriental Jewish communities.

ḥakham bashî H+T: leader of the Jewish community under the Ottomans.

halakhāh H: normative legal and prescriptive part of rabbinic literature.

ḥalāl A: permitted by Islamic law.

ḥalqa A: ruling body of a North African Ibāḍī community.

ḥalūqqāh H: "distribution of alms", collected in the Diaspora (dispersion, exile) for poor scholars returning to and living in Palestine.

ḥalutẓ (*ḥālūṣ*) H: pioneer, working to redeem the land in Palestine.

handžar Serb: a two-edged long knife. From Turkish *hancer* and Arabic *khanjar*.

ḥanīf A: pre-Islamic monotheist in Arabia.

ḥāra A: quarter (of a town). In Tunisia the term is applied specifically to the Jewish quarter.

ḥaram A: sacred enclave.

ḥarām A: prohibited by Islamic law.

ḥarbī A: lit. enemy; any non-Muslim person not subject to Muslim domination (fem. *ḥarbiyya*).

ḥasidism (*ḥasīd*) H: movement of Jewish mystics which originated in Poland and the Ukraine in the eighteenth century, founded by R. Yisrael Baal Shem Tov.

haskālāh H: "enlightenment". Movement for modern enlightenment towards the end of the eighteenth century.

ḥāzān (*ḥazzān*) H: cantor, prayer-leader.

ḥēder (pl. *ḥadarīm*) H: traditional school of elementary Jewish instruction.

hijra A: usually rendered as (*a*) "migration" or "flight" or (*b*) "the breaking of ties of kinship or association", notably by Muḥammad in A.D. 622 when he migrated from Mecca to Medina.

Hijra also means a military-agricultural colony of the Wahhābī Ikhwān in Arabia in the first half of the twentieth century. Only a few of the numerous *hijras* then established still exist.

ḥikma A: wisdom; (*a*) the Druze religious doctrine; (*b*) Shīʿī theosophy.

ḥisba A: market regulations.

hodža Serb: a Muslim religious teacher. From Persian *khwāja* through Turkish *hoca*. Sometimes used interchangeably with *imām*.

hoshanna rabba H: seventh day of Feast of Tabernacles (*sukkōth*).

ḥudūd (pl. of *ḥadd*) A: fixed penalties for seven offences, including theft, consumption of alcoholic beverages and apostasy.

ḥujja A: proof, testimony; a high grade in the Ismāʿīlī hierarchy.

ḥukm (pl. *aḥkām*) A: decision, ruling.

ḥulūl A: incarnation.

ḥurriyya A: freedom.

ʿibādāt A: acts of worship.

ʿīd A: a day of feasting or celebration connected particularly with religious occasions.

ʿīd al-aḍḥā A, *kurban bayramî* T: the feast of sacrifice, greater Bayram.

ʿīd al-fiṭr A, *sheker bayramî* T: the feast of the breaking of the Ramaḍān fast, lesser Bayram.

ʿīd-i ghadīr P: feast of the Shīʿa celebrating the time when, in their belief, ʿAlī was chosen by the Prophet as his successor.

al-ʿīd al-kabīr A: "the great *ʿīd*", i.e. *ʿīd al-aḍḥā*.

al-ʿīd al-ṣaghīr A: "the small *ʿīd*", i.e. *ʿīd al-fiṭr*.

ifṭār—see *fiṭr*.

iftirāq A: schism.

ijāza A: certificate of examination, licence for profession.

ijmāʿ A: consensus; ideally of the Muslim community; in practice of the leading *ʿulamāʾ* of a generation.

ijtihād A: independent legal decision, judgment arrived at by knowledge and reasoning, particularly in matters pertaining to the *sharīʿa*. One who practises *ijtihād* is termed *mujtahid*.

ikhtilāf al-dār A: distinction applied to two Jews or two Christians, one of whom is subject to Muslim and the other to non-Muslim domination. It does not refer to Muslims.

ikhtilāf al-dīn A: difference of religion.

ikhwān A: brethren.

imām A: usually meaning leader in prayer, it is used specifically in Shī'ism to denote those descendants of the Prophet who carry the "Prophetic light" within them by virtue of which they are upholders of the *sharī'a* and revealers of the inner meaning of the Qur'ān as well as intermediaries between man and God.

imāmbārā P: the Ithnā 'Asharī term for the place appointed for the holding of sessions commemorating *imāms*.

īmān A: faith, belief.

in shā'a 'llāh A: *inshallah* T: "if God will". A phrase very commonly used by Muslims in mentioning future events or intentions.

intiẓār A: the awaiting of the appearance of the *mahdī* which implies religious fortitude and patience toward the misfortunes of the world.

'iqqēshīm H: "crooked", obstinate; conservative opponents of *darād'āh*.

'irfān A: gnosis or the way of knowledge which is the heart of Ṣūfī teachings and the means whereby man is led to the realization of the Divine through unitive and illuminative knowledge.

ishhād A (modern): the document granted by a public authority containing an affidavit.

istiqlāl A: autonomy, independence.

i'tiqād A: conviction.

ittifāqāt A: conventions, agreements.

jafr A: cabbalistic word-play.

jahbadh (pl. *jahābidha*) P, A: money-changer, coin-tester, tax-collector.

jāhil—see *juhhāl*.

jāhiliyya A: pre-Islamic times.

jamā'a A: assembly.

jawālī A: synonym of *jizya* q.v.

jihād A: "exertion (in the path of God)", referring especially to the obligation incumbent on Muslims to take up arms against unbelievers for the propagation of the faith, so that the term is often rendered as "holy war".

jinn A: demons.

jizya A: poll-tax, levied on *dhimmīs* q.v.

juhhāl (pl. of *jāhil*) A: ignorant; uninitiated.

kafā'a A: equality of standing between two partners to a marriage.

kāfir A: infidel.

kāhin (pl. *kuhhān*) A: temple priest.

kâhya T: intendant.

kalām A: speech; dialectic, scholastic theology.

kalima A: word; logos.

Kamutay T: Turkish National Assembly.

kanun T: law; code of laws. From Greek *kanōn* through Arabic *qānūn*.

Karaites (*qarā'īm*) H: Jewish sect opposed to the Rabbanites, the adherents of the Oral Law (codified as *halakhāh*).

kāshēr H: ritually fit for human consumption.

kashf A: vision.

khalīfa A: successor, caliph.
khalwa A: solitude, usually accompanied by fasting.
khāniqāh P: the centre of the Ṣūfīs in which the master usually resides and where the gathering of the initiates takes place.
kharāj A: land-tax, but sometimes synonym of *jizya* q.v.
khārijī A: secessionist; rebel; follower of the first heterodox sect in Islam.
khātam al-nabiyyīn A: seal (i.e. last) of the prophets.
khaṭīb A: orator, preacher.
khaṭṭ-i hümayun T, *khaṭṭ-i humāyūn* P: imperial decree.
khaṭṭ-i sherif T, *khaṭṭ-i sharīf* P: noble decree.
khilāf A: dissension.
khilwa (pl. *khilawāt*) A: place for seclusion and prayer.
khums A: a religious tax particular to Shīʿism according to which one fifth of one's excess income should be paid to members of the family of the Prophet (*sādāt*).
khurūj A: a going-out; sortie.
khuṭba A: Muslim Friday sermon.
kibbūsh H: conquest (of Palestine).
kibbutz (*qibbuṣ*) H: Jewish communal settlement on the land in Palestine.
kismet T (from Arabic *qisma*): fatalism.
kitābī (fem. *kitābiyya*) A: one of *ahl al-kitāb*.
kitmān A: concealment.
knesset (*keneseth*) H: assembly, parliament of Israel.
korbana—see *qurbāna*.
Kosmet Serb: abbreviation for the Yugoslav provinces of Kossovo and Metohija.
kouvouklion Gr: edicule built in honour of a saint; in this case the marble construction built over the Holy Sepulchre.
kryegjysh Albanian: "Chief Grandfather"—a clerical rank in the Bekṭāshī order.
kufr A: unbelief.
kurban bayramî—see *ʿīd al-aḍḥā*.
lā ilāha illā Allāh A: there is no god but God.
liqamakuas Eth: aide-de-camp to the kings of Ethiopia.
lise kismî T: supplementary curriculum of secular schooling introduced into Turkish religious schools.
maʿārif A: sciences, knowledge.
madhhab (pl. *madhāhib*) A: school of Islamic law.
madrasa A (*medrese* T): the traditional Muslim schools of higher learning in which both religious and intellectual or philosophical sciences are taught.
Magian—see *Majūs*.
maḥākim (pl. of *maḥkama*) A: courts.
maḥākim sharʿiyya A: *sharīʿa* courts.
maḥalla A: quarter (of a town).
maḥḍar (pl. *maḥāḍir*) A: Qurʾānic school.
mahdī A: a spiritual and temporal leader whose appearance is expected by Muslims.

maḥkama—see *maḥākim*.
mahr A: dowry.
majlis A: council.
majlis millī A: community council.
majlis al-shūrā A: "Consultative Council", an organ of the Saudi government based on the Qur'ānic concept of *shūrā* or consultation (between the ruler and his subjects in this case).
majma' muqaddas A: holy synod.
Majūs A: Magians, Zoroastrians, fire-worshippers.
makārī A: police (in North African Ibāḍī communities).
maktab (pl. *makātib*) A (*mekteb* T): Muslim elementary religious school.
malik A: ruler, used of lay headmen of the Assyrian Community.
mallāḥ A: Moroccan term for the Jewish quarter.
marham-i 'Īsā P, U: ointment of Jesus.
mā shā'a 'llāh A: *mashallah* T: "what God has willed". Very commonly used by Muslims when expressing admiration; often held to avert the evil eye.
mashā'ikh A: doctors of the faith.
al-masīḥ A: Christ, the Messiah.
mawālī—see *mawlā*.
mawlā (pl. *mawālī*) A: master; client; convert to Islam.
mawlāy A: title of ruler in Morocco.
mawlid A, *mevlud* T: birth, particularly the birth of the Prophet Muḥammad; hence, a poem composed in honour of his birth.
medrese—see *madrasa*.
mejelle T: the Ottoman civil code of 1869–76. From Arabic *majalla*.
mekteb—see *maktab*.
mellāḥ—see *mallāḥ*.
metochion Gr: property lying far away from the monastery to which it belongs.
mevlud—see *mawlid*.
midrash H: exposition of the Hebrew Bible, usually aggadic.
millet T (*milla* A): religious community.
mithnagdīm H: name of the opponents of Ḥasidism in Lithuania and Poland.
moshav (*mōshābh*) H: agricultural collective settlement on individual basis.
mu'addib al-ṣibyān A: preceptor.
mu'adhdhin A: muezzin, proclaimer of the *adhān*.
mu'allim A: teacher.
mūbadh P: Zoroastrian priest.
muftī A: a religious scholar empowered to issue *fatwās* or juridical opinions binding on the ruler, who as a Muslim is subject to the *sharī'a*, as well as on other members of the Islamic community.
muḥaddith A: one concerned with the narration of *ḥadīth*.
muhājir (pl. *muhājirūn*) A: one who migrates, makes the *hijra*.
muhibë Albanian: "Lovers", a grade in the Bekṭāshī order. From Arabic *muḥibb*.
muḥtasib A: official, in charge of markets, manners and *dhimmīs*.
mujaddid A: reformer.
mujāhid A: one who takes part in *jihād*.

mujannab A: one who is to be avoided.
mujtahid—see *ijtihād.*
mullā P, T, U (from Arabic *mawlā*): one learned in Islamic theology and law.
mu'min (pl. *mu'minūn*) A: believer.
munāfiqūn A: generally rendered "hypocrites"; the opponents of Muḥammad in Medina.
muqaddam A: leader; officer of the governing board of the Jewish community in Algeria.
murābiṭ A: dweller in a *ribāṭ.*
murīd A: novice in a Dervish order; sometimes used loosely for any mystic.
murtadd A: apostate.
muṣādara A: confiscation.
mushrik A: polytheist, one guilty of *shirk.*
muṣliḥ (religious) reformer.
musta'min A: the recipient of an *amān.*
mut'a A: temporary marriage.
muṭawwa' A: A religious figure in Arabia of lower rank and less learning than the *'ulamā'*, often concerned with enforcement of religious obligations.
nabī A: prophet.
nadhr A: vow.
nafs A: soul; Universal Soul.
nagīdh (pl. *negīdhīm*) H: recognized head of Jewry in Middle Eastern countries.
namaz T: ritual prayer. From Persian *namāz.*
nāmūs A: law; honour (modern Arabic).
naqīb A: headman.
nāsī (pl. *nesī'īm*) H: title of Jewish patriarch in Palestine, of the house of King David in Roman times; of some descendants of David under Islam; later of head of big Jewish community.
naskh A: abrogation.
naskhī A: a variety of Arabic script.
nāṭiq A: gifted with speech, endowed with reason.
nawāfil A: supererogatory prayers.
naw-rūz P: Persian New Year.
neturei karta (*neṭūrēy qartā*) H: "guardians of the city (or Jerusalem)", name of an extremist orthodox group of Jews.
nikāḥ A, *nikâḥ* T: betrothal, marriage.
nizām A: "System or code", a term used in Saudi Arabia for a set of government regulations of a non-religious character. *nizām asāsī* or "fundamental code" is a synonym for *dustūr* or constitution.
nizam-i jedid T: "the new order"; a term current in the Ottoman empire at the beginning of the nineteenth century and meaning military reform in particular.
padishah T: ruler, particularly the Ottoman sultan. From Persian *pādshāh.*
papaz T: priest, monk. From Greek *pappas.*
pardah P, U: veil.

patrik T: patriarch.

pilpul H: dialectical method of studying rabbinic texts, casuistry.

poale zion (*pō'alēy ṣiyyōn*) H: "workers of Zion", name of Jewish socialist (Marxist) party.

polojenye Russian: supreme regulation for governing the affairs of the Armenian Church in Russia.

prindë Albanian: "Fathers", a clerical rank in the Bekṭāshī order.

qabbālāh, *qabbālōth* H: mystical stream in Judaism.

qaḍā' A: adjudication.

qadar A: predestination.

qāḍī (pl. *quḍāt*) A: a religious judge who applies the *sharī'a* as an official of an Islamic state.

qāhāl (pl. *qehālīm*) H: Jewish community, congregation.

qā'id A: chief, leader, head.

qā'im maqām T: originally a deputy of certain high officials; after the nineteenth-century reforms, as a military rank the equivalent of a Lieut. Colonel; in the administration the governor of a Qaḍā'.

qāri'—see qurrā'.

qawmiyya A: nationalism.

qiyāma A: resurrection.

qurbān(*a*) H to Gr, A and Syriac: consecrated offering (see Mark vii and parallels).

qurrā' (pl. of *qāri'*) A; Qur'ān reciters.

qu'ūd A: quietism.

ra'āyā A, *râya* and *reaya* T, *rayah* Serb: flock, the common people; in the Ottoman empire it meant non-Muslim, tributary subjects and came to supersede the term *dhimmī*.

rab̲ akchesi H+T: tax imposed on the Jewish community for the right to religious autonomy.

rabwa A: height (hill).

raḥma A: mercy, loving-kindness.

raḥmān H, A: "All-merciful" as a name for God.

ra'īs al-'ulamā' A: chief of the *'ulamā'* (the class of the Muslim learned).

raj'a A: return, advent (of *mahdī*).

rak'a A: a single prostration in prayer.

ras Eth: literally "head", title usually reserved for rulers of Ethiopian provinces, but now the senior honorary title granted by the emperor.

rasūl A: messenger.

rātib A: devotional excerpt from the Qur'ān.

rawḍa A: literally meaning garden; it refers in Persia to sessions of religious persons at which pious verses are chanted and the tragedy of Karbalā' described.

râya and *rayah*—see *ra'āyā*.

reaya—see *ra'āyā*.

ribāṭ A: fortified religious centre (North Africa).

ridda A: apostasy.

Rum milleti T: Greek community.
sabra H: name given to one born in Israel.
ṣaḥāba A: companions (of the Prophet).
salafiyya A: "Followers of *al-salaf al-ṣāliḥ*", a reformist group centred in Egypt but with considerable influence in other parts of the Islamic world.
al-salaf al-ṣāliḥ A: "The pious predecessors", the earliest generations of Muslims, who set examples for all later generations to imitate.
ṣalāt A: Islamic ritual prayer.
ṣarrāf A: money-lender, money-changer.
sayyid A: lord.
schema Gr: special leather undergarment worn by certain monks and all bishops.
sema' T: mystical dance. From Arabic *simā'*.
serārāh H: hereditary rights to offices.
shahāda A: Muslim profession of faith.
shahīd A: martyr.
sharaf A: nobility.
sharī'a A: divinely revealed; prophetic law of Islam.
sharīf (fem. *sharīfa*, pl. *shurafā'* (*shorfa*) and *ashrāf*) A: "noble", a title given to descendants of the Prophet (see *ahl al-bayt*), notably members of the dynasty which ruled Mecca from the tenth century until 1925.
sharqī (pl. *sharqiyyūn*) A: eastern.
sharṭ—see *shurūṭ*.
shāshiyya A: small red cap worn by men in North Africa.
shaykh A: "an old man", deserving veneration. By extension a tribal chief or a religious dignitary, not necessarily advanced in years.
shaykh al-Islām—see *sheykh ül-Islâm*.
sheḥīṭā H: ritual slaughter of animals for human consumption.
sheker bayramî—see *'īd al-fiṭr*.
shelīaḥ ṣibbūr H: leader in prayer at divine service.
sheykh ül-Islâm T, *shaykh al-Islām* A: head of the Muslim learned corporation in the Ottoman empire and Muftī of Istanbul.
shī'a A: heterodox Islam, followers of 'Alī and his descendants as rightful caliphs.
shī'ī A: following the *shī'a*.
shirk A: syntheism, the association of any person or thing with God in prayers or in other ways.
shorfa A—see *sharīf*.
shuf'a A: right of pre-emption.
shūrā A: consultation, debate.
shurūṭ (pl. of *sharṭ*) A: conditions, provisos.
shurūṭ (or *'ahd* or *'uhūd*) *'Umar* A: discriminatory regulations against non-Muslims, attributed to 'Umar b. al-Khaṭṭāb.
ṣinf—see *aṣnāf*.
siyāsa A: state policy.
sufra A: table laid with food.

sunna A: custom, law, exemplary life of the Prophet Muḥammad; orthodox Islam.
sünnet T: circumcision.
sunnī A: follower of *sunna*, orthodox Muslim.
sūra A: the name given to the chapters of the Qur'ān, but of no other book.
sürgün T: banishment, expulsion.
synaxar Gr: collection of martyrological and hagiological material arranged for daily readings.
ṭabī'iyyūn A: naturalists.
tablīgh A: Muslim missionary activity.
tabshīr A: Christian missionary activity.
tafsīr A: exegesis of the Qur'ān.
ṭāghūt A: pre-Islamic customary law.
tajallī (pl. *tajalliyāt*) A: theophany or the irradiation of divine qualities and names.
takbīr A: the act of saying "Allāhu akbar" (God is very great).
ta'līm al-Islām A: Islamic instruction.
Talmud H: corpus of rabbinical law and lore.
tamṣīr A: Egyptianization.
tanāsukh A: transmigration of souls.
tanẓīmāt A, *tanẓimat* T: reforms (in Ottoman empire dating from 1839).
taqiyya A: religious dissimulation.
taqlīd A: legal decision based on authority of predecessors capable of *ijtihād*; conformity to tradition.
talmud torah, *talmūdēy t.* H: school for traditional instruction in Bible and elementary rabbinics.
ṭarīqa (pl. *ṭuruq*) A, *tarikat* T: literally a road, way or path; a Ṣūfī order.
taṣawwuf A: Ṣūfism.
tawḥīd A: Islamic Unitarianism, the doctrine of the absolute unity of God as Lord of Creation and sole object of worship.
ta'wīl A: allegorical interpretation; in Shī'ism, an esoteric interpretation of both the Qur'ān and the world of nature which is connected with the function of the *imām*.
ta'ziya A: the passion play depicting events of the tragedy of Karbalā'.
tekke T: dervish lodge.
tezkar Eth: literally "memorial". Commemoration service of the Ethiopian church for the souls of the departed.
tihāma A: coast-land, especially the eastern coast of the Red Sea.
tîmar T: an Ottoman feudal estate, a landed fief, with an income of up to 20,000 akçes annually.
tîmarjî T: one who enjoys the benefit from a *tîmar* estate.
tiqqūn H: improvement, restoration; used of the mystical doctrine of the Lurianic Kabbalah about the restoration of the scattered, exiled lights.
tiqqūnīm H: penitential exercises and meditations in order to shorten the process of *tiqqūn*.
topoteretes Gr: lieutenant, vicar, vicegerent.
Torah (*tōrāh*) H: "teaching", term for the Pentateuch.

tugh (*tuğ*) T: horsetail attached to a helmet or flagstaff as a mark of rank.
ṭuruq—see *ṭarīqa.*
ʿuhūd ʿ*Umar*—see *shurūṭ* ʿ*Umar.*
al-ukhuwwa al-waṭaniyya A: patriotic brotherhood.
ʿulamāʾ (pl. of *ʿālim* = learned man), A (*ulema* T): but referring specifically to the body of religious scholars who are authorities in matters of the *sharīʿa* and who have the power of interpreting its rulings by virtue of their acquired knowledge.
umarāʾ—see *amīr.*
umma A: nation, Muslim nation, community of Muslims founded by Muḥammad.
ummī (pl. *ummiyyūn*) A: illiterate.
ʿumrān A: civilization.
ʿuqqāl (pl. of *ʿāqil*) A: Druze initiates.
ʿurūba A: Arabism.
ʿushr (pl. *ʿushūr*) A: tithe.
uṣṭa Yemenite term of addressing a Jew, from *ustādh* = "master" in Arabic.
vaʾad, vaʾad leumi (*waʿad, waʿad leʾummī*) H: council, national council.
varlik vergisi T: taxation of capital (a Turkish law of 1942).
vuzu T (*wuḍūʾ* A): Muslim ritual ablution before prayer.
wafd A: delegation.
waḥy A: divine inspiration, revelation.
wālī A: governor.
walī (pl. *awliyāʾ*) A: legal guardian; saint, holy man (in popular Islam).
waqf (pl. *awqāf*) A (*vakif*, pl. *evkaf* T): Islamic religious endowment by means of which mosques, schools, hospitals, etc., are provided with financial means to continue after their foundation.
waṣī A: guardian whom the *walī* has appointed by will, trustee; legatee.
waṭan (pl. *awṭān*) A: fatherland.
waṭanī A: patriot.
wilāya A: power of administration or of guardianship. The Ibāḍī doctrine of *wilāya* is the obligation of friendliness towards followers of the true faith.
wird A: an excerpt from the Qurʾān recited on the occasion of private worship.
Yahudi milleti T: Jewish community.
yekke: Palestinian term for Jewish immigrants of German origin.
yenafs abbat Eth: literally "father of the soul", father confessor of the Ethiopian church.
yeshiva pl. *yeshivot* (*yeshībhāh*, pl. *yeshībhōth*) H: Talmudic academy, college.
yishuv (*yishūbh*) H: Jewish population of Palestine, the Jews of Israel.
ẓāhir A: exoteric.
ẓahīr (also *ḍahīr*) A: decree of the Moroccan ruler.
zakāt A: the general religious tax stipulated by the *sharīʿa.*
zar Serb: a head covering for women. From Arabic *izār*, through Turkish.
zāwiya A: establishment of a Ṣūfī fraternity.
ẓimmi—see *dhimmī.*
ziyāra A: pilgrimage to a Holy Place, a saint's grave.

BIBLIOGRAPHY

GENERAL BIBLIOGRAPHY

Atlas of the Arab World and the Middle East (introduction by C. F. Beckingham). London, 1960.

BULLARD, Sir R. W. *The Middle East, a Political and Economic Survey*. 3rd ed. London and New York, 1958.

GIBB, H. A. R. and BOWEN, H. *Islamic Society and the West*. Vol. I, parts I–II; Oxford, 1950–7.

GOITEIN, S. D. *Jews and Arabs*. 2nd ed. New York, 1964.

HIRSCHBERG, H. Z. (J. W.). *A History of the Jews in North Africa* (Hebrew). 2 vols. Jerusalem, 1965. An English translation is to be published by E. J. Brill, Leiden.

LANDSHUT, S. *Jewish Communities in the Muslim Countries of the Middle East*. London, 1950.

LEWIS, B. *The Emergence of Modern Turkey*. London, 1961.

—— *The Middle East and the West*. New York, 1964.

RONDOT, P. *Les Chrétiens d'Orient*. Paris, 1955.

ROSENTHAL, E. I. J. *Judaism and Islam*. London, 1961.

—— *Islam in the Modern National State*. Cambridge, 1965.

SMITH, W. C. *Islam in Modern History*. Princeton, 1957.

SPULER, B. *Die morgenländischen Kirchen* (repr. from *Handbuch der Orientalistik*, Abteilung I, Bd VIII, Abschnitt 2, Leiden/Cologne, 1961). Leiden, 1964.

VOLUME 1

PART I: JUDAISM

CHAPTER I: JUDAISM TODAY

AGUS, JACOB B. *Modern Philosophies of Judaism*. New York, 1941.

ALTMANN, ALEXANDER (ed.). *Studies in Nineteenth-century Jewish Intellectual History*. Cambridge, Mass., 1964.

BAECK, LEO. *Von Moses Mendelssohn zu Franz Rosenzweig*. Stuttgart, 1958.

—— *This People Israel: The Meaning of Jewish Existence*. Philadelphia, 1965.

BERGMANN, SAMUEL H. *Faith and Reason*. Washington, D.C., 1961.

BLAU, J. L. *Modern Varieties of Judaism*. New York and London, 1966.

COHEN, ARTHUR A. *The Natural and the Supernatural Jew*. New York, 1962.

Commentary (editors of). *The Condition of Jewish Belief*. New York, 1967.

DAVIS, MOSHE. *The Emergence of Conservative Judaism*. Philadelphia, 1963.

ELBOGEN, ISMAR. *A Century of Jewish Life*. Philadelphia, 1946.

GLAZER, NATHAN. *American Judaism*. Chicago, 1957.

GRAYZEL, SOLOMON. *A History of the Jews*. Philadelphia, 1950.

HERBERG, WILL. *Protestant—Catholic—Jew*. New York, 1955.

HERTZBERG, ARTHUR (ed.). *The Zionist Idea*. Philadelphia, 1960.

JANOWSKY, OSCAR I. (ed.). *The American Jew—A Reappraisal*. Philadelphia, 1964.
Leo Baeck Institute. *Year Book*. London, 1956 ff.
LEVINGER, LEE J. *A History of the Jews in the United States*. Cincinnati, 1932.
LEWKOWITZ, ALBERT. *Das Judentum und die geistigen Strömungen des 19. Jahrhunderts*. Breslau, 1935.
NOVECK, SIMON (ed.). *Contemporary Jewish Thought*. Washington, D.C., 1963.
—— *Great Jewish Thinkers of the Twentieth Century*. Washington, D.C., 1963.
PHILIPSON, DAVID. *The Reform Movement in Judaism*. New York, 1907.
PLAUT, W. GUNTHER. *The Rise of Reform Judaism*. New York, 1963.
—— *The Growth of Reform Judaism*. New York, 1965.
SACHAR, HOWARD M. *The Course of Modern Jewish History*. Cleveland, 1958.
SCHWAB, HERMANN. *The History of Orthodox Jewry in Germany*. London, 1950.
SELIGMANN, CAESAR. *Geschichte der jüdischen Reformbewegung*. Frankfurt, 1922.
SKLARE, MARSHALL. *Conservative Judaism—An American Religious Movement*. Glencoe, 1955.
WAXMAN, MORDECAI (ed.). *Tradition and Change*. New York, 1958.
WIENER, MAX. *Jüdische Religion im Zeitalter der Emanzipation*. Berlin, 1933.
WILHELM, KURT (ed.). *Wissenschaft des Judentums im deutschen Sprachbereich*. Tübingen, 1967.
WOLF, ARNOLD J. (ed.). *Rediscovering Judaism: Reflections on a New Jewish Theology*. Chicago, 1965.

CHAPTER 2: JUDAISM IN ISRAEL

BEN-GURION, D. *Rebirth and Destiny of Israel*. London, 1959.
—— *Ben-Gurion Looks Back*. London, 1965.
—— *The Jews in their Land*. London, 1966.
BEN-ZVI, I. *The Exiled and the Redeemed*. London, 1958.
BENTWICH, J. *Education in Israel*. London, 1964.
—— *Judea Lives Again*. London, 1944.
—— *Israel Resurgent*. London, 1960.
BUBER, M. *Israel and Palestine*. Zurich, 1950.
—— *Paths in Utopia*. London, 1948.
GOLDMANN, E. *Religious Issues in Israel's Political Life*. Jerusalem, 1964.
KAPLAN, M. *Judaism as a Civilisation*. New York, 1934.
PARKES, J. *The End of an Exile*. London, 1954.
RUPPIN, A. *The Jewish Faith and Future*. London, 1940.
SILBERG, J. *The Way of the Talmud*. Jerusalem, 1961 (Hebrew).
WEINER, H. *The Wild Goats of Engedi*. New York, 1961.
WEIZMANN, C. *Trial and Error*. London, 1949.

BIBLIOGRAPHY

CHAPTER 3: THE ORIENTAL JEWISH COMMUNITIES

ANKORI, Z. *Karaites in Byzantium*. New York and Jerusalem, 1959.

BACHER, W. *Les Juifs de Perse au XVIIe et au XVIIIe siècles d'après les Chronicles poétiques de Baboï b. Loutf et de Baboï b. Farhad*. Strasburg, 1906.

BEN-ZVI, I. *The Exiled and the Redeemed*. Philadelphia, 1957.

CABOT-BRIGGS, L. and LAMI GUÈDE, N. *No more for Ever; A Saharan Jewish Town*. Cambridge, Mass., 1964.

CASKEL, W. *Entdeckungen in Arabien*. Cologne, 1954.

CAZÈS, D. *Notes bibliographiques sur la littérature juive-tunisienne*. Tunis, 1893.

CHALOM, JACQUES. *Les Israélites de la Tunisie; leur condition civile et politique*. Paris, 1908.

CHOURAQUI, A. *L'Alliance Israélite Universelle et la renaissance juive contemporaine (1860–1960)*. Paris, 1965.

—— *La Condition juridique de l'Israélite marocain*. Paris, 1950.

COHEN, M. and MORENO, M. M. *Gli Ebrei in Libia*. Rome, n.d.

EISENBETH, M. *Les Juifs de l'Afrique du Nord; démographie et onomastique*. Algiers, 1936.

—— "Les Juifs en Algérie et en Tunisie à l'époque turque (1516–1830)." *Revue Africaine*. Algiers, 1952.

—— *Les Juifs au Maroc*. Algiers, 1948.

EPSTEIN, I. *The Responsa of Rabbi Simon B. Ẓemaḥ Duran as a Source of the History of the Jews in North Africa*. London, 1930.

FISCHEL, W. J. "Israel in Iran" (a survey of Judeo-Persian literature); in *The Jews*, ed. by L. Finkelstein, vol. II, pp. 817–58. New York, 1949.

FRANCO, M. *Essai sur l'histoire des Israélites de l'Empire Ottoman*. Paris, 1897.

GALANTÉ, A. *Documents officiels turcs concernant les Juifs de Turquie*. Istanbul, 1931.

GIBB, H. A. R. and BOWEN, H. *Islamic Society and the West*, vol. I, parts I–II. Oxford, 1950–7.

GOITEIN, S. D. *Jews and Arabs*. New York, 1955.

GOLDZIHER, I. *Mohammedanische Studien*. 2 vols. Halle, 1889–90.

GOODBLATT, M. S. *Jewish Life in Turkey in the XVIth Century*. New York, 1952.

HERSHMAN, A. M. *Rabbi Isaac Ben Sheshet Perfet and His Times*. New York, 1943.

HIRSCHBERG, H. Z. (J. W.). "The Problem of the Judaized Berbers." *Journal of African History*, vol. IV (1963), pp. 313–39.

—— *Jüdische und christliche Lehren im vor- und frühislamischen Arabien*. Krakow, 1939.

—— *Yisrā'ēl be-'Arāb* [Israel in Arabia]. Tel-Aviv, 1946.

—— *Mē-Ereṣ Mebō Ha-Shemash* [Inside Maghrib, The Jews in North Africa]. Jerusalem, 1957.

—— *Toledōt ha-Yehūdīm be-Afriqah ha-Ṣefōnīt* [A History of the Jews in North Africa]. 2 vols. Jerusalem, 1965.

JAPHET, M. D. *The Jews of India*. Bombay, 1960.

KEHIMKAR, H. S. *The History of Bene Israel of India*. Jerusalem, 1937.

KRAUSHAR, A. *Frank i frankiści polscy 1726–1816*. 2 vols. Krakow, 1895.
LANDSHUT, S. *Jewish Communities in the Muslim Countries of the Middle East*. London, 1950.
LEVEN, N. *Cinquante ans d'histoire*. (L'Alliance Israélite Universelle.) 2 vols. Paris, 1911–20.
LEWIS, B. *The Middle East and the West*. New York, 1964.
—— *The Emergence of Modern Turkey*. London, 1961.
—— *Notes and Documents from the Turkish Archives; a contribution to the History of the Jews in the Ottoman Empire*. Jerusalem, 1952.
LOEB, ISIDORE. *La Situation des Israélites en Turquie, en Serbie et en Roumanie*. Paris, 1877.
LUNDIN, A. G. *South Arabia in the VI C* (Russian). Moscow–Leningrad, 1961.
MANN, J. *Karaitica*. (*Texts and Studies*, II.) Philadelphia, 1935.
MARTIN, CL. *Les Israélites algériens de 1830 à 1902*. Paris, 1936.
MICHOFF, N. V. *La Population de la Turquie et de la Bulgarie au XVIIIe et XIXe S*. 3 vols. Sofia, 1915–29.
MILANO, A. *Storia degli ebrei italiani nel levante*. Florence, 1949.
NEDKOFF, B. CH. *Die Gizya* (Kopfsteuer) *im osmanischen Reich*. Leipzig, 1942.
NEHAMA, J. *Histoire des Israélites de Salonique*. 5 vols. Paris, 1935–59.
NEMOY, L. *Karaite Anthology*. New Haven, 1952.
—— "Al-Qirqisānī's Account of the Jewish Sects and Christianity" in *Hebrew Union College Annual*, VII (1930).
NEUMANN, A. A. *The Jews in Spain*. 2 vols. Philadelphia, 1942.
ORTEGA, M. L. *Los Hebreos en Maruecos*. Madrid, 1934.
POLAK, J. E. *Persien; Das Land und seine Bewohner*. 2 vols. Leipzig, 1865.
POZNAŃSKI, S. *Babylonische Geonim im nachgaonaeischen Zeitalter*. Berlin, 1914.
ROBINSON, NEHEMIAH. *The Arab Countries of the Near East and their Jewish Communities*. New York, 1951.
ROSENTHAL, E. I. J. *Judaism and Islam*. London, 1961.
—— *Islam in the Modern National State*. Cambridge, 1965.
SASSOON, DAVID S. *A History of the Jews in Baghdad*. Letchworth, 1949.
SCHECHTER, S. "Safed in the Sixteenth Century" (in his: *Studies in Judaism*; Second Series). Philadelphia, 1938.
SCHOLEM, G. G. *Major Trends in Jewish Mysticism*. New York, 1961.
SZAJKOWSKI, ZOSA. "The Schools of the A.I.U." *Historia Judaica*, vol. XII (1960), pp. 3–22.
TIBI, S. *Le Statut Personnel des Israélites et spécialement des Israélites tunisiens*. 4 vols. Tunis, 1923.
TOPF, E. *Die Staatenbildungen in den arabischen Teilen der Türkei seit dem Weltkriege*. Hamburg, 1929.
TRITTON, A. S. *The Caliphs and their Non-Muslim Subjects*. London, 1930.
UBICINI, A. and PAVET DE COURTEILLE. *Etat présent de l'Empire Ottoman*. (Statistique, gouvernement...communautés non musulmanes, etc.) Paris, 1876.
UHRY, I. *Recueil des Lois, Décrets, Ordonnances...concernant les Israélites; 1850–1903*. Troisième édition. Bordeaux, 1903.

USQUE, SAMUEL. *Consolation for the Tribulations of Israel* [Consolaçam ás tribulaçoens de Israel]; translated from the Portuguese by Martin A. Cohen. Philadelphia, 1965/5725.

VAJDA, G. *Un Recueil de textes historiques Judéo-Marocains*. Paris, 1951.

VÁMBÉRY, H. *Meine Wanderungen und Erlebnisse in Persien*. Budapest, 1867.

VOINOT, L. *Pèlerinages Judéo-Musulmans du Maroc*. Paris, 1948.

WERBLOWSKY, R. J. Z. *Joseph Karo, Lawyer and Mystic*. Oxford, 1962.

WOLFF, J. *Narrative of a Mission to Bokhara in the years 1843–1845*. 2 vols. London, 1845.

YOUNG, G. *Corps de droit ottoman*. 7 vols. Oxford, 1905–6.

CHAPTER 4: THE JEWS OF YEMEN

BRAUER, E. *Ethnologie der Jemenitischen Juden*. Heidelberg, 1934.

GOITEIN, S. D. *Jemenica*. Leipzig, 1934.

—— *Travels in Yemen*. Jerusalem, 1941.

—— *From the Land of Sheba*. New York, 1947.

—— "Portrait of a Yemenite Weavers' Village." *Jewish Social Studies*. New York, 1955.

—— "The Language of Al-Gades." *Le Muséon*. Louvain, 1960.

RATHJENS, C. *Jewish Domestic Architecture in San'a, Yemen*. Jerusalem, 1957.

PART 2: CHRISTIANITY

CHAPTER 5: SURVEY DOWN TO A.D. 1800

As general source-books for Christianity in the Middle East, see A. S. Atiya, *A History of Eastern Christianity*. London, 1968; and B. Spuler, *Die morgenländischen Kirchen* (repr. *Handbuch der Orientalistik*, 1961). Leiden, 1964.

Syria

ATIYA, A. S. *The Crusade in the Later Middle Ages*. London, 1938.

BAR-HEBRAEUS, GREGORY. *Chronicon Ecclesiasticum*, ed. J. B. Abeloos and T. J. Lamy. Paris and Louvain, 1877.

HOURANI, A. H. *Minorities in the Arab World*. Oxford, 1947.

MICHAEL THE SYRIAN. *Chronicle* (ed. J.-B. Chabot, in 3 vols. Paris, 1899–1905). Vol. I reprinted, Brussels, 1963.

RUNCIMAN, S. *A History of the Crusades*. 3 vols. Cambridge, 1951–4.

—— *The Eastern Schism*. Oxford, 1955.

VASILIEV, A. A. *History of the Byzantine Empire*. Madison, 1952.

Armenia

CHAKMAKJIAN, H. A. *Armenian Christology and Evangelisation of Islam*. Leiden, 1965.

DER NERSESSIAN, S. *Armenia and the Byzantine Empire*. Harvard, 1947.

SARKISSIAN, K. *The Council of Chalcedon and the Armenian Church*. London, 1965.

Egypt and Nubia

ABU SALEH. *Churches and Monasteries of Egypt and Some Neighbouring Countries*, trans. B. T. A. Evetts and A. J. Butler. Oxford, 1893.

The History of the Patriarchs of the Egyptian Church, part I, to A.D. 849, trans. B. T. A. Evetts and publ. in *Patrologia Orientalis*, I, V, and X, part II, 849–1102, edited in three sections by A. S. Atiya, Y. Abd al-Masih and O. H. E. Burmester. Cairo, 1942–59.

EVELYN WHITE, H. G. *The Monasteries of the Wadi Natrun*. New York, 1933.

GRIFFITH, F. LL. "Christian Documents from Nubia." *Proc. of the British Academy* (1928).

SHINNIE, P. L. *Mediaeval Nubia*. (Sudan Antiquities Service, Khartoum, 1954.)

WORRELL, W. H. *A Short History of the Copts*. Ann Arbor, 1945.

See also, articles by scholars connected with the salvage of Nubian antiquities from 1960 onwards, published in *Kush*, vols. X–XIV, 1961–4.

North Africa

GAGÉ, J. "Nouveaux aspects de l'Afrique chrétienne." *Annales de l'Ecole des Hautes Etudes de Gand*, vol. I (1937), pp. 183 ff.

MESNAGE, J. *Le Christianisme en Afrique, déclin et extinction*. Paris, 1915.

SESTON, W. "Sur les derniers temps du Christianisme en Afrique." *Mélanges de l'Ecole française à Rome*, vol. LIII (1936), pp. 101–24.

Persia and farther east

JOSEPH, J. *The Nestorians and their Muslim Neighbours*. Princeton, 1961.

LABOURT, J. *Le christianisme dans l'empire perse*. Paris, 1904.

MINGANA, A. "The Early Spread of Christianity in Central Asia and the Far East." *Bulletin of John Rylands Library*, vol. IX, 2 (1927), pp. 297–371.

SPULER, B. *Les Mongoles dans l'histoire*. Paris, 1961.

CHAPTER 6: THE ORTHODOX CHURCH

ATTWATER, DONALD. *The Christian Churches of the East*. 2 vols. Milwaukee, Wis., 1947–8.

BENZ, ERNEST. *The Eastern Orthodox Church: Its Thought and Life*, trans. Richard and Clara Winston. New York, 1963.

BOULGAKOFF, S. *L'Orthodoxie*. Paris, 1959.

THE BROTHERHOOD OF THEOLOGIANS "ZOE" (eds.). *A Sign of God, Orthodoxy 1964, A Pan-Orthodox Symposium*. Athens, 1964.

Calendar of the Greek Church (in Greek). Apostolic Deaconate, Athens, 1964.

CONGAR, M.-J. *Chrétiens Désunis, Principes d'un "Oecuménisme" Catholique*. Paris, 1937.

Creative Tradition in the Middle East, Student World. World Student Christian Federation, Geneva, vol. LVIII, no. 1 (1965).

The Divine Liturgy of St John Chrysostom (Greek and English). London, n.d.

DVORNIK, FRANÇOIS. *Le Schisme de Photius*. Paris, 1950.

The Encyclicals of the Popes on Catholic-Orthodox relations, especially Pius IX's *In suprema Petri* of 1848, Leo XIII's *Praeclara Gratulationis Publicae* of 1894, and Paul VI's *Ecclesiam Suam* of 1964.

The Encyclopaedia of Islam (Leiden), on *umma*, *dhimma*, *naṣārā*, etc.

EVDOKIMOV, P. *L'Orthodoxie*. Neuchâtel-Paris, 1959.

FATTAL, ANTOINE. *Le statut légal des non-musulmans en pays d'Islam*. Beirut, 1958.

HAPGOOD, ISABEL FLORENCE. *Service Book of the Holy Orthodox-Catholic Apostolic Church*, 3rd ed., photo-offset reproduction of the 1922 edition. Syrian Antiochian Orthodox Archdiocese of New York and all North America, 1956.

HOURANI, ALBERT H. *Minorities in the Arab World*. London, 1947.

JESSUP, HENRY HARRIS. *Fifty-three Years in Syria*. 2 vols. New York, 1910.

LOSSKY, V. *The Mystical Theology of the Eastern Church*. London, 1957.

MASTROYIANNOPOULOS, VERY REV. ELIAS. *Nostalgia for Orthodoxy*. Athens, 1959.

MEYENDORFF, JEAN. *L'Église Orthodoxe*. Paris, 1960.

NEALE, JOHN MASON. *A History of the Holy Eastern Church* (The Patriarchate of Antioch). London, 1873.

PAPADOPOULOS, THEODORE H. *Studies and Documents Relating to the History of the Greek Church and People under Turkish Domination*. Brussels, 1952.

PITZIPIOS, JACQUES G. *L'Église Orientale*. Rome, 1855.

RABBATH, PÈRE ANTOINE. *Documents inédits pour servir à l'histoire du Christianisme en Orient*. 2 vols. Paris, 1905 and 1910.

RONDOT, PIERRE. *Les Chrétiens d'Orient*. Paris, 1955.

RUSTUM, ASAD J. *The Church of the City of God Great Antioch*, vol. III. Beirut, 1963; the best for the purposes of this essay. (In Arabic.)

SCHMEMANN, ALEXANDER. *The Historical Road of Eastern Orthodoxy*. New York, 1963.

SPULER, BERTOLD. *Die orthodoxen Kirchen*. Internationale Kirchliche Zeitschrift, Bern, Heft 1, 1965; also the entire series of about 50 volumes by the same author which have appeared twice a year since 1939.

STAVROU, THEOFANIS GEORGE. *Russian Interests in Palestine (1882–1914). A study of* Religious *and Educational Enterprise*. Thessaloniki, 1963.

STRONG, WILLIAM E. *The Story of the American Board*. Boston, 1910.

WARE, TIMOTHY. *The Orthodox Church*. Pelican A 592, 1964.

CHAPTER 7: THE ROMAN CATHOLIC CHURCH

The basic work on which the documentation of this study has been founded is the official publication of the Oriental Congregation in Rome: *Oriente Cattolico. Cenni storici e statistichi*, Vatican City, 1962, which contains an ample bibliography for each of the Eastern Churches, a historical introduction and detailed statistics.

One of the most recent works on these churches is the *Handbuch der Orientalistik, Achter Band: Religion; Zweiter Abschnitt: Religionsgeschichte des Orients in der Zeit der Weltreligionen*, published in 1961 by Brill, Leiden, in which chapters 5–11 are devoted to the different Eastern Churches and have been compiled by Professor Spuler himself. There is an ample bibliography.

Well-documented articles written by experts on each of the Eastern Churches are to be found in the *Dictionary of Catholic Theology*, the *Dictionary of Ecclesiastical History and Geography* and the *Catholic Encyclopedia*. The specialized journals should also be consulted: *Echos d'Orient, Bessarione, Roma e l'Oriente, Irénikon, Proche-Orient chrétien, Istina, Unitas*.

The following is a brief select bibliography of general works:

ATTWATER, DONALD. *The Christian Churches of the East*. 2 vols. Vol. I, *Churches in Communion with Rome*. Milwaukee, 1947.

DE CLERC, CHARLES. *Les Églises unies d'Orient*. Paris, 1934.

DE VRIES, W. *Oriente cristiano ieri e oggi*. Rome, 1949.

EMMI, BENJAMINO. *Introduzione alla teologia orientale*. Rome, 1958.

FORTESCUE, ADRIAN. *The Uniate Eastern Churches*. London, 1923.

HAJJAR, JOSEPH. *Les chrétiens uniates du Proche-Orient*. Paris, 1962.

JANIN, R. *Églises d'Orient*. Paris, 1957.

—— *Les Églises orientales et les rites orientaux*, 4th ed. Paris, 1955.

RONDOT, PIERRE. *Les Chrétiens d'Orient*. Paris, 1955.

CHAPTER 8: THE COPTIC CHURCH IN EGYPT

BUTCHER, E. L. *The Story of the Church of Egypt*. 2 vols. London, 1897.

CRAMER, M. *Das Christlich-Koptische Ägypten einst und heute*. Wiesbaden, 1959.

FOWLER, M. *Christian Egypt, Past, Present and Future*. London, 1902.

JULLIEN, M. *L'Egypte. Souvenirs Bibliques et Chrétiens*. Lille, 1891.

LEEDER, S. H. *Modern Sons of the Pharaohs*. London, 1918.

MEINARDUS, O. *Monks and Monasteries of the Egyptian Deserts*. Cairo, 1961.

—— *Christian Egypt, Ancient and Modern*. Cairo, 1964.

NEALE, J. M. *A History of the Holy Eastern Church*. 2 vols. London, 1847.

SPULER, B. *Die morgenländischen Kirchen*. Leiden, 1964.

STROTHMANN, R. *Die Koptische Kirche in der Neuzeit*. Tübingen, 1932.

WAKIN, E. *A Lonely Minority. The Modern Story of Egypt's Copts*. New York, 1963.

WORRELL, W. H. *A Short Account of the Copts*. Ann Arbor, 1945.

CHAPTER 9: ETHIOPIAN AND SYRIAN ORTHODOX CHURCHES

ALVAREZ, FRANCISCO. *The Prester John of the Indies*. Edited and translated by C. F. Beckingham and G. W. B. Huntingford. 2 vols. London, 1961.

BUDGE, Sir E. A. T. WALLIS. *A History of Ethiopia, Nubia, and Abyssinia*. 2 vols. London, 1928.

CONTI ROSSINI, CARLO. *Storia d'Etiopia*. Milan, 1928.

Coulbeaux, Jean-Baptiste. *Histoire politique et religieuse d'Abyssinie depuis les temps les plus reculés jusqu'à l'avènement de Ménélik II*. 3 vols. Paris, 1929.

Dye, William McEntyre. *Moslem Egypt and Christian Abyssinia*. New York, 1880.

Foreign Office of Great Britain. *Correspondence respecting Abyssinia*. H.M. Stationery Office, London, 1865 (740 pp.).

—— *Further Correspondence respecting British Captives in Abyssinia*. H.M. Stationery Office, London, 1867.

Geddes, Michael. *The Church History of Ethiopia*. London, 1696.

Gobat, S. *Journal of a Three Years' Residence in Abyssinia*. 1834.

Hotten, John Camden (ed.). *Abyssinia and its People or Life in the Land of Prester John*. London, 1868.

Hyatt, Harry M. *The Church of Abyssinia*. London, 1928.

Jones, A. H. M. and Monroe, Elizabeth. *A History of Ethiopia*. Oxford, 1960.

Le-Jean, Guillaume. *Theodore II*. Paris, 1865.

Lipsky, George A. *Ethiopia*. New Haven, 1962.

O'Hanlon, Douglas. *Features of the Abyssinian Church*. London, 1946.

O'Leary, De Lacy. *The Ethiopian Church, Historical Notes*. London, 1936.

Pankhurst, E. Sylvia. *Ethiopia, a Cultural History*. 1955.

Pollera, Alberto. *Lo Stato etiopico e la sua chiesa*. Rome–Milan, 1926.

Trimingham, John Spencer. *The Christian Church and Missions in Ethiopia*. London and New York, 1950/1.

—— *Islam in Ethiopia*. Oxford, 1952.

Ullendorff, Edward. *The Ethiopians*. Oxford, 1960.

CHAPTER 10: THE ARMENIAN CHURCH

Atamian, Sarkis. *The Armenian Community*. New York, 1955.

Arpee, Leon. *A History of Armenian Christianity*. New York, 1946.

—— *A Century of Armenian Protestantism, 1846–1946*. New York, 1946.

Bourdeaux, Michael. *Opium of the People, The Christian Religion in the U.S.S.R.*, chapter vii, "Armenia", pp. 195–201. London, 1965.

Etmekjian, James. *The French Influence on the Western Armenian Renaissance (1843–1915)*. New York, 1964.

Kazarian, Haygaz K. "The Turkish Genocide on the Church Front". *Armenian Review*, vol. xviii, no. 1–69 (1965), pp. 3–9.

Kolarz, Walter. *Religion in the Soviet Union*, ch. v: "The Armenian Church", pp. 150–75. London, 1961.

Lynch, H. F. B. *Armenia, Travels and Studies*, vol. i: *The Russian Province*; vol. ii: *The Turkish Province*. London, 1901. (A new impression by Khayats in the series of Oriental Reprints, no. 15, Beirut, 1965.)

Matossian, M. K. *The Impact of Soviet Policies in Armenia*. Leiden, 1962.

JEAN MÉCÉRIAN, R. P. (S.J.). *Un Tableau de la Diaspora Arménienne* (three extracts from *Proche-Orient Chrétien*, Jerusalem, 1956–62). I. "Les Arméniens de l'Union Soviétique"; II. "Les Arméniens hors de l'Union Soviétique"; III. "Les Organismes d'intérêt général".

—— *Le Génocide du peuple Arménien; Le sort de la population arménienne de l'Empire Ottoman, 1908–23*. Beyrouth, 1965.

NANSEN, FRIDTJOF. *Armenia and the Near East*. New York, 1928.

ORMANIAN, ARCHBISHOP MALACHIA. *The Church of Armenia*. 2nd ed. London, 1955.

PASDERMADJIAN, H. *Histoire de l'Arménie* (revised edition, Paris, 1964). Translated into English and published as a series of articles in *Armenian Review*, starting from vol. XI, nos. 2–42. Boston, 1958.

RONDOT, PIERRE. *Les Chrétiens d'Orient*, ch. IX: "Les Arméniens", pp. 171–99. Paris, 1955.

SARKISSIAN, KAREKIN VARDAPET. "The Ecumenical Problem in Eastern Christendom." *Ecumenical Review*, vol. XII, no. 4 (1960), pp. 436–54. Genoa.

THOROSSIAN, H. *Histoire de l'Arménie et du peuple arménien*. Paris, 1957.

TOYNBEE, ARNOLD. "A Summary of Armenian History up to and Including the Year 1915", in *The Treatment of the Armenians in the Ottoman Empire*. (A voluminous collection of testimonies and documents related to the sufferings of the Armenian people, published by Viscount Bryce, London, 1916.)

—— *Armenian Atrocities—The Murder of a Nation*. London, 1916.

Official publications

The Catholicosate of Cilicia: Her Place and Status in the Armenian Church. Antelias, 1961.

Le Problème religieux en U.R.S.S.

2ème partie: *Données et Documents sur l'Organization actuelle des différentes Eglises et Associations Religieuses*, published by the Présidence du Conseil (*Notes et Etudes Documentaires*, 9 Octobre 1954, no. 1.931).

4ème partie: *La situation de l'Eglise Arménienne*, 8 Octobre 1956, no. 2.239.

Reviews

Echmiadzin, monthly review of the Catholicosate of Echmiadzin, 1944.

Hask, monthly review of the Catholicosate of Cilicia, Antelias, 1931.

Sion, monthly review of the Patriarchate of Jerusalem, New Series, 1927. (All three in Armenian.)

Armenian Review, a quarterly publication, by Hairenik Association, 212 Stuart Street, Boston, 1948.

Ararat, a quarterly publication by the Armenian General Benevolent Union, 109 East 40th St New York, 1959.

CHAPTER II: THE ASSYRIANS

BADGER, G. P. *The Nestorians and their Rituals*. 2 vols. London, 1852.

BETHUNE-BAKER, J. F. *Nestorius and His Teaching*. Cambridge, 1908.

BROWNE, L. E. *The Eclipse of Christianity in Asia*. Cambridge, 1933.
CUTTS, E. L. *Christians under the Crescent in Asia*. London, 1876.
DARMO, MAR THOMAS (Metropolitan of India). *The Assyrian Church and the Hereditary Succession*. Trichur, Kerala.
EMHARDT, W. C. and LAMSA, G. A. *The Oldest Christian People*. New York, 1926.
FOSTER, JOHN. *The Church of the Tang Dynasty*. London, 1939.
HEAZELL, F. N. and MARGOLIOUTH, J. P. *Kurds and Christians*. London, 1913.
JOSEPH, JOHN. *The Nestorians and their Muslim Neighbours*. Princeton, 1961.
MACLEAN, A. J. and BROWNE, W. H. *The Catholicos of the East and His People*. London, 1892.
MACLEAN, A. J. *East Syrian Daily Offices*. London, 1894.
MONTGOMERY, JAMES. *The Story of Yaballaha III*. Columbia, 1927.
SURMA D'BAIT MAR SHIMUN (aunt of the Catholicos-Patriarch). *Assyrian Church Customs and the Murder of Mar Shimun*. London, 1920.
WALLIS BUDGE, SIR E. A. T. (ed.). *The Book of Governors of Thomas of Marga*. 2 vols. London, 1892.
WIGRAM, W. A. *The Doctrinal Position of the Assyrian Church*. London, 1908.
—— *Introduction to the History of the Assyrian Church*. London, 1910.
—— *Our Smallest Ally*. London, 1920.
—— *The Assyrians and their Neighbours*. London, 1929.

CHAPTER 12: THE LUTHERAN AND REFORMED CHURCHES

ANDERSON, RUFUS. *History of the Missions of the A.B. to the Oriental Churches*. 2 vols. Boston, 1872.
ARPEE, LEON. *A Century of Armenian Protestantism*. New York, 1946.
AUDEH, FARID. *The Church of the Reformation in the Bible Lands* (typed thesis). Princeton, 1953.
CRIVELLI, C. *Protestanti i Cristiani orientali*. Rome, 1944.
DE NOVO, JOHN A. *American Interests and Policies in the Middle East, 1900–1939*. Minnesota, 1963.
ELDER, EARL E. *Vindicating a Vision*. Philadelphia, 1958.
ELDER, JOHN. *History of the American Presbyterian Mission to Iran, 1834–1960*. Tehran, 1960.
GRAF, G. *Geschichte der christlichen arabischen Literatur*. 4 vols. Vatican City, 1944–9.
HERTZBERG, HANS WILHELM. *Jerusalem; Geschichte einer Gemeinde*. Kassel, 1965.
HORNUS, JEAN-MICHEL. "Le Protestantisme au Proche-Orient (1) Les origines de la mission jusqu'au partage entre les différentes Sociétés." *POC*, vol. VII (1957), pp. 139–51.
—— "Le Protestantisme au Proche-Orient (2) L'American Board en Turquie et le développement du Protestantisme arménien." *POC*, vol. VIII (1958), pp. 37–68 and 149–67.
—— "Le Protestantisme au Proche-Orient (3) L'American Board puis le Presbyterian Board en Syrie et au Liban; le Synode libano-syrien."

POC, vol. VIII (1958), pp. 243–62; IX (1959), pp. 42–55 and 350–7; X (1960), pp. 26–41 and 146–63; XI (1961), pp. 235–53 and 321–39.

KAWERAU, PETER. *Amerika und die orientalischen Kirchen*. Berlin, 1958.

LINDSAY, RAO H. *Nineteenth Century American Schools in the Levant: a Study of Purposes*. University of Michigan, Comparative Education Dissertation Series number 5, 1965.

LYKO, DIETER. *Gründung, Wachstum und Leben der evangelischen christlichen Kirchen in Iran*. Leiden, 1964.

PUTNEY, ETHEL W. *A Brief History of the American Board Schools in Turkey*. Istanbul, 1964.

RICHTER, JULIUS. *A History of Protestant Missions in the Near East*. Edinburgh and London, 1910. Second German edition: *Missions und Evangelisation im Orient*. Gütersloh, 1930.

RUBYAN, PUZANT ROBERT. *Armenians and Protestant Missions in the Middle East* (typed thesis). Hartford, 1956.

SCHERER, GEORGE H. *Mediterranean Missions, 1808–1870*, a mimeographed undated edition (1939), Beirut.

SOURIAL, SAMUEL HABIB. *The Evangelical Church as a Religious Community in Egypt* (typed thesis). American University of Cairo, 1950.

STRONG, WILLIAM. *The Story of the American Board*. Boston, 1910.

TIBAWI, A. L. *American Interests in Syria 1800–1901, a Study of Educational, Literary and Religious Work*. Oxford, 1966.

TRACY, JOSEPH. "History of the A.B.C.F.M." In the collective volume: *History of American Missions to the Heathen*. Worcester, 1840. (This lengthy contribution had a second separate edition, New York, 1842.)

TRASK, ROGER R. "Unnamed Christianity in Turkey." *Muslim World*, vol. LV (1965), pp. 66–76 and 101–11.

United Presbyterian Church, *Handbook on Foreign Mission*, pp. 1–62 and 131–70. 1953.

CHAPTER 13: THE ANGLICAN CHURCH

ANTONIUS, GEORGE. *The Arab Awakening*. London, 1938.

BIRKS, HERBERT. *Life and Correspondence of Thomas Valpy French*. 2 vols. London, 1895.

BLISS, F. J. *Religions of Modern Syria and Palestine*. Edinburgh, 1912.

CASH, W. WILSON. *The Missionary Church*. London, 1939.

DANBY, H. *Studies in Eastern Church History*. Jerusalem, 1922.

DEHQANI TAFTI, HASSAN. *Design of My World*. London, 1959.

GAIRDNER, W. H. T. *D. M. Thornton: A Study in Missionary Ideals and Methods*. London, 1909.

—— *W.H.T.G. to His Friends*. London, 1930.

GOBAT, SAMUEL. *Biography* (*S. Gobat: His Life and Work*). London, 1884.

HYAMSON, A. M. (ed.). *The British Consulate in Jerusalem* (in relation to the Jews of Palestine, 1838–1914). London, 1939 and 1942.

MACALISTER, R. A. S. *A Century of Excavations*. London, 1925.

PADWICK, CONSTANCE E. *Temple Gairdner of Cairo*. London, 1928.

RICHTER, JULIUS. *A History of Protestant Missions in the Near East*. Edinburgh, 1910. Translated from the German.

SYKES, CHRISTOPHER. *Cross Roads to Israel: Palestine from Balfour to Bevin*. London, 1965.

TIBAWI, A. L. *British Interests in Palestine, 1800–1901*. London, 1961.

TUCHMAN, BARBARA W. *Bible and Sword: England and Palestine from the Bronze Age to Balfour*. New York, 1956; London, 1957.

WAND, J. W. C. *Anglicanism in History and Today*. London, 1961.

WARREN, M. A. C. *The Missionary Movement from Britain in Modern History*. London, 1965.

WEIZMANN, CHAIM. *Trial and Error*. London, 1949.

VOLUME 2

PART I: ISLAM

CHAPTER I: HISTORICAL REVIEW

As pre-Islamic inscriptional data are currently undergoing scrutiny, sifting, and reappraisal, time must elapse before a clear picture of the historical background to Islam emerges, but the following are useful:

BELL, R. *The Origins of Islam in its Christian Environment*. London, 1926.

JAMME, P. "La religion sudarabique." *Histoire des Religions*, vol. IV, ed. M. Brillant and R. Aigrain. Paris, 1953.

O'LEARY, DE LACY. *Arabia before Islam*. London, 1927. (Superficial but useful though too early to include much inscriptional evidence.)

RYCKMANS, G. *Les religions pré-islamiques*. (Bibliothèque du Muséon, XXVI.) 2nd ed. Louvain, 1951.

SMITH, SIDNEY. "Events in Arabia in the 6th century A.D." *Bulletin of the School of Oriental & African Studies*, vol. XVI, pt. 3 (1954), pp. 425–68. (A valuable scholarly assembly and appreciation of materials, though not to be regarded as final or all the conclusions accepted.)

There is no good study of Muḥammad and his career embodying the findings of modern research, though the work of scholars of a previous generation, still with much validity, may be consulted in the *Encyclopaedia of Islam*, 1st ed. (or more conveniently in the *Shorter Encyclopaedia of Islam* (Leiden, 1953)); the 2nd ed. is still in progress.

For factual information. A. Guillaume, *The Life of Muhammad* (Oxford, 1955) has been drawn upon for this essay, though as it is rather inaccurate in detail it has had to be checked invariably against the Arabic (cf. A. Tibawi, review, *Islamic Quarterly*, vol. III, pt. 3 (London, 1956), pp. 196–214). A wide range of Arabic sources, some of which have appeared in fairly recent years for the first time, has been utilized, and occasional acknowledgement made to them in footnotes. For the new approach to this period proposed by the writer, cf. "Ḥaram and ḥawṭah, the sacred enclave in Arabia" in *Mélanges Taha Husain*, ed. Murad Kamil (Cairo, 1962), and for the "holy family", *The Saiyids of Ḥaḍramawt* (London, 1957).

For the Orthodox Caliphs and Umayyad period J. Wellhausen, *The Arab Kingdom and its Fall* (Calcutta, 1927), originally published in 1902, and recently reprinted in Beirut, has, by and large, stood the test of time well. The great Islamic schism has been well studied from various angles in the following works:

LEVI DELLA VIDA, G. "Il califfato di ʿAli secondo il Kitāb ansāb al-ašrāf di al-Balādurī." *Rivista degli studi orientali*, vol. VI (Rome, 1914), pp. 427–507, 923–7.

PETERSEN, E. "ʿAlī and Muʿāwiyah. The rise of the Umayyad Caliphate." *Acta Orientalia*, vol. XXIII (1959), pp. 157–96.

—— *ʿAlī and Muʿāwiya in Early Arabic Tradition* (Copenhagen, 1964), with a full bibliography.

VECCIA VAGLIERI, L. "Il conflitto ʿAli-Muʿāwiya e la secessione khārigita riesaminati alla luce di fonte ibāḍite." *Annali, Istituto orientale di Napoli* n.s. vols. IV (Naples, 1932 and 1953), pp. 1–94 and V, pp. 1–98.

For the full bibliography of the above and subsequent periods see J. Sauvaget and Claude Cahen, *Introduction to the History of the Muslim East* (Berkeley and Los Angeles, 1965); J. D. Pearson, *Index Islamicus* (Cambridge, 1958), and its supplements.

CHAPTER 2: ISLAM IN EGYPT

ABD AL JALIL. *Brève histoire de la littérature arabe*. Paris, 1943.

ADAMS, C. C. *Islam and Modernism in Egypt*. London, 1933.

DODGE, B. *Al-Azhar, a millenium of Muslim Learning*. Washington, 1961.

DUNNE, J. HEYWORTH. *An Introduction to the History of Education in Modern Egypt*. London, 1939.

—— *Religious and Political Trends in Modern Egypt*. Washington, 1950.

GIBB, H. A. R. *Modern Trends in Islam*. Chicago, 1947.

SMITH, WILFRED CANTWELL. *Islam in Modern History*. Princeton, 1957.

CHAPTER 3: ISLAM IN THE COUNTRIES OF THE FERTILE CRESCENT

ʿABD AL-NAṢIR, JAMĀL (GAMAL ABD EL-NASSER). *The Philosophy of the Revolution*. Cairo, 1951.

ATIYAH, EDWARD. *The Arabs*. London, 1955.

Atlas of the Arab World and the Middle East (introduction by C. F. Beckingham). London, 1960.

AL-BAZZAZ, A. *Al-Bazzaz on Arab Nationalism*. London, 1965.

CRAGG, KENNETH. *Counsels in Contemporary Islam*. Edinburgh, 1965.

—— *The Call of the Minaret*. New York, 1956.

ELDER, E. E. *Commentary on the Creed of Islam*. New York, 1950.

FARUQI, ISMA'IL. *On Arabism 'Urubah and Religion*. Amsterdam, 1962.
GIBB, Sir HAMILTON. *Studies in the Civilisation of Islam*. Boston, 1962.
HOLLER, JOANNE E. *Population Growth and Social Change in the Middle East*. Washington, D.C., 1964.
ḤUSAYN, KĀMIL. *City of Wrong* (translation by Kenneth Cragg). London, 1959.
IONIDES, MICHAEL. *Divide and Lose: The Arab Revolt of 1955–58*. London, 1960.
KAMĀL, AḤMAD. *The Sacred Journey*. London, 1964.
NOLIN, KENNETH. "Bibliography of Books on Christianity by Muslim Writers." *Muslim World* (July 1965).
PADWICK, CONSTANCE. *Muslim Devotions*. London, 1961.
PATAI, RAPHAEL. *The Kingdom of Jordan*. Princeton, 1958.
SAYEGH, FAYEZ. *Arab Unity: Hope and Fulfillment*. New York, 1958.
AJ-SIBA'I, MUSTAFA. *Religion and State in Islam* (*This is Islam*, Booklet 2). Beirut, 1953.
SMITH, WILFRED CANTWELL. *Islam in Modern History*. Princeton, 1957.
TIBAWI, A. L. "The Palestine Arab Refugees in Arabic Poetry and Art." *Royal Central Asian Journal* (July/October 1963).

CHAPTER 4: ISLAM IN TURKEY

The reader will feel how much the present writer is indebted to the articles of Professor Dr G. Jäschke, Münster, who has also kindly answered some questions in connexion with modern Turkish politics. Professor Tayib Okiç, Ilâhiyat Fakültesi, Ankara, and Professor Dr M. Hamidullah, Istanbul/Paris, have also kindly provided me with some information about the most recent developments. The impressions of modern Turkish life are based upon five years' activity as professor in the Ilâhiyat Fakültesi, Ankara, and many discussions with Turkish friends.

AKSEKI, AHMED HAMDI. *Islam Dini*. Ankara, 1957.
ALLEN, HENRI E. *The Turkish Transformation*. Chicago, 1935.
ARAZ, NEZIHE. *Anadolu Evliyalarî*. Istanbul, 1960.
AYVERDI, SAMIHA—Nezihe Araz—Safiye Erol—Sofi Huri, *Kenan Rifai ve Yirminci Asrîn Işîgînda Müslümanlîk*. Istanbul, 1951.
—— *Istanbul Geceleri*. Istanbul, 1952.
BECKINGHAM, C. F. "Turkey" (in: Douglas Grant, *The Islamic Near East*, University of Toronto Quarterly Supplements, 4). 1960.
BERKES, NIYAZI. *Turkish Nationalism and Western Civilization*. London, 1959.
BIRGE, J. K. *The Bektashi Order of Dervishes*. London, 1937.
—— "Islam in Modern Turkey" (*Islam in the Modern World*, ed. D. S. Franck). New York, 1951.
CRAGG, KENNETH. *Counsels in Contemporary Islam*. Edinburgh, 1965.
ESIN, EMEL. *Mecca the Radiant, Medina the Glorious*. London, 1963.
FISCHER, AUGUST. *Aus der religiösen Reformbewegung in der Türkei*. Leipzig, 1922.
HEYD, U. *Foundations of Turkish Nationalism*. London, 1950.
—— "Islam in Modern Turkey." R. *Central Asian Journal* (1947).

JÄSCHKE, G. "Nationalismus und Religion im türkischen Befreiungskrieg." *WI*, vol. XVIII (1936).
JÄSCHKE, G. *Die Türkei in den Jahren 1935–1941*. Leipzig, 1943.
—— *Die Türkei in den Jahren 1942–1951*. Wiesbaden, 1955.
—— "Der Islam in der neuen Türkei. Eine rechtsgeschichtliche Untersuchung." *WI*, n.s. vol. I (1951).
—— "Zur Form der Eheschließung in der Türkei." *WI*, n.s. vol. II, pt. 2 (1952).
—— "Die Imam-Ehe in der Türkei." *WI*, n.s. vol. IV, pts. 2–3 (1955).
—— "Vom Kampf der Islamisten und der Kemalisten in der Türkei." *WI*, n.s. vol. VIII, pt. 4 (1963).
—— "Zur Ausbildung der Geistlichen in der Türkei." *WI*, n.s. vol. IX, p. 260.
—— "Bericht der mit der Untersuchung der religiösen Erziehungsprobleme beauftragten Kommission." *WI*, n.s. vol. IX, p. 261.
—— "Die Bedeutung der Religion für Mustafa Kemal (Atatürk)." *Kairos*, vol. V, pt. 2 (1963).
KARPAT, KEMAL H. *Turkey's Politics*. Princeton, 1959.
KÜRKÇÜOĞLU, KEMAL EDIB. *Dinde Reform Meselesi*. Ankara, 1954.
—— *Radyo'da Dini ve Akhlaqi Konuşmalar*. Ankara, 1956.
HARTMANN, R. *Im neuen Anatolien*. Leipzig, 1928.
LEWIS, BERNARD. "Islamic Revival in Turkey" (*International Affairs* XXVIII). 1952.
LEWIS, GEOFFREY. *Turkey*. New York, 1955.
MAKAL, MAHMUD. *Bizim Köy—Köyümden—Memleketin Sahibleri*. Istanbul, 1950, 1952, 1954.
—— *A Village in Anatolia*, trans. by Sir Wyndham Deedes. London, 1953.
MANGO, A. J. A. "Islam in Turkey" (in: D. Grant, *The Islamic Near East*). Toronto, 1960.
REED, HOWARD A. "Revival of Islam in Secular Turkey." *Middle East Journal*, vol. VIII, pt. 3 (1954).
—— "The Religious Life of Modern Turkish Muslims" (*Islam and the West*, ed. R. N. Frye, pp. 108–48). The Hague, 1957.
—— "Turkey's New Imam-Hatip Schools." *WI*, n.s. vol. IV, pts. 2–3 (1955).
—— "The Faculty of Divinity at Ankara", I, II. *The Muslim World*, vols. XLVI, pt. 4, XLVII, pt. 1 (Oct. 1956/Jan. 1957).
RUMMEL, F. VON. *Die Türkei auf dem Weg nach Europa*. Munich, 1952.
RUSTOW, DANKWART A. "Politics and Islam in Turkey 1920–1955" (*Islam and the West*, ed. R. N. Frye, pp. 69–107). The Hague, 1957.
SCHIMMEL, A. "Das Gelübde im türkischen Volksglauben." *WI*, n.s. vol. IV (1956).
—— "Yunus Emre." *Numen*, vol. VIII, pt. 1 (1961).
SMITH, W. C. *Islam in Modern History*. Princeton, 1957.
—— "Modern Turkey—Islamic Reformation" (*Islamic Culture*, XV/XVI). Hyderabad, 1951.
YALMAN, AHMED EMIN. *Turkey in my Time*. Oklahoma, 1956.
YÖRÜKAN, YUSUF ZIYA. *Müslümanlık*. Ankara, Ilahiyat Fakültesi, 1957.

CHAPTER 5: ITHNĀ ʿASHARĪ SHĪʿISM AND IRANIAN ISLAM

L'Âme de l'Iran. Paris, 1951.
ARBERRY, A. J. (ed.). *The Legacy of Persia*. Oxford, 1953.
BELL, G. *Persian Pictures*. London, 1947.
BINDER, L. *Iran: Political Development in a Changing Society*. Los Angeles, 1962.
BROWNE, E. G. *A Literary History of Persia*. Vol. IV. Cambridge, 1928.
—— *A Year amongst the Persians*. London, 1950.
CORBIN, H. (with the collaboration of S. H. Nasr and O. Yahya). *Histoire de la philosophie islamique*. Vol. I. Paris, 1964.
—— *La spiritualité iranienne*. Paris (in press).
—— *Terre céleste et corps de résurrection*. Paris, 1961.
DONALDSON, D. M. *The Shiʿite Religion: A History of Islam in Persia and Irak*. London, 1933.
FRYE, R. N. *Iran*. New York, 1953.
GOBINEAU, A. *Les religions et les philosophies dans l'Asie centrale*. Paris, 1923.
HAAS, W. *Iran*. New York, 1946.
IQBAL, M. *Iran*. Madras, 1946.
LAMBTON, A. K. S. *Islamic Society in Persia*. London, 1954.
MASSÉ, H. *Croyances et coutumes persanes*. 2 vols. Paris, 1938.
NASR, S. H. *Ideals and Realities of Islam*. London, 1966.
—— *Iran*. Paris (UNESCO), 1965.
—— *Three Muslim Sages*. Cambridge, Mass., 1964.
ROSS, E. D. *The Persians*. Oxford, 1931.
SCHUON, F. *Understanding Islam*, trans. D. M. Matheson. London, 1963.
SYKES, P. M. *A History of Persia*. 2 vols. London, 1951.
—— and KHAN BAHADUR, A. K. *The Glory of the Shia World. The Tale of a Pilgrimage*. London, 1910.
WILBUR, D. N. *Iran, Past and Present*. Princeton, 1958.
WILSON, A. T. *Persia*. London, 1932.
YOUNG, T. C. (ed.). *Near Eastern Culture and Society: A Symposium on the Meeting of East and West*. Princeton, 1951.

CHAPTER 6: ISLAM IN AFGHANISTAN, INDIA AND PAKISTAN

ALBIRUNI, A. H. (pseudonym of Shaykh Muḥammad Ikrām). *Makers of Pakistan*. Lahore, 1950.
ARNOLD, T. W. *The Preaching of Islam*. 3rd ed. London, 1935.
AZIZ, AHMED. *Studies in Islamic Culture in the Indian Environment*. Oxford, 1964.
BALJON, J. M. S. *Modern Muslim Koran Interpretation*. Leiden, 1961.
HERKLOTS, G. A. *Qanoon-e-Islam or the Customs of the Moosulmans of India*. London, 1832.
HUSAIN, YUSUF. *Glimpses of Medieval Indian Culture*. Bombay, 1962.
NIZAMI, KHALIQ AHMAD. *Some Aspects of Religion and Politics in India during the 13th Century*. Aligarh, 1961.

Qureshi, Ishtiaq Husain. *The Muslim Community of the Indo-Pakistan Subcontinent.* The Hague, 1962.
Schimmel, Annemarie. *Gabriel's Wing. A Study of the Religious Ideas of Sir Muḥammad Iqbāl.* Leiden, 1963.
—— *Pakistan, ein Schloss mit tausend Toren.* Zürich, 1965.
Shah, Sirdar Ikbal Ali. *Afghanistan of the Afghans.* London, 1920.
Sharma, Sri Ram. *The Religious Policy of the Mughal Emperors.* London, 1962.
Smith, W. Cantwell. *Modern Islam in India.* Rev. ed. London, 1946.
Subhan, John A. *Sufism, its Saints and Shrines.* Lucknow, 1938.
Titus, Murray T. *Islam in India and Pakistan.* Calcutta, 1959.
Wilber, D. N. "The Structure and Position of Islam in Afghanistan." *Middle East Journal*, vol. vi (1952).

CHAPTER 7: ISLAM IN THE USSR

Barthold, V. V. *Four Studies on the History of Central Asia.* 3 vols. Leiden, 1956.
—— *Istoriya Kul'turnoy Zhizni Turkestana* [History of the Cultural Life of Turkestan]. Leningrad, 1927.
—— *Turkestan down to the Mongol Conquest* (English translation). London, 1958.
Belyayev, Ye. A. *Musul'manskoye Sektantstvo* [Muslim Sects]. Moscow, 1957.
Bennigsen, A. and Quelquejay, C. *The Evolution of the Muslim Nationalities of the USSR and their Linguistic Problems* (English translation). London, 1961.
—— *Islam in the Soviet Union.* London, 1967.
—— *La Presse et le mouvement National chez les Musulmans de Russie avant 1920.* Paris, 1964.
—— and Carrere D'Encausse, H. "La littérature anti-Religieuse dans les Républiques Soviétiques Musulmanes", 1957, published in *Revue des Études Islamiques.* Paris, 1958.
Caroe, O. *Soviet Empire.* London, 1953.
Central Asian Review. London, 1953– .
Gibb, H. A. R. *The Arab Conquests in Central Asia.* London, 1923.
Hayit, B. *Turkestan im Zwanzigsten Jahrhundert.* Darmstadt, 1956.
Holdsworth, M. *Turkestan in the 19th Century.* London, 1959.
Pierce, R. *Russian Central Asia, 1867–1917.* Berkeley and Los Angeles, 1960.
Pipes, R. *The Formation of the Soviet Union.* 2nd ed. Cambridge, Mass., 1964.
Schuyler, E. *Turkistan.* London, 1876.
Smirnov, N. A. *Islam and Russia. A detailed analysis of N. A. Smirnov's book "An Outline of the History of Islamic Studies in the USSR" (Moscow 1954) with an introduction by Ann K. S. Lambton.* London, 1956.
Wheeler, G. E. *Racial Problems in Soviet Muslim Asia.* 2nd ed. London, 1962.
—— *The Modern History of Soviet Central Asia.* London, 1964.
Zenkovsky, S. A. *Pan-Turkism and Islam in Russia.* Cambridge, Mass., 1960.

CHAPTER 8: ISLAM IN NORTH-WEST AFRICA

Annuaire de l'Afrique du Nord, published by the Centre National de la Recherche Scientifique, I, 1962; II, 1963.

BEL, A. *La Religion Musulmane en Berbérie*, an outline of the history and religious sociology, I. Paris, 1938.

DEPONT, O. and COPPOLANI, X. *Les confréries religieuses musulmanes*. Algiers, 1897.

IBN 'ABD AL-ḤAKAM. *Conquête de l'Afrique du Nord et de l'Espagne* [Futūḥ Ifrīqiya wa'l-Andalus], Arabic text and French translation with an introduction and notes by A. Gateau. Algiers, 1942.

Initiation à l'Algérie, by a group of eighteen scholars. Paris, 1957.

Initiation au Maroc, by a group of eleven scholars. 2nd ed. Paris, 1945.

Initiation à la Tunisie, by a group of thirteen scholars. Paris, 1950.

JULIEN, C. A. *Histoire de l'Afrique du Nord*, II, 2nd ed., revised and brought up to date by R. Le Tourneau. Paris, 1952.

LE TOURNEAU, R. *Evolution politique de l'Afrique du Nord musulmane 1920–1961*. Paris, 1962.

MARÇAIS, G. *La Berbérie musulmane et l'Orient au Moyen Age*. Paris, 1946.

WESTERMARCK, E. *Survivances païennes dans la civilisation mahometane*. Paris, 1935.

—— *Ritual and Belief in Morocco*. London, 1926.

CHAPTER 9: ISLAM IN THE SUDAN

Notes on Sources

J. S. Trimingham's *Islam in the Sudan* (1949) is the only comprehensive introduction to the subject though parts need readjustment of emphasis and modernizing. The author was formerly secretary of the Church Missionary Society in the Sudan. The best available brief account of the history of Islamic education since 1899 is Kāmil al-Bāqir's paper "Religious education, past and future development" in *Proceedings of the 11th Annual Conference of the Philosophical Society of the Sudan* (dupl. typescr., Khartoum, 1963). The author is now director of the Islamic Seminary (*al-Ma'had al-'Ilmī*), Omdurman, which publishes three journals: a quarterly, *Majallat al-Ma'had al-'Ilmī*, intended for an educated Muslim readership, with *Ishāb al-Din* and *al-Iṣlāḥ*, both monthly journals with a popular appeal.

On the religious issues in the Southern problem the most objective account at present is the chapter entitled "The Problem of the South" in *Sudan Republic*, by K. D. D. Henderson (1965). The fullest source for the administrative history of the problem is the dossier of documents copied and prepared by Muḥammad 'Umar Bashīr for the abortive Round Table Conference held in Khartoum in March 1965. The collection contains copious excerpts from Condominium government files and includes two papers of outstanding worth: "The Administration of the Sudan since 1898" by Karāmallāh 'Awaḍ, and "The Development of British policy in the Southern Sudan, 1899–1947" by Muddaththir 'Abd al-Raḥīm. R. L. Hill's "Government and

Christian missions in the Anglo-Egyptian Sudan, 1889–1914" in *Middle Eastern Studies*, vol. I, 1965, pp. 113–34, discusses the relationship during the earlier years of the Condominium.

Up to the time of writing there is no document available which presents the Islamic policy of the Sudan government in the southern provinces to sophisticated non-Muslim readers. The former military government's justification for its expulsion of foreign missionaries from the south early in 1964 is set out in a "Memorandum on reasons that led to the expulsion of foreign missionaries and priests from the southern provinces of the Sudan" (Ministry of the Interior, Khartoum, March 1964, dupl. typescr.).

The notable contribution to Southern Sudanese religious, anthropological and linguistic studies by the personnel of the Roman Catholic missions listed in S. Santandrea's *Bibliografia di studi africani* (Verona, 1948) needs augmentation to bring it up to date. A dispassionate investigation, "Some aspects of the spread of Islam in the Nuba Mountains" by G. R. C. Stevenson, in *Sudan Notes and Records*, Khartoum, vol. XLIV, 1963, pp. 9–20, deserves to be matched by contributions of the same quality from Muslim investigators on the spread of Christianity in the Southern Sudan.

CHAPTER 10: ISLAM IN EAST AFRICA

Almeida, Manoel de. *Some Records of Ethiopia: (1593–1646)*. Edited and translated by C. F. Beckingham and G. W. B. Huntingford. London, 1954.

Alvarez, Francisco. *The Prester John of the Indies*. Edited and translated by C. F. Beckingham and G. W. B. Huntingford. London, 1961.

Basset, R. *Histoire de la Conquête de l'Abyssinie*, by Chibab ed-din Ahmed ben Abd el-Qader. 2 parts. Paris, 1897–1909.

Castanhoso, M. de. *Historia das cousas que o muy esforçado capitão Dom Cristovão da Gama fez nos Reynos do Presto João*. Lisbon, 1898.

Cerulli, E. "Documenti arabi per la storia dell'Etiopia." *Memoria* R. *Accademia Lincei*, sc. mor. 1931.

—— "Il Sultanato della Scioa nel secolo XIII." *Rassegna di Studi Etiopici*. 1941.

—— *Studi Etiopici*, vol. I: *La storia e la lingua di Harar*. Rome, 1936.

—— "L'Etiopia medievale in alcuni brani di scrittori arabi." *Rassegna di Studi Etiopici*. 1943.

—— *Somalia*. 3 vols. Rome, 1957–64.

Conti Rossini, C. "Storia di Lebna Dengel." *Rendiconti* R. *Accademia Lincei*. 1894.

Conzelman, W. *Chronique de Galâwdêwos, Roi d'Ethiopie*. Paris, 1895.

Trimingham, J. S. *Islam in Ethiopia*. Oxford, 1952.

—— *Islam in East Africa*. Oxford, 1964.

CHAPTER 11: ISLAM IN WEST AFRICA

BOVILL, E. W. *Caravans of the Old Sahara*. London, 1933. (Rewritten as) *The Golden Trade of the Moors*. London, 1958. 2nd ed., rev. R. Hallett, 1968.

FISHER, H. J. *Aḥmadiyyah, A Study in Contemporary Islam on the West African Coast*. Oxford, 1963.

LHOTE, H. *Les Touaregs du Hoggar*. Paris, 1944.

MINER, H. *The Primitive City of Timbuctoo*. Princeton, 1953.

MONTEIL, C. *Djénné*. Paris, 1932.

NADEL, S. F. *Nupe Religion*. London, 1954.

ROUCH, J. *La Religion et la magie Songhay*. Paris, 1960.

SMITH, E. W. and PARRINDER, E. G. (eds.). *African Ideas of God*. 3rd ed. Edinburgh, 1966.

SMITH, M. *Baba of Karo*. London, 1954.

TRIMINGHAM, J. S. *Islam in West Africa*. Oxford, 1959.

—— *A History of Islam in West Africa*. London, 1962.

TYAM, MUḤAMMAD 'ALĪ. *La Vie d'El Hadj Omar*, trans. H. Gaden. Paris, 1935.

CHAPTER 12: ISLAM IN THE BALKANS

ALDERSON, A. D. *The Structure of the Ottoman Dynasty*. Oxford, 1956.

BABINGER, FRANZ. *Die Geschichtsschreiber der Osmanen und ihre Werke*. Leipzig, 1927.

BALDACCI, ANTONIO. *Studi speciali albanesi*. 3 vols. Rome, 1932–8.

BERKES, NIYAZI. *The Development of Secularism in Turkey*. Montreal, 1964.

BIRGE, J. K. *The Bektashi Order of Dervishes*. London, 1937.

CREASY, EDWARD S. *History of the Ottoman Turks*, ed. by Zeine N. Zeine. Beirut, 1961.

DAVISON, RODERIC H. *Reform in the Ottoman Empire 1856–1878*. Princeton, 1963.

DEVEREUX, ROBERT. *The First Ottoman Constitutional Period*. Baltimore, 1963.

GIBB, H. A. R. and BOWEN, HAROLD. *Islamic Society and the West*. Vol. 1, pts 1 and 2. London, 1950–7.

GÖKALP, Z. *Turkish Nationalism and Western Civilization*, ed. and trans. by Niyazi Berkes. New York, 1959.

HAMMER-PURGSTALL, J. VON. *Geschichte der Osmanischen Dichtkunst bis auf unsere Zeit*. 4 vols. Budapest, 1838.

—— *Geschichte des Osmanischen Reiches*. 2nd ed. 4 vols. Budapest, 1835–6.

HEINRICH, HANS. *Der Mensch in Orient und Okzident*. Munich, 1960.

HUREWITZ, J. C. *Diplomacy in the Near and Middle East: a Documentary Record*. 2 vols. Princeton, 1956.

JELAVICH, CHARLES and BARBARA. *The Balkans in Transition*. Berkeley, 1963.

JORGA, N. *Geschichte des Osmanischen Reiches*. 5 vols. Gotha, 1908–13.

KHADDURI, M. and LIEBESNY, H. J. (eds.). *Law in the Middle East*. Washington, 1955.

KHADDURI, MAJID. *War and Peace in the Law of Islam*. Baltimore, 1955.

LEWIS, BERNARD. *The Emergence of Modern Turkey*. London, 1961.
LYBYER, A. H. *The Government of the Ottoman Empire*. Cambridge, Mass., 1913.
MARDIN, ŞERIF. *The Genesis of Young Ottoman Thought*. Princeton, 1962.
MARRIOTT, J. A. R. *The Eastern Question*. Oxford, 1947.
MILLER, BARNETTE. *The Palace School of Muhammad the Conqueror*. Cambridge, Mass., 1941.
MILLER, WILLIAM. *The Ottoman Empire and its Successors, 1801–1927*. Rev. ed. Cambridge, 1936.
ROBINSON, RICHARD. *The First Turkish Republic*. Cambridge, Mass., 1963.
ROSSI, ETTORE. "I musulmani della ex-Jugoslavia." *Oriente Moderno*, vol. XXII (1942), pp. 37–42.
STAVRIANOS, L. S. *The Balkans since 1453*. New York, 1958.
VAUGHAN, DOROTHY M. *Europe and the Turk. A Pattern of Alliances 1350–1700*. Liverpool, 1954.
VUCINICH, WAYNE. *The Ottoman Empire: Its Record and Legacy*. Princeton, 1965.
WITTEK, PAUL. *The Rise of the Ottoman Empire*. London, 1938.
ZINKEISEN, J. W. *Geschichte des Osmanischen Reiches in Europa*. 7 vols. Hamburg and Gotha, 1840–63.

CHAPTER 13: ṢŪFISM

ARBERRY, A. J. *Sufism*. London, 1950.
BALYĀNĪ, 'ABDULLĀH. "An Arabic Manuscript in the Hunterian Collection." *Journal of the Royal Asiatic Society* (1961).
BURCKHARDT, TITUS. *An Introduction to Sufi Doctrine*. Lahore, 1959.
GHAZĀLĪ, AL-. *Mishkāt al-anwār* [The Niche for Lights], trans. W. H. T. Gairdner. London, 1924.
ḤALLĀJ, AL-. *Dīwān d'al-Hallāj*. (Annotated French translation by L. Massignon.) Paris, 1955.
HUJWĪRĪ, AL-. *Kashf al-maḥjūb*, trans. R. A. Nicholson. London, 1936.
IBN 'ARABĪ. *Fuṣūṣ al-ḥikam*. [La Sagesse des Prophètes.] (Annotated French translation by Titus Burckhardt.) Paris, 1955.
IBN AL-FĀRIḌ. *al-Khamriyya*. [Éloge du Vin.] (Annotated French translation by Émile Dermenghem.) Paris, 1931.
—— *The Mystical Poems of Ibn al-Fārid*. (Annotated translation by A. J. Arberry.) Dublin, 1956.
JĪLĪ, AL-. *al-Insān al-kāmil*. [De l'homme universel.] (Extracts in annotated French translation by Titus Burckhardt.) Algiers, 1953. (Extracts in English translation in R. A. Nicholson, *Studies in Islamic Mysticism*, Cambridge, 1921.)
JUNAYD, AL-. *Rasā'il al-Junayd*. (English translation by 'Alī Ḥasan 'Abd al-Qādir in *The Life, Personality and Writings of Al-Junayd*, London, 1962.)
KALĀBĀDHĪ, AL-. *Kitāb al-ta'arruf*. (English translation by A. J. Arberry as *The Doctrine of the Sufis*, Cambridge, 1935.)
KHARRĀZ, AL-. *Kitāb al-ṣidq*. (English translation by A. J. Arberry as *The Book of Truthfulness*, London, 1937.)

LINGS, MARTIN. *A Moslem Saint of the Twentieth Century, Shaikh Ahmad al-'Alawī*. London, 1961.
MASSIGNON, LOUIS. *Essai sur les origines du lexique technique de la mystique musulmane*. Paris, 1922.
—— *La Passion d'Al-Hallāj*. Paris, 1914–21.
NASR, SEYYED HOSSEIN. *Three Muslim Sages—Avicenna, Suhrawardī, Ibn 'Arabī*. Cambridge, Mass., 1964.
NICHOLSON, R. A. *Studies in Islamic Mysticism*. Cambridge, 1921.
RŪMĪ, JALĀL-AL-DĪN. *Discourses of Rumi*, trans. A. J. Arberry. London, 1961.
SARRĀJ, AL-. *Kitāb al-luma'*. Extracts trans. R. A. Nicholson. Leiden, London, 1914.
SCHĀYA, LEO. *La Doctrine soufique de l'unité*. Paris, 1962.
SCHUON, FRITHJOF. *L'Œil du cœur*. Paris, 1950.
—— *The Transcendent Unity of Religions*. London, 1953.
—— *Understanding Islam*. London, 1963.
SIRĀJ AL-DĪN, ABŪ BAKR. *The Book of Certainty*. London, 1952.
—— "The Origins of Sufism." *The Islamic Quarterly*, vol. III, no. 2 (July 1956), pp. 53–64.
SMITH, MARGARET. *An Early Mystic of Baghdad*. London, 1935.
—— *Al-Ghazālī the Mystic*. London, 1944.
—— *Rābi'a the Mystic*. Cambridge, 1928.
—— *Readings from the Mystics of Islam*. London, 1950.
—— *Studies in Early Mysticism in the Near and Middle East*. London, 1931.
—— *The Sufi Path of Love. An Anthology*. London, 1954.
WATT, W. MONTGOMERY. *The Faith and Practice of Al-Ghazali*. London, 1953.

CHAPTER 14: THE WAHHĀBĪS

'ABDUL BARI, MUHAMMAD. "The Politics of Sayyid Ahmad Barelwi.' *Islamic Culture*, vol. XXXI (1957), pp. 156–64.
CASKEL, WERNER. *Altes und neues Wahhabitentum*. Leipzig, 1929.
DIFFELEN, R. W. VAN. *De Leer der Wahhabieten*. Leiden, 1927.
DOUGHTY, CHARLES M. *Travels in Arabia Deserta*. 2 vols. New ed. London, 1936.
HUNTER, W. W. *The Indian Musulmans*. 2nd ed. London, 1872.
HUSAIN, MAHMUD and others (eds.). *A History of the Freedom Movement*. Vol. I. Karachi, 1957.
MUSIL, ALOIS. *Northern Neğd*. New York, 1928.
—— *Zur Zeitgeschichte von Arabien*. Leipzig, 1918.
NALLINO, CARLO A. *L'Arabia Sa'ūdiana*, ed. by Maria Nallino. Rome, 1939.
PHILBY, H. ST JOHN B. *The Heart of Arabia*. 2 vols. London, 1922.
—— *Arabia of the Wahhabis*. London, 1928.
—— *A Pilgrim of the Wahhabis*. London, 1943.
—— *Arabian Jubilee*. London, 1952.
—— *Sa'udi Arabia*. London, 1955.
PRÖBSTER, E. "Die Wahhabiten und der Maġrib." *Islamica*, vol. VII (1935), pp. 66–114.

RIHANI, AMEEN. *Maker of Modern Arabia*. Boston, 1928.

SMITH, H. F. C. "A Neglected Theme of West African History: The Islamic Revolutions of the 19th Century." *Historians in Tropical Africa* (Salisbury, Southern Rhodesia, 1962), pp. 145–58.

SMITH, WILFRED CANTWELL. *Islam in Modern History*. Princeton, 1957.

SULAYMĀN B. SIḤMĀN (ed.). *al-Hadiyya al-sunniya*. Cairo, 1342 A.H.

WAHBA, ḤĀFIẒ. *Jazīrat al-ʻarab*. Cairo, 1935.

CHAPTER 15: THE ZAYDĪS

This sketch has been compiled from the sources cited *infra* combined with the writer's field notes. It is with pleasure that advice and some material supplied by H. E. Sayyid Aḥmad al-Shāmī and his brother Sayyid ʻAbd al-Wahhāb are acknowledged, though of course they are in no way responsible for the views expressed.

ʻABD AL-WĀSIʻ B. YAḤYĀ AL-WĀSIʻĪ. *Tārīkh al-Yaman*. 2nd ed. Cairo, 1947.

ADMIRALTY, NAVAL INTELLIGENCE DIVISION. *Western Arabia and the Red Sea Coast, B.R. 527*. London, 1946.

AL-ʻARSHĪ, ḤUSAIN B. AḤMAD. *Bulūgh al-marām*, ed. Anastase Marie al-Kirmilī. Cairo, 1939.

BOUSQUET, G.-H. and BERQUE, J. *Recueil de la loi musulmane de Zaid ben ʻAlî*. Algiers, 1941.

BROWNE, E. G. *Ibn Isfandiyār's History of Tabaristān*. G.M.S. Leiden, 1905.

FRIEDLAENDER, I. "The Heterodoxies of the Shiites in the Presentation of Ibn Ḥazm." *Journal of the American Oriental Society* (New Haven, 1907 and 1908), vols. XXVIII, pp. 1–80, and XXIX, pp. 1–183.

KAY, H. C. *Yaman, its Early Medieval History*. London, 1892; i.e. the history of ʻUmāra al-Ḥakamī.

KAZI, A. K. "Notes on the Development of Zaidi Law." *Abr-Nahrain* (Leiden, 1962), vol. II, pp. 36–40, based on his edition of *K. al-Muntakhab fi 'l-fiqh*, Ph.D. thesis, S.O.A.S. London University.

MOHAMED MADI. *Jaḥjā b. al-Ḥusain b. al-Mu'ajjad al-Jamanī's "Anbā' az-Zaman fī Aḥbār al-Jaman"*. Berlin–Leipzig, 1936.

MOHAMED SAID EL ATTAR. *Le sous-développement économique et social du Yémen*. Algiers, 1965.

MUḤAMMAD ABŪ ZUHRA. *al-Imām Zaid*. Cairo, 1959.

MUḤAMMAD B. AḤMAD ʻĪSĀ AL-ʻAQĪLĪ. *Tārīkh al-Mikhlāf al-Sulaymānī*. Vol. I, parts I and II, al-Riyāḍ, 1958; Vol. II, Cairo, *c*. 1960.

MUḤAMMAD ḤASAN. *Qalb al-Yaman*. Baghdād, 1947.

MUḤAMMAD B. HĀSHIM. *Tārīkh al-dawlat al-Kathīriyya*. Cairo, 1948.

NASIR, JAMAL J. *The doctrine of Kafā'ah...with a critical edition of the Zaidī MS. Al-Mir'āt al-mubaiyinah...fī mas'alat al-kafā'ah*. Ph.D. thesis, S.O.A.S. London University.

NAZĪH AL-MU'AYYAD AL-ʻAẒM. *Riḥla fī bilād al-ʻArabiyya al-Saʻīda*. Cairo, 1937.

REDHOUSE, J. W. *El-Khazrejiyy; a History of the Resúliyy Dynasty of Yemen*. London, 1906–8.

RIHANI, AMEEN. *Arabian Peak and Desert.* London, 1930.
SERJEANT, R. B. "An Early Zaidi Manual of Ḥisbah." *Rivista degli Studi Orientali*, vol. XXVIII (Rome, 1953), pp. 1–34.
—— *The Saiyids of Ḥaḍramawt.* London, 1957.
STROTHMANN, R. *Kultus der Zaiditen.* Strasbourg, 1912.
—— *Das Staatsrecht der Zaiditen* (Strasbourg, 1912) and articles in *Ency. of Islam*, 1st ed.
TRITTON, A. S. *The Rise of the Imams of Sanaa.* Madras, 1925.
VAN ARENDONK, C. (trans. Jacques Ryckmans). *Les débuts de l'Imāmat Zaidite au Yémen* (Leiden, 1960) with a good bibliography.
ZABĀRA, MUḤ. B. MUḤ. B. YAḤYĀ. *Itḥāf al-mustarshidīn.* Ṣan'ā', 1343 A.H.

CHAPTER 16: THE IBĀḌĪS

AL-BARRĀDĪ. *Kitāb al-jawāhir.* Cairo, 1306 A.H.
CHIKH BEKRI. "Le kharijisme berbère." *Annales de l'Institut d'études orientales.* Vol. XV. Algiers, 1957.
AL-DARJĪNĪ. *Kitāb ṭabaqāt al-mashā'ikh.* MS. in Lvov.
GOICHON, A. M. *La vie féminine au Mzab.* Paris, 1927 (I); 1931 (II).
GOLDZIHER, I. *Le dogme et la loi de l'Islam.* Paris, 1958.
LEVI DELLA VIDA, G. s.v. "Khāridjites" in *Ency. of Islam*, 1st ed.
LEWICKI, T. s.v. "Ibāḍīya" in *Handwörterbuch des Islam.* Leiden, 1941.
—— "La répartition géographique des groupements ibāḍites dans l'Afrique du Nord au moyen-âge." *Rocznik Orientalistyczny*, vol. XXI (Warsaw, 1957), pp. 301–43.
—— "Les subdivisions de l'Ibādiyya." *Studia Islamica*, vol. IX (Paris, 1958), pp. 71–82.
—— *Les Ibāḍites en Tunisie au moyen-âge.* Rome, 1959.
—— "Les Ibāḍites dans l'Arabie du Sud au moyen-âge." *Folia Orientalia*, vol. I (Cracow, 1959), pp. 3–18.
—— s.v. "Ḥalḳa" in *Ency. of Islam*, 2nd ed.
AL-MADANĪ, A. T. *Kitab al-Jazā'ir.* Cairo, 1963.
MASQUERAY, E. *Chronique d'Abou Zakaria.* Algiers–Paris, 1878.
MASSIGNON, L. *Annuaire du monde musulman*, 4th ed. Paris, 1954.
MERCIER, M. M. *La civilisation urbaine au Mzab.* Algiers, 1922.
MILLIOT, L. "Recueil de délibérations des djemā'a du Mzab." *Revue des Études Islamiques*, vol. XXI (Paris, 1930), pp. 17–230.
MORENO, M. M. "Note di teologia ibāḍita." *Annali dell'Istituto Universitario Orientale di Napoli*, n.s. vol. III (Rome, 1949), pp. 299–313.
MOTYLINSKI, A. DE C. "L''aqīda des Ibadhites." *Recueil de Mémoires et de textes en l'honneur du XIVe Congrès International des Orientalistes* (Algiers, 1905), pp. 505–45.
NALLINO, C. A. "Rapporti fra la dommatica mu'tazilita e quella degli Ibaditi dell'Africa Settentrionale." *Rivista degli Studi Orientali*, VII (Rome, 1916–18), pp. 455–60.

RUBINACCI, R. "Il Kitāb al-Ǧawāhir di al-Barrādī." *Annali dell'Istituto Universitario Orientale di Napoli*, n.s. vol. IV (Rome, 1952), pp. 55–110.
—— "Il califfo Abd al-Malik b. Marwān e gl'Ibāḍiti." *Ibid.* vol. V (Rome, 1954), pp. 99–121.
—— "La purità rituale secondo gl'Ibāḍiti." *Ibid.* vol. VI (Rome, 1957), pp. 1–41.
—— "Un antico documento di vita cenobitica musulmana." *Ibid.* vol. X (Rome, 1961), pp. 37–78.
—— "La professione di fede di al-Ǧannāwunī." *Ibid.* vol. XIV (Rome, 1964), pp. 553–95.
SACHAU, E. "Über die religiösen Anschauungen der Ibaditischen Muhammedaner in Oman und Ostafrika." *Mittheilungen des Seminars für orientalische Sprachen*, vol. II (1899), pp. 47–82.
SCHACHT, J. *Origins of Muhammadan Jurisprudence*. Oxford, 1950.
—— "Notes mozabites." *al-Andalus*, vol. XXII (Madrid–Granada, 1957), pp. 1–20
AL-SHAMMĀKHĪ. *Kitāb al-siyar*. Cairo, 1301/1883.
TRIMMINGHAM, J. S. *Islam in East Africa*. Oxford, 1964.
VECCIA VAGLIERI, L. "L'imamato ibāḍita dell''Oman." *Annali dell'Istituto Universitario Orientale di Napoli*, n.s. vol. III (Rome, 1949), pp. 245–82.
—— "Il conflitto Alī-Mu'āwiya e la secessione khārigita riesaminati alla luce di fonti ibāḍite." *Ibid.* vol. IV (Rome, 1952), pp. 1–94.

CHAPTER 17: THE ISMĀ'ĪLĪS

Introductory

FYZEE, ASAF A. A. "Bohoras." *Ency. of Islam*, 2nd ed. (1960), vol. I, p. 1254.
HUART, CL. "Ismā'īlīya." *Ency. of Islam*, 1st ed.
IVANOW, W. "Ismā'īlīya." *Ency. of Islam, Supplement* (1939), p. 98.
—— *Brief Survey of the Evolution of Ismailism*. Bombay, 1952.
MASSIGNON, LOUIS. "Karmaṭians." *Ency. of Islam*, 1st ed.
YUSUF ALI, A. "Khojas." *Ency. of Islam*, 1st ed.

History

'ALĪ, ZĀHID. *Tārīkh-i Fāṭimiyyīn-i Miṣr* (Urdu). Hyderabad, Deccan, 1367/1948.
HODGSON, MARSHALL G. S. *The Order of the Assassins*. The Hague, 1955.
IVANOW, W. *Ibn al-Qaddāḥ*. Bombay, 1957.
—— *Ismaili Tradition concerning the Rise of the Fatimids*. Bombay, 1942.
LEWIS, BERNARD. *The Origins of Ismā'īlism*. Cambridge, 1940.
O'LEARY, DE LACY. *A Short History of the Fatimid Khalifate*. London, 1923.

Doctrine

'ALĪ, ZĀHID. *Hāmarē Ismā'īlī Madhhab kī ḥaqīqat awr us kā Niẓām* (Urdu). Hyderabad, Deccan, 1373/1954.
CORBIN, H. *Histoire de la philosophie islamique*. Paris, 1964.

HOLLISTER, J. N. *The Shī'a of India.* London, 1953.

IVANOW, W. *Kalām-i Pīr* (Persian text), ed. and trans. with an introduction. Bombay, 1936.

Distribution, sociology

MISRA, S. C. *Muslim Communities in Gujerat* (University of Baroda). Bombay, 1964.

Literature

FYZEE, ASAF A. A. "The Study of the Literature of the Fatimid *Da'wa.*" *Arabic and Islamic Studies in Honor of Hamilton A. R. Gibb*, ed. G. Makdisi. Leiden, 1965.

IVANOW, W. *Ismaili Literature.* 2nd ed. Tehran, 1963. (1st ed. London, 1934.)

CHAPTER 18: THE DRUZES

(See also the works cited in the footnotes to this chapter.)

ANDERSON, J. N. D. "The Personal Law of the Druze Community." *The World of Islam, 1953.* Pp. 1–9, 83–94.

BLANC, H. *Studies in North Palestinian Arabic. Linguistic inquiries among the Druzes of Western Galilee and Mt Carmel.* Jerusalem, 1953.

CARALI, P. *Fakhr ad-Din II, principe del Libano e la Corte di Toscana 1605–1635*, I. Rome, 1936.

CHEBLI, M. *Fakhreddine II Maan, Prince du Liban (1572–1635).* Beyrouth, 1946.

Moslems, Christians and Druzes in Israel. State of Israel; Central Bureau of Statistics. Publication no. 17. Jerusalem, 1964.

NIMRI, N. N. "The Warrior People of Djebel Druze." *Journal of the Middle East Society*, vols. I (1946), pp. 47–62; II (1947), pp. 90–6; Jerusalem, 1946–7.

STEEN DE JEHAY, F. VAN DEN. *De la situation légale des sujets ottomans non-Musulmans.* Brussels, 1906.

VATIKIOTIS, P. J. "Al-Hakim Bi-Amrillah: The God-King Idea Realized." *Islamic Culture*, vol. XXIX (1955), pp. 1–8.

WUESTENFELD, F. *Fachr ed-din der Drusenfuerst und seine Zeitgenossen.* Göttingen, 1886.

CHAPTER 19: THE AḤMADĪS

ANALYST. *Facts about the Ahmadiyya Movement.* Lahore, 1962.

BASHĪR AL-DĪN MAḤMŪD AḤMAD (under the auspices of). *The Holy Quran with English Translation and Commentary.* Vol. I. Qadian, 1947.

—— *Introduction to the Study of the Holy Quran* (from the above, separately published). London, 1949.

—— *Ahmadiyyat or the True Islam.* 5th ed. Rabwah, 1959.

Encyclopaedia of Islam, 2nd ed. "Aḥmadiyya", vol. I, pp. 301–3.

FISHER, HUMPHREY J. *Aḥmadiyyah: A Study in Contemporary Islām on the West African Coast.* Oxford, 1963.

Ghulām Aḥmad. *The Teachings of Islam* (Muḥammad 'Alī's trans. of the paper at the 1896 Great Religious Conference). 5th ed. Lahore, 1963.

—— *The Philosophy of the Teachings of Islam* (the above with appendix). Rabwah, 1959.

—— *Phenomenon of Revelation*, trans. and ed. by Maulana Aftabud-Din Ahmad. 2nd ed. Lahore, 1963.

Gibb, H. A. R. (ed.). *Whither Islam?* London, 1932.

Muḥammad 'Alī. *The Religion of Islam*. 3rd ed. Lahore, 1950.

—— *The Holy Qur'ān: Arabic Text, English Translation and Commentary*. 5th ed. Lahore, 1963.

—— *Mirza Ghulam Ahmad of Qadian: A Brief Survey of the Ahmadiyyah Movement*. 3rd ed. Lahore, 1963.

Muḥammad 'Alī. *The Founder of the Ahmadiyya Movement*. Lahore, n.d.

—— *Muhammad the Prophet*. 3rd ed. Lahore, 1951.

—— *The Living Thoughts of the Prophet Muhammad*. London, 1950.

—— *A Manual of Hadith* (Tradition). 2nd ed. Lahore, n.d.

—— *Muhammad and Christ* (reprint). Lahore, 1963.

Muslim World (quarterly), see Index. Note especially H. D. Griswold, vol. II (1912), pp. 373 ff.; H. Kraemer, vol. XXI (1931), pp. 170 f.; S. E. Brush, vol. XLV (1955), pp. 145 ff.; J. M. van der Kroef, vol. LII (1962), pp. 57 f.

Nazir Ahmad. *Jesus in Heaven on Earth*. 4th ed. Woking and Lahore, 1956.

Phoenix. *His Holiness* (a Muslim criticism of the Movement). Lahore, reprint, 1958.

Raḥīm Bakhsh. *The Debt Forgotten*. Lahore, 1960.

Report of the Court of Enquiry constituted under Punjab Act II of 1954 to enquire into the Punjab disturbances of 1953 (commonly called the Munir Report). Lahore, 1954.

Titus, Murray T. *Indian Islam*. Oxford, 1930.

Trimingham, J. S. *Islam in West Africa* (esp. Appendix IV). Oxford, 1959.

Walter, H. A. *The Aḥmadīya Movement*. Oxford, 1918.

Ẓafrulla Khān, M. *Islam, its Meaning for Modern Man*. London, 1962.

Part 2: The Three Religions in Concord and Conflict

CHAPTER 20: DOCTRINE

Books are almost legion in this field and selection an obvious threat to fairness. The author's main indebtedness will be clear from the argument and the footnotes. The following are no more than a venture in further reading, for English readers.

Baeck, Leo. *Judaism and Christianity*, trans. by W. Kaufmann. Philadelphia, 1958.

—— *This People Israel, the Meaning of Jewish Existence*, trans. by A. H. Friedlander. New York, 1965.

Brandon, S. G. F. *Man and his Destiny in the Great Religions*. Manchester, 1962.

BUBER, MARTIN. *Two Types of Faith*, trans. by N. P. Goldhawk. London, 1951.
—— *Israel and the World: Essays in a Time of Crisis*. New York, 1948.
CRAGG, KENNETH. *The Privilege of Man; a Theme in Judaism, Islam and Christianity*. London, 1968.
AL FARUQI, ISMAIL RAGI. *On Arabism: Urubah and Religion*. Amsterdam, 1962.
—— *Christian Ethics*. Montreal, 1967.
HERTZBERG, ARTHUR. *The Zionist Idea*. New York, 1959.
—— *Judaism*. New York, 1961.
HESCHEL, ABRAHAM. *The Prophets*. New York, 1962.
—— *God in Search of Man, a Philosophy of Judaism*. New York, 1955.
IZUTSU, TOSHIHIKO. *Ethico-Religious Concepts in the Qur'an*. Montreal, 1966.
NASR, SEYYED HOSSEIN. *Ideals and Realities of Islam*. London, 1966.
PARKES, JAMES. *Christian and Jew: Foundations of Judaism and Christianity*. London, 1960.
—— *Judaism and Christianity*. Chicago, 1948.
RAHBAR, DAUD. *God of Justice*. Leiden, 1960.
RAHMAN, FAZLUR. *Islam*. London, 1966.
—— *Prophecy in Islam*. London, 1958.
ROSENTHAL, ERWIN I. J. *Islam in the Modern National State*. Cambridge, 1965.
SMITH, WILFRED C. *Islam in Modern History*. Oxford, 1957.
SWEETMAN, J. WINDROW. *Islam and Christian Theology*. Part 1, Part 2 (2 vols.) and Part 3. London, 1949 to 1968.

CHAPTER 21: LAW

HISTORICAL BACKGROUND

CAHEN, C. *L'Islam et les minorités confessionnelles au cours de l'histoire*. Table ronde no. 126, June 1958, pp. 61–72.
—— "Dhimma" in *Encyclopaedia of Islam*. 2nd ed.
EDELBY, N. *Essai sur l'autonomie législative et juridictionnelle des chrétientés d'Orient sous la domination musulmane de 633 à 1517*. Brussels, 1953.
FATTAL, A. *Le statut légal des non-Musulmans en pays d'Islam*. Beirut, 1958.
GOITEIN, S. *Jews and Arabs*. New York, 1955.
HASLUCK, F. W. *Christianity and Islam under the Sultans*. 2 vols. Oxford, 1929.
AL-MĀWARDĪ. *al-Aḥkām al-Sulṭāniyya*. French translation by Fagnan. Algiers, 1915.
PAPADOPOULOS, TH. *Les privilèges du patriarcat œcuménique dans l'Empire ottoman*. Paris, 1924.
PELISSIE DU RAUSAS, G. *Le régime des capitulations dans l'Empire ottoman*. 2 vols. 2nd ed. Paris, 1910–11.
ROY CHOUDHURY SASTRI, M. L. "The status of Dhimmis in Muslim states with special references to Mughal India." *Journal, Greater India Society*, vol. XII (1945), pp. 18–48.
SESOSTRIS, SIDAROUS BEY. *Des patriarcats dans l'Empire ottoman*. Paris, 1907.

Steen de Jehay, F. van den. *De la situation légale des sujets ottomans non-musulmans*. Brussels, 1906.
Tritton, A. S. *The Caliphs and their non-Muslim Subjects*. Oxford, 1930.

WORKS ON ACTUAL CONDITIONS IN THE MIDDLE EAST

Ahmed Safwat. *Courts of Personal Status in Egypt* (in Arabic). 2nd ed. Cairo, 1949.
Anderson, J. N. D. *Islamic Law in the Modern World*. London, 1959.
Cardahi, Choucri. *La conception et la pratique du droit international privé dans l'Islam*. Recueil des cours de l'Acad. de Droit international de la Haye, 1937, vol. II, pp. 511–650.
Decroux, P. *Droit international privé du Maroc*. Rabat–Paris, 1963.
Le droit libanais, by a group of professors of the Faculty of Law at Beirut. Vol. I, Paris, 1963 (Title II).
Fyzee, Asaf A. A. *Outlines of Muhammadan Law*. 3rd ed. London, 1964.
Handbuch der Orientalistik, III, Orientalisches Recht. Leiden–Cologne, 1964.
Hanki, Aziz. "Effets de la divergence de pays sur le droit à la succession." *Revue d'Études Islamiques* (1935), pp. 179–86.
Jambu-Merlin, R. *Le droit privé en Tunisie*. Paris, 1960. Pp. 161–86.
Khadduri. *Law in the Middle East*. Washington, 1955.
Linant de Bellefonds, Y. "Immutabilité du droit musulman et réformes législatives en Égypte." *Revue Internationale de Droit comparé*. Paris (1955), no. I.
—— "La suppression des juridictions du statut personnel en Égypte." *Revue Internationale de Droit comparé*. Paris (1956), no. 3.
—— "La jurisprudence égyptienne et les conflits de lois en matière de statut personnel." *Journal de Droit international*. Paris (1960), no. 3.
—— *Traité de Droit musulman comparé*. Paris–La Haye (1965), tome II, pp. 707 ff.
D'Olivier Farran, C. *Matrimonial Laws of the Sudan*. London, 1963.
Schacht, J. *Introduction to Islamic Law*. Oxford, 1964 (especially chapter 15 and its bibliography).
Travaux et jours. Revue de l'Université St Joseph, Beyrouth. No. 4. January–February 1962 (articles on personal status law).

CHAPTER 22: SOCIETY AND POLITICS

Ammann, Albert. *Storia della Chiesa Russa e dei Paesi limitrofi*. Unione Tipografica Editrice Torinese. Turin, 1948.
Antonius, George. *The Arab Awakening*. Reprint. London, 1955.
Atamian, Sarkis. *The Armenian Community. The Historical Development of a Social and Ideological Conflict*. Philosophical Library, New York, 1955.
Attwater, Donald. *The Christian Churches of the East*. Revd. ed. Milwaukee, 1943.
Berger, Morroe. *The Arab World Today*. London, 1962.
Cromer, Earl of. *Modern Egypt*. 2 vols. London, 1908; New York, 1916.

DAVISON, RODERIC H. *Reform in the Ottoman Empire*. Princeton, 1963.
FISHER, SYDNEY NETTLETON. *Social Forces in the Middle East*. Ithaca, New York, 1958.
HOWARD, HARRY N. *The King–Crane Commission*. Beirut, 1963.
HOURANI, ALBERT. *Arabic Thought in the Liberal Age, 1798–1939*. Oxford, 1962.
LAQUEUR, WALTER Z. *The Middle-East in Transition*. London, 1958.
LEWIS, BERNARD. *The Emergence of Modern Turkey*. Oxford, 1961; reprint 1962.
LEWIS, G. L. *Turkey*. London, 1955.
LLOYD, LORD. *Egypt since Cromer*. 2 vols. London, 1933–4.
LUKE, SIR HARRY. *The Old Turkey and the New*. London, 1955.
Middle East Record. The Israel Oriental Society, Tel Aviv, 1960.
MORRISON, S. A. *Middle East; Tensions, Political, Social and Religious*. New York, 1954.
NASLIAN, JEAN. *Mémoires sur les événements politico-religieux en Proche-Orient de 1914 à 1928*. Beyrouth, 1929?.
PERETZ, DON. *The Middle East Today*. New York, 1963.
RONDOT, PIERRE. *Les Chrétiens d'Orient*. Cahiers de l'Afrique et l'Asie, IV. Paris, 1955.
SANTOS, ANGEL. *Iglesias de Oriente*. 2 vols. Ed. Sal Terrae. Santander, 1963.
SPULER, BERTHOLD. *Die Gegenwartslage der Ostkirchen in ihrer völkischen u. staatlichen Umwelt*. Wiesbaden, 1947.
—— (ed.). *Religionsgeschichte des Orients in der Zeit der Weltreligionen*. Leiden, 1961.
YALE, WILLIAM. *The Near East. A Modern History*. Ann Arbor, 1958.

CHAPTER 23: THE CULTURAL ASPECT

In addition to the works in Arabic cited in footnotes and the text above, reference may be made to the following books in English, arranged in the order of the date of publication:

GIBB, H. A. R. (ed.). *Whither Islam?* London, 1932. (The two articles by the editor are still useful for their assessment of both change and its trends.)
ANTONIUS, G. *The Arab Awakening*. London, 1938. (Very able advocacy. To be used with caution owing to serious omissions and imbalance in emphasis.)
GIBB, H. A. R. *Modern Trends in Islam*. Chicago, 1947. (The standard work on its subject; very little has been added to its ideas by subsequent writers.)
—— and BOWEN, H. *Islamic Society and the West*, I (part 1 published in 1950 and part 2 in 1957 by Oxford). (Although concerned with a period earlier than the one covered by our study, it is an indispensable reference book for background information.)
FARIS, N. A. and HUSAYN, M. T. *Crescent in Crisis*. Kansas, 1955. (A very useful and concise study of Arab nationalism.)
NUSEIBEH, H. Z. *The Ideas of Arab Nationalism*. Ithaca, 1956. (A pioneering work by an Arab scholar and diplomat.)

The place of education in the Arab revival, the contributions of English and American missionaries to the revival, and western attitudes to Islam and Arab nationalism are among the subjects studied in the following works by A. L. Tibawi:

Arab Education in Mandatory Palestine. London, 1956.
British Interests in Palestine 1800–1901. Oxford, 1961.
English Speaking Orientalists. London, 1963.
American Interests in Syria 1800–1901. Oxford, 1966.

CHAPTER 24: RELIGION AND ANTI-RELIGION

ADAMS, CHARLES C. *Islam and Modernism in Egypt*. London, 1933.
BERGER, MORROE. *The Arab World Today*. London, 1962.
BERKES, NIYAZI. *The Development of Secularism in Turkey*. London, 1964.
BINDER, LEONARD. *The Ideological Revolution in the Middle East*. New York, 1964.
CRAGG, KENNETH. *Counsels in Contemporary Islam*. Edinburgh, 1965 (with extensive bibliography).
GIBB, H. A. R. *Modern Trends in Islam*. Chicago, 1947.
GRUNEBAUM, GUSTAV E. VON. *Modern Islam: The Search for Cultural Identity*. Berkeley, 1962.
HAIM, SYLVIA (ed.). *Arab Nationalism*. Berkeley, 1962.
HALPERN, MANFRED. *The Politics of Social Change in the Middle East and North Africa*. Princeton, 1963.
HOURANI, A. H. *Arabic Thought in the Liberal Age, 1798–1939*. London, 1962.
IQBAL, MUHAMMAD. *The Reconstruction of Religious Thought in Islam*. London, 1934.
LAQUEUR, WALTER Z. *Communism and Nationalism in the Middle East*. London, 1956.
LEWIS, BERNARD. *The Emergence of Modern Turkey*. London, 1961.
MORGAN, KENNETH W. (ed.). *Islam the Straight Path*. New York, 1958.
PROCTOR, J. HARRIS (ed.). *Islam and International Relations*. London, 1965.
RUSTOW, DANKWART A. *Politics and Westernization in the Near East*. Princeton, 1956.
SMITH, WILFRED CANTWELL. *Islam in Modern History*. Princeton, 1957.

INDEX

INDEX

(Bold figures indicate volume numbers.)

23-2

INDEX

Basilides, *see* Fasiladas
Basilios, Anba, first Coptic patriarch of Ethiopia, **2**, 509
Basilius IV, Coptic archbishop of Jerusalem, **1**, 445
Basilius, Ethiopian Coptic bishop of Shoa, **1**, 447
Baṣra, **1**, 419; **2**, 23, 309
Ba'th (Syrian Popular party), **1**, 337, 365; **2**, 346
Bāṭinīs, **2**, 294
Bayar, Celal, Turkish president, **2**, 468
Bayezid II, Sultan, **1**, 146
Bayt Ḥamīd al-Dīn, **2**, 293, 296, 297, 299
Bayt at-Takrīs (House of Sanctification), Coptic monastery, **1**, 439
Bayūḍ Ibrāhīm, **2**, 316
Bayūḍī movement, **2**, 316
Bea, Cardinal, **2**, 544, 585
Beckingham, C. F., **2**, 56
Bedouin tribes, **1**, 125; **2**, 13, 59, 174
  and Judaism, **1**, 123
  as *Ikhwān*, **2**, 273, 275, 278
  in Saudi Arabia, **2**, 273
Bedros Saradjian, Catholicos of Sis, **2**, 497
Beirut
  Catholic establishments in, **1**, 418–21 *passim*
  centre for American missions, **1**, 538
  see also American University of Beirut
Bekṭāshīs, Bektaşīs, **2**, 90–1, 93, 236, 244, 245, 250
Belavin, T., *see* Tychon Belavin
Belisarius, general, **1**, 279
Bell, Liqamakuas, missionary, **1**, 461, 464
Belliard, M., **1**, 464
Belmond Monastery (Orthodox), **1**, 343
Belyayev, Y., **2**, 166
Ben Shemen, village, **1**, 67, 106
Bender, –, missionary, **1**, 464
Benedict XIV, Pope, **1**, 369, 373, 375; **2**, 519
Benedict XV, Pope, **1**, 388, 389, 390, 395
Benedictines, **1**, 400, 401, 408
Benedictus (Benediktos) I, Orthodox patriarch of Jerusalem, **1**, 329; **2**, 489
Bengal, Muslims in, **2**, 127–8
Ben-Gurion, David
  and Buddhism, **1**, 113
  and Israeli constitution, **1**, 88
  and Law of Return, **1**, 89
  and religious parties, **1**, 89; **2**, 541
  and the *kibbutz*, **1**, 100
  and Zionism, **1**, 54–5
  as a founder of Israel, **1**, 76
  "belief in miracles", **1**, 109
  opens ideological conference (1957), **1**, 84
Ben Habib, Jacob, **1**, 153
Ben-Horin, Shalom, **1**, 103
Benjamin, Coptic patriarch of Alexandria, **1**, 261, 277
Benjamin I, Orthodox patriarch of Constantinople, **2**, 475
Benjamin Mār Shim'ūn, *see* Shim'ūn XIX
Benjamin of Tudela, **1**, 137; **2**, 339–40
Benni, Behman, Syrian Uniate patriarch, **2**, 527
Bennigsen, Alexandre, **2**, 167
Benson, E. W., archbishop of Canterbury, **1**, 558, 578
Benveniste, Ḥayyim, **1**, 169
Benzinger, O. C. D., bishop of Quilon, **1**, 380
Ben-Zvi, Isaac, **1**, 76
Bérard, Victor, **1**, 496
Berbers, **1**, 281–3; **2**, 171, 173–4
  and Judaism, **1**, 126, 133, 281
  and saint cults, **2**, 179, 182–4
  Christians among, **1**, 282
  converts to Islam, **1**, 264, 282
  paganism of, **1**, 264, 281
Berdyaev, N., **1**, 322
Bergmann, Hugo, **1**, 91, 107
Berlin Reform Congregation (Jewish), **1**, 21, 22
Berlin, Treaty of (1878), **1**, 484, 487, 489; **2**, 238, 422, 495, 499, 611
Bernard, St, **2**, 266
Bernays, Isaac, **1**, 17–18
Berriane, Ibāḍī centre at, **2**, 316
Berron, Paul, **1**, 546
Beser, –, **1**, 246
Bessarabia, **2**, 246
Beth Israel, *see* Falashas
Bēth Lāpāt (Jundayshāpūr), **1**, 287, 292
Bethel Church, **1**, 477
Bethune-Baker, J. F., **1**, 529
Beyrab, Jacob, **1**, 163, 164, 187
Beyt She'ārīm, inscriptions of, **1**, 119
Bhagavadgītā, **2**, 125, 140
Bḥamdūn, Muslim-Christian convocation at, **2**, 53, 65, 635
Bible, the
  and archaeology, **1**, 579–80
  Arabic translation of, **1**, 539, 569, 574; **2**, 58, 532, 561
  Aḥmad Khan's commentary on, **2**, 136
  Assyrian version, **1**, 532
  Jews and, **1**, 11, 16, 76, 82, 117; and German translation, **1**, 11, 30; first polyglot edition, **1**, 167; in Persian-Jewish dialect, **1**, 195; Yemenite Pentateuch, **1**, pl. 7*b*

India (*cont.*)
Jews in, 1, 73, 79, 192, 193, pl. 7*a*
law, 2, 426, 431, 439, 440, 444–5
"Slave Dynasty", 2, 121
Indonesia, Islam in, 2, 24, 26
Ingush, *see* Chechen-Ingush
Innocent III, Pope, 1, 255, 259, 375, 388
Inönü, Ismet, president of Turkey, 2, 467, 468
Institute of Jewish Studies, 1, 79
Interchurch Aid and Service to Refugees, 1, 563
Inter-faith Council, Jerusalem, 1, 112–13
International Missionary Council, 1, 593
Ionides, Michael, 2, 54
Iqbāl, Muḥammad, 2, 28, 68, 76, 94, 129, 130–1, 138, 141, 375, 624
Iraq
and Arab-Israeli war, 1, 78
and Pan-Arabism, 1, 358
British mandate in, 1, 202, 357; 2, 51
Christianity in: Armenian Catholics, 1, 374; Assyrians, Nestorians, 1, 383, 523, 531; Chaldaeans, 2, 525; Latin Catholics, 1, 387; Protestant missions, 1, 542–3, 569; Syrian Catholics, 2, 527; Syrian Orthodox, 1, 480
communism in, 2, 46, 628
guarantees to minorities, 2, 502
Islam in, 2, 21, 60, 281
Jews in, 1, 137, 191–3; 2, 538, 557; and Community Law (1954), 1, 202; graves, 1, 192; migrants from, 1, 70, 192–3; national headgear (*sidara*), 1, 200 n.; pogroms, 1, 211; removal from official positions, 1, 223; under British mandate, 1, 202
law, 2, 427, 429, 439, 447, 449
mixed marriages in, 2, 434
responsibility in Fertile Crescent, 1, 362
Iran, *see* Persia
Iranian peoples in USSR, 2, 170
Irish Presbyterians, 1, 540
ʿĪsā b. Nestorius, 1, 142
Isaac, patriarch of Alexandria, 1, 262
Isenberg, Protestant missionary, 1, 461
al-Iṣfahānī, Abu 'l-Faraj, 1, 267
Ishai Mār Shimʿūn, Assyrian Patriarch, 1, 530
Isḥāq, Adīb, 1, 337; 2, 576–8, 582
Ishmael, son of Abraham, 2, 312
Ishōʿyāb III, Nestorian catholicus, 1, 289
Iskandar Bey Masīḥa, *see* Masīḥa, Iskandar
Iṣlāḥī, Amīn Aḥsan, Mawlānā, 2, 139
Islam
and political power, 2, 25–6, 43, 609
and Zionism, 1, 361; 2, 62, 603
as world faith, 2, 63, 387
conservatism in, 2, 612–14
conversions to, 1, 171, 172, 194; 2, 126–7, 445, 447–52
culture, 2, 45, 54–5, 63, 586–604 *passim*; architecture (mosques), 2, pls. 5, 6, 8, 9*a*, 12*a*, 13, 14*a*, *b*, 15*a*, *b*; centres of, 2, 21; in East Africa, 2, 215–16; westernization, 2, 165; *see also* al-Azhar
distinctive clothing: in Balkans, 2, 237–8; in North Africa (Ibāḍīs), 2, 313; in West Africa, 2, 233
doctrine, 2, 387–412 *passim*; acknowledgement of God, 2, 393, 401; and Messiahship, 2, 380, 384, 387–8, 389; monotheism, 2, 52; oneness of God (monism), 2, 255–6, 271–2; *see also under* Aḥmadīs, Ibāḍīs, Ismāʿīlīs, Shīʿītes, Ṣūfīs, Sunnīs, Wahhābīs, Zaydīs; *and* Jesus, Islamic view of
education, 2, 57, 549, 572–6, 586–91, 602; *see also* ʻ*ulamā*ʼ
"magical" practices, 2, 115
missions, 2, 26, 29; in India, 2, 142; in North Africa, 2, 175
Muḥarram, 2, 105, 113, 115, 185, pl. 10*b*
origins in Arabia, 2, 4–16
pan-Islam, 2, 28, 29, 551, 569–71, 583, 627
Ramaḍān, 2, 15, 32, 33, 56, 62, 260; Druzes and, 2, 338; in Afghanistan, 2, 143; in Persia, 2, 111, 116; in Turkey, 2, 74, 84–5, 86; in Indo-Pakistan subcontinent, 2, 142; in North Africa, 2, 184, 185; in West Africa, 2, 228; Ismāʿīlīs and, 2, 323
relations with Christians: cordiality in Egypt, 2, 189; cultural aspects, 2, 545–604 *passim*; doctrines compared, 2, 65–6, 579; in Ethiopia, 2, 206, 210–11, 216; mixed marriages, 2, 433, 434, 435, 447, 453; rapprochement, 2, 53, 58, 62–3, 65, 547, 551, 553, 564, 581, 634, 635; reaction to missions, 1, 335, 549–51; 2, 197–202, 234; relations with Greek Orthodox, 1, 299, 305, 310, 341; 2, 81; suspicion of Christian thought, 2, 612; *see also* Christian Arabs
resurgence of, 2, 622, 625–7, 631
sharīʿa, *see* law, Islamic
territorial expansion, 2, 25–6
tolerance of, 1, 303, 536; 2, 275–6, 545, 559, 579, 582, 593, 594–5, 603, 631
Tradition (*hadīth*), Traditionists, 1, 129; 2, 22–3, 128, 137–8, 282, 626; Zaydīs and, 2, 289, 292; *see also* Sunnīs